Fullstack React

The Complete Guide to ReactJS and Friends

Anthony Accomazzo
Nate Murray
Ari Lerner
Clay Allsopp
David Guttman
Tyler McGinnis

Fullstack React

The Complete Guide to ReactJS and Friends

Written by Anthony Accomazzo, Ari Lerner, Nate Murray, Clay Allsopp, David Guttman, and Tyler McGinnis

Technical Advisor: Sophia Shoemaker

ISBN: 978-0-9913446-2-8

Typeset using Leanpub.
Cover Art by TJ Fuller.
Published in San Francisco, California by Fullstack.io.

Questions? Email us at: us@fullstack.io

Sample code download available at fullstackreact.com/code

Contents

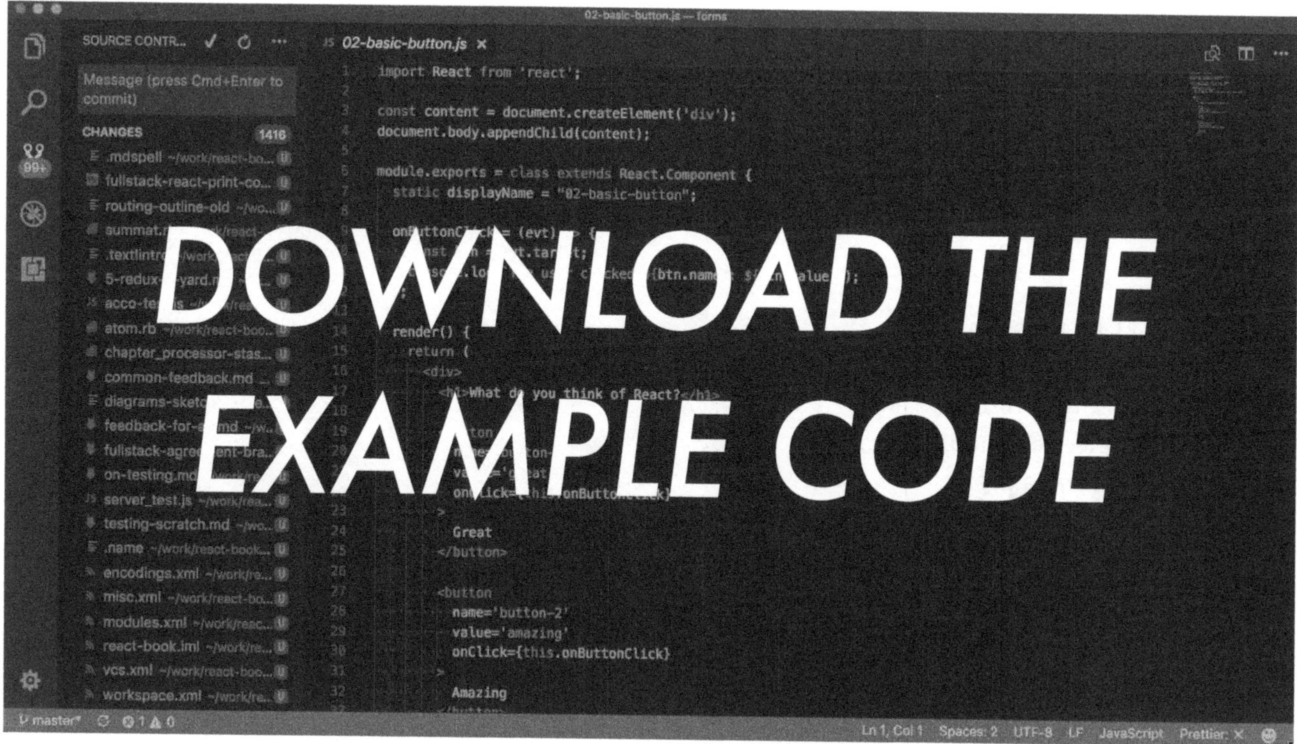

This book contains numerous sample apps and code examples. You can download the code at our website:

URL	https://fullstackreact.com/code
BOOK SERIAL CODE	`AMZ-SmQ7f`

Book Revision

Revision 33 - Supports React 15.5.4

Bug Reports

If you'd like to report any bugs, typos, or suggestions just email us at: `react@fullstack.io`.

Refer to the page `https://fullstackreact.com/print-errata` for notes on any major issues for your revision of the book.

For further help dealing with issues, refer to "How to Get the Most Out of This Book."

Chat With The Community!

There's an unofficial community chat room for this book using Gitter. If you'd like to hang out with other people learning React, come join us on Gitter[1]!

Be notified of updates via Twitter

If you'd like to be notified of updates to the book on Twitter, follow @fullstackio[2]

We'd love to hear from you!

Did you like the book? Did you find it helpful? We'd love to add your face to our list of testimonials on the website! Email us at: `react@fullstack.io`.

[1] https://gitter.im/fullstackreact/fullstackreact

[2] https://twitter.com/fullstackio

book to learn and understand the fundamentals of React. Learning new concepts may feel strange but "give it 5 minutes" and practice them until you feel comfortable.

Then, **try to break the rules**. There is no one best way to build software and React is no exception. React actually embraces this fact by providing you with escape hatches when you want to do things outside of the React-way.

Come up with crazy ideas and who knows, maybe you are going to invent the successor to React!

– Christopher Chedeau @vjeux[3] Front-end Engineer at Facebook

[3] https://twitter.com/Vjeux

How to Get the Most Out of This Book

Overview

This book aims to be the single most useful resource on learning React. By the time you're done reading this book, you (and your team) will have everything you need to build reliable, powerful React apps.

React core is lean and powerful. After the first few chapters, you'll have a solid understanding of React's fundamentals and will be able to build a wide array of rich, interactive web apps with the framework.

But beyond React's core, there are many tools in its ecosystem that you might find helpful for building production apps. Things like client-side routing between pages, managing complex state, and heavy API interaction at scale.

This book consists of two parts.

In Part I, we cover all the fundamentals with a progressive, example-driven approach. You'll create your **first apps**, learn **how to write components**, start **handling user interaction**, manage rich **forms**, and even **interact with servers**.

We bookend the first part by exploring the inner workings of **Create React App** (Facebook's tool for running React apps), writing automated **unit tests**, and building a multi-page app that uses **client-side routing**.

Part II of this book moves into more **advanced concepts** that you'll see used in large, production applications. These concepts explore strategies for *data architecture, transport, and management*:

Redux is a state management paradigm based on Facebook's Flux architecture. Redux provides a structure for large state trees and allows you to decouple user interaction in your app from state changes.

GraphQL is a powerful, typed, REST API alternative where the client describes the data it needs. We also cover how to **write your own GraphQL servers** for your own data.

Relay is the glue between GraphQL and React. Relay is a data-fetching library that makes it easy to write flexible, performant apps without a lot of data-fetching code.

Finally, in the last chapter, we'll talk about how to write native, cross-platform mobile apps using **React Native**.

There are a few guidelines we want to give you **in order to get the most out of this book**.

First, know that you do not need to read this book linearly from cover-to-cover. **However**, we've ordered the contents of the book in a way we feel fits the order you should learn the concepts. We

encourage you to learn all the concepts in Part I of the book first before diving into concepts in Part II.

Second, keep in mind this package is more than just a book - it's a course complete with example code for every chapter. Below, we'll tell you:

- how to approach **the code examples** and
- **how to get help** if something goes wrong

Running Code Examples

This book comes with a library of runnable code examples. The code is available to download from the same place where you purchased this book. If you purchased this book on Amazon, you should have received an email with instructions.

If you have any trouble finding or downloading the code examples, email us at **react@fullstack.io**.

We use the program `npm`[4] to run **every example** in this book. You can boot most apps with the following two commands:

```
npm install
npm start
```

If you're unfamiliar with `npm`, we cover how to get it installed in the "Setting Up" section in the first chapter.

After running `npm start`, you will see some output on your screen that will tell you what URL to open to view your app.

Some apps require a few more commands to setup. **If you're ever unclear on how to run a particular sample app, checkout the `README.md` in that project's directory**. Every sample project contains a `README.md` that will give you the instructions you need to run each app.

Project setups

The first two projects begin with a simple React setup that allows us to quickly write React applications.

From there, with a couple exceptions, every project in this book was built using Create React App[5].

Create React App is based on Webpack, a tool which helps process and bundle our various JavaScript, CSS, HTML, and image files. We explore Create React App in-depth in the chapter "Using Webpack with Create React App." But, **Create React App is not a requirement** for using React. It's simply a wrapper around Webpack (and some other tooling) that makes it easy to get started.

[4] https://www.npmjs.com/

[5] https://github.com/facebookincubator/create-react-app

Code Blocks and Context

Nearly every code block in this book is pulled from a **runnable code example** which you can find in the sample code. For example, here is a code block pulled from the first chapter:

voting_app/public/js/app-2.js

```
class ProductList extends React.Component {
  render() {
    return (
      <div className='ui unstackable items'>
        <Product />
      </div>
    );
  }
}
```

Notice that the header of this code block states the path to the file which contains this code: `voting_app/public/js/app-2.js`.

If you ever feel like you're missing the context for a code example, open up the full code file using your favorite text editor. **This book is written with the expectation that you'll also be looking at the example code alongside the manuscript.**

For example, we often need to `import` libraries to get our code to run. In the early chapters of the book we show these `import` statements, because it's not clear where the libraries are coming from otherwise. However, the later chapters of the book are more advanced and they focus on *key concepts* instead of repeating boilerplate code that was covered earlier in the book. **If at any point you're not clear on the context, open up the code example on disk.**

Code Block Numbering

In this book, we sometimes build up a larger example in steps. If you see a file being loaded that has a numeric suffix, that generally means we're building up to something bigger.

For instance, above the code block has the filename: `app-2.js`. When you see the `-N.js` syntax that means we're building up to a final version of the file. You can jump into that file and see the state of all the code at that particular stage.

Getting Help

While we've made every effort to be clear, precise, and accurate you may find that when you're writing your code you run into a problem.

Generally, there are three types of problems:

- A "bug" in the book (e.g. how we describe something is wrong)
- A "bug" in our code
- A "bug" in your code

If you find an inaccuracy in how we describe something, or you feel a concept isn't clear, email us! We want to make sure that the book is both accurate and clear.

If you suspect a problem with the example code, make sure that your version of the book's code package is up to date. We release code updates periodically.

If you're using the latest code download and you think you've found a bug in our *code* we definitely want to hear about it.

If you're having trouble getting your own app working (and it isn't *our* example code), this case is a bit harder for us to handle.

Your first line of defense, when getting help with your custom app, should be our unofficial community chat room[6]. We (the authors) are there from time-to-time, but there are hundreds of other readers there who may be able to help you faster than we can.

If you're still stuck, we'd still love to hear from you, and here some tips for getting a clear, timely response.

Emailing Us

If you're emailing us asking for technical help, here's what we'd like to know:

- What revision of the book are you referring to?
- What operating system are you on? (e.g. Mac OS X 10.8, Windows 95)
- Which chapter and which example project are you on?
- What were you trying to accomplish?
- What have you tried[7] already?
- What output did you expect?
- What actually happened? (Including relevant log output.)

The **absolute best way to get technical support** is to send us a short, self-contained example of the problem. Our preferred way to receive this would be for you to send us a Plunkr link by using this URL[8].

[6] https://gitter.im/fullstackreact/fullstackreact
[7] http://mattgemmell.com/what-have-you-tried/
[8] http://bit.ly/fsr-plunker

That URL contains a runnable, boilerplate React app. If you can copy and paste your code into that project, reproduce your error, and send it to us **you'll greatly increase the likelihood of a prompt, helpful response**.

When you've written down these things, email us at **react@fullstack.io**. We look forward to hearing from you.

Technical Support Response Time

We perform our free, technical support **once per week**.

If you need a faster response time and help getting **any** of your team's questions answered, then you may consider our premium support option. Email us at `react@fullstack.io`.

Get excited

Writing web apps with React is *fun*. And by using this book, **you're going to learn how to build real React apps** fast. (Much faster than spending hours parsing out-dated blog posts.)

If you've written client-side JavaScript before, you'll find React refreshingly intuitive. If this is your first serious foray into the front-end, you'll be blown away at how quickly you can create something worth sharing.

So hold on tight - you're about to become a React expert and have a lot of fun along the way. Let's dig in!

- Nate (@eigenjoy[9]) & Anthony

---

[9]https://twitter.com/eigenjoy

Part I

Your first React Web Application

Building Product Hunt

In this chapter, you're going to get a crash course on React by building a simple voting application inspired by Product Hunt[10]. You'll become familiar with how React approaches front-end development and all the fundamentals necessary to build an interactive React app from start to finish. Thanks to React's core simplicity, by the end of the chapter you'll already be well on your way to writing a variety of fast, dynamic interfaces.

We'll focus on getting our React app up and running fast. We take a deeper look at concepts covered in this section throughout the book.

Setting up your development environment

Code editor

As you'll be writing code throughout this book, you'll need to make sure you have a code editor you're comfortable working with. If you don't already have a preferred editor, we recommend installing Atom[11] or Sublime Text[12].

Node.js and npm

For all the projects in this book, we'll need to make sure we have a working Node.js[13] development environment along with npm.

There are a couple different ways you can install Node.js so please refer to the Node.js website for detailed information: https://nodejs.org/download/[14]

If you're on a Mac, your best bet is to install Node.js directly from the Node.js website instead of through another package manager (like Homebrew). Installing Node.js via Homebrew is known to cause some issues.

The Node Package Manager (npm for short) is installed as a part of Node.js. To check if npm is available as a part of our development environment, we can open a terminal window and type:

---

[10] http://producthunt.com

[11] http://atom.io

[12] https://www.sublimetext.com/

[13] http://nodejs.org

[14] https://nodejs.org/download/

```
$ npm -v
```

If a version number is not printed out and you receive an error, make sure to download a Node.js installer that includes npm.

Install Git

The app in this chapter requires Git to install some third-party libraries.

If you don't have Git installed, see these instructions[15] for installing Git for your platform.

After installing Git, we recommend restarting your computer.

Browser

Last, we highly recommend using the Google Chrome Web Browser[16] to develop React apps. We'll use the Chrome developer toolkit throughout this book. To follow along with our development and debugging we recommend downloading it now.

Special instruction for Windows users

All the code in this book has been tested on Windows 10 with PowerShell.

Ensure IIS is installed

If you're on a Windows machine and have yet to do any web development on it, you may need to install IIS (Internet Information Services) in order to run web servers locally.

See this tutorial[17] for installing IIS.

JavaScript ES6/ES7

JavaScript is the language of the web. It runs on many different browsers, like Google Chrome, Firefox, Safari, Microsoft Edge, and Internet Explorer. Different browsers have different JavaScript interpreters which execute JavaScript code.

Its widespread adoption as the internet's client-side scripting language led to the formation of a standards body which manages its specification. The specification is called **ECMAScript** or ES.

---

[15] https://git-scm.com/book/en/v2/Getting-Started-Installing-Git

[16] https://www.google.com/chrome/

[17] http://www.howtogeek.com/112455/how-to-install-iis-8-on-windows-8/

The 5th edition of the specification is called ES5. You can think of ES5 as a "version" of the JavaScript programming language. Finalized in 2009, ES5 was adopted by all major browsers within a few years.

The 6th edition of JavaScript is referred to as ES6. Finalized in 2015, the latest versions of major browsers are still finishing adding support for ES6 as of 2017. ES6 is a significant update. It contains a whole host of new features for JavaScript, almost two dozen in total. JavaScript written in ES6 is tangibly different than JavaScript written in ES5.

ES7, a much smaller update that builds on ES6, was ratified in June 2016. ES7 contains only two new features.

As the future of JavaScript, we want to write our code in ES6/ES7 today. But we also want our JavaScript to run on older browsers until they fade out of widespread use. We see later in this chapter how we can enjoy the benefits of ES6/ES7 today while still supporting the vast majority of the world's browsers.

This book is written with JavaScript ES7. Because ES6 ratified a majority of these new features, we'll commonly refer to these new features as ES6 features.

We've included an appendix on the ES6 syntax that we use, "Appendix B: ES6." We'll often refer to the appendix when encountering ES6 syntax for the first time, but if ever syntax seems unfamiliar to you it's worth checking Appendix B to see if it's new ES6 JavaScript syntax.

ES6 is sometimes referred to as ES2015, the year of its finalization. ES7, in turn, is often referred to as ES2016.

Getting started

Sample Code

All the code examples you find in each chapter are available in the code package that came with the book. In that code package you'll find completed versions of each app as well as boilerplates that we will use to build those apps together. Each chapter provides detailed instruction on how to follow along on your own.

While coding along with the book is not necessary, we highly recommend doing so. Playing around with examples and sample code will help solidify and strengthen concepts.

Previewing the application

We'll be building a basic React app that will allow us to touch on React's most important concepts at a high-level before diving into them in subsequent sections. Let's begin by taking a look at a working implementation of the app.

Open up the sample code folder that came with the book. Change to the `voting_app/` directory in the terminal:

```
$ cd voting_app/
```

If you're not familiar with cd, it stands for "change directory." If you're on a Mac, do the following to open terminal and change to the proper directory:

1. Open up `/Applications/Utilities/Terminal.app`.
2. Type `cd`, without hitting enter.
3. Tap the spacebar.
4. In the Finder, drag the `voting_app/` folder on to your terminal window.
5. Hit Enter.

Your terminal is now in the proper directory.

Throughout the book, a code block starting with a `$` signifies a command to be run in your terminal.

First, we'll need to use `npm` to install all our dependencies:

```
$ npm install
```

With our dependencies installed, we can boot the server using the `npm start` command

```
$ npm start
```

The boot process will print some text to the console:

Boot process output

In addition, your browser might automatically launch and open the app. If it doesn't, you can view the running application at the URL `http://localhost:3000`:

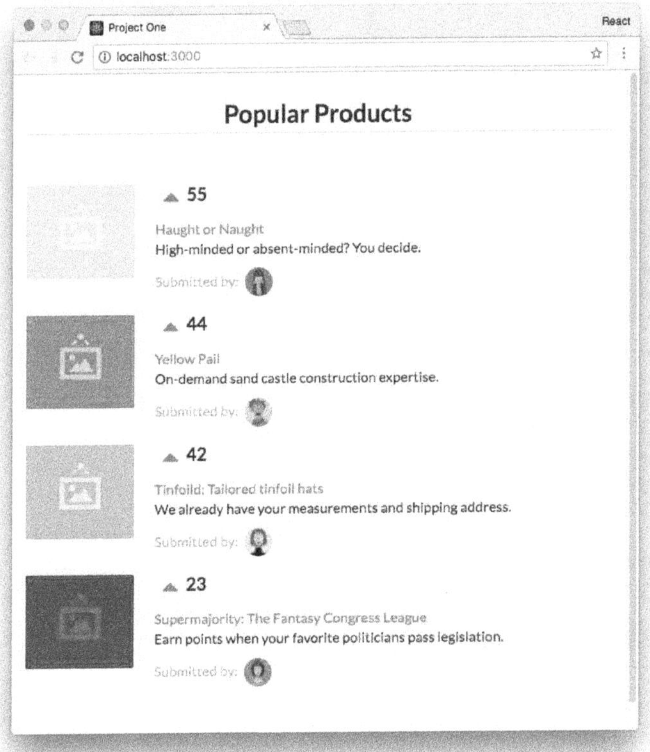

Completed version of the app

This demo app is a site like Product Hunt[18] or Reddit[19]. These sites have lists of links that users can vote on. Like those sites, in our app we can up-vote products. All products are sorted instantaneously by number of votes.

The keyboard command to quit a running Node server is CTRL+C.

Prepare the app

In the terminal, run `ls` to see the project's layout:

[18]http://producthunt.com

[19]http://reddit.com

```
$ ls
README.md
disable-browser-cache.js
nightwatch.json
node_modules/
package.json
public/
semantic.json
tests/
```

If you're running on macOS or Linux, you can run `ls -1p` to format your output as we do above.

Node apps contain a `package.json` which specifies the dependencies of the project. When we ran `npm install`, npm used our `package.json` to determine which dependencies to download and install. It installed them to the folder `node_modules/`.

We explore the format of `package.json` in later chapters.

The code we'll be working with is inside the folder `public/`. Look inside that folder:

```
$ ls public
favicon.ico
images/
index.html
js/
semantic/
style.css
vendor/
```

The general layout here is a common one for web apps. Inside `public/` is `index.html`, the file that we serve to browsers that request our website. As we'll see shortly, `index.html` is the centerpiece of our app. It loads in the rest of our app's assets.

Let's look inside `public/js` next:

```
$ ls public/js
app-1.js
app-2.js
app-3.js
app-4.js
app-5.js
app-6.js
app-7.js
app-8.js
app-9.js
app-complete.js
app.js
seed.js
```

Inside `public/js` is where we'll put our app's JavaScript. We'll be writing our React app inside `app.js`. `app-complete.js` is the completed version of the app that we're working towards, which we viewed a moment ago.

In addition, we've included each version of `app.js` as we build it up throughout this chapter (`app-1.js`, `app-2.js`, etc). Each code block in this chapter will reference which app version you can find it in. You can copy and paste longer code insertions from these app versions into your `app.js`.

All projects include a handy `README.md` that have instructions on how to run them.

To get started, we'll ensure `app-complete.js` is no longer loaded in `index.html`. We'll then have a blank canvas to begin work inside `app.js`.

Open up `public/index.html` in your text editor. It should look like this:

voting_app/public/index.html

```
<!DOCTYPE html>
<html>

  <head>
    <meta charset="utf-8">
    <title>Project One</title>
    <link rel="stylesheet" href="./semantic-dist/semantic.css" />
    <link rel="stylesheet" href="./style.css" />
    <script src="vendor/babel-standalone.js"></script>
    <script src="vendor/react.js"></script>
    <script src="vendor/react-dom.js"></script>
  </head>
```

```
  <body>
    <div class="main ui text container">
      <h1 class="ui dividing centered header">Popular Products</h1>
      <div id="content"></div>
    </div>
    <script src="./js/seed.js"></script>
    <script src="./js/app.js"></script>
    <!-- Delete the script tag below to get started. -->
    <script
      type="text/babel"
      data-plugins="transform-class-properties"
      src="./js/app-complete.js"
    ></script>
  </body>

</html>
```

We'll go over all the dependencies being loaded under the `<head>` tag later. The heart of the HTML document is these few lines here:

voting_app/public/index.html

```
    <div class="main ui text container">
      <h1 class="ui dividing centered header">Popular Products</h1>
      <div id="content"></div>
    </div>
```

For this project, we're using Semantic UI[20] for styling.

Semantic UI is a CSS framework, much like Twitter's Bootstrap[21]. It provides us with a grid system and some simple styling. You don't need to know Semantic UI in order to use this book. We'll provide all the styling code that you need. At some point, you might want to check out the docs Semantic UI docs[22] to get familiar with the framework and explore how you can use it in your own projects.

The `class` attributes here are just concerned with style and are safe to ignore. Stripping those away, our core markup is succinct:

[20] http://semantic-ui.com/

[21] http://getbootstrap.com/

[22] http://semantic-ui.com/introduction/getting-started.html

```
<div>
  <h1>Popular Products</h1>
  <div id="content"></div>
</div>
```

We have a title for the page (`h1`) and a `div` with an `id` of `content`. **This `div` is where we will ultimately mount our React app**. We'll see shortly what that means.

The next few lines tell the browser what JavaScript to load. To start building our own application, let's remove the `./app-complete.js` script tag completely:

```
<script src="./js/seed.js"></script>
<script src="./js/app.js"></script>
<!-- Delete the script tag below to get started. -->
<script
  type="text/babel"
  data-plugins="transform-class-properties"
  src="./js/app-complete.js"
></script>
```

After we save our updated `index.html` and reload the web browser, we'll see that our app has disappeared.

What's a component?

Building a React app is all about **components**. An individual React component can be thought of as a UI component in an app. We can break apart the interface of our app into two classes of components:

The app's components

We have a hierarchy of one parent component and many child components. We'll call these `ProductList` and `Product`, respectively:

1. `ProductList`: Contains a list of product components
2. `Product`: Displays a given product

Not only do React components map cleanly to UI components, but they are self-contained. The markup, view logic, and often component-specific style is all housed in one place. This feature makes React components reusable.

Furthermore, as we'll see in this chapter and throughout this book, React's paradigm for component data flow and interactivity is rigidly defined. In React, when the inputs for a component change, the framework simply re-renders that component. This gives us a robust UI consistency guarantee:

With a given set of inputs, the output (how the component looks on the page) will always be the same.

Our first component

Let's start off by building the `ProductList` component. We'll write all our React code for the rest of this chapter inside the file `public/js/app.js`. Let's open `app.js` and insert the component:

voting_app/public/js/app-1.js

```
class ProductList extends React.Component {
  render() {
    return (
      <div className='ui unstackable items'>
        Hello, friend! I am a basic React component.
      </div>
    );
  }
}
```

React components are **ES6 classes** that extend the class `React.Component`. We're referencing the `React` variable. `index.html` loads the React library for us so we're able to reference it here:

voting_app/public/index.html

```
    <script src="vendor/react.js"></script>
```

Our `ProductList` class has a single method, `render()`. **`render()` is the only required method for a React component**. React uses the return value from this method to determine what to render to the page.

While JavaScript is not a classical language, ES6 introduced a class declaration syntax. ES6 classes are syntactical sugar over JavaScript's prototype-based inheritance model.

We cover the important details you need to know about classes with respect to building React components. If you'd like to learn more about ES6 classes, refer to the docs on MDN[23].

There are two ways to declare React components:

(1) As ES6 classes (as above)

(2) Using the `React.createClass()` method

An example of using an ES6 class:

```
class HelloWorld extends React.Component {
    render() { return(<p>Hello, world!</p>) }
}
```

The same component written using the `createClass` function from the `React` library:

[23] https://developer.mozilla.org/en-US/docs/Web/JavaScript/Reference/Classes

```
const HelloWorld = React.createClass({
    render() { return(<p>Hello, world!</p>) }
})
```

At the time of writing, both types of declarations are in widespread use. The differences between them are minimal. We expose you to both declarations in this book.

If you have some familiarity with JavaScript, the return value may be surprising:

voting_app/public/js/app-1.js

```
    return (
      <div className='ui unstackable items'>
        Hello, friend! I am a basic React component.
      </div>
    );
```

The syntax of the return value doesn't look like traditional JavaScript. We're using **JSX** (JavaScript eXtension syntax), a syntax extension for JavaScript written by Facebook. Using JSX enables us to write the markup for our component views in a familiar, HTML-like syntax. In the end, this JSX code compiles to vanilla JavaScript. Although using JSX is not a necessity, we'll use it in this book as it pairs really well with React.

If you don't have much familiarity with JavaScript, we recommend you follow along and use JSX in your React code too. You'll learn the boundaries between JSX and JavaScript with experience.

JSX

React components ultimately render HTML which is displayed in the browser. As such, the `render()` method of a component needs to describe how the view should be represented as HTML. React builds our apps with a fake representation of the Document Object Model (DOM). React calls this the *virtual DOM*. Without getting deep into details for now, React allows us to describe a component's HTML representation in JavaScript.

The Document Object Model (DOM) refers to the browser's HTML tree that makes up a web page.

JSX was created to make this JavaScript representation of HTML more HTML-like. To understand the difference between HTML and JSX, consider this JavaScript syntax:

```
React.createElement('div', {className: 'ui items'},
  'Hello, friend! I am a basic React component.'
)
```

Which can be represented in JSX as:

```
<div className='ui items'>
  Hello, friend! I am a basic React component.
</div>
```

The code readability is slightly improved in the latter example. This is exacerbated in a nested tree structure:

```
React.createElement('div', {className: 'ui items'},
  React.createElement('p', null, 'Hello, friend! I am a basic React component.')
)
```

In JSX:

```
<div className='ui items'>
  <p>
    Hello, friend! I am a basic React component.
  </p>
</div>
```

JSX presents a light abstraction over the JavaScript version, yet the legibility benefits are huge. Readability boosts our app's longevity and makes it easier to onboard new developers.

Even though the JSX above looks exactly like HTML, it's important to remember that JSX is actually just compiled into JavaScript (ex: `React.createElement('div')`).

During runtime React takes care of rendering the actual HTML in the browser for each component.

The developer console

Our first component is written and we now know that it uses a special flavor of JavaScript called JSX for improved readability.

After editing and saving our `app.js`, let's refresh the page in our web browser and see what changed:

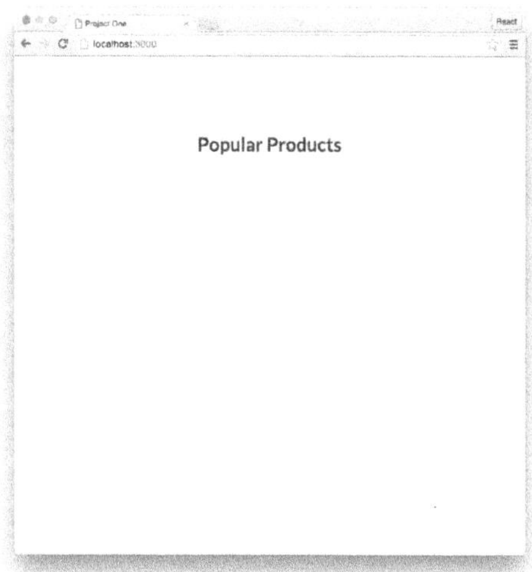

Nothing?

Every major browser comes with a toolkit that helps developers working on JavaScript code. A central part of this toolkit is a console. Think of the console as JavaScript's primary communication medium back to the developer. If JavaScript encounters any errors in its execution, it will alert you in this developer console.

> Our web server, `live-server`, should refresh the page automatically when it detects that `app.js` has changed.

> To open the console in Chrome, navigate to View > Developer > JavaScript Console.
>
> Or, just press `Command` + `Option` + `J` on a Mac or `Control` + `Shift` + `L` on Windows/Linux.

Opening the console, we are given a cryptic clue:

```
Uncaught SyntaxError: Unexpected token <
```

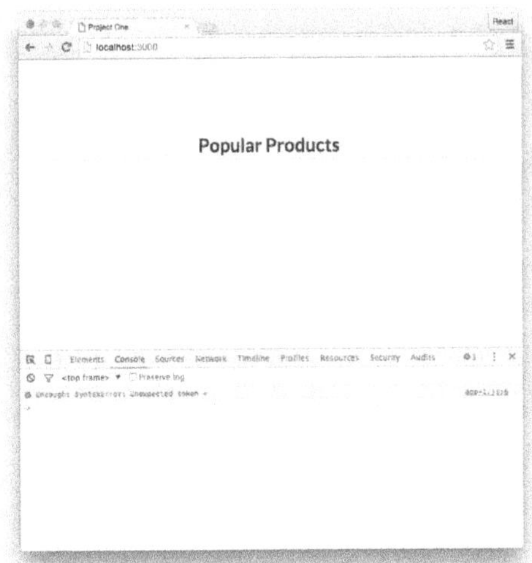

Error in the console

This `SyntaxError` prevented our code from running. A `SyntaxError` is thrown when the JavaScript engine encounters tokens or token order that doesn't conform to the syntax of the language when parsing code. This error type indicates some code is out of place or mistyped.

The issue? **Our browser's JavaScript parser tripped when it encountered the JSX.** The parser doesn't know anything about JSX. As far as it is concerned, this `<` is completely out of place.

As we discussed, JSX is an extension to standard JavaScript. Let's have our browser's JavaScript interpreter use this extension.

Babel

We mentioned at the beginning of the chapter that all the code in the book would be using ES6 JavaScript. However, most browsers in use today do not fully support ES6.

Babel is a JavaScript **transpiler. Babel turns ES6 code into ES5 code**. We call this process **transpiling.** So we can enjoy the features of ES6 today yet ensure our code still runs in browsers that only support ES5.

Another handy feature of Babel is that it understands JSX. Babel compiles our JSX into vanilla ES5 JS that our browser can then interpret and execute. We just need to instruct the browser that we want to use Babel to compile and run our JavaScript code.

The sample code's `index.html` already imports Babel in the `head` tags of `index.html`:

```
<head>
  <!-- ... -->
  <script src="vendor/babel-standalone.js"></script>
  <!-- ... -->
</head>
```

All we need to do is tell our JavaScript runtime that our code should be compiled by Babel. We can do this by setting the `type` attribute when we import the script in `index.html` to `text/babel`.

Open `index.html` and change the script tag that loads `./js/app.js`. We're going to add two attributes:

```
<script src="./js/seed.js"></script>
<script
  type="text/babel"
  data-plugins="transform-class-properties"
  src="./js/app.js"
></script>
```

The attribute `type="text/babel"` indicates to Babel that we would like it to handle the loading of this script. The attribute `data-plugins` specifies a special Babel plugin we use in this book. We discuss this plugin at the end of the chapter.

Save `index.html` and reload the page.

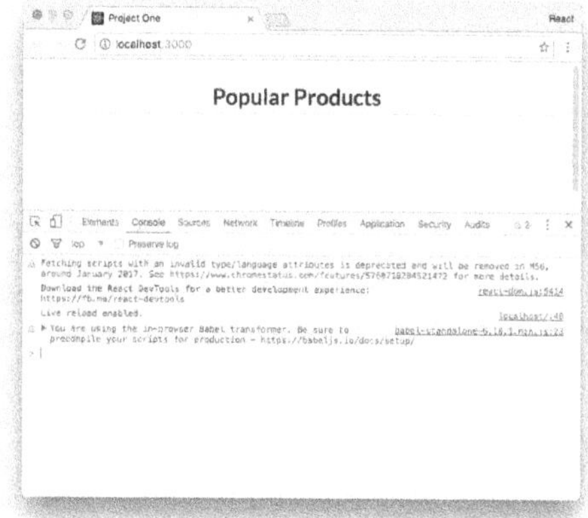

Still nothing. However, the console no longer has the error. Depending on your version of Chrome, you might see some warnings (highlighted in yellow as opposed to red). These warnings are safe to ignore.

Babel successfully compiled our JSX into JavaScript and our browser was able to run that JavaScript without any issues.

So what's happening? We've defined the component, **but we haven't told React to do anything with it yet.** We need to tell the React framework that our component should be inserted on this page.

Depending on your version of Chrome, you might see two errors.

The first:

```
Fetching scripts with an invalid type/language attributes is deprecated and will\
 be removed in M56, around January 2017.
```

This warning is misleading and safe to ignore. The second:

```
You are using the in-browser Babel transformer. Be sure to precompile your scrip\
ts for production
```

Again, safe to ignore. To get up and running quickly, we're having Babel transpile **on-the-fly** in the browser. We explore other JavaScript transpiling strategies later in the book that are more suitable for production.

`ReactDOM.render()`

We need to instruct React to render this `ProductList` inside a specific DOM node.

Add the following code below the component inside `app.js`:

voting_app/public/js/app-1.js

```
class ProductList extends React.Component {
  render() {
    return (
      <div className='ui unstackable items'>
        Hello, friend! I am a basic React component.
      </div>
    );
  }
}

ReactDOM.render(
  <ProductList />,
  document.getElementById('content')
);
```

`ReactDOM` is from the `react-dom` library that we also include in `index.html`. We pass in two arguments to the `ReactDOM.render()` method. The first argument is *what* we'd like to render. The second argument is *where* to render it:

```
ReactDOM.render([what], [where]);
```

Here, for the "what," we're passing in a reference to our React component `ProductList` in JSX. For the "where," you might recall `index.html` contains a `div` tag with an `id` of `content`:

voting_app/public/index.html

```
    <div id="content"></div>
```

We pass in a reference to that DOM node as the second argument to `ReactDOM.render()`.

At this point, it's interesting to note that we use different casing between the different types of React element declarations. We have HTML DOM elements like `<div>` and a React component called `<ProductList />`. In React, native HTML elements *always* start with a lowercase letter whereas React component names *always* start with an uppercase letter.

With `ReactDOM.render()` now at the end of `app.js`, save the file and refresh the page in the browser:

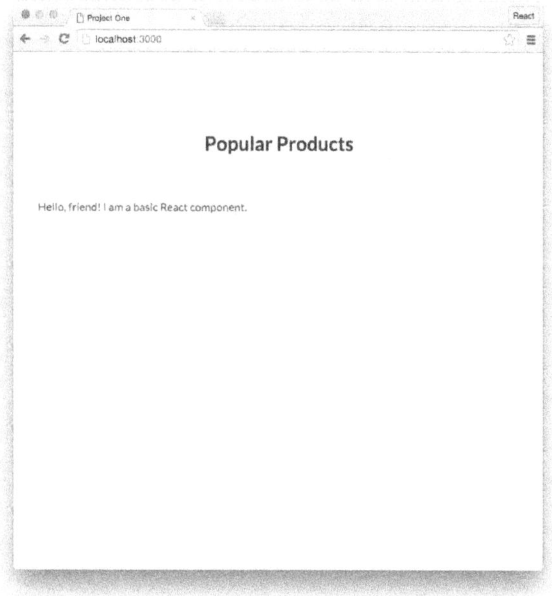

Our component is rendered to the page

To recap, we wrote a React component using an ES6 class as well as JSX. We specified that we wanted Babel to transpile this code to ES5. We then used `ReactDOM.render()` to write this component to the DOM.

While an accomplishment, our current `ProductList` component is rather uninteresting. We eventually want `ProductList` to render a list of products.

Each product will be its own UI element, a fragment of HTML. We can represent each of these elements as their own component, `Product`. Central to its paradigm, React components can render other React components. We'll have `ProductList` render `Product` components, one for each product we'd like to show on the page. Each of these `Product` components will be a **child component** to `ProductList`, the **parent component**.

Building `Product`

Let's build our child component, `Product`, that will contain a product listing. Just like with the `ProductList` component, we'll declare a new ES6 class that extends `React.Component`. We'll define a single method, `render()`:

```
class Product extends React.Component {
  render() {
    return (
      <div>
        {/* ... todo ... */}
      </div>
    );
  }
}

ReactDOM.render(
  // ...
);
```

For every product, we'll add an image, a title, a description, and an avatar of the post author. The markup is below:

voting_app/public/js/app-2.js

```
class Product extends React.Component {
  render() {
    return (
      <div className='item'>
        <div className='image'>
          <img src='images/products/image-aqua.png' />
        </div>
        <div className='middle aligned content'>
```

```
          <div className='description'>
            <a>Fort Knight</a>
            <p>Authentic renaissance actors, delivered in just two weeks.</p>
          </div>
          <div className='extra'>
            <span>Submitted by:</span>
            <img
              className='ui avatar image'
              src='images/avatars/daniel.jpg'
            />
          </div>
        </div>
      </div>
    );
  }
}

ReactDOM.render(
```

The title of the code block above references the location of this example in the book's code download (`voting_app/public/js/app-2.js`). This pattern will be common throughout the book.

If you want to copy and paste the markup into your `app.js`, refer to this file.

Again, we've used a bit of SemanticUI styling in our code here. As we discussed previously, this JSX code will be transpiled to regular JavaScript in the browser. Because it runs in the browser as JavaScript, we cannot use any reserved JavaScript words in JSX. `class` is a reserved word. Therefore, React has us use the attribute name `className`. Later, when the HTML element reaches the page, this attribute name will be written as `class`.

Structurally, the `Product` component is similar to the `ProductList` component. Both have a single `render()` method which returns information about an eventual HTML structure to display.

Remember, the JSX components return is *not* actually the HTML that gets rendered, but is the *representation* that we want React to render in the DOM.

To use the `Product` component, we can modify the render output of our parent `ProductList` component to include the child `Product` component:

voting_app/public/js/app-2.js

```
class ProductList extends React.Component {
  render() {
    return (
      <div className='ui unstackable items'>
        <Product />
      </div>
    );
  }
}
```

Save `app.js` and refresh the web browser.

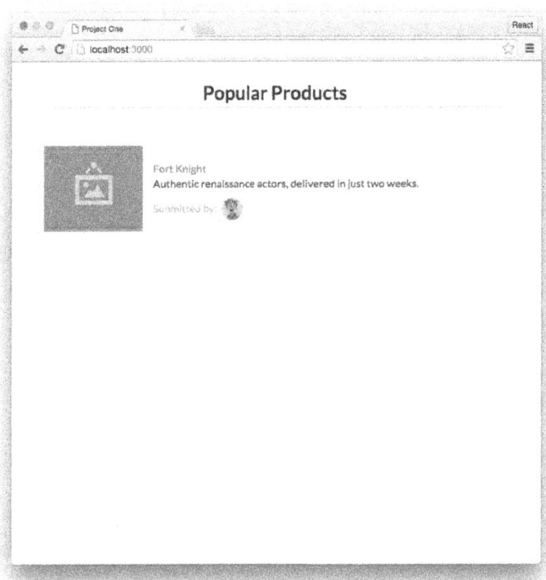

With this update, we now have two React components being rendered in our app. The `ProductList` parent component is rendering the `Product` component as a child nested underneath its root `div` element.

While neat, at the moment the child `Product` component is static. We hard-coded an image, the name, the description, and author details. To use this component in a meaningful way, we'll want to change it to be data-driven and therefore dynamic.

Making `Product` data-driven

Driving the `Product` component with data will allow us to dynamically render the component based upon the data that we give it. Let's familiarize ourselves with the product data model.

The data model

In the sample code, we've included a file inside `public/js` called `seed.js`. `seed.js` contains some example data for our products (it will "seed" our app's data). The `seed.js` file contains a JavaScript object called `Seed.products`. `Seed.products` is an array of JavaScript objects, each representing a product object:

voting_app/public/js/seed.js

```
const products = [
  {
    id: 1,
    title: 'Yellow Pail',
    description: 'On-demand sand castle construction expertise.',
    url: '#',
    votes: generateVoteCount(),
    submitterAvatarUrl: 'images/avatars/daniel.jpg',
    productImageUrl: 'images/products/image-aqua.png',
  },
```

Each product has a unique `id` and a handful of properties including a `title` and `description`. `votes` are randomly generated for each one with the included function `generateVoteCount()`.

We can use the same attribute keys in our React code.

Using props

We want to modify our `Product` component so that it no longer uses static, hard-coded attributes. Instead, we want it to be able to accept data passed down from its parent, `ProductList`. Setting up our component structure in this way enables our `ProductList` component to dynamically render any number of `Product` components that each have their own unique attributes. Data flow will look like this:

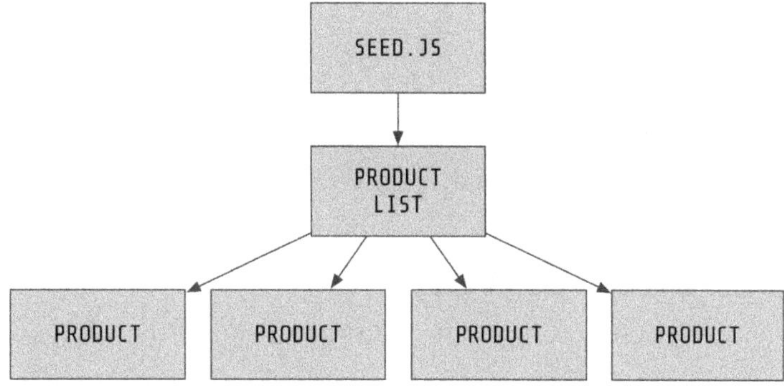

The way data flows from parent to child in React is through **props**. When a parent renders a child, it can send along props the child depends on.

Let's see this in action. First, let's modify `ProductList` to pass down props to `Product`. `seed.js` will save us from having to create a bunch of data manually. Let's pluck the first object off of the `Seed.products` array and use that as data for a single product:

voting_app/public/js/app-3.js

```
class ProductList extends React.Component {
  render() {
    const product = Seed.products[0];
    return (
      <div className='ui unstackable items'>
        <Product
          id={product.id}
          title={product.title}
          description={product.description}
          url={product.url}
          votes={product.votes}
          submitterAvatarUrl={product.submitterAvatarUrl}
          productImageUrl={product.productImageUrl}
        />
      </div>
    );
  }
}
```

Here, the `product` variable is set to a JavaScript object that describes the first of our products. We pass the product's attributes along individually to the `Product` component using the syntax `[propName]=[propValue]`. The syntax of assigning attributes in JSX is exactly the same as HTML and XML.

There are two interesting things here. The first is the braces (`{}`) around each of the property values:

voting_app/public/js/app-3.js

```
          id={product.id}
```

In JSX, braces are a delimiter, signaling to JSX that what resides in-between the braces is a JavaScript expression. The other delimiter is using quotes for strings, like this:

```
id='1'
```

JSX attribute values **must** be delimited by either braces or quotes.

If type is important and we want to pass in something like a Number or a `null`, use braces.

If you've programmed with ES5 JavaScript before, you might be used to using `var` as opposed to `const` or `let`. See "Appendix B" for more on these new declarations.

Now the `ProductList` component is passing props down to `Product`. Our `Product` component isn't using them yet, so let's modify the component to use these props.

In React, a component can access all its props through the object **`this.props`**. Inside of `Product`, the `this.props` object will look like this:

```
{
  "id": 1,
  "title": "Yellow Pail",
  "description": "On-demand sand castle construction expertise.",
  "url": "#",
  "votes": 41,
  "submitterAvatarURL": "images/avatars/daniel.jpg",
  "productImageUrl": "images/products/image-aqua.png"
}
```

Let's swap out everywhere that we hard-coded data and use props instead. While we're here, we'll add a bit more markup like the description and the up-vote icon:

voting_app/public/js/app-3.js

```
class Product extends React.Component {
  render() {
    return (
      <div className='item'>
        <div className='image'>
          <img src={this.props.productImageUrl} />
        </div>
        <div className='middle aligned content'>
          <div className='header'>
            <a>
              <i className='large caret up icon' />
```

```
            </a>
            {this.props.votes}
          </div>
          <div className='description'>
            <a href={this.props.url}>
              {this.props.title}
            </a>
            <p>
              {this.props.description}
            </p>
          </div>
          <div className='extra'>
            <span>Submitted by:</span>
            <img
              className='ui avatar image'
              src={this.props.submitterAvatarUrl}
            />
          </div>
        </div>
      </div>
    );
  }
}
```

Again, everywhere inside of our JSX where we're interpolating a variable we delimit the variable with braces ({}). Note that we're inserting data both as text content inside of tags like this:

voting_app/public/js/app-3.js

```
          <div className='header'>
            <a>
              <i className='large caret up icon' />
            </a>
            {this.props.votes}
          </div>
```

As well as for attributes on HTML elements:

voting_app/public/js/app-3.js

```
          <img src={this.props.productImageUrl} />
```

Interweaving props with HTML elements in this way is how we create dynamic, data-driven React components.

`this` is a special keyword in JavaScript. The details about `this` are a bit nuanced, but for the purposes of the majority of this book, **`this` will be bound to the React component class.** So, when we write `this.props` inside the component, we're accessing the `props` property on the component. When we diverge from this rule in later sections, we'll point it out.

For more details on `this`, check out this page on MDN[24].

With our updated `app.js` file saved, let's refresh the web browser again:

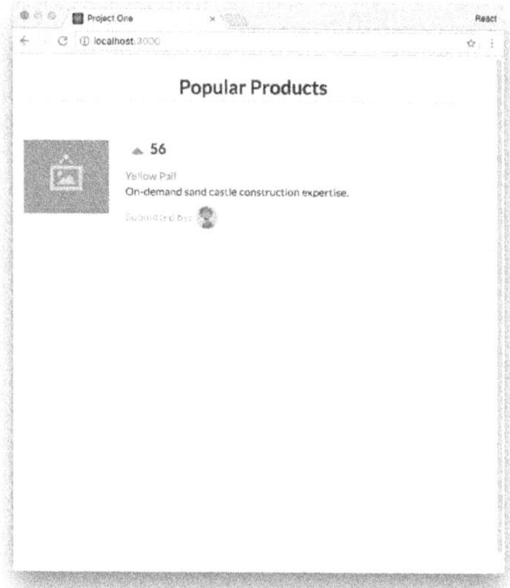

The `ProductList` component now shows a single product listed, the first object pulled from `Seed`.

We're getting somewhere interesting. Our `Product` component is now data-driven. Based on the props it receives it can render any product that we'd like.

Our code is poised to have `ProductList` render any number of products. We just need to configure the component to render some number of `Product` components, one for each product we'd like to represent on the page.

Rendering multiple products

To render multiple products, first we'll have `ProductList` generate an array of `Product` components. Each will be derived from an individual object in the `Seed` array. We'll use map to do so:

[24] https://developer.mozilla.org/en-US/docs/Web/JavaScript/Reference/Operators/this

voting_app/public/js/app-4.js

```
class ProductList extends React.Component {
  render() {
    const productComponents = Seed.products.map((product) => (
      <Product
        key={'product-' + product.id}
        id={product.id}
        title={product.title}
        description={product.description}
        url={product.url}
        votes={product.votes}
        submitterAvatarUrl={product.submitterAvatarUrl}
        productImageUrl={product.productImageUrl}
      />
    ));
```

The function passed to `map` returns a `Product` component. This `Product` is created just as before with props pulled from the object in `Seed`.

We pass an arrow function to `map`. Arrow functions were introduced in ES6. For more info, see "Appendix B."

As such, the `productComponents` variable ends up being an array of `Product` components:

```
// Our `productComponents` array
[
  <Product id={1} ... />,
  <Product id={2} ... />,
  <Product id={3} ... />,
  <Product id={4} ... />
]
```

Notably, we're able to represent the `Product` component instance in JSX inside of `return`. It might seem odd at first that we're able to have a JavaScript array of JSX elements, but remember that Babel will transpile the JSX representation of each `Product` (`<Product />`) into regular JavaScript:

```
// What `productComponents` looks like in JavaScript
[
  React.createElement(Product, { id: 1, ... }),
  React.createElement(Product, { id: 2, ... }),
  React.createElement(Product, { id: 3, ... }),
  React.createElement(Product, { id: 4, ... })
]
```

Array's `map()`

Array's `map` method takes a function as an argument. It calls this function with each item inside of the array (in this case, each object inside `Seed.products`) and builds a **new** array by using the return value from each function call.

Because the `Seed.products` array has four items, `map` will call this function four times, once for each item. When `map` calls this function, it passes in as the first argument an item. The return value from this function call is inserted into the new array that `map` is constructing. After handling the last item, `map` returns this new array. Here, we're storing this new array in the variable `productComponents`.

Note the use of the `key={'product-' + product.id}` prop. React uses this special property to create unique bindings for each instance of the `Product` component. The `key` prop is not used by our `Product` component, but by the React framework. It's a special property that we discuss deeper in the chapter "Advanced Component Configuration." For the time being, it's enough to note that this property needs to be unique per React component in a list.

Now, below the declaration of `productComponents`, we need to modify the return value of `render`. Before, we were rendering a single `Product` component. Now, we can render our array `productComponents`:

voting_app/public/js/app-4.js

```
    return (
      <div className='ui unstackable items'>
        {productComponents}
      </div>
    );
```

Refreshing the page, we'll see all four products from `Seed` listed:

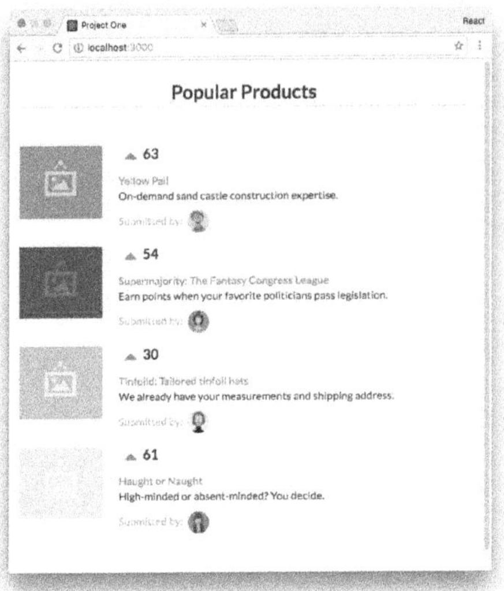

We now have five total React components at work. We have a single parent component, `ProductList`. `ProductList` contains four child `Product` components, one for each product object in the `Seed.products` array in `seed.js`:

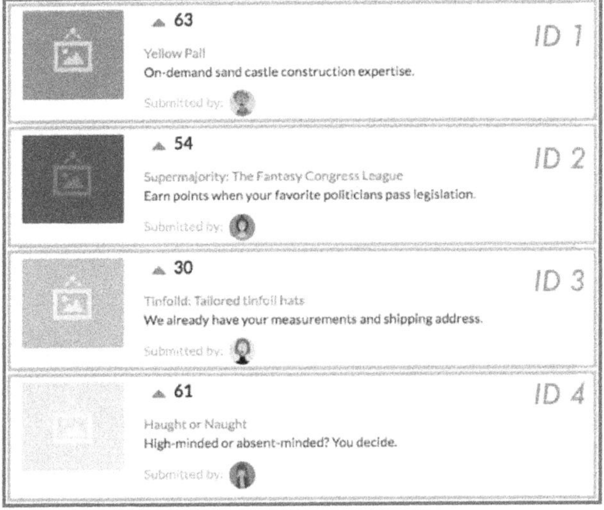

`Product` components inside of the `ProductList` component

At the moment, our products aren't sorted by the number of votes they have. Let's sort them. We'll use Array's sort method to do so. We'll sort the products first before the line where we build our `productComponents` array:

voting_app/public/js/app-5.js

```
class ProductList extends React.Component {
  render() {
    const products = Seed.products.sort((a, b) => (
      b.votes - a.votes
    ));
    const productComponents = products.map((product) => (
      <Product
```

Refreshing the page, we'll see our products are sorted.

`sort()` mutates the original array it was called on. While fine for now, elsewhere in the book we discuss why mutating arrays or objects can be a dangerous pattern.

In the markup for `Product` above, we added an 'up-vote' caret icon. If we click on one of these buttons, we'll see that nothing happens. We've yet to hook up an event to the button.

Although we have a data-driven React app running in our web browser, this page still lacks interactivity. While React has given us an easy and clean way to organize our HTML thus far and enabled us to drive HTML generation based on a flexible, dynamic JavaScript object, we've still yet to tap into its true power: creating dynamic interfaces.

The rest of this book digs deep into this power. Let's start with something simple: the ability to up-vote a given product.

Array's `sort()` method takes an optional function as an argument. If the function is omitted, it will just sort the array by each item's Unicode code point value. This is rarely what a programmer desires. If a function is supplied, elements are sorted according to the function's return value.

On each iteration, the arguments `a` and `b` are two subsequent elements in the array. Sorting depends on the return value of the function:

1. If the return value is less than `0`, `a` should come first (have a lower index).
2. If the return value is greater than `0`, `b` should come first.
3. If the return value is equal to `0`, leave order of `a` and `b` unchanged with respect to each other.

React the vote (your app's first interaction)

When the up-vote button on each one of the `Product` components is clicked, we expect it to update the `votes` attribute for that `Product`, increasing it by one.

But the `Product` component can't modify its `votes`. **`this.props` is immutable.**

While the child can read its props, it can't modify them. A child does not own its props. In our app, **the parent component `ProductList` owns the props given to `Product`.** React favors the idea of *one-way data flow*. This means that data changes come from the "top" of the app and are propagated "downwards" through its various components.

A child component does not own its `props`. Parent components own the `props` of child components.

We need a way for the `Product` component to let `ProductList` know that a click on its up-vote icon occurred. We can then have `ProductList`, the owner of the product's data, update the vote count for that product. The updated data will then flow downward from the `ProductList` component to the `Product` component.

In JavaScript, if we treat an array or object as **immutable** it means we cannot or should not make modifications to it.

Propagating the event

We know that parents communicate data to children through props. Because props are immutable, children need some way to communicate events to parents. The parents could then make whatever data changes might be necessary.

We can pass down *functions* as props too. We can have the `ProductList` component give each `Product` component a function to call when the up-vote button is clicked. Functions passed down through props are the canonical manner in which children communicate events with their parent components.

Let's see this in practice. We'll start by having up-votes log a message to the console. Later, we'll have up-votes increment the `votes` attribute on the target product.

The function `handleProductUpVote` in `ProductList` will accept a single argument, `productId`. The function will log the product's `id` to the console:

voting_app/public/js/app-6.js

```
class ProductList extends React.Component {
  handleProductUpVote(productId) {
    console.log(productId + ' was upvoted.');
  }

  render() {
```

Next, we'll pass this function down as a prop to each `Product` component. We'll name the prop `onVote`:

voting_app/public/js/app-6.js

```
    const productComponents = products.map((product) => (
      <Product
        key={'product-' + product.id}
        id={product.id}
        title={product.title}
        description={product.description}
        url={product.url}
        votes={product.votes}
        submitterAvatarUrl={product.submitterAvatarUrl}
        productImageUrl={product.productImageUrl}
        onVote={this.handleProductUpVote}
      />
    ));
```

We can now access this function inside `Product` via `this.props.onVote`.

Let's write a function inside `Product` that calls this new prop-function. We'll name the function `handleUpVote()`:

voting_app/public/js/app-6.js

```
  // Inside `Product`
  handleUpVote() {
    this.props.onVote(this.props.id);
  }

  render() {
```

We invoke the prop-function `this.props.onVote` with the `id` of the product. Now, we just need to call this function every time the user clicks the caret icon.

In React, we can use the special attribute **`onClick`** to handle mouse click events.

We'll set the `onClick` attribute on the `a` HTML tag that is the up-vote button. We'll instruct it to call `handleUpVote()` whenever it is clicked:

voting_app/public/js/app-6.js

```
        {/* Inside `render` for Product` */}
        <div className='middle aligned content'>
          <div className='header'>
            <a onClick={this.handleUpVote}>
              <i className='large caret up icon' />
            </a>
            {this.props.votes}
          </div>
```

When the user clicks the up-vote icon, it will trigger a chain of function calls:

1. User clicks the up-vote icon.
2. React invokes `Product` component's `handleUpVote`.
3. `handleUpVote` invokes its prop `onVote`. This function lives inside the parent `ProductList` and logs a message to the console.

There's one last thing we need to do to make this work. Inside the function `handleUpVote()` we refer to `this.props`:

voting_app/public/js/app-6.js

```
  handleUpVote() {
    this.props.onVote(this.props.id);
  }
```

Here's the odd part: When working inside `render()`, we've witnessed that `this` is always bound to the component. But inside our custom component method `handleUpVote()`, `this` is actually `null`.

Binding custom component methods

In JavaScript, the special `this` variable has a different **binding** depending on the context. For instance, inside `render()` we say that `this` is "bound" to the component. Put another way, `this` "references" the component.

Understanding the binding of `this` is one of the trickiest parts of learning JavaScript programming. Given this, it's fine for a beginner React programmer to not understand all the nuances at first.

In short, we want `this` inside `handleUpVote()` to reference the component, just like it does inside `render()`. But why does `this` inside `render()` reference the component while `this` inside `handleUpVote()` does not?

For the `render()` function, **React binds `this` to the component for us**. React specifies a default set of special API methods. `render()` is one such method. As we'll see at the end of the chapter, `componentDidMount()` is another. For each of these special React methods, React will bind the `this` variable to the component automatically.

So, **any time we define our own custom component methods, we have to manually bind `this` to the component ourselves**. There's a pattern that we use to do so.

Add the following `constructor()` function to the top of `Product`:

voting_app/public/js/app-6.js

```
class Product extends React.Component {
  constructor(props) {
    super(props);

    this.handleUpVote = this.handleUpVote.bind(this);
  }
```

`constructor()` is a special function in a JavaScript class. JavaScript invokes `constructor()` whenever an object is created via a class. If you've never worked with an object-oriented language before, it's sufficient to know that React invokes `constructor()` first thing when initializing our component. React invokes `constructor()` with the component's props.

Because `constructor()` is called when initializing our component, we'll use it for a couple different types of situations in the book. For our current purposes, it's enough to know that whenever we want to bind custom component methods to a React component class, we can use this pattern:

```
class MyReactComponent extends React.Component {
  constructor(props) {
    super(props); // always call this first

    // custom method bindings here
    this.someFunction = this.someFunction.bind(this);
  }
}
```

If you feel comfortable reading further details on this pattern, see the aside "Binding in `constructor()`".

At the end of the chapter, we'll use an experimental JavaScript feature that allows us to bypass this pattern. However, when working with regular ES7 JavaScript, it's important to keep this pattern in mind:

When defining custom methods on our React component classes, we must perform the binding pattern inside `constructor()` so that `this` references our component.

Saving our updated `app.js`, refreshing our web browser, and clicking an up-vote will log some text to our JavaScript console:

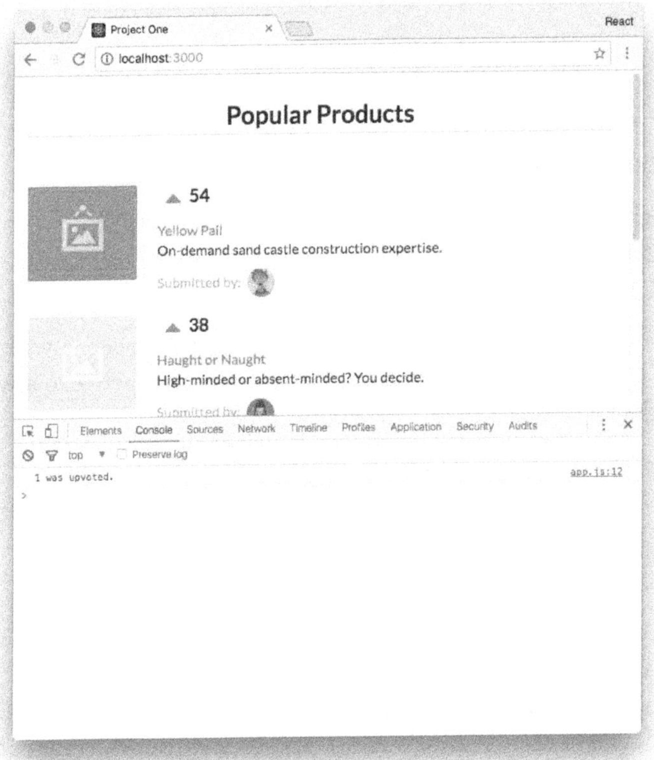

The events are being propagated up to the parent!

`ProductList` is the owner of the product data. And `Product` is now informing its parent whenever a user up-votes a product. Our next task is to update the vote count on the product.

But where do we perform this update? At the moment, our app doesn't have a place to store and manage data. `Seed` should be thought of as a seed of example data, not our app's datastore.

What our app is currently missing is **state**.

In fact, while we might be tempted to update the vote count in `Seed.products` like this:

```
// Would this work?
Seed.products.forEach((product) => {
  if (product.id === productId) {
    product.votes = product.votes + 1;
  }
});
```

Doing so wouldn't work. When updating `Seed`, *our React app would not be informed of the change.* On the user interface there would be no indication that the vote count was incremented.

Binding in `constructor()`

The first thing we do in `constructor()` is call `super(props)`. The `React.Component` class that our `Product` class is extending defines its own `constructor()`. By calling `super(props)`, we're invoking *that* `constructor()` function first.

Importantly, **the `constructor()` function defined by `React.Component` will bind `this` inside *our* `constructor()` to the component**. Because of this, it's a good practice to always call `super()` first whenever you declare a `constructor()` for your component.

After calling `super()`, we call `bind()` on our custom component method:

```
this.handleUpVote = this.handleUpVote.bind(this);
```

Function's `bind()` method allows you to specify what the `this` variable inside a function body should be set to. What we're doing here is a common JavaScript pattern. We're *redefining* the component method `handleUpVote()`, setting it to the same function but bound to `this` (the component). Now, whenever `handleUpVote()` executes, `this` will reference the component as opposed to `null`.

Using state

Whereas props are immutable and owned by a component's parent, **state is owned by the component**. `this.state` is private to the component and as we'll see can be updated with `this.setState()`.

Critically, **when the state or props of a component update, the component will re-render itself.**

Every React component is rendered as a function of its `this.props` and `this.state`. This rendering is deterministic. This means that given a set of props and a set of state, a React component will always render a single way. As we mentioned at the beginning of the chapter, this approach makes for a powerful UI consistency guarantee.

Because we are mutating the data for our products (the number of votes), **we should consider this data to be stateful.** `ProductList` will be the owner of this state. It will then pass this state down as props to `Product`.

At the moment, `ProductList` is reading directly from `Seed` inside `render()` to grab the products. Let's move this data into the component's state.

When adding state to a component, the first thing we do is define what the **initial state** should look like. Because `constructor()` is called when initializing our component, it's the best place to define our initial state.

In React components, state is an object. The shape of our `ProductList` state object will look like this:

```
// Shape of the `ProductList` state object
{
  products: <Array>,
}
```

We'll initialize our state to an object with an empty `products` array. Add this `constructor()` to `ProductList`:

voting_app/public/js/app-7.js

```
class ProductList extends React.Component {
  constructor(props) {
    super(props);

    this.state = {
      products: [],
    };
  }

  componentDidMount() {
    this.setState({ products: Seed.products });
  }
```

Like with our `constructor()` call in `Product`, the first line in `constructor()` is the `super(props)` call. The first line in any `constructor()` functions we write for React components will always be this same line.

Technically, because we don't supply `ProductList` any props, we don't need to propagate the `props` argument to `super()`. But it's a good habit to get into and helps avoid odd bugs in the future.

Next, with our state initialized, let's modify the `ProductList` component's `render` function so that it uses state as opposed to reading from `Seed`. We read the state with `this.state`:

voting_app/public/js/app-7.js

```
  render() {
    const products = this.state.products.sort((a, b) => (
      b.votes - a.votes
    ));
```

`ProductList` is driven by its own state now. If we were to save and refresh now, all our products would be missing. We don't have any mechanisms in `ProductList` that add products to its state.

Setting state with `this.setState()`

It's good practice to initialize components with "empty" state as we've done here. We explore the reasoning behind this when working asynchronously with servers in the chapter "Components & Servers."

However, after our component is initialized, we want to seed the state for `ProductList` with the data in `Seed`.

React specifies a set of **lifecycle methods**. React invokes one lifecycle method, `componentDidMount()`, after our component has mounted to the page. We'll seed the state for `ProductList` inside this method.

We explore the rest of the lifecycle methods in the chapter "Advanced Component Configuration."

Knowing this, we might be tempted to set the state to `Seed.products` inside `componentDidMount()` like this:

```
class ProductList extends React.Component {
  // ...
  // Is this valid ?
  componentDidMount() {
    this.state = Seed.products;
  }
  // ...
}
```

However, this is invalid. The only time we can modify the state in this manner is in `constructor()`. **For all state modifications after the initial state, React provides components the method `this.setState()`.** Among other things, this method triggers the React component to re-render which is essential after the state changes.

Never modify state outside of `this.setState()`. This function has important hooks around state modification that we would be bypassing.

We discuss state management in detail throughout the book.

Add `componentDidMount()` to `ProductList` now. We'll use `setState()` to seed the component's state:

voting_app/public/js/app-8.js

```
class ProductList extends React.Component {
  constructor(props) {
    super(props);

    this.state = {
      products: [],
    };
  }

  componentDidMount() {
    this.setState({ products: Seed.products });
  }
```

The component will mount with an empty state `this.state.products` array. After mounting, we populate the state with data from `Seed`. The component will re-render and our products will be displayed. This happens at a speed that is imperceptible to the user.

If we save and refresh now, we see that the products are back.

Updating state and immutability

Now that `ProductList` is managing the products in state, we're poised to make modifications to this data in response to user input. Specifically, we want to increment the `votes` property on a product when the user votes for it.

We just discussed that we can only make state modifications using `this.setState()`. So while a component can update its state, **we should treat the `this.state` object as immutable.**

As touched on earlier, if we treat an array or object as immutable we never make modifications to it. For example, let's say we have an array of numbers in state:

```
this.setState({ nums: [ 1, 2, 3 ]});
```

If we want to update the state's `nums` array to include a `4`, we might be tempted to use `push()` like this:

```
this.setState({ nums: this.state.nums.push(4) });
```

On the surface, it might appear as though we've treated `this.state` as immutable. However, the `push()` method *modifies the original array*:

```
console.log(this.state.nums);
// [ 1, 2, 3 ]
this.state.nums.push(4);
console.log(this.state.nums);
// [ 1, 2, 3, 4] <-- Uh-oh!
```

Although we invoke `this.setState()` immediately after we push `4` onto the array, we're still modifying `this.state` outside of `setState()` and this is bad practice.

Part of the reason this is bad practice is because **`setState()` is actually asynchronous.** There is no guarantee *when* React will update the state and re-render our component. We touch on this in the "Advanced Component Configuration" chapter.

So, while we eventually called `this.setState()`, we unintentionally modified the state before that.

This next approach doesn't work either:

```
const nextNums = this.state.nums;
nextNums.push(4);
console.log(nextNums);
// [ 1, 2, 3, 4]
console.log(this.state.nums);
// [ 1, 2, 3, 4]  <-- Nope!
```

Our new variable `nextNums` references the same array as `this.state.nums` in memory:

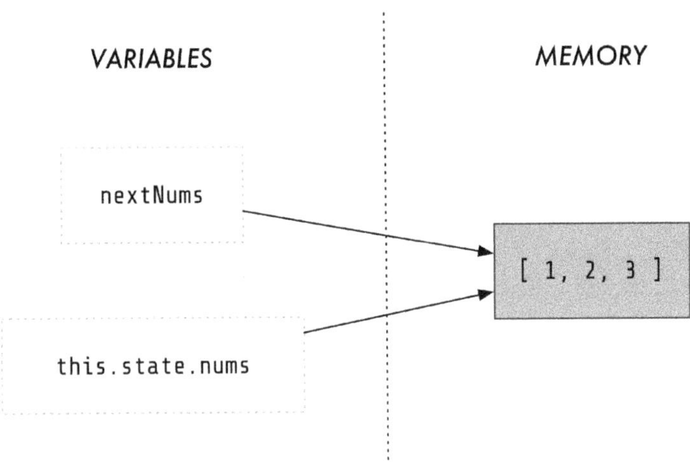

Both variables reference the same array in memory

So when we modify the array with `push()`, we're modifying the same array that `this.state.nums` is pointing to.

Instead, we can use Array's `concat()`. **`concat()` creates a new array** that contains the elements of the array it was called on followed by the elements passed in as arguments.

With `concat()`, we can avoid mutating state:

```
console.log(this.state.nums);
// [ 1, 2, 3 ]
const nextNums = this.state.nums.concat(4);
console.log(nextNums);
// [ 1, 2, 3, 4]
console.log(this.state.nums);
// [ 1, 2, 3 ]  <-- Unmodified!
```

We touch on immutability throughout the book. While you might be able to "get away" with mutating the state in many situations, it's better practice to treat state as immutable.

Treat the state object as immutable. It's important to understand which Array and Object methods modify the objects they are called on.

If an array is passed in as an argument to `concat()`, its elements are appended to the new array. For example:

```
> [ 1, 2, 3 ].concat([ 4, 5 ]);
=> [ 1, 2, 3, 4, 5 ]
```

Knowing that we want to treat the state as immutable, the following approach to handling up-votes would be problematic:

```
// Inside `ProductList`
// Invalid
handleProductUpVote(productId) {
  const products = this.state.products;
  products.forEach((product) => {
    if (product.id === productId) {
      product.votes = product.votes + 1;
    }
  });
  this.setState({
    products: products,
  });
}
```

When we initialize `products` to `this.state.products`, `product` references the same array in memory as `this.state.products`:

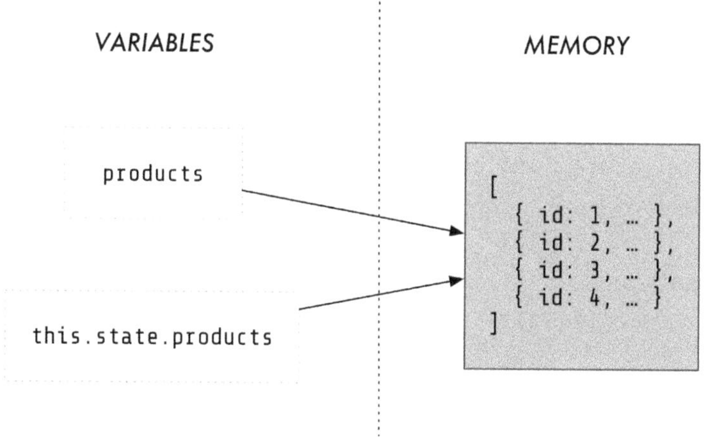

Both variables reference the same array in memory

So, when we modify a `product` object by incrementing its vote count inside `forEach()`, *we're modifying the original product object in state.*

Instead, we should create a *new* array of products. And if we modify one of the product objects, we should modify a *clone* of the object as opposed to the original one.

Let's see what a `handleProductUpVote()` implementation looks like that treats state as immutable. We'll see it in full then break it down:

voting_app/public/js/app-9.js

```
// Inside `ProductList`
handleProductUpVote(productId) {
  const nextProducts = this.state.products.map((product) => {
    if (product.id === productId) {
      return Object.assign({}, product, {
        votes: product.votes + 1,
      });
    } else {
      return product;
    }
  });
  this.setState({
    products: nextProducts,
  });
}
```

First, we use `map()` to traverse the `products` array. Importantly, `map()` returns a *new* array as opposed to modifying the array `this.state.products`.

Next, we check if the current `product` matches `productId`. If it does, we create a *new* object, copying over the properties from the original product object. We then *overwrite* the `votes` property on our new product object. We set it to the incremented vote count. We do this using Object's `assign()` method:

voting_app/public/js/app-9.js

```
    if (product.id === productId) {
      return Object.assign({}, product, {
        votes: product.votes + 1,
      });
```

We use `Object.assign()` a lot for avoiding mutating objects. For more details on the method, check out "Appendix B."

If the current `product` is not the one specified by `productId`, we return it unmodified:

voting_app/public/js/app-9.js

```
      } else {
        return product;
      }
```

Finally, we use `setState()` to update the state.

`map()` is creating a new array. So you might ask: Why can't we modify the `product` object directly? Like this:

```
if (product.id === productId) {
  product.votes = product.votes + 1;
}
```

While we're creating a new array, **the variable `product` here still references the product object sitting on the original array in state**. Therefore, if we make changes to it we'll be modifying the object in state. So we use `Object.assign()` to clone the original into a new object and then modify the `votes` property on that new object.

Our state update for up-votes is in place. There's one last thing we have to do: Our custom component method `handleProductUpVote()` is now referencing `this`. We need to add a `bind()` call like the one we have for `handleUpVote()` in `Product`:

voting_app/public/js/app-9.js

```
class ProductList extends React.Component {
  constructor(props) {
    super(props);

    this.state = {
      products: [],
    };

    this.handleProductUpVote = this.handleProductUpVote.bind(this);
  }
```

Now `this` in `handleProductUpVote()` references our component.

Our app should finally be responsive to user interaction. Save `app.js`, refresh the browser, and cross your fingers:

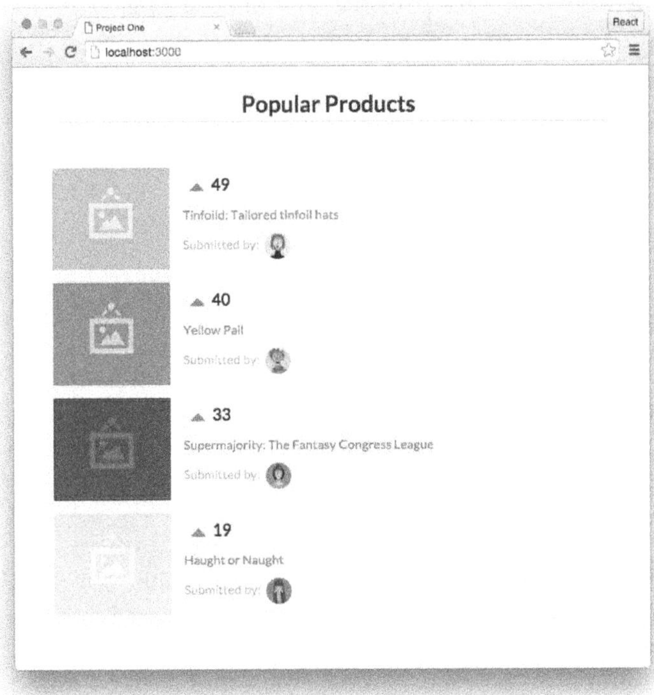

At last, the vote counters are working! Try up-voting a product a bunch of times and notice how it immediately jumps above products with lower vote counts.

Refactoring with the Babel plugin `transform-class-properties`

In this last section, we'll explore a possible refactor that we can make to our class components using an experimental JavaScript feature. For reasons you'll soon see, this feature is popular among React developers. Because the community is still adopting this feature, we expose you to both class component styles throughout the book.

We're able to access this feature using Babel's library of **plugins and presets.**

Babel plugins and presets

We've been using Babel in this project to give us the ability to write modern JavaScript that will run in a majority of browsers on the web. Specifically, our code has been using Babel to convert ES6 syntax and JSX into vanilla ES5 JavaScript.

There's a few ways to integrate Babel into your project. We've been using `babel-standalone` which allows us to setup Babel quickly for use directly in the browser.

`babel-standalone` by default uses two **presets**. In Babel, **a *preset* is a set of *plugins* used to support particular language features**. The two presets Babel has been using by default:

- `es2015`[25]: Adds support for ES2015 (or ES6) JavaScript
- `react`[26]: Adds support for JSX

Remember: ES2015 is just another name used for ES6. We let Babel use the default `es2015` preset for this project because we don't need or use either of ES7's two new features.

JavaScript is an ever-changing language. At its current pace, new syntax will be ratified for adoption on a yearly basis.

Because JavaScript will continue to evolve, tools like Babel are here to stay. Developers want to take advantage of the latest language features. But it takes time for browsers to update their JavaScript engines. And it takes even more time for the majority of the public to upgrade their browsers to the latest versions. Babel closes this gap. It enables a codebase to evolve along with JavaScript without leaving older browsers behind.

Beyond ES7, proposed JavaScript features can exist in various **stages**. A feature can be an experimental proposal, one that the community is still working out the details for ("stage 1"). Experimental proposals are at risk of being dropped or modified at any time. Or a feature might already be "ratified," which means it will be included in the next release of JavaScript ("stage 4").

We can customize Babel with presets and plugins to take advantage of these upcoming or experimental features.

In this book, we generally avoid features that are experimental. However, there is one feature that looks to be ratified that we make an exception for: property initializers.

We avoid features that are experimental because we don't want to teach features that might be modified or dropped. For your own projects, it's up to you and your team to decide how "strict" you want to be about the JavaScript features that you use.

If you'd like to read more about the various Babel presets and plugins, check out the docs[27].

Property initializers

Property initializers are detailed in the proposal "ES Class Fields & Static Properties[28]." While an experimental feature that has yet to be ratified, property initializers offer a compelling syntax that

[25] https://babeljs.io/docs/plugins/preset-es2015/
[26] https://babeljs.io/docs/plugins/preset-react/
[27] https://babeljs.io/docs/plugins/
[28] https://github.com/tc39/proposal-class-public-fields

greatly simplify React class components. This feature works so well with React that the Facebook team has written about using it internally[29].

Property initializers are available in the Babel plugin `transform-class-properties`. Recall that we specified this plugin for `app.js` inside `index.html`:

```
<script
  type="text/babel"
  data-plugins="transform-class-properties"
  src="./js/app.js"
></script>
```

Therefore, we're ready to use this feature in our code. The best way to understand what this feature gives us is to see it in action.

Refactoring `Product`

Inside `Product`, we defined the custom component method `handleUpVote`. As we discussed, because `handleUpVote` is not part of the standard React component API, React does not bind `this` inside the method to our component. So we had to perform a manual binding trick inside `constructor`:

voting_app/public/js/app-9.js

```
class Product extends React.Component {
  constructor(props) {
    super(props);

    this.handleUpVote = this.handleUpVote.bind(this);
  }

  handleUpVote() {
    this.props.onVote(this.props.id);
  }

  render() {
```

With the `transform-class-properties` plugin, **we can write `handleUpVote` as an arrow function. This will ensure `this` inside the function is bound to the component**, as expected:

[29] https://babeljs.io/blog/2015/06/07/react-on-es6-plus

voting_app/public/js/app-complete.js

```
class Product extends React.Component {
  handleUpVote = () => (
    this.props.onVote(this.props.id)
  );

  render() {
```

Using this feature, we can drop `constructor()`. There is no need for the manual binding call.

Note that methods that are part of the standard React API, like `render()`, will remain as class methods. If we write a custom component method in which we want `this` bound to the component, we write it as an arrow function.

Refactoring `ProductList`

We can give the same treatment to `handleProductUpVote` inside `ProductList`. In addition, property initializers give us an alternative way to define the initial state of a component.

Before, we used `constructor()` in `ProductList` to both bind `handleProductUpVote` to the component and define the component's initial state:

```
class ProductList extends React.Component {
  constructor(props) {
    super(props);

    this.state = {
      products: [],
    };

    this.handleProductUpVote = this.handleProductUpVote.bind(this);
  }
```

With property initializers, we no longer need to use `constructor`. Instead, we can define the initial state like this:

voting_app/public/js/app-complete.js

```
class ProductList extends React.Component {
  state = {
    products: [],
  };
```

And, if we define `handleProductUpVote` as an arrow function, `this` will be bound to the component as desired:

voting_app/public/js/app-complete.js

```
  handleProductUpVote = (productId) => {
    const nextProducts = this.state.products.map((product) => {
      if (product.id === productId) {
        return Object.assign({}, product, {
          votes: product.votes + 1,
        });
      } else {
        return product;
      }
    });
    this.setState({
      products: nextProducts,
    });
  }
```

In sum, we can use property initializers to make two refactors to our React components:

1. We can use arrow functions for custom component methods (and avoid having to bind `this`)
2. We can define the initial state outside of `constructor()`

We expose you to both approaches in this book as both are in widespread use. Each project will be consistent as to whether or not it uses `transform-class-properties`. You're welcome to continue to use vanilla ES6 in your own projects. However, the terseness afforded by `transform-class-properties` is often too attractive to pass up.

Using ES6/ES7 with additional presets or plugins is sometimes referred to by the community as "ES6+/ES7+."

Congratulations!

We just wrote our first React app. There are a ton of powerful features we've yet to go over, yet all of them build upon the core fundamentals we just covered:

1. We think about and organize our React apps as components
2. Using JSX inside the `render` method
3. Data flows from parent to children through props
4. Event flows from children to parent through functions
5. Utilizing React lifecycle methods
6. Stateful components and how state is different from props
7. How to manipulate state while treating it as immutable

Onward!

Components

A time-logging app

In the last chapter, we described how React organizes apps into components and how data flows between parent and child components. And we discussed core concepts such as how we manage **state** and pass data between components using **props**.

In this chapter, we construct a more intricate application. We investigate a pattern that you can use to build React apps from scratch and then put those steps to work to build an interface for managing timers.

In this time-tracking app, a user can add, delete, and modify various timers. Each timer corresponds to a different task that the user would like to keep time for:

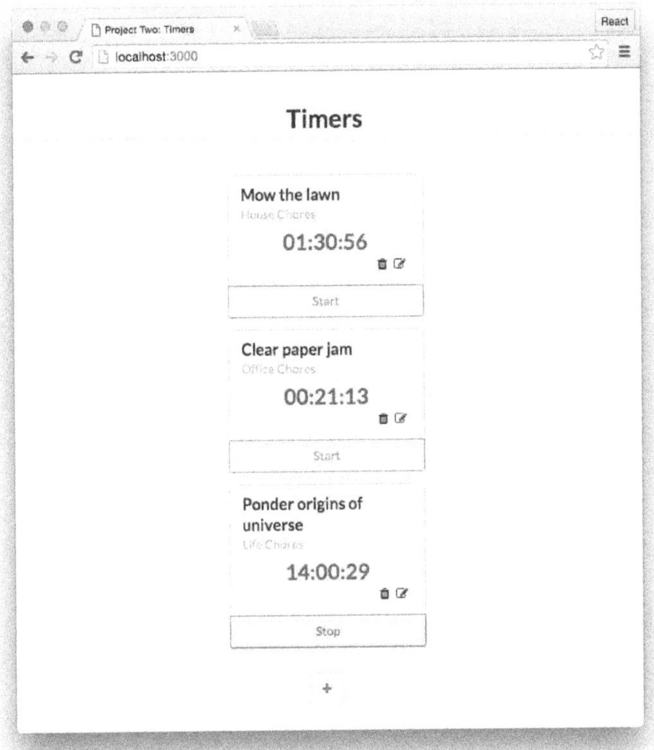

This app will have significantly more interactive capabilities than the one built in the last chapter. This will present us with some interesting challenges that will deepen our familiarity with React's core concepts.

Getting started

As with all chapters, before beginning make sure you've downloaded the book's sample code and have it at the ready.

Previewing the app

Let's begin by playing around with a completed implementation of the app.

In your terminal, `cd` into the `time_tracking_app` directory:

```
$ cd time_tracking_app
```

Use npm to install all the dependencies:

```
$ npm install
```

Then boot the server:

```
$ npm start
```

Now you can view the app in your browser. Open your browser and enter the URL `http://localhost:3000`.

Play around with it for a few minutes to get a feel for all the functionality. Refresh and note that your changes have been persisted.

Note that this app uses a different web server than the one used in the voting app. The app won't automatically launch in your browser or automatically refresh when you make changes.

Prepare the app

In your terminal, run `ls` to see the project's layout:

```
$ ls
README.md
data.json
nightwatch.json
node_modules/
package.json
public/
semantic.json
server.js
tests/
```

There are a few organizational changes from the last project.

First, notice that there is now a `server.js` in this project. In the last chapter, we used a pre-built Node package (called `live-server`) to serve our assets.

This time we have a custom-built server which serves our assets and also adds a persistence layer. We will cover the server in detail in the next chapter.

When you visit a website, **assets** are the files that your browser downloads and uses to display the page. `index.html` is delivered to the browser and inside its `head` tags it specifies which additional files from the server the browser needs to download.

In the last project, our assets were `index.html` as well as our stylesheets and images.

In this project, everything under `public/` is an asset.

In the voting app, we loaded all of our app's initial data from a JavaScript variable, loaded in the file `seed.js`.

This time, we're going to eventually store it in the text file `data.json`. This brings the behavior a bit closer to a database. By using a JSON file, we can make edits to our data that will be persisted even if the app is closed.

JSON stands for JavaScript Object Notation. JSON enables us to serialize a JavaScript object and read/write it from a text file.

If you're not familiar with JSON, take a look at `data.json`. Pretty recognizable, right? JavaScript has a built-in mechanism to parse the contents of this file and initialize a JavaScript object with its data.

Peek inside `public`:

```
$ cd public
$ ls
```

The structure here is the same as the last project:

```
favicon.ico
index.html
js/
semantic/
style.css
vendor/
```

Again, `index.html` is the centerpiece of the app. It's where we include all of our JavaScript and CSS files and where we specify the DOM node where we'll ultimately mount our React app.

We're using SemanticUI again here for styling. All of SemanticUI's assets are underneath `semantic/`.

All our JavaScript files are inside of `js/`:

```
$ ls js/
app-1.js
app-2.js
app-3.js
app-4.js
app-5.js
app-6.js
app-7.js
app-8.js
app-9.js
app-complete.js
app.js
client.js
helpers.js
```

We'll be building the app inside `app.js`. The completed version of the app which we reach in the next chapter is inside `app-complete.js`. Each step we take along the way is included here: `app-1.js`, `app-2.js`, and so forth. Like the last chapter, code examples in the book are titled with the file in which you can find that example.

Furthermore, we'll be using a couple additional JavaScript files for this project. As we'll see, `client.js` contains functions that we'll use to interface with our server in the next chapter. `helpers.js` contains some helper functions that our components will use.

As before, our first step is to ensure `app-complete.js` is no longer loaded in `index.html`. We'll instead load the empty file `app.js`.

Open up `index.html`:

time_tracking_app/public/index.html

```
<!DOCTYPE html>
<html>

  <head>
    <meta charset="utf-8">
    <title>Project Two: Timers</title>
    <link rel="stylesheet" href="./semantic-dist/semantic.css" />
    <link rel="stylesheet" href="style.css" />
    <script src="vendor/babel-standalone.js"></script>
    <script src="vendor/react.js"></script>
    <script src="vendor/react-dom.js"></script>
    <script src="vendor/uuid.js"></script>
    <script src="vendor/fetch.js"></script>
  </head>

  <body>
    <div id="main" class="main ui">
      <h1 class="ui dividing centered header">Timers</h1>
      <div id="content"></div>
    </div>
    <script type="text/babel" src="./js/client.js"></script>
    <script type="text/babel" src="./js/helpers.js"></script>
    <script
      type="text/babel"
      data-plugins="transform-class-properties"
      src="./js/app.js"
    ></script>
    <!-- Delete the script tag below to get started. -->
    <script
      type="text/babel"
      data-plugins="transform-class-properties"
      src="./js/app-complete.js"
    ></script>
  </body>

</html>
```

Overall, this file is very similar to the one we used in our voting app. We load in our dependencies within the `head` tags (the assets). Inside of `body` we have a few elements. This `div` is where we will ultimately mount our React app:

time_tracking_app/public/index.html

```
      <div id="content"></div>
```

And this `script` tag is where we instruct the browser to load `app.js` into the page:

time_tracking_app/public/index.html

```
    <script
      type="text/babel"
      data-plugins="transform-class-properties"
      src="./js/app.js"
    ></script>
```

We're using the Babel plugin `transform-class-properties` again in this chapter. We discussed this plugin at the end of the previous chapter.

Do as the comment says and delete the `script` tag that loads `app-complete.js`:

```
<script
  type="text/babel"
  data-plugins="transform-class-properties"
  src="./js/app.js"
></script>
<!-- Delete the script tag below to get started. -->
<script
  type="text/babel"
  data-plugins="transform-class-properties"
  src="./js/app-complete.js"
></script>
```

Save `index.html`. If you reload the page now, you'll see the app has disappeared.

Breaking the app into components

As we did with our last project, we begin by breaking our app down into its components. Again, visual components often map tightly to their respective React components. Let's examine the interface of our app:

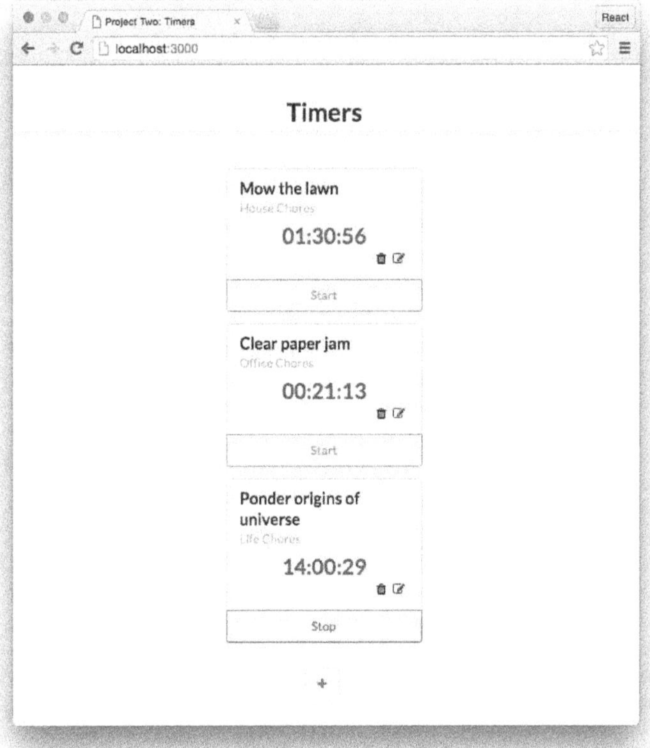

In the last project, we had `ProductList` and `Product` components. The first contained instances of the second. Here, we spot the same pattern, this time with `TimerList` and `Timer` components:

However, there's one subtle difference: This list of timers has a little "+" icon at the bottom. As we saw, we're able to add new timers to the list using this button. So, in reality, the `TimerList` component isn't just a list of timers. It also contains a widget to create new timers.

Think about components as you would functions or objects. The single responsibility principle[30] applies. A component should, ideally, **only be responsible for one piece of functionality**. So, the proper response here is for us to shrink `TimerList` back into its responsibility of just listing timers and to nest it under a parent component. We'll call the parent `TimersDashboard`. `TimersDashboard` will have `TimerList` and the "+"/create form widget as children:

[30]https://en.wikipedia.org/wiki/Single_responsibility_principle

Not only does this separation of responsibilities keep components simple, but it often also improves their re-usability. In the future, we can now drop the `TimerList` component anywhere in the app where we just want to display a list of timers. This component no longer carries the responsibility of also creating timers, which might be a behavior we want to have for just this dashboard view.

How you name your components is indeed up to you, but having some consistent rules around language as we do here will greatly improve code clarity.

In this case, developers can quickly reason that any component they come across that ends in the word `List` simply renders a list of children and no more.

The "+"/create form widget is interesting because it has two distinct representations. When the "+" button is clicked, the widget transmutes into a form. When the form is closed, the widget transmutes back into a "+" button.

There are two approaches we could take. The first one is to have the parent component, `TimersDashboard`, decide whether or not to render a "+" component or a form component based on some piece of stateful data. It could swap between the two children. However, this adds more responsibility to `TimersDashboard`. The alternative is to have a new child component own the single responsibility of determining whether or not to display a "+" button or a create timer form. We'll call it `ToggleableTimerForm`. As a child, it can either render the component `TimerForm` or the HTML markup for the "+" button.

At this point, we've carved out four components:

Now that we have a sharp eye for identifying overburdened components, another candidate should catch our eye:

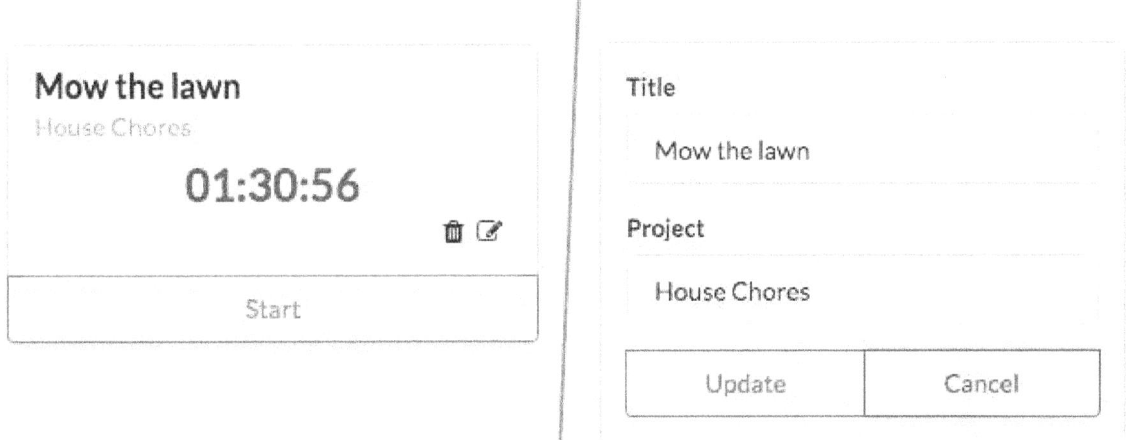

A single timer: Displaying time (left) vs. edit form (right)

The timer itself has a fair bit of functionality. It can transform into an edit form, delete itself, and start and stop itself. Do we need to break this up? And if so, how?

Displaying a timer and editing a timer are indeed two distinct UI elements. They should be two distinct React components. Like `ToggleableTimerForm`, we need some container component that renders either the timer's face or its edit form depending on if the timer is being edited.

We'll call this `EditableTimer`. The child of `EditableTimer` will then be either a `Timer` component or the edit form component. The form for creating and editing timers is very similar, so let's assume that we can use the component `TimerForm` in both contexts:

As for the other functionality of the timer, like the start and stop buttons, it's a bit tough to determine at this point whether or not they should be their own components. We can trust that the answers will be more apparent after we've written some code.

Working back up the component tree, we can see that the name `TimerList` would be a misnomer. It really is a `EditableTimerList`. Everything else looks good.

So, we have our final component hierarchy, with some ambiguity around the final state of the timer component:

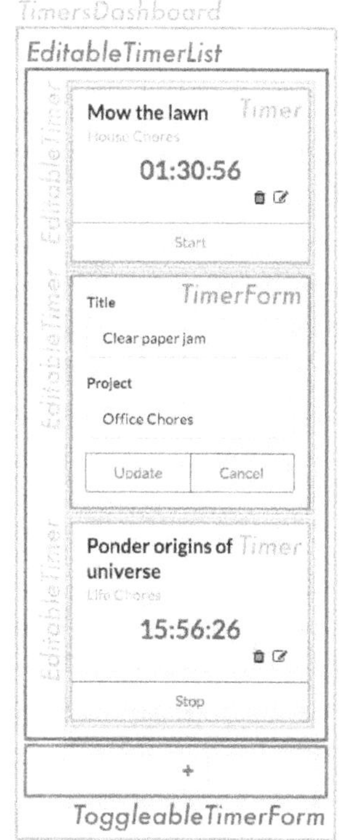

- `TimersDashboard`: Parent container
  - `EditableTimerList`: Displays a list of timer containers
    * `EditableTimer`: Displays either a timer or a timer's edit form
      · `Timer`: Displays a given timer
      · `TimerForm`: Displays a given timer's edit form
  - `ToggleableTimerForm`: Displays a form to create a new timer
    * `TimerForm` (not displayed): Displays a new timer's create form

Represented as a hierarchical tree:

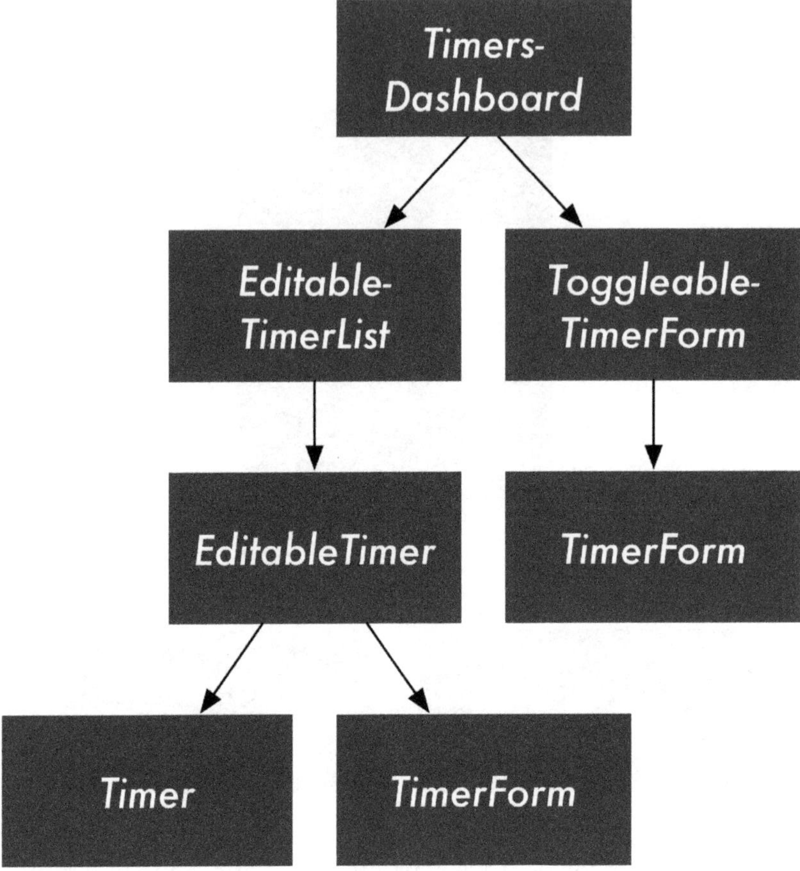

In our previous app, `ProductList` handled not only rendering components, but also the responsibility of handling up-votes and talking to the store. While this worked for that app, you can imagine that as a codebase expands, there may come a day where we'd want to free `ProductList` of this responsibility.

For example, imagine if we added a "sort by votes" feature to `ProductList`. What if we wanted some pages to be sortable (category pages) but other pages to be static (top 10)? We'd want to "hoist" sort responsibility up to a parent component and make `ProductList` the straightforward list renderer that it should be.

This new parent component could then include the sorting-widget component and then pass down the ordered products to the `ProductList` component.

The steps for building React apps from scratch

Now that we have a good understanding of the composition of our components, we're ready to build a static version of our app. Ultimately, our top-level component will communicate with a server. The

server will be the initial source of state, and React will render itself according to the data the server provides. Our app will also send updates to the server, like when a timer is started:

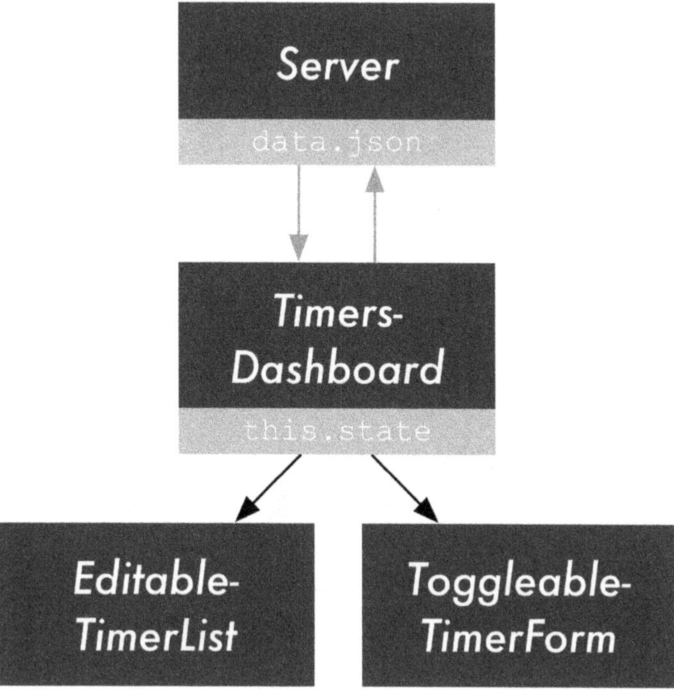

However, it will simplify things for us if we start off with static components, as we did in the last chapter. Our React components will do little more than render HTML. Clicking on buttons won't yield any behavior as we will not have wired up any interactivity. This will enable us to lay the framework for the app, getting a clear idea of how the component tree is organized.

Next, we can determine what the **state** should be for the app and in which component it should live. We'll start off by just hard-coding the state into the components instead of loading it from the server.

At that point, we'll have the data flow **from parent to child** in place. Then we can add inverse data flow, propagating events **from child to parent**.

Finally, we'll modify the top-level component to have it communicate with the server.

In fact, this follows from a handy framework for developing a React app from scratch:

1. Break the app into components
2. Build a static version of the app
3. Determine what should be stateful
4. Determine in which component each piece of state should live
5. Hard-code initial states
6. Add inverse data flow

7. Add server communication

We followed this pattern in the last project:

1. Break the app into components

We looked at the desired UI and determined we wanted `ProductList` and `Product` components.

2. Build a static version of the app

Our components started off without using `state`. Instead, we had `ProductList` pass down static props to `Product`.

3. Determine what should be stateful

In order for our application to become interactive, we had to be able to modify the vote property on each product. Each product had to be mutable and therefore stateful.

4. Determine in which component each piece of state should live

`ProductList` managed the voting state using React component class methods.

5. Hard-code initial state

When we re-wrote `ProductList` to use `this.state`, we seeded it from `Seed.products`.

6. Add inverse data flow

We defined the `handleUpVote` function in `ProductList` and passed it down in props so that each `Product` could inform `ProductList` of up-vote events.

7. Add server communication

We did not add a server component to our last app, but we will be doing so in this one.

If steps in this process aren't completely clear right now, don't worry. The purpose of this chapter is to familiarize yourself with this procedure.

We've already covered step (1) and have a good understanding of all of our components, save for some uncertainty down at the `Timer` component. Step (2) is to build a static version of the app. As in the last project, this amounts to defining React components, their hierarchy, and their HTML representation. We completely avoid state for now.

Step 2: Build a static version of the app

`TimersDashboard`

Let's start off with the `TimersDashboard` component. Again, all of our React code for this chapter will be inside of the file `public/app.js`.

We'll begin by defining a familiar function, `render()`:

time_tracking_app/public/js/app-1.js

```
class TimersDashboard extends React.Component {
  render() {
    return (
      <div className='ui three column centered grid'>
        <div className='column'>
          <EditableTimerList />
          <ToggleableTimerForm
            isOpen={true}
          />
        </div>
      </div>
    );
  }
}
```

This component renders its two child components nested under `div` tags. `TimersDashboard` passes down one prop to `ToggleableTimerForm`: `isOpen`. This is used by the child component to determine whether to render a "+" or `TimerForm`. When `ToggleableTimerForm` is "open" the form is being displayed.

As in the last chapter, don't worry about the `className` attribute on the `div` tags. This will ultimately define the `class` on HTML `div` elements and is purely for styling purposes.

In this example, classes like `ui three column centered grid` all come from the CSS framework Semantic UI[31]. The framework is included in the `head` of `index.html`.

We will define `EditableTimerList` next. We'll have it render two `EditableTimer` components. One will end up rendering a timer's face. The other will render a timer's edit form:

time_tracking_app/public/js/app-1.js

```
class EditableTimerList extends React.Component {
  render() {
    return (
      <div id='timers'>
        <EditableTimer
          title='Learn React'
          project='Web Domination'
          elapsed='8986300'
          runningSince={null}
```

[31] http://semantic-ui.com

```
          editFormOpen={false}
        />
        <EditableTimer
          title='Learn extreme ironing'
          project='World Domination'
          elapsed='3890985'
          runningSince={null}
          editFormOpen={true}
        />
      </div>
    );
  }
}
```

We're passing five props to each child component. The key difference between the two `EditableTimer` components is the value being set for `editFormOpen`. We'll use this boolean to instruct `EditableTimer` which sub-component to render.

The purpose of the prop `runningSince` will be covered later on in the app's development.

EditableTimer

`EditableTimer` returns either a `TimerForm` or a `Timer` based on the prop `editFormOpen`:

time_tracking_app/public/js/app-1.js

```
class EditableTimer extends React.Component {
  render() {
    if (this.props.editFormOpen) {
      return (
        <TimerForm
          title={this.props.title}
          project={this.props.project}
        />
      );
    } else {
      return (
        <Timer
          title={this.props.title}
          project={this.props.project}
```

```
          elapsed={this.props.elapsed}
          runningSince={this.props.runningSince}
        />
      );
    }
  }
}
```

Note that `title` and `project` are passed down as props to `TimerForm`. This will enable the component to fill in these fields with the timer's current values.

`TimerForm`

We'll build an HTML form that will have two input fields. The first input field is for the title and the second is for the project. It also has a pair of buttons at the bottom:

time_tracking_app/public/js/app-1.js

```
class TimerForm extends React.Component {
  render() {
    const submitText = this.props.title ? 'Update' : 'Create';
    return (
      <div className='ui centered card'>
        <div className='content'>
          <div className='ui form'>
            <div className='field'>
              <label>Title</label>
              <input type='text' defaultValue={this.props.title} />
            </div>
            <div className='field'>
              <label>Project</label>
              <input type='text' defaultValue={this.props.project} />
            </div>
            <div className='ui two bottom attached buttons'>
              <button className='ui basic blue button'>
                {submitText}
              </button>
              <button className='ui basic red button'>
                Cancel
              </button>
            </div>
          </div>
```

```
        </div>
      </div>
    );
  }
}
```

Look at the `input` tags. We're specifying that they have `type` of `text` and then we are using the React property `defaultValue`. When the form is used for editing as it is here, this sets the fields to the current values of the timer as desired.

Later, we'll use `TimerForm` again within `ToggleableTimerForm` for *creating* timers. `ToggleableTimerForm` will not pass `TimerForm` any props. `this.props.title` and `this.props.project` will therefore return `undefined` and the fields will be left empty.

At the beginning of `render()`, before the `return` statement, we define a variable `submitText`. This variable uses the presence of `this.props.title` to determine what text the submit button at the bottom of the form should display. If `title` is present, we know we're editing an existing timer, so it displays "Update." Otherwise, it displays "Create."

With all of this logic in place, `TimerForm` is prepared to render a form for creating a new timer or editing an existing one.

We used an expression with the **ternary operator** to set the value of `submitText`. The syntax is:

```
condition ? expression1 : expression2
```

If the `condition` is true, the operator returns the value of `expression1`. Otherwise, it returns the value of `expression2`. In our example, the variable `submitText` is set to the returned expression.

`ToggleableTimerForm`

Let's turn our attention next to `ToggleableTimerForm`. Recall that this is a wrapper component around `TimerForm`. It will display either a "+" or a `TimerForm`. Right now, it accepts a single prop, `isOpen`, from its parent that instructs its behavior:

time_tracking_app/public/js/app-1.js

```
class ToggleableTimerForm extends React.Component {
  render() {
    if (this.props.isOpen) {
      return (
        <TimerForm />
      );
    } else {
      return (
        <div className='ui basic content center aligned segment'>
          <button className='ui basic button icon'>
            <i className='plus icon' />
          </button>
        </div>
      );
    }
  }
}
```

As noted earlier, `TimerForm` does not receive any props from `ToggleableTimerForm`. As such, its `title` and `project` fields will be rendered empty.

The return statement under the `else` block is the markup to render a "+" button. You could make a case that this should be its own React component (say `PlusButton`) but at present we'll keep the code inside `ToggleableTimerForm`.

`Timer`

Time for the `Timer` component. Again, don't worry about all the `div` and `span` elements and `className` attributes. We've provided these for styling purposes:

time_tracking_app/public/js/app-1.js

```
class Timer extends React.Component {
  render() {
    const elapsedString = helpers.renderElapsedString(this.props.elapsed);
    return (
      <div className='ui centered card'>
        <div className='content'>
          <div className='header'>
            {this.props.title}
          </div>
```

```
          <div className='meta'>
            {this.props.project}
          </div>
          <div className='center aligned description'>
            <h2>
              {elapsedString}
            </h2>
          </div>
          <div className='extra content'>
            <span className='right floated edit icon'>
              <i className='edit icon' />
            </span>
            <span className='right floated trash icon'>
              <i className='trash icon' />
            </span>
          </div>
        </div>
        <div className='ui bottom attached blue basic button'>
          Start
        </div>
      </div>
    );
  }
}
```

`elapsed` in this app is in milliseconds. This is the representation of the data that React will keep. This is a good representation for machines, but we want to show our carbon-based users a more readable format.

We use a function defined in `helpers.js`, `renderElapsedString()`. You can pop open that file if you're curious about how it's implemented. The string it renders is in the format 'HH:MM:SS'.

Note that we could store `elapsed` in seconds as opposed to milliseconds, but JavaScript's time functionality is all in milliseconds. We keep `elapsed` consistent with this for simplicity. As a bonus, our timers are also slightly more accurate, even though they round to seconds when displayed to the user.

Render the app

With all of the components defined, the last step before we can view our static app is to ensure we call `ReactDOM#render()`. Put this at the bottom of the file:

time_tracking_app/public/js/app-1.js

```
ReactDOM.render(
  <TimersDashboard />,
  document.getElementById('content')
);
```

Again, we specify with `ReactDOM#render()` *which* React component we want to render and *where* in our HTML document (`index.html`) to render it.

In this case, we're rendering `TimersDashboard` at the `div` with the `id` of `content`.

Try it out

Save `app.js` and boot the server (`npm start`). Find it at `localhost:3000`:

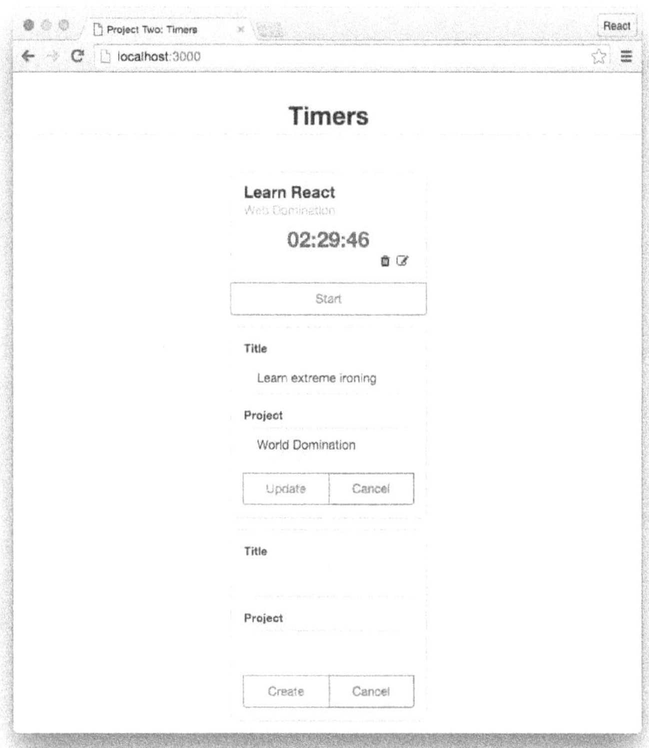

Tweak some of the props and refresh to see the results. For example:

- Flip the prop passed down to `ToggleableTimerForm` from `true` to `false` and see the "+" button render.

- Flip parameters on `editFormOpen` and witness `EditableTimer` flip the child it renders accordingly.

Let's review all of the components represented on the page:

Inside `TimersDashboard` are two child components: `EditableTimerList` and `ToggleableTimerForm`.

`EditableTimerList` contains two `EditableTimer` components. The first of these has a `Timer` component as a child and the second a `TimerForm`. These bottom-level components — also known as **leaf components** — hold the majority of the page's HTML. This is generally the case. The components above leaf components are primarily concerned with orchestration.

`ToggleableTimerForm` renders a `TimerForm`. Notice how the two forms on the page have different language for their buttons, as the first is updating and the second is creating.

Step 3: Determine what should be stateful

In order to bestow our app with interactivity, we must evolve it from its static existence to a mutable one. The first step is determining *what*, exactly, should be mutable. Let's start by collecting all of the data that's employed by each component in our static app. In our static app, data will be wherever we are defining or using props. We will then determine which of that data should be stateful.

`TimersDashboard`

In our static app, this declares two child components. It sets one prop, which is the `isOpen` boolean that is passed down to `ToggleableTimerForm`.

`EditableTimerList`

This declares two child components, each which have props corresponding to a given timer's properties.

`EditableTimer`

This uses the prop `editFormOpen`.

`Timer`

This uses all the props for a timer.

`TimerForm`

This has two interactive input fields, one for `title` and one for `project`. When editing an existing timer, these fields are initialized with the timer's current values.

State criteria

We can apply criteria to determine if data should be stateful:

These questions are from the excellent article by Facebook called "Thinking In React". You can read the original article here[32].

1. Is it passed in from a parent via props? If so, it probably isn't state.

A lot of the data used in our child components are already listed in their parents. This criterion helps us de-duplicate.

For example, "timer properties" is listed multiple times. When we see the properties declared in `EditableTimerList`, we can consider it state. But when we see it elsewhere, it's not.

2. Does it change over time? If not, it probably isn't state.

This is a key criterion of stateful data: it changes.

3. Can you compute it based on any other state or props in your component? If so, it's not state.

For simplicity, we want to strive to represent state with as few data points as possible.

Applying the criteria

`TimersDashboard`

- `isOpen` boolean for `ToggleableTimerForm`

Stateful. The data is defined here. It changes over time. And it cannot be computed from other state or props.

`EditableTimerList`

- Timer properties

Stateful. The data is defined in this component, changes over time, and cannot be computed from other state or props.

`EditableTimer`

- `editFormOpen` for a given timer

Stateful. The data is defined in this component, changes over time, and cannot be computed from other state or props.

`Timer`

[32] https://facebook.github.io/react/docs/thinking-in-react.html

- Timer properties

In this context, **not stateful**. Properties are passed down from the parent.

`TimerForm`

We might be tempted to conclude that `TimerForm` doesn't manage any stateful data, as `title` and `project` are props passed down from the parent. However, as we'll see, forms are special state managers in their own right.

So, outside of `TimerForm`, we've identified our stateful data:

- The list of timers and properties of each timer
- Whether or not the edit form of a timer is open
- Whether or not the create form is open

Step 4: Determine in which component each piece of state should live

While the data we've determined to be stateful might live in certain components in our static app, this does not indicate the best position for it in our stateful app. Our next task is to determine the optimal place for each of our three discrete pieces of state to live.

This can be challenging at times but, again, we can apply the following steps from Facebook's guide "Thinking in React[33]" to help us with the process:

> For each piece of state:
>
> - Identify every component that renders something based on that state.
> - Find a common owner component (a single component above all the components that need the state in the hierarchy).
> - Either the common owner or another component higher up in the hierarchy should own the state.
> - If you can't find a component where it makes sense to own the state, create a new component simply for holding the state and add it somewhere in the hierarchy above the common owner component.

Let's apply this method to our application:

[33] https://facebook.github.io/react/docs/thinking-in-react.html

The list of timers and properties of each timer

At first glance, we may be tempted to conclude that `TimersDashboard` does not appear to use this state. Instead, the first component that uses it is `EditableTimerList`. This matches the location of the declaration of this data in our static app. Because `ToggleableTimerForm` doesn't appear to use the state either, we might deduce that `EditableTimerList` must then be the common owner.

While this may be the case for displaying timers, modifying them, and deleting them, what about creates? `ToggleableTimerForm` does not need the state to render, but it *can* affect state. It needs to be able to insert a new timer. It will propagate the data for the new timer up to `TimersDashboard`.

Therefore, `TimersDashboard` is truly the common owner. It will render `EditableTimerList` by passing down the timer state. It can handle modifications from `EditableTimerList` and creates from `ToggleableTimerForm`, mutating the state. The new state will flow downward through `EditableTimerList`.

Whether or not the edit form of a timer is open

In our static app, `EditableTimerList` specifies whether or not an `EditableTimer` should be rendered with its edit form open. Technically, though, this state could just live in each individual `EditableTimer`. No parent component in the hierarchy depends on this data.

Storing the state in `EditableTimer` will be fine for our current needs. But there are a few requirements that might require us to "hoist" this state up higher in the component hierarchy in the future.

For instance, what if we wanted to impose a restriction such that only one edit form could be open at a time? Then it would make sense for `EditableTimerList` to own the state, as it would need to inspect it to determine whether to allow a new "edit form open" event to succeed. If we wanted to allow only one form open at all, including the create form, then we'd hoist the state up to `TimersDashboard`.

Visibility of the create form

`TimersDashboard` doesn't appear to care about whether `ToggleableTimerForm` is open or closed. It feels safe to reason that the state can just live inside `ToggleableTimerForm` itself.

So, in summary, we'll have three pieces of state each in three different components:

- **Timer data** will be owned and managed by `TimersDashboard`.
- Each `EditableTimer` will manage the state of its **timer edit form**.
- The `ToggleableTimerForm` will manage the state of its **form visibility**.

Step 5: Hard-code initial states

We're now well prepared to make our app stateful. At this stage, we won't yet communicate with the server. Instead, we'll define our initial states within the components themselves. This means hard-coding a list of timers in the top-level component, `TimersDashboard`. For our two other pieces of state, we'll have the components' forms closed by default.

After we've added initial state to a parent component, we'll make sure our props are properly established in its children.

Adding state to `TimersDashboard`

Start by modifying `TimersDashboard` to hold the timer data directly inside the component:

time_tracking_app/public/js/app-2.js

```
class TimersDashboard extends React.Component {
  state = {
    timers: [
      {
        title: 'Practice squat',
        project: 'Gym Chores',
        id: uuid.v4(),
        elapsed: 5456099,
        runningSince: Date.now(),
      },
      {
        title: 'Bake squash',
        project: 'Kitchen Chores',
        id: uuid.v4(),
        elapsed: 1273998,
        runningSince: null,
      },
    ],
  };

  render() {
    return (
      <div className='ui three column centered grid'>
        <div className='column'>
          <EditableTimerList
            timers={this.state.timers}
          />
```

```
          <ToggleableTimerForm />
        </div>
      </div>
    );
  }
}
```

We're leaning on the Babel plugin `transform-class-properties` to give us the property initializers syntax. We set the initial state to an object with the key `timers`. `timers` points to an array with two hard-coded timer objects.

We discuss property initializers in the previous chapter.

Below, in `render`, we pass down `state.timers` to `EditableTimerList`.

For the `id` property, we're using a library called `uuid`. We load this library in `index.html`. We use `uuid.v4()` to randomly generate a Universally Unique IDentifier[34] for each item.

A UUID is a string that looks like this:

```
2030efbd-a32f-4fcc-8637-7c410896b3e3
```

Receiving props in `EditableTimerList`

`EditableTimerList` receives the list of timers as a prop, `timers`. Modify that component to use those props:

time_tracking_app/public/js/app-2.js

```
class EditableTimerList extends React.Component {
  render() {
    const timers = this.props.timers.map((timer) => (
      <EditableTimer
        key={timer.id}
        id={timer.id}
        title={timer.title}
        project={timer.project}
```

[34] https://en.wikipedia.org/wiki/Universally_unique_identifier

```
        elapsed={timer.elapsed}
        runningSince={timer.runningSince}
      />
    ));
    return (
      <div id='timers'>
        {timers}
      </div>
    );
  }
}
```

Hopefully this looks familiar. We're using `map` on the `timers` array to build a list of `EditableTimer` components. This is exactly how we built our list of `Product` components inside `ProductList` in the last chapter.

We pass the `id` down to `EditableTimer` as well. This is a bit of eager preparation. Remember how `Product` communicated up to `ProductList` by calling a function and passing in its `id`? It's safe to assume we'll be doing this again.

Props vs. state

With your renewed understanding of React's state paradigm, let's reflect on props again.

Remember, **props are state's immutable accomplice**. What existed as mutable state in `TimersDashboard` is passed down as immutable props to `EditableTimerList`.

We talked at length about what qualifies as state and where state should live. Mercifully, we do not need to have an equally lengthy discussion about props. Once you understand state, you can see how props act as its **one-way data pipeline**. State is managed in some select parent components and then that data flows down through children as props.

If state is updated, the component managing that state re-renders by calling `render()`. This, in turn, causes any of its children to re-render as well. And the children of those children. And on and on down the chain.

Let's continue our own march down the chain.

Adding state to `EditableTimer`

In the static version of our app, `EditableTimer` relied on `editFormOpen` as a prop to be passed down from the parent. We decided that this state could actually live here in the component itself.

We'll set the initial value of `editFormOpen` to `false`, which means that the form starts off as closed. We'll also pass the `id` property down the chain:

time_tracking_app/public/js/app-2.js

```
class EditableTimer extends React.Component {
  state = {
    editFormOpen: false,
  };

  render() {
    if (this.state.editFormOpen) {
      return (
        <TimerForm
          id={this.props.id}
          title={this.props.title}
          project={this.props.project}
        />
      );
    } else {
      return (
        <Timer
          id={this.props.id}
          title={this.props.title}
          project={this.props.project}
          elapsed={this.props.elapsed}
          runningSince={this.props.runningSince}
        />
      );
    }
  }
}
```

`Timer` remains stateless

If you look at `Timer`, you'll see that it does not need to be modified. It has been using exclusively props and is so far unaffected by our refactor.

Adding state to `ToggleableTimerForm`

We know that we'll need to tweak `ToggleableTimerForm` as we've assigned it some stateful responsibility. We want to have the component manage the state `isOpen`. Because this state is isolated to this component, let's also add our app's first bit of interactivity while we're here.

Let's start by initializing the state. We want the component to initialize to a closed state:

time_tracking_app/public/js/app-2.js

```
class ToggleableTimerForm extends React.Component {
  state = {
    isOpen: false,
  };
```

Next, let's define a function that will toggle the state of the form to open:

time_tracking_app/public/js/app-2.js

```
  handleFormOpen = () => {
    this.setState({ isOpen: true });
  };

  render() {
```

As we explored at the end of the last chapter, we need to write this function as an *arrow* function in order to ensure `this` inside the function is bound to the component. React will automatically bind class methods corresponding to the component API (like `render` and `componentDidMount`) to the component for us.

> As a refresher, without the property initializer feature we'd write our custom component method like this:
>
> ```
> handleFormOpen() {
>   this.setState({ isOpen: true });
> }
> ```
>
> Our next step would be to bind this method to the component inside the constructor, like this:
>
> ```
> constructor(props) {
>   super(props);
>
>   this.handleFormOpen = this.handleFormOpen.bind(this);
> }
> ```
>
> This is a perfectly valid approach and does not use any features beyond ES7. However, we'll be using property initializers for this project.

While we're here, we can also add a little bit of interactivity:

time_tracking_app/public/js/app-2.js

```
  render() {
    if (this.state.isOpen) {
      return (
        <TimerForm />
      );
    } else {
      return (
        <div className='ui basic content center aligned segment'>
          <button
            className='ui basic button icon'
            onClick={this.handleFormOpen}
          >
            <i className='plus icon' />
          </button>
        </div>
      );
    }
  }
```

Like the up-vote button in the last app, we use the `onClick` property on `button` to invoke the function `handleFormOpen()`. `handleFormOpen()` modifies the state, setting `isOpen` to `true`. This causes the component to re-render. When `render()` is called this second time around, `this.state.isOpen` is `true` and `ToggleableTimerForm` renders `TimerForm`. Neat.

Adding state to `TimerForm`

We mentioned earlier that `TimerForm` would manage state as it includes a form. In React, **forms are stateful**.

Recall that `TimerForm` includes two input fields:

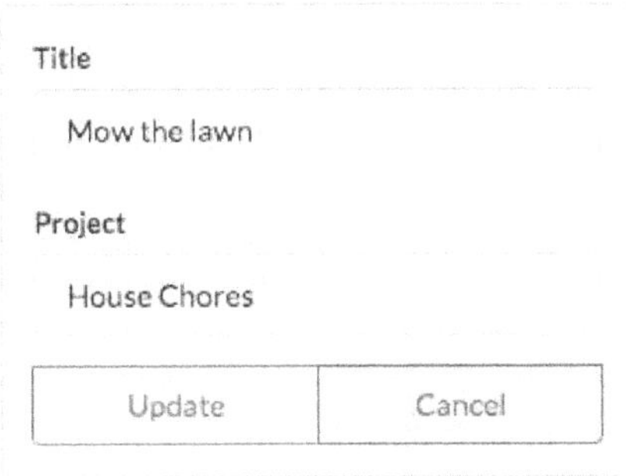

These input fields are modifiable by the user. In React, **all** modifications that are made to a component should be handled by React and kept in state. This includes changes like the modification of an input field. By having React manage all modifications, we guarantee that the visual component that the user is interacting with on the DOM matches the state of the React component behind the scenes.

The best way to understand this is to see what it looks like.

To make these input fields stateful, let's first initialize `state` at the top of the component:

time_tracking_app/public/js/app-2.js

```
class TimerForm extends React.Component {
  state = {
    title: this.props.title || '',
    project: this.props.project || '',
  };
```

Our state object has two properties, each corresponding to an input field that `TimerForm` manages. We set the initial state of these properties to the values passed down via props. If `TimerForm` is *creating* a new timer as opposed to editing an existing one, those props would be `undefined`. In that case, we initialize both to a blank string (`''`).

We want to avoid initializing `title` or `project` to `undefined`. That's because the value of an input field can't technically ever be `undefined`. If it's empty, its value in JavaScript is a blank string. In fact, if you initialize the `value` of an input field to `undefined`, React will complain.

`defaultValue` only sets the value of the input field for the *initial* render. Instead of using `defaultValue`, we can connect our input fields directly to our component's state using `value`. We could do something like this:

```
<div className='field'>
  <label>Title</label>
  <input
    type='text'
    value={this.state.title}
  />
</div>
```

With this change, our input fields would be driven by state. Whenever the state properties `title` or `project` change, our input fields would be updated to reflect the new value.

However, this misses a key ingredient: **We don't currently have any way for the user to *modify* this state.** The input field will start off in-sync with the component's state. But the moment the user makes a modification, **the input field will become out-of-sync with the component's state.**

We can fix this by using React's **onChange** attribute for input elements. Like onClick for button or a elements, we can set onChange to a function. Whenever the input field is changed, React will invoke the function specified.

Let's set the onChange attributes on both input fields to functions we'll define next:

time_tracking_app/public/js/app-2.js

```
            <div className='field'>
              <label>Title</label>
              <input
                type='text'
                value={this.state.title}
                onChange={this.handleTitleChange}
              />
            </div>
            <div className='field'>
              <label>Project</label>
              <input
                type='text'
                value={this.state.project}
                onChange={this.handleProjectChange}
              />
            </div>
```

The functions handleTitleChange and handleProjectChange will both modify their respective properties in state. Here's what they look like:

time_tracking_app/public/js/app-2.js

```
  handleTitleChange = (e) => {
    this.setState({ title: e.target.value });
  };

  handleProjectChange = (e) => {
    this.setState({ project: e.target.value });
  };
```

When React invokes the function passed to onChange, it invokes the function with an event object. We call this argument e. The event object includes the updated value of the field under target.value. We update the state to the new value of the input field.

Using a combination of state, the value attribute, and the onChange attribute is the canonical method we use to write form elements in React. We explore forms in depth in the chapter "Forms." We explore this topic specifically in the section "Uncontrolled vs. Controlled Components."

To recap, here's an example of the lifecycle of `TimerForm`:

1. On the page is a timer with the title "Mow the lawn."
2. The user toggles open the edit form for this timer, mounting `TimerForm` to the page.
3. `TimerForm` initializes the state property `title` to the string `"Mow the lawn"`.
4. The user modifies the input field, changing it to the value `"Cut the grass"`.
5. With every keystroke, React invokes `handleTitleChange`. The internal state of `title` is kept in-sync with what the user sees on the page.

With `TimerForm` refactored, we've finished establishing our stateful data inside our elected components. Our downward data pipeline, props, is assembled.

We're ready — and perhaps a bit eager — to build out interactivity using inverse data flow. But before we do, let's save and reload the app to ensure everything is working. We expect to see new example timers based on the hard-coded data in `TimersDashboard`. We also expect clicking the "+" button toggles open a form:

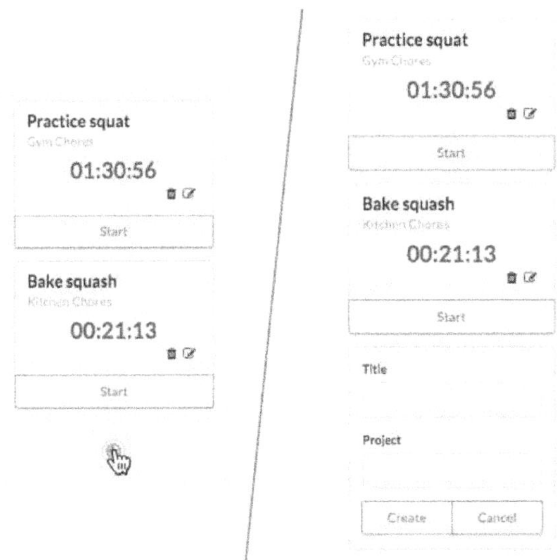

Step 6: Add inverse data flow

As we saw in the last chapter, children communicate with parents by calling functions that are handed to them via props. In the ProductHunt app, when an up-vote was clicked `Product` didn't do any data management. It was not the owner of its state. Instead, it called a function given to it by `ProductList`, passing in its `id`. `ProductList` was then able to manage state accordingly.

We are going to need inverse data flow in two areas:

- `TimerForm` needs to propagate **create** and **update** events (create while under `ToggleableTimerForm` and update while under `EditableTimer`). Both events will eventually reach `TimersDashboard`.
- `Timer` has a fair amount of behavior. It needs to handle **delete** and **edit** clicks, as well as the **start** and **stop** timer logic.

Let's start with `TimerForm`.

`TimerForm`

To get a clear idea of what exactly `TimerForm` will require, we'll start by adding event handlers to it and then work our way backwards up the hierarchy.

`TimerForm` needs two **event handlers**:

- When the form is submitted (creating or updating a timer)
- When the "Cancel" button is clicked (closing the form)

`TimerForm` will receive two functions as props to handle each event. The parent component that uses `TimerForm` is responsible for providing these functions:

- `props.onFormSubmit()`: called when the form is submitted
- `props.onFormClose()`: called when the "Cancel" button is clicked

As we'll see soon, this empowers the parent component to dictate what the behavior should be when these events occur.

Let's first modify the buttons on `TimerForm`. We'll specify `onClick` attributes for each:

time_tracking_app/public/js/app-3.js

```
          <div className='ui two bottom attached buttons'>
            <button
              className='ui basic blue button'
              onClick={this.handleSubmit}
            >
              {submitText}
            </button>
            <button
              className='ui basic red button'
              onClick={this.props.onFormClose}
            >
              Cancel
            </button>
          </div>
```

The `onClick` attribute for the "Submit" button specifies the function `this.handleSubmit`, which we'll define next. The `onClick` attribute for the "Cancel" button specifies the prop `onFormClose` directly.

Let's see what `handleSubmit` looks like:

time_tracking_app/public/js/app-3.js

```
  handleSubmit = () => {
    this.props.onFormSubmit({
      id: this.props.id,
      title: this.state.title,
      project: this.state.project,
    });
  };

  render() {
```

`handleSubmit()` calls a yet-to-be-defined function, `onFormSubmit()`. It passes in a data object with `id`, `title`, and `project` attributes. This means `id` will be `undefined` for creates, as no id exists yet.

Before moving on, let's make one last tweak to `TimerForm`:

time_tracking_app/public/js/app-3.js

```
  render() {
    const submitText = this.props.id ? 'Update' : 'Create';
```

We have `submitText` switch on `id` as opposed to `title`. Using the `id` property to determine whether or not an object has been created is a more common practice.

`ToggleableTimerForm`

Let's chase the submit event from `TimerForm` as it bubbles up the component hierarchy. First, we'll modify `ToggleableTimerForm`. We need it to pass down two prop-functions to `TimerForm`, `onFormClose()` and `onFormSubmit()`:

time_tracking_app/public/js/app-3.js

```
// Inside ToggleableTimerForm
handleFormOpen = () => {
  this.setState({ isOpen: true });
};

handleFormClose = () => {
  this.setState({ isOpen: false });
};

handleFormSubmit = (timer) => {
  this.props.onFormSubmit(timer);
  this.setState({ isOpen: false });
};

render() {
  if (this.state.isOpen) {
    return (
      <TimerForm
        onFormSubmit={this.handleFormSubmit}
        onFormClose={this.handleFormClose}
      />
    );
  } else {
```

Looking first at the `render()` function, we can see we pass in the two functions as props. Functions are just like any other prop.

Of most interest here is `handleFormSubmit()`. Remember, `ToggleableTimerForm` is not the manager of timer state. `TimerForm` has an event it's emitting, in this case the submission of a new timer. `ToggleableTimerForm` is just a proxy of this message. So, when the form is submitted, it calls its own prop-function `props.onFormSubmit()`. We'll eventually define this function in `TimersDashboard`.

`handleFormSubmit()` accepts the argument `timer`. Recall that in `TimerForm` this argument is an object containing the desired timer properties. We just pass that argument along here.

After invoking `onFormSubmit()`, `handleFormSubmit()` calls `setState()` to close its form.

Note that the *result* of `onFormSubmit()` will not impact whether or not the form is closed. We invoke `onFormSubmit()`, which may eventually create an **asynchronous** call to a server. Execution will continue before we hear back from the server which means `setState()` will be called.

If `onFormSubmit()` fails — such as if the server is temporarily unreachable — we'd ideally have some way to display an error message and re-open the form.

TimersDashboard

We've reached the top of the hierarchy, `TimersDashboard`. As this component will be responsible for the data for the timers, it is here that we will define the logic for handling the events we're capturing down at the leaf components.

The first event we're concerned with is the submission of a form. When this happens, either a new timer is being *created* or an existing one is being *updated*. We'll use two separate functions to handle the two distinct events:

- `handleCreateFormSubmit()` will handle creates and will be the function passed to `ToggleableTimerForm`
- `handleEditFormSubmit()` will handle updates and will be the function passed to `EditableTimerList`

Both functions travel down their respective component hierarchies until they reach `TimerForm` as the prop `onFormSubmit()`.

Let's start with `handleCreateFormSubmit`, which inserts a new timer into our timer list state:

time_tracking_app/public/js/app-3.js

```
// Inside TimersDashboard
handleCreateFormSubmit = (timer) => {
  this.createTimer(timer);
};

createTimer = (timer) => {
  const t = helpers.newTimer(timer);
  this.setState({
    timers: this.state.timers.concat(t),
  });
};

render() {
  return (
    <div className='ui three column centered grid'>
      <div className='column'>
        <EditableTimerList
          timers={this.state.timers}
        />
        <ToggleableTimerForm
          onFormSubmit={this.handleCreateFormSubmit}
        />
```

```
        </div>
      </div>
    );
  }
```

We create the timer object with `helpers.newTimer()`. You can peek at the implementation inside of `helpers.js`. We pass in the object that originated down in `TimerForm`. This object has `title` and `project` properties. `helpers.newTimer()` returns an object with those `title` and `project` properties as well as a generated `id`.

The next line calls `setState()`, appending the new timer to our array of timers held under `timers`. We pass the whole state object to `setState()`.

You might wonder: why separate `handleCreateFormSubmit()` and `createTimer()`? While not strictly required, the idea here is that we have one function for handling the event (`handleCreateFormSubmit()`) and another for performing the operation of creating a timer (`createTimer()`).

This separation follows from the Single Responsibility Principle and enables us to call `createTimer()` from elsewhere if needed.

We've finished wiring up the create timer flow from the form down in `TimerForm` up to the state managed in `TimersDashboard`. Save `app.js` and reload your browser. Toggle open the create form and create some new timers:

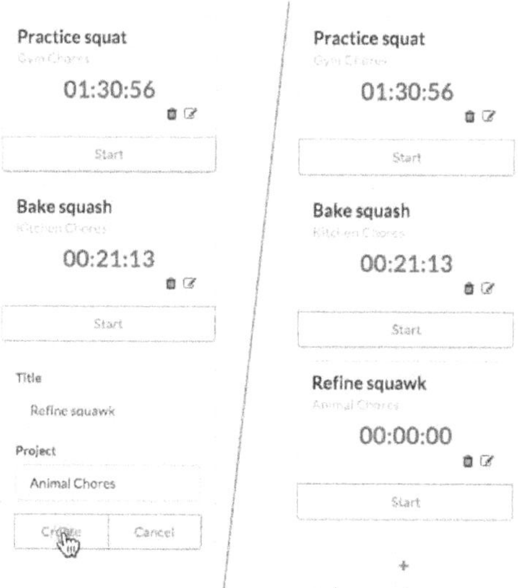

Updating timers

We need to give the same treatment to the update timer flow. However, as you can see in the current state of the app, we haven't yet added the ability for a timer to be edited. So we don't have a way

to display an edit form, which will be a prerequisite to submitting one.

To display an edit form, the user clicks on the edit icon on a `Timer`. This should propagate an event up to `EditableTimer` and tell it to flip its child component, opening the form.

Adding editability to `Timer`

To notify our app that the user wants to edit a timer we need to add an `onClick` attribute to the `span` tag of the edit button. We anticipate a prop-function, `onEditClick()`:

time_tracking_app/public/js/app-4.js

```
          {/* Inside Timer.render() */}
          <div className='extra content'>
            <span
              className='right floated edit icon'
              onClick={this.props.onEditClick}
            >
              <i className='edit icon' />
            </span>
            <span className='right floated trash icon'>
              <i className='trash icon' />
            </span>
          </div>
```

Updating `EditableTimer`

Now we're prepared to update `EditableTimer`. Again, it will display either the `TimerForm` (if we're editing) or an individual `Timer` (if we're not editing).

Let's add event handlers for both possible child components. For `TimerForm`, we want to handle the form being closed or submitted. For `Timer`, we want to handle the edit icon being pressed:

time_tracking_app/public/js/app-4.js

```
  // Inside EditableTimer
  handleEditClick = () => {
    this.openForm();
  };

  handleFormClose = () => {
    this.closeForm();
  };
```

```
  handleSubmit = (timer) => {
    this.props.onFormSubmit(timer);
    this.closeForm();
  };

  closeForm = () => {
    this.setState({ editFormOpen: false });
  };

  openForm = () => {
    this.setState({ editFormOpen: true });
  };
```

We pass these event handlers down as props:

time_tracking_app/public/js/app-4.js

```
  render() {
    if (this.state.editFormOpen) {
      return (
        <TimerForm
          id={this.props.id}
          title={this.props.title}
          project={this.props.project}
          onFormSubmit={this.handleSubmit}
          onFormClose={this.handleFormClose}
        />
      );
    } else {
      return (
        <Timer
          id={this.props.id}
          title={this.props.title}
          project={this.props.project}
          elapsed={this.props.elapsed}
          runningSince={this.props.runningSince}
          onEditClick={this.handleEditClick}
        />
      );
    }
  }
```

Look a bit familiar? `EditableTimer` handles the same events emitted from `TimerForm` in a very similar manner as `ToggleableTimerForm`. This makes sense. Both `EditableTimer` and `ToggleableTimerForm` are just intermediaries between `TimerForm` and `TimersDashboard`. `TimersDashboard` is the one that defines the submit function handlers and assigns them to a given component tree.

Like `ToggleableTimerForm`, `EditableTimer` doesn't do anything with the incoming `timer`. In `handleSubmit()`, it just blindly passes this object along to its prop-function `onFormSubmit()`. It then closes the form with `closeForm()`.

We pass along a new prop to `Timer`, `onEditClick`. The behavior for this function is defined in `handleEditClick`, which modifies the state for `EditableTimer`, opening the form.

Updating `EditableTimerList`

Moving up a level, we make a one-line addition to `EditableTimerList` to send the submit function from `TimersDashboard` to each `EditableTimer`:

time_tracking_app/public/js/app-4.js

```
// Inside EditableTimerList
const timers = this.props.timers.map((timer) => (
  <EditableTimer
    key={timer.id}
    id={timer.id}
    title={timer.title}
    project={timer.project}
    elapsed={timer.elapsed}
    runningSince={timer.runningSince}
    onFormSubmit={this.props.onFormSubmit}
  />
));
// ...
```

`EditableTimerList` doesn't need to do anything with this event so again we just pass the function on directly.

Defining `onEditFormSubmit()` in `TimersDashboard`

Last step with this pipeline is to define and pass down the submit function for edit forms in `TimersDashboard`.

For creates, we have a function that creates a new timer object with the specified attributes and we append this new object to the end of the `timers` array in the state.

For updates, we need to hunt through the `timers` array until we find the timer object that is being updated. As mentioned in the last chapter, the state object **cannot** be updated directly. We have to use `setState()`.

Therefore, we'll use `map()` to traverse the array of timer objects. If the timer's `id` matches that of the form submitted, we'll return a new object that contains the timer with the updated attributes. Otherwise we'll just return the original timer. This new array of timer objects will be passed to `setState()`:

time_tracking_app/public/js/app-4.js

```
  // Inside TimersDashboard
  handleEditFormSubmit = (attrs) => {
    this.updateTimer(attrs);
  };

  createTimer = (timer) => {
    const t = helpers.newTimer(timer);
    this.setState({
      timers: this.state.timers.concat(t),
    });
  };

  updateTimer = (attrs) => {
    this.setState({
      timers: this.state.timers.map((timer) => {
        if (timer.id === attrs.id) {
          return Object.assign({}, timer, {
            title: attrs.title,
            project: attrs.project,
          });
        } else {
          return timer;
        }
      }),
    });
  };
```

We pass this down as a prop inside `render()`:

time_tracking_app/public/js/app-4.js

```
        { /* Inside TimersDashboard.render() */}
        <EditableTimerList
          timers={this.state.timers}
          onFormSubmit={this.handleEditFormSubmit}
        />
```

Note that we can call `map()` on `this.state.timers` from *within* the JavaScript object we're passing to `setState()`. This is an often used pattern. The call is evaluated and then the property `timers` is set to the result.

Inside of the `map()` function we check if the `timer` matches the one being updated. If not, we just return the `timer`. Otherwise, we use `Object#assign()` to return a new object with the timer's updated attributes.

Remember, it's important here that we **treat state as immutable**. By creating a *new* timers object and then using `Object#assign()` to populate it, we're not modifying any of the objects sitting in state.

We discuss the `Object#assign()` method in the last chapter.

As we did with `ToggleableTimerForm` and `handleCreateFormSubmit`, we pass down `handleEditFormSubmit` as the prop `onFormSubmit`. `TimerForm` calls this prop, oblivious to the fact that this function is entirely different when it is rendered underneath `EditableTimer` as opposed to `ToggleableTimerForm`.

Both of the forms are wired up! Save `app.js`, reload the page, and try both creating and updating timers. You can also click "Cancel" on an open form to close it:

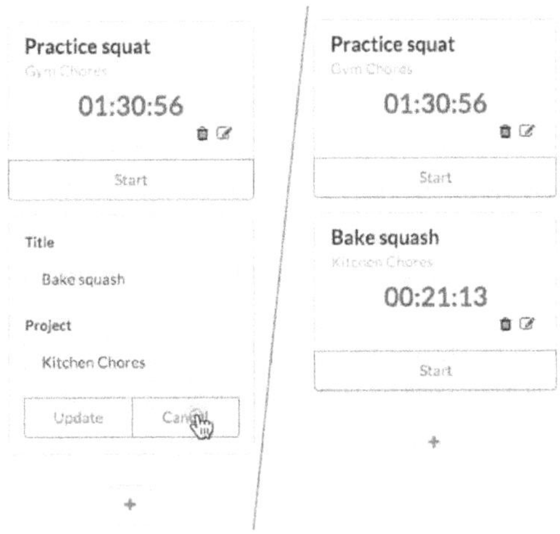

The rest of our work resides within the timer. We need to:

- Wire up the trash button (deleting a timer)
- Implement the start/stop buttons and the timing logic itself

At that point, we'll have a complete server-less solution.

Try it yourself: Before moving on to the next section, see how far you can get wiring up the trash button by yourself. Move ahead afterwards and verify your solution is sound.

Deleting timers

Adding the event handler to `Timer`

In `Timer`, we define a function to handle trash button click events:

time_tracking_app/public/js/app-5.js

```
class Timer extends React.Component {
  handleTrashClick = () => {
    this.props.onTrashClick(this.props.id);
  };

  render() {
```

And then use `onClick` to connect that function to the trash icon:

time_tracking_app/public/js/app-5.js

```
          {/* Inside Timer.render() */}
          <div className='extra content'>
            <span
              className='right floated edit icon'
              onClick={this.props.onEditClick}
            >
              <i className='edit icon' />
            </span>
            <span
              className='right floated trash icon'
              onClick={this.handleTrashClick}
            >
              <i className='trash icon' />
            </span>
          </div>
```

We've yet to define the function that will be set as the prop `onTrashClick()`. But you can imagine that when this event reaches the top (`TimersDashboard`), we're going to need the `id` to sort out which timer is being deleted. `handleTrashClick()` provides the `id` to this function.

Routing through `EditableTimer`

`EditableTimer` just proxies the function:

time_tracking_app/public/js/app-5.js

```
// Inside EditableTimer
} else {
  return (
    <Timer
      id={this.props.id}
      title={this.props.title}
      project={this.props.project}
      elapsed={this.props.elapsed}
      runningSince={this.props.runningSince}
      onEditClick={this.handleEditClick}
      onTrashClick={this.props.onTrashClick}
    />
  );
}
```

Routing through `EditableTimerList`

As does `EditableTimerList`:

time_tracking_app/public/js/app-5.js

```
// Inside EditableTimerList.render()
const timers = this.props.timers.map((timer) => (
  <EditableTimer
    key={timer.id}
    id={timer.id}
    title={timer.title}
    project={timer.project}
    elapsed={timer.elapsed}
    runningSince={timer.runningSince}
    onFormSubmit={this.props.onFormSubmit}
    onTrashClick={this.props.onTrashClick}
  />
));
```

Implementing the delete function in `TimersDashboard`

The last step is to define the function in `TimersDashboard` that deletes the desired timer from the state array. There are many ways to accomplish this in JavaScript. Don't sweat it if your solution was not the same or if you didn't quite work one out.

We add our handler function that we ultimately pass down as a prop:

time_tracking_app/public/js/app-5.js

```
// Inside TimersDashboard
handleEditFormSubmit = (attrs) => {
  this.updateTimer(attrs);
};

handleTrashClick = (timerId) => {
  this.deleteTimer(timerId);
};
```

`deleteTimer()` uses Array's `filter()` method to return a new array with the timer object that has an `id` matching `timerId` removed:

time_tracking_app/public/js/app-5.js

```
// Inside TimersDashboard
deleteTimer = (timerId) => {
  this.setState({
    timers: this.state.timers.filter(t => t.id !== timerId),
  });
};
```

Finally, we pass down `handleTrashClick()` as a prop:

time_tracking_app/public/js/app-5.js

```
        {/* Inside TimersDashboard.render() */}
        <EditableTimerList
          timers={this.state.timers}
          onFormSubmit={this.handleEditFormSubmit}
          onTrashClick={this.handleTrashClick}
        />
```

Array's `filter()` method accepts a function that is used to "test" each element in the array. It returns a new array containing all the elements that "passed" the test. If the function returns `true`, the element is kept.

Save `app.js` and reload the app. Low and behold, you can delete timers:

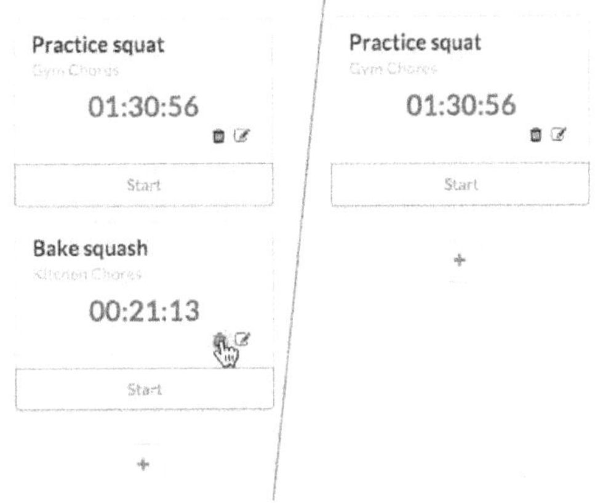

Adding timing functionality

Create, update, and delete (CRUD) capability is now in place for our timers. The next challenge: making these timers functional.

There are several different ways we can implement a timer system. The simplest approach would be to have a function update the `elapsed` property on each timer every second. But this is severely limited. What happens when the app is closed? The timer should continue "running."

This is why we've included the timer property `runningSince`. A timer is initialized with `elapsed` equal to `0`. When a user clicks "Start", we do not increment `elapsed`. Instead, we just set `runningSince` to the start time.

We can then use the difference between the start time and the current time to render the time for the user. When the user clicks "Stop", the difference between the start time and the current time is added to `elapsed`. `runningSince` is set to `null`.

Therefore, at any given time, we can derive how long the timer has been running by taking `Date.now() - runningSince` and adding it to the total accumulated time (`elapsed`). We'll calculate this inside the `Timer` component.

For the app to truly feel like a running timer, we want React to constantly perform this operation and re-render the timers. But `elapsed` and `runningSince` *will not be changing while the timer is running*. So the one mechanism we've seen so far to trigger a `render()` call will not be sufficient.

Instead, we can use React's `forceUpdate()` method. This forces a React component to re-render. We can call it on an interval to yield the smooth appearance of a live timer.

Adding a `forceUpdate()` interval to `Timer`

`helpers.renderElapsedString()` accepts an optional second argument, `runningSince`. It will add the delta of `Date.now() - runningSince` to `elapsed` and use the function `millisecondsToHuman()` to return a string formatted as `HH:MM:SS`.

We will establish an interval to run `forceUpdate()` after the component mounts:

time_tracking_app/public/js/app-6.js

```
class Timer extends React.Component {
  componentDidMount() {
    this.forceUpdateInterval = setInterval(() => this.forceUpdate(), 50);
  }

  componentWillUnmount() {
    clearInterval(this.forceUpdateInterval);
  }

  handleTrashClick = () => {
    this.props.onTrashClick(this.props.id);
  };

  render() {
    const elapsedString = helpers.renderElapsedString(
      this.props.elapsed, this.props.runningSince
    );
    return (
```

In `componentDidMount()`, we use the JavaScript function `setInterval()`. This will invoke the function `forceUpdate()` once every 50 ms, causing the component to re-render. We set the return of `setInterval()` to `this.forceUpdateInterval`.

In `componentWillUnmount()`, we use `clearInterval()` to stop the interval `this.forceUpdateInterval`. `componentWillUnmount()` is called before a component is removed from the app. This will happen if a timer is deleted. We want to ensure we do not continue calling `forceUpdate()` after the timer has been removed from the page. React will throw errors.

`setInterval()` accepts two arguments. The first is the function you would like to call repeatedly. The second is the interval on which to call that function (in milliseconds).

`setInterval()` returns a unique interval ID. You can pass this interval ID to `clearInterval()` at any time to halt the interval.

You might ask: Wouldn't it be more efficient if we did not continuously call `forceUpdate()` on timers that are not running?

Indeed, we would save a few cycles. But it would not be worth the added code complexity. React will call `render()` which performs some inexpensive operations in JavaScript. It will then compare this result to the previous call to `render()` and see that nothing has changed. It stops there — it won't attempt any DOM manipulation.

The 50 ms interval was not derived scientifically. Selecting an interval that's too high will make the timer look unnatural. It would jump unevenly between values. Selecting an interval that's too low would just be an unnecessary amount of work. A 50 ms interval looks good to humans and is ages in computerland.

Try it out

Save `app.js` and reload. The first timer should be running.

We've begun to carve out the app's real utility! We need only wire up the start/stop button and our server-less app will be feature complete.

Add start and stop functionality

The action button at the bottom of each timer should display "Start" if the timer is paused and "Stop" if the timer is running. It should also propagate events when clicked, depending on if the timer is being stopped or started.

We could build all of this functionality into `Timer`. We could have `Timer` decide to render one HTML snippet or another depending on if it is running. But that would be adding more responsibility and complexity to `Timer`. Instead, let's make the button its own React component.

Add timer action events to `Timer`

Let's modify `Timer`, anticipating a new component called `TimerActionButton`. This button just needs to know if the timer is running. It also needs to be able to propagate two events, `onStartClick()` and `onStopClick()`. These events will eventually need to make it all the way up to `TimersDashboard`, which can modify `runningSince` on the timer.

First, the event handlers:

time_tracking_app/public/js/app-7.js

```
// Inside Timer
componentWillUnmount() {
  clearInterval(this.forceUpdateInterval);
}

handleStartClick = () => {
  this.props.onStartClick(this.props.id);
};

handleStopClick = () => {
  this.props.onStopClick(this.props.id);
};
// ...
```

Then, inside `render()`, we'll declare `TimerActionButton` at the bottom of the outermost `div`:

time_tracking_app/public/js/app-7.js

```
      {/* At the bottom of `Timer.render()`` */}
      <TimerActionButton
        timerIsRunning={!!this.props.runningSince}
        onStartClick={this.handleStartClick}
        onStopClick={this.handleStopClick}
      />
    </div>
  );
```

We use the same technique used in other click-handlers: `onClick` on the HTML element specifies a handler function in the component that invokes a prop-function, passing in the timer's id.

We use `!!` here to derive the boolean prop `timerIsRunning` for `TimerActionButton`. `!!` returns `false` when `runningSince` is `null`.

Create `TimerActionButton`

Create the `TimerActionButton` component now:

time_tracking_app/public/js/app-7.js

```
class TimerActionButton extends React.Component {
  render() {
    if (this.props.timerIsRunning) {
      return (
        <div
          className='ui bottom attached red basic button'
          onClick={this.props.onStopClick}
        >
          Stop
        </div>
      );
    } else {
      return (
        <div
          className='ui bottom attached green basic button'
          onClick={this.props.onStartClick}
        >
          Start
        </div>
      );
    }
  }
}
```

We render one HTML snippet or another based on `this.props.timerIsRunning`.

You know the drill. Now we run these events up the component hierarchy, all the way up to `TimersDashboard` where we're managing state:

Run the events through `EditableTimer` and `EditableTimerList`

First `EditableTimer`:

time_tracking_app/public/js/app-7.js

```
      // Inside EditableTimer
    } else {
      return (
        <Timer
          id={this.props.id}
          title={this.props.title}
          project={this.props.project}
          elapsed={this.props.elapsed}
          runningSince={this.props.runningSince}
          onEditClick={this.handleEditClick}
          onTrashClick={this.props.onTrashClick}
          onStartClick={this.props.onStartClick}
          onStopClick={this.props.onStopClick}
        />
      );
    }
```

And then `EditableTimerList`:

time_tracking_app/public/js/app-7.js

```
    // Inside EditableTimerList
    const timers = this.props.timers.map((timer) => (
      <EditableTimer
        key={timer.id}
        id={timer.id}
        title={timer.title}
        project={timer.project}
        elapsed={timer.elapsed}
        runningSince={timer.runningSince}
        onFormSubmit={this.props.onFormSubmit}
        onTrashClick={this.props.onTrashClick}
        onStartClick={this.props.onStartClick}
        onStopClick={this.props.onStopClick}
      />
    ));
```

Finally, we define these functions in `TimersDashboard`. They should hunt through the state timers array using `map`, setting `runningSince` appropriately when they find the matching timer.

First we define the handling functions:

time_tracking_app/public/js/app-7.js

```
// Inside TimersDashboard
handleTrashClick = (timerId) => {
  this.deleteTimer(timerId);
};

handleStartClick = (timerId) => {
  this.startTimer(timerId);
};

handleStopClick = (timerId) => {
  this.stopTimer(timerId);
};
```

And then `startTimer()` and `stopTimer()`:

time_tracking_app/public/js/app-7.js

```
deleteTimer = (timerId) => {
  this.setState({
    timers: this.state.timers.filter(t => t.id !== timerId),
  });
};

startTimer = (timerId) => {
  const now = Date.now();

  this.setState({
    timers: this.state.timers.map((timer) => {
      if (timer.id === timerId) {
        return Object.assign({}, timer, {
          runningSince: now,
        });
      } else {
        return timer;
      }
    }),
  });
};

stopTimer = (timerId) => {
  const now = Date.now();
```

```
    this.setState({
      timers: this.state.timers.map((timer) => {
        if (timer.id === timerId) {
          const lastElapsed = now - timer.runningSince;
          return Object.assign({}, timer, {
            elapsed: timer.elapsed + lastElapsed,
            runningSince: null,
          });
        } else {
          return timer;
        }
      }),
    });
  };
```

Finally, we pass them down as props:

time_tracking_app/public/js/app-7.js

```
        {/* Inside TimerDashboard.render() */}
        <EditableTimerList
          timers={this.state.timers}
          onFormSubmit={this.handleEditFormSubmit}
          onTrashClick={this.handleTrashClick}
          onStartClick={this.handleStartClick}
          onStopClick={this.handleStopClick}
        />
```

When `startTimer` comes across the relevant timer within its `map` call, it sets the property `runningSince` to the current time.

`stopTimer` calculates `lastElapsed`, the amount of time that the timer has been running for since it was started. It adds this amount to `elapsed` and sets `runningSince` to `null`, "stopping" the timer.

Try it out

Save `app.js`, reload, and behold! You can now create, update, and delete timers as well as actually use them to time things:

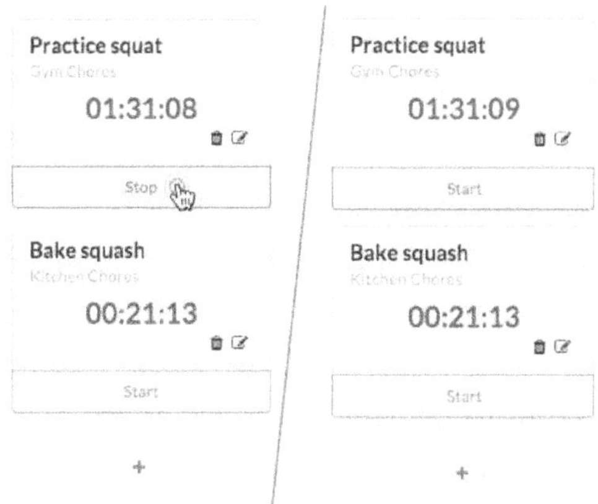

This is excellent progress. But, without a connection to a server, our app is ephemeral. If we refresh the page, we lose all of our timer data. Our app does not have any persistence.

A server can give us persistence. We'll have our server write all changes to timer data to a file. Instead of hard-coding state inside of the `TimersDashboard` component, when our app loads it will query the server and construct its timer state based on the data the server provides. We'll then have our React app notify the server about any state changes, like when a timer is started.

Communicating with a server is the last big major building block you'll need to develop and distribute real-world web applications with React.

Methodology review

While building our time-logging app, we learned and applied a methodology for building React apps. Again, those steps were:

1. Break the app into components

   We mapped out the component structure of our app by examining the app's working UI. We then applied the single-responsibility principle to break components down so that each had minimal viable functionality.
2. Build a static version of the app

   Our bottom-level (user-visible) components rendered HTML based on static props, passed down from parents.
3. Determine what should be stateful

   We used a series of questions to deduce what data should be stateful. This data was represented in our static app as props.
4. Determine in which component each piece of state should live

   We used another series of questions to determine which component should own each piece of state. `TimersDashboard` owned timer state data and `ToggleableTimerForm` and `EditableTimer` both held state pertaining to whether or not to render a `TimerForm`.

5. Hard-code initial states

   We then initialized state-owners' `state` properties with hard-coded values.

6. Add inverse data flow

   We added interactivity by decorating buttons with `onClick` handlers. These called functions that were passed in as props down the hierarchy from whichever component owned the relevant state being manipulated.

The final step is 7. **Add server communication**. We'll tackle this in the next chapter.

Components & Servers

Introduction

In the last chapter, we used a methodology to construct a React app. State management of timers takes place in the top-level component `TimersDashboard`. As in all React apps, data flows from the top down through the component tree to leaf components. Leaf components communicate events to state managers by calling prop-functions.

At the moment, `TimersDashboard` has a hard-coded initial state. Any mutations to the state will only live as long as the browser window is open. That's because all state changes are happening in-memory inside of React. We need our React app to communicate with a server. The server will be in charge of persisting the data. In this app, data persistence happens inside of a file, `data.json`.

`EditableTimer` and `ToggleableTimerForm` also have hard-coded initial state. But because this state is just whether or not their forms are open, we don't need to communicate these state changes to the server. We're OK with the forms starting off closed every time the app boots.

Preparation

To help you get familiar with the API for this project and working with APIs in general, we have a short section where we make requests to the API outside of React.

curl

We'll use a tool called curl to make more involved requests from the command line.

OS X users should already have curl installed.

Windows users can download and install curl here: https://curl.haxx.se/download.html[35].

`server.js`

Included in the root of your project folder is a file called `server.js`. This is a Node.js server specifically designed for our time-tracking app.

You don't have to know anything about Node.js or about servers in general to work with the server we've supplied. We'll provide the guidance that you need.

[35]https://curl.haxx.se/download.html

`server.js` uses the file `data.json` as its "store." The server will read and write to this file to persist data. You can take a look at that file to see the initial state of the store that we've provided.

`server.js` will return the contents of `data.json` when asked for all items. When notified, the server will reflect any updates, deletes, or timer stops and starts in `data.json`. This is how data will be persisted even if the browser is reloaded or closed.

Before we start working with the server, let's briefly cover its **API**. Again, don't be concerned if this outline is a bit perplexing. It will hopefully become clearer as we start writing some code.

The Server API

Our ultimate goal in this chapter is to **replicate state changes on the server**. We're not going to move all state management exclusively to the server. Instead, the server will maintain its state (in `data.json`) and React will maintain its state (in this case, within `this.state` in `TimersDashboard`). We'll demonstrate later why keeping state in both places is desirable.

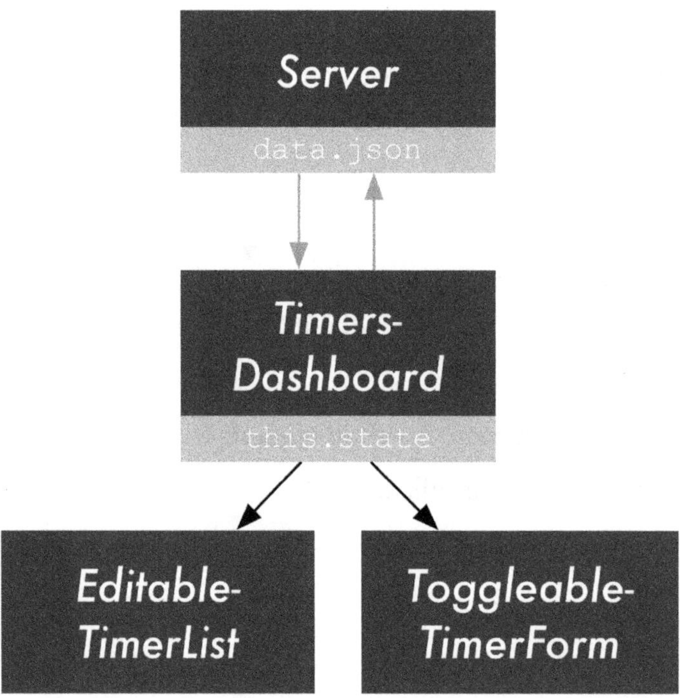

`TimersDashboard` communicates with the server

If we perform an operation on the React ("client") state that we want to be persisted, then we also need to notify the server of that state change. This will keep the two states in sync. We'll consider these our "write" operations. The write operations we want to send to the server are:

- A timer is created

- A timer is updated
- A timer is deleted
- A timer is started
- A timer is stopped

We'll have just one read operation: requesting all of the timers from the server.

HTTP APIs

This section assumes a little familiarity with HTTP APIs. If you're not familiar with HTTP APIs, you may want to read up on them[36] at some point.

However, don't be deterred from continuing with this chapter for the time being. Essentially what we're doing is making a "call" from our browser out to a local server and conforming to a specified format.

`text/html` endpoint

GET /

This entire time, `server.js` has actually been responsible for serving the app. When your browser requests `localhost:3000/`, the server returns the file `index.html`. `index.html` loads in all of our JavaScript/React code.

Note that React never makes a request to the server at this path. This is just used by the browser to load the app. React only communicates with the JSON endpoints.

JSON endpoints

`data.json` is a JSON document. As touched on in the last chapter, JSON is a format for storing human-readable data objects. We can serialize JavaScript objects into JSON. This enables JavaScript objects to be stored in text files and transported over the network.

`data.json` contains an array of objects. While not strictly JavaScript, the data in this array can be readily loaded into JavaScript.

In `server.js`, we see lines like this:

[36] http://www.andrewhavens.com/posts/20/beginners-guide-to-creating-a-rest-api/

```
fs.readFile(DATA_FILE, function(err, data) {
  const timers = JSON.parse(data);
  // ...
});
```

`data` is a string, the JSON. `JSON.parse()` converts this string into an actual JavaScript array of objects.

`GET /api/timers`

Returns a list of all timers.

`POST /api/timers`

Accepts a JSON body with `title`, `project`, and `id` attributes. Will insert a new timer object into its store.

`POST /api/timers/start`

Accepts a JSON body with the attribute `id` and `start` (a timestamp). Hunts through its store and finds the timer with the matching `id`. Sets its `runningSince` to `start`.

`POST /api/timers/stop`

Accepts a JSON body with the attribute `id` and `stop` (a timestamp). Hunts through its store and finds the timer with the matching `id`. Updates `elapsed` according to how long the timer has been running (`stop - runningSince`). Sets `runningSince` to `null`.

`PUT /api/timers`

Accepts a JSON body with the attributes `id` and `title` and/or `project`. Hunts through its store and finds the timer with the matching `id`. Updates `title` and/or `project` to new attributes.

`DELETE /api/timers`

Accepts a JSON body with the attribute `id`. Hunts through its store and deletes the timer with the matching `id`.

Playing with the API

If your server is not booted, make sure to boot it:

```
npm start
```

You can visit the endpoint `/api/timers` endpoint in your browser and see the JSON response (`localhost:3000/api/timers`). When you visit a new URL in your browser, your browser makes a GET request. So our browser calls `GET /api/timers` and the server returns all of the timers:

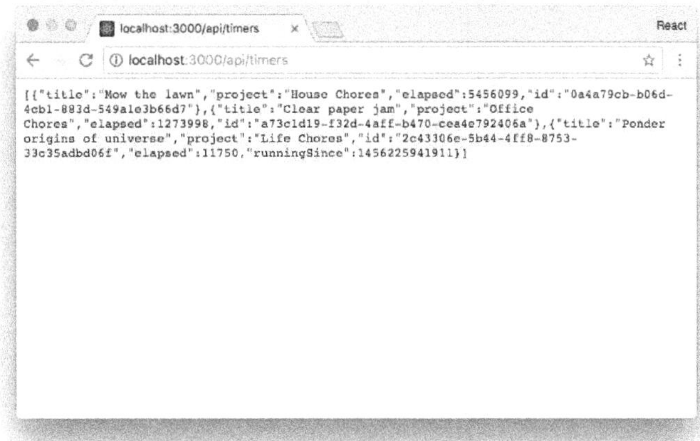

Note that the server stripped all of the extraneous whitespace in `data.json`, including newlines, to keep the payload as small as possible. Those only exist in `data.json` to make it human-readable.

We can use a Chrome extension like JSONView[37] to "humanize" the raw JSON. JSONView takes these raw JSON chunks and adds back in the whitespace for readability:

```
[
  - {
      title: "Mow the lawn",
      project: "House Chores",
      elapsed: 5456099,
      id: "0a4a79cb-b06d-4cb1-883d-549a1e3b66d7"
    },
  - {
      title: "Clear paper jam",
      project: "Office Chores",
      elapsed: 1273998,
      id: "a73c1d19-f32d-4aff-b470-cea4e792406a"
    },
  - {
      title: "Ponder origins of universe",
      project: "Life Chores",
      id: "2c43306e-5b44-4ff8-8753-33c35adbd06f",
      elapsed: 11750,
      runningSince: 1456225941911
    }
]
```

Visiting the endpoint after installing JSONView

We can only easily use the browser to make GET requests. For *writing* data — like starting and stopping timers — we'll have to make POST, PUT, or DELETE requests. We'll use curl to play around with writing data.

Run the following command from the command line:

[37] https://chrome.google.com/webstore/detail/jsonview/chklaanhfefbnpoihckbnefhakgolnmc

```
$ curl -X GET localhost:3000/api/timers
```

The `-X` flag specifies which HTTP method to use. It should return a response that looks a bit like this:


```
[{"title":"Mow the lawn","project":"House Chores","elapsed":5456099,"id":"0a4a79\
cb-b06d-4cb1-883d-549a1e3b66d7"},{"title":"Clear paper jam","project":"Office Ch\
ores","elapsed":1273998,"id":"a73c1d19-f32d-4aff-b470-cea4e792406a"},{"title":"P\
onder origins of universe","project":"Life Chores","id":"2c43306e-5b44-4ff8-8753\
-33c35adbd06f","elapsed":11750,"runningSince":"1456225941911"}]
```


You can start one of the timers by issuing a PUT request to the `/api/timers/start` endpoint. We need to send along the id of one of the timers and a start timestamp:

```
$ curl -X POST \
-H 'Content-Type: application/json' \
-d '{"start":1456468632194,"id":"a73c1d19-f32d-4aff-b470-cea4e792406a"}' \
localhost:3000/api/timers/start
```

The `-H` flag sets a header for our HTTP request, `Content-Type`. We're informing the server that the body of the request is JSON.

The `-d` flag sets the body of our request. Inside of single-quotes `''` is the JSON data.

When you press enter, curl will quickly return without any output. The server doesn't return anything on success for this endpoint. If you open up `data.json`, you will see that the timer you specified now has a `runningSince` property, set to the value we specified as `start` in our request.

If you'd like, you can play around with the other endpoints to get a feel for how they work. Just be sure to set the appropriate method with `-X` and to pass along the JSON `Content-Type` for the write endpoints.

We've written a small library, `client`, to aid you in interfacing with the API in JavaScript.

Note that the backslash \ above is only used to break the command out over multiple lines for readability. This only works on macOS and Linux. Windows users can just type it out as one long string.

Tool tip: jq

macOS and Linux users: If you want to parse and process JSON on the command line, we highly recommend the tool "jq."

You can pipe curl responses directly into jq to have the response pretty-formatted:

```
curl -X GET localhost:3000/api/timers | jq '.'
```

You can also do some powerful manipulation of JSON, like iterating over all objects in the response and returning a particular field. In this example, we extract just the `id` property of every object in an array:

```
curl -X GET localhost:3000/api/timers | jq '.[] | { id }'
```

You can download jq here: https://stedolan.github.io/jq/[a].

[a]https://stedolan.github.io/jq/

Loading state from the server

Right now, we set initial state in `TimersDashboard` by hardcoding a JavaScript object, an array of timers. Let's modify this function to load data from the server instead.

We've written the client library that your React app will use to interact with the server, `client`. The library is defined in `public/js/client.js`. We'll use it first and then take a look at how it works in the next section.

The `GET /api/timers` endpoint provides a list of all timers, as represented in `data.json`. We can use `client.getTimers()` to call this endpoint from our React app. We'll do this to "hydrate" the state kept by `TimersDashboard`.

When we call `client.getTimers()`, the network request is made *asynchronously*. The function call itself is not going to return anything useful:

```
// Wrong
// `getTimers()` does not return the list of timers
const timers = client.getTimers();
```

Instead, we can pass `getTimers()` a success function. `getTimers()` will invoke that function after it hears back from the server if the server successfully returned a result. `getTimers()` will invoke the function with a single argument, the list of timers returned by the server:

```
// Passing `getTimers()` a success function
client.getTimers((serverTimers) => (
  // do something with the array of timers, `serverTimers`
));
```

`client.getTimers()` uses the Fetch API, which we cover in the next section. For our purposes, the important thing to know is that when `getTimers()` is invoked, it fires off the request to the server and then returns control flow *immediately*. The execution of our program does not wait for the server's response. This is why `getTimers()` is called an **asynchronous function**.

The success function we pass to `getTimers()` is called a **callback**. We're saying: "When you finally hear back from the server, if it's a successful response, invoke this function." This asynchronous paradigm ensures that execution of our JavaScript is not **blocked by I/O**.

We'll initialize our component's state with the `timers` property set to a blank array. This will allow all components to mount and perform their initial render. Then, we can populate the app by making a request to the server and setting the state:

time_tracking_app/public/js/app-8.js

```
class TimersDashboard extends React.Component {
  state = {
    timers: [],
  };

  componentDidMount() {
    this.loadTimersFromServer();
    setInterval(this.loadTimersFromServer, 5000);
  }

  loadTimersFromServer = () => {
    client.getTimers((serverTimers) => (
        this.setState({ timers: serverTimers })
      )
    );
  };
  // ...
```

A timeline is the best medium for illustrating what happens:

1. Before initial render

   React initializes the component. `state` is set to an object with the property `timers`, a blank array, is returned.
2. The initial render

   React then calls `render()` on `TimersDashboard`. In order for the render to complete, `EditableTimerList` and `ToggleableTimerForm` — its two children — must be rendered.

3. Children are rendered

   `EditableTimerList` has its render method called. Because it was passed a blank data array, it simply produces the following HTML output:

   ```
   <div id='timers'>
   </div>
   ```

   `ToggleableTimerForm` renders its HTML, which is the "+" button.

4. Initial render is finished

   With its children rendered, the initial render of `TimersDashboard` is finished and the HTML is written to the DOM.

5. `componentDidMount` is invoked

   Now that the component is mounted, `componentDidMount()` is called on `TimersDashboard`.

   This method calls `loadTimersFromServer()`. In turn, that function calls `client.getTimers()`. That will make the HTTP request to our server, requesting the list of timers. When `client` hears back, it invokes our success function.

   On invocation, the success function is passed one argument, `serverTimers`. This is the array of timers returned by the server. We then call `setState()`, which will trigger a new render. The new render populates our app with `EditableTimer` children and all of their children. The app is fully loaded and at an imperceptibly fast speed for the end user.

We also do one other interesting thing in `componentDidMount`. We use `setInterval()` to ensure `loadTimersFromServer()` is called every 5 seconds. While we will be doing our best to mirror state changes between client and server, this hard-refresh of state from the server will ensure our client will always be correct should it shift from the server.

The server is considered the master holder of state. Our client is a mere replica. This becomes incredibly powerful in a multi-instance scenario. If you have two instances of your app running — in two different tabs or two different computers — changes in one will be pushed to the other within five seconds.

Try it out

Let's have fun with this now. Save `app.js` and reload the app. You should see a whole new list of timers, driven by `data.json`. Any action you take will be wiped out within five seconds. Every five seconds, state is restored from the server. For instance, try deleting a timer and witness it resiliently spring back unscathed. Because we're not telling the server about these actions, its state remains unchanged.

On the flip-side, you can try modifying `data.json`. Notice how any modifications to `data.json` will be propagated to your app in under five seconds. Neat.

We're loading the initial state from the server. We have an interval function in place to ensure the client app's state does not drift from the server's in a multi-instance scenario.

We'll need to inform our server of the rest of our state changes: creates, updates (including starts and stops), and deletes. But first, let's pop open the logic behind `client` to see how it works.

While it is indeed neat that changes to our server data is seamlessly propagated to our view, in certain applications — like messaging — five seconds is almost an eternity. We'll cover the concept of **long-polling** in a future app. Long-polling enables changes to be pushed to clients near instantly.

`client`

If you open up `client.js`, the first method defined in the library is `getTimers()`:

time_tracking_app/public/js/client.js

```
function getTimers(success) {
  return fetch('/api/timers', {
    headers: {
      Accept: 'application/json',
    },
  }).then(checkStatus)
    .then(parseJSON)
    .then(success);
}
```

We are using the new **Fetch API** to perform all of our HTTP requests. Fetch's interface should look relatively familiar if you've ever used `XMLHttpRequest` or jQuery's `ajax()`.

Fetch

Until Fetch, JavaScript developers had two options for making web requests: Use `XMLHttpRequest` which is supported natively in all browsers or import a library that provides a wrapper around it (like jQuery's `ajax()`). Fetch provides a better interface than `XMLHttpRequest`. And while Fetch is still undergoing standardization, it is already supported by a few major browsers. At the time of writing, Fetch is turned on by default in Firefox 39 and above and Chrome 42 and above.

Until Fetch is more widely adopted by browsers, it's a good idea to include the library just in case. We've already done so inside `index.html`:

```
<!-- inside `head` tags index.html -->
<script src="vendor/fetch.js"></script>
```

As we can see in `client.getTimers()`, `fetch()` accepts two arguments:

- The path to the resource we want to fetch
- An object of request parameters

By default, Fetch makes a `GET` request, so we're telling Fetch to make a `GET` request to `/api/timers`. We also pass along one parameter: `headers`, the HTTP headers in our request. We're telling the server we'll *accept* only a JSON response.

Attached to the end of our call to `fetch()`, we have a chain of `.then()` statements:

time_tracking_app/public/js/client.js

```
    }).then(checkStatus)
      .then(parseJSON)
      .then(success);
```

To understand how this works, let's first review the functions that we pass to each `.then()` statement:

- **`checkStatus()`**: This function is defined inside of `client.js`. It checks if the server returned an error. If the server returned an error, `checkStatus()` logs the error to the console.
- **`parseJSON()`**: This function is also defined inside of `client.js`. It takes the response object emitted by `fetch()` and returns a JavaScript object.
- **`success()`**: This is the function we pass as an argument to `getTimers()`. `getTimers()` will invoke this function if the server successfully returned a response.

Fetch returns a **promise**. While we won't go into detail about promises, as you can see here a promise allows you to chain `.then()` statements. We pass each `.then()` statement a function. What we're essentially saying here is: "Fetching the timers from `/api/timers` *then* check the status code returned by the server. *Then*, extract the JavaScript object from the response. *Then*, pass that object to the success function."

At each stage of the pipeline, the result of the previous statement is passed as the argument to the next one:

1. When `checkStatus()` is invoked, it's passed a Fetch response object that `fetch()` returns.
2. `checkStatus()`, after verifying the response, returns the same response object.
3. `parseJSON()` is invoked and passed the response object returned by `checkStatus()`.
4. `parseJSON()` returns the JavaScript array of timers returned by the server.

5. `success()` is invoked with the array of timers returned by `parseJSON()`.

We could attach an infinite number of `.then()` statements to our pipeline. This pattern enables us to chain multiple function calls together in an easy-to-read format that supports asynchronous functions like `fetch()`.

It's OK if you're still uncomfortable with the concept of promises. We've written all the client code for this chapter for you, so you won't have trouble completing this chapter. You can come back afterwards to play around with `client.js` and get a feel for how it works.

You can read more about JavaScript's Fetch here[38] and promises here[39].

Looking at the rest of the functions in `client.js`, you'll note the methods contain much of the same boilerplate with small differences based on the endpoint of the API we are calling.

We just looked at `getTimers()` which demonstrates *reading* from the server. We'll look at one more function, one that *writes* to the server.

`startTimer()` makes a `POST` request to the `/api/timers/start` endpoint. The server needs the `id` of the timer and the `start` time. That request method looks like:

time_tracking_app/public/js/client.js

```
function startTimer(data) {
  return fetch('/api/timers/start', {
    method: 'post',
    body: JSON.stringify(data),
    headers: {
      'Accept': 'application/json',
      'Content-Type': 'application/json',
    },
  }).then(checkStatus);
}
```

In addition to `headers`, the request parameters object that we pass to `fetch()` has two more properties:

[38] https://developer.mozilla.org/en-US/docs/Web/API/Fetch_API

[39] https://developer.mozilla.org/en-US/docs/Web/JavaScript/Reference/Global_Objects/Promise

time_tracking_app/public/js/client.js

```
      method: 'post',
      body: JSON.stringify(data),
```

Those are:

- `method`: The HTTP request method. `fetch()` defaults to a `GET` request, so we specify we'd like a `POST` here.
- `body`: The body of our HTTP request, the data we're sending to the server.

`startTimer()` expects an argument, `data`. This is the object that will be sent along in the body of our request. It contains the properties `id` and `start`. An invocation of `startTimer()` might look like this:

```
// Example invocation of `startTimer()`
startTimer(
  {
    id: "bc5ea63b-9a21-4233-8a76-f4bca9d0a042",
    start: 1455584369113,
  }
);
```

In this example, the body of our request to the server will look like this:

```
{
  "id": "bc5ea63b-9a21-4233-8a76-f4bca9d0a042",
  "start": 1455584369113
}
```

The server will extract the id and start timestamp from the body and "start" the timer.

We don't pass `startTimers()` a success function. Our app does not need data from the server for this request and indeed our server will not return anything besides an "OK" anyway.

`getTimers()` is our only read operation and therefore the only one we'll pass a success function. The rest of our calls to the server are writes. Let's implement those now.

Sending starts and stops to the server

We can use the methods `startTimer()` and `stopTimer()` on `client` to make calls to the appropriate endpoints on the server. We just need to pass in an object that includes the `id` of the timer as well as the time it was started/stopped:

time_tracking_app/public/js/app-9.js

```
// Inside TimersDashboard
// ...
startTimer = (timerId) => {
  const now = Date.now();

  this.setState({
    timers: this.state.timers.map((timer) => {
      if (timer.id === timerId) {
        return Object.assign({}, timer, {
          runningSince: now,
        });
      } else {
        return timer;
      }
    }),
  });

  client.startTimer(
    { id: timerId, start: now }
  );
};

stopTimer = (timerId) => {
  const now = Date.now();

  this.setState({
    timers: this.state.timers.map((timer) => {
      if (timer.id === timerId) {
        const lastElapsed = now - timer.runningSince;
        return Object.assign({}, timer, {
          elapsed: timer.elapsed + lastElapsed,
          runningSince: null,
        });
      } else {
        return timer;
      }
    }),
  });

  client.stopTimer(
    { id: timerId, stop: now }
```

```
    );
  };

  render() {
```

You might ask: Why do we still manually make the state change within React? Can't we just inform the server of the action taken and then update state based on the server, the source of truth? Indeed, the following implementation is valid:

```
startTimer: function (timerId) {
  const now = Date.now();

  client.startTimer(
    { id: timerId, start: now }
  ).then(loadTimersFromServer);
},
```

We can chain a `.then()` to `startTimer()` as that function returns our original promise object. The last stage of the `startTimer()` pipeline would then be invoking the function `loadTimersFromServer()`. So immediately after the server processes our start timer request, we would make a subsequent request asking for the latest list of timers. This response would contain the now-running timer. React's state updates and the running timer would then be reflected in the UI.

Again, this is valid. However, the user experience will leave something to be desired. Right now, clicking the start/stop button gives *instantaneous* feedback because the state changes locally and React immediately re-renders. If we waited to hear back from the server, there might be a noticeable delay between the action (mouse click) and the response (timer starts running). You can try it yourself locally, but the delay would be most noticeable if the request had to go out over the internet.

What we're doing here is called **optimistic updating**. We're updating the client locally before waiting to hear from the server. This duplicates our state update efforts, as we perform updates on both the client and the server. But it makes our app as responsive as possible.

The "optimism" we have here is that the request will succeed and not fail with an error.

Using the same pattern as we did with starts and stops, see if you can implement creates, updates, and deletes on your own. Come back and compare your work with the next section.

Optimistic updating: Validations

Whenever we optimistic update, we always try to replicate whatever restrictions the server would have. This way, our client state changes under the same conditions as our server state.

For example, imagine if our server enforced that a timer's title cannot contain symbols. But the client did not enforce such a restriction. What would happen?

A user has a timer named `Gardening`. He feels a bit cheeky and renames it `Gardening :P`. The UI immediately reflects his changes, displaying `Gardening :P` as the new name of the timer. Satisfied, the user is about to get up and grab his shears. But wait! His timer's name suddenly snaps back to `Gardening`.

To successfully pull off eager updating, we must diligently replicate the code that manages state changes on both the client and the server. Furthermore, in a production app we should surface any errors the request to the server returns in the event that there is an inconsistency in the code or a fluke (the server is down).

Sending creates, updates, and deletes to the server

time_tracking_app/public/js/app-complete.js

```
// Inside TimersDashboard
// ...
createTimer = (timer) => {
  const t = helpers.newTimer(timer);
  this.setState({
    timers: this.state.timers.concat(t),
  });

  client.createTimer(t);
};

updateTimer = (attrs) => {
  this.setState({
    timers: this.state.timers.map((timer) => {
      if (timer.id === attrs.id) {
        return Object.assign({}, timer, {
          title: attrs.title,
          project: attrs.project,
        });
      } else {
```

```
          return timer;
        }
      }),
    });

    client.updateTimer(attrs);
  };

  deleteTimer = (timerId) => {
    this.setState({
      timers: this.state.timers.filter(t => t.id !== timerId),
    });

    client.deleteTimer(
      { id: timerId }
    );
  };

  startTimer = (timerId) => {
```

Recall that, in `createTimer()` and `updateTimer()` respectively, the `timer` and `attrs` objects contain an `id` property, as required by the server.

For creates, we need to send a full timer object. It should have an `id`, a `title`, and a `project`. For updates, we can send an `id` along with just whatever attributes are being updated. Right now, we always send along `title` and `project` regardless of what has changed. But it's worth noting this difference as it's reflected in the variable names that we are using (`timer` vs `attrs`).

Give it a spin

We are now sending all of our state changes to the server. Save `app.js` and reload the app. Add some timers, start some timers, and refresh and note that everything is persisted. You can even make changes to your app in one browser tab and see the changes propagate to another tab.

Next up

We've worked through a reusable methodology for building React apps and now have an understanding of how we connect a React app to a web server. Armed with these concepts, you're already equipped to build a variety of dynamic web applications.

In imminent chapters, we'll cover a variety of different component types that you encounter across the web (like forms and date pickers). We'll also explore state management paradigms for more complex applications.

JSX and the Virtual DOM

React Uses a Virtual DOM

React works differently than many earlier front-end JavaScript frameworks in that instead of working with the **browser's DOM**, it builds a **virtual representation** of the DOM. By **virtual**, we mean a tree of JavaScript objects that *represent* the "actual DOM". More on this in a minute.

In React, we *do not directly manipulate the actual DOM*. Instead, we must manipulate the virtual representation and let React take care of changing the browser's DOM.

As we'll see in this chapter, this is a very powerful feature but it requires us to think differently about how we build web apps.

Why Not Modify the Actual DOM?

It's worth asking: why do we need a Virtual DOM? Can't we just use the "actual-DOM"?

When we do "classic-" (e.g. jQuery-) style web development, we would typically:

1. locate an element (using `document.querySelector` or `document.getElementById`) and then
2. modify that element directly (say, by setting `.innerHTML` on the element).

This style of development is problematic in that:

- **It's hard to keep track of changes** - it can become difficult to keep track of current (and prior) state of the DOM to manipulate it into the form we need
- **It can be slow** - modifying the actual-DOM is a costly operation, and modifying the DOM on every change can cause poor performance

What is a Virtual DOM?

The Virtual DOM was created to deal with these issues. But *what is the Virtual DOM anyway*?

The Virtual DOM is a tree of JavaScript objects that represents the actual DOM.

One of the interesting reasons to use the Virtual DOM is the API it gives us. When using the Virtual DOM we code as if we're **recreating the entire DOM on every update**.

This idea of re-creating the entire DOM results in an easy-to-comprehend development model: instead of the developer keeping track of all DOM state changes, the developer simply returns the DOM *they wish to see*. React takes care of the transformation behind the scenes.

This idea of re-creating the Virtual DOM every update might sound like a bad idea: isn't it going to be slow? In fact, React's Virtual DOM implementation comes with important performance optimizations that make it very fast.

The Virtual DOM will:

- use **efficient diffing algorithms**, in order to know what changed
- **update subtrees** of the DOM simultaneously
- **batch updates** to the DOM

All of this results in an easy-to-use and optimized way to build web apps.

Virtual DOM Pieces

Again, when building a web app in React, we're not working directly with the browser's "actual DOM" directly, but instead a *virtual representation* of it. Our job is to provide React with enough information to build a **JavaScript object** that *represents* what the browser will render.

But what does this Virtual DOM JavaScript object actually consist of?

React's Virtual DOM is a tree of `ReactElements`.

Understanding the Virtual DOM, `ReactElements`, and how they interact with the "actual DOM" is a lot easier to understand by working through some examples, which we'll do below.

Q: Virtual DOM vs. Shadow DOM, are they the same thing? (A: No)

Maybe you've heard of the "Shadow DOM" and you're wondering, is the Shadow DOM the same thing as the Virtual DOM? The answer is **no**.

The *Virtual DOM* is a tree of JavaScript objects that represent the real DOM elements.

The *Shadow DOM* is a form of encapsulation on our elements. Think about using the `<video>` tag in your browser. In a `video` tag, your browser will create a set of video controls such as a play button, a timecode number, a scrubber progress bar etc. These elements aren't part of your "regular DOM", but instead, part of the "Shadow DOM".

Talking about the Shadow DOM is outside the scope of this chapter. But if you want to learn more about the Shadow DOM checkout this article: Introduction to Shadow DOM[40]

[40]http://webcomponents.org/articles/introduction-to-shadow-dom/

`ReactElement`

A `ReactElement` is a representation of a DOM element in the Virtual DOM.

React will take these `ReactElements` and place them into the "actual DOM" for us.

One of the best ways to get an intuition about `ReactElement` is to play around with it in our browser, so let's do that now.

Experimenting with `ReactElement`

Try this in your browser

For this section, open up the file `code/jsx/basic/index.html` (from the code download) in your browser.

Then open up your developer console and type commands into the console. You can access the console in Chrome by right-clicking and picking "Inspect" and then clicking on "Console" in the inspector.

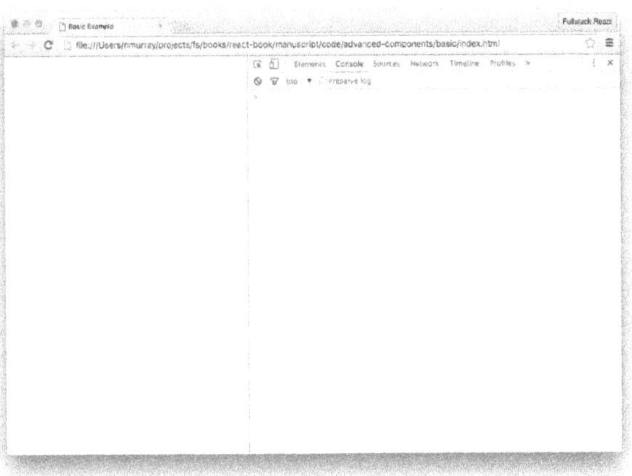

Basic Console

We'll start by using a simple HTML template that includes one `<div>` element with an id tag:

```
<div id='root' />
```

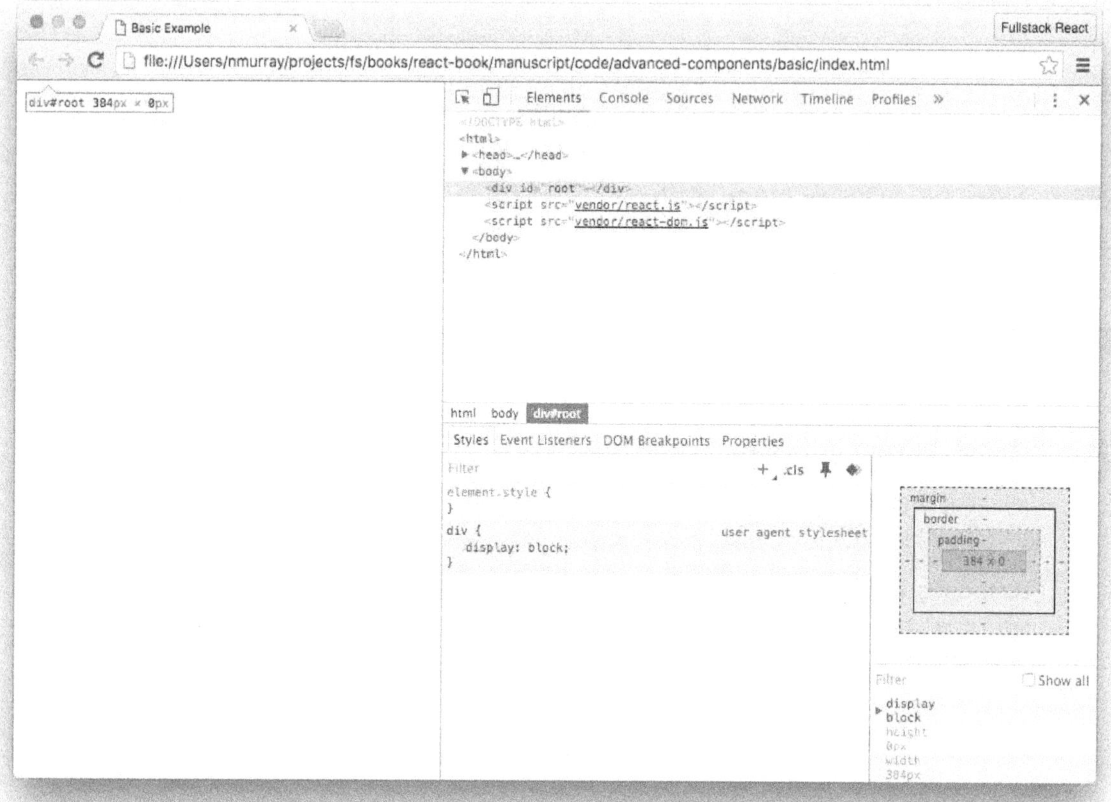

Root Element

Let's walk through how we render a <b></b> tag in our (actual) DOM using React. Of course, we **are not** going to create a <b> tag directly in the DOM (like we might if we were using jQuery).

Instead, React expects us to provide a **Virtual DOM tree**. That is, we're going to give React a set of JavaScript objects which **React will turn into a real DOM tree.**

The objects that make up the tree will be `ReactElements`. To create a `ReactElement`, we use the `createElement` method provided by React.

For instance, to create a `ReactElement` that represents a <b> (bold) element in React, type the following in the browser console:

```
var boldElement = React.createElement('b');
```

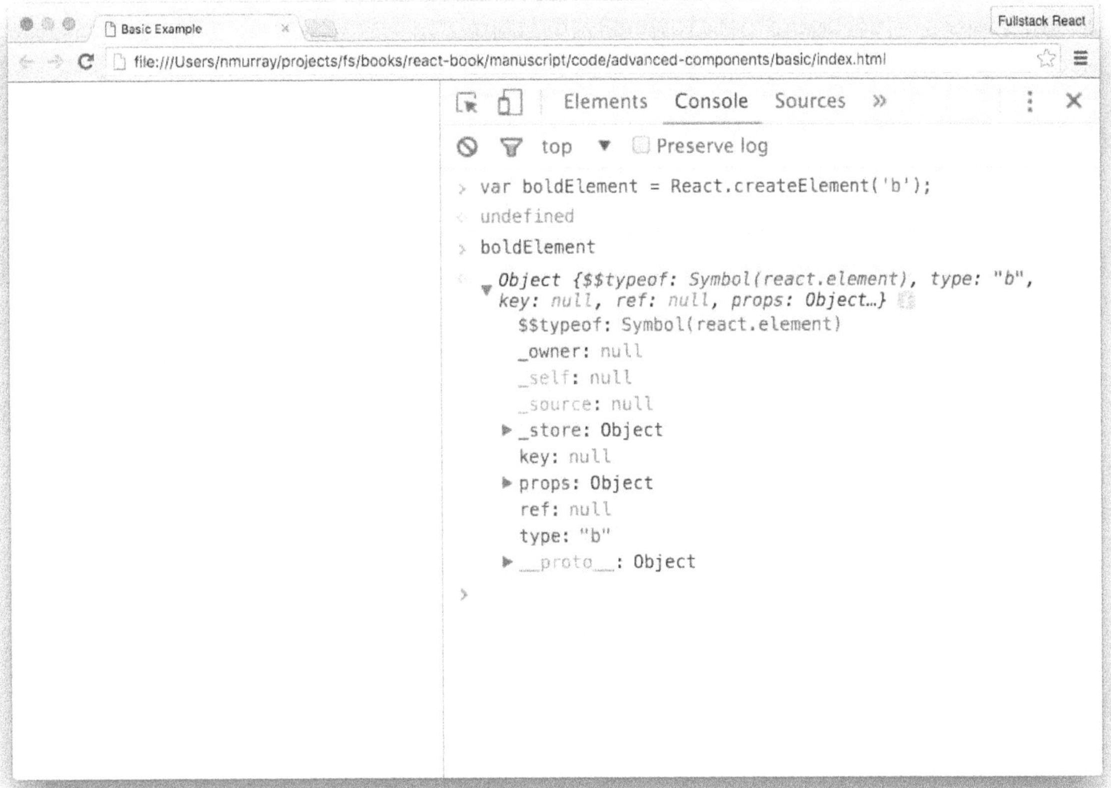

```
> var boldElement = React.createElement('b');
< undefined
> boldElement
< ▼Object {$$typeof: Symbol(react.element), type: "b",
   key: null, ref: null, props: Object…}
    $$typeof: Symbol(react.element)
    _owner: null
    _self: null
    _source: null
   ▶_store: Object
    key: null
   ▶props: Object
    ref: null
    type: "b"
   ▶__proto__: Object
>
```

`boldElement` is a `ReactElement`

Our `boldElement` above is an instance of a `ReactElement`. Now, we have this `boldElement`, but it's not visible without giving it to React to render in the actual DOM tree.

Rendering Our `ReactElement`

In order to render this element to the actual DOM tree we need to use `ReactDOM.render()` (which we cover in more detail a bit later in this chapter. `ReactDOM.render()` requires two things:

1. The *root* of our virtual tree
2. the *mount location* where we want React write to the *actual* browser DOM

In our simple template we want to get access to the `div` tag with an `id` of `root`. To get a reference to our actual DOM `root` element, we use one of the following:

```
// Either of these will work
var mountElement = document.getElementById('root');
var mountElement = document.querySelector('#root');

// if we were using jQuery this would work too
var mountElement = $('#root')
```

With our `mountElement` retrieved from the DOM, we can give React a point to insert its own rendered DOM.

```
var boldElement = React.createElement('b');
var mountElement = document.querySelector('#root');
// Render the boldElement in the DOM tree
ReactDOM.render(boldElement, mountElement);
```

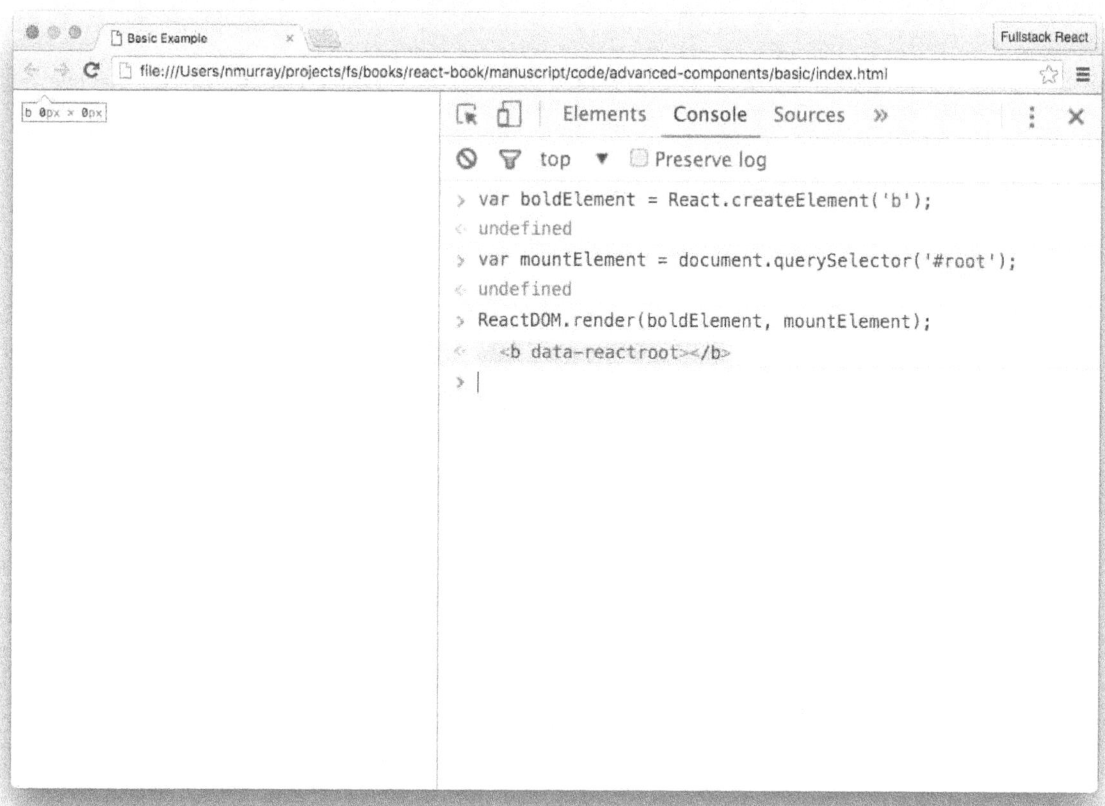

Despite the fact that nothing appears in the DOM, a new empty element has been inserted into the document as a child of the `mountElement`.

If we click the "Elements" tab in the Chrome inspector, we can see that a `b` tag was created in the actual DOM.

Adding Text (with children)

Although we now have a `b` tag in our DOM, it would be nice if we could add some text in the tag. Because text is in-between the opening and closing `b` tags, adding text is a matter of creating a *child* of the element.

Above, we used `React.createElement` with only a single argument (`'b'` for the `b` tag), however the `React.createElement()` function accepts three arguments:

1. The DOM element type
2. The element `props`
3. The children of the element

We'll walk through `props` in detail later in this section, so for now we'll set this parameter to `null`.

The `children` of the DOM element must be a `ReactNode` object, which is any of the following:

1. `ReactElement`
2. A string or a number (a `ReactText` object)
3. An array of `ReactNodes`

For example, to place text in our `boldElement`, we can pass a string as the third argument in the `createElement()` function from above:

```
var mountElement = document.querySelector('#root');
// Third argument is the inner text
var boldElement = React.createElement('b', null, "Text (as a string)");
ReactDOM.render(boldElement, mountElement);
```

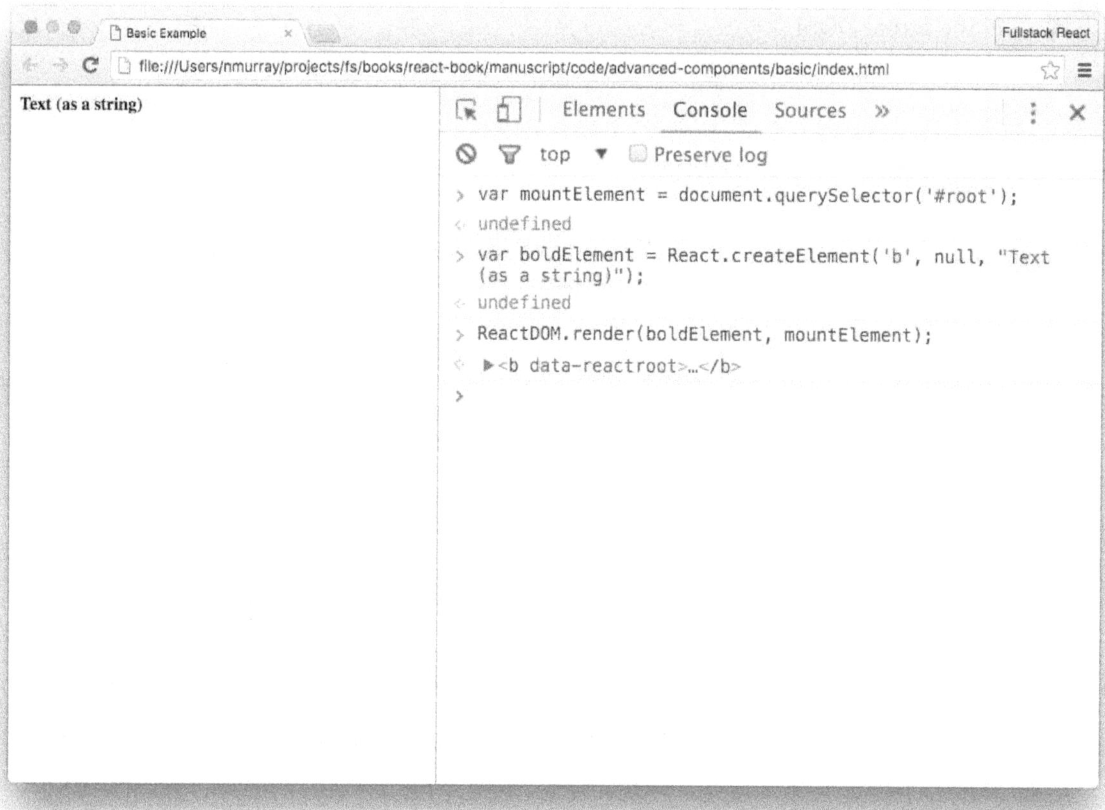

`ReactDOM.render()`

As we've seen, we use a React renderer places the virtual tree into a "hard" browser view (the "actual" DOM).

But there's a neat side effect of React using its own virtual representation of the view-tree: it can render this tree in **multiple types of canvases.**

That is, not only can React render into the browser's DOM, but it can also be used to **render views in other frameworks such as mobile apps**. In React Native (which we talk about later in this book), this tree is rendered into *native mobile views.*

That said, in this section we'll spend most of our time in the DOM, so we'll use the `ReactDOM` renderer to manage elements in the browser DOM.

As we've seen `ReactDOM.render()` is the way we get our React app into the DOM:

```
// ...
const component = ReactDOM.render(boldElement, mountElement);
```

We can call the `ReactDOM.render()` function multiple times and it will only perform updates (mutations) to the DOM as necessary.

The `ReactDOM.render` function accepts a 3rd argument: a callback argument that is executed after the component is rendered/updated. We can use this callback as a way to run functions after our app has started:

```
ReactDOM.render(boldElement, mountElement, function() {
  // The React app has been rendered/updated
});
```

JSX

JSX Creates Elements

When we created our `ReactElement` earlier, we used `React.createElement` like this:

```
var boldElement = React.createElement('b', null, "Text (as a string)");
```

This works fine as we had a small component, but if we had many nested components the syntax could get messy very quickly. Our DOM is hierarchical and our React component tree is hierarchical as well.

We can think of it this way: to describe pages to our browser we write HTML; the HTML is parsed by the browser to create HTML Elements which become the DOM.

HTML works very well for specifying tag hierarchies. It would be nice to represent our React component tree using markup, much like we do for HTML.

This is the idea behind `JSX`.

When using JSX, creating the `ReactElement` objects are handled for us. Instead of calling `React.createElement` for each element, the equivalent structure in JSX is:

```
var boldElement = <b>Text (as a string)</b>;
// => boldElement is now a ReactElement
```

The JSX parser will read that string and call `React.createElement` *for us*.

JSX stands for **JavaScript Syntax Extension**, and it is a syntax React provides that looks a lot like HTML/XML. Rather than building our component trees using normal JavaScript directly, we write our components almost as if we were writing HTML.

JSX provides a syntax that is similar to HTML. However, in JSX we can create our own tags (which encapsulate functionality of other components).

Although it has a scary-sounding name, writing JSX is not much more difficult than writing HTML. For instance, here is a JSX component:

```
const element = <div>Hello world</div>;
```

One difference between React components and HTML tags is in the naming. HTML tags start with a lowercase letter, while React components start with an uppercase. For example:

```
// html tag
const htmlElement = (<div>Hello world</div>);

// React component
const Message = props => (<div>{props.text}</div>)

// Use our React component with a `Message` tag
const reactComponent = (<Message text="Hello world" />);
```

We often surround JSX with parenthesis `()`. Although this is not always technically required, it helps us set apart JSX from JavaScript.

Our browser doesn't know how to read JSX, so how is JSX possible?

JSX is transformed into JavaScript by using a pre-processor build-tool before we load it with the browser.

When we write JSX, we pass it through a "compiler" (sometimes we say the code is *transpiled*) that converts the JSX to JavaScript. The most common tool for this is a plugin to `babel`, which we'll cover later.

Besides being able to write HTML-like component trees, JSX provides another advantage: we can mix JavaScript with our JSX markup. This lets us add logic inline with our views.

We've seen basic examples of JSX several times in this book already. What is different in this section is that we're going to take a more structured look at the different ways we can use JSX. We'll cover tips for using JSX and then talk about how to handle some tricky cases.

Let's look at:

- attribute expressions
- child expressions
- boolean attributes
- and comments

JSX Attribute Expressions

In order to use a JavaScript expression in a component's attribute, we wrap it in curly braces {} instead of quotes "".

```
// ...
const warningLevel = 'debug';
const component = (<Alert
                   color={warningLevel === 'debug' ? 'gray' : 'red'}
                   log={true} />)
```

This example uses the ternary operator[41] on the `color` prop.

If the `warningLevel` variable is set to `debug`, then the `color` prop will be `'gray'`, otherwise it will be `'red'`.

JSX Conditional Child Expressions

Another common pattern is to use a boolean checking expression and then render another element conditionally.

For instance, if we're building a menu that shows options for an `admin` user, we might write:

```
// ...
const renderAdminMenu = function() {
  return (<MenuLink to="/users">User accounts</MenuLink>)
}
// ...
const userLevel = this.props.userLevel;
return (
  <ul>
    <li>Menu</li>
    {userLevel === 'admin' && renderAdminMenu()}
  </ul>
)
```

We can also use the ternary operator to render one component or another.

For instance, if we want to show a `<UserMenu>` component for a logged in user and a `<LoginLink>` for an anonymous user, we can use this expression:

[41] https://developer.mozilla.org/en-US/docs/Web/JavaScript/Reference/Operators/Conditional_Operator

```
const Menu = (<ul>{loggedInUser ? <UserMenu /> : <LoginLink />}</ul>)
```

JSX Boolean Attributes

In HTML, the presence of some attributes sets the attribute to true. For instance, a disabled `<input>` HTML element can be defined:

```
<input name='Name' disabled />
```

In React we need to set these as booleans. That is, we need to pass a `true` or `false` explicitly as an attribute:

```
// Set the boolean in brackets directly
<input name='Name' disabled={true} />

// ... or use JavaScript variables
let formDisabled = true;
<input name='Name' disabled={formDisabled} />
```

If we ever need to *enable* the `input` above, then we set `formDisabled` to `false`.

JSX Comments

We can define comments inside of JSX by using the curly braces (`{}`) with comment delimiters (`/* */`):

```
let userLevel = 'admin';
{/*
  Show the admin menu if the userLevel is 'admin'
*/}
{userLevel === 'admin' && <AdminMenu />}
```

JSX Spread Syntax

Sometimes when we have many props to pass to a component, it can be cumbersome to list each one individually. Thankfully, JSX has a shortcut syntax that makes this easier.

For instance, if we have a `props` object that has two keys:

```
const props = {msg: "Hello", recipient: "World"}
```

We *could* pass each prop individually like this:

```
<Component msg={"Hello"} recipient={"World"} />
```

But by using the JSX *spread syntax* we can do it like this instead:

```
<Component {...props} />
<!-- essentially the same as this: -->
<Component msg={"Hello"} recipient={"World"} />
```

JSX Gotchas

Although JSX mimics HTML, there are a few important differences to pay attention to.

Here's a few things to keep in mind:

JSX Gotcha: `class` and `className`

When we want to set the CSS class of an HTML element, we normally use the `class` attribute in the tag:

```
<div class='box'></div>
```

Since JSX is so closely tied to JavaScript, we cannot use identifiers that JavaScript uses in our tag attributes. Attributes such as `for` and `class` conflict with the JavaScript keywords `for` and `class`.

Instead of using `class` to identify a class, JSX uses `className`:

```
<!-- Same as <div class='box'></div> -->
<div className='box'></div>
```

The `className` attributes works similarly to the `class` attribute in HTML. It expects to receive a string that identifies the class (or classes) associated with a CSS class.

To pass multiple classes in JSX, we can join an array to convert it to a string:

```
var cssNames = ['box', 'alert']
// and use the array of cssNames in JSX
(<div className={cssNames.join(' ')}></div>)
```

Tip: Managing `className` with `classnames`

The `classnames` npm package[42] is a great extension that we use to help manage css classes. It can take a list of strings or objects and allows us to conditionally apply classes to an element.

The `classnames` package takes the arguments, converts them to an object and conditionally applies a CSS class if the value is truthy.

code/jsx/basic/app.js

```
class App extends React.Component {
  render() {
    const klass = classnames({
      box: true, // always apply the box class
      alert: this.props.isAlert, // if a prop is set
      severity: this.state.onHighAlert, // with a state
      timed: false // never apply this class
    });
    return (<div className={klass} />)
  }
}
```

The package readme[43] provides alternate examples for more complex environments.

JSX Gotcha: `for` and `htmlFor`

For the same reason we cannot use the `class` attribute, we cannot apply the `for` attribute to a `<label>` element. Instead, we must use the attribute `htmlFor`. The property is a pass-through property in that it applies the attribute as `for`:

```
<!-- ... -->
<label htmlFor='email'>Email</label>
<input name='email' type='email' />
<!-- ... -->
```

JSX Gotcha: HTML Entities and Emoji

Entities are reserved characters in HTML which include characters such as less-than `<`, greater-than `>`, the copyright symbol, etc. In order to display entities, we can just place the entity code in literal text.

[42] https://www.npmjs.com/package/classnames

[43] https://github.com/JedWatson/classnames/blob/master/README.md

```
<ul>
  <li>phone: &phone;</li>
  <li>star: &star;</li>
</ul>
```

In order to display entities in dynamic data, we need to surround them in a string inside of curly braces ({}). Using unicode directly in JS works as expected. Just as we can send our JS to the browser as UTF-8 text directly. Our browser knows how to display UTF-8 code natively.

Alternatively, instead of using the entity character code, we can use unicode version instead.

```
return (
  <ul>
    <li>phone: {'\u0260e'}</li>
    <li>star: {'\u2606'}</li>
  </ul>
)
```

Emoji are just unicode character sequences, so we can add emoji the same way:

```
return(
  <ul>
    <li>dolphin: {'\uD83D\uDC2C'}</li>
    <li>dolphin: {'\uD83D\uDC2C'}</li>
    <li>dolphin: {'\uD83D\uDC2C'}</li>
  </ul>
)
```

- dolphin: 🐬
- dolphin: 🐬
- dolphin: 🐬

Everyone needs more dolphins

JSX Gotcha: `data-anything`

If we want to apply our own attributes that the HTML spec does not cover, we have to prefix the attribute key with the string `data-`.

```
<div className='box' data-dismissible={true} />
<span data-highlight={true} />
```

This requirement *only* applies to DOM components that are native to HTML and does not mean custom components cannot accept arbitrary keys as props. That is, we can accept *any* attribute on a custom component:

```
<Message dismissible={true} />
<Note highlight={true} />
```

There are a standard set of web accessibility[44] attributes[45] and its a good idea to use them because there are many people who will have a hard time using our site without them. We can use any of these attributes on an element with the key prepended with the string `aria-`. For instance, to set the `hidden` attribute:

```
<div aria-hidden={true} />
```

JSX Summary

JSX isn't magic. The key thing to keep in mind is that JSX is syntactic sugar to call `React.createElement`.

JSX is going to parse the tags we write and then create JavaScript objects. JSX is a convenience syntax to help build the component tree.

As we saw earlier, when we use JSX tags in our code, it gets converted to a `ReactElement`:

```
var boldElement = <b>Text (as a string)</b>;
// => boldElement is now a ReactElement
```

We can pass that `ReactElement` to `ReactDOM.render` and see our code rendered on the page.

There's one problem though: `ReactElement` is stateless and immutable. If we want to add interactivity (with state) into our app, we need another piece of the puzzle: `ReactComponent`.

In the next chapter, we'll talk about `ReactComponents` in depth.

[44] https://www.w3.org/WAI/intro/aria
[45] https://www.w3.org/TR/wai-aria/

References

Here are some places to read more about JSX and the Virtual DOM:

- JSX in Depth[46] - (Facebook)
- If-Else in JSX[47] - (Facebook)
- React (Virtual) DOM Terminology[48] - (Facebook)
- What is Virtual DOM[49] - (Jack Bishop)

---

[46]https://facebook.github.io/react/docs/jsx-in-depth.html
[47]https://facebook.github.io/react/tips/if-else-in-JSX.html
[48]https://facebook.github.io/react/docs/glossary.html
[49]http://jbi.sh/what-is-virtual-dom/

Advanced Component Configuration with `props`, `state`, and `children`

Unlike the rest of the chapters in this book, this chapter is intended on being read as an in-depth, deep dive into the different features of React, from an encylopedia-like perspective. For this reason, we did not include a step-by-step follow-along style project in this section of the book.

Intro

In this chapter we're going to dig deep into the configuration of components.

A `ReactComponent` is a JavaScript object that, at a minimum, has a `render()` function. `render()` is expected to **return a `ReactElement`**.

Recall that `ReactElement` is a representation of a DOM element in the Virtual DOM.

In the chapter "JSX and the Virtual DOM" we talked about `ReactElement` extensively. Checkout that chapter if you want to understand `ReactElement` better.

The goal of a `ReactComponent` is to

- `render()` a `ReactElement` (which will eventually become the real DOM) and
- attach functionality to this section of the page

"Attaching functionality" is a bit ambiguous; it includes attaching event handlers, managing state, interacting with children, etc. In this chapter we're going to cover:

- `render()` - the one required function on every `ReactComponent`
- `props` - the "input parameters" to our components
- `context` - a "global variable" for our components
- `state` - a way to hold data that is local to a component (that affects rendering)
- Stateless components - a simplified way to write reusable components
- `children` - how to interact and manipulate child components
- `statics` - how to create "class methods" on our components

Let's get started!

How to use this chapter

This chapter is built using a specific tool called `styleguidist`. In the code included with this course is a section called `components-cookbook`, which accompanies this chapter with the `styleguidist` tool bundled in with it. To use the `styleguidist` tool, which allows introspection into the components themselves, we can boot up the section through the chapter.

In order to get it started, change into the directory in terminal and issue the following commands. First, we'll need to get the dependencies for the project using `npm install`:

```
npm install
```

To start the application, issue the `npm start` command:

```
npm start
```

Once the server is running, we can navigate to our browser and head to the URL of `http://localhost:3000`. We'll see the styleguide running with all the components exposed by this chapter, where we can navigate through running examples of the components executing in real-time.

ReactComponent

Creating `ReactComponent`s - `createClass` or ES6 Classes

As discussed in the first chapter, there are two ways to define a `ReactComponent` instance:

1. `React.createClass()` or
2. ES6 classes

As we've seen, the two methods of creating components are roughly equivalent:

advanced-components/components-cookbook/src/components/Component/CreateClassApp.js

```
import React from 'react'

// React.createClass
const App = React.createClass({
  render: function() {} // required method
});

export default App
```

and

advanced-components/components-cookbook/src/components/Component/Components.js

```
import React from 'react'

// ES6 class-style
class App extends React.Component {
  render() {} // required
}

export default App
```

Regardless of the method we used to define the `ReactComponent`, React expects us to define the `render()` function.

`render()` Returns a `ReactElement` Tree

The `render()` method is the only required method to be defined on a `ReactComponent`.

After the component is **mounted** and **initialized**, `render()` will be called. The `render()` function's job is to provide React a *virtual representation* of a native DOM component.

An example of using `React.createClass` with the `render` function might look like this

advanced-components/components-cookbook/src/components/Component/CreateClassHeading.js

```
const CreateClassHeading = React.createClass({
  render: function() {
    return (
      <h1>Hello</h1>
    )
  }
});
```

Or with ES6 class-style components:

advanced-components/components-cookbook/src/components/Component/Header.js

```
class Heading extends React.Component {
  render() {
    return (
      <h1>Hello</h1>
    )
  }
};
```

The above code should look familiar. It describes a `Heading` component class with a single `render()` method that returns a simple, single Virtual DOM representation of a `<h1>` tag.

Remember that this `render()` method returns a `ReactElement` which isn't part of the "actual DOM", but instead a description of the Virtual DOM.

React expects the method to return a *single* child element. It can be a virtual representation of a DOM component or can return the falsy value of `null` or `false`. React handles the falsy value by rendering an empty element (a `<noscript />` tag). This is used to remove the tag from the page.

Keeping the `render()` method side-effect free provides an important optimization and makes our code easier to understand.

Getting Data into `render()`

Of course, while `render` is the only required method, it isn't very interesting if the only data we can render is known at compile time. That is, we need a way to:

- input "arguments" into our components and
- maintain state within a component.

React provides ways to do both of these things, with `props` and `state`, respectively.

Understanding these are crucial to making our components dynamic and *useable* within a larger app.

In React, `props` are immutable pieces of data that are passed into child components from parents.

Component `state` is where we hold data, local to a component. Typically, when our component's `state` changes, the component needs to be re-rendered. Unlike props, `state` is private to a component and is mutable.

We'll look at both `props` and `state` in detail below. Along the way we'll also talk about `context`, a sort of "implicit `props`" that gets passed through the whole component tree.

Let's look at each of these in more detail.

`props` are the parameters

`props` are the inputs to your components. If we think of our component as a function, we can think of the props as the arguments.

Let's look at an example:

```
<div>
  <Header headerText="Hello world" />
</div>
```

In the example code, we're creating both a `<div>` and a `<Header>` element, where the `<div>` is a usual DOM element, while `<Header>` is an instance of our `Header` component.

In this example, we're passing data from the component (the string `"Hello world"`) through the attribute `headerText` to the component.

Passing data through attributes to the component is often called *passing props*.

When we pass data to a component through an attribute it becomes available to the component through the `this.props` property. So in this case, we can access our `headerText` through the property `this.props.headerText`:

```
import React from 'react';

export class Header extends React.Component {
  render() {
    return (
      <h1>{this.props.headerText}</h1>
    );
  }
}
```

While we can access the `headerText` property, we *cannot* change it.

By using `props` we've taken our static component and allowed it to dynamically render whatever `headerText` is passed into it. The `<Header>` component cannot change the `headerText`, but it can use the `headerText` itself or pass it on to its children.

We can pass any JavaScript object through `props`. We can pass primitives, simple JavaScript objects, atoms, functions etc. We can even pass other React elements and Virtual DOM nodes.

We can document the functionality of our components using `props` and we can specify the *type* of each prop by using `PropTypes`.

PropTypes

`PropTypes` are a way to validate the values that are passed in through our `props`. Well-defined interfaces provide us with a layer of safety at the run time of our apps. They also provide a layer of documentation to the consumer of our components.

We include the `prop-types` package in our `package.json`.

We define `PropTypes` by setting a *static* (class) property `propTypes`. This object should be a map of prop-name keys to `PropTypes` values:

```
class Map extends React.Component {
  static propTypes = {
    lat: PropTypes.number,
    lng: PropTypes.number,
    zoom: PropTypes.number,
    place: PropTypes.object,
    markers: PropTypes.array,
  };
```

If using `createClass`, we define `PropTypes` by passing them as an option to `createClass()`:

```
const Map = React.createClass({
  propTypes: {
    lat: PropTypes.number,
    lng: PropTypes.number
    // ...
  },
})
```

In the example above, our component will validate that `lat`, `lng`, and `zoom` are all numbers, while `place` is an object and `marker` is an array.

There are a number of built-in `PropTypes`, and we can define our own.

We've written a code example for many of the `PropTypes` validators in "Appendix A: `PropTypes`." For more details on `PropTypes`, check out that appendix.

For now, we need to know that there are validators for scalar types:

- `string`
- `number`
- `boolean`

We can also validate complex types such as:

- `function`
- `object`
- `array`
- `arrayOf` - expects an array of a particular type
- `node`
- `element`

We can also validate a particular `shape` of an input object, or validate that it is an `instanceOf` a particular class.

Default `props` with `getDefaultProps()`

Sometimes we want our `props` to have defaults. We can use the static property `defaultProps` to do this.

For instance, create a `Counter` component definition and tell the component that if no `initialValue` is set in the `props` to set it to 1 using `defaultProps`:

```
class Counter extends React.Component {
  static defaultProps = {
    initialValue: 1
  };
  // ...
};
```

Now the component can be used without setting the `initialValue` prop. The two usages of the component are functionally equivalent:

```
<Counter />
<Counter initialValue={1} />
```

context

Sometimes we might find that we have a prop which we want to expose "globally". In this case, we might find it cumbersome to pass this particular prop down from the root, to every leaf, through every intermediate component.

Instead, specifying `context` allows us to automatically pass down variables from component to component, rather than needing to pass down our props at every level,

The `context` feature is experimental and it's similar to using a global variable to handle state in an application - i.e. minimize the use of `context` as relying on it too frequently is a code smell.

That is, `context` works best for things that truly are global, such as the central store in Redux.

When we specify a `context`, React will take care of passing down `context` from component to component so that at any point in the tree hierarchy, any component can reach up to the "global" context where it's defined and get access to the parent's variables.

In order to tell React we want to pass context from a parent component to the rest of its children we need to define two attributes in the parent class:

- `childContextTypes` and
- `getChildContext`

To retrieve the context inside a child component, we need to define the `contextTypes` in the child.

To illustrate, let's look at a possible message reader implementation:

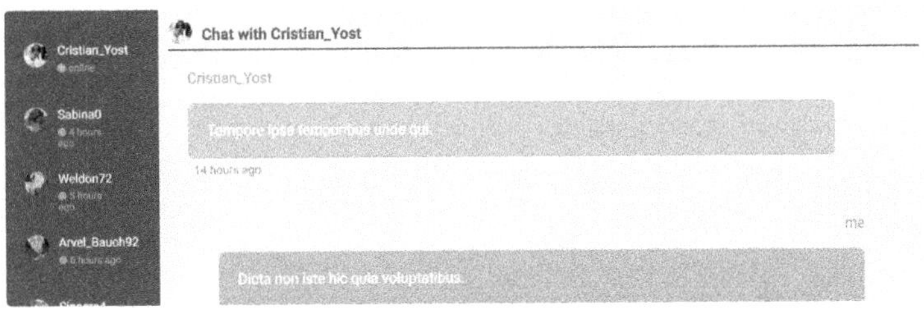


```
class Messages extends React.Component {
  static propTypes = {
    users: PropTypes.array.isRequired,
    messages: PropTypes.array.isRequired
  };

  render() {
    return (
      <div>
         <ThreadList />
         <ChatWindow />
      </div>
    )
  }
});

// ThreadList and ChatWindow are also React.Components
```

Without context, our `Messages` will have to pass the users along with the messages to the two child components (which in turn pass them to their children). Let's set up our hierarchy to accept `context` instead of needing to pass down `this.props.users` and `this.props.messages` along with every component.

In the `Messages` component, we'll define the two required properties. First, we need to tell React what the types are of our context.

We define this with the `childContextTypes` key. Similar to `propTypes`, the `childContextTypes` is a key-value object that lists the keys as the name of a context item and the value is a `PropType`.

Implementing `childContextTypes` in our `Messages` component looks like the following:

advanced-components/components-cookbook/src/components/Messages/Messages.js

```
class Messages extends React.Component {
  static propTypes = {
    users: PropTypes.array.isRequired,
    initialActiveChatIdx: PropTypes.number,
    messages: PropTypes.array.isRequired,
  };

  static childContextTypes = {
    users: PropTypes.array,
    userMap: PropTypes.object,
  };
```

Just like `propTypes`, the `childContextTypes` doesn't populate the context, it just defines it. In order to fill in the `this.context` object, we need to define the second required function: `getChildContext()`.

With `getChildContext()` we can set the initial value of our context with the return value of the function. Back in our `Messages` component, we will set our `users` context object to the value of the `this.props.users` given to the component.

advanced-components/components-cookbook/src/components/Messages/Messages.js

```
class Messages extends React.Component {
  // ...
  static childContextTypes = {
    users: PropTypes.array,
    userMap: PropTypes.object,
  };
  // ...
  getChildContext() {
    return {
      users: this.getUsers(),
      userMap: this.getUserMap(),
    };
  }
  // ...
}
```

Since the `state` and `props` of a component can change, the `context` can change as well. The `getChildContext()` method in the parent component gets called every time the `state` or `props` change on the parent component. If the `context` is updated, then the children will receive the updated context and will subsequently be re-rendered.

With the two required properties set on the parent component, React *automatically* passes the object down its subtree where any component can reach into it. In order to grab the context in a child component, we need to tell React we want access to it. We communicate this to React using the `contextTypes` definition in the child.

Without the `contextTypes` property on the child React component, React won't know what to send our component. Let's give our child components access to the context of our `Messages`.

advanced-components/components-cookbook/src/components/Messages/ThreadList.js

```
class ThreadList extends React.Component {
  // ...
  static contextTypes = {
    users: PropTypes.array,
  };
  // ...
}
```

advanced-components/components-cookbook/src/components/Messages/ChatWindow.js

```
class ChatWindow extends React.Component {
  // ...
  static contextTypes = {
    userMap: PropTypes.object,
  };
  // ...
}
```

advanced-components/components-cookbook/src/components/Messages/ChatMessage.js

```
class ChatMessage extends React.Component {
  // ...
  static contextTypes = {
    userMap: PropTypes.object,
  };
  // ...
}
```

Now anywhere in any one of our child components (that have `contextTypes` defined), we can reach into the parent and grab the `users` without needing to pass them along manually via `props`. The `context` data is set on the `this.context` object of the component with `contextTypes` defined.

For instance, our complete `ThreadList` might look something like:

advanced-components/components-cookbook/src/components/Messages/ThreadList.js

```
class ThreadList extends React.Component {
  // ...
  render() {
    return (
      <div className={styles.threadList}>
        <ul className={styles.list}>
          {this.context.users.map((u, idx) => {
            return (
              <UserListing
                onClick={this.props.onClick}
                key={idx}
                index={idx}
                user={u}
              />
            );
          })}
        </ul>
      </div>
    );
  }
```

If `contextTypes` is defined on a component, then several of its lifecycle methods will get passed an additional argument of `nextContext`:

advanced-components/components-cookbook/src/components/Messages/ThreadList.js

```
class ThreadList extends React.Component {
  // ...
  static contextTypes = {
    users: PropTypes.array,
  };
  // ...
  componentWillReceiveProps(nextProps, nextContext) {
    // ...
  }
  // ...
  shouldComponentUpdate(nextProps, nextState, nextContext) {
    // ...
  }
  // ...
  componentWillUpdate(nextProps, nextState, nextContext) {
```

```
    // ...
  }
  // ...
  componentDidUpdate(prevProps, prevState, prevContext) {
    // ...
  }
```

In a functional stateless component, `context` will get passed as the second argument:

We talk about stateless components below

advanced-components/components-cookbook/src/components/Messages/ChatHeader.js

```
const ChatHeader = (props, context) => {
  // ...
};
```

Using global variables in JavaScript is usually never a good idea and `context` is usually best reserved for limited situations where a global variable needs to be retrieved, such as a logged-in user. We err on the side of caution in terms of using `context` in our production apps and tend to prefer `props`.

`state`

The second type of data we'll deal with in our components is `state`. To know when to apply state, we need to understand the concept of *stateful* components. Any time a component needs to *hold on to a dynamic piece of data*, that component can be considered stateful.

For instance, when a light switch is turned on, that light switch is holding the state of "on." Turning a light off can be described as flipping the state of the light to "off."

In building our apps, we might have a switch that describes a particular setting, such as an input that requires validation, or a presence value for a particular user in a chat application. These are all cases for keeping state about a component within it.

We'll refer to components that hold local-mutable data as *stateful* components. We'll talk a bit more below about when we should use component state. For now, know that it's a good idea to have as **few stateful components as possible**. This is because state introduces complexity and makes composing components more difficult. That said, sometimes we need component-local state, so let's look at how to implement it, and we'll discuss *when* to use it later..

Using `state`: Building a Custom Radio Button

In this example, we're going to use internal state to build a radio button to switch between payment methods. Here's what the form will look like when we're done:

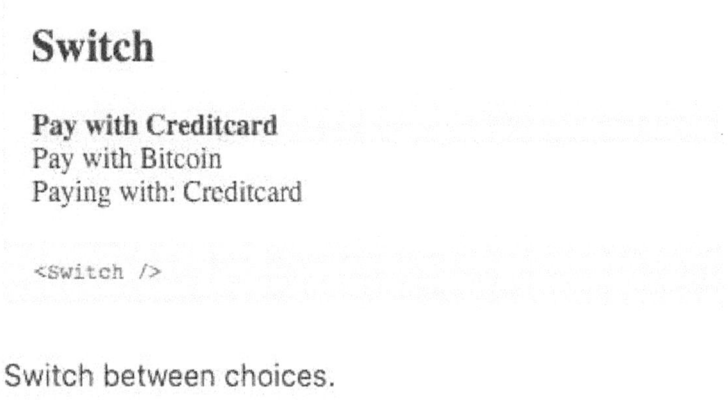

Switch

Pay with Creditcard
Pay with Bitcoin
Paying with: Creditcard

<Switch />

Switch between choices.

Simple Switch

Let's look at how to make a component stateful:

advanced-components/components-cookbook/src/components/Switch/steps/Switch1.js

```
class Switch extends React.Component {
  state = {};

  render() {
    return <div><em>Template will be here</em></div>;
  }
}

module.exports = Switch;
```

That's it! Of course, just setting state on the component isn't all that interesting. To *use* the state on our component, we'll reference it using `this.state`.

advanced-components/components-cookbook/src/components/Switch/steps/Switch2.js

```
const CREDITCARD = 'Creditcard';
const BTC = 'Bitcoin';

class Switch extends React.Component {
  state = {
    payMethod: BTC,
  };

  render() {
    return (
      <div className='switch'>
        <div className='choice'>Creditcard</div>
        <div className='choice'>Bitcoin</div>
        Pay with: {this.state.payMethod}
      </div>
    );
  }
}

module.exports = Switch;
```

In our render function, we can see the choices our users can pick from (although we can't change a method of payment yet) and their current choice stored in the component's `state`. This `Switch` component is now stateful as it's keeping track of the user's preferred method of payment.

Our payment switch isn't yet interactive; we cannot change the state of the component. Let's hook up our first bit of interactivity by adding an event handler to run when our user selects a different payment method.

In order to add interaction, we'll want to respond to a click event. To add a callback handler to *any* component, we can use the `onClick` attribute on a component. The `onClick` handler will be fired anytime the component it's defined on is clicked.

advanced-components/components-cookbook/src/components/Switch/steps/Switch3.js

```
    return (
      <div className='switch'>
        <div
          className='choice'
          onClick={this.select(CREDITCARD)} // add this
        >Creditcard</div>
        <div
          className='choice'
          onClick={this.select(BTC)} // ... and this
        >Bitcoin</div>
        Pay with: {this.state.payMethod}
      </div>
    );
```

Using the `onClick` attribute, we've attached a callback handler that will be called every time either one of the `<div>` elements are clicked.

The `onClick` handler expects to receive a *function* that it will call when the click event occurs. Let's look at the `select` function:

advanced-components/components-cookbook/src/components/Switch/steps/Switch3.js

```
class Switch extends React.Component {
  state = {
    payMethod: BTC,
  };

  select = (choice) => {
    return (evt) => {
      // <-- handler starts here
      this.setState({
        payMethod: choice,
      });
    };
  };
```

Notice two things about `select`:

1. It returns a function
2. It uses `setState`

Returning a New Function

Notice something interesting about `select` and `onClick`: the attribute `onClick` expects a *function* to be passed in, but we're *calling* a function first. That's because the `select` function will *return* a function itself.

This is a common pattern for passing arguments to handlers. We *close over* the `choice` argument when we call `select`. `select` returns a new function that will call `setState` with the appropriate `choice`.

When one of the child `<div>` elements are clicked, the handler function will be called. Note that `select` is actually called during `render`, and it's the *return value* of `select` that gets called `onClick`.

Updating the State

When the handler function is called, the component will call `setState` on itself. Calling `setState` triggers a refresh, which means the `render` function will be called again, and we'll be able to see the current `state.payMethod` in our view.

`setState` has performance implications

Since the `setState` method triggers a refresh, we want to be careful about how often we call it.

Modifying the actual-DOM is slow so we don't want to cause a cascade of `setStates` to be called, as that could result it poor performance for our user.

Viewing the Choice

In our component we don't (yet) have a way to indicate which choice has been selected other than the accompanying text.

It would be nice if the choice itself had a visual indication of being the selected one. We usually do this with CSS by applying an `active` class. In our example, we use the `className` attribute.

In order to do this, we'll need to add some logic around which CSS classes to add depending upon the current state of the component.

But before we add too much logic around the CSS, let's refactor component to use a function to render each choice:

advanced-components/components-cookbook/src/components/Switch/steps/Switch4.js

```
      <div className='choice' onClick={this.select(choice)}>
        {choice}
      </div>
    );
  };

  render() {
    return (
      <div className='switch'>
        {this.renderChoice(CREDITCARD)}
        {this.renderChoice(BTC)}
        Pay with: {this.state.payMethod}
      </div>
    );
  }
}

module.exports = Switch;
```

Now, instead of putting all render code into `render()` function, we isolate the choice rendering into its own function.

Lastly, let's add the `.active` class to the `<div>` choice component.

advanced-components/components-cookbook/src/components/Switch/steps/Switch5.js

```
    const cssClasses = [];

    if (this.state.payMethod === choice) {
      cssClasses.push(styles.active); // add .active class
    }

    return (
      <div
        className='choice'
        onClick={this.select(choice)}
        className={cssClasses}
      >
        {choice}
      </div>
    );
```

```
  };

  render() {
    return (
      <div className='switch'>
        {this.renderChoice(CREDITCARD)}
        {this.renderChoice(BTC)}
        Pay with: {this.state.payMethod}
      </div>
    );
  }
```

Notice that we push the style `styles.active` onto the `cssClassses` array. Where did `styles` come from?

For this code example, we're using a webpack loader to import the CSS. Diving in to how webpack works is beyond the scope of this chapter. But just so you know how we're using it, there are two things to know:

1. We're importing the styles like this: `import styles from '../Switch.css';`
2. This means all of the styles in that file are accessible like an object - e.g. `styles.active` gives us a reference to the `.active` class from `Switch.css`

We do it this way because it's a form of *CSS encapsulation*. That is, the *actual* CSS class won't actually be `.active`, which means we won't conflict with other components that might use the same class name.

Stateful components

Defining state on our component requires us to set an instance variable called `this.state` in the object prototype class. In order to do this, it requires us to set the state in one of two places, either as a property of the class or in the constructor.

Setting up a stateful component in this way:

1. Allows us to define the *initial* state of our component.
2. Tells React that our component will be stateful. Without this method defined, our component will be considered to be stateless.

For a component, this looks like:

advanced-components/components-cookbook/src/components/InitialState/Component.js

```
class InitialStateComponent extends React.Component {
  // ...
  constructor(props) {
    super(props)

    this.state = {
      currentValue: 1,
      currentUser: {
        name: 'Ari'
      }
    }
  }
  // ...
}
```

In this example, the `state` object is just a JavaScript object, but we can return anything in this function. For instance, we may want to set it to a single value:

advanced-components/components-cookbook/src/components/InitialState/Component.js

```
class Counter extends React.Component {
  constructor(props) {
    super(props)

    this.state = 0
  }
}
```

Setting `props` inside of our component is always a bad idea. Setting the initial value of the `state` property is the *only* time we should ever use props when dealing with a component's state. That is, if we ever want to set the value of a prop to the state, we should do it here.

For instance, if we have a component where the `prop` indicates a `value` of the component, we should apply that value to the `state` in the `constructor()` method. A better name for the value as a prop is `initialValue`, indicating that the initial state of the value will be set.

For example, consider a `Counter` component that displays some count and contains an increment and decrement button. We can set the initial value of the counter like this:

advanced-components/components-cookbook/src/components/Counter/CounterWrapper.js

```
const CounterWrapper = props => (
  <div>
    <Counter initialValue={125} />
  </div>
)
```

From the usage of the `<Counter>` component, we know that the value of the `Counter` will change simply by the name `initialValue`. The `Counter` component can use this prop in `constructor()`, like so:

advanced-components/components-cookbook/src/components/Counter/Counter.js

```
class Counter extends Component {
  constructor(props) {
    super(props);

    this.state = {
      value: this.props.initialValue
    };
  }
  // ...
}
```

Since the constructor is run once and only once before the component itself is mounted, we can use it to establish our initial state.

State updates that depend on the current state

`Counter` has buttons for incrementing and decrementing the count:

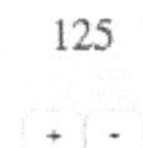

The `Counter` component

When the "-" button is pressed, React will invoke `decrement()`. `decrement()` will subtract `1` from state's `value`. Something like this would appear to be sufficient:

advanced-components/components-cookbook/src/components/Counter/Counter1.js

```
decrement = () => {
  // Appears correct, but there is a better way
  const nextValue = this.state.value - 1;
  this.setState({
    value: nextValue,
  });
}
```

However, **whenever a state update depends on the current state, it is preferable to pass a function to `setState()`**. We can do so like this:

advanced-components/components-cookbook/src/components/Counter/Counter.js

```
decrement = () => {
  this.setState(prevState => {
    return {
      value: prevState.value - 1,
    };
  });
}
```

`setState()` will invoke this function with the previous version of the state as the first argument.

Why is setting state this way necessary? Because **`setState()` is asynchronous**.

Here's an example. Let's say we're using the first `decrement()` method where we pass an object to `setState()`. When we invoke `decrement()` for the first time, `value` is `125`. We'd then invoke `setState()`, passing an object with a `value` of `124`.

However, **the state will not necessarily be updated immediately**. Instead, React will add our requested state update to its queue.

Let's say that the user is particularly fast with her mouse and her computer is particularly slow with its processing. The user manages to click the decrement button *again* before React gets around to our previous state update. Responding to user interactions are high-priority, so React invokes `decrement()`. The `value` in state is *still* `125`. So, we enqueue *another* state update, again setting `value` to `124`.

React then commits both state updates. To the dismay of our astute and quick-fingered user, instead of the correct `value` of `123` the app shows a count of `124`.

In our simple example, there's a thin chance this bug would occur. But as a React app grows in complexity, React might encounter periods where it is overloaded with high-priority work, like animations. And it is conceivable that state updates might be queued for consequential lengths of time.

Whenever a state transition depends on the current state, using a function to set the state helps to avoid the chance for such enigmatic bugs to materialize.

For further reading on this topic, see our own Sophia Shoemaker's post Using a function in `setState` instead of an object[50].

Thinking About State

Spreading state throughout our app can make it difficult to reason about. When building stateful components, we should be mindful about **what** we put in state and **why** we're using state.

Generally, we want to minimize the number of components in our apps that keep component-local state.

If we have a component that has UI states which:

1. cannot be "fetched" from outside or
2. cannot be passed into the component,

that's usually a case for building state into the component.

However, any data that can be passed in through `props` or by other components is usually best to leave untouched. The *only* information we should ever put in state are values that are not computed and do not need to be *sync'd* across the app.

> The decision to put state in our components or not is deeply related to the tension between "object-oriented programming" and "functional programming".
>
> In functional programming, if you have a pure function, then calling the same function, with the same arguments, will always return the same value for a given set of inputs. This makes the behavior of a pure function easy to reason about, because the output is consistent at all times, with respect to the inputs.
>
> In object-oriented programming you have objects which hold on to state within that object. The object state then becomes implicit parameters to the methods on the object. The state can change and so calling the same function, with the same arguments, at different times in your program can return different answers.
>
> This is related to `props` and `state` in React components because you can think of `props` as "arguments" to our components and `state` as "instance variables" to an object.
>
> If our component uses only `props` for configuring a component (and it does not use `state` or any

[50] https://medium.com/@shopsifter/using-a-function-in-setstate-instead-of-an-object-1f5cfd6e55d1

other outside variables) then we can easily predict how a particular component will render.

However, if we use mutable, component-local state then it becomes more difficult to understand what a component will render at a particular time.

So while carrying "implicit arguments" through state can be convenient, it can also make the system difficult to reason about.

That said, state can't be avoided entirely. The real world has state: when you flip a light switch the world has now changed - our programs have to be able to deal with state in order to operate in the real world.

The good news is that there are a variety of tools and patterns that have emerged for dealing with state in React (notably Flux and its variants), which we talk about elsewhere in the book. The rule of thumb you should work with is to **minimize the number of components with `state`**.

Keeping state is usually good to enforce and maintain consistent UI that wouldn't otherwise be updated. Additionally, one more thing to keep in mind is that we should try to minimize the amount of information we put into our state. The smaller and more serializable we can keep it (i.e. can we easily turn it into JSON), the better. Not only will our app be faster, but it will be easier to reason about. It's usually a red-flag when our state gets large and/or unmanageable.

One way that we can mitigate and minimize the complex states is by building our apps with a single stateful component composed of stateless components: components that do not keep state.

Stateless Components

An alternative approach to building *stateful* components would be to use *stateless* components. Stateless components are intended to be lightweight components that do not need any special handling around the component.

Stateless components are React's lightweight way of building components that only need the `render()` method.

Let's look an example of a stateless component:

advanced-components/components-cookbook/src/components/Header/StatelessHeader.js

```
const Header = function(props) {
  return (<h1>{props.headerText}</h1>)
}
```

Notice that we don't reference `this` when accessing our props as they are simply passed into the function. The stateless component here isn't actually a class in the sense that it isn't a `ReactElement`.

We won't reference `this` when working with functional, stateless components. They are just functions and do not have a backing instance. These components *cannot* contain state and do not get called with the normal component lifecycle methods.

React **does** allow us to use `propTypes` and `defaultProps` on stateless components.

With so many constraints, why would we want to use stateless components? There are two reasons:

First, as we discussed above, stateful components often spread complexity throughout a system. Using stateless components where possible can help contain the state in fewer locations. This makes our programs easier to reason about.

Second, using functional components can have performance benefits. There's less "ceremony" around component setup and tear-down. The React core team has mentioned that more performance improvements may be introduced for functional components in the future.

A good rule of thumb is to use stateless components as much as we can. If we don't need any lifecycle methods and can get away with only a rendering function, using a stateless component is a great choice.

`Switch`ing to Stateless

Can we convert our `Switch` component above to a stateless component? Well, the currently selected payment choice *is* state and so it has to be kept somewhere.

While we can't remove state completely, we could at least isolate it. This is a common pattern in React apps: try to pull the state into a few parent components.

In our `Switch` component we pulled each choice out into the `renderChoice` function. This indicates that this is a good candidate for pulling into its own stateless component. There's one problem: `renderChoice` is the function that calls `select`, which means that it indirectly is the function that calls `setState`. Let's take a look at how to handle this issue:

advanced-components/components-cookbook/src/components/Switch/steps/Switch6.js

```
const Choice = function (props) {
  const cssClasses = [];

  if (props.active) {
    // <-- check props, not state
    cssClasses.push(styles.active);
  }

  return (
    <div
      className='choice'
      onClick={props.onClick}
```

```
        className={cssClasses}
      >
        {props.label} {/* <-- allow any label */}
```

Here we've created a `Choice` function which is *a stateless component*. But we have a problem: if our component is stateless then we can't read from `state`. What do we do instead? **Pass the arguments down through `props`.**

In `Choice` we make three changes (which is marked by comments in the code above):

1. We determine if this choice is the active one by reading `props.active`
2. When a `Choice` is clicked, we call whatever function that is on `props.onClick`
3. The label is determined by `props.label`

All of these changes mean that `Choice` is *decoupled* from the `Switch` statement. We could now conceivably use `Choice` anywhere, as long as we pass `active`, `onClick`, and `label` through the props.

Let's look at how this changes `Switch`:

advanced-components/components-cookbook/src/components/Switch/steps/Switch6.js

```
  render() {
    return (
      <div className='switch'>
        <Choice
          onClick={this.select(CREDITCARD)}
          active={this.state.payMethod === CREDITCARD}
          label='Pay with Creditcard'
        />

        <Choice
          onClick={this.select(BTC)}
          active={this.state.payMethod === BTC}
          label='Pay with Bitcoin'
        />

        Paying with: {this.state.payMethod}
```

Here we're using our `Choice` component and passing the three props (parameters) `active`, `onClick`, and `label`. What's neat about this is that we could easily:

1. Change what happens when we click this choice by changing the input to `onClick`

2. Change the condition by which a particular choice is considered active by changing the `active` prop
3. Change what the label is to any arbitrary string

By creating a stateless component `Choice` we're able to make `Choice` reusable and not be tied to any particular `state`.

Stateless Encourages Reuse

Stateless components are a great way to create reusable components. Because stateless components need to have all of their configuration passed from the outside, we can often reuse stateless components in nearly any project, provided that we supply the right hooks.

Now that we've covered both `props`, `context`, and `state` we're going to cover a couple more advanced features we can use with components.

Our components exist in a hierarchy and sometimes we need to communicate (or manipulate) the children components. The the next section, we're going to discuss how to do this.

Talking to Children Components with `props.children`

While we generally specify `props` ourselves, React provides provides some special `props` for us. In our components, we can refer to child components in the tree using `this.props.children`.

For instance, say we have a `Newspaper` component that holds an `Article`:

advanced-components/components-cookbook/src/components/Article/Newspaper.js

```
const Newspaper = props => {
  return (
    <Container>
      <Article headline="An interesting Article">
        Content Here
      </Article>
    </Container>
  )
}
```

The container component above contains a single child, the `Article` component. How many children does the `Article` component contain? It contains a single child, the text `Content Here`.

In the `Container` component, say that we want to add markup *around* whatever the `Article` component renders. To do this, we write our JSX in the `Container` component, and then place `this.props.children`:

advanced-components/components-cookbook/src/components/Article/Container.js

```
class Container extends React.Component {
  // ...
  render() {
    return (
      <div className='container'>
        {this.props.children}
      </div>
    )
  }
```

The `Container` component above will create a `div` with `class='container'` and the children of this React tree will render within that `div`.

Generally, React will pass the `this.props.children` prop as a list of components if there are multiple children, whereas it will pass a single element if there is only one component.

Now that we know how `this.props.children` works, we should rewrite the previous `Container` component to use `propTypes` to document the API of our component. We can expect that our `Container` is likely to contain multiple `Article` components, but it might also contain only a single `Article`. So let's specify that the `children` prop can be either an element or an array.

If `PropTypes.oneOfType` seems unfamiliar, refer to "Appendix A: `PropTypes`](#appendix_-prop_types)" which explains how it works.

advanced-components/components-cookbook/src/components/Article/DocumentedContainer.js

```
class Container extends React.Component {
  static propTypes = {
    children: PropTypes.oneOf([
      PropTypes.element,
      PropTypes.array
    ])
  }
  // ...
  render() {
    return (
      <div className="container">
        {this.props.children}
      </div>
    )
  }
}
```

It can become cumbersome to check what type our `children` prop is every time we want to use `children` in a component. We can handle this a few different ways:

1. Require `children` to be a single child every time (e.g., wrap our children in their own element).
2. Use the `Children` helper provided by React.

The first method of requiring a child to be a single element is straightforward. Rather than defining the children above as `oneOfType()`, we can set the children to a be a single element.

advanced-components/components-cookbook/src/components/Article/SingleChildContainer.js

```
class Container extends React.Component {
  static propTypes = {
    children: PropTypes.element.isRequired,
  }
  // ...
  render() {
    return (
      <div className="container">
        {this.props.children}
      </div>
    )
  }
}
```

Inside the `Container` component we can deal with the children *always* being able to be rendered as a single leaf of the hierarchy.

The second method of is to use the `React.Children` utility helper for dealing with the child components. There are a number of helper methods for handling children, let's look at them now.

`React.Children.map()` & `React.Children.forEach()`

The most common operation we'll use on children is mapping over the list of them. We'll often use a `map` to call `React.cloneElement()` or `React.createElement()` along the children.

map() and forEach()

Both the `map()` and `forEach()` function execute a provided function once per each element in an iterable (either an object or array).

```
[1, 2, 3].forEach(function(n) {
  console.log("The number is: " + n);
  return n; // we won't see this
})
[1, 2, 3].map(function(n) {
  console.log("The number is: " + n);
  return n; // we will get these
})
```

The difference between `map()` and `forEach()` is that the *return* value of `map()` is an array of the result of the callback function, whereas `forEach()` does not collect results.

So in this case, while both `map()` and `forEach()` will print the `console.log` statements, `map()` will return the array `[1, 2, 3]` whereas `forEach()` will not.

Let's rewrite the previous `Container` to allow a **configurable wrapper component for each child.** The idea here is that this component takes:

1. A prop `component` which is going to wrap each child
2. A prop `children` which is the list of children we're going to wrap

To do this, we call `React.createElement()` to generate a new `ReactElement` for each child:

advanced-components/components-cookbook/src/components/Article/MultiChildContainer.js

```
class Container extends React.Component {
  static propTypes = {
    component: PropTypes.element.isRequired,
    children: PropTypes.element.isRequired
  }
  // ...
  renderChild = (childData, index) => {
    return React.createElement(
      this.props.component,
      {}, // <~ child props
      childData // <~ child's children
    )
  }
  // ...
```

```
  render() {
    return (
      <div className='container'>
        {React.Children.map(
          this.props.children,
          this.renderChild
        )}
      </div>
    )
  }
}
```

Again, the difference between `React.Children.map()` and `React.Children.forEach()` is that the former creates an array and returns the result of each function and the latter does not. We'll mostly use `.map()` when we render a child collection.

`React.Children.toArray()`

`props.children` returns a data structure that can be tricky to work with. Often when dealing with children, we'll want to convert our `props.children` object into a regular array, for instance when we want to re-sort the ordering of the children elements. `React.Children.toArray()` converts the `props.children` data structure into an array of the children.

advanced-components/components-cookbook/src/components/Article/ArrayContainer.js

```
class Container extends React.Component {
  static propTypes = {
    component: PropTypes.element.isRequired,
    children: PropTypes.element.isRequired
  }
  // ...
  render() {
    const arr =
      React.Children.toArray(this.props.children);

    return (
      <div className="container">
        {arr.sort((a, b) => a.id < b.id )}
      </div>
    )
  }
}
```

Summary

By using props and context we get data into our components and by using PropTypes we can specify clear expectations about what we require that data to be.

By using state we hold on to component-local data, and we tell our components to re-render whenever that state changes. However state can be tricky! One technique to minimize stateful components is to use stateless, functional components.

Using these tools we can create powerful interactive components. However there is one important set of configurations that we did not cover here: lifecycle methods.

Lifecycle methods like componentDidMount and componentWillUpdate provide us with powerful hooks into the application process. In the next chapter, we're going to dig deep into component lifecycle and show how we can use those hooks to validate forms, hook in to external APIs, and build sophisticated components.

References

- React Top-Level API Docs[51]
- React Component API Docs[52]

[51] https://facebook.github.io/react/docs/top-level-api.html
[52] https://facebook.github.io/react/docs/component-api.html

Forms

Forms 101

Forms are one of the most crucial parts of our application. While we get some interaction through clicks and mouse moves, it's really through forms where we'll get the majority of our rich input from our users.

In a sense, it's where the rubber meets the road. It's through a form that a user can add their payment info, search for results, edit their profile, upload a photo, or send a message. Forms transform your web **site** into a web **app**.

Forms can be deceptively simple. All you really need are some `input` tags and a `submit` tag wrapped up in a `form` tag. However, creating a rich, interactive, easy to use form can often involve a significant amount of programming:

- Form inputs modify data, both on the page and the server.
- Changes often have to be kept in sync with data elsewhere on the page.
- Users can enter unpredictable values, some that we'll want to modify or reject outright.
- The UI needs to clearly state expectations and errors in the case of validation failures.
- Fields can depend on each other and have complex logic.
- Data collected in forms is often sent asynchronously to a back-end server, and we need to keep the user informed of what's happening.
- We want to be able to test our forms.

If this sounds daunting, don't worry! This is exactly why React was created: to handle the complicated forms that needed to be built at Facebook.

We're going to explore how to handle these challenges with React by building a sign up app. We'll start simple and add more functionality in each step.

Preparation

Inside the code download that came with this book, navigate to `forms`:

```
$ cd forms
```

This folder contains all the code examples for this chapter. To view them in your browser install the dependencies by running `npm install` (or `npm i` for short):

```
$ npm i
```

Once that's finished, you can start the app with `npm start`:

```
$ npm start
```

You should expect to see the following in your terminal:

```
$ npm start

Compiled successfully!

The app is running at:

  http://localhost:3000/
```

You should now be able to see the app in your browser if you go to `http://localhost:3000`.

This app is powered by Create React App, which we cover in the next chapter.

The Basic Button

At their core, forms are a conversation with the user. Fields are the app's questions, and the values that the user inputs are the answers.

Let's ask the user what they think of React.

We could present the user with a text box, but we'll start even simpler. In this example, we'll constrain the response to just one of two possible answers. We want to know whether the user thinks React is either "great" or "amazing", and the simplest way to do that is to give them two buttons to choose from.

Here's what the first example looks like:

What do you think of React?

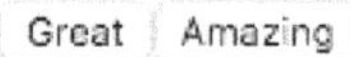

Basic Buttons

To get our app to this stage we create a component with a `render()` method that returns a `div` with three child elements: an `h1` with the question, and two `button` elements for the answers. This will look like the following:

forms/src/01-basic-button.js

```
  render() {
    return (
      <div>
        <h1>What do you think of React?</h1>

        <button
          name='button-1'
          value='great'
          onClick={this.onGreatClick}
        >
          Great
        </button>

        <button
          name='button-2'
          value='amazing'
          onClick={this.onAmazingClick}
        >
          Amazing
        </button>
      </div>
    );
  }
```

So far this looks a lot like how you'd handle a form with vanilla HTML. The important part to pay attention to is the `onClick` prop of the `button` elements. When a `button` is clicked, if it has a function set as its `onClick` prop, that function will be called. We'll use this behavior to know what our user's answer is.

To know what our user's answer is, we pass a different function to each button. Specifically, we'll create function `onGreatClick()` and provide it to the "Great" button and create function `onAmazingClick()` and provide it to the "Amazing" button.

Here's what those functions look like:

forms/src/01-basic-button.js

```
  onGreatClick = (evt) => {
    console.log('The user clicked button-1: great', evt);
  };

  onAmazingClick = (evt) => {
    console.log('The user clicked button-2: amazing', evt);
  };
```

When the user clicks on the "Amazing" button, the associated `onClick` function will run (`onAmazingClick()` in this case). If, instead, the user clicked the "Great" button, `onGreatClick()` would be run instead.

Notice that in the `onClick` handler we pass `this.onGreatClick` and *not* `this.onGreatClick()`.

What's the difference?

In the first case (without parens), we're passing the *function* `onGreatClick`, whereas in the second case we're passing the *result of calling the function* `onGreatClick` (which isn't what we want right now).

This becomes the foundation of our app's ability to respond to a user's input. Our app can do different things depending on the user's response. In this case, we log different messages to the `console`.

Events and Event Handlers

Note that our `onClick` functions (`onAmazingClick()` and `onGreatClick()`) accept an argument, `evt`. This is because these functions are *event handlers.*

Handling events is central to working with forms in React. When we provide a function to an element's `onClick prop`, that function becomes an event handler. The function will be called when that event occurs, and it will receive **an event object as its argument**.

In the above example, when the `button` element is clicked, the corresponding event handler function is called (`onAmazingClick()` or `onGreatClick()`) and it is provided with a mouse click event object (`evt` in this case). This object is a `SyntheticMouseEvent`. This `SyntheticMouseEvent` is just a cross-browser wrapper around the browser's native `MouseEvent`, and you'll be able to use it the same way you would a native DOM event. In addition, if you need the original native event you can access it via the `nativeEvent` attribute (e.g. `evt.nativeEvent`).

Event objects contain lots of useful information about the action that occurred. A `MouseEvent` for example, will let you see the x and y coordinates of the mouse at the time of the click, whether or not the shift key was pressed, and (most useful for this example) a reference to the element that was clicked. We'll use this information to simplify things in the next section.

Instead, if we were interested in mouse movement, we could have created an event handler and provided it to the `onMouseMove` prop. In fact, there are many such element `props` that you can provide mouse event handlers to:, `onClick`, `onContextMenu`, `onDoubleClick`, `onDrag`, `onDragEnd`, `onDragEnter`, `onDragExit`, `onDragLeave`, `onDragOver`, `onDragStart`, `onDrop`, `onMouseDown`, `onMouseEnter`, `onMouseLeave`, `onMouseMove`, `onMouseOut`, `onMouseOver`, and `onMouseUp`.

And those are only the mouse events. There are also clipboard, composition, keyboard, focus, form, selection, touch, ui, wheel, media, image, animation, and transition event groups. Each group has its own types of events, and not all events are appropriate for all elements. For example, here we will mainly work with the form events, `onChange` and `onSubmit`, which are related to `form` and `input` elements.

For more information on events in React, see React's documentation on the Event System[53].

Back to the Button

In the previous section, we were able to perform different actions (log different messages) depending on the action of the user. However, the way that we set it up, we'd need to create a separate function for each action. Instead, it would be much cleaner if we provided the same event handler to both buttons, and used information from the event itself to determine our response.

To do this, we replace the two event handlers `onGreatClick()` and `onAmazingClick()` with a new single event handler, `onButtonClick()`.

forms/src/02-basic-button.js

```
  onButtonClick = (evt) => {
    const btn = evt.target;
    console.log(`The user clicked ${btn.name}: ${btn.value}`);
  };
```

Our click handler function receives an event object, `evt`. `evt` has an attribute `target` that is a reference to the button that the user clicked. This way we can access the button that the user clicked without creating a function for each button. We can then log out different messages for different user behavior.

Next we update our `render()` function so that our `button` elements both use the same event handler, our new `onButtonClick()` function.

[53] https://facebook.github.io/react/docs/events.html

forms/src/02-basic-button.js

```
  render() {
    return (
      <div>
        <h1>What do you think of React?</h1>

        <button
          name='button-1'
          value='great'
          onClick={this.onButtonClick}
        >
          Great
        </button>

        <button
          name='button-2'
          value='amazing'
          onClick={this.onButtonClick}
        >
          Amazing
        </button>
      </div>
    );
  }
```

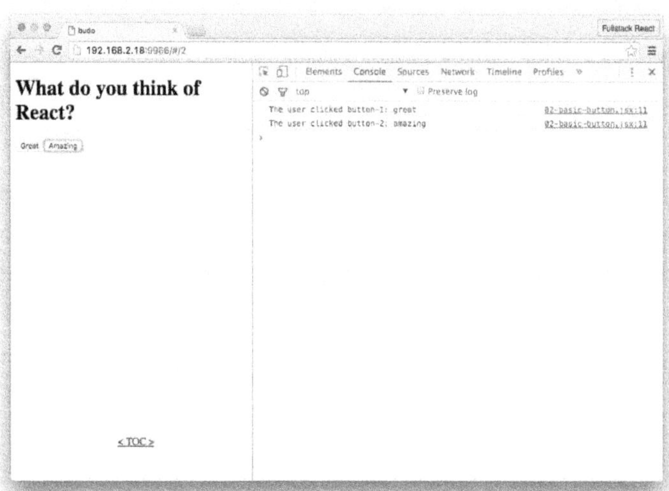

One Event Handler for Both Buttons

By taking advantage of the event object and using a shared event handler, we could add 100 new buttons, and we wouldn't have to make any other changes to our app.

Text Input

In the previous example, we constrained our user's response to only one of two possibilities. Now that we know how to take advantage of event objects and handlers in React, we're going to accept a much wider range of responses and move on to a more typical use of forms: text input.

To showcase text input we'll create a "sign-up sheet" app. The purpose of this app is to allow a user to record a list of names of people who want to sign up for an event.

The app presents the user a text field where they can input a name and hit "Submit". When they enter a name, it is added to a list, that list is displayed, and the text box is cleared so they can enter a new name.

Here's what it will look like:

Sign-Up Adding to a List

Accessing User Input With `refs`

We want to be able to read the contents of the text field when the user submits the form. A simple way to do this is to wait until the user submits the form, find the text field in the DOM, and finally grab its `value`.

To begin we'll start by creating a form element with two child elements: a text input field and a submit button:

forms/src/03-basic-input.js

```
  render() {
    return (
      <div>
        <h1>Sign Up Sheet</h1>

        <form onSubmit={this.onFormSubmit}>
          <input
            placeholder='Name'
            ref='name'
          />

          <input type='submit' />
        </form>
      </div>
    );
  }
```

This is very similar to the previous example, but instead of two `button` elements, we now have a `form` element with two child elements: a text field and a submit button.

There are two things to notice. First, we've added an `onSubmit` event handler to the `form` element. Second, we've given the text field a `ref` prop of `'name'`.

By using an `onSubmit` event handler on the `form` element this example will behave a little differently than before. One change is that the handler will be called either by clicking the "Submit" button, or by pressing "enter"/"return" while the `form` has focus. This is more user-friendly than forcing the user to click the "Submit" button.

However, because our event handler is tied to the `form`, the event object argument to the handler is less useful than it was in the previous example. Before, we were able to use the `target` prop of the event to reference the `button` and get its value. This time, we're interested in the text field's value. One option would be to use the event's `target` to reference the `form` and from there we could find the child `input` we're interested in, but there's a simpler way.

In React, if we want to easily access a DOM element in a component we can use `refs` (references). Above, we gave our text field a `ref` property of `'name'`. Later when the `onSubmit` handler is called, we have the ability to access `this.refs.name` to get a reference to that text field. Here's what that looks like in our `onFormSubmit()` event handler:

forms/src/03-basic-input.js

```
  onFormSubmit = (evt) => {
    evt.preventDefault();
    console.log(this.refs.name.value);
  };
```

Use `preventDefault()` with the `onSubmit` handler to prevent the browser's default action of submitting the form.

As you can see, by using `this.refs.name` we gain a reference to our text field element and we can access its `value` property. That `value` property contains the text that was entered into the field.

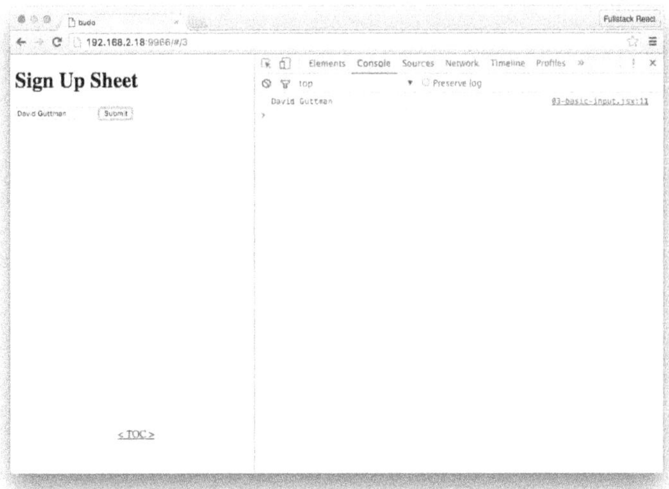

Logging The Name

With just the two functions `render()` and `onFormSubmit()`, we should now be able to see the `value` of the text field in our console when we click "Submit". In the next step we'll take that `value` and display it on the page.

Using User Input

Now that we've shown that we can get user submitted names, we can begin to use this information to change the app's state and UI.

The goal of this example is to show a list with all of the names that the user has entered. React makes this easy. We will have an array in our state to hold the names, and in `render()` we will use that array to populate a list.

When our app loads, the array will be empty, and each time the user submits a new name, we will add it to the array. To do this, we'll make a few additions to our component.

First, we'll create a `names` array in our state. In React, when we're using ES6 component classes we can set the initial value of our `state` object by defining a property of `state`.

Here's what that looks like:

forms/src/04-basic-input.js

```
module.exports = class extends React.Component {
  static displayName = "04-basic-input";
  state = { names: [] }; // <-- initial state
```

`static` belongs to the class

Notice in this component we have the line:

```
static displayName = "04-basic-input";
```

This means that this component class has a *static* property `displayName`. When a property is static, that means it is a class property (instead of an instance property). In this case, we're going to use this `displayName` when we show the list of examples on the demo listing page.

Next, we'll modify `render()` to show this list. Below our `form` element, we'll create a new `div`. This new container `div` will hold a heading, `h3`, and our names list, a `ul` parent with a `li` child for each name. Here's our updated `render()` method:

forms/src/04-basic-input.js

```
  render() {
    return (
      <div>
        <h1>Sign Up Sheet</h1>

        <form onSubmit={this.onFormSubmit}>
          <input
            placeholder='Name'
            ref='name'
          />

          <input type='submit' />
        </form>

```

```
      <div>
        <h3>Names</h3>
        <ul>
          { this.state.names.map((name, i) => <li key={i}>{name}</li>) }
        </ul>
      </div>
    </div>
  );
}
```

ES2015 gives us a compact way to insert `li` children. Since `this.state.names` is an array, we can take advantage of its `map()` method to return a `li` child element for each name in the array. Also, by using "arrow" syntax, for our iterator function in `map()`, the `li` element is returned without us explicitly using `return`.

One other thing to note here is that we provide a `key prop` to the `li` element. React will complain when we have children in an array or iterator (like we do here) and they don't have a `key prop`. React wants this information to keep track of the child and make sure that it can be reused between render passes.

We won't be removing or reordering the list here, so it is sufficient to identify each child by its index. If we wanted to optimize rendering for a more complex use-case, we could assign an immutable id to each name that was not tied to its value or order in the array. This would allow React to reuse the element even if its position or value was changed.

See React's documentation on Multiple Components and Dynamic Children[54] for more information.

Now that `render()` is updated, the `onFormSubmit()` method needs to update the `state` with the new name. To add a name to the `names` array in our `state` we might be tempted to try to do something like `this.state.names.push(name)`. However, React relies on `this.setState()` to mutate our `state` object, which will then trigger a new call to `render()`.

The way to do this properly is to:

1. create a new variable that copies our current `names`
2. add our new name to that array, and finally
3. use that variable in a call to `this.setState()`.

We also want to clear the text field so that it's ready to accept additional user input. It would not be very user friendly to require the user to delete their input before adding a new name. Since we already have access to the text field via `refs`, we can set its `value` to an empty string to clear it.

This is what `onFormSubmit()` should look like now:

[54] https://facebook.github.io/react/docs/multiple-components.html#dynamic-children

forms/src/04-basic-input.js

```
  onFormSubmit = (evt) => {
    const name = this.refs.name.value;
    const names = [ ...this.state.names, name ];
    this.setState({ names: names });
    this.refs.name.value = '';
    evt.preventDefault();
  };
```

At this point, our sign-up app is functional. Here's a rundown of the application flow:

1. User enters a name and clicks "Submit".
2. `onFormSubmit` is called.
3. `this.refs.name` is used to access the value of the text field (a name).
4. The name is added to our `names` list in the `state`.
5. The text field is cleared so that it is ready for more input.
6. `render` is called and displays the updated list of names.

So far so good! In the next sections we'll improve it further.

Uncontrolled vs. Controlled Components

In the previous sections we took advantage of `refs` to access the user's input. When we created our `render()` method we added an `input` field with a `ref` attribute. We later used that attribute to get a reference to the rendered `input` so that we could access and modify its `value`.

We covered using `refs` with forms because it is conceptually similar to how one might deal with forms without React. However, by using `refs` this way, we opt out of a primary advantage of using React.

In the previous example we access the DOM directly to retrieve the name from the text field, as well as manipulate the DOM directly by resetting the field after a name has been submitted.

With React we shouldn't have to worry about modifying the DOM to match application state. We should concentrate only on altering `state` and rely on React's ability to efficiently manipulate the DOM to match. This provides us with the certainty that for any given value of `state`, we can predict what `render()` will return and therefore know what our app will look like.

In the previous example, our text field is what we would call an "uncontrolled component". This is another way of saying that React does not "control" how it is rendered – specifically its value. In other words, React is hands-off, and allows it to be freely influenced by user interaction. This means that knowing the application state is not enough to predict what the page (and specifically the `input` field) looks like. Because the user could have typed (or not typed) input into the field, the only way to know what the `input` field looks like is to access it via `refs` and check its `value`.

There is another way. By converting this field to a "controlled component", we give React control over it. It's `value` will always be specified by `render()` and our application state. When we do this, we can predict how our application will look by examining our `state` object.

By directly tying our view to our application state we get certain features for very little work. For example, imagine a long `form` where the user must answer many questions by filling out lots of `input` fields. If the user is halfway through and accidentally reloads the page that would ordinarily clear out all the fields. If these were controlled components and our application state was persisted to `localStorage`, we would be able to come back exactly where they left off. Later, we'll get to another important feature that controlled components pave the way for: validation.

Accessing User Input With `state`

Converting an uncontrolled `input` component to a controlled one requires three things. First, we need a place in `state` to store its value. Second, we provide that location in `state` as its `value prop`. Finally, we add an `onChange` handler that will update its value in `state`. The flow for a controlled component looks like this:

1. The user enters/changes the input.
2. The `onChange` handler is called with the "change" event.
3. Using `event.target.value` we update the `input` element's `value` in `state`.
4. `render()` is called and the `input` is updated with the new value in `state`.

Here's what our `render()` looks like after converting the `input` to a controlled component:

forms/src/05-state-input.js

```
  render() {
    return (
      <div>
        <h1>Sign Up Sheet</h1>

        <form onSubmit={this.onFormSubmit}>
          <input
            placeholder='Name'
            value={this.state.name}
            onChange={this.onNameChange}
          />

          <input type='submit' />
```

```
        </form>

        <div>
          <h3>Names</h3>
          <ul>
            { this.state.names.map((name, i) => <li key={i}>{name}</li>) }
          </ul>
        </div>
      </div>
    );
  }
```

The only difference in our input is that we've removed the ref prop and replaced it with both a value and an onChange prop.

Now that the input is "controlled", its value will always be set equal to a property of our state. In this case, that property is name, so the value of the input is this.state.name.

While not strictly necessary, it's a good habit to provide sane defaults for any properties of state that will be used in our component. Because we now use state.name for the value of our input, we'll want to choose what value it will have before the user has had a chance to provide one. In our case, we want the field to be empty, so the default value will be an empty string, '':

forms/src/05-state-input.js

```
  state = {
    name: '',
    names: [],
  };
```

If we had just stopped there, the input would effectively be disabled. No matter what the user types into it, its value wouldn't change. In fact, if we left it like this, React would give us a warning in our console.

To make our input operational, we'll need to listen to its onChange events and use those to update the state. To achieve this, we've created an event handler for onChange. This handler is responsible for updating our state so that state.name will always be updated with what the user has typed into the field. We've created the method onNameChange() for that purpose.

Here's what onNameChange() looks like now:

forms/src/05-state-input.js

```
  onNameChange = (evt) => {
    this.setState({ name: evt.target.value });
  };
```

`onNameChange()` is a very simple function. Like we did in a previous section, we use the event passed to the handler to reference the field and get its `value`. We then update `state.name` with that `value`.

Now the controlled component cycle is complete. The user interacts with the field. This triggers an `onChange` event which calls our `onNameChange()` handler. Our `onNameChange()` handler updates the `state`, and this in turn triggers `render()` to update the field with the new `value`.

Our app still needs one more change, however. When the user submits the form, `onFormSubmit()` is called, and we need that method to add the entered name (`state.name`) to the names list (`state.names`). When we last saw `onFormSubmit()` it did this using `this.refs`. Since we're no longer using `refs`, we've updated it to the following:

forms/src/05-state-input.js

```
  onFormSubmit = (evt) => {
    const names = [ ...this.state.names, this.state.name ];
    this.setState({ names: names, name: '' });
    evt.preventDefault();
  };
```

Notice that to get the current entered name, we simply access `this.state.name` because it will be continually updated by our `onNameChange()` handler. We then append that to our names list, `this.state.names` and update the `state`. We also clear `this.state.name` so that the field is empty and ready for a new name.

While our app didn't gain any new features in this section, we've both paved the way for better functionality (like validation and persistence) while also taking greater advantage of the React paradigm.

Multiple Fields

Our sign-up sheet is looking good, but what would happen if we wanted to add more fields? If our sign-up sheet is like most projects, it's only a matter of time before we want to add to it. With forms, we'll often want to add inputs.

If we continue our current approach and create more controlled components, each with a corresponding state property and an `onChange` handler, our component will become quite verbose. Having a one-to-one-to-one relationship between our inputs, state, and handlers is not ideal.

Let's explore how we can modify our app to allow for additional inputs in a clean, maintainable way. To illustrate this, let's add email address to our sign-up sheet.

In the previous section our `input` field has a dedicated property on the root of our `state` object. If we were to do that here, we would add another property, `email`. To avoid adding a property for each input on `state`, let's instead add a `fields` object to store the values for all of our fields in one place. Here's our new initial `state`:

forms/src/06-state-input-multi.js

```
  state = {
    fields: {
      name: '',
      email: ''
    },
    people: [],
  };
```

This `fields` object can store state for as many inputs as we'd like. Here we've specified that we want to store fields for `name` and `email`. Now, we will find those values at `state.fields.name` and `state.fields.email` instead of `state.name` and `state.email`.

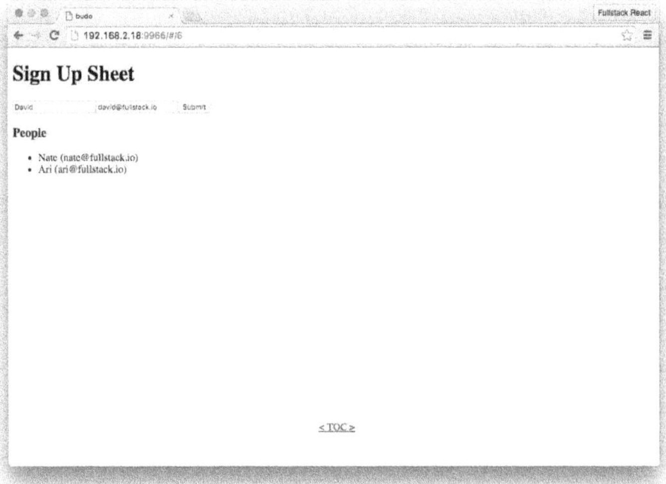

Name and Email Fields

Of course, those values will need to be updated by an event handler. We *could* create an event handler for each field we have in the form, but that would involve a lot of copy/paste and needlessly bloat our component. Also it would make maintainability more difficult, as any change to a form would need to be made in multiple places.

Instead of creating an `onChange` handler for each input, we can create a single method that accepts change events from **all** of our inputs. The trick is to write this method in such a way that it updates the correct property in `state` depending on the `input` field that triggered the event. To pull this off, the method uses the `event` argument to determine which input was changed and update our `state.fields` object accordingly. For example, if we have an `input` field and we were to give it a `name` prop of `"email"`, when that field triggers an event, we would be able to know that it was email field, because `event.target.name` would be `"email"`.

To see what this looks like in practice, here's the updated `render()`:

forms/src/06-state-input-multi.js

```
  render() {
    return (
      <div>
        <h1>Sign Up Sheet</h1>

        <form onSubmit={this.onFormSubmit}>
          <input
            placeholder='Name'
            name='name'
            value={this.state.fields.name}
            onChange={this.onInputChange}
          />

          <input
            placeholder='Email'
            name='email'
            value={this.state.fields.email}
            onChange={this.onInputChange}
          />

          <input type='submit' />
        </form>

        <div>
          <h3>People</h3>
          <ul>
            { this.state.people.map(({ name, email }, i) =>
              <li key={i}>{name} ({ email })</li>
            ) }
          </ul>
        </div>
      </div>
    );
  }
```

There are a several things to note: first, we've added a second `input` to handle email addresses.

Second, we've changed the `value` `prop` of the `input` fields so that they don't access attributes on the root of the `state` object. Instead they access the attributes of `state.fields`. Looking at the code above, the `input` for name now has its `value` set to `this.state.fields.name`.

Third, both `input` fields have their `onChange` `prop` set to the same event handler, `onInputChange()`. We'll see below how we modified `onNameChange()` to be a more general event handler that can accept events from any field, not just "name".

Fourth, our `input` fields now have a `name` `prop`. This is related to the last point. To allow our general event handler, `onInputChange()`, to be able to tell where the change event came from and where we should store it in our state (e.g. if the change comes from the "email" `input` the new value should be stored at `state.fields.email`), we provide that `name` `prop` so that it can be pulled off of the event via its `target` attribute.

Finally, we modify how our people list is rendered. Because it's no longer just a list of names, we modify our `li` element to display both the previous `name` attribute as well as the new `email` data we plan to have.

To make sure that all the data winds up in the right place, we'll need to make sure that our event handlers are properly modified. Here's what the `onInputChange()` event handler (that gets called when any field's input changes) should look like:

forms/src/06-state-input-multi.js

```
  onInputChange = (evt) => {
    const fields = this.state.fields;
    fields[evt.target.name] = evt.target.value;
    this.setState({ fields });
  };
```

At its core this is similar to what we did before in `onNameChange()` in the last section. The two key differences are that:

1. we are updating a value nested in the `state` (e.g. updating `state.fields.email` instead of `state.email`), and
2. we're using `evt.target.name` to inform which attribute of `state.fields` needs to be updated.

To properly update our state, we first grab a local reference to `state.fields`. Then, we use information from the event (`evt.target.name` and `evt.target.value`) to update the local reference. Lastly, we `setState()` with the modified local reference.

To get concrete, let's go through what would happen if the user enters "someone@somewhere.com" into the "email" field.

First, `onInputChange()` would be called with the `evt` object as an argument. `evt.target.name` would be `"email"` (because `"email"` is set as its `name` prop in `render()`) and `evt.target.value` would be `"someone@somewhere.com"` (because that's what they entered into the field).

Next, `onInputChange()` would grab a local reference to `state.fields`. If this is the first time there was input, `state.fields` and our local reference will be the default `fields` in `state`, `{ name: '', email: '' }`. Then, the local reference would be modified so that it becomes `{ name: '', email: "someone@somewhere.com" }`.

And finally, `setState()` is called with that change.

At this point, `this.state.fields` will always be in sync with any text in the `input` fields. However, `onFormSubmit()` will need to be changed to get that information into the list of people who have signed up. Here's what the updated `onFormSubmit()` looks like:

forms/src/06-state-input-multi.js

```
  onFormSubmit = (evt) => {
    const people = [
      ...this.state.people,
      this.state.fields,
    ];
    this.setState({
      people,
      fields: {
        name: '',
        email: ''
      }
    });
    evt.preventDefault();
  };
```

In `onFormSubmit()` we first obtain a local reference to the list of people who have signed up, `this.state.people`. Then, we add our `this.state.fields` object (an object representing the name and email currently entered into the fields) onto the `people` list. Finally, we use `this.setState()` to simultaneously update our list with the new information and clear all the fields by returning `state.fields` to the empty defaults, `{ name: '', email: '' }`.

The great thing about this is that we can easily add as many input fields as we want with very minimal changes. In fact, only the `render()` method would need to change. For each new field, all we would have to do is add another `input` field and change how the list is rendered to display the new field.

For example, if we wanted to add a field for phone number, we would add a new `input` with appropriate `name` and `value` props: `name` would be `phone` and `value` would be `this.state.fields.phone`. `onChange`, like the others, would be our existing `onInputChange()` handler.

After doing that our `state` will automatically keep track of the phone field and will add it to the `state.people` array and we could change how the view (e.g. the `li`) displays the information.

At this point we have a functional app that's well situated to be extended and modified as requirements evolve. However, it is missing one crucial aspect that almost all forms need: validation.

On Validation

Validation is so central to building forms that it's rare to have a form without it. Validation can be both on the level of the **individual field** and on the **form as a whole**.

When you validate on an individual field, you're making sure that the user has entered data that conforms to your application's expectations and constraints as it relates to that piece of data.

For example, if we want a user to enter an email address, we expect their input to look like a valid email address. If the input does not look like an email address, they might have made a mistake and we're likely to run into trouble down the line (e.g. they won't be able to activate their account). Other common examples are making sure that a zip code has exactly five (or nine) numerical characters and enforcing a password length of at least some minimum length.

Validation on the form as a whole is slightly different. Here is where you'll make sure that all required fields have been entered. This is also a good place to check for internal consistency. For example you might have an order form where specific options are required for specific products.

Additionally, there are trade-offs for "how" and "when" we validate. On some fields we might want to give validation feedback in real-time. For example, we might want to show password strength (by looking at length and characters used) while the user is typing. However, if we want to validate the availability of a username, we might want to wait until the user has finished typing before we make a request to the server/database to find out.

We also have options for how we display validation errors. We might style the field differently (e.g. a red outline), show text near the field (e.g. "Please enter a valid email."), and/or disable the form's submit button to prevent the user from progressing with invalid information.

As for our app, we can begin with validation of the form as a whole and

1. make sure that we have both a name and email and
2. make sure that the email is a valid address.

Adding Validation to Our App

To add validation to our sign-up app we've made some changes. At a high level these changes are

1. add a place in `state` to store validation errors if they exist,
2. change our `render()` method so it will show validation error messages (if they exist) with red text next to each field,

3. add a new `validate()` method that takes our `fields` object as an argument and returns a `fieldErrors` object, and
4. `onFormSubmit()` will call the new `validate()` method to get the `fieldErrors` object, and if there are errors it will add them to the state (so that they can be shown in `render()`) and return early without adding the "person" to the list, `state.people`.

First, we've changed our initial `state`:

forms/src/07-basic-validation.js

```
  state = {
    fields: {
      name: '',
      email: '',
    },
    fieldErrors: {},
    people: [],
  };
```

The only change here is that we've created a default value for the `fieldErrors` property. This is where we'll store errors for each of the field if they exist.

Next, here's what the updated `render()` method looks like:

forms/src/07-basic-validation.js

```
  render() {
    return (
      <div>
        <h1>Sign Up Sheet</h1>

        <form onSubmit={this.onFormSubmit}>

          <input
            placeholder='Name'
            name='name'
            value={this.state.fields.name}
            onChange={this.onInputChange}
          />

          <span style={{ color: 'red' }}>{ this.state.fieldErrors.name }</span>

          <br />

```

```
        <input
          placeholder='Email'
          name='email'
          value={this.state.fields.email}
          onChange={this.onInputChange}
        />

        <span style={{ color: 'red' }}>{ this.state.fieldErrors.email }</span>

        <br />

        <input type='submit' />
      </form>

      <div>
        <h3>People</h3>
        <ul>
          { this.state.people.map(({ name, email }, i) =>
            <li key={i}>{name} ({ email })</li>
          ) }
        </ul>
      </div>
    </div>
  );
}
```

The only differences here are two new `span` elements, one for each field. Each `span` will look in the appropriate place in `state.fieldErrors` for an error message. If one is found it will be displayed in red next to the field. Next up, we'll see how those error messages can get into the `state`.

It is after the user submits the form that we will check the validity of their input. So the appropriate place to begin validation is in the `onFormSubmit()` method. However, we'll want to create a standalone function for that method to call. We've created the pure function, `validate()` method for this:

forms/src/07-basic-validation.js

```
  validate = (person) => {
    const errors = {};
    if (!person.name) errors.name = 'Name Required';
    if (!person.email) errors.email = 'Email Required';
    if (person.email && !isEmail(person.email)) errors.email = 'Invalid Email';
    return errors;
  };
```

Our `validate()` method is pretty simple and has two goals. First, we want to make sure that both name and email are present. By checking their truthiness we can know that they are defined and not empty strings. Second, we want to know that the provided email address looks valid. This is actually a bit of a thorny issue, so we rely on `validator`[55] to let us know. If any of these conditions are not met, we add a corresponding key to our errors object and set an error message as the value.

Afterwards, we've updated our `onFormSubmit()` to use this new `validate()` method and act on the returned error object:

forms/src/07-basic-validation.js

```
  onFormSubmit = (evt) => {
    const people = [ ...this.state.people ];
    const person = this.state.fields;
    const fieldErrors = this.validate(person);
    this.setState({ fieldErrors });
    evt.preventDefault();

    if (Object.keys(fieldErrors).length) return;

    this.setState({
      people: people.concat(person),
      fields: {
        name: '',
        email: '',
      },
    });
  };
```

To use the `validate()` method, we get the current values of our fields from `this.state.fields` and provide it as the argument. `validate()` will either return an empty object if there are no issues, or

[55] http://npm.im/validator

if there are issues, it will return an object with keys corresponding to each field name and values corresponding to each error message. In either case, we want to update our `state.fieldErrors` object so that `render()` can display or hide the messages as necessary.

If the validation errors object has any keys (`Object.keys(fieldErrors).length > 0`) we know there are issues. If there are no validation issues, the logic is the same as in previous sections – we add the new information and clear the fields. However, if there are any errors, we return early. This prevents the new information from being added to the list.

Email Required

Email Invalid

At this point we've covered the fundamentals of creating a form with validation in React. In the next section we'll take things a bit further and show how we can validate in real-time at the field level and we'll create a `Field` component to improve the maintainability when an app has multiple fields with different validation requirements.

Creating the Field Component

In the last section we added validation to our form. However, our form component is responsible for running the validations on the form as a whole as well as **the individual validation rules for each field**.

It would be ideal if *each field* was responsible for identifying validation errors on *its own input*, and the parent form was only responsible for identifying issues at the form-level. This comes with several advantages:

1. an email field created in this way could check the format of its input while the user types in real-time.

2. the field could incorporate its validation error message, freeing the parent form from having to keep track of it.

To do this we're first going to create a new separate `Field` component, and we will use it instead of `input` elements in the form. This will let us combine a normal `input` with both validation logic and error messaging.

Before we get into the creation of this new component, it will be useful to think of it at a high level in terms of inputs and outputs. In other words, "what information do we need to provide this component?", and "what kinds of things would we expect in return?"

These inputs are going to become this component's `props` and the output will be used by any event handlers we pass into it.

Because our `Field` component will contain a child `input`, we'll need to provide the same baseline information so that it can be passed on. For example, if we want a `Field` component rendered with a specific `placeholder prop` on its child `input`, we'll have to provide it as a `prop` when we create the `Field` component in our form's `render()` method.

Two other `props` we'll want to provide are `name`, and `value`. `name` will allow us to share an event handler between components like we've done before, and `value` allows the parent form to pre-populate `Field` as well as keep it updated.

Additionally, this new `Field` component is responsible for its own validation. Therefore we'll need to provide it rules specific to data it contains. For example, if this is the "email" `Field`, we'll provide it a function as its `validate prop`. Internally it will run this function to determine if its input is a valid email address.

Lastly, we'll provide an event handler for `onChange` events. The function we provide as the `onChange prop` will be called every time the input in the `Field` changes, and it will be called with an event argument that we get to define. This event argument should have three properties that we're interested in: (1) the name of the `Field`, (2) the current `value` of the `input`, and (3) the current validation error (if present).

To quickly review, for the new `Field` component to do its job it will need the following:

- `placeholder`: This will be passed straight through to the `input` child element. Similar to a label, this tells the user what data to the `Field` expects.
- `name`: We want this for the same reason we provide `name` to `input` elements: we'll use this in the event handler decide where to store input data and validation errors.
- `value`: This is how our parent form can initialize the `Field` with a value, or it can use this to update the `Field` with a new value. This is similar to how the `value prop` is used on an `input`.
- `validate`: A function that returns validation errors (if any) when run.
- `onChange`: An event handler to be run when the `Field` changes. This function will accept an event object as an argument.

Following this, we're able to set up `propTypes` on our new `Field` component:

forms/src/08-field-component-field.js

```
  static propTypes = {
    placeholder: PropTypes.string,
    name: PropTypes.string.isRequired,
    value: PropTypes.string,
    validate: PropTypes.func,
    onChange: PropTypes.func.isRequired,
  };
```

Next, we can think about the `state` that `Field` will need to keep track of. There are only two pieces of data that `Field` will need, the current `value` and `error`. Like in previous sections where our form component needed that data for its `render()` method, so too does our `Field` component. Here's how we'll set up our initial `state`:

forms/src/08-field-component-field.js

```
  state = {
    value: this.props.value,
    error: false,
  };
```

One key difference is that our `Field` has a parent, and sometimes this parent will want to update the `value` `prop` of our `Field`. To allow this, we'll need to create a new lifecycle method, `componentWillReceiveProps()` to accept the new `value` and update the `state`. Here's what that looks like:

forms/src/08-field-component-field.js

```
  componentWillReceiveProps(update) {
    this.setState({ value: update.value });
  }
```

The `render()` method of `Field` should be pretty simple. It's just the `input` and the corresponding `span` that will hold the error message:

forms/src/08-field-component-field.js

```
  render() {
    return (
      <div>
        <input
          placeholder={this.props.placeholder}
          value={this.state.value}
          onChange={this.onChange}
        />
        <span style={{ color: 'red' }}>{ this.state.error }</span>
      </div>
    );
  }
```

For the `input` element, the `placeholder` will be passed in from the parent and is available from `this.props.placeholder`. As mentioned above, the `value` of the `input` and the error message in the `span` will both be stored in the `state`. `value` comes from `this.state.value` and the error message is at `this.state.error`. And lastly, we'll set an `onChange` event handler that will be responsible for accepting user input, validating, updating state, *and calling the parent's event handler as well.* The method that will take care of that is `this.onChange`:

```
  onChange (evt) {
    const name = this.props.name;
    const value = evt.target.value;
    const error = this.props.validate ? this.props.validate(value) : false;

    this.setState({value, error});

    this.props.onChange({name, value, error});
  }
```

`this.onChange` is a pretty efficient function. It handles four different responsibilities in as many lines. As in previous sections, the event object gives us the current text in the `input` via its `target.value` property. Once we have that, we see if it passes validation. If `Field` was given a function for its `validate` prop, we use it here. If one was not given, we don't have to validate the input and `error` sets to `false`. Once we have both the `value` and `error` we can update our `state` so that they both appear in `render()`. However, it's not just the `Field` component that needs to be updated with this information.

When `Field` is used by a parent component, it passes in its own event handler in as the `onChange` prop. We call this function so that we can pass information up the parent. Here in `this.onChange()`, it is available as `this.props.onChange()`, and we call it with three pieces of information: the `name`, `value`, and `error` of the `Field`.

This might be a little confusing since "onChange" appears in multiple places. You can think of it as carrying information in a chain of event handlers. The form contains the `Field` which contains an `input`. Events occur on the `input` and the information passes first to the `Field` and finally to the form.

At this point our `Field` component is ready to go, and can be used in place of the `input` and error message combos in our app.

Using our new Field Component

Now that we're ready to use our brand new `Field` component, we can make some changes to our app. The most obvious change is that `Field` will take the place of both the `input` and error message `span` elements in our `render()` method. This is great because `Field` can take care of validation at the field level. But what about at the form level?

If you remember, we can employ two different levels of validation, one at the field level, and one at the form level. Our new `Field` component will let us validate the format of each field in real-time. What they won't do, however, is validate the entire form to make sure we have all the data we need. For that, we also want form-level validation.

Another nice feature we'll add here is disabling/enabling the form submit button in real-time as the form passes/fails validation. This is a nice bit of feedback that can improve a form's UX and make it feel more responsive.

Here's how our update `render()` looks:

forms/src/08-field-component-form.js

```
  render() {
    return (
      <div>
        <h1>Sign Up Sheet</h1>

        <form onSubmit={this.onFormSubmit}>

          <Field
            placeholder='Name'
            name='name'
            value={this.state.fields.name}
            onChange={this.onInputChange}
            validate={(val) => (val ? false : 'Name Required')}
          />

```

```
            <br />

            <Field
              placeholder='Email'
              name='email'
              value={this.state.fields.email}
              onChange={this.onInputChange}
              validate={(val) => (isEmail(val) ? false : 'Invalid Email')}
            />

            <br />

            <input type='submit' disabled={this.validate()} />
          </form>

          <div>
            <h3>People</h3>
            <ul>
              { this.state.people.map(({ name, email }, i) =>
                <li key={i}>{name} ({email})</li>
              ) }
            </ul>
          </div>
        </div>
      );
    }
```

You can see that `Field` is a drop-in replacement for `input`. All the `props` are the same as they were on `input`, except we have one additional `prop` this time: `validate`.

Above in the `Field` component's `onChange()` method, we make a call to the `this.props.validate()` function. What we provide as the `validate` `prop` to `Field`, will be that function. Its goal is to take user provided input as its argument and give a return value that corresponds to the validity of that input. If the input is not valid, `validate` should return an error message. Otherwise, it should return `false`.

For the "name" `Field` the `validate` `prop` is pretty simple. We're just checking for a truthy value. As long as there are characters in the box, validation will pass, otherwise we return the `'Name Required'` error message.

For the "email" `Field`, we're going to use the `isEmail()` function that we imported from the `validator` module. If that function returns `true`, we know it's a valid-looking email and validation passes. If not, we return the `'Invalid Email'` message.

Notice that we left their `onChange` prop alone, it is still set to `this.onInputChange`. However, since `Field` uses the function differently than `input`, we must update `onInputChange()`.

Before we move on, notice the only other change that we've made to `render()`: we conditionally disable the submit button. To do this, we set the value of the `disabled` prop to the return value of `this.validate()`. Because `this.validate()` will have a truthy return value if there are validation errors, the button will be disabled if the form is not valid. We'll show what the `this.validate()` function looks like in a bit.

Disabled Submit Button

As mentioned, both `Field` components have their `onChange` props set to `this.onInputChange`. We've had to make some changes to match the difference between `input` and our `Field`. Here's the updated version:

forms/src/08-field-component-form.js

```
  onInputChange = ({ name, value, error }) => {
    const fields = this.state.fields;
    const fieldErrors = this.state.fieldErrors;

    fields[name] = value;
    fieldErrors[name] = error;

    this.setState({ fields, fieldErrors });
  };
```

Previously, the job of `onInputChange()` was to update `this.state.fields` with the current user input values. In other words, when an a text field was edited, `onInputChange()` would be called with an event object. That event object had a `target` property that referenced the `input` element. Using that reference, we could get the `name` and `value` of the `input`, and with those, we would update `state.fields`.

This time around `onInputChange()` has the same responsibility, but it is our `Field` component that calls this function, not `input`. In the previous section, we show the `onChange()` method of

`Field`, and that's where `this.props.onChange()` is called. When it is called, it's called like this: ' this.props.onChange({name, value, error})'.

This means that instead of using `evt.target.name` or `evt.target.value` as we did before, we get `name` and `value` directly from the argument object. In addition, we also get the validation error for each field. This is necessary – for our form component to prevent submission, it will need to know about field-level validation errors.

Once we have the `name`, `value`, and `error`, we can update two objects in our `state`, the `state.fields` object we used before, and a new object, `state.fieldErrors`. Soon, we will show how `state.fieldErrors` will be used to either prevent or allow the form submit depending on the presence or absence of field-level validation errors.

With both `render()` and `onInputChange()` updated, we again have a nice feedback loop set up for our `Field` components:

- First, the user types into the `Field`.
- Then, the event handler of the `Field` is called, `onInputChange()`.
- Next, `onInputChange()` updates the `state`.
- After, the form is rendered again, and the `Field` passed an updated `value` `prop`.
- Then, `componentWillReceiveProps()` is called in `Field` with the new `value`, and its state is updated.
- Finally, `Field.render()` is called again, and the text field shows the appropriate input and (if applicable) validation error.

At this point, our form's `state` and appearance are in sync. Next, we need to change how we handle the submit event. Here's the updated event handler for the form, `onFormSubmit()`:

forms/src/08-field-component-form.js

```
  onFormSubmit = (evt) => {
    const people = this.state.people;
    const person = this.state.fields;

    evt.preventDefault();

    if (this.validate()) return;

    this.setState({
      people: people.concat(person),
      fields: {
        name: '',
        email: '',
      },
```

```
    });
  };
```

The objective of `onFormSubmit()` hasn't changed. It is still responsible for either adding a person to the list, or preventing that behavior if there are validation issues. To check for validation errors, we call `this.validate()`, and if there are any, we return early before adding the new person to the list.

Here's what the current version of `validate()` looks like:

```
  validate () {
    const person = this.state.fields;
    const fieldErrors = this.state.fieldErrors;
    const errMessages = Object.keys(fieldErrors).filter((k) => fieldErrors[k])

    if (!person.name) return true;
    if (!person.email) return true;
    if (errMessages.length) return true;

    return false
  },
```

Put simply, `validate()` is checking to make sure the data is valid at the form level. For the form to pass validation at this level it must satisfy two requirements: (1) neither field may be empty and (2) there must not be any field-level validation errors.

To satisfy the first requirement, we access `this.state.fields` and ensure that both `state.fields.name` and `state.fields.email` are truthy. These are kept up to date by `onInputChange()`, so it will always match what is in the text fields. If either `name` or `email` are missing, we return `true`, signaling that there is a validation error.

For the second requirement, we look at `this.state.fieldErrors`. `onInputChange()` will set any field-level validation error messages on this object. We use `Object.keys` and `Array.filter` to get an array of all present error messages. If there are any field-level validation issues, there will be corresponding error messages in the array, and its length will be non-zero and truthy. If that's the case, we also return `true` to signal the existence of a validation error.

`validate()` is a simple method that can be called at any time to check if the data is valid at the form-level. We use it both in `onFormSubmit()` to prevent adding invalid data to the list and in `render()` to disable the submit button, providing nice feedback in the UI.

And that's it. We're now using our custom `Field` component to do field-level validation on the fly, and we also use form-level validation to toggle the submit button in real-time.

Remote Data

Our form app is coming along. A user can sign up with their name and email, and we validate their information before accepting the input. But now we're going to kick it up a notch. We're going to explore how to allow a user to select from hierarchical, asynchronous options.

The most common example is to allow the user to select a car by year, make, and model. First the user selects a year, then the manufacturer, then the model. After choosing an option in one `select`, the next one becomes available. There are two interesting facets to building a component like this.

First, not all combinations make sense. There's no reason to allow your user to choose a 1965 Tesla Model T. Each option list (beyond the first) depends on a previously selected value.

Second, we don't want to send the entire database of valid choices to the browser. Instead, the browser only knows the top level of choices (e.g. years in a specific range). When the user makes a selection, we provide the selected value to the server and ask for next level (e.g. manufacturers available for a given year). Because the next level of options come from the server, this is an asynchronous activity.

Our app won't be interested in the user's car, but we will want to know what they're signing up for. Let's make this an app for users to learn more JavaScript by choosing a NodeSchool[56] workshop to attend.

A NodeSchool workshop can be either "core" or "elective". We can think of these as "departments" of NodeSchool. Therefore, depending on which department the user is interested in, we can allow them to choose a corresponding workshop. This is similar to the above example where a user chooses a car's year before its manufacturer.

If a user chooses the core department, we would enable them to choose from a list of core workshops like `learnyounode` and `stream-adventure`. If instead, they choose the elective department, we would allow them to pick workshops like `Functional JavaScript` or `Shader School`. Similar to the car example, the course list is provided asynchronously and depends on which department was selected.

The simplest way to achieve this is with two `select` elements, one for choosing the department and the other for choosing the course. However, we will hide the second `select` until: (1) the user has selected a department, and (2) we've received the appropriate course list from the server.

Instead of building this functionality directly into our form. We'll create a custom component to handle both the hierarchical and asynchronous nature of these fields. By using a custom component, our form will barely have to change. Any logic specific to the workshop selection will be hidden in the component.

Building the Custom Component

The purpose of this component is to allow the user to select a NodeSchool course. From now on we'll refer to it as our `CourseSelect` component.

[56] http://nodeschool.io

However, before starting on our new `CourseSelect` component, we should think about how we want it to communicate with its form parent. This will determine the component's `props`.

The most obvious `prop` is `onChange()`. The purpose of this component is to help the user make a department/course selection and to make that data available to the form. Additionally, we'll want to be sure that `onChange()` is called with the same arguments we're expecting from the other field components. That way we don't have to create any special handling for this component.

We also want the form to be able to set this component's state if need be. This is particularly useful when we want to clear the selections after the user has submitted their info. For this we'll accept two props. One for `department` and one for `course`.

And that's all we need. This component will accept three `props`. Here's how they'll look in our new `CourseSelect` component:

forms/src/09-course-select.js

```
  static propTypes = {
    department: PropTypes.string,
    course: PropTypes.string,
    onChange: PropTypes.func.isRequired,
  };
```

Next, we can think about the `state` that `CourseSelect` will need to keep track of. The two most obvious pieces of state are `department` and `course`. Those will change when the user makes selections, and when the form parent clears them on a submit.

`CourseSelect` will also need to keep track of available courses for a given department. When a user selects a department, we'll asynchronously fetch the corresponding course list. Once we have that list we'll want to store it in our `state` as `courses`.

Lastly, when dealing with asynchronous fetching, it's nice to inform the user that data is loading behind the scenes. We will also keep track of whether or not data is "loading" in our `state` as `_loading`.

The underscore prefix of `_loading` is just a convention to highlight that it is purely presentational. Presentational state is only used for UI effects. In this case it will be used to hide/show the loading indicator image.

Here's what our initial `state` looks like:

forms/src/09-course-select.js

```
  state = {
    department: null,
    course: null,
    courses: [],
    _loading: false,
  };
```

As mentioned above, this component's form parent will want to update the `department` and `course` `props`. Our `componentWillReceiveProps()` method will use the update to appropriately modify the `state`:

forms/src/09-course-select.js

```
  componentWillReceiveProps(update) {
    this.setState({
      department: update.department,
      course: update.course,
    });
  }
```

Now that we have a good idea of what our data looks like, we can get into how the component is rendered. This component is a little more complicated than our previous examples, so we take advantage of composition to keep things tidy. You will notice that our `render()` method is mainly composed of two functions, `renderDepartmentSelect()` and `renderCourseSelect()`:

forms/src/09-course-select.js

```
  render() {
    return (
      <div>
        { this.renderDepartmentSelect() }
        <br />
        { this.renderCourseSelect() }
      </div>
    );
  }
```

Aside from those two functions, `render()` doesn't have much. But this nicely illustrates the two "halves" of our component: the "department" half and the "course" half. Let's first take a look at the "department" half. Starting with `renderDepartmentSelect()`:

forms/src/09-course-select.js

```
        { this.renderDepartmentSelect() }
```

This method returns a `select` element that displays one of three options. The currently displayed option depends on the `value` prop of the `select`. The option whose `value` matches the `select` will be shown. The options are:

- "Which department?" (value: *empty string*)
- "NodeSchool: Core" (value: `"core"`)
- "NodeSchool: Electives" (value: `"electives"`)

The value of `select` is `this.state.department || ''`. In other words, if `this.state.department` is falsy (it is by default), the `value` will be an *empty string* and will match "Which department?". Otherwise, if `this.state.department` is either `"core"` or `"electives"`, it will display one of the other options.

Because `this.onSelectDepartment` is set as the `onChange` prop of the `select`, when the user changes the option, `onSelectDepartment()` is called with the change event. Here's what that looks like:

forms/src/09-course-select.js

```
  onSelectDepartment = (evt) => {
    const department = evt.target.value;
    const course = null;
    this.setState({ department, course });
    this.props.onChange({ name: 'department', value: department });
    this.props.onChange({ name: 'course', value: course });

    if (department) this.fetch(department);
  };
```

When the department is changed, we want three things to happen. First, we want to update `state` to match the selected department option. Second, we want to propagate the change via the `onChange` handler provided in the `props` of `CourseSelect`. Third, we want to fetch the available courses for the department.

When we update the `state`, we update it to the value of the event's `target`, the `select`. The value of the `select` is the value of the chosen `option`, either `''`, `"core"`, or `"electives"`. After the `state` is set with a new value, `render()` and `renderDepartmentSelect()` are run and a new option is displayed.

Notice that we also reset the course. Each course is only valid for its department. If the department changes, it will no longer be a valid choice. Therefore, we set it back to its initial value, `null`.

After updating `state`, we propagate the change to the component's change handler, `this.props.onChange`. Because we use the arguments as we have previously, this component can be used just like `Field` and can be given the same handler function. The only trick is that we need to call it twice, once for each input.

Finally, if a department was selected, we fetch the course list for it. Here's the method it calls, `fetch()`:

forms/src/09-course-select.js

```
  fetch = (department) => {
    this.setState({ _loading: true, courses: [] });
    apiClient(department).then((courses) => {
      this.setState({ _loading: false, courses: courses });
    });
  };
```

The responsibility of this method is to take a `department` string, use it to asynchronously get the corresponding course list, `courses`, and update the `state` with it. However, we also want to be sure to affect the `state` for a better user experience.

We do this by updating the `state` *before* the `apiClient` call. We know that we'll be waiting for the response with the new course list, and in that time we should show the user a loading indicator. To do that, we need our `state` to reflect our fetch status. Right before the `apiClient` call, we set the `state` of `_loading` to `true`. Once the operation completes, we set `_loading` back to `false` and update our course list.

Previously, we mentioned that this component had two "halves" illustrated by our `render()` method:

forms/src/09-course-select.js

```
  render() {
    return (
      <div>
        { this.renderDepartmentSelect() }
        <br />
        { this.renderCourseSelect() }
      </div>
    );
  }
```

We've already covered the "department" half. Let's now take a look at the "course" half starting with `renderCourseSelect()`:

forms/src/09-course-select.js

```
        { this.renderCourseSelect() }
```

The first thing that you'll notice is that `renderCourseSelect()` returns a different root element depending on particular conditions.

If `state._loading` is true, `renderCourseSelect()` only returns a single `img`: a loading indicator. Alternatively, if we're not loading, but a department has not been selected (and therefore `state.department` is falsy), an empty `span` is returned – effectively hiding this half of the component.

However, if we're not loading, and the user *has* selected a department, `renderCourseSelect()` returns a `select` similar to `renderDepartmentSelect()`.

The biggest difference between `renderCourseSelect()` and `renderDepartmentSelect()` is that `renderCourseSelect()` dynamically populates the `option` children of the `select`.

The first option in this `select` is "Which course?" which has an empty string as its value. If the user has not yet selected a course, this is what they should see (just like "Which department?" in the other `select`). The options that follow the first come from the course list stored in `state.courses`.

To provide all the child `option` elements to the `select` at once, the `select` is given a single array as its child. The first item in the array is an element for our "Which course?" option. Then, we use the spread operator combined with `map()` so that from the second item on, the array contains the course options from `state`.

Each item in the array is an `option` element. Like before, each element has text that it displays (like "Which course?") as well as a value `prop`. If the `value` of the `select` matches the `value` of the `option`, that `option` will be displayed. By default, the `value` of the `select` will be an empty string, so it will match the "Which course?" `option`. Once the user chooses a course and we are able to update `state.course`, the corresponding course will be shown.

This is a dynamic collection, we must also provide a `key prop` to each `option` to avoid warnings from React.

Lastly, we provide a change handler function, `onSelectCourse()` to the `select` prop `onChange`. When the user chooses a course, that function will be called with a related event object. We will then use information from that event to update the state and notify the parent.

Here's `onSelectCourse()`:

forms/src/09-course-select.js

```
  onSelectCourse = (evt) => {
    const course = evt.target.value;
    this.setState({ course });
    this.props.onChange({ name: 'course', value: course });
  };
```

Like we've done before, we get the `value` of the `target` element from the event. This `value` is the `value` of whichever `option` the user picked in the courses `select`. Once we update `state.course` with this `value`, the `select` will display the appropriate `option`.

After the `state` is updated, we call the change handler provided by the component's parent. Same as with the department selection, we provide `this.props.onChange()` an object argument with the `name/value` structure the handler expects.

And that's it for our `CourseSelect` component! As we'll see in the next part, integration with the form requires very minimal changes.

Adding CourseSelect

Now that our new `CourseSelect` component is ready, we can add it to our form. Only three small changes are necessary:

1. We add the `CourseSelect` component to `render()`.
2. We update our "People" list in `render()` to show the new fields (department and course).
3. Since department and course are required fields, we modify our `validate()` method to ensure their presence.

Because we were careful to call the change handler from within `CourseSelect` (`this.props.onChange`) with a `{name, value}` object the way that `onInputChange()` expects, we're able to reuse that handler. When `onInputChange()` is called by `CourseSelect`, it can appropriately update `state` with the new department and course information – just like it does with calls from the `Field` components.

Here's the updated `render()`:

forms/src/09-async-fetch.js

```
  render() {
    return (
      <div>
        <h1>Sign Up Sheet</h1>

        <form onSubmit={this.onFormSubmit}>

          <Field
            placeholder='Name'
            name='name'
            value={this.state.fields.name}
            onChange={this.onInputChange}
            validate={(val) => (val ? false : 'Name Required')}
          />

          <br />

          <Field
            placeholder='Email'
            name='email'
            value={this.state.fields.email}
            onChange={this.onInputChange}
            validate={(val) => (isEmail(val) ? false : 'Invalid Email')}
          />

          <br />

          <CourseSelect
            department={this.state.fields.department}
            course={this.state.fields.course}
            onChange={this.onInputChange}
          />

          <br />

          <input type='submit' disabled={this.validate()} />
        </form>

        <div>
          <h3>People</h3>
          <ul>
```

```
            { this.state.people.map(({ name, email, department, course }, i) =>
              <li key={i}>{[ name, email, department, course ].join(' - ')}</li>
            ) }
          </ul>
        </div>
      </div>
    );
  }
```

When adding `CourseSelect` we provide three `props`:

1. The current department from `state` (if one is present)
2. The current course from `state` (if one is present)
3. The `onInputChange()` handler (same function used by `Field`)

Here it is by itself:

```
<CourseSelect
  department={this.state.fields.department}
  course={this.state.fields.course}
  onChange={this.onInputChange} />
```

The other change we make in `render()` is we add the new department and course fields to the "People" list. Once a user submits sign-up information, they appear on this list. To show the department and course information, we need to get that data from `state` and display it:

```
<h3>People</h3>
<ul>
  { this.state.people.map( ({name, email, department, course}, i) =>
    <li key={i}>{[name, email, department, course].join(' - ')}</li>
  ) }
</ul>
```

This is as simple as pulling more properties from each item in the `state.people` array.

The only thing left to do is add these fields to our form-level validation. Our `CourseSelect` controls the UI to ensure that we won't get invalid data, so we don't need to worry about field-level errors. However, department and course are required fields, we should make sure that they are present before allowing the user to submit. We do this by updating our `validate()` method to include them:

forms/src/09-async-fetch.js

```
  validate = () => {
    const person = this.state.fields;
    const fieldErrors = this.state.fieldErrors;
    const errMessages = Object.keys(fieldErrors).filter((k) => fieldErrors[k]);

    if (!person.name) return true;
    if (!person.email) return true;
    if (!person.course) return true;
    if (!person.department) return true;
    if (errMessages.length) return true;

    return false;
  };
```

Once `validate()` is updated, our app will keep the submit button disabled until we have both department and course selected (in addition to our other validation requirements).

Thanks to the power of React and composition our form was able to take on complicated functionality while keeping high maintainability.

Separation of View and State

Once we've received information from the user and we've decided that it's valid, we then need to convert the information to JavaScript objects. Depending on the form, this could involve casting input values from strings to numbers, dates, or booleans, or it could be more involved if you need to impose a hierarchy by corralling the values into arrays or nested objects.

After we have the information as JavaScript objects, we then have to decide how to use them. The objects might be sent to a server as JSON to be stored in a database, encoded in a url to be used as a search query, or maybe only used to configure how the UI looks.

The information in those objects will almost always affect the UI and in many cases will also affect your application's behavior. It's up to us to determine how to store that info in our app.

Async Persistence

At this point our app is pretty useful. You could imagine having the app open on a kiosk where people can come up to it and sign up for things. However, there's one big shortcoming: if the browser is closed or reloaded, all data is lost.

In most web apps, when a user inputs data, that data should be sent to a server for safe keeping in a database. When the user returns to the app, the data can be fetched, and the app can pick back up right where it left off.

In this example, we'll cover three aspects of persistence: saving, loading, and handling errors. While we won't be sending the data to a remote server or storing it in a database (we'll be using `localStorage` instead), we'll treat it as an asynchronous operation to illustrate how almost any persistence strategy could be used.

To persist the sign up list (`state.people`), we'll only need to make a few changes to our parent form component. At a high level they are:

1. Modify `state` to keep track of persistence status. Basically, we'll want to know if the app is currently loading, is currently saving, or encountered an error during either operation.
2. Make a request using our API client to get any previously persisted data and load it into our `state`.
3. Update our `onFormSubmit()` event handler to trigger a save.
4. Change our `render()` method so that the "submit" button both reflects the current save status and prevents the user from performing an unwanted action like a double-save.

First, we'll want to modify our `state` keep track of our "loading" and "saving" status. This is useful to both accurately communicate the status of persistence and to prevent unwanted user actions. For example, if we know that the app is in the process of "saving", we can disable the submit button. Here's the updated `state` method with the two new properties:

forms/src/10-remote-persist.js

```
  state = {
    fields: {
      name: '',
      email: '',
      course: null,
      department: null
    },
    fieldErrors: {},
    people: [],
    _loading: false,
    _saveStatus: 'READY',
  };
```

The two new properties are `_loading` and `_saveStatus`. As before, we use the underscore prefix convention to signal that they are private to this component. There's no reason for a parent or child component to ever know their values.

_saveStatus is initialized with the value "READY", but we will have four possible values: "READY", "SAVING", "SUCCESS", and "ERROR". If the _saveStatus is either "SAVING" or "SUCCESS", we'll want to prevent the user from making an additional save.

Next, when the component has been successfully loaded and is about to be added to the DOM, we'll want to request any previously saved data. To do this we'll add the lifecycle method componentWillMount() which is automatically called by React at the appropriate time. Here's what that looks like:

forms/src/10-remote-persist.js

```
  componentWillMount() {
    this.setState({ _loading: true });
    apiClient.loadPeople().then((people) => {
      this.setState({ _loading: false, people: people });
    });
  }
```

Before we start the fetch with apiClient, we set state._loading to true. We'll use this in render() to show a loading indicator. Once the fetch returns, we update our state.people list with the previously persisted list and set _loading back to false.

apiClient is a simple object we created to simulate asynchronous loading and saving. If you look at the code for this chapter, you'll see that the "save" and "load" methods are thin async wrappers around localStorage. In your own apps you could create your own apiClient with similar methods to perform network requests.

Unfortunately, our app doesn't yet have a way to persist data. At this point there won't be any data to load. However, we can fix that by updating onFormSubmit().

As in the previous sections, we'll want our user to be able to fill out each field and hit "submit" to add a person to the list. When they do that, onFormSubmit() is called. We'll make a change so that we not only perform the previous behavior (validation, updating state.people), but we *also* persist that list using apiClient.savePeople():

forms/src/10-remote-persist.js

```
  onFormSubmit = (evt) => {
    const person = this.state.fields;

    evt.preventDefault();

    if (this.validate()) return;

    const people = [ ...this.state.people, person ];

    this.setState({ _saveStatus: 'SAVING' });
    apiClient.savePeople(people)
      .then(() => {
        this.setState({
          people: people,
          fields: {
            name: '',
            email: '',
            course: null,
            department: null
          },
          _saveStatus: 'SUCCESS',
        });
      })
      .catch((err) => {
        console.error(err);
        this.setState({ _saveStatus: 'ERROR' });
      });
  };
```

In the previous sections, if the data passed validation, we would just update our `state.people` list to include it. This time we'll also add the `person` to the `people` list, but we only want to update our `state` if `apiClient` can successfully persist. The order of operations looks like this:

1. Create a new array, `people` with both the contents of `state.people` and the new `person` object.
2. Update `state._saveStatus` to `"SAVING"`
3. Use `apiClient` to begin persisting the new `people` array from #1.
4. If `apiClient` is successful, update `state` with our new `people` array, an empty fields object, and `_saveStatus: "SUCCESS"`. If `apiClient` is *not* successful, leave everything as is, but set `state._saveStatus` to `"ERROR"`.

Put simply, we set the `_saveStatus` to `"SAVING"` while the `apiClient` request is "in-flight". If the request is successful, we set the `_saveStatus` to `"SUCCESS"` and perform the same actions as before. If not, the only update is to set `_saveStatus` to `"ERROR"`. This way, our local state does not get out of sync with our persisted copy. Also, since we don't clear the fields, we give the user an opportunity to try again without having to re-input their information.

For this example we are being conservative with our UI updates. We only add the new person to the list *if `apiClient` is successful.* This is in contrast to an optimistic update, where we would add the person to the list locally *first*, and later make adjustments if there was a failure. To do an optimistic update we could keep track of which `person` objects were added before which `apiClient` calls. Then if an `apiClient` call fails, we could selectively remove the particular `person` object associated with that call. We would also want to display a message to the user explaining the issue.

Our last change is to modify our `render()` method so that the UI accurately reflects our status with respect to loading and saving. As mentioned, we'll want the user to know if we're in the middle of a load or a save, or if there was a problem saving. We can also control the UI to prevent them from performing unwanted actions such as a double save.

Here's the updated `render()` method:

forms/src/10-remote-persist.js

```
  render() {
    if (this.state._loading) {
      return <img alt='loading' src='/img/loading.gif' />;
    }

    return (
      <div>
        <h1>Sign Up Sheet</h1>

        <form onSubmit={this.onFormSubmit}>

          <Field
            placeholder='Name'
            name='name'
            value={this.state.fields.name}
            onChange={this.onInputChange}
            validate={(val) => (val ? false : 'Name Required')}
          />

          <br />

```

```
          <Field
            placeholder='Email'
            name='email'
            value={this.state.fields.email}
            onChange={this.onInputChange}
            validate={(val) => (isEmail(val) ? false : 'Invalid Email')}
          />

          <br />

          <CourseSelect
            department={this.state.fields.department}
            course={this.state.fields.course}
            onChange={this.onInputChange}
          />

          <br />

          {{
            SAVING: <input value='Saving...' type='submit' disabled />,
            SUCCESS: <input value='Saved!' type='submit' disabled />,
            ERROR: <input
              value='Save Failed - Retry?'
              type='submit'
              disabled={this.validate()}
            />,
            READY: <input
              value='Submit'
              type='submit'
              disabled={this.validate()}
            />,
          }[this.state._saveStatus]}

        </form>

        <div>
          <h3>People</h3>
          <ul>
            { this.state.people.map(({ name, email, department, course }, i) =>
              <li key={i}>{[ name, email, department, course ].join(' - ')}</li>
            ) }
          </ul>
```

```
      </div>
    </div>
  );
}
```

First, we want to show the user a loading indicator while we are loading previously persisted data. Like the previous section, this is done on the first line of `render()` with a conditional and an early return. While we are loading (`state._loading` is truthy), we won't render the form, only the loading indicator:

```
  if (this.state._loading) return <img src='/img/loading.gif' />
```

Next, we want the submit button to communicate the current save status. If no save request is in-flight, we want the button to be enabled if the field data is valid. If we are in the process of saving, we want the button to read "Saving..." and to be disabled. The user will know that the app is busy, and since the button is disabled, they won't be able to submit duplicate save requests. If the save request resulted in an error, we use the button text to communicate that and indicate that they can try again. The button will be enabled if the input data is still valid. Finally, if the save request completed successfully, we use the button text to communicate that. Here's how we render the button:

```
{{
  SAVING: <input value='Saving...' type='submit' disabled />,
  SUCCESS: <input value='Saved!' type='submit' disabled/>,
  ERROR: <input value='Save Failed - Retry?' type='submit' disabled={this.valida\
te()}/>,
  READY: <input value='Submit' type='submit' disabled={this.validate()}/>
}[this.state._saveStatus]}
```

What we have here are four different buttons – one for each possible `state._saveStatus`. Each button is the value of an object keyed by its corresponding status. By accessing the key of the current save status, this expression will evaluate to the appropriate button.

The last thing that we have to do is related to the `"SUCCESS"` case. We want to show the user that the addition was a success, and we do that by changing the text of the button. However, "Saved!" is not a call to action. If the user enters another person's information and wants to add it to the list, our button would still say "Saved!". It should say "Submit" to more accurately reflect its purpose.

The easy fix for this is to change our `state._saveStatus` back to `"READY"` as soon as they start entering information again. To do this, we update our `onInputChange()` handler:

forms/src/10-remote-persist.js

```
  onInputChange = ({ name, value, error }) => {
    const fields = this.state.fields;
    const fieldErrors = this.state.fieldErrors;

    fields[name] = value;
    fieldErrors[name] = error;

    this.setState({ fields, fieldErrors, _saveStatus: 'READY' });
  };
```

Now instead of just updating `state.fields` and `state.fieldErrors`, we also set `state._saveStatus` to `'READY'`. This way after the user acknowledges their previous submit was a success and starts to interact with the app again, the button reverts to its "ready" state and invites the user to submit again.

At this point our sign-up app is a nice illustration of the features and issues that you'll want to cover in your own forms using React.

Redux

In this section we'll show how you we can modify the form app we've built up so that it can work within a larger app using Redux.

Chronologically we haven't talked about Redux in this book. The next two chapters are all about Redux in depth. If you're unfamiliar with Redux, hop over to those chapters and come back here when you need to deal with forms in Redux.

Our form, which used to be our entire app, will now become a component. In addition, we'll adapt it to fit within the Redux paradigm. At a high level, this involves moving state and functionality from our form component to Redux reducers and actions. For example, we will no longer call API functions from within the form component – we use Redux async actions for that instead. Similarly, data that used to be held as `state` in our form will become read-only `props` – it will now be held in the Redux store.

When building with Redux, it is very helpful to start by thinking about the "shape" your state will take. In our case, we have a pretty good idea already since our functionality has been built. When using Redux, you'll want to centralize state as much as possible – this will be the `store`, accessible by all components in the app. Here's what our `initialState` should look like:

forms/src/11-redux-reducer.js

```
const initialState = {
  people: [],
  isLoading: false,
  saveStatus: 'READY',
  person: {
    name: '',
    email: '',
    course: null,
    department: null
  },
};
```

No surprises here. Our app cares about the list of people who have signed up, the current person being typed in the form, whether or not we're loading, and the status of our save attempt.

Now that we know the shape of our state, we can think of different actions that would mutate it. For example, since we're keeping track of the list of people, we can imagine one action to retrieve the list from the server when the app starts. This action would affect multiple properties of our state. When the request to the server returns with the list, we'll want to update our state with it, and we'll also want to update `isLoading`. In fact, we'll want to set `isLoading` to `true` when we *start* the request, and we'll want to set it to `false` when the request finishes. With Redux, it's important to realize that we can often split one objective into multiple actions.

For our Redux app, we'll have five action types. The first two are related to the objective just mentioned, they are `FETCH_PEOPLE_REQUEST` and `FETCH_PEOPLE_SUCCESS`. Here are those action types with their corresponding action creator functions:

forms/src/11-redux-actions.js

```
/* eslint-disable no-use-before-define */
export const FETCH_PEOPLE_REQUEST = 'FETCH_PEOPLE_REQUEST';
function fetchPeopleRequest () {
  return {type: FETCH_PEOPLE_REQUEST};
}

export const FETCH_PEOPLE_SUCCESS = 'FETCH_PEOPLE_SUCCESS';
function fetchPeopleSuccess (people) {
  return {type: FETCH_PEOPLE_SUCCESS, people};
}
```

When we start the request we don't need to provide any information beyond the action type to the reducer. The reducer will know that the request started just from the type and can update `isLoading` to `true`. When the request is successful, the reducer will know to set it to `false`, but we'll need to provide the people list for that update. This is why `people` is on the second action, `FETCH_PEOPLE_-SUCCESS`.

We skip `FETCH_PEOPLE_FAILURE` only for expediency, but you'll want to handle fetch failures in your own app. See below for how to do that for saving the list.

We can now imagine dispatching these actions and having our state updated appropriately. To get the people list from the server we would dispatch the `FETCH_PEOPLE_REQUEST` action, use our API client to get the list, and finally dispatch the `FETCH_PEOPLE_SUCCESS` action (with the people list on it). With Redux, we'll use an asynchronous action creator, `fetchPeople()` to perform those actions:

forms/src/11-redux-actions.js

```
export function fetchPeople () {
  return function (dispatch) {
    dispatch(fetchPeopleRequest())
    apiClient.loadPeople().then((people) => {
      dispatch(fetchPeopleSuccess(people))
    })
  }
}
```

Instead of returning an action object, asynchronous action creators return functions that dispatch actions.

Asynchronous action creators are not supported by default with Redux. To be able to dispatch functions instead of action objects, we'll need to use the `redux-thunk` middleware when we create our store.

We'll also want to create actions for *saving* our list to the server. Here's what they look like:

forms/src/11-redux-actions.js

```
export const SAVE_PEOPLE_REQUEST = 'SAVE_PEOPLE_REQUEST';
function savePeopleRequest () {
  return {type: SAVE_PEOPLE_REQUEST};
}

export const SAVE_PEOPLE_FAILURE = 'SAVE_PEOPLE_FAILURE';
function savePeopleFailure (error) {
  return {type: SAVE_PEOPLE_FAILURE, error};
}
```

```

export const SAVE_PEOPLE_SUCCESS = 'SAVE_PEOPLE_SUCCESS';
function savePeopleSuccess (people) {
  return {type: SAVE_PEOPLE_SUCCESS, people};
```

Just like the fetch we have `SAVE_PEOPLE_REQUEST` and `SAVE_PEOPLE_SUCCESS`, but we also have `SAVE_PEOPLE_FAILURE`. The `SAVE_PEOPLE_REQUEST` action happens when we start the request, and like before we don't need to provide any data besides the action type. The reducer will see this type and know to update `saveStatus` to `'SAVING'`. Once the request resolves, we can trigger either `SAVE_PEOPLE_SUCCESS` or `SAVE_PEOPLE_FAILURE` depending on the outcome. We will want to pass additional data with these though – `people` on a successful save and `error` on a failure.

Here's how we use those together within an asynchronous action creator, `savePeople()`:

forms/src/11-redux-actions.js

```
export function savePeople (people) {
  return function (dispatch) {
    dispatch(savePeopleRequest())
    apiClient.savePeople(people)
      .then((resp) => { dispatch(savePeopleSuccess(people)) })
      .catch((err) => { dispatch(savePeopleFailure(err)) })
  }
}
```

Notice that this action creator delegates the 'work' of making the API request to our API client. We can define our API client like this:

forms/src/11-redux-actions.js

```
const apiClient = {
  loadPeople: function () {
    return {
      then: function (cb) {
        setTimeout( () => {
          cb(JSON.parse(localStorage.people || '[]'))
        }, 1000);
      }
    }
  },

  savePeople: function (people) {
    const success = !!(this.count++ % 2);
```

```
  return new Promise(function (resolve, reject) {
    setTimeout( () => {
      if (!success) return reject({success});

      localStorage.people = JSON.stringify(people);
      resolve({success});
    }, 1000);
  })
},

count: 1
}
```

Now that we've defined all of our action creators, we have everything we need for our reducer. By using the two asynchronous action creators above, the reducer can make all the updates to our state that our app will need. Here's what our reducer looks like:

forms/src/11-redux-reducer.js

```
const initialState = {
  people: [],
  isLoading: false,
  saveStatus: 'READY',
  person: {
    name: '',
    email: '',
    course: null,
    department: null
  },
};

export function reducer (state = initialState, action) {
  switch (action.type) {
    case FETCH_PEOPLE_REQUEST:
      return Object.assign({}, state, {
        isLoading: true
      });
    case FETCH_PEOPLE_SUCCESS:
      return Object.assign({}, state, {
        people: action.people,
        isLoading: false
      });
```

```
      case SAVE_PEOPLE_REQUEST:
        return Object.assign({}, state, {
          saveStatus: 'SAVING'
        });
      case SAVE_PEOPLE_FAILURE:
        return Object.assign({}, state, {
          saveStatus: 'ERROR'
        });
      case SAVE_PEOPLE_SUCCESS:
        return Object.assign({}, state, {
          people: action.people,
          person: {
            name: '',
            email: '',
            course: null,
            department: null
          },
          saveStatus: 'SUCCESS'
        });
      default:
        return state;
    }
}
```

By just looking at the actions and the reducer you should be able to see all the ways our state can be updated. This is one of the great things about Redux. Because everything is so explicit, state becomes very easy to reason about and test.

Now that we've established the shape of our state and how it can change, we'll create a store. Then we'll want to make some changes so that our form can connect to it properly.

Form Component

Now that we've created the foundation of our app's data architecture with Redux, we can adapt our form component to fit in. In broad strokes, we need to remove any interaction with the API client (our asynchronous action creators handle this now) and shift dependence from component-level `state` to `props` (Redux state will be passed in as `props`).

The first thing we need to do is set up `propTypes` that will align with the data we expect to get from Redux:

forms/src/11-redux-form.js

```
  static propTypes = {
    people: PropTypes.array.isRequired,
    isLoading: PropTypes.bool.isRequired,
    saveStatus: PropTypes.string.isRequired,
    fields: PropTypes.object,
    onSubmit: PropTypes.func.isRequired,
  };
```

We will require one additional `prop` that is not related to data in our Redux store, `onSubmit()`. When the user submits a new person, instead of using the API client, our form component will call this function instead. Later we'll show how we hook this up to our asynchronous action creator `savePeople()`.

Next, we limit the amount of data that we'll keep in `state`. We keep `fields` and `fieldErrors`, but we remove `people`, `_loading`, and `_saveStatus` – those will come in on `props`. Here's the updated `state`

forms/src/11-redux-form.js

```
  state = {
    fields: this.props.fields || {
      name: '',
      email: '',
      course: null,
      department: null
    },
    fieldErrors: {},
  };
```

`state.fields` will be initialized to `props.fields` (or the default fields, if not provided). Additionally, if a new `fields` object comes in on `props`, we will update our `state`:

forms/src/11-redux-form.js

```
  componentWillReceiveProps(update) {
    console.log('this.props.fields', this.props.fields, update);

    this.setState({ fields: update.fields });
  }
```

Now that our props and state are in order, we can remove any usage of apiClient since that will be handled by our asynchronous action creators. The two places that we used the API client were in componentWillMount() and onFormSubmit().

Since the only purpose of componentWillMount() was to use the API client, we have removed it entirely. In onFormSubmit(), we remove the block related to the API and replace it with a call to props.onSubmit():

forms/src/11-redux-form.js

```
  onFormSubmit = (evt) => {
    const person = this.state.fields;

    evt.preventDefault();

    if (this.validate()) return;

    this.props.onSubmit([ ...this.props.people, person ]);
  };
```

With all of that out of the way, we can make a few minor updates to render(). In fact, the only modifications we have to make to render() are to replace references to state._loading, state._saveStatus, and state.people with their counterparts on props.

forms/src/11-redux-form.js

```
  render() {
    if (this.props.isLoading) {
      return <img alt='loading' src='/img/loading.gif' />;
    }

    const dirty = Object.keys(this.state.fields).length;
    let status = this.props.saveStatus;
    if (status === 'SUCCESS' && dirty) status = 'READY';

    return (
      <div>
        <h1>Sign Up Sheet</h1>

        <form onSubmit={this.onFormSubmit}>

          <Field
            placeholder='Name'
            name='name'
```

```
            value={this.state.fields.name}
            onChange={this.onInputChange}
            validate={(val) => (val ? false : 'Name Required')}
          />

          <br />

          <Field
            placeholder='Email'
            name='email'
            value={this.state.fields.email}
            onChange={this.onInputChange}
            validate={(val) => (isEmail(val) ? false : 'Invalid Email')}
          />

          <br />

          <CourseSelect
            department={this.state.fields.department}
            course={this.state.fields.course}
            onChange={this.onInputChange}
          />

          <br />

          {{
            SAVING: <input value='Saving...' type='submit' disabled />,
            SUCCESS: <input value='Saved!' type='submit' disabled />,
            ERROR: <input
              value='Save Failed - Retry?'
              type='submit'
              disabled={this.validate()}
            />,
            READY: <input
              value='Submit'
              type='submit'
              disabled={this.validate()}
            />,
          }[status]}

        </form>
```

```
        <div>
          <h3>People</h3>
          <ul>
            {this.props.people.map(({ name, email, department, course }, i) =>
              <li key={i}>{[ name, email, department, course ].join(' - ')}</li>
            ) }
          </ul>
        </div>
      </div>
    );
  }
```

You may notice that we handle `saveStatus` a bit differently. In the previous iteration, our form component was able to control `state._saveStatus` and could set it to `'READY'` on a field change. In this version, we get that information from `props.saveStatus` and it is read-only. The solution is to check if `state.fields` has any keys – if it does, we know the user has entered data and we can set the button back to the "ready" state.

Connect the Store

At this point we have our actions, our reducer, and our streamlined form component. All that's left is to connect them together.

First, we will use Redux's `createStore()` method to create a `store` from our `reducer`. Because we want to be able to dispatch asynchronous actions, we will also use `thunkMiddleware` from the `redux-thunk` module. To use middleware in our `store`, we'll use Redux's `applyMiddleware()` method. Here's what that looks like:

forms/src/11-redux-app.js

```
const store = createStore(reducer, applyMiddleware(thunkMiddleware));
```

Next, we will use the `connect()` method from `react-redux` to optimize our form component for use with Redux. We do this by providing it two methods: `mapStateToProps` and `mapDispatchToProps`.

When using Redux, we want our components to subscribe to the `store`. However, with `react-redux` it will do that for us. All we need to do is provide a `mapStateToProps` function that defines the mapping between data in the `store` and `props` for the component. In our app, they line up neatly:

forms/src/11-redux-app.js

```
function mapStateToProps(state) {
  return {
    isLoading: state.isLoading,
    fields: state.person,
    people: state.people,
    saveStatus: state.saveStatus,
  };
}
```

From within our form component, we call `props.onSubmit()` when the user submits and validation passes. We want this behavior to dispatch our `savePeople()` asynchronous action creator. To do this, we provide `mapDispatchToProps()` to define the connection between the `props.onSubmit()` function and the dispatch of our action creator:

forms/src/11-redux-app.js

```
function mapDispatchToProps(dispatch) {
  return {
    onSubmit: (people) => {
      dispatch(savePeople(people));
    },
  };
}
```

With both of those functions created, we use the `connect()` method from `react-redux` to give us an optimized `ReduxForm` component:

forms/src/11-redux-app.js

```
const ReduxForm = connect(mapStateToProps, mapDispatchToProps)(Form);
```

The final step is to incorporate the `store` and the `ReduxForm` into our app. At this point our app is a very simple component with only two methods, `componentWillMount()` and `render()`.

In `componentWillMount()` we dispatch our `fetchPeople()` asynchronous action to load the people list from the server:

forms/src/11-redux-app.js

```
  componentWillMount() {
    store.dispatch(fetchPeople());
  }
```

In `render()` we use a helpful component `Provider` that we get from `react-redux`. `Provider` will make the store available to all of its child components. We simply place `ReduxForm` as a child of `Provider` and our app is good to go:

forms/src/11-redux-app.js

```
  render() {
    return (
      <Provider store={store}>
        <ReduxForm />
      </Provider>
    );
  }
```

And that's it! Our form now fits neatly inside a Redux-based data architecture.

After reading this chapter, you should have a good handle on the fundamentals of forms in React. That said, if you'd like to outsource some portion of your form handling to an external module, there are several available. Read on for a list of some of the more popular options.

Form Modules

formsy-react

https://github.com/christianalfoni/formsy-react[57]

`formsy-react` tries to strike a balance between flexibility and reusability. This is a worthwhile goal as the author of this module acknowledges that forms, inputs, and validation are handled quite differently across projects.

The general pattern is that you use the `Formsy.Form` component as your form element, and provide your own input components as children (using the `Formsy.Mixin`). The `Formsy.Form` component has handlers like `onValidSubmit()` and `onInvalid()` that you can use to alter state on the form's parent, and the mixin provides some validation and other general purpose helpers.

react-input-enhancements

http://alexkuz.github.io/react-input-enhancements[58]

[57] https://github.com/christianalfoni/formsy-react

[58] http://alexkuz.github.io/react-input-enhancements

`react-input-enhancements` is a collection of five rich components that you can use to augment forms. This module has a nice demo to showcase how you can use the `Autosize`, `Autocomplete`, `Dropdown`, `Mask`, and `DatePicker` components. The author does make a note that they aren't quite ready for production and are more conceptual. That said, they might be useful if you're looking for a drop-in datepicker or autocomplete element.

tcomb-form

http://gcanti.github.io/tcomb-form[59]

`tcomb-form` is meant to be used with `tcomb` models (https://github.com/gcanti/tcomb[60]) which center around Domain Driven Design. The idea is that once you create a model, the corresponding form can be automatically generated. In theory, the benefits are that you don't have to write as much markup, you get usability and accessibility for free (e.g. automatic labels and inline validation), and your forms will automatically stay in sync with changes to your model. If `tcomb` models seem to be a good fit for your app, this `tcomb-form` is worth considering.

winterfell

https://github.com/andrewhathaway/winterfell[61]

If the idea of defining your forms and fields entirely with JSON, `winterfell` might be for you. With `winterfell`, you sketch out your entire form in a JSON schema. This schema is a large object where you can define things like CSS class names, section headers, labels, validation requirements, field types, and conditional branching. `winterfell` is organized into "form panels", "question panels", and "question sets". Each panel has an ID and that ID is used to assign sets to it. One benefit of this approach is that if you find yourself creating/modifying lots of forms, you could create a UI to create/modify these schema objects and persist them to a database.

react-redux-form

https://github.com/davidkpiano/react-redux-form[62]

If Redux is more your style `react-redux-form` is a "collection of action creators and reducer creators" to simplify "building complex and custom forms with React and Redux". In practice, this module provides a `modelReducer` and a `formReducer` helper to use when creating your Redux `store`. Then within your form you can use the provided `Form`, `Field`, and `Error` components to help connect your `label` and `input` elements to the appropriate reducers, set validation requirements, and display appropriate errors. In short, this is a nice thin wrapper to help you build forms using Redux.

[59] http://gcanti.github.io/tcomb-form
[60] https://github.com/gcanti/tcomb
[61] https://github.com/andrewhathaway/winterfell
[62] https://github.com/davidkpiano/react-redux-form

Using Webpack with Create React App

In most of our earlier projects, we loaded React with `script` tags in our apps' `index.html` files:

```
<script src='vendor/react.js'></script>
<script src='vendor/react-dom.js'></script>
```

Because we've been using ES6, we've also been loading the Babel library with `script` tags:

```
<script src='vendor/babel-standalone.js'></script>
```

With this setup we've been able to load in any ES6 JavaScript file we wanted in `index.html`, specifying that its type is `text/babel`:

```
<script type='text/babel' src='./client.js'></script>
```

Babel would handle the loading of the file, transpiling our ES6 JavaScript to browser-ready ES5 JavaScript.

If you need a refresher on our setup strategy so far, we detail it in Chapter 1.

We began with this setup strategy because it's the simplest. You can begin writing React components in ES6 with little setup.

However, this approach has limitations. For our purposes, the most pressing limitation is the lack of support for **JavaScript modules**.

JavaScript modules

We saw modules in earlier apps. For instance, the time tracking app had a Client module. That module's file defined a few functions, like `getTimers()`. It then set `window.client` to an object that "exposed" each function as a property. That object looked like this:

```
// `window.client` was set to this object
// Each property is a function
{
  getTimers,
  createTimer,
  updateTimer,
  startTimer,
  stopTimer,
  deleteTimer,
};
```

This Client module only exposed these functions. These are the Client module's **public methods**. The file `public/js/client.js` also contained other function definitions, like `checkStatus()`, which verifies that the server returned a 2xx response code. While each of the public methods uses `checkStatus()` internally, `checkStatus()` is kept **private**. It is only accessible from within the module.

That's the idea behind a module in software. You have some self-contained component of a software system that is responsible for some discrete functionality. The module exposes a limited interface to the rest of the system, ideally the minimum viable interface the rest of the system needs to effectively use the module.

In React, **we can think of each of our individual components as their own modules**. Each component is responsible for some discrete part of our interface. React components might contain their own state or perform complex operations, but the interface for all of them is the same: they accept inputs (props) and output their DOM representation (`render`). Users of a React component need not know any of the internal details.

In order for our React components to be truly modular, we'd ideally have them live in their own files. In the upper scope of that file, the component might define a styles object or helper functions that only the component uses. But we want our component-module to only expose the component itself.

Until ES6, modules were not natively supported in JavaScript. Developers would use a variety of different techniques to make modular JavaScript. Some solutions only work in the browser, relying on the browser environment (like the presence of `window`). Others only work in Node.js.

Browsers don't yet support ES6 modules. But ES6 modules are the future. The syntax is intuitive, we avoid bizarre tactics employed in ES5, and they work both in and outside of the browser. Because of this, the React community has quickly adopted ES6 modules.

If you look at `time_tracking_app/public/js/client.js`, you'll get an idea of how strange the techniques for creating ES5 JavaScript modules are.

However, due to the complexity of module systems, we can't simply use ES6's import/export syntax and expect it to "just work" in the browser, even with Babel. More tooling is needed.

For this reason and more, the JavaScript community has widely adopted **JavaScript bundlers**. As we'll see, JavaScript bundlers allow us to write modular ES6 JavaScript that works seamlessly in the browser. But that's not all. Bundlers pack numerous advantages. Bundlers provide a strategy for both organizing and distributing web apps. They have powerful toolchains for both iterating in development and producing production-optimized builds.

While there are several options for JavaScript bundlers, the React community's favorite is **Webpack**.

However, bundlers like Webpack come with a significant trade-off: They add complexity to the setup of your web application. Initial configuration can be difficult and you ultimately end up with an app that has more moving pieces.

In response to setup and configuration woes, the community has created loads of boilerplates and libraries developers can use to get started with more advanced React apps. But the React core team recognized that as long as there wasn't a core team sanctioned solution, the community was likely to remain splintered. The first steps for a bundler-powered React setup can be confusing for novice and experienced developers alike.

The React core team responded by producing the **Create React App** project.

Create React App

The create-react-app[63] library provides a command you can use to initiate a new **Webpack-powered React app**:

```
$ create-react-app my-app-name
```

The library will configure a "black box" Webpack setup for you. It provides you with the benefits of a Webpack setup while abstracting away the configuration details.

Create React App is a great way to get started with a Webpack-React app using standard conventions. Therefore, we'll use it in all of our forthcoming Webpack-React apps.

In this chapter, we'll:

- See what a React component looks like when represented as an ES6 module
- Examine the setup of an app managed by Create React App
- Take a close look at how Webpack works
- Explore some of the numerous advantages that Webpack provides for both development and production use
- Peek under the hood of Create React App
- Figure out how to get a Webpack-React app to work alongside an API

---

[63] https://github.com/facebookincubator/create-react-app

The idea of a "black box" controlling the inner-workings of your app might be scary. This is a valid concern. Later in the chapter, we'll explore a feature of Create React App, `eject`, which should hopefully assuage some of this fear.

Exploring Create React App

Let's install Create React App and then use it to initialize a Webpack-React app. We can install it globally from the command line using the `-g` flag. You can run this command anywhere on your system:

```
$ npm i -g create-react-app@0.5.0
```

The `@0.5.0` above is used to specify a version number and is important.

create-react-app is a very new project. It is moving quickly in its early stages. To avoid possible discrepancies, be sure to use the same version we have specified here.

Now, anywhere on your system, you can run the `create-react-app` command to initiate the setup for a new Webpack-powered React app.

Let's create a new app. We'll do this inside of the code download that came with the book. From the root of the code folder, change into the directory for this chapter:

```
$ cd webpack
```

That directory already has three folders:

```
$ ls
es6-modules/
food-lookup/
heart-webpack-complete/
```

The completed version of the code for this next section is available in `heart-webpack-complete`.

Run the following command to initiate a new React app in a folder called `heart-webpack`:

```
$ create-react-app heart-webpack
```

This will create the boilerplate for the new app and install the app's dependencies. This might take a while.

When Create React App is finished, `cd` into the new directory:

```
$ cd heart-webpack
```

Before exploring, we want to ensure your `react-scripts` version is the same as the one we're using here in the book. We'll see what the `react-scripts` package is in a moment. Run this command inside `heart-webpack` to lock in version `0.7.0`:

```
npm install --save-dev --save-exact react-scripts@0.7.0
```

Now let's take a look at what's inside:

```
$ ls
README.md
node_modules/
package.json
public/
src/
```

Inside `src/` is a sample React app that Create React App has provided for demonstration purposes. Inside of `public/` is an `index.html`, which we'll look at first.

`public/index.html`

Opening `public/index.html` in a text editor:

```
<!doctype html>
<html lang="en">
<head>
    <meta charset="utf-8">
    <meta name="viewport" content="width=device-width, initial-scale=1">
    <link rel="shortcut icon" href="%PUBLIC_URL%/favicon.ico">
    <!--
    ... comment omitted ...
    -->
    <title>React App</title>
</head>
    <body>
        <div id="root"></div>
        <!--
        ... comment omitted ...
        -->
    </body>
</html>
```

The stark difference from the `index.html` we've used in previous apps: there are no `script` tags here. That means this file is not loading any external JavaScript files. We'll see why this is soon.

`package.json`

Looking inside of the project's `package.json`, we see a few dependencies and some script definitions:

webpack/heart-webpack-complete/package.json

```
{
  "name": "heart-webpack",
  "version": "0.1.0",
  "private": true,
  "devDependencies": {
    "react-scripts": "0.9.5"
  },
  "dependencies": {
    "react": "15.5.4",
    "react-dom": "15.5.4"
  },
  "scripts": {
    "start": "react-scripts start",
    "build": "react-scripts build",
    "test": "react-scripts test --env=jsdom",
    "eject": "react-scripts eject"
  }
}
```

Let's break it down.

`react-scripts`

`package.json` specifies a single development dependency, `react-scripts`:

webpack/heart-webpack-complete/package.json

```
  "devDependencies": {
    "react-scripts": "0.9.5"
  },
```

Create React App is just a boilerplate generator. That command produced the folder structure of our new React app, inserted a sample app, and specified our `package.json`. It's actually the `react-scripts` package that makes everything work.

`react-scripts` specifies all of our app's development dependencies, like Webpack and Babel. Furthermore, it contains scripts that "glue" all of these dependencies together in a conventional manner.

Create React App is just a boilerplate generator. The `react-scripts` package, specified in `package.json`, is the engine that will make everything work.

Even though `react-scripts` is the engine, throughout the chapter we'll continue to refer to the overall *project* as Create React App.

`react` and `react-dom`

Under `dependencies`, we see `react` and `react-dom` listed:

webpack/heart-webpack-complete/package.json

```
  "dependencies": {
    "react": "15.5.4",
    "react-dom": "15.5.4"
  },
```

In our first two projects, we loaded in `react` and `react-dom` via script tags in `index.html`. As we saw, those libraries were not specified in this project's `index.html`.

Webpack gives us the ability to use npm packages in the browser. We can specify external libraries that we'd like to use in `package.json`. This is incredibly helpful. Not only do we now have easy access to a vast library of packages. We also get to use npm to manage **all** the libraries that our app uses. We'll see in a bit how this all works.

Scripts

`package.json` specifies four commands under `scripts`. Each executes a command with `react-scripts`. Over this chapter and the next we'll cover each of these commands in depth, but at a high-level:

- `start`: Boots the Webpack development HTTP server. This server will handle requests from our web browser.
- `build`: For use in production, this command creates an optimized, static bundle of all our assets.
- `test`: Executes the app's test suite, if present.
- `eject`: Moves the innards of `react-scripts` into your project's directory. This enables you to abandon the configuration that `react-scripts` provides, tweaking the configuration to your liking.

For those weary of the black box that `react-scripts` provides, that last command is comforting. You have an escape hatch should your project "outgrow" `react-scripts` or should you need some special configuration.

In a `package.json`, you can specify which packages are necessary in which environment. Note that `react-scripts` is specified under `devDependencies`.

When you run `npm i`, npm will check the environment variable `NODE_ENV` to see if it's installing packages in a production environment. In production, npm only installs packages listed under `dependencies` (in our case, `react` and `react-dom`). In development, npm installs all packages. This speeds the process in production, foregoing the installation of unneeded packages like linters or testing libraries.

Given this, you might wonder: Why is `react-scripts` listed as a development dependency? How will the app work in a production environment without it? We'll see why this is after taking a look at how Webpack prepares production builds.

`src/`

Inside of `src/`, we see some JavaScript files:

```
$ ls src
App.css
App.js
App.test.js
index.css
index.js
logo.svg
```

Create React App has created a boilerplate React app to demonstrate how files can be organized. This app has a single component, `App`, which lives inside `App.js`.

`App.js`

Looking inside `src/App.js`:

webpack/heart-webpack-complete/src/App.js

```
import React, { Component } from 'react';
import logo from './logo.svg';
import './App.css';

class App extends Component {
  render() {
    return (
      <div className="App">
        <div className="App-header">
          <img src={logo} className="App-logo" alt="logo" />
          <h2>Welcome to React</h2>
        </div>
        <p className="App-intro">
          To get started, edit <code>src/App.js</code> and save to reload.
        </p>
      </div>
    );
  }
}

export default App;
```

There are a few noteworthy features here.

The import statements

We import `React` and `Component` at the top of the file:

webpack/heart-webpack-complete/src/App.js

```
import React, { Component } from 'react';
```

This is the ES6 module import syntax. Webpack will infer that by `'react'` we are referring to the npm package specified in our `package.json`.

If ES6 modules are new to you, check out the entry in "Appendix B."

The next two imports may have surprised you:

webpack/heart-webpack-complete/src/App.js

```
import logo from './logo.svg';
import './App.css';
```

We're using `import` on files that aren't JavaScript! Webpack has you specify *all* your dependencies using this syntax. We'll see later how this comes into play. Because the paths are relative (they are preceded with `./`), Webpack knows we're referring to local files and not npm packages.

`App` is an ES6 module

The `App` component itself is simple and does not employ state or props. Its return method is just markup, which we'll see rendered in a moment.

What's special about the `App` component is that it's an ES6 module. Our `App` component lives inside its own dedicated `App.js`. At the top of this file, it specifies its dependencies and at the bottom it specifies its export:

webpack/heart-webpack-complete/src/App.js

```
export default App;
```

Our React component is entirely self-contained in this module. Any additional libraries, styles, and images could be specified at the top. Any developer could open this file and quickly reason what dependencies this component has. We could define helper functions that are private to the component, inaccessible to the outside.

Furthermore, recall that there is another file in `src/` related to `App` besides `App.css`: `App.test.js`. So, we have three files corresponding to our component: The component itself (an ES6 module), a dedicated stylesheet, and a dedicated test file.

Create React App has suggested a powerful organization paradigm for our React app. While perhaps not obvious in our single-component app, you can imagine how this modular component model is intended to scale well as the number of components grows to the hundreds or thousands.

We know where our modular component is defined. But we're missing a critical piece: Where is the component written to the DOM?

The answer lies inside `src/index.js`.

`index.js`

Open `src/index.js` now:

webpack/heart-webpack-complete/src/index.js

```
import React from 'react';
import ReactDOM from 'react-dom';
import App from './App';
import './index.css';

ReactDOM.render(
  <App />,
  document.getElementById('root')
);
```

Stepping through this file, we first import both `react` and `react-dom`. Because we specified `App` as the default export from `App.js`, we can import it here. Note again that the relative path (`./App`) signals to Webpack that we're referring to a local file, not an npm package.

At this point, we can use our `App` component just as we have in the past. We make a call to `ReactDOM.render()`, rendering the component to the DOM on the `root` div. This div tag is the one and only div present in `index.html`.

This layout is certainly more complicated than the one we used in our first couple of projects. Instead of just rendering `App` right below where we define it, we have another file that we're importing `App` into and making the `ReactDOM.render()` call in. Again, this setup is intended to keep our code modular. `App.js` is restricted to only defining a React component. It does not carry the additional responsibility of rendering that component. Following from this pattern, we could comfortably import and render this component anywhere in our app.

We now know where the `ReactDOM.render()` call is located. But the way this new setup works is still opaque. `index.html` does not appear to load in any JavaScript. How do our JavaScript modules make it to the browser?

Let's boot the app and then explore how everything fits together.

Why do we import `React` at the top of the file? It doesn't apparently get referenced anywhere.

`React` actually *is* referenced later in the file, we just can't see it because of a layer of indirection. We're referencing `App` using JSX. So this line in JSX:

```
<App />
```

Is actually this underneath the JSX abstraction:

```
React.createElement(App, null);
```

Booting the app

From the root of `heart-webpack`, run the start command:

```
$ npm start
```

This boots the **Webpack development server**. We dig into the details of this server momentarily.

Visiting `http://localhost:3000/`, we see the interface for the sample app that Create React App has provided:

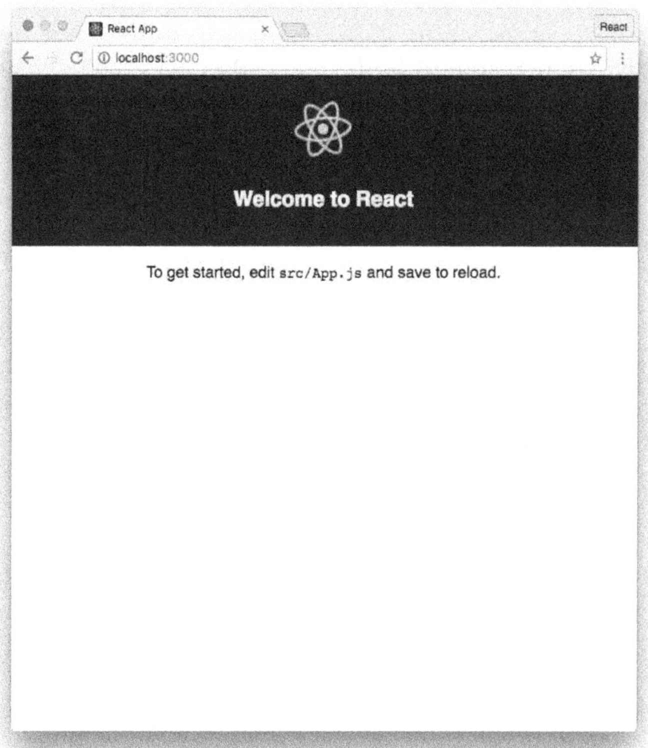

The sample app

The `App` component is clearly present on the page. We see both the logo and text that the component specifies. How did it get there?

Let's view the source code behind this page. In both Chrome and Firefox, you can type `view-source:http://localhost:3000/` into the address bar to do so:

```
<!doctype html>
<html lang="en">
  <head>
    <meta charset="utf-8">
    <meta name="viewport" content="width=device-width, initial-scale=1">
    <link rel="shortcut icon" href="/favicon.ico">
    <!--
      ... comment omitted ...
    -->
    <title>React App</title>
  </head>
  <body>
    <div id="root"></div>
    <!--
      ... comment omitted ...
    -->
  <script type="text/javascript" src="/static/js/bundle.js"></script></body>
</html>
```

This `index.html` looks the same as the one we looked at earlier, save for one key difference: **There is a `script` tag appended to the bottom of the `body`**. This script tag references a `bundle.js`. As we'll see, the `App` component from `App.js` and the `ReactDOM.render()` call from `index.js` both live inside of that file.

The Webpack development server inserted this line into our `index.html`. To understand what `bundle.js` is, let's dig into how Webpack works.

This script defaults the server's port to `3000`. However, if it detects that `3000` is occupied, it will choose another. The script will tell you where the server is running, so check the console if it appears that it is not on `http://localhost:3000/`.

If you're running OS X, this script will automatically open a browser window pointing to `http://localhost:3000/`.

Webpack basics

In our first app (the voting app), we used the library `http-server` to serve our static assets, like `index.html`, our JavaScript files, and our images.

In the second app (the timers app), we used a small Node server to serve our static assets. We defined a server in `server.js` which both provided a set of API endpoints and served all assets under `public/`. Our API server and our static asset server were one in the same.

With Create React App, our static assets are served by the **Webpack development server** that is booted when we run `npm start`. At the moment, we're not working with an API.

As we saw, the original `index.html` did not contain any references to the React app. Webpack inserted a reference to `bundle.js` in `index.html` before serving it to our browser. If you look around on disk, `bundle.js` doesn't exist anywhere. **The Webpack development server produces this file on the fly and keeps it in memory**. When our browser makes a request to `localhost:3000/`, Webpack is serving its modified version of `index.html` and `bundle.js` from memory.

From the page `view-source:http://localhost:3000/`, you can click on `/static/js/bundle.js` to open that file in your browser. It will probably take a few seconds to open. It's a gigantic file.

`bundle.js` contains *all* the JavaScript code that our app needs to run. Not only does it contain the entire source for `App.js` — it contains the entire source for the React library!

You can search for the string `./src/App.js` in this file. Webpack demarcates each separate file it has included with a special comment. What you'll find is quite messy:

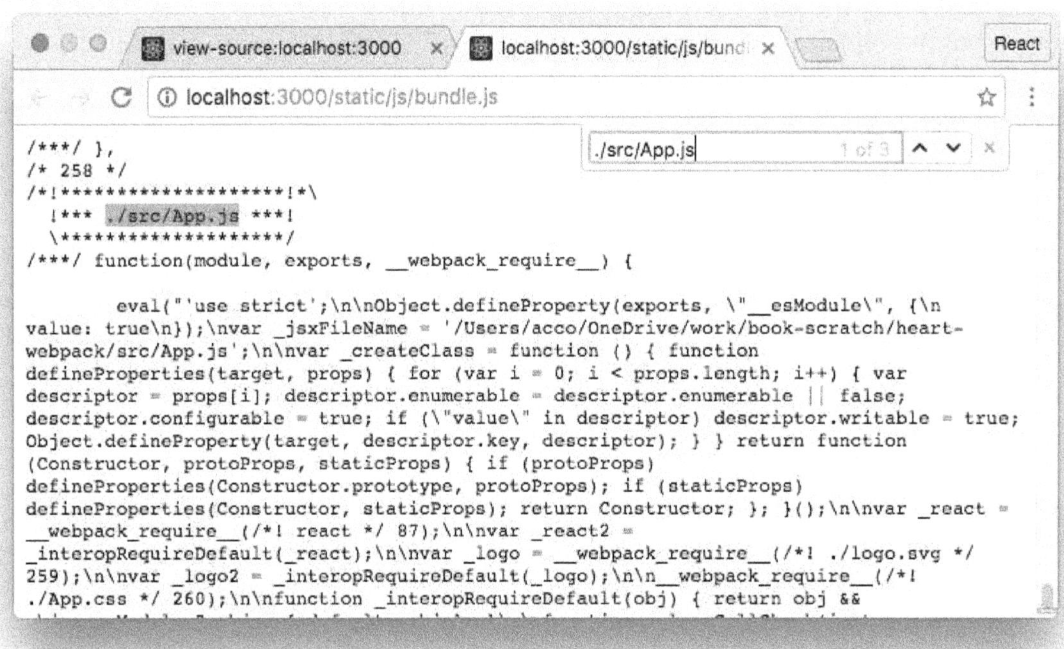

If you do a little hunting, you can see recognizable bits and pieces of `App.js` amidst the chaos. This is indeed our component. But it looks nothing like it.

Webpack has performed some transformation on all the included JavaScript. Notably, it used Babel to transpile our ES6 code to an ES5-compatible format.

If you look at the comment header for `App.js`, it has a number. In the screenshot above, that number was 258:

```
/* 258 */
/*!********************!*\
  !*** ./src/App.js ***!
  \********************/
```

Your module IDs might be different than the ones here in the text.

The module itself is encapsulated inside of a function that looks like this:

```
function(module, exports, __webpack_require__) {
  // The chaotic `App.js` code here
}
```

Each module of our web app is encapsulated inside of a function with this signature. Webpack has given each of our app's modules this function container as well as a module ID (in the case of `App.js`, 258).

But "module" here is not limited to JavaScript modules.

Remember how we imported the logo in `App.js`, like this:

webpack/heart-webpack-complete/src/App.js

```
import logo from './logo.svg';
```

And then in the component's markup it was used to set the `src` on an `img` tag:

webpack/heart-webpack-complete/src/App.js

```
          <img src={logo} className="App-logo" alt="logo" />
```

Here's what the variable declaration of `logo` looks like inside the chaos of the `App.js` Webpack module:

```
var _logo = __webpack_require__(/*! ./logo.svg */ 259);
```

This looks quite strange, mostly due to the in-line comment that Webpack provides for debugging purposes. Removing that comment:

```
var _logo = __webpack_require__(259);
```

Instead of an `import` statement, we have plain old ES5 code. What is this doing though?

To find the answer, search for `./src/logo.svg` in this file. (It should appear directly below `App.js`). The SVG is represented inside `bundle.js`, too!

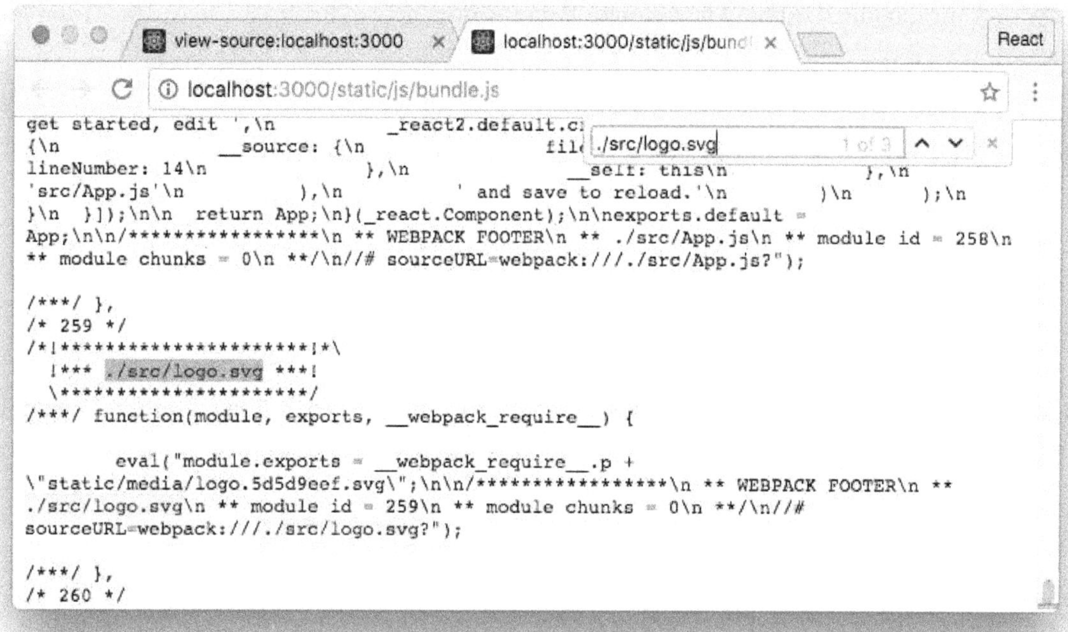

Looking at the header for this module:

```
/* 259 */
/*!**********************!*\
  !*** ./src/logo.svg ***!
  \**********************/
```

Note that its module ID is 259, the same integer passed to `__webpack_require__()` above.

Webpack treats *everything* as a module, including image assets like `logo.svg`. We can get an idea of what's going on by picking out a path in the mess of the `logo.svg` module. Your path might be different, but it will look like this:

```
static/media/logo.5d5d9eef.svg
```

If you open a new browser tab and plug in this address:

```
http://localhost:3000/static/media/logo.5d5d9eef.svg
```

You should get the React logo:

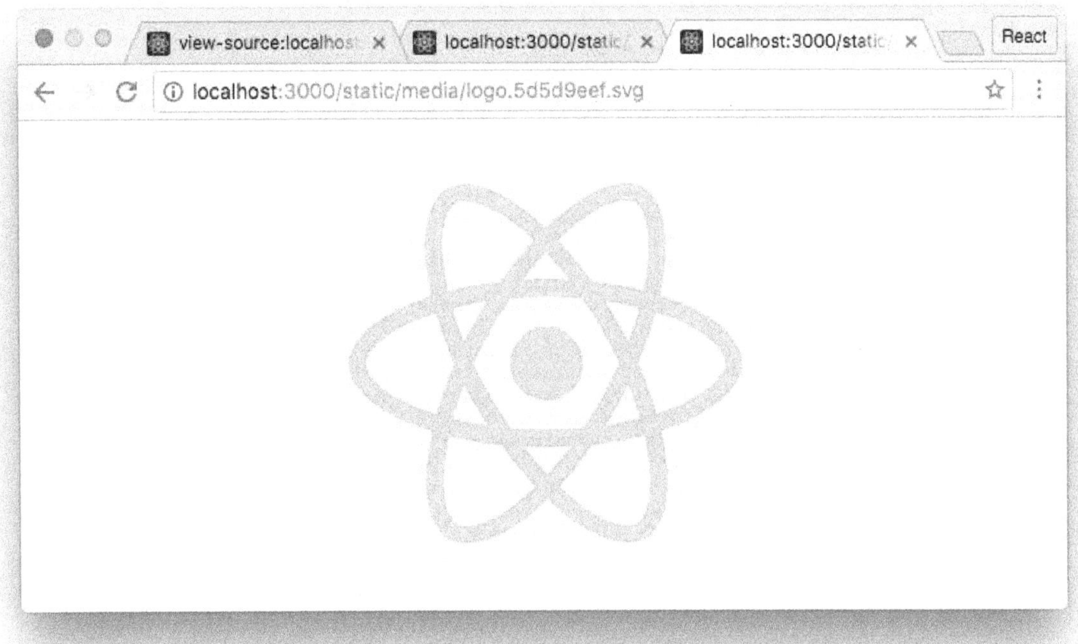

So Webpack created a Webpack module for `logo.svg` by defining a function. While the implementation details of this function are opaque, we know it refers to the path to the SVG on the Webpack development server. Because of this modular paradigm, it was able to intelligently compile a statement like this:

```
import logo from './logo.svg';
```

Into this ES5 statement:

```
var _logo = __webpack_require__(259);
```

`__webpack_require__()` is Webpack's special module loader. This call refers to the Webpack module corresponding to `logo.svg`, number `259`. That module returns the string path to the logo's location on the Webpack development server, `static/media/logo.5d5d9eef.svg`:

```
var _logo = __webpack_require__(259);
console.log(_logo);
// -> "static/media/logo.5d5d9eef.svg"
```

What about our CSS assets? Yep, *everything* is a module in Webpack. Search for the string `./src/App.css`:

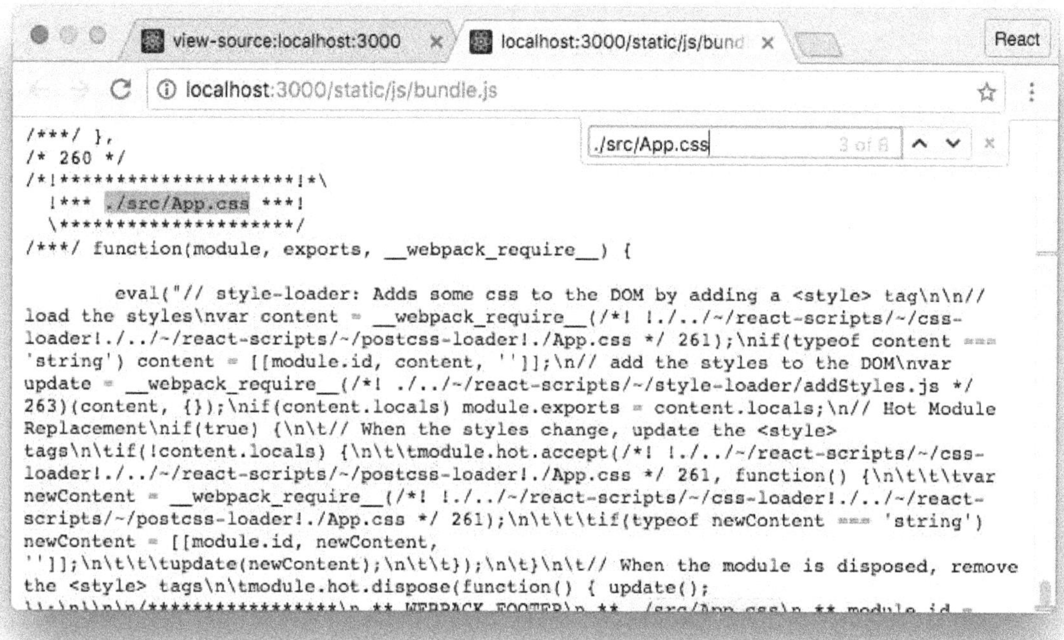

Webpack's `index.html` didn't include any references to CSS. That's because Webpack is including our CSS here via `bundle.js`. When our app loads, this cryptic Webpack module function dumps the contents of `App.css` into `style` tags on the page.

So we know *what* is happening: Webpack has rolled up every conceivable "module" for our app into `bundle.js`. You might be asking: Why?

The first motivation is universal to JavaScript bundlers. Webpack has converted all our ES6 modules into its own bespoke ES5-compatible module syntax.

Furthermore, Webpack, like other bundlers, consolidated all our JavaScript modules into a single file. While it *could* keep JavaScript modules in separate files, having a single file maximizes performance. The initiation and conclusion of each file transfer over HTTP adds overhead. Bundling up hundreds or thousands of smaller files into one bigger one produces a notable speed-up.

Webpack takes this module paradigm further than other bundlers, however. As we saw, it applies the same modular treatment to image assets, CSS, and npm packages (like React and ReactDOM).

This modular paradigm unleashes a lot of power. We touch on aspects of that power throughout the rest of this chapter.

With our nascent understanding of how Webpack works, let's turn our attention back to the sample app. We'll make some modifications and see first-hand how the Webpack development process works.

Making modifications to the sample app

We've been checking out the `bundle.js` produced by the Webpack development server in our browser. Recall that to boot this server, we ran the following command:

```
$ npm start
```

As we saw, this command was defined in `package.json`:

```
"start": "react-scripts start",
```

What exactly is going on here?

The `react-scripts` package defines a start script. Think of this start script as a special interface to Webpack that contains some features and conventions provided by Create React App. At a high-level, the start script:

- Sets up the Webpack configuration
- Provides some nice formatting and coloring for Webpack's console output
- Launches a web browser if you're on OS X

Let's take a look at what the development cycle of our Webpack-powered React app looks like.

Hot reloading

If the server is not already running, go ahead and run the start command to boot it:

```
$ npm start
```

Again, our app launches at `http://localhost:3000/`. The Webpack development server is listening on this port and serves the development bundle when our server makes a request.

One compelling development feature Webpack gives us is **hot reloading**. Hot reloading enables certain files in a web app to be hot-swapped on the fly whenever changes are detected without requiring a full page reload.

At the moment, Create React App only sets up hot reloading for CSS. This is because the React-specific hot reloader is not considered stable enough for the default setup.

Hot reloading for CSS is wonderful. With your browser window open, make an edit to `App.css` and witness as the app updates without a refresh.

For example, you can change the speed at which the logo spins. Here, we changed it from `20s` to `1s`:

```
.App-logo {
  animation: App-logo-spin infinite 1s linear;
  height: 80px;
}
```

Or you can change the color of the header's text. Here, we changed it from `white` to `purple`:

```
.App-header {
  background-color: #222;
  height: 150px;
  padding: 20px;
  color: purple;
}
```

How hot reloading works

Webpack includes client-side code to perform hot reloading inside `bundle.js`. The Webpack client maintains an open socket with the server. Whenever the bundle is modified, the client is notified via this websocket. The client then makes a request to the server, asking for a *patch* to the bundle. Instead of fetching the whole bundle, the server will just send the client the code that client needs to execute to "hot swap" the asset.

Webpack's modular paradigm makes hot reloading of assets possible. Recall that Webpack inserts CSS into the DOM inside `style` tags. To swap out a modified CSS asset, the client removes the previous `style` tags and inserts the new one. The browser renders the modification for the user, all without a page reload.

Auto-reloading

Even though hot reloading is not supported for our JavaScript files, Webpack will still auto-reload the page whenever it detects changes.

With our browser window still open, let's make a minor edit to `src/App.js`. We'll change the text in the `p` tag:

```
<p className="App-intro">
  I just made a change to <code>src/App.js</code>!
</p>
```

Save the file. You'll note the page refreshes shortly after you save and your change is reflected.

Because Webpack is at heart a platform for JavaScript development and deployment, there is an ever-growing ecosystem of plug-ins and tools for Webpack-powered apps.

For development, hot- and auto-reloading are two of the most compelling plug-ins that come configured with Create React App. In the later section on `eject` ("Ejecting"), we'll point to the Create React App configuration file that sets up Webpack for development so that you can see the rest.

For deployment, Create React App has configured Webpack with a variety of plug-ins that produce a production-level optimized build. We'll take a look at the production build process next.

Creating a production build

So far, we've been using the Webpack development server. In our investigation, we saw that this server produces a modified `index.html` which loads a `bundle.js`. Webpack produces and serves this file from memory — nothing is written to disk.

For production, we want Webpack to write a bundle to disk. We'll end up with a production-optimized build of our HTML, CSS, and JavaScript. We could then serve these assets using whatever HTTP server we wanted. To share our app with the world, we'd just need to upload this build to an asset host, like Amazon's S3.

Let's take a look at what a production build looks like.

Quit the server if it's running with `CTRL+C`. From the command line, run the `build` command that we saw in `package.json` earlier:

```
$ npm run build
```

When this finishes, you'll note a new folder is created in the project's root: `build`. `cd` into that directory and see what's inside:

```
$ cd build
$ ls
favicon.ico
index.html
static/
```

If you look at this `index.html`, you'll note that Webpack has performed some additional processing that it did not perform in development. Most notably: there are no newlines. The entire file is on a single line. Newlines are not necessary in HTML and are just extra bytes. We don't need them in production.

Here's what that exact file looks like in a human readable format:

```
<!DOCTYPE html>
<html lang="en">
  <head>
    <meta charset="utf-8">
    <meta content="width=device-width,initial-scale=1" name="viewport">
    <link href="/favicon.ico?fd73a6eb" rel="shortcut icon">
    <title>React App</title>
    <link href="/static/css/main.9a0fe4f1.css" rel="stylesheet">
  </head>
  <body>
    <div id="root"></div>
    <script src="/static/js/main.590bf8bb.js" type="text/javascript">
    </script>
  </body>
</html>
```

Instead of referencing a `bundle.js`, this `index.html` references a file in `static/` which we'll look at momentarily. What's more, this production `index.html` now has a `link` tag to a CSS bundle. As we saw, in development Webpack inserts CSS via `bundle.js`. This feature enables hot reloading. In production, hot reloading capability is irrelevant. Therefore, Webpack deploys CSS normally.

Webpack versions assets. We can see above that our JavaScript bundle has a different name and is versioned (`main.<version>.js`).

Asset versioning is useful when dealing with browser caches in production. If a file is changed, the version of that file will be changed as well. Client browsers will be forced to fetch the latest version.

Note that your versions (or digests) for the files above may be different.

The `static/` folder is organized as follows:

```
$ ls static
css/
js/
media/
```

Checking out the folders individually:

```
$ ls static/css
main.9a0fe4f1.css
main.9a0fe4f1.css.map

$ ls static/js
main.f7b2704e.js
main.f7b2704e.js.map

$ ls static/media
logo.5d5d9eef.svg
```

Feel free to open up both the `.css` file and the `.js` file in your text editor. We refrain from printing them here in the book due to their size.

Be careful about opening these files — you might crash your editor due to their size!

If you open the CSS file, you'll see it's just two lines: The first line is *all* of our app's CSS, stripped of all superfluous whitespace. We could have hundreds of different CSS files in our app and they would end up on this single line. The second line is a special comment declaring the location of the map file.

The JavaScript file is even more packed. In development, `bundle.js` has some structure. You can pick apart where the individual modules live. The production build does not have this structure. What's more, our code has been both minified and uglified. If you're unfamiliar with minification or uglification, see the aside "Minification, uglification, and source maps."

Last, the media folder will contain all of our app's other static files, like images and videos. This app only has one image, the React logo SVG file.

Again, this bundle is entirely self-contained and ready to go. If we wanted to, we could install the same `http-server` package that we used in the first application and use it to serve this folder, like this:

```
http-server ./build -p 3000
```

Without the Webpack development server, you can imagine the development cycle would be a bit painful:

1. Modify the app
2. Run `npm run build` to generate the Webpack bundle
3. Boot/restart the HTTP server

This is why there is no way to "build" anything other than a bundle intended for production. The Webpack server services our needs for development.

Minification, uglification, and source maps

For production environments, we can significantly reduce the size of JavaScript files by converting them from a human-readable format to a more compact one that behaves exactly the same. The basic strategy is stripping all excess characters, like spaces. This process is called **minification**.

Uglification (or **obfuscation**) is the process of deliberately modifying JavaScript files so that they are harder for humans to read. Again, the actual behavior of the app is unchanged. Ideally, this process slows down the ability for outside developers to understand your codebase.

Both the `.css` and `.js` files are accompanied by a companion file ending in `.map`. The `.map` file is a **source map** that provides debugging assistance for production builds. Because they've been minified and uglified, the CSS and JavaScript for a production app are difficult to work with. If you encounter a JavaScript bug on production, for example, your browser will direct you to a cryptic line of this obscure code.

Through a source map, you can map this puzzling area of the codebase back to its original, un-built form. For more info on source maps and how to use them, see the blog post "Introduction to JavaScript Source Maps[a]."

[a] http://www.html5rocks.com/en/tutorials/developertools/sourcemaps/

Ejecting

When first introducing Create React App at the beginning of this chapter, we noted that the project provided a mechanism for "ejecting" your app.

This is comforting. You might find yourself in a position in the future where you would like further control over your React-Webpack setup. An eject will copy all the scripts and configuration encapsulated in `react-scripts` into your project's directory. It opens up the "black box," handing full control of your app back over to you.

Performing an eject is also a nice way to strip some of the "magic" from Create React App. We'll perform an eject in this section and take a quick look around.

There is no backing out from an eject. Be careful when using this command. Should you decide to eject in the future, make sure your app is checked in to source control.

If you've been adding to the app inside `heart-webpack`, you might consider duplicating that directory before proceeding. For example, you can do this:

```
cp -r heart-webpack heart-webpack-ejected
```

The `node_modules` folder does not behave well when it's moved wholesale like this, so you'll need to remove `node_modules` and re-install:

```
cd heart-webpack-ejected
rm -rf node_modules
npm i
```

You can then perform the steps in this section inside of `heart-webpack-ejected` and preserve `heart-webpack`.

Buckle up

From the root of `heart-webpack`, run the eject command:

```
$ npm run eject
```

Confirm you'd like to eject by typing `y` and hitting enter.

After all the files are copied from `react-scripts` into your directory, `npm install` will run. This is because, as we'll see, all the dependencies for `react-scripts` have been dumped into our `package.json`.

When the npm install is finished, take a look at our project's directory:

```
$ ls
README.md
build/
config/
node_modules/
package.json
public/
scripts/
src/
```

We have two new folders: `config/` and `scripts/`. If you looked inside `src/` you'd note that, as expected, it is unchanged.

Take a look at `package.json`. There are *loads* of dependencies. Some of these dependencies are necessary, like Babel and React. Others — like `eslint` and `whatwg-fetch` — are more "nice-to-haves." This reflects the ethos of the Create React App project: an opinionated starter kit for the React developer.

Check out `scripts/` next:

```
$ ls scripts
build.js
start.js
test.js
```

When we ran `npm start` and `npm run build` earlier, we were executing the scripts `start.js` and `build.js`, respectively. We won't look at these files here in the book, but feel free to peruse them. While complicated, they are well-annotated with comments. Simply reading through the comments can give you a good idea of what each of these scripts are doing (and what they are giving you "for free").

Finally, check out `config/` next:

```
$ ls config
env.js
jest/
paths.js
polyfills.js
webpack.config.dev.js
webpack.config.prod.js
```

`react-scripts` provided sensible defaults for the tools that it provides. In `package.json`, it specifies configuration for Babel. Here, it specifies configuration for Webpack and Jest (the testing library we use in the next chapter).

Of particular noteworthiness are the configuration files for Webpack. Again, we won't dive into those here. But these files are well-commented. Reading through the comments can give you a good idea of what the Webpack development and production pipelines look like and what plug-ins are used. In the future, if you're ever curious about how `react-scripts` has configured Webpack in development or production, you can refer to the comments inside these files.

Hopefully seeing the "guts" of `react-scripts` reduces a bit of its mysticism. Testing out eject as we have here gives you an idea of what the process looks like to abandon `react-scripts` should you need to in the future.

So far in this chapter, we've covered the fundamentals of Webpack and Create React App's interface to it. Specifically, we've seen:

- How the interface for Create React App works
- The general layout for a Webpack-powered React app
- How Webpack works (and some of the power it provides)
- How Create React App and Webpack help us generate production-optimized builds
- What an ejected Create React App project looks like

There's one essential element our demo Webpack-React app is missing, however.

In our second project (the timers app) we had a React app that interfaced with an API. The node server both served our static assets (HTML/CSS/JS) and provided a set of API endpoints that we used to persist data about our running timers.

As we've seen in this chapter, when using Webpack via Create React App we boot a Webpack development server. This server is responsible for serving our static assets.

What if we wanted our React app to interface with an API? We'd still want the Webpack development server to serve our static assets. Therefore, we can imagine we'd boot our API and Webpack servers separately. Our challenge then is getting the two to cooperate.

Using Create React App with an API server

In this section, we'll investigate a strategy for running a Webpack development server alongside an API server. Before digging into this strategy, let's take a look at the app we'll be working with.

The completed app

`food-lookup-complete` is in the root of the book's code download. Getting there from `heart-webpack`:

```
$ cd ../..
$ cd food-lookup-complete
```

Take a look at the folder's structure:

```
$ ls
README.md
client/
db/
node_modules/
package.json
server.js
start-client.js
start-server.js
```

In the root of the project is where the *server* lives. There's a `package.json` here along with a `server.js` file. Inside of `client/` is where the *React app* lives. The `client/` folder was generated with Create React App.

Look inside of `client/` now:

If you're on macOS or Linux run:

```
$ ls -a client
```

Windows users can run:

```
$ ls client
```

And you'll see:

```
.babelrc
.gitignore
node_modules/
package.json
public/
src/
tests/
```

In OSX and Unix, the `-a` flag for the `ls` command displays *all* files, including "hidden" files that are preceded by a `.` like `.babelrc`. Windows displays hidden files by default.

So, we have *two* `package.json` files. One sits in the root and specifies the packages that the server needs. And the other lives in `client/` and specifies the packages that the React app needs. While co-existing in this folder, we have two entirely independent apps.

`.babelrc`

A noteworthy file inside `cilent/` is `.babelrc`. The contents of that file:

```
// client/.babelrc
{
  "plugins": ["transform-class-properties"]
}
```

As you may recall, this plugin gives us the property initializer syntax which we used at the end of the first chapter. In that project, we specified we wanted to use this plugin by setting the `data-plugins` attribute on the script tag for `app.js`, like this:

```
<script
  type="text/babel"
  data-plugins="transform-class-properties"
  src="./js/app.js"
></script>
```

Now, for this project, Babel is being included and managed by `react-scripts`. To specify plugins we'd like Babel to use for our Create React App projects, we must first include the plugin in our `package.json`. It's already included:

food-lookup-complete/client/package.json

```
    "babel-plugin-transform-class-properties": "6.22.0",
```

We then just have to specify we'd like Babel to use the plugin in our `.babelrc`.

Running the app

In order to boot our app, we need to install the packages for both the server and client. We'll run `npm i` inside both directories:

```
$ npm i
$ cd client
$ npm i
$ cd ..
```

With the packages for both the server and client installed, we can run the app. Be sure to do this from the top-level directory of the project (where the server lives):

```
$ npm start
```

As things are booting, you'll see some console output from both the server and the client. Once the app is booted, you can visit `localhost:3000` to see the app:

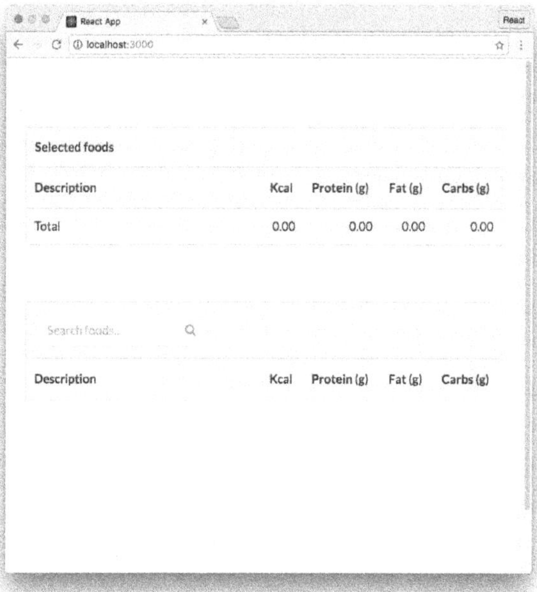

The app provides a search field for looking up nutritional info in a food database. Typing a value into the search field performs a live search. You can click on food items to add them to the top table of totals:

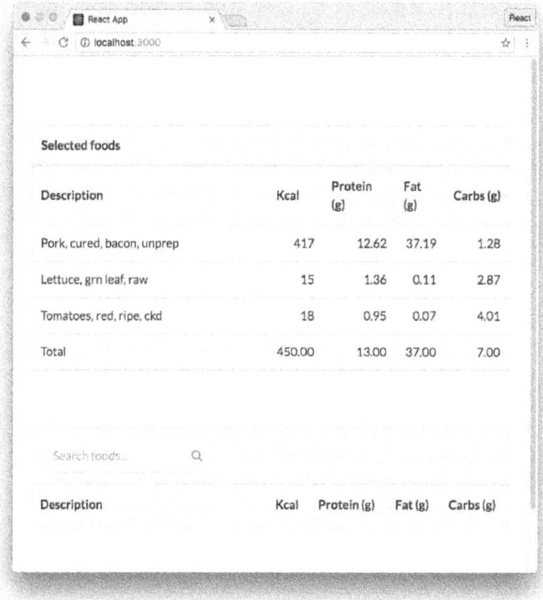

The app's components

The app consists of three components:

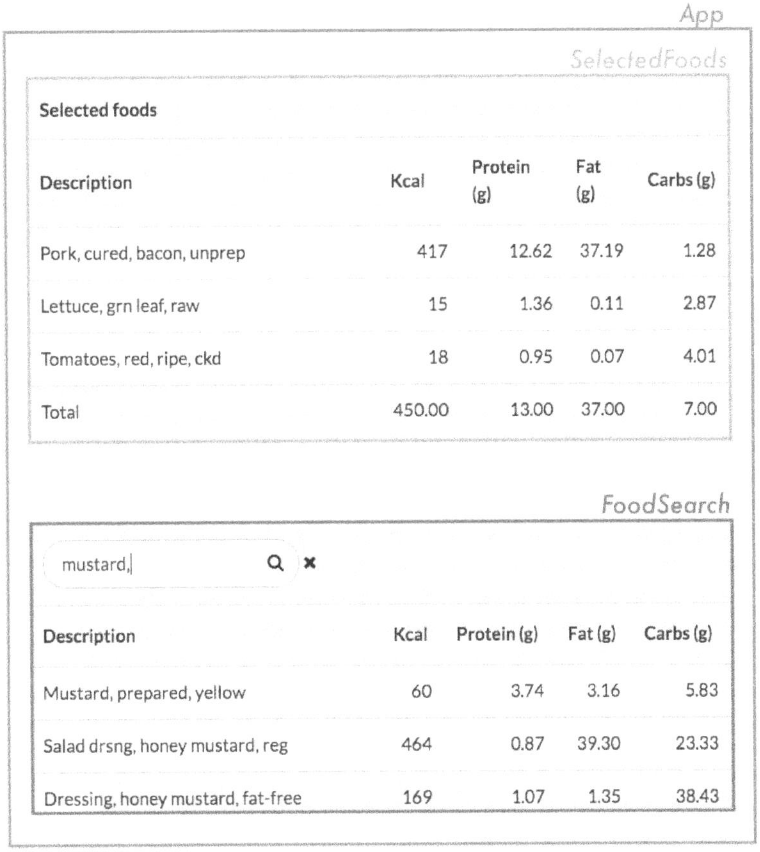

App

SelectedFoods

Selected foods

Description	Kcal	Protein (g)	Fat (g)	Carbs (g)
Pork, cured, bacon, unprep	417	12.62	37.19	1.28
Lettuce, grn leaf, raw	15	1.36	0.11	2.87
Tomatoes, red, ripe, ckd	18	0.95	0.07	4.01
Total	450.00	13.00	37.00	7.00

FoodSearch

mustard,

Description	Kcal	Protein (g)	Fat (g)	Carbs (g)
Mustard, prepared, yellow	60	3.74	3.16	5.83
Salad drsng, honey mustard, reg	464	0.87	39.30	23.33
Dressing, honey mustard, fat-free	169	1.07	1.35	38.43

- **App**: The parent container for the application.
- **SelectedFoods**: A table that lists selected foods. Clicking on a food item removes it.
- **FoodSearch**: Table that provides a live search field. Clicking on a food item in the table adds it to the total (`SelectedFoods`).

In this chapter, we won't dig into the details of any of these components. Instead, we're just going to focus on how we got this existing Webpack-React app to cooperate with a Node server.

How the app is organized

Now that we've seen the completed app, let's see how we got this to work.

Kill the app if it's running then change to the `food-lookup` directory (the non-complete version) inside `webpack`. Getting there from `food-lookup-complete`:

```
cd webpack/food-lookup
```

Again, we have to install the npm packages for both server and client:

```
$ npm i
$ cd client
$ npm i
$ cd ..
```

The server

Let's boot just the server and see how that works. In the completed version, we used `npm start` to start both the server and the client. If you check `package.json` in this directory, you'll see that this command is not yet defined. We can boot just the server with this:

```
$ npm run server
```

This server provides a single API endpoint, `/api/food`. It expects a single parameter, `q`, the food we are searching for.

You can give it a whirl yourself. You can use your browser to perform a search or use `curl`:

```
$ curl localhost:3001/api/food?q=hash+browns
```


```
[
  {
    "description": "Fast foods, potatoes, hash browns, rnd pieces or patty",
    "kcal": 272,
    "protein_g": 2.58,
    "carbohydrate_g": 28.88,
    "sugar_g": 0.56
  },
  {
    "description": "Chick-fil-a, hash browns",
    "kcal": 301,
    "protein_g": 3,
    "carbohydrate_g": 30.51,
    "sugar_g": 0.54
  },
  {
    "description": "Denny's, hash browns",
    "kcal": 197,
```

```
    "protein_g": 2.49,
    "carbohydrate_g": 26.59,
    "sugar_g": 1.38
  },
  {
    "description": "Restaurant, family style, hash browns",
    "kcal": 197,
    "protein_g": 2.49,
    "carbohydrate_g": 26.59,
    "sugar_g": 1.38
  }
]
```


Now that we understand how this endpoint works, let's take a look at the one area it is called in the client. Kill the server with CTRL+C.

Client

The `FoodSearch` component makes the call to `/api/foods`. It performs a request every time the user changes the search field. It uses a library, `Client`, to make the request.

The `Client` module is defined in `client/src/Client.js`. It exports an object with one method, `search()`. Looking just at the `search()` function:

webpack/food-lookup/client/src/Client.js

```
function search(query, cb) {
  return fetch(`http://localhost:3001/api/food?q=${query}`, {
    accept: 'application/json',
  }).then(checkStatus)
    .then(parseJSON)
    .then(cb);
}
```

The `search()` function is the one touch point between the client and the server. `search()` makes a call to `localhost:3001`, the default location of the server.

So, we have two different servers we need to have running in order for our app to work. We need the API server running (at `localhost:3001`) and the Webpack development server running (at `localhost:3000`). If we have both servers running, they should presumably be able to communicate.

We could use two terminal windows, but there's a better solution.

If you need a review on the Fetch API, we use it in Chapter 3: Components and Servers.

Concurrently

Concurrently[64] is a utility for running multiple processes. We'll see how it works by implementing it.

Concurrently is already included in the server's `package.json`:

webpack/food-lookup/package.json

```
  },
  "devDependencies": {
    "concurrently": "3.1.0"
```

We want concurrently to execute two commands, one to boot the API server and one to boot the Webpack development server. You boot multiple commands by passing them to concurrently in quotes like this:

```
# Example of using `concurrently`
$ concurrently "command1" "command2"
```

If you were writing your app to just work on Mac or Unix machines, you could do something like this:

```
$ concurrently "npm run server" "cd client && npm start"
```

Note the second command for booting the client changes into the `client` directory and then runs `npm start`.

However, the `&&` operator is not cross-platform and won't work on Windows. As such, we've included a `start-client.js` script with the project. This script will boot the client from the top-level directory.

Given this start script, you can boot the client app from the top-level directory like this:

```
$ babel-node start-client.js
```

We'll add a `client` command to our `package.json`. That way, the method for booting the server and the client will look the same:

[64] https://github.com/kimmobrunfeldt/concurrently

```
# Boot the server
$ npm run server
# Boot the client
$ npm run client
```

Therefore, using `concurrently` will look like this:

```
$ concurrently "npm run server" "npm run client"
```

Let's add the `start` and `client` commands to our `package.json` now:

food-lookup-complete/package.json

```
  "scripts": {
    "start": "concurrently \"npm run server\" \"npm run client\"",
    "server": "babel-node start-server.js",
    "client": "babel-node start-client.js"
  },
```

For `start`, we execute both commands, **escaping the quotes** because we're in a JSON file.

Save and close `package.json`. Now we can boot both servers by running `npm start`. Go ahead and do this now:

```
$ npm start
```

You'll see output for both the server and the client logged to the console. Concurrently has executed both run commands simultaneously.

When it appears everything has booted, visit `localhost:3000`. And then start typing some stuff in. Strangely, nothing appears to happen:

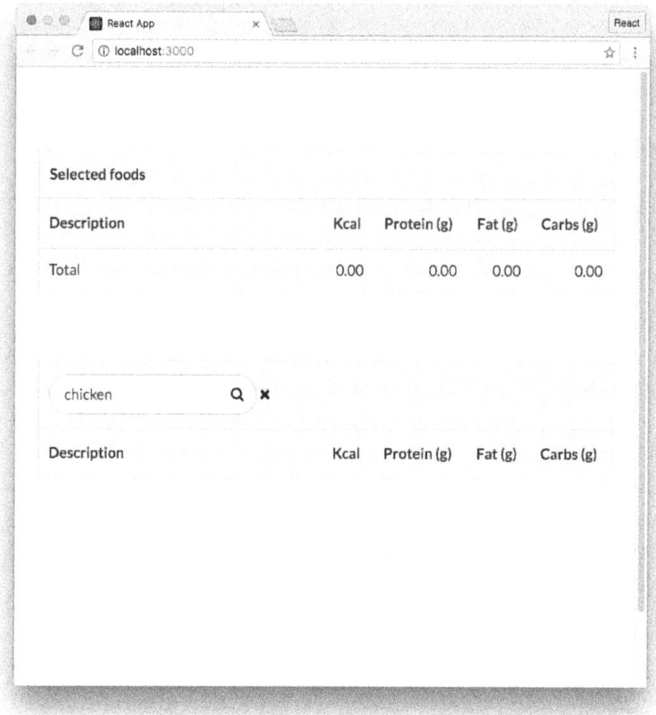

Popping open the developer console, we see that it is littered with errors:

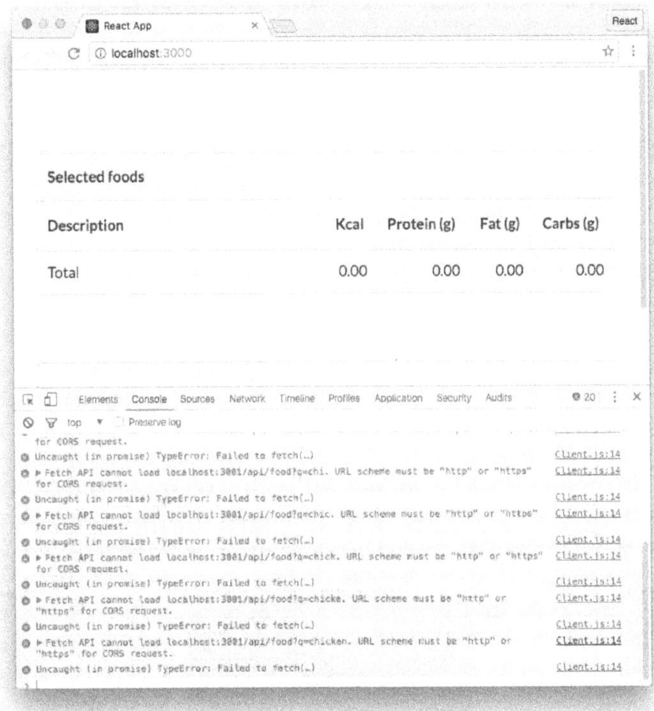

Picking out one of them:

```
Fetch API cannot load http://localhost:3001/api/food?q=c. No 'Access-Control-All\
ow-Origin' header is present on the requested resource. Origin 'http://localhost\
:3000' is therefore not allowed access. If an opaque response serves your needs,\
 set the request's mode to 'no-cors' to fetch the resource with CORS disabled.
```

Our browser prevented our React app (hosted at `localhost:3000`) from loading a resource from a different origin (`localhost:3001`). We attempted to perform **Cross-Origin Resource Sharing** (or CORS). The browser prevents these types of requests from scripts for security reasons.

Note: If this issue didn't occur for you, you may want to verify your browser security settings are sound. Not restricting CORS leaves you open to significant security risk.

This is the primary difficulty with our two-server solution. But the two-server setup is common in development. Common enough that Create React App has a solution readily available for us to use.

Using the Webpack development proxy

Create React App enables you to setup the Webpack development server **to proxy requests to your API**. Instead of making a request to the API server at `localhost:3001`, our React app can make requests to `localhost:3000`. We can then have Webpack proxy those requests to our API server.

So, our original approach was to have the user's browser interact directly with both servers, like this:

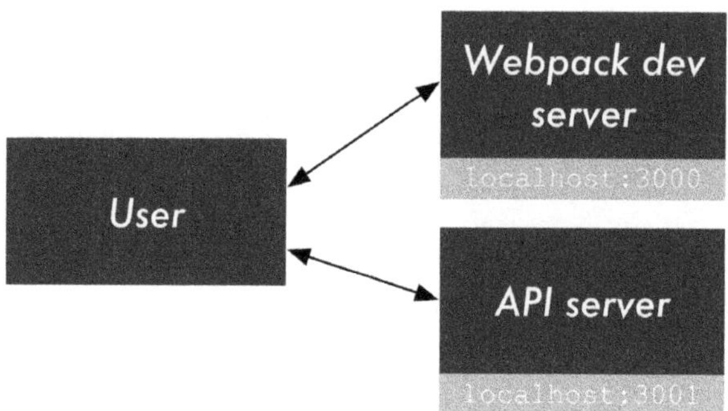

However, we want the browser to just interact with the Webpack development server at `localhost:3000`. Webpack will forward along requests intended for the API, like this:

This proxy feature allows our React app to interact exclusively with the Webpack development server, eliminating any issues with CORS.

To do this, let's first modify `client/src/Client.js`. Remove the base URL, `localhost:3001`:

food-lookup-complete/client/src/Client.js

```
function search(query, cb) {
  return fetch(`/api/food?q=${query}`, {
    accept: 'application/json',
  }).then(checkStatus)
```

Now, `search()` will make calls to `localhost:3000`.

Next, in our client's `package.json`, we can set a special property, `proxy`. Add this property to `client/package.json` now:

```
// Inside client/package.json
"proxy": "http://localhost:3001/",
```

Make sure to add that line to the **client's** `package.json`, not the server's.

This property is special to Create React App, and instructs Create React App to setup our Webpack development server to proxy API requests to `localhost:3001`. The Webpack development server will infer what traffic to proxy. It will proxy a request to our API if the URL is not recognized or if the request is not loading static assets (like HTML, CSS, or JavaScript).

Try it out

Use Concurrently to boot both processes:

```
$ npm start
```

Visiting `localhost:3000`, we see everything working. Because our browser is interfacing with the API through `localhost:3000`, we have no issues with CORS.

Webpack at large

As a platform for JavaScript applications, Webpack packs numerous features. We witnessed some of these features in this chapter. Webpack's abilities can be considered more broadly underneath two categories:

Optimization

Webpack's optimization toolset for production environments is vast.

One immediate optimization Webpack provides is reducing the number of files the client browser has to fetch. For large JavaScript apps composed of many different files, serving a handful of bundle files (like `bundle.js`) is faster than serving tons of small files.

Code splitting is another optimization which builds off of the concept of a bundle. You can configure Webpack so that it only serves the JavaScript and CSS assets that are relevant to the page that a user is viewing. While your multi-page app might have hundreds of React components, you can have Webpack only serve the necessary components and CSS that the client needs to render whatever page that they are on.

Tooling

As with optimization, the ecosystem around Webpack's tooling is vast.

For development, we saw Webpack's handy hot- and auto-reloading features. In addition, Create React App configures other niceties in the development pipeline, like auto-linting your JavaScript code.

For production, we saw how we can configure Webpack to execute plug-ins that optimize our production build.

When to use Webpack/Create React App

So, given Webpack's power, you might ask: Should I just use Webpack/Create React App for all my future React projects?

It depends.

Loading React and Babel in `script` tags as we did in the first couple of chapters is still a completely sane approach. For some projects, the simplicity of this setup might be preferable. Plus, you can always start simple and then move a project to the more complex Webpack setup in the future.

What's more, if you're looking to roll React out inside an existing application this simple approach is your best bet. You don't have to adopt an entirely new build or deployment pipeline for your app. Instead, you can roll React components out one-by-one, all by simply ensuring that the React library is included in your app.

But, for many developers and many types of projects, Webpack is a compelling option with features that are too good to miss. If you're planning on writing a sizeable React application with many different components, Webpack's support for ES6 modules will help keep your codebase sensible. Support for npm packages is great. And thanks to Create React App, you get tons of tooling for development and production for free.

There is one additional deal breaker in favor of Webpack: testing. In the next chapter, we learn how to write tests for our React apps. As we'll see, Webpack provides a platform for easily executing our test suite in the console, outside of a browser.

Unit Testing

A robust test suite is a vital constituent of quality software. With a good test suite at his or her disposal, a developer can more confidently refactor or add features to an application. Test suites are an upfront investment that pay dividends over the lifetime of a system.

Testing user interfaces is notoriously difficult. Thankfully, testing React components is not. With the right tools and the right methodology, the interface for your web app can be just as fortified with tests as every other part of the system.

We'll begin by writing a small test suite without using any testing libraries. After getting a feel for a test suite's essence, we'll introduce the Jest testing framework to alleviate a lot of boilerplate and easily allow our tests to be much more expressive.

While using Jest, we'll see how we can organize our test suite in a behavior-driven style. Once we're comfortable with the basics, we'll take a look at how to approach testing React components in particular. We'll introduce Enzyme, a library for working with React components in a testing environment.

Finally, in the last section of this chapter, we work with a more complex React component that sits inside of a larger app. We use the concept of a mock to isolate the API-driven component we are testing.

Writing tests without a framework

If you're already familiar with JavaScript testing, you can skip ahead to the next section.

However, you might still find this section to be a useful reflection on what testing frameworks are doing behind the scenes.

The projects for this chapter are located inside of the folder `testing` that was provided with this book's code download.

We'll start in the `basics` folder:

```
$ cd testing/basics
```

The structure of this project:

```
$ ls
Modash.js
Modash.test.js
complete/
package.json
```

Inside of `complete/` you'll find files corresponding to each iteration of `Modash.test.js` as well as the completed version of `Modash.js`.

We'll be using `babel-node` to run our test suite from the command-line. `babel-node` is included in this folder's `package.json`. Go ahead and install the packages in `package.json` now:

```
$ npm install
```

In order to write tests, we need to have a library to test. Let's write a little utility library that we can test.

Preparing `Modash`

We'll write a small library in `Modash.js`. Modash will have some methods that might prove useful when working with JavaScript strings. We'll write the following three methods. Each returns a string:

`truncate(string, length)`

Truncates `string` if it's longer than the supplied `length`. If the string is truncated, it will end with `...`:

```
const s = 'All code and no tests makes Jack a precarious boy.';
Modash.truncate(s, 21);
  // => 'All code and no tests...'
Modash.truncate(s, 100);
  // => 'All code and no tests makes Jack a precarious boy.'
```

`capitalize(string)`

Capitalizes the first letter of `string` and lower cases the rest:

```
const s = 'stability was practically ASSURED.';
Modash.capitalize(s);
  // => 'Stability was practically assured.'
```

`camelCase(string)`

Takes a string of words delimited by spaces, dashes, or underscores and returns a camel-cased representation:

```
let s = 'started at';
Modash.camelCase(s);
  // => 'startedAt'
s = 'started_at';
Modash.camelCase(s);
  // => 'startedAt'
```

The name "Modash" is a play on the popular JavaScript utility library Lodash[65].

We'll write Modash as an ES6 module. For more details on how this works with Babel, see the aside "ES6: Import/export with Babel." If you need a refresher on ES6 modules, refer to the previous chapter "Using Webpack with create-react-app.".

Open up `Modash.js` now. We'll write our library's three functions then export our interface at the bottom of this file.

First, we'll write the function for `truncate()`. There are many ways to do this. Here's one approach:

testing/basics/complete/Modash.js

```
function truncate(string, length) {
  if (string.length > length) {
    return string.slice(0, length) + '...';
  } else {
    return string;
  }
}
```

Next, here's the implementation for `capitalize()`:

testing/basics/complete/Modash.js

```
function capitalize(string) {
  return (
    string.charAt(0).toUpperCase() + string.slice(1).toLowerCase()
  );
}
```

Finally, we'll write `camelCase()`. This one's slightly trickier. Again, there are multiple ways to implement this but here's the strategy that follows:

[65] https://lodash.com/

1. Use `split` to get an array of the words in the string. Spaces, dashes, and underscores will be considered delimiters.
2. Create a new array. The first entry of this array will be the lower-cased version of the first word. The rest of the entries will be the capitalized version of each subsequent word.
3. Join that array with `join`.

That looks like this:

testing/basics/complete/Modash.js

```
function camelCase(string) {
  const words = string.split(/[\s|\-|_]+/);
  return [
    words[0].toLowerCase(),
    ...words.slice(1).map((w) => capitalize(w)),
  ].join('');
}
```

String's `split()` splits a string into an array of strings. It accepts as an argument the character(s) you would like to split on. The argument can be either a string or a regular expression. You can read more about `split()` here[66].

Array's `join()` combines all the members of an array into a string. You can read more about `join()` here[67].

With those three functions defined in `Modash.js`, we're ready to export our module.

At the bottom of `Modash.js`, we first create the object that encapsulates our methods:

testing/basics/complete/Modash.js

```
const Modash = {
  truncate,
  capitalize,
  camelCase,
};
```

And then we export it:

[66] https://developer.mozilla.org/en-US/docs/Web/JavaScript/Reference/Global_Objects/String/split
[67] https://developer.mozilla.org/en-US/docs/Web/JavaScript/Reference/Global_Objects/Array/join

testing/basics/complete/Modash.js

```
export default Modash;
```

We'll write our testing code for this section inside of the file `Modash.test.js`. Open up that file in your text editor now.

ES6: Import/export with Babel

Our `package.json` already includes Babel. In addition, we're including a Babel plug-in, `babel-plugin-transform-e`

This package will let us use the ES6 import/export syntax. Importantly, we specify it as a Babel plugin inside the project's `.babelrc`:

```
// basics/.babelrc
{
  "plugins": ["transform-es2015-modules-commonjs"]
}
```

With this plugin in place, we can now export a module from one file and import it into another.

However, note that this solution **won't work in the browser**. It works locally in the Node runtime, which is fine for the purposes of writing tests for our Modash library. But to support this in the browser requires additional tooling. As we mentioned in the last chapter, ES6 module support in the browser is one of our primary motivations for using Webpack.

Writing the first spec

Our test suite will import the library we're writing tests for, `Modash`. We'll call methods on that library and make **assertions** on how the methods should behave.

At the top of `Modash.test.js`, let's first import our library:

testing/basics/complete/Modash.test-1.js

```
import Modash from './Modash';
```

Our first assertion will be for the method `truncate`. We're going to **assert** that when given a string over the supplied length, `truncate` returns a truncated string.

First, we setup the test:

testing/basics/complete/Modash.test-1.js

```
const string = 'there was one catch, and that was CATCH-22';
const actual = Modash.truncate(string, 19);
const expected = 'there was one catch...';
```

We're declaring our sample test string, `string`. We then set two variables: `actual` and `expected`. In test suites, **actual** is what we call the behavior that was observed. In this case, it's what `Modash.truncate` actually returned. **expected** is the value we are expecting.

Next, we make our test's assertion. We'll print a message indicating whether `truncate` passed or failed:

testing/basics/complete/Modash.test-1.js

```
if (actual !== expected) {
  console.log(
    `[FAIL] Expected \`truncate()\` to return '${expected}', got '${actual}'`
  );
} else {
  console.log('[PASS] `truncate()`.');
}
```

Try it out

We can run our test suite at this stage in the command line. Save the file `Modash.test.js` and run the following from the `testing/basics` folder:

```
./node_modules/.bin/babel-node Modash.test.js
```

Executing this, we see a `[PASS]` message printed to the console. If you'd like, you can modify the `truncate` function in `Modash.js` to observe this test failing:

```
bash

 in ~/fullstack-react-code/testing/basics
$ ./node_modules/.bin/babel-node Modash.test.js
[PASS] `truncate()`.

 in ~/fullstack-react-code/testing/basics
$
```

Test passing

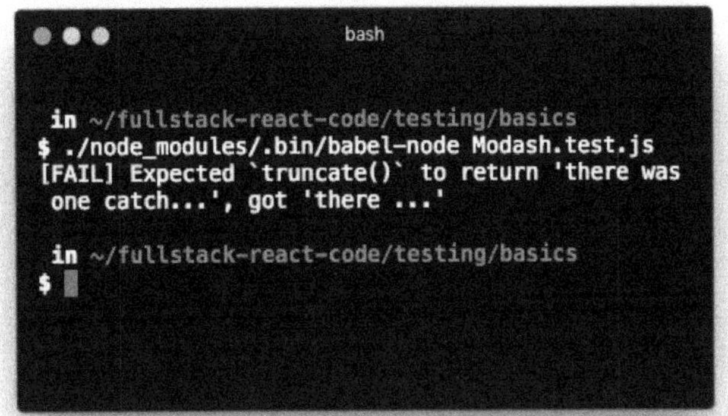

```
bash

 in ~/fullstack-react-code/testing/basics
$ ./node_modules/.bin/babel-node Modash.test.js
[FAIL] Expected `truncate()` to return 'there was
 one catch...', got 'there ...'

 in ~/fullstack-react-code/testing/basics
$
```

Example of what it looks like when test fails

The `assertEqual()` function

Let's write some tests for the other two methods in `Modash`.

For all our tests, we're going to be following a similar pattern. We're going to have some assertion that checks if `actual` equals `expected`. We'll print a message to the console that indicates whether the function under test passed or failed.

To avoid this code duplication, we'll write a helper function, `assertEqual()`. `assertEqual()` will check equality between both its arguments. The function will then write a console message, indicating if the spec passed or failed.

At the top of `Modash.test.js`, below the import statement for `Modash`, declare `assertEqual`:

testing/basics/complete/Modash.test-2.js

```
import Modash from './Modash';

function assertEqual(description, actual, expected) {
  if (actual === expected) {
    console.log(`[PASS] ${description}`);
  } else {
    console.log(`[FAIL] ${description}`);
    console.log(`\tactual: '${actual}'`);
    console.log(`\texpected: '${expected}'`);
  }
}
```

A tab is represented as the `\t` character in JavaScript.

With `assertEqual` defined, let's re-write our first test spec. We're going to re-use the variables `actual`, `expected`, and `string` throughout the test suite, so we'll use the `let` declaration so that we can redefine them:

testing/basics/complete/Modash.test-2.js

```
let actual;
let expected;
let string;

string = 'there was one catch, and that was CATCH-22';
actual = Modash.truncate(string, 19);
expected = 'there was one catch...';

assertEqual('`truncate()`: truncates a string', actual, expected);
```

If you were to run `Modash.test.js` now, you'd note that things are working just as before. The console output is just slightly different:

Test passing

With our assert function written, let's write some more tests.

Let's write one more assertion for `truncate`. The function should return a string as-is if it's less than the supplied length. We'll use the same `string`. Write this assertion below the current one:

testing/basics/complete/Modash.test-2.js

```
actual = Modash.truncate(string, string.length);
expected = string;

assertEqual('`truncate()`: no-ops if <= length', actual, expected);
```

Next, let's write an assertion for `capitalize`. We can continue to use the same `string`:

testing/basics/complete/Modash.test-2.js

```
actual = Modash.capitalize(string);
expected = 'There was one catch, and that was catch-22';

assertEqual('`capitalize()`: capitalizes the string', actual, expected);
```

Given the example string we're using, this assertion tests both aspects of `capitalize`: That it capitalizes the first letter in the string and that it converts the rest to lowercase.

Last, we'll write our assertions for `camelCase`. We'll test this function with two different strings. One will be delimited by spaces and the other by underscores.

The assertion for spaces:

testing/basics/complete/Modash.test-2.js

```
string = 'customer responded at';
actual = Modash.camelCase(string);
expected = 'customerRespondedAt';

assertEqual('`camelCase()`: string with spaces', actual, expected);
```

And for underscores:

testing/basics/complete/Modash.test-2.js

```
string = 'customer_responded_at';
actual = Modash.camelCase(string);
expected = 'customerRespondedAt';

assertEqual('`camelCase()`: string with underscores', actual, expected);
```

Try it out

Save `Modash.test.js`. From the console, run the test suite:

```
./node_modules/.bin/babel-node Modash.test.js
```

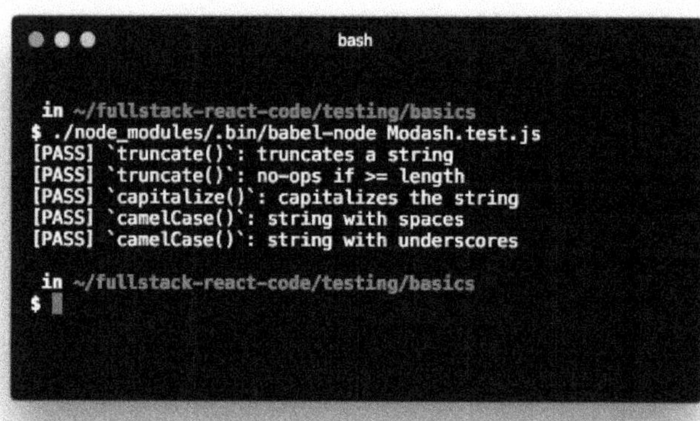

Tests passing

Feel free to tweak either the `expected` values for each assertion or break the library and watch the tests fail.

Our miniature assertion framework is clear but limited. It's hard to imagine how it would be both maintainable and scalable for a more complex app or module. And while `assertEqual()` works fine for checking the equality of strings, we'll want to make more complex assertions when working with objects or arrays. For instance, we might want to check if an object contains a particular property or an array a particular element.

What is Jest?

JavaScript has a variety of testing libraries that pack a bunch of great features. These libraries help us organize our test suite in a robust, maintainable manner. Many of these libraries accomplish the same domain of tasks but with different approaches.

An example of testing libraries you may have heard of or worked with are Mocha, Jasmine, QUnit, Chai, and Tape.

We like to think of testing libraries as having three major components:

- The test runner. This is what you execute in the command-line. The test runner is responsible for finding your tests, running them, and reporting results back to you in the console.
- A domain-specific language for organizing your tests. As we'll see, these functions help us perform common tasks like orchestrating setup and teardown before and after tests run.
- An assertion library. The assert functions provided by these libraries help us easily make otherwise complex assertions, like checking equality between JavaScript objects or the presence of certain elements in an array.

React developers have the option to use any JavaScript testing framework they'd like for their tests. In this book, we'll focus on one in particular: **Jest**.

Facebook created and maintains Jest. If you've used other JavaScript testing frameworks or even testing frameworks in other programming languages, you'll likely find Jest quite familiar.

For assertions, Jest uses **Jasmine's assertion library**. If you've used Jasmine before, you'll be pleased to know the syntax is exactly the same.

Later in the chapter, we explore what's arguably Jest's biggest difference from other JavaScript testing frameworks: mocking.

Using Jest

Inside of `testing/basics/package.json`, you'll note that Jest is already included.

As of Jest 15, Jest will consider any file that ends with `*.test.js` or `*.spec.js` a test. Because our file is named `Modash.test.js`, we don't have to do anything special to instruct Jest that this is a test file.

We'll rewrite the specs for `Modash` using Jest.

Jest 15

If you've used an older version of Jest before, you might be surprised that our tests do not have to be inside a `__tests__/` folder. Furthermore, later in the chapter, you'll notice that Jest's auto-mocking appears to be turned off.

Jest 15 shipped new defaults for Jest. These changes were motivated by a desire to make Jest easier for new developers to begin using while maintaining Jest's philosophy to require as little configuration as necessary.

You can read about all the changes in this blog post[a]. Relevant to this chapter:

- In addition to looking under `__tests__/` for test files Jest also looks for files matching `*.test.js` or `*.spec.js`
- Auto-mocking is disabled by default

[a]https://facebook.github.io/jest/blog/2016/09/01/jest-15.html

`expect()`

In Jest, we use `expect()` statements to make assertions. As you'll see, the syntax is different than the assert function we wrote before.

Because Jest uses the Jasmine assertion library, these matchers are technically a feature of *Jasmine*, not *Jest*. However, to avoid confusion, throughout this chapter we'll refer to everything that ships with Jest – including the Jasmine assertion library – as Jest.

Here's an example of using the `expect` syntax to assert that `true` is... `true`:

```
expect(true).toBe(true)
```

`toBe` is a **matcher**. Jest ships with a few different matchers. Under the hood, the `toBe` matcher uses the === operator to check equality. So these all work as expected:

```
expect(1).toBe(1); // pass
const a = 5;
expect(a).toBe(5); // pass
```

Because it just uses the === operator, `toBe` has its limitations. For instance, while we can use `toBe` to check if an object is the *exact same* object:

```
const a = { espresso: '60ml' };
const b = a;
expect(a).toBe(b); // pass
```

What if we wanted to check if two *different* objects were identical?

```
const a = { espresso: '60ml' };
expect(a).toBe({ espresso: '60ml' }) // fail
```

Jest has another matcher, `toEqual`. `toEqual` is more sophisticated than `toBe`. For our purposes, it will allow us to assert that two objects are identical, even if they aren't the exact same object:

```
const a = { espresso: '60ml' };
expect(a).toEqual({ espresso: '60ml' }) // pass
```

We'll use both `toBe` and `toEqual` in this chapter. We tend to use `toBe` for boolean and numeric assertions and `toEqual` for everything else. We could just use `toEqual` for everything. But we use `toBe` in certain situations as we like how it reads in English. It's a matter of preference. The important part is that you understand the difference between the two.

With Jest, like in many other test frameworks, we organize our code into **describe blocks** and **it blocks**. To get a feel for this organization, let's write our first Jasmine test. Replace the contents of `Modash.test.js` with the following:

testing/basics/complete/Modash.test-3.js

```
describe('My test suite', () => {
  it('`true` should be `true`', () => {
    expect(true).toBe(true);
  });

  it('`false` should be `false`', () => {
    expect(false).toBe(false);
  });
});
```

Both `describe` and `it` take a string and a function. The string is just a human-friendly description, which we'll see printed to the console in a moment.

As we'll see throughout this chapter, `describe` is used to organize assertions that all pertain to the same feature or context. `it` blocks are our individual assertions or **specs**.

Jest requires that you always have a top-level `describe` that encapsulates all your code. Here, our top-level `describe` is titled "My test suite." The two `it` blocks nested inside of this `describe` are our specs. This organization is standard: `describe` blocks don't contain assertions, `it` blocks do.

Throughout the rest of this chapter, an "assertion" refers to a call to `expect()`. A "spec" is an `it` block.

Try it out

Inside of `package.json`, we already have a `test` script defined. So we can run the following command to run our test suite:

```
$ npm test
```

```
bash

 in ~/fullstack-react-code/testing/basics
$ npm test
 PASS  ./Modash.test.js
  My test suite
    ✓ `true` should be `true` (3ms)
    ✓ `false` should be `false` (2ms)

Test Summary
 › Ran all tests.
 › 2 tests passed (2 total in 1 test suite, run time 1.444s)

 in ~/fullstack-react-code/testing/basics
$
```

Both tests passing

The first Jest test for `Modash`

Let's replace this test suite with something useful that tests `Modash`.

Open `Modash.test.js` again and clear it out. At the top, import the library:

testing/basics/complete/Modash.test-4.js

```
import Modash from './Modash';
```

We'll title our `describe` block `'Modash'`:

```
describe('Modash', () => {
  // assertions will go here
});
```

It's conventional to title the top-level `describe` whatever module is currently under test.

Let's make our first assertion. We're asserting that `truncate()` works:

testing/basics/complete/Modash.test-4.js

```
describe('Modash', () => {
  it('`truncate()`: truncates a string', () => {
    const string = 'there was one catch, and that was CATCH-22';
    expect(
      Modash.truncate(string, 19)
    ).toEqual('there was one catch...');
  });
});
```

We organized our assertion differently, but the logic and end result are the same as before. Note how `expect` and `toEqual` provide a human-readable format for expressing what we are testing and how we expect it to behave.

Try it out

Save `Modash.test.js`. Run the single-spec test suite:

```
$ npm test
```

Test passing

The other `truncate()` spec

We have a second assertion for `truncate()`. We assert that `truncate()` returns the same string if it's below the specified length.

Because both of these assertions correspond to the same method on Modash, it makes sense to wrap them together inside their own `describe`. Let's add the next spec, wrapping both our specs inside of a new `describe`:

testing/basics/complete/Modash.test-5.js

```
describe('Modash', () => {
  describe('`truncate()`', () => {
    const string = 'there was one catch, and that was CATCH-22';

    it('truncates a string', () => {
      expect(
        Modash.truncate(string, 19)
      ).toEqual('there was one catch...');
    });

    it('no-ops if <= length', () => {
      expect(
        Modash.truncate(string, string.length)
      ).toEqual(string);
    });
  });
});
```

It's conventional to group tests using `describe` blocks like this.

Note that we declared the `string` under test at the top of the `truncate()` describe block:

testing/basics/complete/Modash.test-5.js

```
describe('Modash', () => {
  describe('`truncate()`', () => {
    const string = 'there was one catch, and that was CATCH-22';
```

When variables are declared inside `describe` in this manner, they are in scope for each of the `it` blocks.

Furthermore, we slightly changed the title of each spec. We were able to drop the `truncate():` at the beginning. Because these specs are under the `describe` block titled `'truncate()'`, if one of these specs were to fail Jest would present the failure like this:

```
- Modash > `truncate()` > no-ops if less than length
```

This gives us all the context we need.

The rest of the specs

We'll wrap the specs for our other two methods inside their own `describe` blocks, like this:

```
describe('Modash', () => {
  describe('`truncate()`', () => {
    // ... `truncate()` specs
  });
  describe('`capitalize()`', () => {
    // ... `capitalize()` specs
  });
  describe('`camelCase()`', () => {
    // ... `camelCase()` specs
  });
});
```

First, our `capitalize()` spec:

testing/basics/complete/Modash.test-6.js

```
describe('capitalize()', () => {
  it('capitalizes first letter, lowercases rest', () => {
    const string = 'there was one catch, and that was CATCH-22';
    expect(
      Modash.capitalize(string)
    ).toEqual(
      'There was one catch, and that was catch-22'
    );
  });
});
```

Note that the `string` inside the `truncate()` `describe` block is not in scope here, so we declare `string` at the top of this spec.

Last, our set of `camelCase()` specs:

testing/basics/complete/Modash.test-6.js

```
describe('camelCase()', () => {
  it('camelizes string with spaces', () => {
    const string = 'customer responded at';
    expect(
      Modash.camelCase(string)
    ).toEqual('customerRespondedAt');
  });

  it('camelizes string with underscores', () => {
    const string = 'customer_responded_at';
    expect(
      Modash.camelCase(string)
    ).toEqual('customerRespondedAt');
  });
});
```

Try it out

Save `Modash.test.js`. Fire up Jest from the command-line:

```
$ npm test
```

And you'll see everything pass:

```
bash

PASS  ./Modash.test.js
  Modash
    `truncate()`
      ✓ truncates a string (4ms)
      ✓ no-ops if less than length (1ms)
    capitalize()
      ✓ capitalizes first letter, lowercases rest
    camelCase()
      ✓ camelizes string with spaces (1ms)
      ✓ camelizes string with underscores

Test Summary
 › Ran all tests.
 › 5 tests passed (5 total in 1 test suite, run time 2.395s)

 in ~/fullstack-react-code/testing/basics
$
```

Tests passing

We've covered the basics of assertions, organizing code into `describe` and `it` blocks, and using the Jest test runner. Let's see how these pieces come together for testing React applications. Along the way, we'll dig even deeper into Jest's assertion library and best practices for behavior-driven test suite organization.

Testing strategies for React applications

In software testing, there are two primary categories that tests fall into: *integration tests* and *unit tests*.

Integration vs Unit Testing

Integration tests are tests where multiple modules or parts of a software system are tested together. For a React app, we can think of each component as an individual module. Therefore, an integration test would involve testing our app as a whole.

Integration tests might go even further. If our React app was communicating with an API server, integration tests could involve communicating with that server as well. Developers often like to call these types of integration tests **end-to-end** tests.

There are a few ways to drive end-to-end tests. One popular method is to use a driver like Selenium to programatically load your app in a browser and automatically navigate your app's interface. You might have your program click on buttons or fill out forms, asserting what the page looks like after these interactions. Or you might make assertions on the resulting state of the datastore over on the server.

Integration tests are an important component of a comprehensive test suite for a large software system. However, in this book, we'll focus exclusively on **unit testing** for our React applications.

In a unit test, modules of a software system are tested **in isolation**.

For React components, we'll make two kinds of assertions:

1. Given a set of inputs (state & props), assert what a component should output (render).
2. Given a user action, assert how the component behaves. The component might make a state update or call a prop-function passed to it by a parent.

Shallow rendering

When rendered in the browser, our React components are written to the DOM. While we typically see a DOM visually in a browser, we could load a "headless" one into our test suite. We could use the DOM's API to write and read React components as if we were working directly with a browser. But there's an alternative: **shallow rendering**.

Normally, when a React component renders it first produces its virtual DOM representation. This virtual DOM representation is then used to make updates to an actual DOM.

When a component is shallow rendered, it does not write to a DOM. Instead, it maintains its virtual DOM representation. You can then make assertions against this virtual DOM much like you would an actual one.

Furthermore, your component is rendered only one level deep (hence "shallow"). So if the render function of your component contains children, those children won't actually be rendered. Instead, the virtual DOM representation will just contain references to the un-rendered child components.

React provides a library for shallow rendering React components, **`react-test-renderer`**. This library is useful, but is a bit low-level and can be verbose.

Enzyme is a library that wraps `react-test-renderer`, providing lots of handy functionality that is helpful for writing React component tests.

Enzyme

Enzyme was initially developed by Airbnb and is gaining widespread adoption among the React open-source community. In fact, Facebook recommends the utility in its documentation for `react-test-renderer`. Following this trend, we'll be using Enzyme as opposed to `react-test-renderer` throughout this chapter.

Enzyme, through `react-test-renderer`, allows you to shallow render a component. Instead of using `ReactDOM.render()` to render a component to a real DOM, you use Enzyme's `shallow()` to shallow render it:

```
const wrapper = Enzyme.shallow(
  <App />
);
```

As we'll see soon, `shallow()` returns an `EnzymeWrapper` object. Nested inside of this object is our shallow-rendered component in its virtual DOM representation. `EnzymeWrapper` gives us a bunch of useful methods for traversing and writing assertions against the component's virtual DOM.

If you ever want to use `react-test-renderer` directly in the future, you'll find knowing Enzyme helps. Because Enzyme is a lightweight wrapper on top of `react-test-renderer`, the APIs have a lot in common.

There are a two primary advantages to shallow rendering:

It tests components in isolation

This is preferable for unit tests. When we are writing tests for a parent component, we don't have to worry about dependencies on child components. A change made to a child component might break the child component's unit tests but it won't break that of any parents.

It's faster

Another nice benefit is that your tests will be faster. Rendering to, manipulating, and reading from an actual DOM adds overhead. With shallow rendering, you avoid the DOM entirely.

As we'll see, Enzyme has an API for simulating DOM events for shallow rendered components. These allow us to, for example, "click" a component even though no DOM is present.

Testing a basic React component with Enzyme

We'll get familiar with Enzyme by writing tests for a basic React component.

Setup

Inside the folder `testing/react-basics` is an app created with create-react-app. From the `testing/basics` folder, `cd` into that directory:

```
$ cd ../react-basics
```

And install the packages:

```
$ npm i
```

We cover create-react-app in detail in the previous chapter, "Using Webpack with create-react-app".

Take a look at the directory:

```
$ ls
public
node_modules/
package.json
src/
```

And `src/`:

```
$ ls src/
App.css
App.js
App.test.js
complete/
index.css
index.js
semantic/
```

The basic organization of this create-react-app app is the same that we saw in the last chapter. `App.js` defines an `App` component. `index.js` calls `ReactDOM.render()`. Semantic UI is included for styling.

The `App` component

Before looking at `App`, let's see it in the browser. Boot the app:

```
$ npm start
```

The app is simple. There is a field coupled with a button that adds items to a list. There is no way to delete items in the list:

The completed list app

Open up `App.js`. As we see in the initialization of `state`, `App` has two state properties:

testing/react-basics/src/App.js

```
class App extends React.Component {
  state = {
    items: [],
    item: '',
  };
```

`items` is the list of items. `item` is the state property that is tied to our controlled input, which we'll see in a moment.

Inside of `render()`, `App` iterates over `this.state.items` to render all items in a table:

testing/react-basics/src/App.js

```
          <tbody>
            {
              this.state.items.map((item, idx) => (
                <tr
                  key={idx}
                >
                  <td>{item}</td>
                </tr>
              ))
            }
          </tbody>
```

The controlled input is standard. It resides inside of a form:

testing/react-basics/src/App.js

```
                <form
                  className='ui form'
                  onSubmit={this.addItem}
                >
                <div className='field'>
                  <input
                    className='prompt'
                    type='text'
                    placeholder='Add item...'
                    value={this.state.item}
                    onChange={this.onItemChange}
                  />
```

For more info on controlled inputs, see the section "Uncontrolled vs. Controlled Components" in the "Forms" chapter.

For the `input`, `onItemChange()` sets `item` in state as expected:

testing/react-basics/src/App.js

```
  onItemChange = (e) => {
    this.setState({
      item: e.target.value,
    });
  };
```

For the form, `onSubmit` calls `addItem()`. This function adds the new item to state and clears `item`:

testing/react-basics/src/App.js

```
  addItem = (e) => {
    e.preventDefault();

    this.setState({
      items: this.state.items.concat(
        this.state.item
      ),
      item: '',
    });
  };
```

Finally, the button:

testing/react-basics/src/App.js

```
              <button
                className='ui button'
                type='submit'
                disabled={submitDisabled}
              >
                Add item
              </button>
```

We set the attribute `disabled` on the button. This variable (`submitDisabled`) is defined at the top of `render` and depends on whether or not the input field is populated:

testing/react-basics/src/App.js

```
  render() {
    const submitDisabled = !this.state.item;
    return(
```

The first spec for `App`

In order to write our first spec, we need to have two libraries in place: Jest and Enzyme.

In the last chapter, we noted that create-react-app sets up a few commands in `package.json`. One of those was `test`.

`react-scripts` already specifies Jest as a dependency. To boot Jest, we just need to run `npm test`. Like other commands that create-react-app creates for us, `test` runs a script in `react-scripts`. This script configures and executes Jest.

To see all of the packages that `react-scripts` includes, see the file `./node_modules/react-scripts/package.json`.

create-react-app sets up a dummy test for us in `App.test.js`. Let's execute Jest from inside `testing/react-basics` and see what happens:

```
$ npm test
```

Jest runs, emitting a well-formatted report of our test suite's results:

```
node

 PASS  src/App.test.js
  ✓ renders without crashing (58ms)

Test Summary
 › Ran all tests.
 › 1 test passed (1 total in 1 test suite, run time 3.057s)

Watch Usage
 › Press p to filter by a filename regex pattern.
 › Press q to quit watch mode.
 › Press Enter to trigger a test run.
```

The sample test run

`react-scripts` has provided some additional configuration to Jest. One configuration is **booting Jest in watch mode**. In this mode, Jest does not quit after the test suite finishes. Instead, it watches the whole project for changes. When a change is detected, it re-runs the test suite.

Throughout this chapter, we'll continue to instruct you to execute the test suite with `npm test`. However, you can just keep a console window open with Jest running in watch mode if you'd like.

`react-scripts` does not include `enzyme`. So we've included it in our `package.json`.

`enzyme` wraps `react-test-renderer`. As a result, it depends on that package to be installed too. You'll see that dependency in the `package.json` as well.

Let's replace the spec in `App.test.js` with something more useful.

Open up `App.test.js` and clear out the file. At the top of that file, we first import the React component that is under test:

testing/react-basics/src/complete/App.test.complete-1.js

```
import App from './App';
```

Next, we'll import `React` from `react` and `shallow()` from `enzyme`:

testing/react-basics/src/complete/App.test.complete-1.js

```
import React from 'react';
import { shallow } from 'enzyme';
```

`shallow()` is the only function we'll use from Enzyme, so we explicitly specify it in our import. As you may have guessed, `shallow()` is the function we'll use to shallow render components.

If you need a refresher on the ES6 import syntax, refer to the previous chapter "Using Webpack with create-react-app."

We'll title our `describe` after the module under test:

```
describe('App', () => {
  // assertions will go here
});
```

Let's write our first spec. We'll assert that our table should render with a table header of "Items":

```
describe('App', () => {
  it('should have the `th` "Items"', () => {
    // our assertion will go here
  });

  // the rest of our assertions will go here
});
```

In order to write this assertion, we'll need to:

- Shallow render the component
- Traverse the virtual DOM, picking out the first `th` element
- Assert that that element encloses a text value of "Items"

We first shallow render the component:

testing/react-basics/src/complete/App.test.complete-1.js

```
  it('should have the `th` "Items"', () => {
    const wrapper = shallow(
      <App />
    );
```

As mentioned earlier, the `shallow()` function returns what Enzyme calls a "wrapper" object, `ShallowWrapper`. This wrapper contains the shallow-rendered component. Remember, there is no actual DOM here. Instead, the component is kept inside of the wrapper in its virtual DOM representation.

The wrapper object that Enzyme provides us with has loads of useful methods that we can use to write our assertions. In general, these helper methods **help us traverse and select elements on the virtual DOM**.

Let's see how this works in practice. One helper method is `contains()`. We'll use it to assert the presence of our table header:

testing/react-basics/src/complete/App.test.complete-1.js

```
  it('should have the `th` "Items"', () => {
    const wrapper = shallow(
      <App />
    );
    expect(
      wrapper.contains(<th>Items</th>)
    ).toBe(true);
  });
```

`contains()` accepts a ReactElement, in this case JSX representing an HTML element. It returns a boolean, indicating whether or not the rendered component contains that HTML.

Try it out

With our first Enzyme spec written, let's verify everything works. Save `App.test.js` and run the test command from the console:

```
$ npm test
```

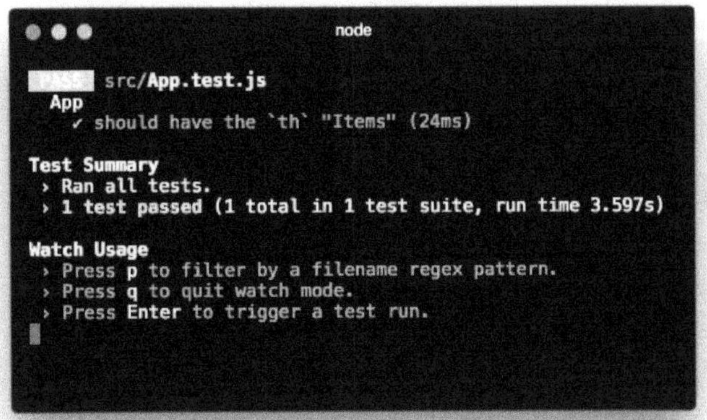

Enzyme spec passes

Let's write some more assertions, exploring the API for Enzyme in the process.

We import React at the top of our test file. Yet, we don't reference React anywhere in the file. Why do we need it?

You can try removing this import statement and see what happens. You'll get the following error:

```
ReferenceError: React is not defined
```

We can't readily see the reference to React, but it's there. We're using JSX in our test suite. When we specify a th component with <th>Items</th> this compiles to:

```
React.createElement('th', null, 'Items');
```

More assertions for App

Next, let's assert that the component contains a button element, the button that says "Add item." We might expect we could just do something like this:

```
wrapper.contains(<button>Add Item</button>)
```

But, contains() matches *all the attributes* on an element. Our button inside of render() looks like this:

testing/react-basics/src/App.js

```
<button
  className='ui button'
  type='submit'
  disabled={submitDisabled}
>
  Add item
</button>
```

We need to pass contains() a ReactElement that has the exact same set of attributes. But usually this is excessive. For this spec, it's sufficient to just assert that the button is on the page.

We can use Enzyme's containsMatchingElement() method. This will check if anything in the component's output **looks like** the expected element. We don't have to match attribute-for-attribute.

Using containsMatchingElement(), let's assert that the rendered component also includes a button element. Write this spec below the last one:

testing/react-basics/src/complete/App.test.complete-2.js

```
it('should have a `button` element', () => {
  const wrapper = shallow(
    <App />
  );
  expect(
    wrapper.containsMatchingElement(
      <button>Add item</button>
    )
  ).toBe(true);
});
```

`containsMatchingElement()` allows us to write a "looser" spec that's closer to the assertion we want: that there's a button on the page. It doesn't tie our specs to style attributes like `className`. While the attributes `onClick` and `disabled` are important, we'll write specs later that cover these.

Let's write another assertion with `containsMatchingElement()`. We'll assert that the `input` field is present as well:

testing/react-basics/src/complete/App.test.complete-2.js

```
it('should have an `input` element', () => {
  const wrapper = shallow(
    <App />
  );
  expect(
    wrapper.containsMatchingElement(
      <input />
    )
  ).toBe(true);
});
```

Our specs at this point assert that certain key elements are present in the component's output after the initial render. As we'll see shortly, we're laying the foundation for the rest of our specs. Subsequent specs will assert what happens after we make changes to the component, like populating its input or clicking its button. These fundamental specs assert that the elements we will be interacting with are present on the page to begin with.

In this initial state, there is one more important assertion we should make: that the button on the page is disabled. The button should only be enabled if there is text inside the input.

We actually could modify our previous spec to include this particular attribute, like this:

```
expect(
  wrapper.containsMatchingElement(
    <button disabled={true}>
      Add item
    </button>
  )
).toBe(true);
```

This spec would then be making two assertions: (1) That the `button` is present and (2) that it is disabled.

This is a perfectly valid approach. However, we like to split these two assertions into two different specs. When you limit the scope of the assertion in a given spec, test failures are much more expressive. If this dual-assertion spec were to fail, it would not be obvious why. Is the button missing? Or is the button not disabled?

This discussion on how to limit assertions per spec touches on the art of unit testing. There are many different strategies and styles for composing unit tests which are highly dependent on the codebase you're working with. There is usually more than one "right way" to structure a test suite.

Throughout this chapter, we'll be exhibiting our particular style. But as you get comfortable with unit testing, feel free to experiment to find a style that works best for you or your codebase. Just be sure to aim to keep your style consistent.

Our three specs so far have asserted that elements are present in the output of our component. This spec is different. We'll first "find" the component and then make an assertion on its `disabled` attribute. Let's take a look at it then break it down:

testing/react-basics/src/complete/App.test.complete-2.js

```
  it('`button` should be disabled', () => {
    const wrapper = shallow(
      <App />
    );
    const button = wrapper.find('button').first();
    expect(
      button.props().disabled
    ).toBe(true);
  });
```

`find()` is another EnzymeWrapper method. It expects as an argument an **Enzyme selector**. The selector in this case is a CSS selector, `'button'`. A CSS selector is just one supported type of Enzyme selector. We'll only use CSS selectors in this chapter, but Enzyme selectors can also refer directly to React components. For more info on Enzyme selectors, see the Enzyme docs[68].

`find()` returns another Enzyme `ShallowWrapper`. This object contains a list of all matching elements. The object behaves a bit like an array, with methods like `length`. The object has a method, `first()`, which we use here to return the first matching element. `first()` returns another `ShallowWrapper` object which references the `button` element.

As you find and select various elements within a shallow rendered component, all of those elements will be Enzyme `ShallowWrapper` objects. That means you can expect the same API of methods to be available to you, whether you're working with a shallow-rendered React component or a div tag.

To read the `disabled` attribute on the button, we use `props()`. `props()` returns an object that specifies either the attributes on an HTML element or the props set on a React component.

CSS selectors

CSS files use selectors to specify which HTML elements a set of styles refers to. JavaScript applications also use this syntax to select HTML elements on a page. Check out this MDN section[69] for more info on CSS selectors.

Using `beforeEach`

At this point, our test suite has some repetitious code. We shallow render the component before each assertion. This is ripe for refactor.

We *could* just shallow render the component at the top of our `describe` block:

```
describe('the "App" component', () => {
  const wrapper = shallow(
    <App />
  );
  // specs here ...
})
```

Due to JavaScript's scoping rules, `wrapper` would be available inside of each of our `it` blocks.

But there are problems that can arise with this approach. For instance, what if one of our specs modifies the component? We might change the component's state or simulate an event. This would **cause state to leak between specs**. At the start of the next spec, our component's state would be unpredictable.

[68] http://airbnb.io/enzyme/docs/api/selector.html

[69] https://developer.mozilla.org/en-US/docs/Web/Guide/CSS/Getting_started/Selectors

It would instead be preferable to re-render the component between each spec, ensuring that each spec is working with the component in a predictable, fresh state.

In all popular JavaScript test frameworks, there's a function we can use to aid in test setup: `beforeEach`. `beforeEach` is a block of code that will run **before each `it` block**. We can use this function to render our component before each spec.

When writing a test, you'll often need to perform some setup to get your environment into the proper context to make an assertion. In addition to shallow rendering a component as we do above, we'll soon write tests that will demand even richer context. By setting up the context inside of a `beforeEach`, you guarantee that each spec will receive a fresh set of context.

Setting up fresh context before each spec helps prevent state from leaking between tests.

When writing tests, we strive to keep our individual specs (our `it` blocks) as terse as possible. We'll rely on `beforeEach` to establish context, like the state or props for a component or even events like an element being clicked. Our `it` blocks, then, will almost always contain exclusively assertions.

Let's use a `beforeEach` block to render our component. We can then remove the rendering from each of our assertions:

testing/react-basics/src/complete/App.test.complete-3.js

```
describe('App', () => {
  let wrapper;

  beforeEach(() => {
    wrapper = shallow(
      <App />
    );
  });
```

We had to first declare `wrapper` using a `let` declaration at the top of the `describe` block. This is because if we had declared `wrapper` inside of the `beforeEach` block like this:

```
// ...
beforeEach(() => {
  const wrapper = shallow(
    <App />
  );
})
// ...
```

`wrapper` would not have been in scope for our specs. By declaring `wrapper` at the top of our `describe` block, we've ensured it's in scope for all of our assertions.

We can now safely remove the declaration of `wrapper` from each of our assertions:

testing/react-basics/src/complete/App.test.complete-3.js

```
  it('should have the `th` "Items"', () => {
    expect(
      wrapper.contains(<th>Items</th>)
    ).toBe(true);
  });

  it('should have a `button` element', () => {
    expect(
      wrapper.containsMatchingElement(
        <button>Add item</button>
      )
    ).toBe(true);
  });

  it('should have an `input` element', () => {
    expect(
      wrapper.containsMatchingElement(
        <input />
      )
    ).toBe(true);
  });

  it('`button` should be disabled', () => {
    const button = wrapper.find('button').first();
    expect(
      button.props().disabled
    ).toBe(true);
  });
```

Much better. Our `it` blocks are no longer setting up context and we've removed redundant code.

Try it out

Save `App.test.js`. Run the test suite:

```
$ npm test
```

All four tests pass:

```
Test Summary
 › Ran all tests.
 PASS  src/App.test.js
  App
    ✓ should have the `th` "Items" (6ms)
    ✓ should have a `button` element (6ms)
    ✓ should have an `input` element (3ms)
    ✓ `button` should be disabled (3ms)

Test Summary
 › Ran all tests.
 › 4 tests passed (4 total in 1 test suite, run time 0.636s)

Watch Usage
 › Press p to filter by a filename regex pattern.
 › Press q to quit watch mode.
 › Press Enter to trigger a test run.
```

All four passing tests

While limited, these specs set the foundation for our next set of specs. By asserting the presence of certain elements in the initial render as we have so far, we're asserting what the user will see on the page when the app loads. We asserted that there will be a table header, an input, and a button. We also asserted that the button should be disabled.

For the rest of this chapter, we're going to use a **behavior-driven** style to drive the development of our test suite. With this style, we'll use `beforeEach` to set up some context. We'll simulate interactions with the component much like we were a user navigating the interface. We'll then write assertions on how the component should have behaved.

After loading the app, the first thing we'd envision a user would do is fill in the input. When the input is filled, they will click the "Add item" button. We would then expect the new item to be in state and on the page.

We'll step through these behaviors, writing assertions about the component after each user interaction.

Simulating a change

The first interaction the user can have with our app is filling out the input field for adding a new item. In addition to shallow rendering our component, we want to simulate this behavior before the next set of specs.

While we could perform this setup inside of the `it` blocks, as we noted before it's better if we perform as much of our setup as possible inside of `beforeEach` blocks. Not only does this help us organize our code, this practice makes it easy to have multiple specs that rely on the same setup.

However, we don't need this particular piece of setup for our other four existing specs. What we should do is declare another `describe` block inside of our current one. `describe` blocks are how we "group" specs that all require the same context:

```
describe('App', () => {
  // ... the assertions we've written so far

  describe('the user populates the input', () => {
    beforeEach(() => {
      // ... setup context
    })

    // ... assertions
  });
});
```

The `beforeEach` that we write for our inner `describe` will be run *after* the `beforeEach` declared in the outer context. Therefore, the `wrapper` will already be shallow rendered by the time this `beforeEach` runs. As expected, this `beforeEach` will only be run for `it` blocks inside our inner `describe` block.

Here's what our inner `describe` with our `beforeEach` setup looks like for the next spec group:

testing/react-basics/src/complete/App.test.complete-4.js

```
  describe('the user populates the input', () => {
    const item = 'Vancouver';

    beforeEach(() => {
      const input = wrapper.find('input').first();
      input.simulate('change', {
        target: { value: item }
      })
    });
```

We first declare `item` at the top of `describe`. As we'll see soon, this will enable us to reference the variable in our specs.

The `beforeEach` first uses the `find()` method on `EnzymeWrapper` to grab the input. Recall that `find()` returns another `EnzymeWrapper` object, in this case a list with a single item, our input. We call `first()` to get the `EnzymeWrapper` object corresponding to the input element.

We then use `simulate()` on the input. `simulate()` is how we simulate user interactions on components. The method accepts two arguments:

1. The event to simulate (like `'change'` or `'click'`). This determines which event handler to use (like `onChange` or `onClick`).
2. The event object (optional).

Here, we're specifying a `'change'` event for the input. We then pass in our desired event object. Note that this event object looks exactly the same as the event object that React passes an `onChange` handler. Here's the method `onItemChange` on `App` again, which expects an object of this shape:

testing/react-basics/src/App.js

```
onItemChange = (e) => {
  this.setState({
    item: e.target.value,
  });
};
```

With this setup written, we can now write specs related to the context where the user has just populated the input field. We'll write two:

1. That the state property `item` was updated to match the input field
2. That the button is no longer disabled

Here's what the `describe` looks like, in full:

testing/react-basics/src/complete/App.test.complete-4.js

```
describe('the user populates the input', () => {
  const item = 'Vancouver';

  beforeEach(() => {
    const input = wrapper.find('input').first();
    input.simulate('change', {
      target: { value: item }
    })
  });

  it('should update the state property `item`', () => {
    expect(
      wrapper.state().item
```

```
    ).toEqual(item);
  });

  it('should enable `button`', () => {
    const button = wrapper.find('button').first();
    expect(
      button.props().disabled
    ).toBe(false);
  });
});
```

In the first spec, we used `wrapper.state()` to grab the state object. Note that it is a function and not a property. Remember, `wrapper` is an EnzymeWrapper so we're not interacting with the component directly. We use the `state()` method which retrieves the `state` property from the component.

In the second, we used `props()` again to read the `disabled` attribute on the button.

Continuing our behavior-driven approach, we now envision our component in the following state:

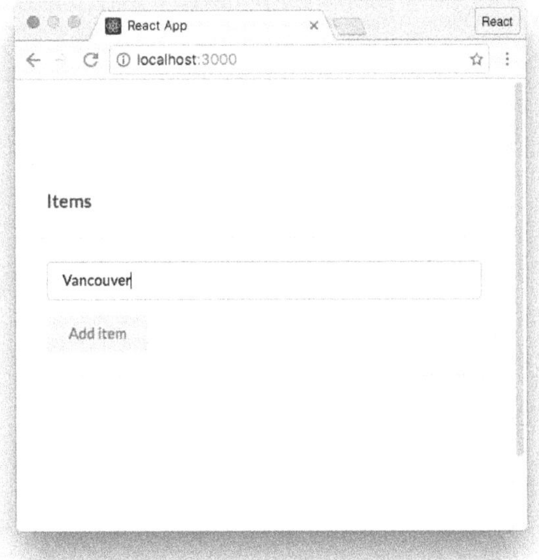

Imagined state of the component

The user has filled in the input field. There are two actions the user can take from here that we can write specs for:

1. The user clears the input field
2. The user clicks the "Add item" button

Clearing the input field

When the user clears the input field, we expect the button to become disabled again. We can build on our existing context for the `describe` "the user populates the input" by nesting our new `describe` inside of it:

```
describe('App', () => {
  // ... initial state assertions

  describe('the user populates the input', () => {
    // ... populated field assertions

    describe('and then clears the input', () => {
      // ... assert the button is disabled again

    });
  });
});
```

We'll use `beforeEach` to simulate a change event again, this time setting `value` to a blank string. We'll write one assertion: that the button is disabled again.

Remember to compose this `describe` block underneath "the user populates the input." Our "user clears the input" `describe` block, in full:

testing/react-basics/src/complete/App.test.complete-5.js

```
    it('should enable `button`', () => {
      const button = wrapper.find('button').first();
      expect(
        button.props().disabled
      ).toBe(false);
    });

    describe('and then clears the input', () => {
      beforeEach(() => {
        const input = wrapper.find('input').first();
        input.simulate('change', {
          target: { value: '' }
        })
      });

      it('should disable `button`', () => {
```

```
        const button = wrapper.find('button').first();
        expect(
          button.props().disabled
        ).toBe(true);
      });
    });
  });
});
```

Notice how we're building on existing context, getting deeper into a workflow through our app. We're three layers deep. The app has rendered, the user filled in the input field, and then the user cleared the input field.

Now's a good time to verify all our tests pass.

Try it out

Save `App.test.js`. Running the test suite:

```
$ npm test
```

We see everything passes:

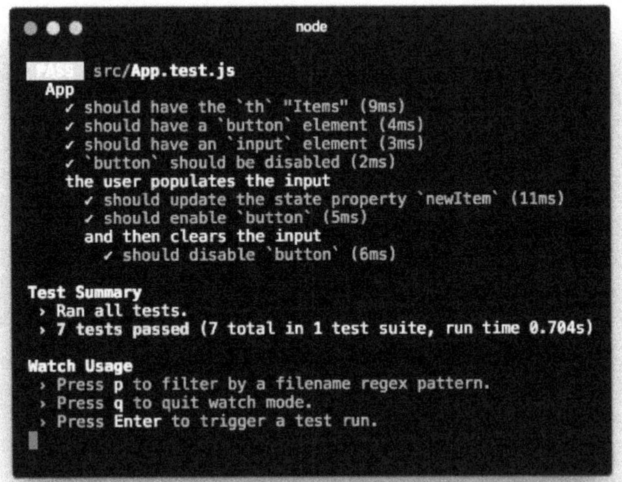

```
PASS  src/App.test.js
  App
    ✓ should have the `th` "Items" (9ms)
    ✓ should have a `button` element (4ms)
    ✓ should have an `input` element (3ms)
    ✓ `button` should be disabled (2ms)
    the user populates the input
      ✓ should update the state property `newItem` (11ms)
      ✓ should enable `button` (5ms)
      and then clears the input
        ✓ should disable `button` (6ms)

Test Summary
 › Ran all tests.
 › 7 tests passed (7 total in 1 test suite, run time 0.704s)

Watch Usage
 › Press p to filter by a filename regex pattern.
 › Press q to quit watch mode.
 › Press Enter to trigger a test run.
```

Next, we'll simulate the user submitting the form. This should cause a few changes to our app which we'll write assertions for.

Simulating a form submission

After the user has submitted the form, we expect the app to look like this:

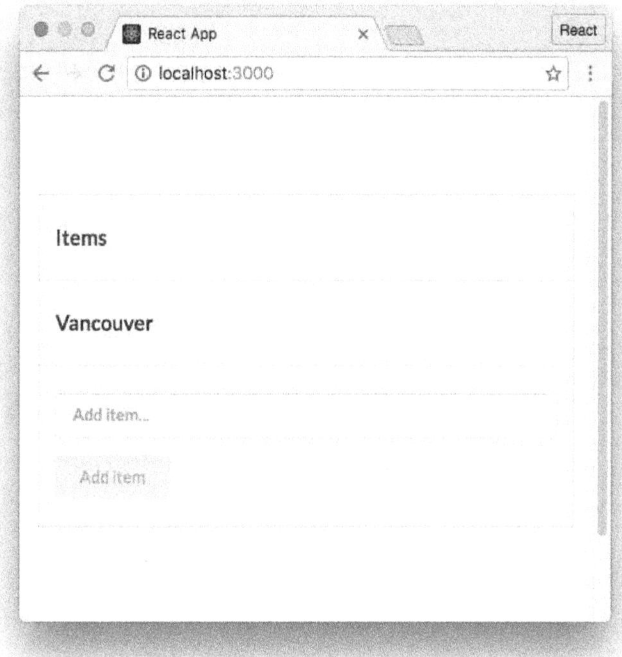

We'll assert that:

1. The new item is in state (`items`)
2. The new item is inside the rendered table
3. The input field is empty
4. The "Add item" button is disabled

To reach this context, we'll build on the previous context where the user has populated the input. So we'll write our `describe` inside "the user populates the input" as a sibling to "and then clears the input":

```
describe('App', () => {
  // ... initial state assertions

  describe('the user populates the input', () => {
    // ... populated field assertions

    describe('and then clears the input', () => {
      // ... assert the button is disabled again

    });

    describe('and then submits the form', () => {
      // ... upcoming assertions
    });
  });
});
```

Our `beforeEach` will simulate a form submission. Recall that `addItem` expects an object that has a method `preventDefault()`:

testing/react-basics/src/App.js

```
  addItem = (e) => {
    e.preventDefault();

    this.setState({
      items: this.state.items.concat(
        this.state.item
      ),
      item: '',
    });
  };
```

We'll simulate an event type of `submit`, passing in an object that has the shape that `addItem` expects. We can just set `preventDefault` to an empty function:

testing/react-basics/src/complete/App.test.complete-6.js

```
    describe('and then submits the form', () => {
      beforeEach(() => {
        const form = wrapper.find('form').first();
        form.simulate('submit', {
          preventDefault: () => {},
        });
      });
```

With our setup in place, we first assert that the new item is in state:

testing/react-basics/src/complete/App.test.complete-6.js

```
      it('should add the item to state', () => {
        expect(
          wrapper.state().items
        ).toContain(item);
      });
```

Jest comes with a few special matchers for working with arrays. We use the matcher `toContain()` to assert that the array `items` contains `item`.

Remember, `wrapper` is an `EnzymeWrapper` object with a React component inside. We retrieve the state with `state()` (a method).

Next, let's assert that the item is inside the table. There's a few ways to do this, here's one:

testing/react-basics/src/complete/App.test.complete-6.js

```
      it('should render the item in the table', () => {
        expect(
          wrapper.containsMatchingElement(
            <td>{item}</td>
          )
        ).toBe(true);
      });
```

`contains()` would work for this spec as well, but we tend to use `containsMatchingElement()` more often to keep our tests from being too brittle. For instance, if we added a `class` to each of our `td` elements, a spec using `containsMatchingElement()` would not break.

Next, we'll assert that the input field has been cleared. We have the option of checking the state property `item` or checking the actual input field in the virtual DOM. We'll do the latter as it's a bit more comprehensive:

testing/react-basics/src/complete/App.test.complete-6.js

```
      it('should clear the input field', () => {
        const input = wrapper.find('input').first();
        expect(
          input.props().value
        ).toEqual('');
      });
```

Finally, we'll assert that the button is again disabled:

testing/react-basics/src/complete/App.test.complete-6.js

```
      it('should disable `button`', () => {
        const button = wrapper.find('button').first();
        expect(
          button.props().disabled
        ).toBe(true);
      });
```

Our "and then submits the form" `describe`, in full:

testing/react-basics/src/complete/App.test.complete-6.js

```
      it('should disable `button`', () => {
        const button = wrapper.find('button').first();
        expect(
          button.props().disabled
        ).toBe(true);
      });
    });

    describe('and then submits the form', () => {
      beforeEach(() => {
        const form = wrapper.find('form').first();
        form.simulate('submit', {
          preventDefault: () => {},
        });
      });
```

```
      it('should add the item to state', () => {
        expect(
          wrapper.state().items
        ).toContain(item);
      });

      it('should render the item in the table', () => {
        expect(
          wrapper.containsMatchingElement(
            <td>{item}</td>
          )
        ).toBe(true);
      });

      it('should clear the input field', () => {
        const input = wrapper.find('input').first();
        expect(
          input.props().value
        ).toEqual('');
      });

      it('should disable `button`', () => {
        const button = wrapper.find('button').first();
        expect(
          button.props().disabled
        ).toBe(true);
      });
    });
  });
});
```

It might appear we have another possible refactor we can do. We have a lot of these declarations throughout our test suite:

```
const input = wrapper.find('input').first();
const button = wrapper.find('button').first();
```

You might wonder if it's possible to declare these variables at the top of our test suite's scope, alongside `wrapper`. We could then set them in our top-most `beforeEach`, like this:

```
// Valid refactor?
describe('App', () => {
  let wrapper;
  let input;
  let button;

  beforeEach(() => {
    wrapper = shallow(
      <App />
    );
    const input = wrapper.find('input').first();
    const button = wrapper.find('button').first();
  });
  // ...
});
```

Then, you'd be able to reference `input` and `button` throughout the test suite without re-declaring them.

However, if you were to try this, you'd note some test failures. This is because throughout the test suite, `input` and `button` would reference HTML elements *from the initial render*. When we call a `simulate()` event, like this:

```
input.simulate('change', {
  target: { value: item }
});
```

Under the hood, the React component re-renders. This is what we'd expect. Therefore, an entirely new virtual DOM object is created with new `input` and `button` elements inside. We need to perform a `find()` to pick out those elements inside the new virtual DOM object, which we do here.

Try it out

Save `App.test.js`. Run the test suite:

```
$ npm test
```

Everything passes:

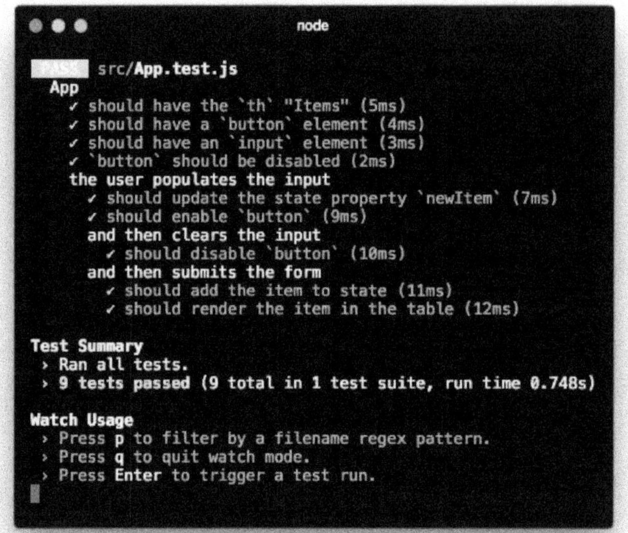

```
node

PASS  src/App.test.js
 App
   ✓ should have the `th` "Items" (5ms)
   ✓ should have a `button` element (4ms)
   ✓ should have an `input` element (3ms)
   ✓ `button` should be disabled (2ms)
   the user populates the input
     ✓ should update the state property `newItem` (7ms)
     ✓ should enable `button` (9ms)
     and then clears the input
       ✓ should disable `button` (10ms)
     and then submits the form
       ✓ should add the item to state (11ms)
       ✓ should render the item in the table (12ms)

Test Summary
 › Ran all tests.
 › 9 tests passed (9 total in 1 test suite, run time 0.748s)

Watch Usage
 › Press p to filter by a filename regex pattern.
 › Press q to quit watch mode.
 › Press Enter to trigger a test run.
```

You might try breaking various parts of `App` and witness the test suite catch these failures.

Our test suite for `App` is sufficiently comprehensive. We saw how we can use a behavioral-driven approach to drive the composition of a test suite. This style encourages completeness. We establish layers of context based on real-world workflows. And with the context established, it's easy to assert the component's desired behavior.

In total, so far we've covered:

- The basics of assertions
- The Jest testing library (with Jasmine assertions)
- Organizing testing code in a behavioral-driven manner
- Shallow rendering with Enzyme
- `ShallowWrapper` methods for traversing the virtual DOM
- Jest/Jasmine matchers for writing different kinds of assertions (like `toContain()` for arrays)

In the next section, we'll advance our understanding of writing React unit tests with Jest and Enzyme. We'll write specs for a component that exists inside of a larger React app. Specifically, we'll cover:

- What happens when an app has multiple components
- What happens when an app relies on a web request to an API
- Some additional methods for both Jest and Enzyme

Writing tests for the food lookup app

In the previous chapter on Webpack and create-react-app, we set up a Webpack-powered food lookup app:

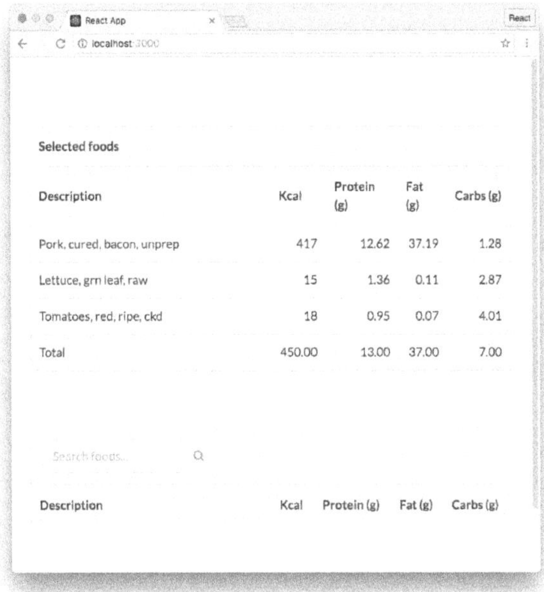

The food lookup app

We'll work inside the completed version of this app. It's in the top-level folder `food-lookup-complete`. To get to it from the `testing/react-basics` folder, run the following command:

```
$ cd ../../food-lookup-complete
```

It's not necessary that you've completed the chapter on Webpack to proceed. We describe this app's layout and the `FoodSearch` component before writing our specs.

Install the npm packages for both the server and the client if they are not installed already:

```
$ npm i
$ cd client
$ npm i
$ cd ..
```

And start up the app to play around with it if you'd like with:

```
$ npm start
```

We'll be writing tests for just the component `FoodSearch` in this chapter. We won't dig into the code for the other components in the app. Instead, it's sufficient to understand how the app is broken down into components at a high-level:

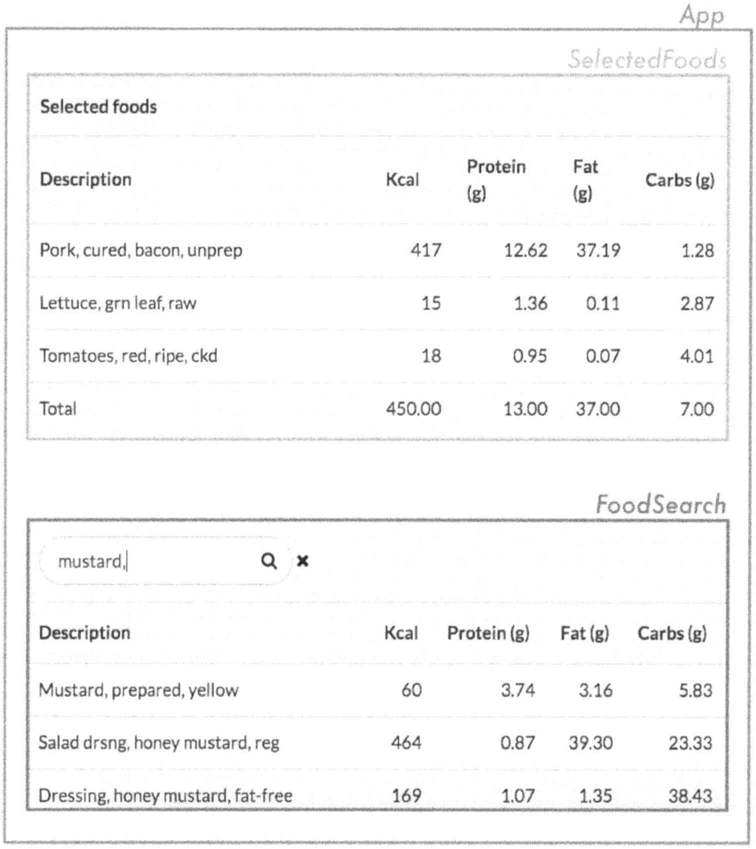

App

SelectedFoods

Selected foods

Description	Kcal	Protein (g)	Fat (g)	Carbs (g)
Pork, cured, bacon, unprep	417	12.62	37.19	1.28
Lettuce, grn leaf, raw	15	1.36	0.11	2.87
Tomatoes, red, ripe, ckd	18	0.95	0.07	4.01
Total	450.00	13.00	37.00	7.00

FoodSearch

mustard,

Description	Kcal	Protein (g)	Fat (g)	Carbs (g)
Mustard, prepared, yellow	60	3.74	3.16	5.83
Salad drsng, honey mustard, reg	464	0.87	39.30	23.33
Dressing, honey mustard, fat-free	169	1.07	1.35	38.43

- **App**: The parent container for the application.
- **SelectedFoods**: A table that lists selected foods. Clicking on a food item removes it.
- **FoodSearch**: Table that provides a live search field. Clicking on a food item in the table adds it to the total (`SelectedFoods`).

Kill the app if you started it. Change into the `client/` directory. We'll be working solely in this directory for this chapter:

```
$ cd client
```

For this app, instead of having the tests alongside the components in `src` we've placed them inside a dedicated folder, `tests`. Inside of `tests`, you'll see that tests already exist for the other components in our app:

```
$ ls tests/
  App.test.js
  SelectedFoods.test.js
  complete/
```

Feel free to peruse the other tests after we've finished writing tests for `FoodSearch`. All the other tests re-use the same concepts that we use for testing `FoodSearch`.

Before writing tests for the component, let's walk through how `FoodSearch` works. You can pop open the `FoodSearch` component and follow along if you'd like (`src/FoodSearch.js`).

`complete/` contains each version of the completed `FoodSearch.test.js` that we write in this section, for your reference.

FoodSearch

The `FoodSearch` component has a search field. As the user types, a table of matching foods is updated below the search field:

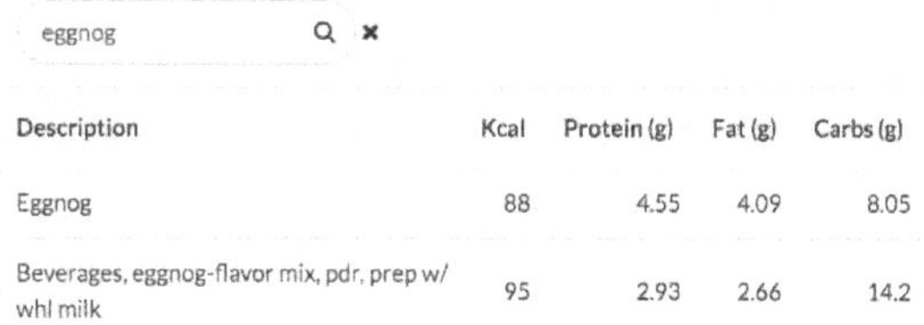

The `FoodSearch` component

When the search field is changed, the `FoodSearch` component makes a request to the app's API server. If the user has typed in the string `truffle`, the request to the server looks like this:

```
GET localhost:3001/api/food?q=truffle
```

The API server then returns an array of matching food items:

```
[
  {
    "description": "Pate  truffle flavor",
    "kcal": 327,
    "fat_g": 27.12,
    "protein_g": 11.2,
    "carbohydrate_g": 6.3
  },
  {
    "description": "Candies, truffles, prepared-from-recipe",
    "kcal": 510,
    "fat_g": 32.14,
    "protein_g": 6.21,
    "carbohydrate_g": 44.88
  },
  {
    "description": "Candies, m  m mars 3 musketeers truffle crisp",
    "kcal": 538,
    "fat_g": 25.86,
    "protein_g": 6.41,
    "carbohydrate_g": 63.15
  }
]
```

`FoodSearch` populates its table with these items.

`FoodSearch` has three pieces of state:

`foods`

This is an array of all of the foods returned by the server. It defaults to a blank array.

`showRemoveIcon`

When the user starts typing into the search field, an X appears next to the field:

The remove icon

This X provides a quick way to clear the search field. When the field is empty, `showRemoveIcon` should be `false`. When the field is populated, `showRemoveIcon` should be `true`.

`searchValue`

`searchValue` is the state that's tied to the controlled input, the search field.

Exploring FoodSearch

Armed with the knowledge of how FoodSearch behaves and what state it keeps, let's explore the actual code. We'll include the code snippets here, but feel free to follow along by opening src/FoodSearch.js.

At the top of the component are import statements:

food-lookup-complete/client/src/FoodSearch.js

```
import React from 'react';
import Client from './Client';
```

We also have a constant that defines the maximum number of search results to show on the page. We use this inside of the component:

food-lookup-complete/client/src/FoodSearch.js

```
const MATCHING_ITEM_LIMIT = 25;
```

Then we define the component.

state initialization for our three pieces of state:

food-lookup-complete/client/src/FoodSearch.js

```
class FoodSearch extends React.Component {
  state = {
    foods: [],
    showRemoveIcon: false,
    searchValue: '',
  };
```

Let's step through the interactive elements in the component's render method along with each element's handling function.

The input search field

The input field at the top of FoodSearch drives the search functionality. The table body updates with search results as the user modifies the input field.

The input element:

food-lookup-complete/client/src/FoodSearch.js

```
              <input
                className='prompt'
                type='text'
                placeholder='Search foods...'
                value={this.state.searchValue}
                onChange={this.onSearchChange}
              />
```

`className` is set for SemanticUI styling purposes. `value` ties this controlled input to `this.state.searchValue`.

`onSearchChange()` accepts an event object. Let's step through the code. Here's the first half of the function:

food-lookup-complete/client/src/FoodSearch.js

```
  onSearchChange = (e) => {
    const value = e.target.value;

    this.setState({
      searchValue: value,
    });

    if (value === '') {
      this.setState({
        foods: [],
        showRemoveIcon: false,
      });
```

We grab the `value` off of the event object. We then set `searchValue` in state to this value, following the pattern for handling the change for a controlled input.

If the `value` is blank, we set `foods` to a blank array (clearing the search results table) and set `showRemoveIcon` to `false` (hiding the "X" that's used to clear the search field).

If the `value` is not blank, we need to:

- Ensure that the `showRemoveIcon` is set to `true`
- Make a call to the server with the latest search value to get the list of matching foods

Here's that code:

food-lookup-complete/client/src/FoodSearch.js

```
    } else {
      this.setState({
        showRemoveIcon: true,
      });

      Client.search(value, (foods) => {
        this.setState({
          foods: foods.slice(0, MATCHING_ITEM_LIMIT),
        });
      });
    }
  };
```

`Client` uses the Fetch API under the hood, the same web request interface that we used in Chapter 3. `Client.search()` makes the web request to the server and then invokes the callback with the array of matching foods.

If you need a refresher on working with a client library driven by Fetch, see Chapter 3: Components & Servers.

We then set `foods` in state to the returned foods, truncating this list so that it's within the bounds of `MATCHING_ITEM_LIMIT` (which is 25).

In full, `onSearchChange()` looks like this:

food-lookup-complete/client/src/FoodSearch.js

```
  onSearchChange = (e) => {
    const value = e.target.value;

    this.setState({
      searchValue: value,
    });

    if (value === '') {
      this.setState({
        foods: [],
        showRemoveIcon: false,
      });
    } else {
      this.setState({
```

```
      showRemoveIcon: true,
    });

    Client.search(value, (foods) => {
      this.setState({
        foods: foods.slice(0, MATCHING_ITEM_LIMIT),
      });
    });
  }
};
```

The remove icon

As we've seen, the remove icon is the little X that appears next to the search field whenever the field is populated. Clicking this X should clear the search field.

We perform the logic for whether or not to show the remove icon in-line. The icon element has the `onClick` attribute:

food-lookup-complete/client/src/FoodSearch.js

```
                  this.state.showRemoveIcon ? (
                    <i
                      className='remove icon'
                      onClick={this.onRemoveIconClick}
                    />
                  ) : ''
                }
```

The code for `onRemoveIconClick()`:

food-lookup-complete/client/src/FoodSearch.js

```
  onRemoveIconClick = () => {
    this.setState({
      foods: [],
      showRemoveIcon: false,
      searchValue: '',
    });
  };
```

We reset everything, including `foods`.

`props.onFoodClick`

The final bit of interactivity is on each food item. When the user clicks a food item, we add it to the list of selected foods on the interface:

food-lookup-complete/client/src/FoodSearch.js

```
          <tbody>
          {
            this.state.foods.map((food, idx) => (
              <tr
                key={idx}
                onClick={() => this.props.onFoodClick(food)}
              >
                <td>{food.description}</td>
                <td className='right aligned'>
                  {food.kcal}
                </td>
                <td className='right aligned'>
                  {food.protein_g}
                </td>
                <td className='right aligned'>
                  {food.fat_g}
                </td>
                <td className='right aligned'>
                  {food.carbohydrate_g}
                </td>
              </tr>
            ))
          }
          </tbody>
```

Under the hood, when the user clicks a food item we invoke `this.props.onFoodClick()`. The parent of `FoodSearch` (`App`) specifies this prop-function. It expects the full food object.

As we'll see, for the purpose of writing unit tests for `FoodSearch`, we don't need to know anything about what the prop-function `onFoodClick()` actually *does*. We just care about what it *wants* (a full food object).

Shallow rendering helps us achieve this desirable isolation. While this app is relatively small, these isolation benefits are huge for larger teams with larger codebases.

Writing `FoodSearch.test.js`

We're ready to write unit tests for the `FoodSearch` component.

The file `client/tests/FoodSearch.test.js` contains the scaffold for the test suite. At the top are the `import` statements:

food-lookup-complete/client/tests/FoodSearch.test.js

```
import { shallow } from 'enzyme';
import React from 'react';
import FoodSearch from '../src/FoodSearch';
```

Next is the scaffolding for the test suite. Don't be intimidated, we'll be filling out each of these `describe` and `beforeEach` blocks one-by-one:

food-lookup-complete/client/tests/FoodSearch.test.js

```
describe('FoodSearch', () => {
  // ... initial state specs

  describe('user populates search field', () => {
    beforeEach(() => {
      // ... simulate user typing "brocc" in input
    });

    // ... specs

    describe('and API returns results', () => {
      beforeEach(() => {
        // ... simulate API returning results
      });

      // ... specs

      describe('then user clicks food item', () => {
        beforeEach(() => {
          // ... simulate user clicking food item
        });

        // ... specs
      });

      describe('then user types more', () => {
        beforeEach(() => {
          // ... simulate user typing "x"
        });
```

```
        describe('and API returns no results', () => {
          beforeEach(() => {
            // ... simulate API returning no results
          });

          // ... specs
        });
      });
    });
  });
});
```

As in the previous section, we'll establish different contexts by using `beforeEach` to perform setup. Each of our contexts will be contained inside `describe`.

In initial state

Our first series of specs will involve the component in its initial state. Our `beforeEach` will simply shallow render the component. We'll then write assertions on this initial state:

food-lookup-complete/client/tests/complete/FoodSearch.test.complete-1.js

```
describe('FoodSearch', () => {
  let wrapper;

  beforeEach(() => {
    wrapper = shallow(
      <FoodSearch />
    );
  });
```

As in our first round of component tests in the last section, we declare `wrapper` in the upper scope. In our `beforeEach`, we use Enzyme's `shallow()` to shallow-render the component.

Let's write two assertions:

1. That the remove icon is not in the DOM
2. That the table doesn't have any entries

For our first test, there are multiple ways we can write it. Here's one:

food-lookup-complete/client/tests/complete/FoodSearch.test.complete-1.js

```
  it('should not display the remove icon', () => {
    expect(
      wrapper.find('.remove.icon').length
    ).toBe(0);
  });
```

We pass a selector to wrapper's `find()` method. If you recall, the remove icon has the following `className` attribute:

food-lookup-complete/client/src/FoodSearch.js

```
                      <i
                        className='remove icon'
                        onClick={this.onRemoveIconClick}
                      />
```

So, we're selecting it here based on its class. `find()` returns a `ShallowWrapper` object. This object is array-like, containing a list of all matches for the specified selector. Just like an array, it has the property `length` which we assert should be `0`.

We could also have used one of the contains methods, like this:

```
it('should not display the remove icon', () => {
  expect(
    wrapper.containsAnyMatchingElements(
      <i className='remove icon' />
    )
  ).toBe(false);
});
```

We'll primarily be driving our tests with `find()` for the rest of this chapter, as we like using the CSS selector syntax. But it's a matter of preference.

Next, we'll assert that in this initial state the table does not have any entries.

For this spec, we can just assert that this component did not output any `tr` elements inside of `tbody`, like so:

food-lookup-complete/client/tests/complete/FoodSearch.test.complete-1.js

```
  it('should display zero rows', () => {
    expect(
      wrapper.find('tbody tr').length
    ).toEqual(0);
  });
```

If we were to run this test suite now, both of our specs would pass.

However, this doesn't lend us much assurance that our specs are composed correctly. When asserting that an element is *not* present on the DOM, you expose yourself to the error where you're simply not selecting the element properly. We'll address this shortly when we use the exact same selectors to assert that the elements *are* present.

How comprehensive should my assertions be?

In the last section, we wrote assertions around the presence of key elements in the component's initial output. We asserted that the input field and button were present, setting the stage for interacting with them later.

In this section, we're skipping this class of assertions. We omit them here as they are repetitive. But, in general, you or your team will have to decide how comprehensive you want your test suite to be. There's a balance to strike; your test suite is there to service development of your app. It is possible to go overboard and compose a test suite that ultimately slows you down.

A user has typed a value into the search field

Guided by our behavior-driven approach, our next step is to simulate a user interaction. We'll then write assertions given this new layer of context.

There's only one interaction the user can have with the `FoodSearch` component after it loads: entering a value into the search field. When this happens, there are two further possibilities:

1. The search matches food in the database and the API returns a list of those foods
2. The search does not match any food in the database and the API returns an empty array

This branch happens at the bottom of `onSearchChange()` when we call `Client.search()`:

food-lookup-complete/client/src/FoodSearch.js

```
      Client.search(value, (foods) => {
        this.setState({
          foods: foods.slice(0, MATCHING_ITEM_LIMIT),
        });
      });
```

For our app, the API is queried and results are displayed with every keystroke. Therefore, situation 2 (no results) will almost always happen after situation 1.

We'll setup our test context to mirror this state transition. We'll simulate the user typing `'brocc'` into the search field, yielding two results (two kinds of broccoli):

brocc

Description	Kcal	Protein (g)	Fat (g)	Carbs (g)
Broccolini	100	11	21	31
Broccoli rabe	200	12	22	32

What our component might look like after the user types 'brocc'

We'll write assertions against this context.

Next, we'll build on this context by simulating the user typing an "x" (`'broccx'`). This will yield no results:

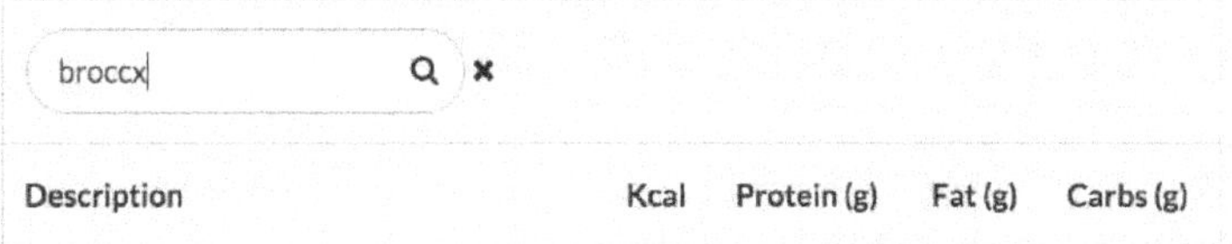

What our component might look like after the user types 'brocc'

We'll then write assertions against this context.

There are exceptions to situation 2 always following situation 1. For instance, this user overestimated the capabilities of our app:

Welp

However, the state transition of foods in state to no foods in state is much more interesting than verifying that `foods` in state remained blank after the API returned empty results.

Regardless of what `Client.search()` returns, we expect the component to both update `searchValue` in state and display the remove icon. Those specs will exist up top inside "user populates search field." We'll start with these, only writing specs for the search field itself and leaving assertions based on what the API returned for later:

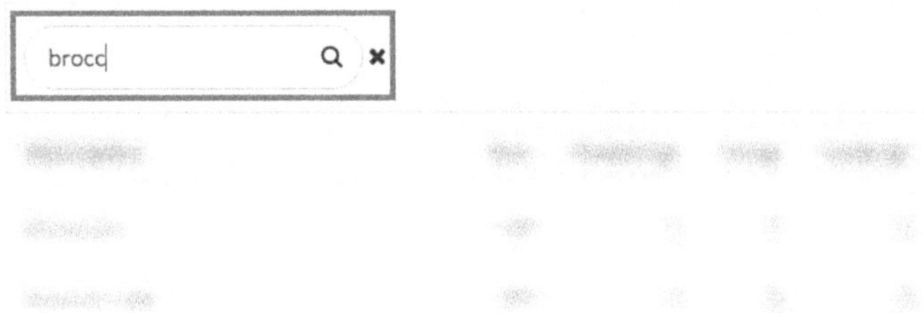

First set of specs focus on the search field

After writing these specs, we'll see how to establish the context for the API returning results.

We first simulate the user interaction inside a `beforeEach`. We'll declare `value` at the top of the `describe` so we can reference it later in our tests:

food-lookup-complete/client/tests/complete/FoodSearch.test.complete-2.js

```
describe('user populates search field', () => {
  const value = 'brocc';

  beforeEach(() => {
    const input = wrapper.find('input').first();
    input.simulate('change', {
      target: { value: value },
    });
  });
```

Next, we assert that `searchValue` has been updated in state to match this new value:

food-lookup-complete/client/tests/complete/FoodSearch.test.complete-2.js

```
    it('should update state property `searchValue`', () => {
      expect(
        wrapper.state().searchValue
      ).toEqual(value);
    });
```

We assert next that the remove icon is present on the DOM:

food-lookup-complete/client/tests/complete/FoodSearch.test.complete-2.js

```
    it('should display the remove icon', () => {
      expect(
        wrapper.find('.remove.icon').length
      ).toBe(1);
    });
```

We use the same selector that we used in our earlier assertion that the remove icon was *not* present on the DOM. This is important, as it assures us that our earlier assertion is valid and isn't just using the wrong selector.

Our assertions for "user populates search field" are in place. Before moving on, let's save and make sure our test suite passes.

Try it out

Save `FoodSearch.test.js`. From your console:

```
# inside client/
$ npm test
```

Everything should pass:

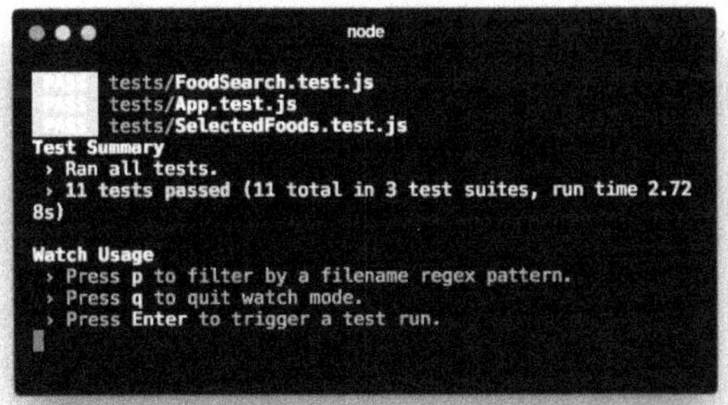

```
tests/FoodSearch.test.js
tests/App.test.js
tests/SelectedFoods.test.js
Test Summary
 › Ran all tests.
 › 11 tests passed (11 total in 3 test suites, run time 2.72
8s)

Watch Usage
 › Press p to filter by a filename regex pattern.
 › Press q to quit watch mode.
 › Press Enter to trigger a test run.
```

Tests pass

From here, the next layer of context will be the API returning results.

If we were writing integration tests, we'd take one of two approaches. If we wanted a full end-to-end test, we'd have `Client.search()` make an actual call to the API. Otherwise, we could use a Node library to "fake" the HTTP request. There are plenty of libraries that can intercept JavaScript's attempt to make an HTTP request. You can supply these libraries with a fake response object to provide to the caller.

However, as we're writing unit tests, we want to remove any dependency on both the API and the implementation details of `Client.search()`. We're exclusively testing the `FoodSearch` component, a single unit in our application. We only care about how `FoodSearch` uses `Client.search()`, nothing deeper.

As such, we want to intercept the call to `Client.search()` at the surface. We don't want `Client` to get involved at all. Instead, we want to assert that `Client.search()` was invoked with the proper parameter (the value of the search field). And then we want to invoke the callback passed to `Client.search()` with our own result set.

What we'd like to do is **mock the `Client` library**.

Mocking with Jest

When writing unit tests, we'll often find that the module we're testing depends on other modules in our application. There are multiple strategies for dealing with this, but they mostly center around the idea of a **test double**. A test double is a pretend object that "stands in" for a real one.

For instance, we could write a fake version of the `Client` library for use in our tests. The simplest version would look like this:

```
const Client = {
  search: () => {},
};
```

We could "inject" this fake `Client` as opposed to the real one into `FoodSearch` for testing purposes. `FoodSearch` could call `Client.search()` anywhere it wanted and it would invoke an empty function as opposed to performing an HTTP request.

We could take it a step further by injecting a fake `Client` that always returns a certain result. This would prove even more useful, as we'd be able to assert how the state for `FoodSearch` updates based on the behavior of `Client`:

```
const Client = {
  search: (_, cb) => {
    const result = [
      {
        description: 'Hummus',
        kcal: '166',
        protein_g: '8',
        fat_g: '10',
        carbohydrate_g: '14',
      },
    ];
    cb(result);
  },
};
```

This test double implements a `search()` method that immediately invokes the callback passed as the second argument. It invokes the callback with a hard-coded array that has a single food object.

But the implementation details of the test double are irrelevant. What's important is that this test double is mimicking the API returning the same, one-entry result set every time. With this fake client inserted into the app, we can readily write assertions on how `FoodSearch` handles this "response": that there's now a single entry in the table, that the description of that entry is "Hummus", etc.

We use _ as the first argument above to signify that we "don't care" about this argument. This is purely a stylistic choice.

It would be even better if our test double allowed us to dynamically specify what `result` to use. That way we wouldn't need to define a completely different double to test what happens if the API doesn't return any results. Furthermore, the simple test double above doesn't care about the search term passed to it. It would be nice to ensure that `FoodSearch` is invoking `Client.search()` with the appropriate value (the value of the input field).

Jest ships with a generator for a powerful flavor of test doubles: **mocks**. We'll use Jest's mocks as our test double. The best way to understand mocks is to see them in action.

You generate a Jest mock like this:

```
const myMockFunction = jest.fn();
```

This mock function can be invoked like any other function. By default, it will not have a return value:

```
console.log(myMockFunction()); // undefined
```

When you invoke a vanilla mock function nothing appears to happen. However, what's special about this function is that it will **keep track of invocations**. Jest's mock functions have methods you can use to introspect what happened.

For example, you can ask a mock function how many times it was called:

```
const myMock = jest.fn();
console.log(myMock.mock.calls.length);
// -> 0
myMock('Paris');
console.log(myMock.mock.calls.length);
// -> 1
myMock('Paris', 'Amsterdam');
console.log(myMock.mock.calls.length);
// -> 2
```

All of the introspective methods for a mock are underneath the property `mock`. By calling `myMock.mock.calls`, we receive an array of arrays. Each entry in the array corresponds to the arguments of each invocation:

```
const myMock = jest.fn();
console.log(myMock.mock.calls);
// -> []
myMock('Paris');
console.log(myMock.mock.calls);
// -> [ [ 'Paris' ] ]
myMock('Paris', 'Amsterdam');
console.log(myMock.mock.calls);
// -> [ [ 'Paris' ], [ 'Paris', 'Amsterdam' ] ]
```

This simple feature unlocks tons of power that we'll soon witness. We could declare our own `Client` double, using a Jest mock function:

```
const Client = {
  search: jest.fn(),
};
```

But Jest can take care of this for us. Jest has a mock generator for entire modules. By calling this method:

```
jest.mock('../src/Client')
```

Jest will look at our `Client` module. It will notice that it exports an object with a `search()` method. It will then create a fake object – a test double – that has a `search()` method that is a mock function. Jest will then ensure that the fake `Client` is used everywhere in the app as opposed to the real one.

Mocking `Client`

Let's use `jest.mock()` to mock `Client`. Using the special properties of mock functions, we'll then be able to write an assertion that `search()` was invoked with the proper argument.

At the top of `FoodSearch.test.js`, below the `import` statement for `FoodSearch`, let's import `Client` as we'll be referencing it later in the test suite. In addition, we tell Jest we'd like to mock it:

food-lookup-complete/client/tests/complete/FoodSearch.test.complete-3.js

```
import FoodSearch from '../src/FoodSearch';
import Client from '../src/Client';

jest.mock('../src/Client');

describe('FoodSearch', () => {
```

Now, let's consider what will happen. In our `beforeEach` block, when we simulate the change:

food-lookup-complete/client/tests/complete/FoodSearch.test.complete-3.js

```
  beforeEach(() => {
    const input = wrapper.find('input').first();
    input.simulate('change', {
      target: { value: value },
    });
  });
```

This will trigger the call to `Client.search()` at the bottom of `onSearchChange()`:

food-lookup-complete/client/src/FoodSearch.js

```
      Client.search(value, (foods) => {
        this.setState({
          foods: foods.slice(0, MATCHING_ITEM_LIMIT),
        });
      });
```

Except, instead of calling the method on the real `Client`, it's calling the method on the mock that Jest has injected. `Client.search()` is a mock function and has **done nothing** except log that it was called.

Let's declare a new spec below "should display the remove icon." Before writing the assertion, let's just log a few things out to the console to see what's happening:

food-lookup-complete/client/tests/complete/FoodSearch.test.complete-3.js

```
    it('should display the remove icon', () => {
      expect(
        wrapper.find('.remove.icon').length
      ).toBe(1);
    });

    it('...todo...', () => {
      const firstInvocation = Client.search.mock.calls[0];
      console.log('First invocation:');
      console.log(firstInvocation);
      console.log('All invocations: ');
      console.log(Client.search.mock.calls);
    });

    describe('and API returns results', () => {
```

We read the `mock.calls` property on the mock function. Each entry in the calls array corresponds to an invocation of the mock function `Client.search()`.

If you were to save `FoodSearch.test.js` and run the test suite, you'd be able to see the log statements in the console:

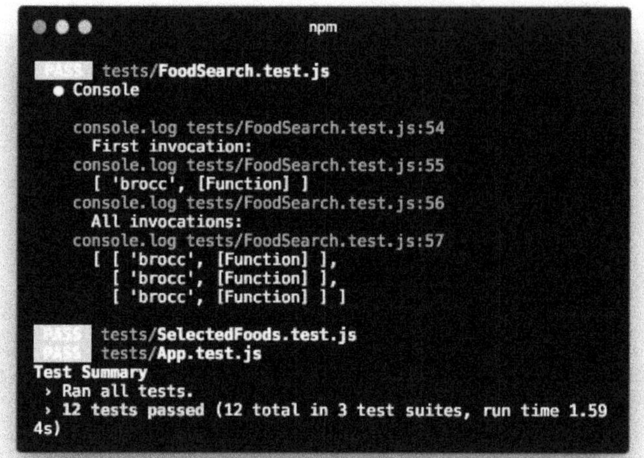

```
PASS tests/FoodSearch.test.js
  ● Console

    console.log tests/FoodSearch.test.js:54
      First invocation:
    console.log tests/FoodSearch.test.js:55
      [ 'brocc', [Function] ]
    console.log tests/FoodSearch.test.js:56
      All invocations:
    console.log tests/FoodSearch.test.js:57
      [ [ 'brocc', [Function] ],
        [ 'brocc', [Function] ],
        [ 'brocc', [Function] ] ]

PASS tests/SelectedFoods.test.js
PASS tests/App.test.js
Test Summary
 › Ran all tests.
 › 12 tests passed (12 total in 3 test suites, run time 1.59
4s)
```

Log statements in the test run

Picking out the first one:

```
First invocation:
[ 'brocc', [Function] ]
```

The mock captured the invocation that occurred in the `beforeEach` block. The first argument of the invocation is what we'd expect, `'brocc'`. And the second argument is our callback function. Importantly, **the callback function has yet to be invoked**. `search()` has captured the function but not done anything with it.

If you were to fence the call to `Client.search()` with `console.log()` statements, like this:

```
// Example of "fencing" `Client.search()`
console.log('Before `search()`');
Client.search(value, (foods) => {
  console.log('Inside the callback');
  this.setState({
    foods: foods.slice(0, MATCHING_ITEM_LIMIT),
  });
});
console.log('After `search()`');
```

You'd see this output in the console when running the test suite:

```
Before `search()`
After `search()`
```

The mock function `search()` is invoked but all it does is capture the arguments. The line that logs "Inside the callback" has not been called.

So, the console output for "First invocation" makes sense. However, check out the console output for "All invocations":

```
All invocations:
[ [ 'brocc', [Function] ],
[ 'brocc', [Function] ],
[ 'brocc', [Function] ] ]
```

Reformatting that array:

```
[
  [ 'brocc', [Function] ],
  [ 'brocc', [Function] ],
  [ 'brocc', [Function] ]
]
```

We see *three* invocations in total. Why is this?

We have three `it` blocks that correspond to our `beforeEach` that simulates a change. Remember, a `beforeEach` is run once before each related `it`. Therefore, **our `beforeEach` that simulates a search is executed three times**. Which means the mock function `Client.search()` is invoked three times as well.

While this makes sense, it's undesirable. State is **leaking between specs**. We want each `it` to receive a fresh version of the `Client` mock.

Jest mock functions have a method for this, `mockClear()`. We'll invoke this method after each spec is executed using the antipode of `beforeEach`, `afterEach`. This will ensure the mock is in a pristine state before each spec run. We'll do this inside the top-level `describe`, below the `beforeEach` where we shallow-render the component:

food-lookup-complete/client/tests/complete/FoodSearch.test.complete-4.js

```
describe('FoodSearch', () => {
  let wrapper;

  beforeEach(() => {
    wrapper = shallow(
      <FoodSearch />
    );
  });

  afterEach(() => {
    Client.search.mockClear();
  });

  it('should not display the remove icon', () => {
```

We could have used a `beforeEach` block here as well, but it usually makes sense to perform any "tidying up" in `afterEach` blocks.

Now, if we run our test suite again:

```
First invocation:
[ 'brocc', [Function] ]
All invocations:
[ [ 'brocc', [Function] ] ]
```

We've succeeded in resetting the mock between test runs. There's only a single invocation logged, the invocation that occurred right before this last `it` was executed.

With our mock behaving as desired, let's convert our dummy spec into a real one. We'll assert that the first argument passed to `Client.search()` is the same value the user typed into the search field:

food-lookup-complete/client/tests/complete/FoodSearch.test.complete-5.js

```
    it('should display the remove icon', () => {
      expect(
        wrapper.find('.remove.icon').length
      ).toBe(1);
    });

    it('...todo...', () => {
      const firstInvocation = Client.search.mock.calls[0];
      console.log('First invocation:');
      console.log(firstInvocation);
      console.log('All invocations: ');
      console.log(Client.search.mock.calls);
    });

    it('should call `Client.search() with `value`', () => {
      const invocationArgs = Client.search.mock.calls[0];
      expect(
        invocationArgs[0]
      ).toEqual(value);
    });

    describe('and API returns results', () => {
```

We're asserting that the zeroeth argument of the invocation matches `value`, in this case `brocc`.

Try it out

With `Client` mocked, we can run our test suite assured that `FoodSearch` is in total isolation. Save `FoodSearch.test.js` and run the test suite from the console:

```
$ npm test
```

The result:

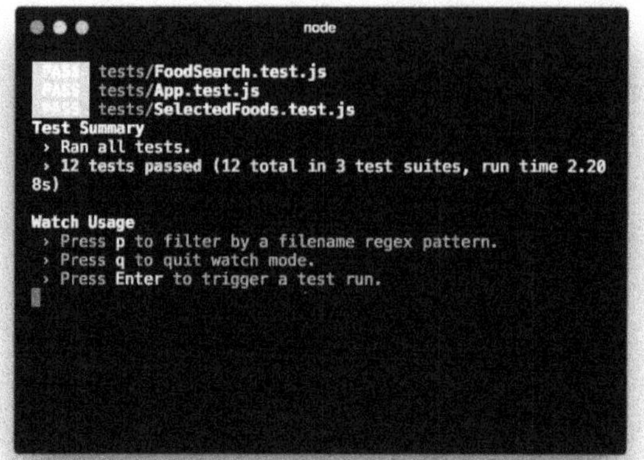

All specs pass

We used a Jest mock function to both capture and introspect the `Client.search()` invocation. Now, let's see how we can use it to establish behavior for our next layer of context: when the API returns results.

The API returns results

As we can see in the pre-existing test scaffolding, we'll write the specs pertaining to this context inside of their own `describe`:

```
describe('FoodSearch', () => {
  // ...

  describe('user populates search field', () => {
    // ...

    describe('and API returns results', () => {
      beforeEach(() => {
        // ... simulate API returning results
      });

      // ... specs
    });

    describe('then user types more', () => {
      // ...

    });
  });
});
```

In our `beforeEach` for this `describe`, we want to simulate the API returning results. We can do this by **manually invoking the callback function** passed to `Client.search()` with whatever we'd like to simulate the API returning.

We'll fake Client returning two matches. We can picture our component in this state:

Description	Kcal	Protein (g)	Fat (g)	Carbs (g)
Broccolini	100	11	21	31
Broccoli rabe	200	12	22	32

Visual representation of desired state for component

Let's look at the code first then we'll break it down:

food-lookup-complete/client/tests/complete/FoodSearch.test.complete-6.js

```
    it('should call `Client.search() with `value`', () => {
      const invocationArgs = Client.search.mock.calls[0];
      expect(
        invocationArgs[0]
      ).toEqual(value);
    });

    describe('and API returns results', () => {
      const foods = [
        {
          description: 'Broccolini',
          kcal: '100',
          protein_g: '11',
          fat_g: '21',
          carbohydrate_g: '31',
        },
        {
          description: 'Broccoli rabe',
          kcal: '200',
          protein_g: '12',
          fat_g: '22',
          carbohydrate_g: '32',
        },
      ];
      beforeEach(() => {
```

```
    const invocationArgs = Client.search.mock.calls[0];
    const cb = invocationArgs[1];
    cb(foods);
    wrapper.update();
  });
```

First, we declare an array, `foods`, which we use as the fake result set returned by `Client.search()`.

Second, in our `beforeEach`, we grab the second argument that `Client.search()` was invoked with, in this case our callback function. We then invoke it with our array of food objects. **By manually invoking callbacks passed to a mock, we can simulate desired behavior of asynchronous resources.**

Last, we call `wrapper.update()` after invoking the callback. This will cause our component to re-render. When a component is shallow-rendered, the usual re-rendering hooks do not apply. Therefore, when `setState()` is called within our callback, a re-render is not triggered.

If that's the case, you might wonder why this is the first time we've needed to use `wrapper.update()`. Enzyme has actually been automatically calling `update()` after every one of our `simulate()` calls. `simulate()` invokes an event handler. Immediately after that event handler returns, Enzyme will call `wrapper.update()`.

Because we're invoking our callback asynchronously some time *after* the event handler returns, we need to manually call `wrapper.update()` to re-render the component.

When a component is shallow-rendered, the usual re-rendering hooks do not apply. If any state changes instigated by a `simulate()` are made asynchronously, you must call `update()` to re-render the component.

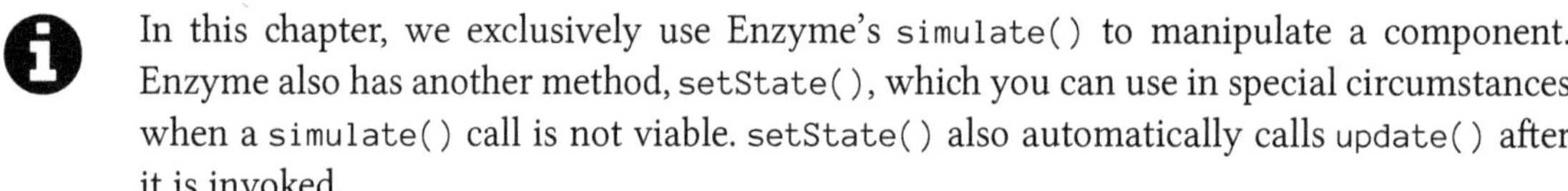

In this chapter, we exclusively use Enzyme's `simulate()` to manipulate a component. Enzyme also has another method, `setState()`, which you can use in special circumstances when a `simulate()` call is not viable. `setState()` also automatically calls `update()` after it is invoked.

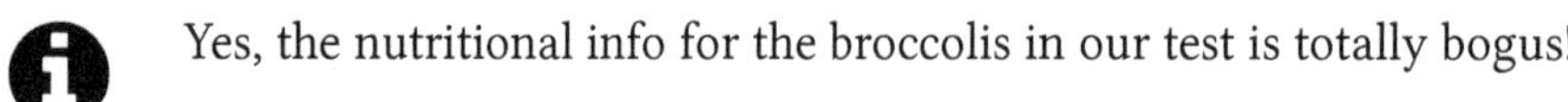

Yes, the nutritional info for the broccolis in our test is totally bogus!

With our callback invoked, let's write our first spec. We'll assert that the `foods` property in state matches our array of foods:

food-lookup-complete/client/tests/complete/FoodSearch.test.complete-6.js

```
    it('should set the state property `foods`', () => {
      expect(
        wrapper.state().foods
      ).toEqual(foods);
    });
```

Again, we use the `state()` method when reading state from an `EnzymeWrapper`.

Next, we'll assert that the table has two rows:

food-lookup-complete/client/tests/complete/FoodSearch.test.complete-6.js

```
    it('should display two rows', () => {
      expect(
        wrapper.find('tbody tr').length
      ).toEqual(2);
    });
```

Because this spec uses the same selector as our previous spec "should display zero rows," this gives us assurance that the previous spec uses the proper selector.

Finally, let's take it a step further and assert that both of our foods are actually printed in the table. There are many ways to do this. Because the `description` of each is so unique, we can actually just hunt for each food's description in the HTML output, like this:

food-lookup-complete/client/tests/complete/FoodSearch.test.complete-6.js

```
    it('should render the description of first food', () => {
      expect(
        wrapper.html()
      ).toContain(foods[0].description);
    });

    it('should render the description of second food', () => {
      expect(
        wrapper.html()
      ).toContain(foods[1].description);
    });

    describe('then user clicks food item', () => {
```

Because we're hunting for a unique string, there's no need to use Enzyme's selector API. Instead, we use Enzyme's `html()` to yield a string of the component's HTML output. We then use Jest's `toContain()` matcher, this time on a string as opposed to an array.

`html()` is also a great method for debugging shallow-rendered components. For instance, seeing the full HTML output of a component can help you determine if an assertion issue is due to an erroneous selector or an erroneous component.

For this set of specs, we're working with two food items returned from the API (and subsequently entered into state).

Our assertions would have been robust even if we'd only used one item. However, when writing assertions against arrays some developers prefer that the array has more than one item. This can help catch certain classes of bugs and asserts that the variable under test is the appropriate data structure.

Try it out

Save `FoodSearch.test.js`. From your console:

```
$ npm test
```

Everything passes:

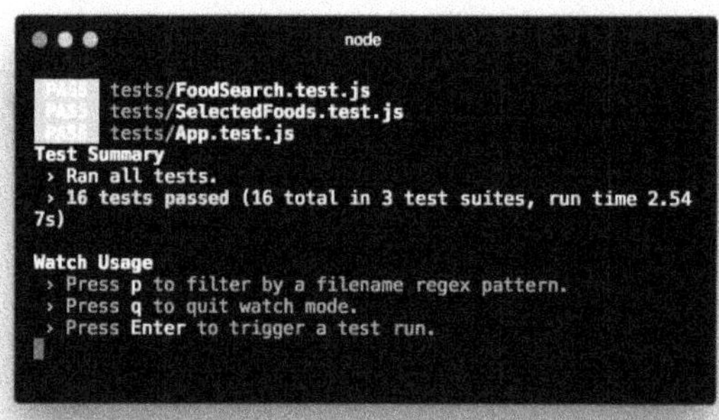

Tests pass

From here, there are a few behaviors the user can take with respect to the `FoodSearch` component:

- They can click on a food item to add it to their total
- They can type an additional character, appending to their search string

- They can hit backspace to remove a character or the entire string of text
- They can click on the "X" (remove icon) to clear the search field

We're going to write specs for the first two behaviors together. The last two behaviors are left as exercises at the end of this chapter.

We'll start with simulating the user clicking on a food item.

The user clicks on a food item

When the user clicks on a food item, that item is added to their list of totals. Those totals are displayed by the `SelectedFoods` component at the top of the app:

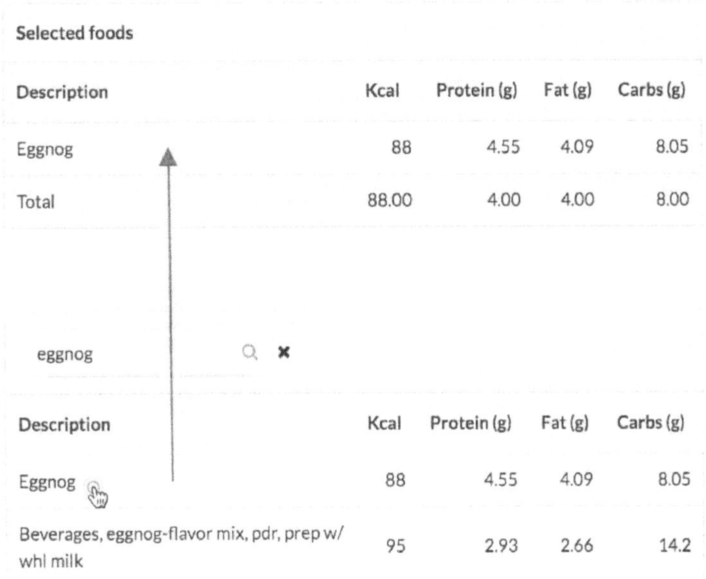

Selected foods

Description	Kcal	Protein (g)	Fat (g)	Carbs (g)
Eggnog	88	4.55	4.09	8.05
Total	88.00	4.00	4.00	8.00

eggnog

Description	Kcal	Protein (g)	Fat (g)	Carbs (g)
Eggnog	88	4.55	4.09	8.05
Beverages, eggnog-flavor mix, pdr, prep w/ whl milk	95	2.93	2.66	14.2

Clicking on an item

As you may recall, each food item is displayed in a `tr` element that has an `onClick` handler. That `onClick` handler is set to a prop-function that `App` passes to `FoodSearch`:

food-lookup-complete/client/src/FoodSearch.js

```
          <tbody>
          {
            this.state.foods.map((food, idx) => (
              <tr
                key={idx}
                onClick={() => this.props.onFoodClick(food)}
              >
```

We want to simulate a click and assert that `FoodSearch` calls this prop-function.

Because we're unit testing, we don't want `App` to be involved. Instead, we can set the prop `onFoodClick` to a mock function.

At the moment, we're rendering `FoodSearch` without setting any props:

food-lookup-complete/client/tests/complete/FoodSearch.test.complete-6.js

```
  beforeEach(() => {
    wrapper = shallow(
      <FoodSearch />
    );
  });
```

We'll begin by setting the prop `onFoodClick` inside our shallow render call to a new mock function:

food-lookup-complete/client/tests/complete/FoodSearch.test.complete-7.js

```
describe('FoodSearch', () => {
  let wrapper;
  const onFoodClick = jest.fn();

  beforeEach(() => {
    wrapper = shallow(
      <FoodSearch
        onFoodClick={onFoodClick}
      />
    );
  });
```

We declare `onFoodClick`, a mock function, at the top of our test suite's scope and pass it as a prop to `FoodSearch`.

While we're at it, let's make sure to clear our new mock between spec runs. This is always good practice:

food-lookup-complete/client/tests/complete/FoodSearch.test.complete-7.js

```
  afterEach(() => {
    Client.search.mockClear();
    onFoodClick.mockClear();
  });
```

Next, we'll setup the `describe` 'then user clicks food item.' This `describe` is a child of "and API returns results."

```
describe('FoodSearch', () => {
  // ...

  describe('user populates search field', () => {
    // ...

    describe('and API returns results', () => {
      // ...

      describe('then user clicks food item', () => {
        beforeEach(() => {
          // ... simulate the click
        });

        // ... specs
      });
    });
  });
});
```

Our `beforeEach` block simulates a click on the first food item in the table:

food-lookup-complete/client/tests/complete/FoodSearch.test.complete-7.js

```
      describe('then user clicks food item', () => {
        beforeEach(() => {
          const foodRow = wrapper.find('tbody tr').first();
          foodRow.simulate('click');
        });
```

We first use `find()` to select the first element that matches `tbody tr`. We then simulate a click on the row. Note that we do not need to pass an event object to `simulate()`.

By using a mock function as our prop `onFoodClick`, we are able to keep `FoodSearch` in total isolation. With respect to unit tests for `FoodSearch`, we don't care how `App` implements `onFoodClick()`. We only care that `FoodSearch` invokes this function at the right time with the right arguments.

Our spec asserts that `onFoodClick` was invoked with the first food object in the `foods` array:

food-lookup-complete/client/tests/complete/FoodSearch.test.complete-7.js

```
it('should call prop `onFoodClick` with `food`', () => {
  const food = foods[0];
  expect(
    onFoodClick.mock.calls[0]
  ).toEqual([ food ]);
});
```

In full, this `describe` block:

food-lookup-complete/client/tests/complete/FoodSearch.test.complete-7.js

```
it('should render the description of second food', () => {
  expect(
    wrapper.html()
  ).toContain(foods[1].description);
});

describe('then user clicks food item', () => {
  beforeEach(() => {
    const foodRow = wrapper.find('tbody tr').first();
    foodRow.simulate('click');
  });

  it('should call prop `onFoodClick` with `food`', () => {
    const food = foods[0];
    expect(
      onFoodClick.mock.calls[0]
    ).toEqual([ food ]);
  });
});

describe('then user types more', () => {
```

Try it out

Save `FoodSearch.test.js` and run the suite:

```
$ npm test
```

Our new spec passes:

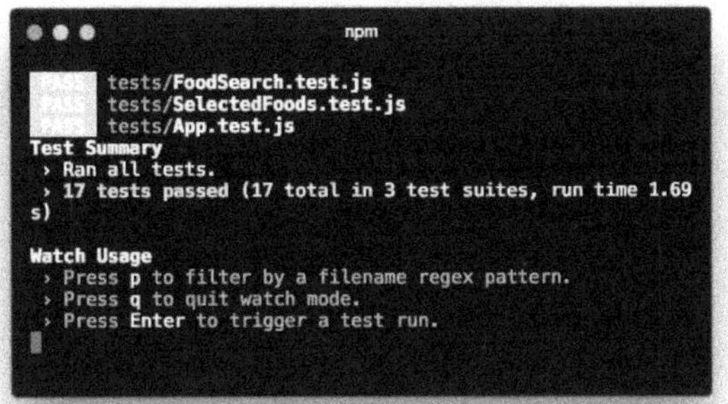

```
npm

PASS tests/FoodSearch.test.js
PASS tests/SelectedFoods.test.js
PASS tests/App.test.js
Test Summary
 › Ran all tests.
 › 17 tests passed (17 total in 3 test suites, run time 1.69
s)

Watch Usage
 › Press p to filter by a filename regex pattern.
 › Press q to quit watch mode.
 › Press Enter to trigger a test run.
```

Tests pass

With our spec for the user clicking on a food item completed, let's return to the context of "and API returns results." The user has typed `'brocc'` and sees two results. The next behavior we want to simulate is the user typing an additional character into the search field. This will cause our (mocked) API to return an empty result set (no results).

The API returns empty result set

As you can see in the scaffold, our last `describe` blocks are children to "and API returns results," siblings to "then user clicks food item":

```
describe('FoodSearch', () => {
  // ...

  describe('user populates search field', () => {
    // ...

    describe('and API returns results', () => {
      // ...

      describe('then user clicks food item', () => {
        // ...
      });

      describe('then user types more', () => {
        beforeEach(() => {
          // ... simulate user typing "x"
```

```
        });

        describe('and API returns no results', () => {
          beforeEach(() => {
            // ... simulate API returning no results
          });

          // ... specs
        });
      });
    });
  });
});
```

We could have combined "then user types more" and "and API returns no results" into one `describe` with one `beforeEach`. But we like organizing our contextual setup in this manner, both for readability and to leave room for future specs.

After establishing the context in both `beforeEach` blocks, we'll write one assertion: that the `foods` property in state is now a blank array.

If you're feeling comfortable, try composing these `describe` blocks yourself and come back to verify your solution.

Our first `beforeEach` block first simulates the user typing an "x," meaning the event object now carries the value `'broccx'`:

food-lookup-complete/client/tests/complete/FoodSearch.test.complete-8.js

```
      describe('then user types more', () => {
        const value = 'broccx';

        beforeEach(() => {
          const input = wrapper.find('input').first();
          input.simulate('change', {
            target: { value: value },
          });
        });
```

We won't write any specs specific to this `describe`. Our next `describe`, "and API returns no results," will simulate `Client.search()` yielding a blank array:

```
describe('and API returns no results', () => {
  beforeEach(() => {
    // ... simulate search returning no results
  });
});
```

Here's the tricky part: By the time we've reached this `beforeEach` block, **we've simulated the user changing the input twice**. As a result, `Client.search()` has been invoked twice.

Another way to look at it: If we were to insert a log statement in this `beforeEach` for `Client.search.mock.calls`

```
describe('and API returns no results', () => {
  beforeEach(() => {
    // What happens if we log the mock calls here?
    console.log(Client.search.mock.calls);
  });
});
```

We would see in the console that it has been invoked twice:

```
[
  [ 'brocc', [Function] ],
  [ 'broccx', [Function] ],
]
```

This is because the `beforeEach` blocks for "user populates search field" *and* "then user types more" simulate changing the input which in turn eventually calls `Client.search()`.

We want to invoke the callback function passed to the *second* invocation. That corresponds to the most recent input field change that the user made. Therefore, we'll grab the second invocation and invoke the callback passed to it with a blank array:

food-lookup-complete/client/tests/complete/FoodSearch.test.complete-8.js

```
        describe('and API returns no results', () => {
          beforeEach(() => {
            const secondInvocationArgs = Client.search.mock.calls[1];
            const cb = secondInvocationArgs[1];
            cb([]);
            wrapper.update();
          });
```

We did not need to call `wrapper.update()` in the `beforeEach` block as we're not making any assertions against the virtual DOM. However, it's good practice to follow an async state change with an `update()` call. It will avoid possibly bewildering behavior should you add specs that assert against the DOM in the future.

Finally, we're ready for our spec. We assert that the state property `foods` is now an empty array:

food-lookup-complete/client/tests/complete/FoodSearch.test.complete-8.js

```
          it('should set the state property `foods`', () => {
            expect(
              wrapper.state().foods
            ).toEqual([]);
          });
```

The "then user types more" `describe`, in full:

food-lookup-complete/client/tests/complete/FoodSearch.test.complete-8.js

```
        it('should call prop `onFoodClick` with `food`', () => {
          const food = foods[0];
          expect(
            onFoodClick.mock.calls[0]
          ).toEqual([ food ]);
        });
      });

      describe('then user types more', () => {
        const value = 'broccx';

        beforeEach(() => {
          const input = wrapper.find('input').first();
          input.simulate('change', {
            target: { value: value },
          });
        });

        describe('and API returns no results', () => {
          beforeEach(() => {
            const secondInvocationArgs = Client.search.mock.calls[1];
            const cb = secondInvocationArgs[1];
            cb([]);
            wrapper.update();
```

```
          });

          it('should set the state property `foods`', () => {
            expect(
              wrapper.state().foods
            ).toEqual([]);
          });
        });
      });
    });
  });
});
```

> Assertions on the component's output, like that it should not contain any rows, aren't strictly necessary here. Our assertions against the initial state (like "should display zero rows") already provide assurance that when `foods` is empty in state no rows are rendered.

> As you recall, both callback functions look like this:
>
> ```
> (foods) => {
>     this.setState({
>       foods: foods.slice(0, MATCHING_ITEM_LIMIT),
>     });
>   };
> ```
>
> Because the callback function does not reference any variables inside `onSearchChange()`, we could technically invoke either callback function and the spec we just wrote would pass. However, this is bad practice and would likely set you up for a puzzling bug in the future.

Further reading

In this chapter, we:

1. Demystified JavaScript testing frameworks, building from the ground up.
2. Introduced Jest, a testing framework for JavaScript, to give us some handy features like `expect` and `beforeEach`.
3. Learned how to organize code in a behavior-driven style.

4. Introduced Enzyme, a library for working with React components in a testing environment.
5. Used the idea of mocks to write assertions for a React component that makes a request to an API.

Armed with this knowledge, you're prepared to isolate React components in a variety of different contexts and effectively write unit tests for them. These unit tests will give you peace of mind as the number and complexity of components in your app grows.

A few resources outside of this chapter will aid you greatly as you compose unit tests:

Jest API reference[70]

These docs will help you discover rich matchers that can both save you time and elevate the expressiveness of your test suite. We used some handy matchers in this chapter, like `toEqual` and `toContain`. Here are a few more examples:

- You can assert that one number is close to another with `toBeCloseTo()`
- You can match a string against a regular expression with `toMatch()`
- You can control time, allowing you to work with `setTimeout` or `setInterval`

create-react-app configures Jest for you. However, if you use Jest outside of create-react-app, you'll also find the reference for Jest configuration useful. You can configure settings like test watching or instruct Jest where to find test files.

Jasmine docs[71]

Jest uses Jasmine assertions, so the docs for Jasmine also apply. You can use that as another reference point to understand matchers.

Furthermore, you can use some additional functionality that's not mentioned in the Jest API reference. For example:

- You can assert that an array contains a specific subset of members with `jasmine.arrayContaining()`
- You can assert that an object contains a specific subset of key/value pairs with `jasmine.objectContaining()`

Enzyme `ShallowWrapper` API docs[72]

We explored a few methods for traversing the virtual DOM (with `find()`) and making assertions on the virtual DOM's contents (like with `contains()`). `ShallowWrapper` has many more methods that you might find useful. Some examples:

[70] http://facebook.github.io/jest/docs/api.html

[71] http://jasmine.github.io/2.5/introduction.html

[72] http://airbnb.io/enzyme/docs/api/shallow.html

- As we saw in this chapter, `ShallowWrapper` is array-like. A `find()` call might match more than one element in a component's output. You can perform operations on this list of matching elements that mirror Array's methods, like `map()`.
- You can grab the actual React component itself with `instance()`. You can use this to unit test particular methods on the component.
- You can set the state of the underlying component with `setState()`. When possible, we like to use `simulate()` or call the component's methods directly to invoke state changes. But when that's not practical, `setState()` is useful.

Earlier, we saw that `find()` accepts an Enzyme selector. The docs contain a reference page for what constitutes a valid Enzyme selector that you'll find helpful.

End-to-end tests

We have end-to-end tests that we use for the code in this book. We use the tool Nightwatch.js[73] to drive these.

[73] http://nightwatchjs.org/

Routing

What's in a URL?

A URL is a reference to a web resource. A typical URL looks something like this:

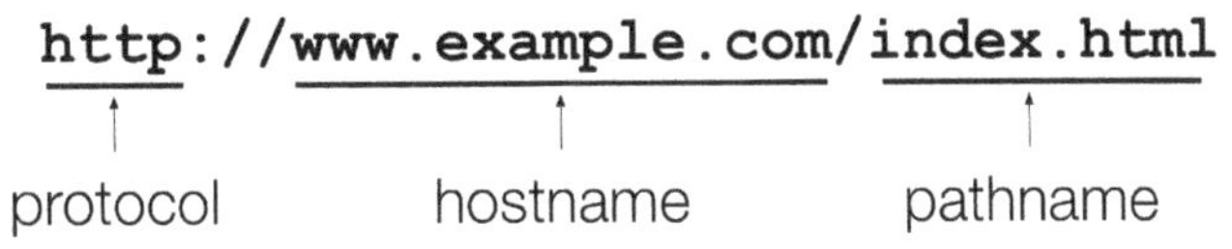

```
http://www.example.com/index.html
```

protocol — `http:`
hostname — `www.example.com`
pathname — `index.html`

While a combination of the protocol and the hostname direct us to a certain website, it's the **pathname** that references a specific resource on that site. Another way to think about it: the pathname references a specific **location** in our application.

For example, consider a URL for some music website:

```
https://example.com.com/artists/87589/albums/1758221
```

This location refers to a specific album by an artist. The URL contains identifiers for both the artist and album desired:

```
example.com/artists/:artistId/albums/:albumId
```

We can think of the URL as being an **external keeper of state**, in this case the album the user is viewing. By storing pieces of app state up at the level of the browser's location, we can enable users to bookmark the link, refresh the page, and share it with others.

In a traditional web application with minimal JavaScript, the request flow for this page might look like this:

1. Browser makes a request to the server for this page.
2. The server uses the identifiers in the URL to retrieve data about the artist and the album from its database.
3. The server populates a template with this data.
4. The server returns this populated HTML document along with any other assets like CSS and images.
5. The browser renders these assets.

When using a rich JavaScript framework like React, we want React to generate the page. So an evolution of that request flow using React might look like this:

1. Browser makes a request to the server for this page.
2. **The server doesn't care about the pathname.** Instead, it just returns a standard `index.html` that includes the React app and any static assets.
3. The React app mounts.
4. The React app extracts the identifiers from the URL and uses these identifiers to make an API call to fetch the data for the artist and the album. It might make this call to the same server.
5. The React app renders the page using data it received from the API call.

Projects elsewhere in the book have mirrored this second request flow. One example is the timers app in "Components & Servers." The same `server.js` served both the static assets (the React app) and an API that fed that React app data.

This initial request flow for React is slightly more inefficient than the first. Instead of one round-trip from the browser to the server, there will be two or more: One to fetch the React app and then however many API calls the React app has to make to get all the data it needs to render the page.

However, the gains come after the initial page load. The user experience of our timers app with React is much better than it would be without. Without JavaScript, each time the user wanted to stop, start, or edit a timer, their browser would have to fetch a brand new page from the server. This adds noticeable delay and an unpleasant "blink" between page loads.

Single-page applications (SPAs) are web apps that load once and then dynamically update elements on the page using JavaScript. Every React app we've built so far has been a type of SPA.

So we've seen how to use React to make interface elements on a page fluid and dynamic. But other apps in the book have had only a single location. For instance, the product voting app had a single view: the list of products to vote on. What if we wanted to add a different page, like a product view page at the location `/products/:productId`? This page would use a completely different set of components.

Back to our music website example, imagine the user is looking at the React-powered album view page. They then click on an "Account" button at the top right of the app to view their account information. A request flow to support this might look like:

1. User clicks on the "Account" button which is a link to `/account`.
2. Browser makes a request to `/account`.
3. The server, again, doesn't care about the pathname. Again, it returns the same `index.html` that includes the full React app and static assets.
4. The React app mounts. It checks the URL and sees that the user is looking at the `/accounts` page.

5. The top-level React component, say `App`, might have a switch for what component to render based on the URL. Before, it was rendering `AlbumView`. But now it renders `AccountView`.
6. The React app renders and populates itself with an API request to the server (say `/api/account`).

This approach works and we can see examples of it across the web. But for many types of applications, there's a more efficient approach.

When the user clicks on the "Account" button, we could prevent the browser from fetching the next page from `/account`. Instead, we could instruct the React app to switch out the `AlbumView` component for the `AccountView` component. In full, that flow would look like this:

1. User visits `https://example.com.com/artists/87589/albums/1758221`.
2. The server delivers the standard `index.html` that includes the React app and assets.
3. The React app mounts and populates itself by making an API call to the server.
4. User clicks on the "Account" button.
5. The React app captures this click event. React updates the URL to `https://example.com/account` and re-renders.
6. When the React app re-renders, it checks the URL. It sees the user is viewing `/account` and it swaps in the `AccountView` component.
7. The React app makes an API call to populate the `AccountView` component.

When the user clicks on the "Account" button, the browser already contains the full React app. There's no need to have the browser make a new request to fetch the same app again from the server and re-mount it. The React app just needs to update the URL and then re-render itself with a new component-tree (`AccountView`).

This is the idea of a **JavaScript router**. As we'll see first hand, **routing** involves two primary pieces of functionality: (1) Modifying the location of the app (the URL) and (2) determining what React components to render at a given location.

There are many routing libraries for React, but the community's clear favorite is **React Router**. React Router gives us a wonderful foundation for building rich applications that have hundreds or thousands of React components across many different views and URLs.

React Router's core components

For *modifying* the location of an app, we use links and redirects. In React Router, links and redirects are managed by two React components, `Link` and `Redirect`.

For *determining what to render* at a given location, we also use two React Router components, `Route` and `Switch`.

To best understand React Router, we'll start out by building basic versions of React Router's core components. In doing so, we'll get a feel for what routing looks like in a component-driven paradigm.

We'll then swap out our components for those provided by the `react-router` library. We'll explore a few more components and features of the library.

In the second half of the chapter, we'll see React Router at work in a slightly larger application. The app we build will have multiple pages with dynamic URLs. The app will communicate with a server that is protected by an API token. We'll explore a strategy for handling logging and logging out inside a React Router app.

React Router v4

The latest version of React Router, v4, is a major shift from its predecessors. The authors of React Router state that the most compelling aspect of this version of the library is that it's "just React."

We agree. And while v4 was just released at the time of writing, we find its paradigm so compelling that we wanted to ensure we covered v4 as opposed to v3 here in the book. We believe v4 will be rapidly adopted by the community.

Because v4 is so new, it's possible the next few months will see some changes. But the essence of v4 is settled, and this chapter focuses on those core concepts.

Building the components of `react-router`

The completed app

All the example code for this chapter is inside the folder `routing` in the code download. We'll start off with the `basics` app:

```
$ cd routing/basics
```

Taking a look inside this directory, we see that this app is powered by create-react-app:

```
$ ls
README.md
nightwatch.json
package.json
public/
src/
tests/
```

If you need a refresher on create-react-app, refer to the chapter "Using Webpack with create-react-app."

Our React app lives inside `src/`:

```
$ ls src
App.css
App.js
SelectableApp.js
complete/
index-complete.js
index.css
index.js
logo.svg
```

`complete/` contains the completed version of `App.js`. The folder also contains each iteration of `App.js` that we build up throughout this section.

Install the npm packages:

```
$ npm i
```

At the moment, `index.js` is loading `index-complete.js`. `index-complete.js` uses `SelectableApp` to give us the ability to toggle between the app's various iterations. `SelectableApp` is just for demo purposes.

If we boot the app, we'll see the completed version:

```
$ npm start
```

The app consists of three links. Clicking on a link displays a blurb about the selected body of water below the application:

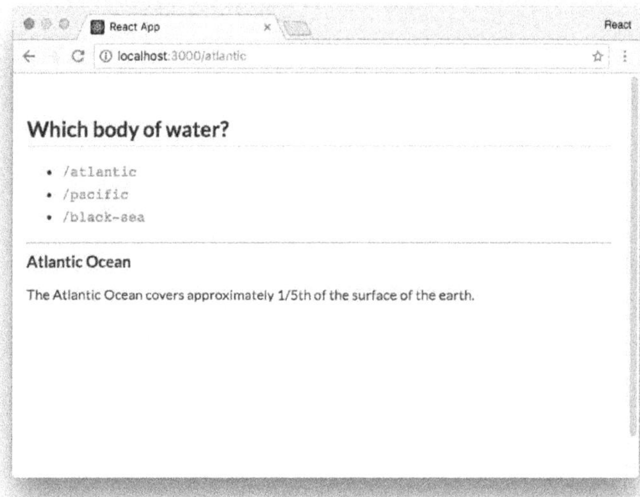

The completed app

Notice that clicking on a link *changes the location of the app.* Clicking on the link `/atlantic` updates the URL to `/atlantic`. Importantly, the browser *does not make a request* when we click on a link. The blurb about the Atlantic Ocean appears and the browser's URL bar updates to `/atlantic` instantly.

Clicking on the link `/black-sea` displays a countdown. When the countdown finishes, the app redirects the browser to `/`.

The routing in this app is powered by the `react-router` library. We'll build a version of the app ourselves by constructing our own React Router components.

We'll be working inside the file `App.js` throughout this section.

Building `Route`

We'll start off by building React Router's `Route` component. We'll see what it does shortly.

Let's open the file `src/App.js`. Inside is a skeletal version of `App`. Below the import statement for `React`, we define a simple `App` component with two `<a>` tag links:

routing/basics/src/App.js

```
class App extends React.Component {
  render() {
    return (
      <div
        className='ui text container'
      >
        <h2 className='ui dividing header'>
          Which body of water?
        </h2>

        <ul>
          <li>
            <a href='/atlantic'>
              <code>/atlantic</code>
            </a>
          </li>
          <li>
            <a href='/pacific'>
              <code>/pacific</code>
            </a>
          </li>
        </ul>

        <hr />

        {/* We'll insert the Route components here */}
      </div>
    );
  }
}
```

We have two regular HTML anchor tags pointing to the paths `/atlantic` and `/pacific`.

Below `App` are two stateless functional components:

routing/basics/src/App.js

```
const Atlantic = () => (
  <div>
    <h3>Atlantic Ocean</h3>
    <p>
      The Atlantic Ocean covers approximately 1/5th of the
      surface of the earth.
    </p>
  </div>
);

const Pacific = () => (
  <div>
    <h3>Pacific Ocean</h3>
    <p>
      Ferdinand Magellan, a Portuguese explorer, named the ocean
      'mar pacifico' in 1521, which means peaceful sea.
    </p>
  </div>
);
```

These components render some facts about the two oceans. Eventually, we want to render these components inside `App`. We want to have `App` render `Atlantic` when the browser's location is `/atlantic` and `Pacific` when the location is `/pacific`.

Recall that `index.js` is currently deferring to `index-complete.js` to load the completed version of the app to the DOM. Before we can take a look at the app so far, we need to ensure `index.js` mounts the `App` component we're working on here in `./App.js` instead.

Open up `index.js`. First, comment out the line that imports `index-complete`:

```
// [STEP 1] Comment out this line:
// import "./index-complete";
```

As in other create-react-app apps, the mounting of the React app to the DOM will take place here in `index.js`. Let's un-comment the line that mounts `App`:

```
// [STEP 2] Un-comment this line:
ReactDOM.render(<App />, document.getElementById("root"));
```

From the root of the project's folder, we can boot the app with the `start` command:

```
$ npm start
```

We see the two links rendered on the page. We can click on them and note the browser makes a page request. The URL bar is updated but nothing in the app changes:

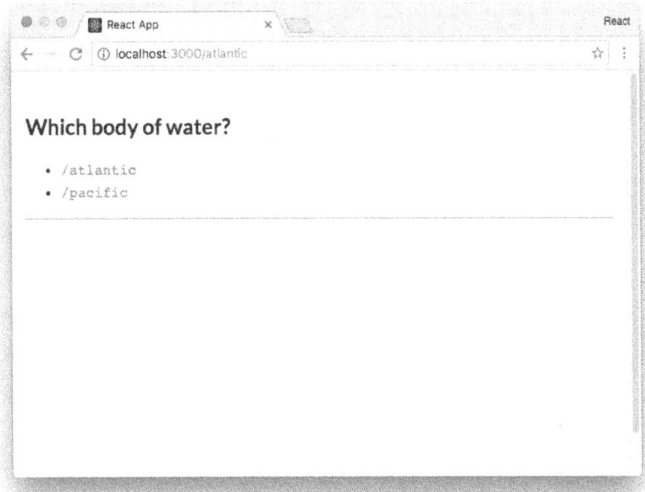

We see neither `Atlantic` nor `Pacific` rendered, which makes sense because we haven't yet included them in `App`. Despite this, it's interesting that at the moment **our app doesn't care about the state of the pathname**. No matter what path the browser requests from our server, the server will return the same `index.html` with the same exact JavaScript bundle.

This is a desirable foundation. We want our browser to load React in the same way in each location and defer to React on what to do at each location.

Let's have our app render the appropriate component, `Atlantic` or `Pacific`, based on the location of the app (`/atlantic` or `/pacific`). To implement this behavior, we'll write and use a `Route` component.

In React Router, `Route` is a component that **determines whether or not to render a specified component based on the app's location**. We'll need to supply `Route` with two arguments as `props`:

- The `path` to *match* against the location
- The `component` to render when the location matches `path`

Let's look at how we might use this component before we write it. In the `render()` function of our `App` component, we'll use `Route` like so:

routing/basics/src/complete/App-1.js

```
        <ul>
          <li>
            <a href='/atlantic'>
              <code>/atlantic</code>
            </a>
          </li>
          <li>
            <a href='/pacific'>
              <code>/pacific</code>
            </a>
          </li>
        </ul>

        <hr />

        <Route path='/atlantic' component={Atlantic} />
        <Route path='/pacific' component={Pacific} />
      </div>
    );
```

`Route`, like everything else in React Router, is a component. The supplied `path` prop is matched against the browser's location. If it matches, `Route` will return the component. If not, `Route` will return `null`, rendering nothing.

At the top of the file above `App`, let's write the `Route` component as a stateless function. We'll take a look at the code then break it down:

routing/basics/src/complete/App-1.js

```
import React from 'react';

const Route = ({ path, component }) => {
  const pathname = window.location.pathname;
  if (pathname.match(path)) {
    return (
      React.createElement(component)
    );
  } else {
    return null;
  }
};
```

```
class App extends React.Component {
```

We use the ES6 destructuring syntax to extract our two props, `path` and `component`, from the arguments:

routing/basics/src/complete/App-1.js

```
const Route = ({ path, component }) => {
```

Next, we instantiate the `pathname` variable:

routing/basics/src/complete/App-1.js

```
  const pathname = window.location.pathname;
```

Inside a browser environment, `window.location` is a special object containing the properties of the browser's current location. We grab the `pathname` from this object which is the path of the URL.

Last, if the `path` supplied to `Route` matches the `pathname`, we return the component. Otherwise, we return `null`:

routing/basics/src/complete/App-1.js

```
  if (pathname.match(path)) {
    return (
      React.createElement(component)
    );
  } else {
    return null;
  }
```

While the `Route` that ships with React Router is more complex, this is the component's heart. The component matches `path` against the app's location to determine whether or not the specified component should be rendered.

Let's take a look at the app at this stage.

You can also render components passed as props like this:

```
const Route = ({ pattern, component: Component }) => {
  const pathname = window.location.pathname;
  if (pathname.match(pattern)) {
    return (
      <Component />
    );
```

It's imperative when you do this that the component name is capitalized, which is why we extract the component as `Component` in the arguments. But when a component class is a dynamic variable as it is here, oftentimes React developers prefer to just use `React.createElement()` as opposed to JSX.

Try it out

Save `App.js`. Ensure the Webpack development server is running if it isn't already:

```
$ npm start
```

Head to the browser and visit the app. Notice that we're now rendering the appropriate component when we visit each location:

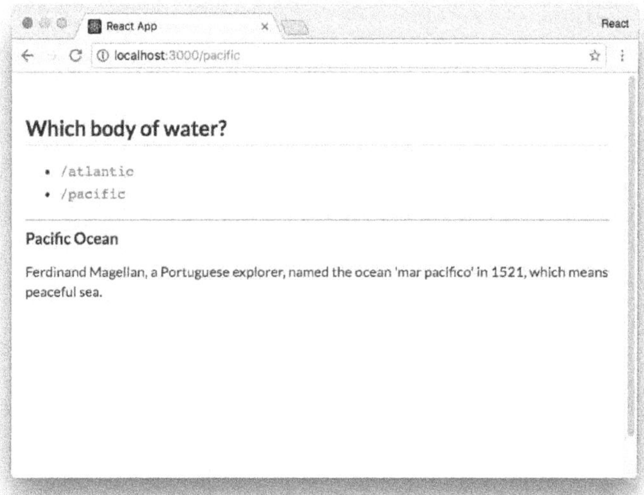

`/pacific` now renders `Pacific`

Our app is responding to some external state, the location of the browser. Each `Route` determines whether its component should be displayed based on the app's location. Note that when the browser visits `/`, neither component matches. The space both `Route` components occupy is left empty.

When we click on a link, we see that the browser is doing a full page load:

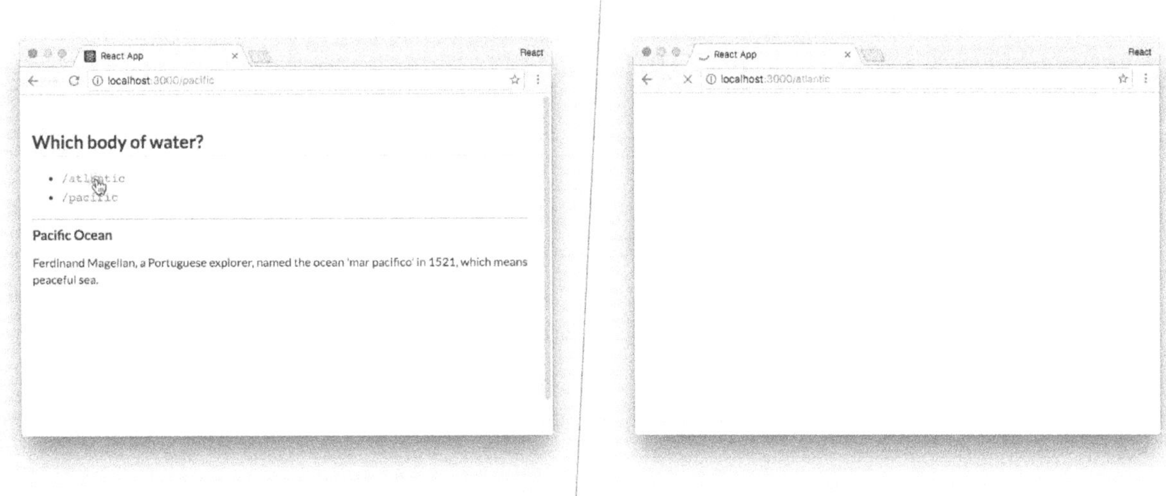

Clicking on `/atlantic` triggers a full page load

By default, our browser makes a fresh request to the Webpack development server every time we click a link. The server returns the `index.html` and our browser needs to perform the work of mounting the React app again.

As highlighted in the intro, this cycle is unnecessary. When switching between `/pacific` and `/atlantic`, there's no need to involve the server. Our client app already has all the components loaded and ready to go. We just need to swap in the `Atlantic` component for the `Pacific` one when clicking on the `/atlantic` link.

What we'd like clicking the links to do is **change the location of the browser without making a web request**. With the location updated, we can re-render our React app and rely on `Route` to appropriately determine which components to render.

To do so, we'll build our own version of another component that ships with React Router.

Building `Link`

In web interfaces, we use HTML `<a>` tags to create links. What we want here is a special type of `<a>` tag. When the user clicks on this tag, we'll want the browser to skip its default routine of making a web request to fetch the next page. Instead, we just want to manually update the browser's location.

Most browsers supply an API for managing the history of the current session, `window.history`. We encourage trying it out in a JavaScript console inside the browser. It has methods like `history.back()` and `history.forward()` that allow you to navigate the history stack. Of immediate interest, it has a method `history.pushState()` which allows you to navigate the browser to a desired location.

For more info on the history API, check out the docs on MDN[74].

The `history` API received some updates with HTML5. To maximize compatibility across browsers, `react-router` interfaces with this API using a library called `History.js`. This `history` package is already included in this project's `package.json`:

routing/basics/package.json

```
    "history": "4.3.0",
```

Let's update our `App.js` file and import the `createBrowserHistory` function from the `history` library. We'll use this function to create an object, called `history`, which we'll use to interact with the browser's history API:

routing/basics/src/complete/App-2.js

```
import React from 'react';

import createHistory from 'history/createBrowserHistory';

const history = createHistory();

const Route = ({ path, component }) => {
```

Let's compose a `Link` component that produces an `<a>` tag with a special `onClick` binding. When the user clicks on the `Link` component, we'll want to prevent the browser from making a request. Instead, we'll use the history API to update the browser's location.

Just like we did with the `Route` component, let's see how we'll use this component before we implement it. Inside of the `render()` function of our `App` component, let's replace the `<a>` tags with our upcoming `Link` component. Rather than using the `href` attribute, we'll specify the desired location of the link with the `to` prop:

[74] https://developer.mozilla.org/en-US/docs/Web/API/History_API

routing/basics/src/complete/App-2.js

```
        <ul>
          <li>
            <Link to='/atlantic'>
              <code>/atlantic</code>
            </Link>
          </li>
          <li>
            <Link to='/pacific'>
              <code>/pacific</code>
            </Link>
          </li>
        </ul>
```

Our `Link` component will be a stateless function that renders an `<a>` tag with an `onClick` handler attribute. Let's see the component in its entirety and then walk through it:

routing/basics/src/complete/App-2.js

```
const Link = ({ to, children }) => (
  <a
    onClick={(e) => {
      e.preventDefault();
      history.push(to);
    }}
    href={to}
  >
    {children}
  </a>
);

class App extends React.Component {
```

Stepping through this:

`onClick`

The `onClick` handler for the `<a>` tag first calls `preventDefault()` on the event object. Recall that the first argument passed to an `onClick` handler is always the event object. Calling `preventDefault()` prevents the browser from making a web request for the new location.

Using the `history.push()` API, we're "pushing" the new location onto the browser's history stack. Doing so will update the location of the app. This will be reflected in the URL bar.

`href`

We set the `href` attribute on the `<a>` tag to the value of the `to` prop.

When a user clicks a traditional `<a>` tag, the browser uses `href` to determine the next location to visit. As we're changing the location manually in our `onClick` handler, the `href` isn't strictly necessary. However, we should always set it anyway. It enables a user to hover over our links and see where they lead or open up links in new tabs:

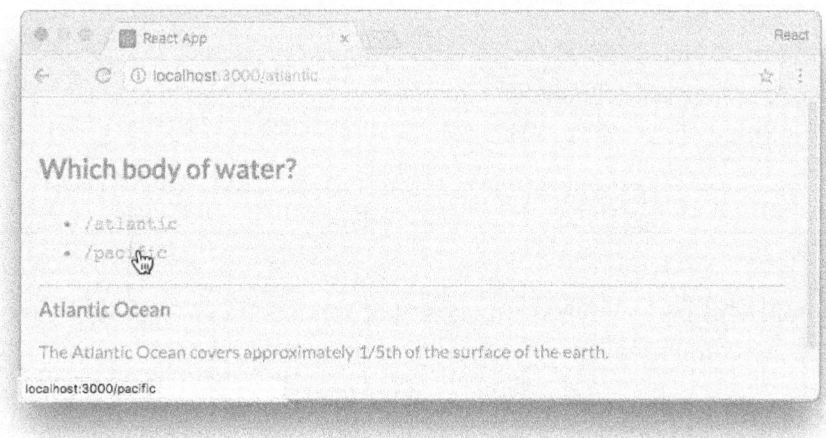

Hovering over a link

`children`

Inside of the `<a>` tag we render the prop `children`. As covered in the chapter "Advanced Component Configuration," the `children` prop is a special prop. It is a reference to all React elements contained inside of our `Link` component. This is the text or HTML that we're turning into a link. In our case, this will be either `<code>/atlantic</code>` or `<code>/pacific</code>`.

With our app using our `Link` component instead of vanilla `<a>` tags, we're modifying the location of the browser without performing a web request whenever the user clicks on one of our links.

If we save and run the app now, we'll see that the functionality isn't quite working as we expect. We can click on the links and the URL bar will update with the new location without refreshing the page, yet our app does not respond to the change:

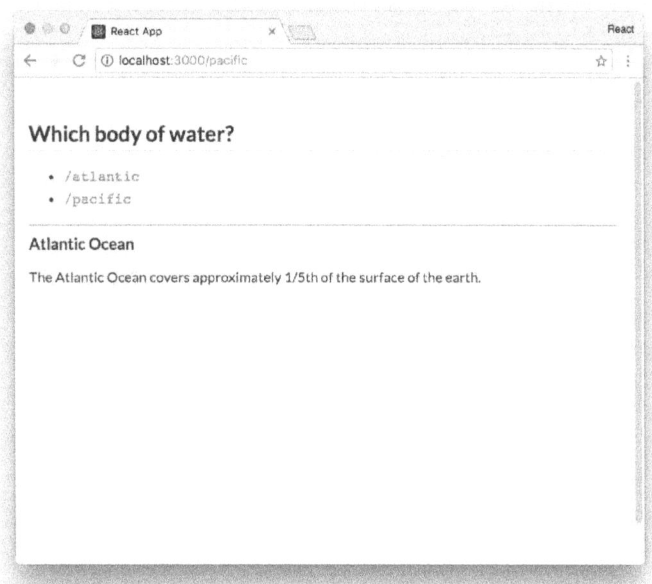

After clicking the link `/pacific`, URL bar says `/pacific` but we still see `Atlantic`

While `Link` is updating the location of the browser, our React app is not alerted of the change. We'll need to trigger our React app to re-render whenever the location changes.

The `history` object provides a `listen()` function which we can use here. We can pass `listen()` a function that it will invoke every time the history stack is modified. We can set up the `listen()` handler inside of `componentDidMount()`, subscribing to `history` with a function that calls `forceUpdate()`:

routing/basics/src/complete/App-2.js

```
class App extends React.Component {
  componentDidMount() {
    history.listen(() => this.forceUpdate());
  }

  render() {
```

When the browser's location changes, this listening function will be invoked, re-rendering `App`. Our `Route` components will then re-render, matching against the latest URL.

Try it out

Let's save our updated `App.js` and visit the app in the browser. Notice that the browser doesn't perform any full page loads as we navigate between the two routes `/pacific` and `/atlantic`!

Even with the tiny size of our app we can enjoy a noticeable performance improvement. Avoiding a full page load saves hundreds of milliseconds and prevents our app from "blinking" during the page change. Given this is a superior user experience now, it's easy to imagine how these benefits scale as the size and complexity of our app does.

Between the `Link` and `Route` components, we're getting an understanding of how we can use a component-driven routing paradigm to make updates to the browser's location and have our app respond to this state change.

We still have two more components to cover: `Redirect` and `Switch`. These will give us even more control over the routing in our app.

Before building these components, however, we'll build a basic version of React Router's `Router` component. `react-router` supplies a `Router` component which is the top-most component in every `react-router` app. As we'll see, it's responsible for triggering re-renders whenever the location changes. It also supplies all of React Router's other components with APIs they can use to both read and modify the browser's location.

Building `Router`

Our basic version of `Router` should do two things:

1. Supply its children with **context** for both `location` and `history`
2. Re-render the app whenever the history changes

Regarding the first requirement, at the moment our `Route` and `Link` components are using two external APIs directly. `Route` uses `window.location` to read the location and `Link` uses `history` to modify the location. `Redirect` will need to access the same APIs. The `Router` supplied by `react-router` makes these APIs available to child components via context. This is a cleaner pattern and means you can easily inject your own `location` or `history` object into your app for testing purposes.

If you need a refresher on context, we cover this React feature in the chapter "Advanced Component Configuration."

Regarding the second requirement, right now `App` subscribes to `history` in `componentDidMount()`. We'll move this responsibility up to `Router`, which will be our app's top-most component.

Let's use `Router` inside `App` before building it. Because we will no longer need to use `componentDidMount()` in `App`, we can turn the component into a stateless function.

At the top of `App`, we'll convert the component to a function, remove `componentDidMount()`, and add the opening tag for `<Router>`:

routing/basics/src/complete/App-3.js

```
const App = () => (
  <Router>
    <div
      className='ui text container'
    >
```

And close both off at the bottom:

routing/basics/src/complete/App-3.js

```
      <Route path='/atlantic' component={Atlantic} />
      <Route path='/pacific' component={Pacific} />
    </div>
  </Router>
);
```

We'll declare Router above App. Let's see what it looks like in full before walking through the component:

routing/basics/src/complete/App-3.js

```
class Router extends React.Component {

  static childContextTypes = {
    history: PropTypes.object,
    location: PropTypes.object,
  };

  constructor(props) {
    super(props);

    this.history = createHistory();
    this.history.listen(() => this.forceUpdate());
  }

  getChildContext() {
    return {
      history: this.history,
      location: window.location,
    };
  }
```

```
  render() {
    return this.props.children;
  }
}
```

Subscribing to `history`

Inside of the constructor for our new `Router` component, we initialize `this.history`. We then subscribe to changes, which is the same thing we did inside the `App` component:

routing/basics/src/complete/App-3.js

```
  constructor(props) {
    super(props);

    this.history = createHistory();
    this.history.listen(() => this.forceUpdate());
  }
```

Exposing context

As we mentioned earlier, we want `Router` to expose two properties to its child components. We can use the context feature of React components. Let's add the two properties we want to pass down, `history` and `location`, to the child context.

In order to expose context to children, we must specify the type of each context. We do that by defining `childContextTypes`.

First, we import the `prop-types` package at the top of the file:

routing/basics/src/complete/App-3.js

```
import PropTypes from 'prop-types';
```

Then we can define `childContextTypes`:

routing/basics/src/complete/App-3.js

```
class Router extends React.Component {

  static childContextTypes = {
    history: PropTypes.object,
    location: PropTypes.object,
  };
```

JavaScript classes: `static`

The line defining `childContextTypes` inside the class is identical to doing this below the class definition:

```
Router.childContextTypes = {
  history: PropTypes.object,
  location: PropTypes.object,
};
```

This keyword allows us to define a property on the class `Router` itself as opposed to instances of `Router`.

Then, in `getChildContext()`, we return the context object:

routing/basics/src/complete/App-3.js

```
  getChildContext() {
    return {
      history: this.history,
      location: window.location,
    };
  }
```

Finally, we render the children wrapped by our new `Router` component in the `render()` function:

routing/basics/src/complete/App-3.js

```
  render() {
    return this.props.children;
  }
```

Because we're initializing `history` inside of `Router`, we can remove the declaration that we had at the top of the file:

routing/basics/src/complete/App-3.js

```
import React from 'react';

import createHistory from 'history/createBrowserHistory';

~~const history = createHistory();~~
```

Since we now have a `Router` component that is passing the `history` and `location` in the context, we can update our `Route` and `Link` components to use these variables from our context.

Let's first tackle the `Route` component. The second argument passed to a stateless functional component is the context object. Rather than using the location on `window.location`, we'll grab `location` from that `context` object in the arguments of the component:

routing/basics/src/complete/App-3.js

```
const Route = ({ path, component }, { location }) => {
  const pathname = location.pathname;
  if (pathname.match(path)) {
    return (
      React.createElement(component)
    );
  } else {
    return null;
  }
};

Route.contextTypes = {
  location: PropTypes.object,
};
```

Below `Route`, we set the property `contextTypes`. Remember, to receive context a component must white-list which parts of the context it should receive.

Let's also update our `Link` component in a similar manner. `Link` can use the `history` property from the context object:

routing/basics/src/complete/App-3.js

```
const Link = ({ to, children }, { history }) => (
  <a
    onClick={(e) => {
      e.preventDefault();
      history.push(to);
    }}
    href={to}
  >
    {children}
  </a>
);

Link.contextTypes = {
  history: PropTypes.object,
};
```

Our app is now wrapped in a `Router` component. While it lacks lots of the features provided by the actual `Router` supplied by `react-router`, it gives us an idea of how the `Router` component works: It supplies location-management APIs to child components and forces the app to re-render when the location changes.

Let's save our updated `App.js` and head to the app in our browser. We see that everything is working exactly as before.

With our `Router` in place, we can now roll our own `Redirect` component that uses `history` from context to manipulate the browser's location.

Building `Redirect`

The `Redirect` component is a cousin of `Link`. Whereas `Link` produces a link that the user can click on to modify the location, `Redirect` will immediately modify the location whenever it is rendered.

Like `Link`, we'll expect this component to be supplied with a `to` prop. And, like `Link`, we'll grab `history` from context and use that object to modify the browser's location.

However, *where* we do this is different. Above `Router`, let's write the `Redirect` component and see how it works:

routing/basics/src/complete/App-4.js

```
class Redirect extends React.Component {

  static contextTypes = {
    history: PropTypes.object,
  }

  componentDidMount() {
    const history = this.context.history;
    const to = this.props.to;
    history.push(to);
  }

  render() {
    return null;
  }
}

class Router extends React.Component {
```

We've placed the `history.push()` *inside* `componentDidMount()`! The moment this component is mounted to the page, it calls out to the `history` API to modify the app's location.

If you're familiar with routing paradigms from other web development frameworks, the `Redirect` component might appear particularly curious. Most developers are used to things like an imperative routing table to handle redirects.

Instead, `react-router` furnishes a *declarative* paradigm consisting of composable components. Here, a `Redirect` is represented as nothing more than a React component. Want to redirect? Just render a `Redirect` component.

Because we're defining `Redirect` as a JavaScript class, we can define `contextTypes` inside the class declaration with `static`.

In the completed version of the app, we saw a third route, `black-sea`. When this location was visited, the app displayed a countdown timer before redirecting to `/`. Let's build this now.

First, we'll add a new `Link` and `Route` for the component that we'll soon define, `BlackSea`:

routing/basics/src/complete/App-4.js

```
      <ul>
        <li>
          <Link to='/atlantic'>
            <code>/atlantic</code>
          </Link>
        </li>
        <li>
          <Link to='/pacific'>
            <code>/pacific</code>
          </Link>
        </li>
        <li>
          <Link to='/black-sea'>
            <code>/black-sea</code>
          </Link>
        </li>
      </ul>

      <hr />

      <Route path='/atlantic' component={Atlantic} />
      <Route path='/pacific' component={Pacific} />
      <Route path='/black-sea' component={BlackSea} />
    </div>
  </Router>
```

Let's go ahead and define `BlackSea` at the bottom of `App.js`.

First, let's implement the counting logic. We'll initialize `state.counter` to `3`. Then, inside `componentDidMount()`, we'll perform the countdown using JavaScript's built-in `setInterval()` function:

routing/basics/src/complete/App-4.js

```
class BlackSea extends React.Component {
  state = {
    counter: 3,
  };

  componentDidMount() {
    this.interval = setInterval(() => (
      this.setState(prevState => {
```

```
        return {
          counter: prevState.counter - 1,
        };
      }
    )), 1000);
  }
```

The `setInterval()` function will decrease `state.counter` by one every second.

Because the state update depends on the current version of state, we're passing `setState()` a *function* as opposed to an *object*. We discuss this technique in the "Advanced Component Configuration" chapter.

We have to remember to clear the interval when the component is unmounted. This is the same strategy we used in the timers app in the second chapter:

routing/basics/src/complete/App-4.js

```
  componentWillUnmount() {
    clearInterval(this.interval);
  }
```

Last, let's focus on the redirect logic. We'll handle the redirect logic inside our `render()` function. When the `render()` function is called, we'll want to check if the counter is less than `1`. If it is, we want to perform a redirect. We do this by including the `Redirect` component in our render output:

routing/basics/src/complete/App-4.js

```
  render() {
    return (
      <div>
        <h3>Black Sea</h3>
        <p>Nothing to sea [sic] here ...</p>
        <p>Redirecting in {this.state.counter}...</p>
        {
          (this.state.counter < 1) ? (
            <Redirect to='/' />
          ) : null
        }
      </div>
    );
  }
}
```

Three seconds after `BlackSea` mounts, our interval function decrements our `state.counter` to `0`. The `setState()` function triggers a re-render of the `BlackSea` component. Its output will include the `Redirect` component. When the `Redirect` component mounts, it will trigger the redirect.

In the `BlackSea` component, we use a ternary operator to control whether or not we render the `Redirect` component. Using ternary operators inside of JSX is common in React. This is because we can't embed multi-line statements like an if/else clause inside our JSX.

This mechanism for triggering a redirect might seem peculiar at first. But this paradigm is powerful. We have complete control of routing by rendering components and passing props. Again, the React Router team prides itself on the fact that the interface to the library is *just React*. As we'll explore more in the second half of the chapter, this property gives us lots of flexibility.

Try it out

With `Redirect` built and in use, let's try it out. Save `App.js`. Visiting `/black-sea` in the browser, we witness the component rendering before it performs the redirect:

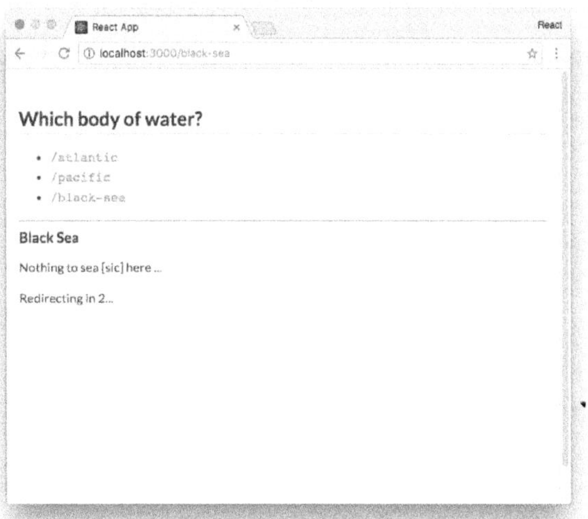

The Black Sea countdown

At this point, we have an understanding of how three of React Router's fundamental components work to read and update the browser's location state. We also see how they work with the context of the top-most `Router` component.

Let's scrap our hand-rolled React Router components and instead use the library's routing components. After doing so, we can explore a couple more features of the `Route` component supplied by `react-router`. Further, we'll see how `Switch` provides one last key piece of functionality.

Using react-router

We'll import the components that we want to use from the react-router package and remove the ones we've written so far.

The react-router *library* encompasses a few different npm *packages* such as react-router-dom and react-router-native. Each corresponds to a supported environment for React. Because we're building a web app, we'll use the react-router-dom npm package.

react-router-dom is already included in this project's package.json.

At the top of our App.js file, remove the import statement for createBrowserHistory. React Router will take care of history management:

```
import React from 'react';
import createHistory from 'history/createBrowserHistory';
```

We'll add an import statement that includes each of the components we want to use. Then, we'll delete all our custom react-router components. All our other components, like App, can remain unchanged:

routing/basics/src/complete/App-5.js

```
import React from 'react';

import {
  BrowserRouter as Router,
  Route,
  Link,
  Redirect,
} from 'react-router-dom'

const App = () => (
```

react-router-dom exports its router under the name BrowserRouter to distinguish it from the routers included in other environments, like NativeRouter. It is common practice to use the alias Router by using the as keyword as we do here.

Save App.js. After this change, we'll see that everything is still working as it was before we switched to using React Router.

More Route

Now that we're using the `react-router` library, our imported `Route` component has several additional features.

So far, we've used the prop `component` to instruct `Route` which component to render when the `path` matches the current location. `Route` also accepts the prop `render`. We can use this prop to define a render function in-line.

To see an example of this, let's add another `Route` declaration to `App`. We'll insert it above the rest of our existing `Route` components. This time, we'll use `render`:

routing/basics/src/complete/App-5.js

```
<Route path='/atlantic/ocean' render={() => (
  <div>
    <h3>Atlantic Ocean — Again!</h3>
    <p>
      Also known as "The Pond."
    </p>
  </div>
)} />
<Route path='/atlantic' component={Atlantic} />
<Route path='/pacific' component={Pacific} />
<Route path='/black-sea' component={BlackSea} />
```

Save `App.js`. If we visit the app at `/atlantic` we see just the `Atlantic` component, as expected:

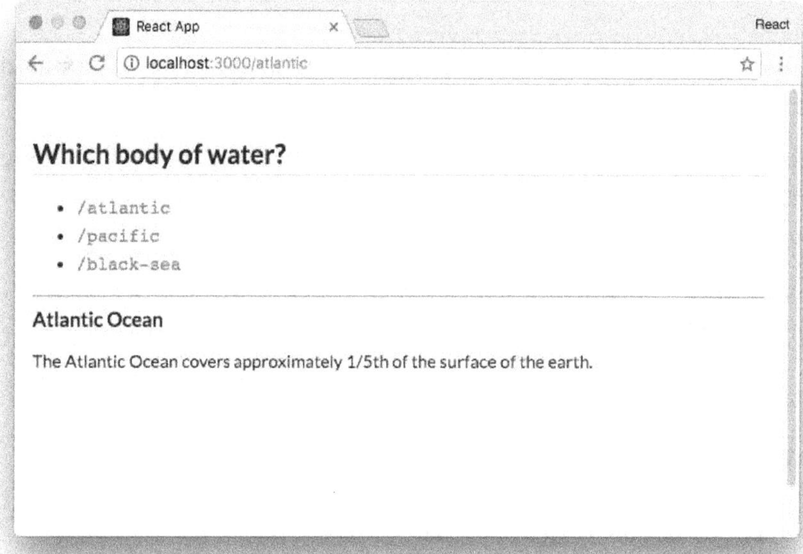

Just `Atlantic` shows on `/atlantic`

What happens if we visit `/atlantic/ocean`? We don't have a `Link` to this path so type it into the address bar. We notice *both* the `Atlantic` component and our new anonymous render function, one stacked atop the other:

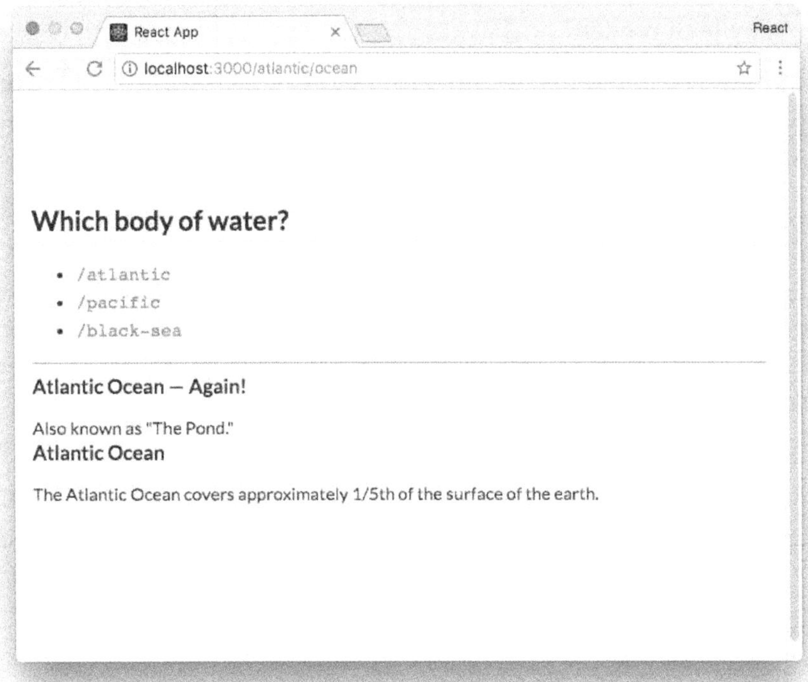

Both Atlantic components appear on `/atlantic/ocean`

Why do we see both components? Because of how `Route` matches `path` against the location. Recall that our `Route` component performed the match like this:

routing/basics/src/complete/App-1.js

```
  if (pathname.match(path)) {
```

Consider how that behaves:

```
const routePath = '/atlantic';

let browserPath = '/atl';
browserPath.match(routePath); // -> no match

browserPath = '/atlantic';
browserPath.match(routePath); // -> matches

browserPath = '/atlantic/ocean'
browserPath.match(routePath); // -> matches
```

Therefore, both `Route` declarations for our two Atlantic components match the location `/atlantic/ocean`. So they both render.

We hadn't observed this behavior of `Route` up until now. But given how `Route` works, this behavior makes sense. **Any number of components might match a given location and they will all render.** `Route` does not impose any kind of exclusivity.

Sometimes, this behavior is undesirable. We'll see a strategy for managing this a bit later.

The example above and our implementation of pathname matching are not strictly accurate. As you might expect, `Route` matches against the *start* of the pathname. Therefore, `/atlantic/ocean/pacific` will *not* match for the component `Pacific` even though that path contains the `/pacific` substring.

With this behavior in mind, what if we wanted to add a component that renders when the user visits the root (/)? It would be nice to have some text that instructs the user to click on one of the links.

We now know that a solution like this would be problematic:

routing/basics/src/complete/App-5.js

```
        {/* This solution is problematic */}
        <Route path='/' render={() => (
          <h3>
            Welcome! Select a body of saline water above.
          </h3>
        )} />
```

Given that `/` matches paths like `/atlantic` and `/pacific`, this component would render on every page of the app:

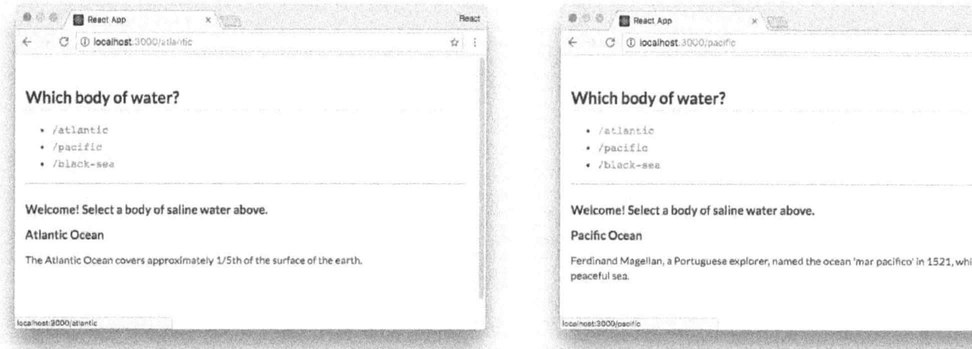

The `Route` for `/` matches every location

This behavior is not quite what we want. By adding the prop `exact` to the `Route` component, we can specify that the path must **exactly** match the location. Add the `Route` for `/` now:

routing/basics/src/complete/App-6.js

```
      <Route path='/atlantic/ocean' render={() => (
        <div>
          <h3>Atlantic Ocean — Again!</h3>
          <p>
            Also known as "The Pond."
          </p>
        </div>
      )} />
      <Route path='/atlantic' component={Atlantic} />
      <Route path='/pacific' component={Pacific} />
      <Route path='/black-sea' component={BlackSea} />

      <Route exact path='/' render={() => (
        <h3>
          Welcome! Select a body of saline water above.
        </h3>
      )} />
```

We're using some JSX syntactic sugar here. While we could set the prop explicitly like this:

```
<Route exact={true} path='/' render={() => (
  // ...
)}
```

In JSX, if the prop is listed but not assigned to a value it defaults the value to `true`.

Try it out

Save `App.js`. Visiting `/` in our browser, we see our welcome component. Importantly, the welcome component does not appear on any other path:

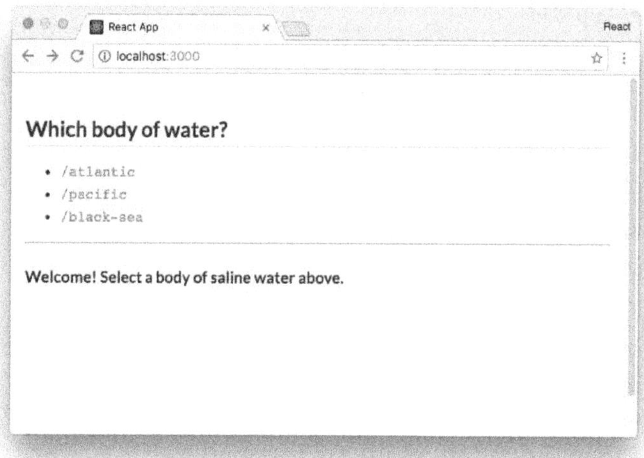

We welcome the user at /

We now have a proper handler for when the user visits `/`.

The `Route` component is a powerful yet simple way to declare which components we'd like to appear on which routes. However, `Route` alone has some limitations:

1. As we saw earlier with the route `/atlantic/ocean`, we'll often want only one `Route` to match a given path.
2. Furthermore, we don't yet have a strategy for handling the situation where a user visits a location that our app doesn't specify a match for.

To work around these, we can wrap our `Route` components in a **`Switch`** component.

Using `Switch`

When `Route` components are wrapped in a `Switch` component, only the first matching `Route` will be displayed.

This means we can use `Switch` to overcome the two limitations we've witnessed so far with `Route`:

1. When the user visits `/atlantic/ocean`, the first `Route` will match and the subsequent `Route` matching `/atlantic` will be ignored.
2. We can include a catch-all `Route` at the bottom of our `Switch` container. If none of the other `Route` components match, this component will be rendered.

Let's see this in practice.

In order to use the `Switch` component, let's import the `Switch` component from `react-router`:

routing/basics/src/complete/App-7.js

```
import React from 'react';

import {
  BrowserRouter as Router,
  Route,
  Link,
  Redirect,
  Switch,
} from 'react-router-dom'

const App = () => (
```

We'll wrap all of our `Route` components in a `Switch` component. Add the opening `Switch` component tag above the first `Route`:

routing/basics/src/complete/App-7.js

```
      <hr />
      <Switch>
        <Route path='/atlantic/ocean' render={() => (
```

Next, we'll add our "catch-all" `Route` beneath our existing `Route` components. Because we don't specify a `path` prop, this `Route` will match every path:

routing/basics/src/complete/App-7.js

```
        <Route exact path='/' render={() => (
          <h3>
            Welcome! Select a body of saline water above.
          </h3>
        )} />

        <Route render={({ location }) => (
          <div className='ui inverted red segment'>
            <h3>
              Error! No matches for <code>{location.pathname}</code>
            </h3>
          </div>
        )} />
      </Switch>
    </div>
```

```
  </Router>
);
```

`Route` passes the prop `location` to the render function. `Route` always passes this prop to its target. We'll explore this more in the second half of this chapter.

Try it out

Save `App.js`. Visit `/atlantic/ocean` and note that the component matching `/atlantic` is gone. Next, manually enter a path for the app that doesn't exist. Our catch-all `Route` component will render:

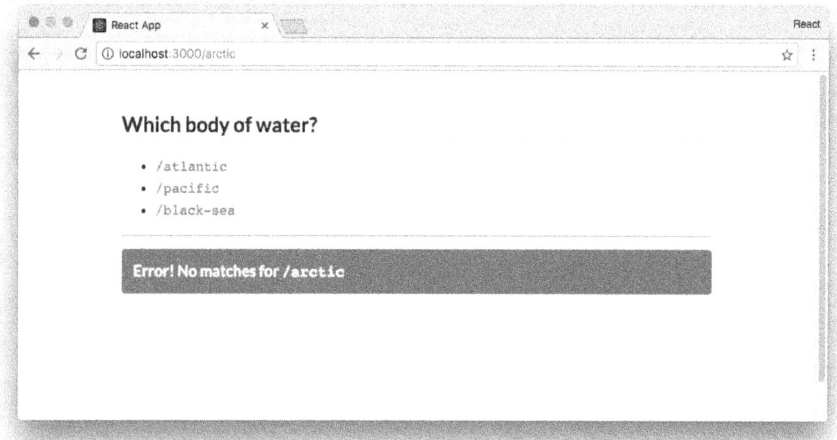

No matches for `/arctic`

At this point, we're familiar with React Router's fundamental components. We wrap our app in `Router`, which supplies any React Router components in the tree with location and history APIs and ensures our React app is re-rendered whenever the location is changed. `Route` and `Switch` both help us control what React components are displayed at a given location. And `Link` and `Redirect` give us the ability to modify the location of the app without a full page load.

In the second half of this chapter, we'll apply these fundamentals to a more complex application.

Dynamic routing with React Router

In this section, we'll build off the foundations established in the last. We'll see how React Router's fundamental components work together inside of a slightly larger app, and explore a few different strategies for programming in its unique component-driven routing paradigm.

The app in this section has multiple pages. The app's main page has a vertical menu where the user can choose between five different music albums. Choosing an album immediately shows album information in the main panel. All album information is pulled from Spotify's API[75].

The server that our React app communicates with is protected by a token that requires a login. While not a genuine authentication flow, the setup will give us a feel for how to use React Router inside of an application that requires users to login.

The completed app

The code for this section is inside `routing/music`. From the root of the book's code folder, navigate to that directory:

```
$ cd routing/music
```

Let's take a look at this project's structure:

```
$ ls
SpotifyClient.js
client/
nightwatch.json
package.json
server.js
server.test.js
start-client.js
start-server.js
tests/
```

In the root of the project is a Node API server (`server.js`). Inside `client` is a React app powered by create-react-app:

```
$ ls client
package.json
public/
semantic/
semantic.json
src/
```

[75] https://developer.spotify.com/web-api/

This project's structure is identical to the food lookup app at the end of the chapter "Using Webpack with create-react-app." When in development, we boot two servers: `server.js` and the Webpack development server. The Webpack development server will serve our React app. Our React app interfaces with `server.js` to fetch data about a given album. `server.js`, in turn, communicates with the Spotify API to get the album data:

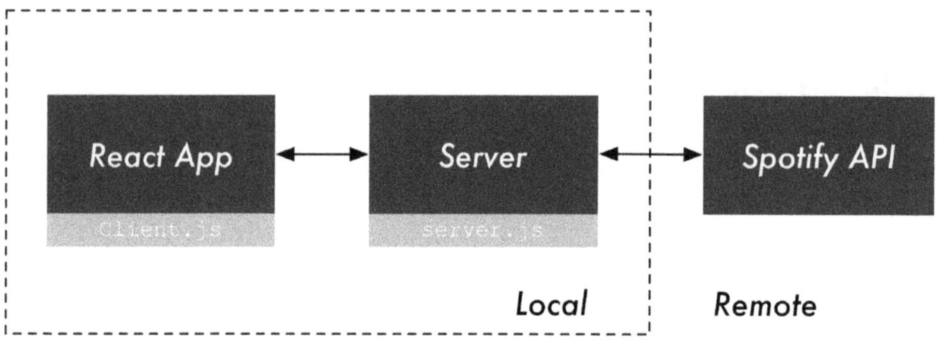

Communication diagram

Let's install the dependencies and see the running app. We have two `package.json` files, one for `server.js` and one for the React app. We'll run `npm i` for both:

```
$ npm i
$ cd client
$ npm i
$ cd ..
```

We can boot the app with `npm start` in the top-level directory. This uses Concurrently to boot both servers simultaneously:

```
$ npm start
```

Find the app at `http://localhost:3000`.

The app will prompt you with a login button. Click login to "login." We are not prompted for a user name or password.

After logging in, we can see a list of albums in a vertical side menu:

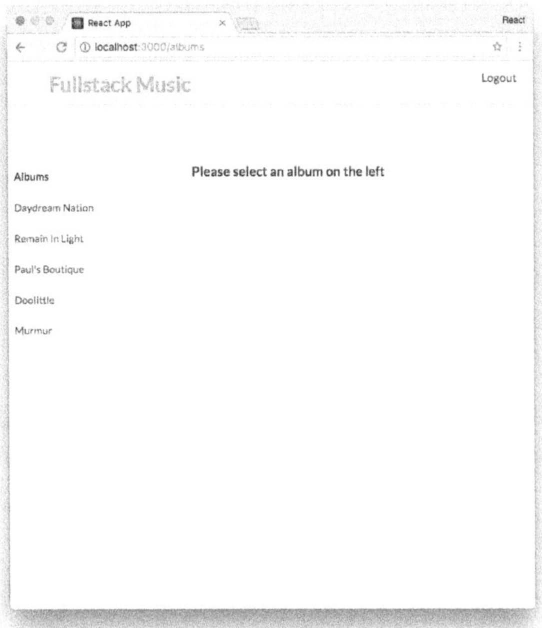

Clicking on one of these albums displays it to the right of the vertical side menu. Furthermore, the URL of the app is updated:

The URL follows the scheme `/albums/:albumId` where `:albumId` is the **dynamic part** of the URL.

Clicking the "Logout" button in the top right, we're redirected to the login page at `/login`. If we try to manually navigate back to /albums by typing that address into the URL bar, we are prevented from reaching that page. Instead, we are redirected back to /login.

Before digging into the React app, let's take a look at the server's API.

The server's API

POST /api/login

The server provides an endpoint for retrieving an API token, /api/login. This token is required for the endpoint /api/albums.

Unlike a real-world login endpoint, the /api/login endpoint does not require a user name or a password. server.js will always return a hard-coded API token when this endpoint is requested. That hard-coded token is a variable inside server.js:

routing/music/server.js

```
// A fake API token our server validates
export const API_TOKEN = 'D6W69PRgCoDKgHZGJmRUNA';
```

To test this endpoint yourself, with the server running you can use curl to make a POST request to that endpoint:

```
$ curl -X POST http://localhost:3001/api/login
{
  "success": true,
  "token": "D6W69PRgCoDKgHZGJmRUNA"
}
```

The React app stores this API token in localStorage. React will include this token in all subsequent requests to the API. Clicking the "Logout" button in the app removes the token from React and localStorage. The user will have to "login" again to access the app.

We interact with both the API and localStorage using the Client library declared in client/src/Client.js. We discuss this library more later.

The `localStorage` API allows you to read and write to a key-value store in the user's browser. You can store items to `localStorage` with `setItem()`:

```
localStorage.setItem('gas', 'pop');
```

And retrieve them later with `getItem()`:

```
localStorage.getItem('gas');
// => 'pop'
```

Note that items stored in `localStorage` have no expiry.

Security and client-side API tokens

Security on the web is a huge topic. And managing client-side API tokens is a delicate task. To build a truly secure web application, it's important to understand the intricacies of the topic. Unfortunately, it's far too easy to miss subtle practices which can end up leaving giant security holes in your implementation.

While using `localStorage` to store client-side API tokens works fine for hobby projects, there are significant risks. Your users' API tokens are exposed to cross-site scripting attacks. And tokens stored in `localStorage` impose no requirement on their safe transfer. If someone on your development team accidentally inserts code that makes requests over `http` as opposed to `https`, your tokens will be transferred over the wire exposed.

As a developer, you are obligated to be careful and deliberate when users entrust you with sensitive data. There are strategies you can use to protect your app and your users, like using JSON Web Tokens (JWTs) or cookies or both. Should you find yourself in this fortunate position, take the necessary time to carefully research and implement your token management solution.

GET `/api/albums`

The `/api/albums` endpoint returns data supplied by the Spotify API for a given list of albums. We supply the endpoint with a query parameter, `ids`, which we set to the list of desired album IDs:

```
/api/albums?ids=<id1>,<id2>
```

Note that IDs are comma-separated.

This endpoint also expects the API token to be included as the query param `token`. Including both the `ids` and `token` query params looks like this:

```
/api/albums?ids=<id1>,<id2>&token=<token>
```

Here's an example of querying the `/api/albums` endpoint with `curl`:

```
$ curl -X GET \
"http://localhost:3001/api/albums"\
"?ids=1DWWb4Q39mp1T3NgyscowF,2ANVost0y2y52ema1E9xAZ"\
"&token=D6W69PRgCoDKgHZGJmRUNA"
```

In bash, the \ character allows us to split our command over multiple lines. Strings can be split over multiple lines in a similar manner:

```
$ echo "part1"\
"part2"
-> part1part2
```

We do this above for readability. Importantly, there is no whitespace between the " and \ characters. Furthermore, `"part2"` does not have any whitespace ahead of it. If there was any whitespace, the strings would not concatenate properly.

If you're using Windows, you can just write this command as a single line.

The information for each album is extensive, so we refrain from including an example response here.

Starting point of the app

The completed components and the steps we take to get to them are located under `client/src/components-complete`. We'll be writing all the code for the rest of this chapter in `client/src/components`.

Touring around the existing code, our first stop is `index.js`. Check out its `import` statements:

routing/music/client/src/index.js

```
import React from "react";
import ReactDOM from "react-dom";

import { BrowserRouter as Router } from "react-router-dom";

import App from './components/App';

import "./styles/index.css";
import "./semantic-dist/semantic.css";

// [STEP 1] Comment out this line:
import './index-complete';
```

Note that we're importing `Router` here.

Like the last project, `index.js` includes `index-complete.js` which allows us to traverse each iteration of `App` inside `components/complete`. Let's comment out that import statement:

```
// [STEP 1] Comment out this line:
// import './index-complete';
```

Then, at the bottom of `index.js`, un-comment the call to `ReactDOM.render()`. Note that we wrap `<App>` in `<Router>`:

```
// [STEP 2] Un-comment these lines:
ReactDOM.render(
  <Router>
    <App />
  </Router>,
  document.getElementById("root")
);
```

Wrapping your `App` in `index.js` with `<Router>` is a common pattern for React Router apps.

Save `index.js`. With our development server still running, we'll see that our starting point is a stripped-down interface:

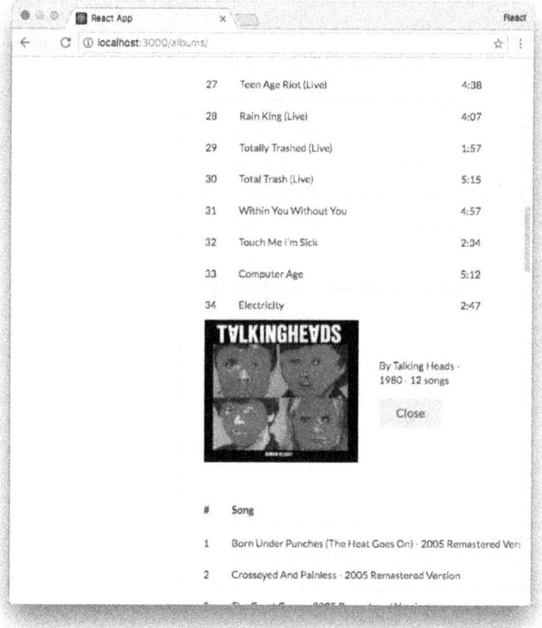

Initial App

Our starting point doesn't use React Router at all. The app lists out all the albums on one page. There is a "Logout" button and clicking it changes the URL but doesn't appear to do anything else. The "Close" buttons don't work either.

Next, let's take a look at `App.js`:

routing/music/client/src/components/App.js

```
import React from 'react';

import TopBar from './TopBar';
import AlbumsContainer from './AlbumsContainer';

import '../styles/App.css';

const App = () => (
  <div className='ui grid'>
    <TopBar />
    <div className='spacer row' />
    <div className='row'>
      <AlbumsContainer />
    </div>
  </div>
);
```

```
export default App;
```

App renders both our TopBar and AlbumsContainer.

As always, the div and className elements throughout the app are present just for structure and styling. As in other projects, this app uses SemanticUI[76].

We won't look at TopBar right now.

AlbumsContainer is the component that interfaces with our API to fetch the data for the albums. It then renders Album components for each album.

At the top of AlbumsContainer, we define our import statements. We also have a hard-coded list of ALBUM_IDS that AlbumsContainer uses to fetch the desired albums from the API:

routing/music/client/src/components/AlbumsContainer.js

```
import React, { Component } from 'react';

import Album from './Album';
import { client } from '../Client';

const ALBUM_IDS = [
  '23O4F21GDWiGd33tFN3ZgI',
  '3AQgdwMNCiN7awXch5fAaG',
  '1kmyirVya5fRxdjsPFDM05',
  '6ymZBbRSmzAvoSGmwAFoxm',
  '4Mw9Gcu1LT7JaipXdwrq1Q',
];
```

AlbumsContainer is a stateful component with two state properties:

- fetched: Whether or not AlbumsContainer has successfully fetched the album data from the API yet
- albums: An array of all the album objects

Stepping through the component, we'll start with its initial state:

[76] http://semantic-ui.com

routing/music/client/src/components/AlbumsContainer.js

```
class AlbumsContainer extends Component {
  state = {
    fetched: false,
    albums: [],
  };
```

We use the `fetched` boolean to keep track of whether or not the albums have been retrieved from the server.

After our `AlbumsContainer` component mounts, we call the `this.getAlbums()` function. This populates the `albums` in state:

routing/music/client/src/components/AlbumsContainer.js

```
  componentDidMount() {
    this.getAlbums();
  }
```

In our `getAlbums()` function, we use the `Client` library (inside `src/Client.js`) to make a request to the API to grab the data for the albums specified in `ALBUM_IDS`. We use the method `getAlbums()` from the library, which expects as an argument an array of album IDs.

When we get the data back, we update the state to set `fetched` to `true` and `albums` to the result:

routing/music/client/src/components/AlbumsContainer.js

```
  getAlbums = () => {
    client.setToken('D6W69PRgCoDKgHZGJmRUNA');
    client.getAlbums(ALBUM_IDS)
      .then((albums) => (
        this.setState({
          fetched: true,
          albums: albums,
        })
      ));
  };
```

We introduce Fetch and promises in the chapter "Components & Servers."

Notice that before calling `client.getAlbums()` we call `client.setToken()`. As mentioned earlier, our API expects a token in the request to `/api/albums`. Since we don't yet have the login and logout functionality implemented in the app, we cheat by setting the token manually before making our request. This is the same token expected by `server.js`:

routing/music/server.js

```
export const API_TOKEN = 'D6W69PRgCoDKgHZGJmRUNA';
```

Finally, the `render` method for `AlbumsContainer` switches on `this.state.fetched`. If the data has yet to be fetched, we render the loading icon. Otherwise, we render all the albums in `this.state.albums`:

routing/music/client/src/components/AlbumsContainer.js

```
  render() {
    if (!this.state.fetched) {
      return (
        <div className='ui active centered inline loader' />
      );
    } else {
      return (
        <div className='ui two column divided grid'>
          <div
            className='ui six wide column'
            style={{ maxWidth: 250 }}
          >
            {/* VerticalMenu will go here */}
          </div>
          <div className='ui ten wide column'>
            {
              this.state.albums.map((a) => (
                <div
                  className='row'
                  key={a.id}
                >
                  <Album album={a} />
                </div>
              ))
            }
          </div>
        </div>
      );
    }
  }
```

Our first update will be to add the vertical menu that we saw in the completed version of the app. This vertical menu should allow us to choose which album we'd like to view. When an album in the vertical menu is selected, the album should be displayed and the location of the app updated to `/albums/:albumId`.

Using URL params

At the moment, our `App` component is rendering both `TopBar` and `AlbumsContainer`:

routing/music/client/src/components/App.js

```
const App = () => (
  <div className='ui grid'>
    <TopBar />
    <div className='spacer row' />
    <div className='row'>
      <AlbumsContainer />
    </div>
  </div>
);
```

As we saw, we'll eventually have login and logout pages. We can keep `TopBar` in `App` as we want `TopBar` to appear on every page. Since we want the album listing page to appear on a route, we should nest `AlbumsContainer` inside a `Route`. We'll have it only render at the location `/albums`. This will prepare us for adding `/login` and `/logout` soon.

First, inside `App.js`, let's import the `Route` component:

routing/music/client/src/components-complete/App-1.js

```
import React from 'react';

import { Route } from 'react-router-dom';
```

Then, we'll use `Route` on the path `/albums`:

routing/music/client/src/components-complete/App-1.js

```
const App = () => (
  <div className='ui grid'>
    <TopBar />
    <div className='spacer row' />
    <div className='row'>
      <Route path='/albums' component={AlbumsContainer} />
    </div>
  </div>
);
```

Now, `AlbumsContainer` will only render when we visit the app at `/albums`.

We'll have `AlbumsContainer` render a child component, `VerticalMenu`. We'll have the parent (`AlbumsContainer`) pass the child (`VerticalMenu`) the list of `albums`. Let's first compose `VerticalMenu` and then we'll update `AlbumsContainer` to use it.

Open the file `src/components/VerticalMenu.js`. The current file contains the scaffold for the component:

routing/music/client/src/components/VerticalMenu.js

```
import React from 'react';

import '../styles/VerticalMenu.css';

const VerticalMenu = ({ albums }) => (
  <div className='ui secondary vertical menu'>
    <div className='header item'>
      Albums
    </div>
    {/* Render album menu here */}
  </div>
);

export default VerticalMenu;
```

As we can see, `VerticalMenu` expects the prop `albums`. We want to iterate over the `albums` prop, rendering a `Link` for each album. First, we'll import `Link` from `react-router`:

routing/music/client/src/components-complete/VerticalMenu-1.js

```
import React from 'react';

import { Link } from 'react-router-dom';

import '../styles/VerticalMenu.css';
```

We'll use `map` to compose our list of `Link` components. The `to` prop for each `Link` will be `/albums/:albumId`:

routing/music/client/src/components-complete/VerticalMenu-1.js

```
const VerticalMenu = ({ albums }) => (
  <div className='ui secondary vertical menu'>
    <div className='header item'>
      Albums
    </div>
    {
      albums.map((album) => (
        <Link
          to={`/albums/${album.id}`}
          className='item'
          key={album.id}
        >
          {album.name}
        </Link>
      ))
    }
  </div>
);
```

We set the `className` to `item` for styling. We're using SemanticUI's vertical menu.

`VerticalMenu` will now update the location of the app whenever the user clicks on one of its menu items. Let's update `AlbumsContainer` to both use `VerticalMenu` and render a single album based on the location of the app.

Open `src/components/AlbumsContainer.js`. Add `VerticalMenu` to the list of imports:

```
import Album from './Album';
import VerticalMenu from './VerticalMenu';
import { client } from '../Client';
```

Then, inside the `render` method, we'll add `VerticalMenu` nested inside a column:

routing/music/client/src/components-complete/AlbumsContainer-1.js

```
  render() {
    if (!this.state.fetched) {
      return (
        <div className='ui active centered inline loader' />
      );
    } else {
      return (
        <div className='ui two column divided grid'>
          <div
            className='ui six wide column'
            style={{ maxWidth: 250 }}
          >
            <VerticalMenu
              albums={this.state.albums}
            />
          </div>
          <div className='ui ten wide column'>
```

> Because `VerticalMenu` does not need full album objects, it would indeed be cleaner to pass the component subset objects that look like this:
>
> ```
> [{ name: 'Madonna', id: '1DWWb4Q39mp1T3NgyscowF' }]
> ```
>
> This would also make `VerticalMenu` more flexible, as we could write it such that it can be a side menu for any list of items.

In the output for `AlbumsContainer`, in the column adjacent to `VerticalMenu`, we want to render a single album now as opposed to a list of all of them. We know that `VerticalMenu` is going to modify the location according to the scheme `/albums/:albumId`. We can use a `Route` component to match against this pattern and extract the parameter `:albumId` from the URL.

Still in `AlbumsContainer.js`, first add `Route` to the component's imports:

routing/music/client/src/components-complete/AlbumsContainer-1.js

```
import React, { Component } from 'react';

import { Route } from 'react-router-dom';
```

Then, inside `render` in the `div` tags below `VerticalMenu`, we'll replace the `map` call that renders all the albums. Instead, we'll define a `Route` component with a `render` prop. We'll take a look at it in full then break it down:

routing/music/client/src/components-complete/AlbumsContainer-1.js

```
        <div className='ui ten wide column'>
          <Route
            path='/albums/:albumId'
            render={({ match }) => {
              const album = this.state.albums.find(
                (a) => a.id === match.params.albumId
              );
              return (
                <Album
                  album={album}
                />
              );
            }}
          />
        </div>
```

`path`

The string we're matching against is `/albums/:albumId`. The `:` is how we indicate to React Router that this part of the URL is a **dynamic parameter**. Importantly, **any value** will match this dynamic parameter.

`render`

We set a `render` prop on this `Route` to a function. `Route` invokes the render function with a few arguments, like `match`. We explore `match` more in a bit. Here, we're interested in the **`params`** property on `match`.

`Route` extracts all the dynamic parameters from the URL and passes them to the target component inside the object `match.params`. In our case, `params` will contain the property `albumId` which will correspond to the value of the `:albumId` part of the current URL (`/albums/:albumId`).

We use `find` to get the album that matches `params.albumId`, rendering a single `Album`.

The user can now modify the location of the app with the links in `VerticalMenu`. And `AlbumsContainer` uses `Route` to read the location and extract the desired `albumId`, rendering the desired album.

Try it out

Save `AlbumsContainer.js`. If the app isn't still running, be sure to boot it from the top-level directory using the `npm start` command:

```
$ npm start
```

Currently only the `TopBar` will be visible when we visit `http://localhost:3000` in our browser:

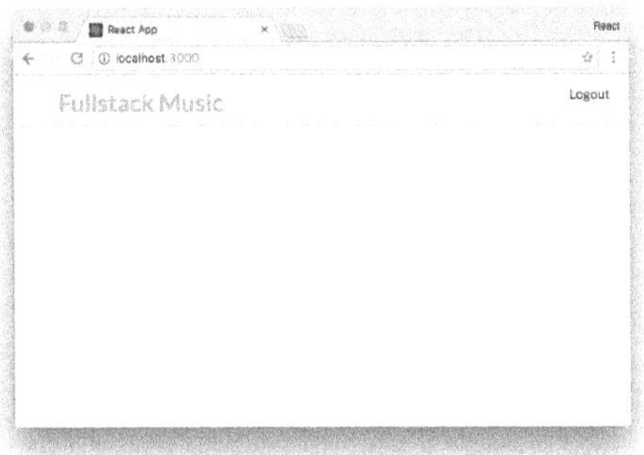

Nothing matches at /

Recall that in `App` we wrapped `AlbumsContainer` in a `Route` for the pattern `/albums`. It doesn't match `/`, so the body of `App` remains empty.

Let's manually visit the `/albums` path by typing it in the browser URL bar and we'll see our `VerticalMenu` rendered:

`VerticalMenu` appears

Nothing is rendered in the column adjacent to `VerticalMenu` as that column is awaiting a URL matching `/albums/:albumId`. Clicking on one of the albums changes the location of the app:

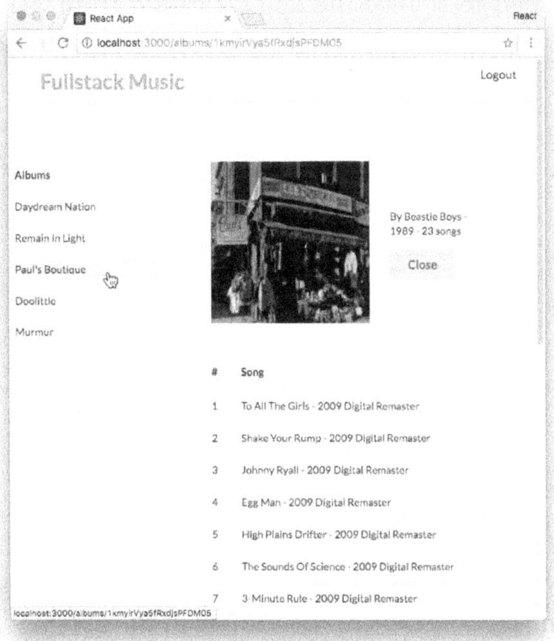

Selecting an album

We're getting somewhere! While the "Close" and "Logout" buttons still don't work, we can switch between albums. The app's location updates without refreshing the page.

Let's wire up the "Close" button next.

Propagating pathnames as props

Inside `Album.js`, we render a "Close" button inside the album's header:

routing/music/client/src/components-complete/Album-1.js

```
        <div className='six wide column'>
          <p>
            {
              `By ${album.artist.name}
              - ${album.year}
              - ${album.tracks.length} songs`
            }
          </p>
          <div
            className='ui left floated large button'
          >
            Close
          </div>
```

To “close” the album, we need to change the app’s location from `/albums/:albumId` to `/albums`. Knowing what we know about routing through this point, we could create a link to handle this behavior for us, like this:

```
// Valid "close" button
<Link
  to='/albums'
  className='ui left floated large button'
>
  Close
</Link>
```

This is perfectly valid. However, one consideration we have to make as we add routing to our apps is flexibility.

For example, what if we wanted to modify the app so that our albums page existed on `/` and not `/albums`? We’d have to change all references to `/albums` in the app.

More compelling, what if we wanted to display an album in different locations within the app? For example, we might add artist pages at `/artists/:artistId`. The user can then drill down to an individual album, opening the URL `/artists/:artistId/albums/:albumId`. We’d want a “Close” button in this situation to link to `/artists/:artistId`, not `/albums`.

A simple way to maintain some flexibility is to pass pathnames through the app as props. Let’s see this in action.

Recall that inside `App.js`, we specify the path for `AlbumsContainer` is `/albums`:

routing/music/client/src/components-complete/App-1.js

```
      <Route path='/albums' component={AlbumsContainer} />
```

We just saw that `Route` invokes a function passed as a `render` prop with the argument `match`. `Route` also sets this prop on components rendered via the `component` prop. Regardless of how `Route` renders its component, it will always set three props:

- `match`
- `location`
- `history`

According to the React Router docs[77], the `match` object contains the following properties:

[77] https://reacttraining.com/react-router/web/api/Route

- `params` - (object) Key/value pairs parsed from the URL corresponding to the dynamic segments of the path
- `isExact` - true if the entire URL was matched (no trailing characters)
- `path` - (string) The path pattern used to match. Useful for building nested `<Route>`s
- `url` - (string) The matched portion of the URL. Useful for building nested `<Link>`s

Of interest to us is the property `path`. Inside `AlbumsContainer`, `this.props.match.path` will be `/albums`.

We can update the `Route` inside `AlbumsContainer` that wraps `Album`. Before, the `path` prop was `/albums/:albumId`. We can replace the root of the path (`/albums`) with the variable `this.props.match.path`.

First, let's declare a new variable, `matchPath`:

routing/music/client/src/components-complete/AlbumsContainer-2.js

```
  render() {
    if (!this.state.fetched) {
      return (
        <div className='ui active centered inline loader' />
      );
    } else {
      const matchPath = this.props.match.path;
```

Then, we can change the `path` prop on `Route` to use this variable:

routing/music/client/src/components-complete/AlbumsContainer-2.js

```
          <div className='ui ten wide column'>
            <Route
              path={`${matchPath}/:albumId`}
              render={({ match }) => {
                const album = this.state.albums.find(
                  (a) => a.id === match.params.albumId
                );
                return (
```

With this approach, `AlbumsContainer` doesn't make any assumptions about its location. We could, for example, update `App` so that `AlbumsContainer` matches at `/` instead of `/albums` and `AlbumsContainer` would need no changes.

We want the "Close" button in `Album` to link to this same path. "Closing" an album means changing the location back to `/albums`. Let's propagate the prop down to `Album`:

routing/music/client/src/components-complete/AlbumsContainer-2.js

```
            return (
              <Album
                album={album}
                albumsPathname={matchPath}
              />
            );
```

Then, inside `Album.js` we can extract the `albumsPathname` from the props object:

routing/music/client/src/components-complete/Album.js

```
const Album = ({ album, albumsPathname }) => (
```

Now, we can change the `div` element to a `Link` component. We'll set the `to` prop to `albumsPathname`:

routing/music/client/src/components-complete/Album.js

```
        <div className='six wide column'>
          <p>
            {
              `By ${album.artist.name}
              - ${album.year}
              - ${album.tracks.length} songs`
            }
          </p>
          <Link
            to={albumsPathname}
            className='ui left floated large button'
          >
            Close
          </Link>
```

Let's apply the same approach to `VerticalMenu`. Switch back to `AlbumsContainer.js`. We'll pass `VerticalMenu` the prop `albumsPathname`:

routing/music/client/src/components-complete/AlbumsContainer-2.js

```
          <div
            className='ui six wide column'
            style={{ maxWidth: 250 }}
          >
            <VerticalMenu
              albums={this.state.albums}
              albumsPathname={matchPath}
            />
          </div>
```

Now we can use this prop to compose the `to` attribute for `Link`:

routing/music/client/src/components-complete/VerticalMenu-2.js

```
const VerticalMenu = ({ albums, albumsPathname }) => (
  <div className='ui secondary vertical menu'>
    <div className='header item'>
      Albums
    </div>
    {
      albums.map((album) => (
        <Link
          to={`${albumsPathname}/${album.id}`}
          className='item'
          key={album.id}
        >
          {album.name}
        </Link>
      ))
    }
  </div>
);
```

By isolating the number of places we specify pathnames we make our app more flexible for routing changes in the future. With this update, the only place in our app where we specify the path `/albums` is in `App`.

Try it out

Save `Album.js`. With the app running, visit `/albums`. Clicking on an album opens it. Clicking on "Close" closes it by changing the location back to `/albums`.

With the "Close" button working, there's an interface improvement we can make before moving on to implementing login and logout.

When an album is open, it would be nice if the sidebar indicated which album was active:

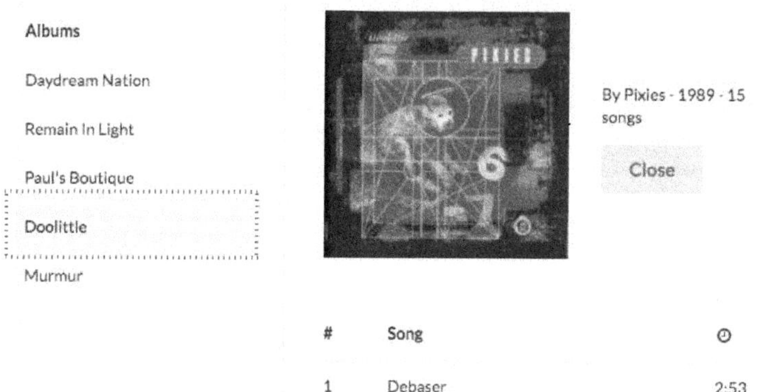

`VerticalMenu` indicating which album is active with a light highlight

We'll solve this next.

Dynamic menu items with `NavLink`

At the moment, all the menu items in our vertical menu have the class `item`. In SemanticUI's vertical menus, we can set the class of the active item to `active item` to have it show up as highlighted.

How will we know if an album is "active"? This state is maintained in the URL. If the album's `id` matches that of `:albumId` in the URL, we'd know that album was active.

Given this, we could drum up the following solution:

```
albums.map((album) => {
  const to = `${albumsPathname}/${album.id}`;
  const active = window.location.pathname === to;
  <Link
    to={to}
    className={active ? 'active item' : 'item'}
    key={album.id}
  >
    {album.name}
  </Link>
})
```

We grab the URL's pathname through the browser's `window.location` API. If the browser's location matches that of the link, we set its class to `active item`.

Styling active links is a common need. While the solution above would work, `react-router` provides a built-in strategy to handle this situation.

We can use another link component, **`NavLink`**. `NavLink` is a special version of `Link` that is intended for just this purpose. When a `NavLink` component's target location matches the current URL, it will add style attributes to the rendered element.

We can use `NavLink` like this:

routing/music/client/src/components-complete/VerticalMenu-3.js

```
        <NavLink
          to={`${albumsPathname}/${album.id}`}
          activeClassName='active'
          className='item'
          key={album.id}
        >
```

When the `to` prop on a `NavLink` matches the current location, the class applied to the element will be a combination of `className` and `activeClassName`. Here, that will render the class `active item` as desired.

In this instance, however, we don't need to set the prop `activeClassName`. The default value of `activeClassName` is the string `'active'`. So, we can omit it.

Import `NavLink` at the top of the file:

routing/music/client/src/components-complete/VerticalMenu.js

```
import { NavLink } from 'react-router-dom';
```

Then swap out `Link` for `NavLink`:

routing/music/client/src/components-complete/VerticalMenu.js

```
const VerticalMenu = ({ albums, albumsPathname }) => (
  <div className='ui secondary vertical menu'>
    <div className='header item'>
      Albums
    </div>
    {
      albums.map((album) => (
        <NavLink
          to={`${albumsPathname}/${album.id}`}
          className='item'
          key={album.id}
```

```
        >
          {album.name}
        </NavLink>
      ))
    }
  </div>
);
```

NavLink makes styling links easy. Use NavLink when you need this feature but stick to Link when you don't.

Try it out

Save VerticalMenu.js. In our browser, the vertical menu will now reflect the active album with a gray background:

Menu highlights the active album

Let's handle one last thing before moving on to login and logout. AlbumsContainer matches on /albums. If the user visits /, it would be nice if they were redirected to /albums. We'll add that now.

Adding a redirect for the root path

Inside App.js, we first import Redirect:

routing/music/client/src/components-complete/App-3.js

```
import { Route, Redirect } from 'react-router-dom';
```

We'll then be able to add the `Redirect` component to the output of `App`. We want to `Route` the path / **exactly**:

routing/music/client/src/components-complete/App-3.js

```
    <div className='row'>
      <Route path='/albums' component={AlbumsContainer} />

      <Route exact path='/' render={() => (
        <Redirect
          to='/albums'
        />
      )} />
    </div>
```

Recall that the `exact` attribute is necessary here. Otherwise, the pattern / would match against every route, including `/albums` and `/login`.

Try it out

Save `App.js`. In your browser, visiting / redirects to `/albums` and the vertical menu of albums renders.

We've gotten to see some of React Router's components at work inside a slightly more complex interface:

- We matched a component against a dynamic URL
- We used some of the properties in the `match` argument that `Route` sets on its target component
- We propagated the pathname `/albums` down from `App`, a best practice
- We used `NavLink` to render styled link elements

Let's take this a bit further. In the next section, we'll implement a fake authentication system for our app. We'll explore a strategy for elegantly preventing a user from accessing certain locations without logging in first.

Supporting authenticated routes

As we saw when we explored the API endpoint `/api/albums` earlier, this endpoint requires a token to access. At the moment, we're cheating by manually setting the token before every request in `getAlbums()`:

routing/music/client/src/components-complete/AlbumsContainer-2.js

```
getAlbums = () => {
  client.setToken('D6W69PRgCoDKgHZGJmRUNA');
  client.getAlbums(ALBUM_IDS)
```

To mimic a more real-world authentication flow, we want to remove the token string literal from our client app. Instead, we should have our app make a request to the API's `/api/login` endpoint. As we saw, to keep things simple our API doesn't require a user name or password. But, mimicking an actual login endpoint, it will return a token that we can store locally and use in subsequent requests.

The `Client` library

Packaged with our app is a client library inside `client/src/Client.js`. The `Client` library has all the methods we need to interact with the server's API.

The `Client` library has a method, `login()`, that will both perform a request to `/api/login` and store the token. This `login()` function executes the request, checks to make sure it's the expected `201` status, parses the `json` response value, and stores the token by using the `setToken()` function:

routing/music/client/src/Client.js

```
login() {
  return fetch('/api/login', {
    method: 'post',
    headers: {
      accept: 'application/json',
    },
  }).then(this.checkStatus)
    .then(this.parseJson)
    .then((json) => this.setToken(json.token));
}
```

`setToken()` stores the token in `localStorage`:

routing/music/client/src/Client.js

```
  setToken(token) {
    this.token = token;

    if (this.useLocalStorage) {
      localStorage.setItem(LOCAL_STORAGE_KEY, token);
    }
  }
```

When the app loads, `Client` first tries to load the token from `localStorage`. The token is kept in `localStorage` indefinitely and has no expiry. Therefore, the user will only ever be logged out of our app when they perform a logout.

To logout, we can use the `logout()` function implemented in the `Client` library:

routing/music/client/src/Client.js

```
  logout() {
    this.removeToken();
  }
```

`removeToken()` nullifies the token and removes it from `localStorage`:

routing/music/client/src/Client.js

```
  removeToken() {
    this.token = null;

    if (this.useLocalStorage) {
      localStorage.removeItem(LOCAL_STORAGE_KEY);
    }
  }
```

With an idea of the functions we'll use in `Client`, let's begin by adding a new login component.

Implementing login

As we saw in the completed version of the app, the `Login` component displays a single "Login" button. Clicking this button fires off the login process. We want to display the loading indicator while the login is in process:

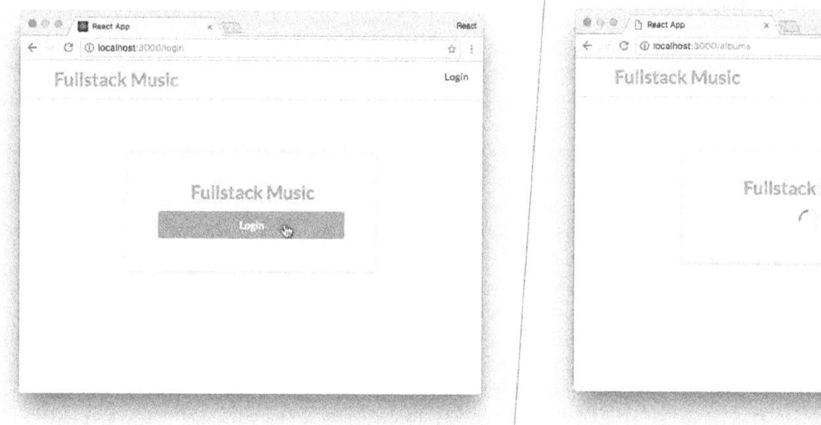

Clicking the "Login" button on `Login`

Open up `Login.js`. This file contains the scaffold for the component. We'll use a state property `loginInProgress` to indicate whether the login is underway. We'll use another property in state, `shouldRedirect`, to indicate if the login process has completed and the component should redirect to `/albums`. Let's declare both the initial state and the `performLogin()` function now:

routing/music/client/src/components-complete/Login-1.js

```
class Login extends Component {
  state = {
    loginInProgress: false,
    shouldRedirect: false,
  };

  performLogin = () => {
    this.setState({ loginInProgress: true });
    client.login().then(() => (
      this.setState({ shouldRedirect: true })
    ));
  };
```

We set the state properties `loginInProgress` and `shouldRedirect` initially to `false`.

In `performLogin()`, we first flip `loginInProgress` to `true`. When `client.login()` completes, we flip the state property `shouldRedirect` to `true`. We don't need to flip `loginInProgress` back to `false` as the component will be redirecting immediately anyway.

In `render()`, we first check to see if the component should redirect. If it should, we render a `Redirect` component. Otherwise, we can use `loginInProgress` to determine whether to show the "Login" button or the loading indicator:

routing/music/client/src/components-complete/Login-1.js

```
render() {
  if (this.state.shouldRedirect) {
    return (
      <Redirect to='/albums' />
    );
  } else {
    return (
      <div className='ui one column centered grid'>
        <div className='ten wide column'>
          <div
            className='ui raised very padded text container segment'
            style={{ textAlign: 'center' }}
          >
            <h2 className='ui green header'>
              Fullstack Music
            </h2>
            {
              this.state.loginInProgress ? (
                <div className='ui active centered inline loader' />
              ) : (
                <div
                  className='ui large green submit button'
                  onClick={this.performLogin}
                >
                  Login
                </div>
              )
            }
          </div>
        </div>
      </div>
    );
  }
}
```

Save `Login.js`. In order to test `Login`, we'll need to add our `Logout` component.

Logging out doesn't require an API request. We just need to call `client.logout()` which instantly removes the token stored locally. We can perform this call in `constructor()`. We'll then redirect to the login path, which will be `/login`.

First, inside `Logout.js`, import `Redirect` from `react-router`:

routing/music/client/src/components-complete/Logout.js

```
import React, { Component } from 'react';

import { Redirect } from 'react-router-dom';
```

Then we'll fill in the `Logout` component:

routing/music/client/src/components-complete/Logout.js

```
class Logout extends Component {

  constructor(props) {
    super(props);

    client.logout();
  }

  render() {
    return (
      <Redirect
        to='/login'
      />
    );
  }
}
```

Save `Logout.js`. With `Login` and `Logout` composed, we just need to add them to `App`.

First, we import the components:

```
// Top of `App.js`
import TopBar from './TopBar';
import AlbumsContainer from './AlbumsContainer';
import Login from './Login';
import Logout from './Logout';
```

And then we add `Route` components for each of them:

routing/music/client/src/components-complete/App-4.js

```
    <div className='row'>
      <Route path='/albums' component={AlbumsContainer} />

      <Route path='/login' component={Login} />
      <Route path='/logout' component={Logout} />

      <Route exact path='/' render={() => (
        <Redirect
          to='/albums'
        />
      )} />
    </div>
```

Finally, let's remove the manual `setToken()` call from inside `getAlbums()` in `AlbumsContainer`:

```
getAlbums() {
  client.setToken('D6W69PRgCoDKgHZGJmRUNA');
  client.getAlbums(ALBUM_IDS)
  // ...
};
```

Save `AlbumsContainer.js`. With `setToken()` removed, we can now test that our login functionality works. When we click the "Login" button at `/login`, it should trigger an API call to `/api/login` and set the token given in the response.

The component `TopBar` has been responsible for rendering the menu bar at the top of the page. The far right button has said "Logout" thus far as we've always been logged in. `TopBar` uses a function on `Client`, `isLoggedIn()`, to check if the user is logged in. This function checks if the token is present. We render either a "Login" link or a "Logout" link based on this boolean value:

routing/music/client/src/components/TopBar.js

```
    <div className='right menu'>
      {
        client.isLoggedIn() ? (
          <Link className='ui item' to='/logout'>
            Logout
          </Link>
        ) : (
          <Link className='ui item' to='/login'>
            Login
```

```
        </Link>
      )
    }
  </div>
```

With this in mind, let's test the app out.

Try it out

We'll take some steps to make sure that login and logout are working properly.

1. Load the page at `/albums`. We can see all the albums. In the top right, we see the "Logout" button.
2. Click the "Logout" button. We should be redirected to `/login`.
3. Without clicking the "Login" button, manually enter the path `/albums`.

When we visit `/albums` after logging out, we see the spinner on the page, indefinitely:

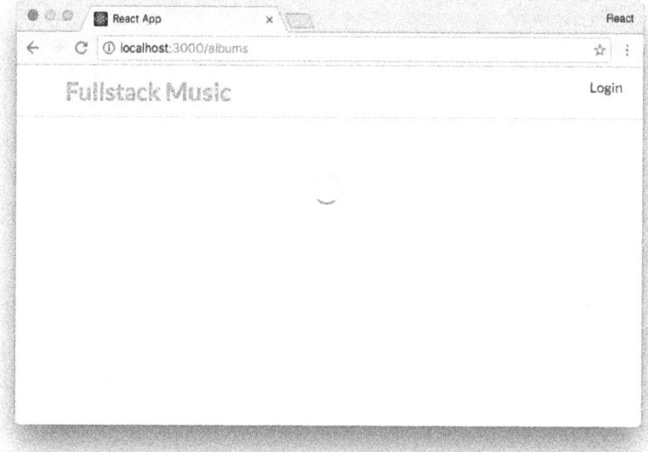

Page hangs indefinitely

Opening up the console, we see that our app is complaining that it received a `403` from the API:

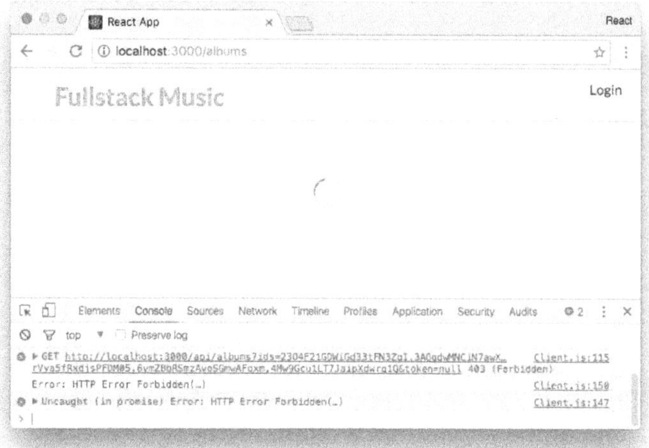

Error in the console

Great. The API rejected our request because it didn't include a token. The `Logout` component did its job and removed the token.

Now, we should be able to log in and view this page again:

1. Click the "Login" button in the top right.
2. On the `/login` page, click the "Login" button.
3. We'll be redirected to `/albums`. The albums should now be visible again.

Our app is close! We're converging on a real-world authentication flow. But we just identified an improvement we need to make. When the user visits `/albums` without being logged in, the app silently fails. Instead, we should redirect the user to `/login`.

What will happen if the user visits another page, say `/albums/1DWWb`? We should redirect the user to `/login` in that instance as well. And, when the login completes, the best experience would be if we redirected the user back to where they came from (`/albums/1DWWb`).

We'll address each of these in turn.

`PrivateRoute`, a higher-order component

If the user visits a page under `/albums` and is not logged in, we want to redirect them to the login page.

Using the client library's `isLoggedIn()`, we could implement something like this in `AlbumsContainer`:

```
// In AlbumsContainer
render() {
  // Something like this would work fine
  if (!client.isLoggedIn()) {
    return (
      <Redirect to='/login' />
    );
  }
}
```

This would work fine for our purposes right now. But, as our app grows, we'd likely need many pages and their constituent components to be wrapped with this redirect.

This is where React Router's **composability** comes in handy. Because everything in React Router is a component, we can write **higher-order components** that wrap React Router's elements in custom functionality.

A higher-order component is a React component that wraps another one. This pattern is a powerful mechanism for extending or altering the functionality of a pre-existing component.

As we saw when we wrote `Route`, this component is an example of a higher-order component.

In this case, we can write a new component, `PrivateRoute`. `PrivateRoute` will be like our own custom flavor of the `Route` component. As we'll see, we'll use it to extend and focus the functionality of `Route`. We can interchange it with `Route` anywhere in our app where we want to assert that the user is logged in. Under the hood, it will use both `Route` and `Redirect` to operate.

Open up `App.js`. Let's import and use `PrivateRoute` to see what using it will look like. We'll then build the component.

Import it at the top of `App.js`:

routing/music/client/src/components-complete/App-5.js

```
import TopBar from './TopBar';
import PrivateRoute from './PrivateRoute';
import AlbumsContainer from './AlbumsContainer';
import Login from './Login';
import Logout from './Logout';
```

We want `PrivateRoute` to have the same interface as `Route`. `/albums` will be the only route that requires the user to be logged in. For `/albums`, we'll swap out `Route` for `PrivateRoute`:

routing/music/client/src/components-complete/App-5.js

```
      <Switch>
        <PrivateRoute path='/albums' component={AlbumsContainer} />
        <Route path='/login' component={Login} />
        <Route path='/logout' component={Logout} />
```

Open up `PrivateRoute.js`. A scaffold for the component already exists.

Again, higher-order components are functions that return components wrapped with new functionality. To wrap our head around this, let's consider what `PrivateRoute` would look like if all it did was return `Route`. This implementation is the same as using `Route` directly:

routing/music/client/src/components-complete/PrivateRoute-1.js

```
const PrivateRoute = (props) => (
  <Route {...props} />
);
```

In this example, `PrivateRoute` returns a `Route` component, passing along all its props to `Route`. While not useful, this version of `PrivateRoute` is the simplest implementation of a higher-order component.

Because all that `PrivateRoute` does is render a `Route` component, if you were to save `PrivateRoute.js` and reload the app, everything would be working just as before.

What we want to eventually do is have our component either render the component that `PrivateRoute` was given (the prop `component`) or redirect if the user is not logged in. Something like this:

routing/music/client/src/components-complete/PrivateRoute-2.js

```
const PrivateRoute = (props) => (
  <Route {...props} render={(props) => (
    client.isLoggedIn() ? (
      // render the component
      todo
    ) : (
      // render the redirect
      todo
    )
  )} />
);
```

We pass along all the props to `Route` as before. Except this time, we specify a `render` function. Remember, you can either set the prop `component` on `Route` or pass a function to `render`.

Inside of this render function, we would switch off of `client.isLoggedIn()`. This boolean value will tell us if we should render the component given to `PrivateRoute` or perform a redirect.

Here's one approach to doing this. First, we can use the destructuring syntax to grab our arguments:

routing/music/client/src/components-complete/PrivateRoute-3.js

```
const PrivateRoute = ({ component, ...rest }) => (
```

We grab the `component` prop then use the spread syntax to grab `...rest`, which is all the rest of the props set on `PrivateRoute`.

Next, we pass along all the props (`rest`) to `Route`:

routing/music/client/src/components-complete/PrivateRoute-3.js

```
const PrivateRoute = ({ component, ...rest }) => (
  <Route {...rest} render={(props) => (
```

If the user is logged in, we want to render the component:

routing/music/client/src/components-complete/PrivateRoute-3.js

```
  <Route {...rest} render={(props) => (
    client.isLoggedIn() ? (
      React.createElement(component, props)
    ) : (
```

Otherwise, we want to perform a redirect:

routing/music/client/src/components-complete/PrivateRoute-3.js

```
    ) : (
      <Redirect to={{
        pathname: '/login',
      }} />
    )
```

Our `PrivateRoute` component, in full:

routing/music/client/src/components-complete/PrivateRoute-3.js

```
const PrivateRoute = ({ component, ...rest }) => (
  <Route {...rest} render={(props) => (
    client.isLoggedIn() ? (
      React.createElement(component, props)
    ) : (
      <Redirect to={{
        pathname: '/login',
      }} />
    )
  )} />
);
```

Save `PrivateRoute.js`. Because we're already using the component in `App` to match the `/albums` endpoint, we're ready to test it out in the browser.

Higher-order components can be difficult to parse at first. If you're struggling with `PrivateRoute`, we recommend returning to the component later and playing around with it.

Try it out

With the app open, perform the following steps to verify things work:

1. Click the "Logout" button in the top right
2. We are redirected to `/login`
3. Now, when visiting `/albums` the app should redirect you to `/login`
4. When we login, we'll be redirected to `/albums` and this time it renders

We're almost finished tying things together. There's one last piece that we mentioned would be nice to have.

Redirect state

If the user visits a page on the site they can't access because they're not logged in, we redirect them to `/login`. When they log in, we should send them back to whichever page they came from. In order to do this, `Login` needs some way to know where the user came from.

React Router's `Redirect` allows us to set some state when we perform our redirect. That state will be available at the next location. We can have the `Redirect` in `PrivateRoute` set this state according to the user's location. We'll see how we can have `Login` read from this state to figure out where to send the user.

Open up `PrivateRoute.js`. Passing this `state` along in a `Redirect` looks like this:

routing/music/client/src/components-complete/PrivateRoute.js

```
      <Redirect to={{
        pathname: '/login',
        state: { from: props.location },
      }} />
```

We can set this state to whatever we want. We set the property `from` to the location of the app before the redirect. So, if the user tried to access `/albums/1DWWb4Q39mp1T3NgyscowF`, `state.from` would be set to this value.

Now, let's use this state in `Login.js` to determine where to redirect the user after they log in.

The `state` will be available to us here under the `location` prop that `Route` provides. Let's make a new class function on our `Login` component we'll call `redirectPath()` that reads this state:

routing/music/client/src/components-complete/Login.js

```
  redirectPath = () => {
    const locationState = this.props.location.state;
    const pathname = (
      locationState && locationState.from && locationState.from.pathname
    );
    return pathname || '/albums';
  };

  render() {
```

This function reads the location's `state` variable. If it sees a `from` property, it will return that string. Otherwise, it will default to `/albums`.

Now we can use it in our `Redirect`:

routing/music/client/src/components-complete/Login.js

```
    if (this.state.shouldRedirect) {
      return (
        <Redirect to={this.redirectPath()} />
```

Try it out

Now that we're including state in our redirect, logged-out users will be sent to whichever page they were trying to access after they log in.

To test this out, in the browser we:

1. Visit one of the albums.
2. Copy the full URL (e.g. `http://localhost:3000/albums/2304F21GDWiGd33tFN3ZgI`).
3. Click "Logout."
4. Paste the full URL and hit enter (we can also hit the back button).
5. Our browser is trying to access a page protected by `PrivateRoute`. We're redirected to `/login`.
6. Click the "Login" button.
7. After the login completes, instead of being redirected to `/albums` we're redirected to the location we were trying to access.

Recap

In this chapter, we saw how we can use components from React Router to provide fast, JavaScript-powered navigation around our web apps. We can prevent the user's browser from doing full page loads when navigating around our site. We can build user-friendly URLs that are shareable. And the added complexity to our application is minimal.

React Router's declarative, component-driven paradigm is unique in the routing landscape. While it often means that we have to re-think how to approach routing solutions, the reward is that we're working with familiar React components. This limits the surface area of React Router's API and minimizes any "magic."

Further Reading

The React Router docs[78] contain several focused examples on a variety of React Router's concepts. At the time of writing, examples included common patterns like query params and ambiguous route matching. All those examples build on the foundations established in this chapter.

[78]https://reacttraining.com/react-router/

Part II

Intro to Flux and Redux

Why Flux?

In our projects so far, we've managed state inside of React components. The top-level React component managed our primary state. In this type of data architecture, data flows downward to child components. To make changes to state, child components propagate events up to their parent components by calling prop-functions. Any state mutations took place at the top and then flowed downward again.

Managing application state with React components works fine for a wide variety of applications. However, as apps grow in size and complexity, managing state inside of React components (or the *component-state paradigm*) can become cumbersome.

A common pain point is the **tight coupling between user interactions and state changes**. For complex web applications, oftentimes a single user interaction can affect many different, discrete parts of the state.

For example, consider an app for managing email. Clicking an email must:

1. Replace the "inbox view" (the list of emails) with the "email view" (the email the user clicked)
2. Mark the email as read locally
3. Reduce the total unread counter locally
4. Change the URL of the browser
5. Send a web request to mark the email as read on the server

The function in the top-level component that handles a user clicking on an email must describe all of the state changes that occur. This loads a single function with lots of complexity and responsibility. Wading through all of this logic for managing many disparate parts of an app's state tree can make updates difficult to manage and error-prone.

Facebook was running into this and other architectural problems with their apps. This motivated them to invent Flux.

Flux is a Design Pattern

Flux is a design pattern. The predecessor to Flux at Facebook was another design pattern, Model-View-Controller[79] (MVC). MVC is a popular design pattern for both desktop and web applications.

[79] https://en.wikipedia.org/wiki/Model-view-controller

In MVC, user interactions with the View trigger logic in the Controller. The Controller instructs the Model how to update itself. After the Model updates, the View re-renders.

While React does not have three discrete "actors" like a traditional MVC implementation, it suffers from the same coupling between user interactions and state changes.

Flux overview

The Flux design pattern is made up of four parts, organized as a one-way data pipeline:

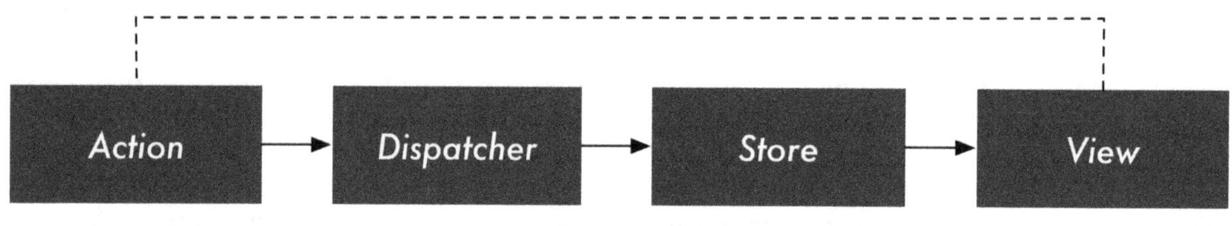

Flux diagram

The **view** dispatches **actions** that describe what happened. The **store** receives these actions and determines what state changes should occur. After the state updates, the new state is pushed to the View.

Returning to our email example, in Flux, we no longer have a single function handling email clicks that describes all of the state changes. Instead, React notifies the store (through an action) that the user clicked on an email. As we'll see over the next few chapters, we can organize the store such that each discrete part of the state has its own logic for handling updates.

In addition to decoupling interaction handling and state changes, Flux also provides the following benefits:

Breaking up state management logic

As parts of the state tree become interdependent, most of an app's state usually gets rolled up to a top-level component. Flux relieves the top-level component of state management responsibility and allows you to break up state management into isolated, smaller, and testable parts.

React components are simpler

Certain component-managed state is fine, like activating certain buttons on mouse hover. But by managing all other state externally, React components become simple HTML rendering functions. This makes them smaller, easier to understand, and more composable.

Mis-match between the state tree and the DOM tree

Oftentimes, we want to store our state with a different representation than how we want to display it. For example, we might want to have our app store a timestamp for a message (`createdAt`) but in the view we want to display a human-friendly representation, like "23 minutes ago." Instead of having components hold all this computational logic for *derived data*, we'll see how Flux enables us to perform these computations *before* providing state to React components.

We'll reflect on these benefits as we dig deep into the design of a complex application in the next chapter. Before that, we'll implement the Flux design pattern in a basic application so that we can review Flux's fundamentals.

Flux implementations

Flux is a design pattern, not a specific library or implementation. Facebook has open-sourced a library they use[80]. This library provides the interface for a dispatcher and a store that you can use in your application.

But Facebook's implementation is not the exclusive option. Since Facebook started sharing Flux with the community, the community has responded by writing tons of different Flux implementations[81]. A developer has many compelling choices.

While the available choices can be overwhelming, one community favorite has emerged: Redux[82].

Redux

Redux has gained widespread popularity and respect in the React community. The library has even won the endorsement of the creator of Flux[83].

Redux's best feature is its simplicity. Stripped of its comments and sanity checks, Redux is only about 100 lines of code.

Because of this simplicity, throughout this chapter we'll be implementing the Redux core library ourselves. We'll use small example applications to see how everything fits together.

In the following chapters, we'll build on this foundation by constructing a feature-rich messaging application that mirrors Facebook's. We'll see how using Redux as the backbone of our application equips our app to handle increasing feature complexity.

Redux's key ideas

Throughout this chapter, we'll become familiar with each of Redux's key ideas. Those ideas are:

- All of your application's data is in a single data structure called the **state** which is held in the **store**

[80] https://github.com/facebook/flux
[81] https://github.com/voronianski/flux-comparison
[82] https://github.com/reactjs/redux
[83] https://twitter.com/jingc/status/616608251463909376

- Your app reads the **state** from this **store**
- The **state** is never mutated directly outside the **store**
- The **views** emit **actions** that describe what happened
- A **new state** is created by combining the **old state** and the **action** by a function called the **reducer**

These key ideas are probably a bit cryptic at the moment, but you'll come to understand each of them over the course of this chapter.

Throughout the rest of the chapter, we'll be referring to Redux. Because Redux is an implementation of Flux, many of the concepts that apply to Redux apply to Flux as well.

While the Flux creators approve of Redux, Redux is arguably not a "strict" Flux implementation. You can read about the nuances on the Redux website[84].

Building a counter

We'll explore Redux's core ideas by building a simple counter. For now, we'll focus only on Redux and state management. We'll see later how Redux connects to React views.

Preparation

Inside of the code download that came with this book, navigate to `redux/counter`:

```
$ cd redux/counter
```

All the code for the counter will go inside `app.js`.

Because we're focusing on Redux and state management to start, we'll be running our code in the terminal as opposed to the browser.

The `package.json` for both of the projects contains the package `babel-cli`. As we'll indicate in the **Try it out** sections below, we'll be using the `babel-node` command that comes with `babel-cli` to run our code examples:

```
# example of using `babel-node` to run code in the terminal
$ ./node_modules/.bin/babel-node app.js
```

Run `npm install` now inside of `redux/counter` to install `babel-cli`:

[84] http://redux.js.org/docs/introduction/PriorArt.html

```
$ npm install
```

Overview

Our state will be a number. The number will start off as `0`. Our actions will either be to **increment** or **decrement** the state. We know from our Redux diagram that the views would dispatch these actions to the store:

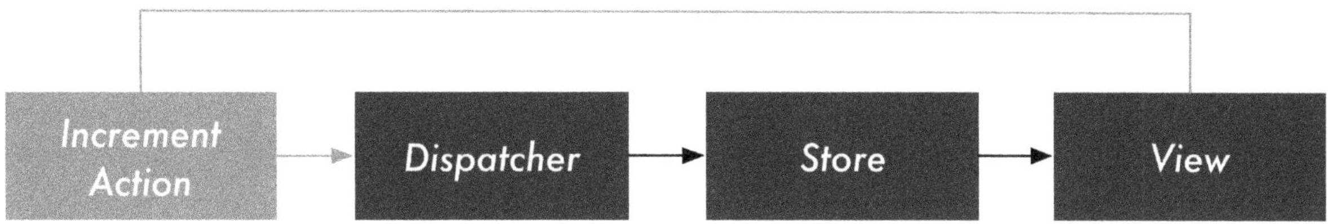

View emits "Increment" action

When the store receives an action from the views, the store uses a **reducer function** to process the action. The store provides the reducer function with the current state and the action. The reducer function returns the new state:

```
// Inside the store, receives `action` from the view
state = reducer(state, action);
```

For example, consider a store with a current state of `5`. The store receives an increment action. The store uses its reducer to derive the next state:

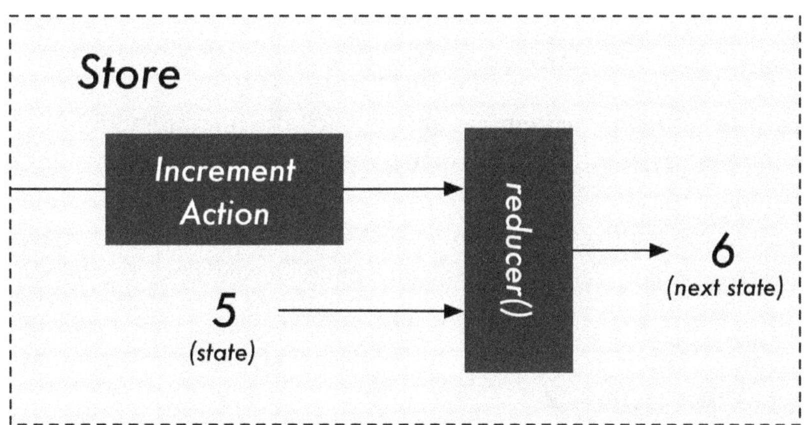

Inside an example store

We'll start building our Redux counter by constructing its reducer. We'll then work our way up to see what a Redux store looks like. Our store will be the maintainer of state, accepting actions and using the reducer to determine the next version of the state.

While we're starting with a simple representation of state (a number), we'll be working with much more complicated state in the next chapter.

The counter's actions

We know the reducer function for our counter will accept two arguments, `state` and `action`. We know `state` for our counter will be an integer. But how are actions represented in Redux?

Actions in Redux are objects. Actions always have a `type` property.

Our increment actions will look like this:

```
{
  type: 'INCREMENT',
}
```

And decrement actions like this:

```
{
  type: 'DECREMENT',
}
```

We can envision what a simple interface for this counter app might look like:

An example counter interface

When the user clicks the "+" icon, the view would dispatch the increment action to the store. When the user clicks the "-" icon, the view would dispatch the decrement action to the store.

The image of the interface for the counter app is provided as just an example of what the view *might* look like. We will not be implementing a view layer for this app.

Incrementing the counter

Let's begin writing our reducer function. We'll start by handling the increment action.

The reducer function for our counter accepts two arguments, `state` and `action`, and returns the next version of the state. When the reducer receives an `INCREMENT` action, it should return `state + 1`.

Inside of `app.js`, add the code for our counter's reducer:

redux/counter/complete/initial-reducer.js

```
function reducer(state, action) {
  if (action.type === 'INCREMENT') {
    return state + 1;
  } else {
    return state;
  }
}
```

If the `action.type` is `INCREMENT`, we return the incremented state. Otherwise, our reducer returns the state unmodified.

You might be wondering if it would be a better idea to raise an error if our reducer receives an `action.type` that it does not recognize.

In the next chapter, we'll see how **reducer composition** "breaks up" state management into smaller, more focused functions. These smaller reducers might only handle a subset of the app's state and actions. As such, if they receive an action they do not recognize, they should just ignore it and return the state unmodified.

Try it out

At the bottom of `app.js`, let's add some code to test our reducer.

We'll call our reducer, passing in integers for state and seeing how the reducer increments the number. If we pass in an unknown action type, our reducer returns the state unchanged:

redux/counter/complete/initial-reducer.js

```
const incrementAction = { type: 'INCREMENT' };

console.log(reducer(0, incrementAction)); // -> 1
console.log(reducer(1, incrementAction)); // -> 2
console.log(reducer(5, incrementAction)); // -> 6

const unknownAction = { type: 'UNKNOWN' };

console.log(reducer(5, unknownAction)); // -> 5
console.log(reducer(8, unknownAction)); // -> 8
```

Save `app.js` and run it with `./node_modules/.bin/babel-node`:

```
$ ./node_modules/.bin/babel-node app.js
```

And your output should look like this:

```
1
2
6
5
8
```

Decrementing the counter

Again, decrement actions have a `type` of `DECREMENT`:

```
{
  type: 'DECREMENT',
}
```

To support decrement actions, we add another clause to our reducer:

redux/counter/complete/initial-reducer-w-dec.js

```
function reducer(state, action) {
  if (action.type === 'INCREMENT') {
    return state + 1;
  } else if (action.type === 'DECREMENT') {
    return state - 1;
  } else {
    return state;
  }
}
```

Try it out

At the bottom of `app.js`, below the code where we dispatched increment actions, add some code to dispatch decrement actions:

redux/counter/complete/initial-reducer-w-dec.js

```
const decrementAction = { type: 'DECREMENT' };

console.log(reducer(10, decrementAction)); // -> 9
console.log(reducer(9, decrementAction)); // -> 8
console.log(reducer(5, decrementAction)); // -> 4
```

Run `app.js` with `./node_modules/.bin/babel-node`:

```
$ ./node_modules/.bin/babel-node app.js
```

And your output should look like this:

```
1
2
6
5
8
9
8
4
```

Supporting additional parameters on actions

In the last example, our actions contained only a `type` which told our reducer either to increment or decrement the state. But often behavior in our app can't be described by a single value. In these cases, we need additional parameters to describe the change.

For example, what if we wanted our app to allow the user to specify an *amount* to increment or decrement by?

An example counter interface with an amount field

We'll have our actions carry the additional property `amount`. An `INCREMENT` action would then look like this:

```
{
  type: 'INCREMENT',
  amount: 7,
}
```

We modify our reducer to increment and decrement by `action.amount`, expecting all actions to now carry this property:

redux/counter/complete/reducer-w-amount.js

```
function reducer(state, action) {
  if (action.type === 'INCREMENT') {
    return state + action.amount;
  } else if (action.type === 'DECREMENT') {
    return state - action.amount;
  } else {
    return state;
  }
}
```

Try it out

Clear out the code we used to test out `reducer()` in `app.js` previously.

This time, we'll test calling the reducer with our modified actions that now carry the `amount` property:

redux/counter/complete/reducer-w-amount.js

```
const incrementAction = {
  type: 'INCREMENT',
  amount: 5,
};

console.log(reducer(0, incrementAction)); // -> 5
console.log(reducer(1, incrementAction)); // -> 6

const decrementAction = {
  type: 'DECREMENT',
  amount: 11,
};

console.log(reducer(100, decrementAction)); // -> 89
```

Run `app.js` with `./node_modules/.bin/babel-node`:

```
$ ./node_modules/.bin/babel-node app.js
```

And note the output:

```
5
6
89
```

Building the store

So far, we've been calling our reducer and manually supplying the last version of the state along with an action.

In Redux, the store is responsible for both maintaining the state and accepting actions from the view. Only the store has access to the reducer:

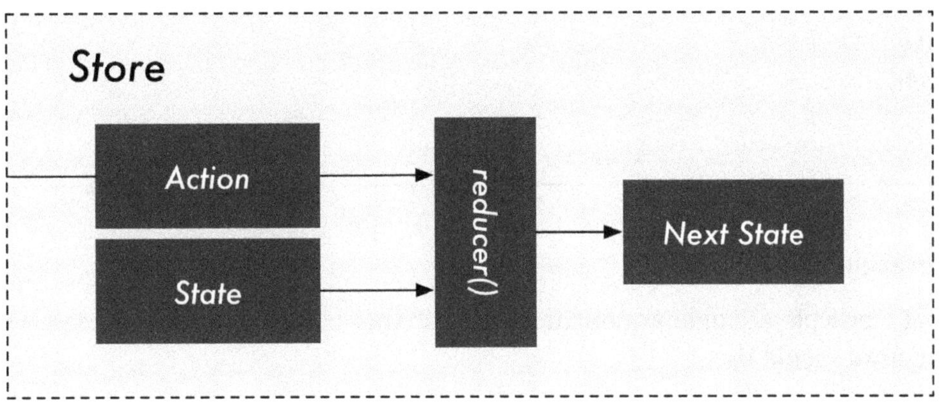

Inside the store

The Redux library provides a function for creating stores, `createStore()`. This function returns a store object that keeps an internal variable, `state`. In addition, it provides a few methods for interacting with the store.

We will write our own version of `createStore()` so that we fully understand how Redux stores work. By the end of this chapter, our code for `createStore()` will behave almost exactly like the one provided by the Redux library.

At the moment, our store will provide two methods:

- `dispatch`: The method we'll use to send the store actions
- `getState`: The method we'll use to read the current value of `state`

Inside of app.js, clear out the code we used to test out reducer() previously. Below the definition of reducer(), let's define createStore(). createStore() will accept a single argument, the desired reducer for the store.

Let's take a look at the full createStore() function. We'll break it down piece-by-piece below the code block:

redux/counter/complete/reducer-w-store-v1.js

```
function createStore(reducer) {
  let state = 0;

  const getState = () => (state);

  const dispatch = (action) => {
    state = reducer(state, action);
  };

  return {
    getState,
    dispatch,
  };
}
```

The reducer argument

createStore() accepts a single argument, reducer. This is how we will indicate what reducer function our store should use.

state

We initialize the state to 0 at the top of createStore(). Note that we close over the state variable. This makes state private and inaccessible outside of createStore().

For more info on closures, see the aside "The Factory Pattern."

getState

To get read access to the state from outside createStore(), we have the method getState which returns state.

dispatch

The dispatch method is how we send actions to the store. We'll call it like this:

```
store.dispatch({ type: 'INCREMENT', amount: 7 });
```

`dispatch` calls the `reducer` function passed in as an argument with the current state and the action. `dispatch` sets `state` to the reducer's return value.

Note that `dispatch` **does not return the state**. Dispatching actions in Redux are "fire-and-forget." When we call `dispatch`, we're sending a notification to the store with no expectation on when or how that action will be processed.

Dispatching actions to the store is decoupled from reading the latest version of the state. We'll see how this works in practice when we connect the store to React views at the end of this chapter.

The return object

At the bottom of `createStore()`, we return a new object. This object has `getState` and `dispatch` as methods.

The Factory Pattern

In `createStore()` above, we're using a pattern called the "Factory Pattern." This is a ubiquitous pattern in JavaScript for creating complex objects like our store object.

The Factory Pattern provides a **closure** for variables declared inside the factory function.

At the top of `createStore()`, we declare the variable `state`:

```
function createStore(reducer) {
  let state = 0;
  // ...
```

`state` is a **private variable**. Only the functions declared inside of `createStore()` have access to it. Furthermore, because `state` is inside of this closure, the variable "lives on" between function calls.

As an example, consider the following factory function:

```
function createAdder() {
  let value = 0;

  const add = (amount) => (value = value + amount);
  const getValue = () => (value);

  return {
    add,
    getValue,
  }
}
```

We first call the factory to instantiate our `adder` object. The private variable `value` is initialized to `0`:

```
const adder = createAdder();
```

While `createAdder()` has returned our new object and exited, the variable `value` lives on in memory as `0`. Whenever we call `add()`, we are modifying this same `value`:

```
adder.add(1);
adder.getValue();
// => 1
adder.add(1);
adder.getValue();
// => 2
adder.add(5);
adder.getValue();
// => 7
```

Importantly, `value` is *only accessible to the functions inside the factory.* This prevents unintended reads or writes.

In the case with our store, this prevents any modifications from being made to `state` outside of the `dispatch()` function.

Try it out

We'll write the code to test out our store in `app.js` below `createStore()`.

We'll create our store object with `createStore()`. Then, instead of calling `reducer()` with a state and an action, we'll dispatch actions to the store. Because our store is keeping the internal variable `state`, our `state` persists between dispatches.

We can use `getState()` to read `state` between dispatches:

redux/counter/complete/reducer-w-store-v1.js

```
const store = createStore(reducer);

const incrementAction = {
  type: 'INCREMENT',
  amount: 3,
};

store.dispatch(incrementAction);
console.log(store.getState()); // -> 3
store.dispatch(incrementAction);
console.log(store.getState()); // -> 6

const decrementAction = {
  type: 'DECREMENT',
  amount: 4,
};

store.dispatch(decrementAction);
console.log(store.getState()); // -> 2
```

Run `app.js` with `./node_modules/.bin/babel-node`:

```
$ ./node_modules/.bin/babel-node app.js
```

And note the output:

```
3
6
2
```

The core of Redux

As it stands, our `createStore()` function closely resembles the `createStore()` function that ships with the Redux library. By the end of this chapter, we'll have made just a couple of tweaks and additions to `createStore()` to bring it closer to that of the Redux library.

Now that we've seen a Redux store in action, let's recap Redux's key ideas:

All of your application's data is in a single data structure called the state which is held in the store.

We saw that the store has a single private variable for the state, `state`.

Your app reads the state from this store.

We use `getState()` to access the store's state.

The state is never mutated directly outside the store.

Because `state` is a private variable, it cannot be mutated outside of the store.

The views emit actions that describe what happened.

We use `dispatch()` to send these actions to the store.

A new state is created by combining the old state and the action by a function called the reducer.

Inside of `dispatch()`, our store uses `reducer()` to get the new state, passing in the current state and the action.

There is one more key idea of Redux we have yet to cover:

Reducer functions must be pure functions.

We will explore this idea in the next app.

Next up

In the next app and over the next two chapters, we'll work with examples of increasing complexity. All the ideas we cover are patterns that flow from this core: a single store controls state, making updates by using a reducer. This reducer takes the current state and an action and returns a new state.

If you understand the ideas presented above, it's likely you'd be able to invent many of the patterns and libraries we'll be discussing.

To see how Redux operates inside of a feature-rich web application, we'll cover:

- How to carefully handle more complex data structures in our state
- How to be notified when our state changes without having to poll the store with `getState()` (with *subscriptions*)
- How to split up large reducers into more manageable, smaller ones (and recombine them)
- How to organize our React components in a Redux-powered app

Let's first deal with handling more complex data structures in our state. For the remainder of this chapter, we'll switch gears from our counter app to the beginnings of a chat app. In subsequent chapters, the interface for our chat app will begin to mirror the richness and complexity of Facebook's.

The beginnings of a chat app

Previewing

We'll build our chat app inside of the folder `redux/chat_simple`. From inside of the `redux/counter` directory, you can type:

```
$ cd ../chat_simple
```

First, run `npm install`:

```
$ npm install
```

Run `ls` to see the contents of this folder:

```
$ ls
README.md
nightwatch.json
node_modules
package.json
public
semantic
semantic.json
src
tests
yarn.lock
```

The structure of this app was generated with create-react-app.

For more on create-react-app, see the chapter "Using Webpack with create-react-app."

Inside of `src/` is `App.js`, the file we'll be working with in this chapter:

```
$ ls src/
App.js
complete
index.css
index.js
```

As is the case with apps generated by create-react-app, `index.js` is where we mount `<App />` to the DOM. Inside of `complete/` are the iterations of `App` as we build it up through the chapter.

At the moment, `index.js` is mounting `complete/App-5.js`, the completed version of the app that we reach at the end of this chapter. We can boot our app to see it:

```
$ npm start
```

Navigate to `localhost:3000`:

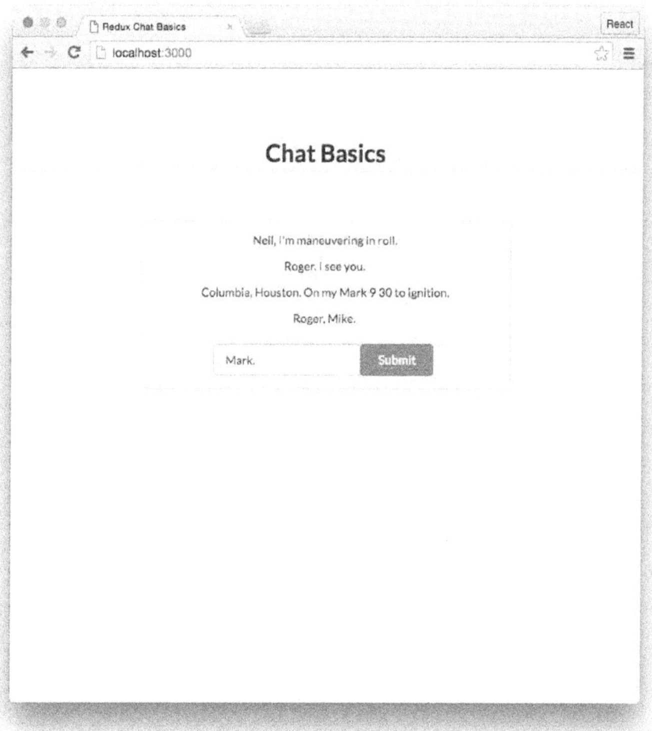

The iteration of the chat app that we build in this chapter

Over the next few chapters, we'll be enhancing the feature-set (and complexity) of this app. For now, we can add messages using the input box and delete messages by clicking on them.

While it's on our mind, let's modify `index.js` so that it includes `./App` instead of `./complete/App-5`:

```
import React from "react";
import ReactDOM from "react-dom";
import App from "./App";
```

Open up `src/App.js`. You'll see that the same `createStore()` that we built for the counter app is already present.

As with the counter app, we'll start by building the chat app's reducer. Once our reducer is built, we'll see how we connect our Redux store to React views.

Before we build our reducer, though, we should examine how the chat app will represent both its state and its actions.

State

The state in our counter app was a single number. In our chat app, the state is going to be an object.

This state object will have a single property, `messages`. `messages` will be an array of strings, with each string representing an individual message in the application. For example:

```
// an example `state` value
{
  messages: [
    'here is message one',
    'here is message two',
  ],
}
```

Actions

Our app will process two actions: `ADD_MESSAGE` and `DELETE_MESSAGE`.

The `ADD_MESSAGE` action object will always have the property `message`, the message to be added to the state. The `ADD_MESSAGE` action object has this shape:

```
{
  type: 'ADD_MESSAGE',
  message: 'Whatever message is being added here',
}
```

The `DELETE_MESSAGE` action object will delete a specified message from the state.

If each of our messages were objects, we could assign each message an `id` property when it is created. `DELETE_MESSAGE` could then specify the message to delete with an `id` property.

However, for simplicity, our messages at the moment are strings. To specify the message to be removed from state, we can use the index of the message in the array.

With that in mind, the `DELETE_MESSAGE` action object has this shape:

```
{
  type: 'DELETE_MESSAGE',
  index: 2, // <- index of whichever message is being removed here
}
```

Building the `reducer()`

Initializing `state`

Right now, we initialize `state` at the top of `createStore()` to `0`:

```
function createStore(reducer) {
  let state = 0;
  // ...
}
```

While this works fine for our counter app, we want the initial state for our messaging app to look like this:

```
{                    // an object
  messages: [],      // no messages
}
```

We'll need to modify `createStore()` so that it will work for this and any representation of state.

We'll have `createStore()` accept a second argument, `initialState`. The function will initialize `state` to this value.

Inside of `App.js`, edit `createStore()` now:

redux/chat_simple/src/complete/App-1.js

```
function createStore(reducer, initialState) {
  let state = initialState;
  // ...
```

We'll pass in `initialState` when we initialize the store a bit later.

Handling the `ADD_MESSAGE` action

Begin writing the `reducer()` inside of `App.js`, below `createStore()`:

redux/chat_simple/src/complete/App-1.js

```
function reducer(state, action) {
  if (action.type === 'ADD_MESSAGE') {
    return {
      messages: state.messages.concat(action.message),
    };
  } else {
    return state;
  }
}
```

When our reducer receives the `ADD_MESSAGE` action we want to append the new message to the end of the `messages` array in state. Otherwise, we return state unmodified.

We might be tempted to use Array's `push` to append the new message to `messages`:

```
// tempting, but flawed
if (action.type === 'ADD_MESSAGE') {
  state.messages.push(action.messages);
  return state;
}
```

This would yield the desired result: `state.messages` would contain the new message.

However, this violates a principle of Redux reducers, our last key idea of Redux from our list above: **reducers must be pure functions**.

A **pure function**[85] is one that:

- Will always return the same value given the same set of arguments.
- Does not alter the "world" around it in any way. **This includes mutating variables external to the function** or altering an entry in a database.

Because `state` is a variable external to `reducer()` and passed in as an argument, `reducer()` does not "own" this variable. Modifying `state`, as we do with `push` above, would make `reducer()` impure.

When writing Redux reducers, our pure reducer functions will always return a new array or object in the event that `state` has to be modified. This follows from the practice of treating component state as immutable as we discussed in the first few chapters. Reducers should treat the state object as **immutable** or read-only.

---

[85] https://en.wikipedia.org/wiki/Pure_function

Reducers should treat the state object as **immutable**.

Because we do not want to modify the `state` argument, `ADD_MESSAGE` should instead create a *new* state object with a *new* `messages` array. The new array should have the desired message appended to it.

Look again at how we produce the next state in `ADD_MESSAGE`:

redux/chat_simple/src/complete/App-1.js

```
    return {
      messages: state.messages.concat(action.message),
    };
```

Crucially, Array's `concat` does *not* modify the original array. Instead, it creates a *new* copy of the array that includes `action.message` appended to it.

In general, writing functions purely can help reduce surprises or enigmatic bugs in your code. We explore the specific motivations and benefits of Redux's insistence on pure reducer functions in a subsequent chapter.

Try it out

We'll write our testing code at the bottom of `App.js`, below the definition for `reducer()`.

Our `createStore()` function now accepts `initialState` as an argument. Let's first define this variable:

redux/chat_simple/src/complete/App-1.js

```
const initialState = { messages: [] };
```

And then initialize the store:

redux/chat_simple/src/complete/App-1.js

```
const store = createStore(reducer, initialState);
```

Let's add code to dispatch add message actions to the store. This time, we'll save each state "version" in two variables, `stateV1` and `stateV2`. We'll print out the two versions of our state at the end:

redux/chat_simple/src/complete/App-1.js

```
const addMessageAction1 = {
  type: 'ADD_MESSAGE',
  message: 'How does it look, Neil?',
};

store.dispatch(addMessageAction1);
const stateV1 = store.getState();

const addMessageAction2 = {
  type: 'ADD_MESSAGE',
  message: 'Looking good.',
};

store.dispatch(addMessageAction2);
const stateV2 = store.getState();

console.log('State v1:');
console.log(stateV1);
console.log('State v2:');
console.log(stateV2);
```

While we're inside of a create-react-app project, we don't yet have any React components. So we'll just run `App.js` with `babel-node`:

```
./node_modules/.bin/babel-node src/App.js
```

Which yields the following result:

```
State v1:
{ messages: [ 'How does it look, Neil?' ] }
State v2:
{ messages: [ 'How does it look, Neil?', 'Looking good.' ] }
```

Importantly, the **`state` object was not modified between dispatches**. We saved the first version of the state as the variable `stateV1`. Although this object was passed into `reducer()`, `reducer()` did not modify it. Instead, it created a new object with our second message appended. This new object was returned and set to the variable `stateV2`.

Handling the `DELETE_MESSAGE` action

As discussed, the `DELETE_MESSAGE` action object has the following shape:

```
{
  type: 'DELETE_MESSAGE',
  index: 2, // <- index of whichever message is being removed here
}
```

To support this action, we need to add a new `else if` statement to handle an action with a `type` of `'DELETE_MESSAGE'`. When the reducer receives this action, it should return an object with a `messages` array that contains every message **except** the one specified by the action's `index` property.

The most succinct solution might seem to be Array's `splice` method[86]. The first argument for `splice` is the starting index of the element(s) you want to remove. The second is the number of elements to remove:

```
// tempting, but flawed
case 'DELETE_MESSAGE':
  state.messages.splice(action.index, 1);
  return state;
```

However, like `push`, **`splice` modifies the original array**. This would make `reducer()` impure. Again, we cannot modify `state` — we must treat it as read-only.

Instead, we can create a new object as we did in `ADD_MESSAGE`. That new object will contain a new `messages` array that includes all of the elements in `state.messages` *except* the one being removed.

To do this in JavaScript, we can create a new array that contains:

- All of the elements from `0` to `action.index`
- All of the elements from `action.index + 1` to the end of the array

We use Array's `slice` to grab the desired "chunks" of the array:

redux/chat_simple/src/complete/App-2.js

```
function reducer(state, action) {
  if (action.type === 'ADD_MESSAGE') {
    return {
      messages: state.messages.concat(action.message),
    };
  } else if (action.type === 'DELETE_MESSAGE') {
    return {
      messages: [
        ...state.messages.slice(0, action.index),
```

[86] https://developer.mozilla.org/en-US/docs/Web/JavaScript/Reference/Global_Objects/Array/splice

```
        ...state.messages.slice(
          action.index + 1, state.messages.length
        ),
      ],
    };
  } else {
    return state;
  }
}
```

Importantly, `slice` does not modify the original array. Instead, it returns a new array with the elements in the range you specify. We create a new array that combines two ranges: up to and excluding `action.index` and every element after `action.index`.

For more info on the ES6 spread operator (...) see "Appendix B."

Try it out

At the very bottom of `App.js`, we'll add on to our code that tested the `ADD_MESSAGE` action. Write the following below the last `console.log()` statement in the file:

redux/chat_simple/src/complete/App-2.js

```
const deleteMessageAction = {
  type: 'DELETE_MESSAGE',
  index: 0,
};

store.dispatch(deleteMessageAction);
const stateV3 = store.getState();

console.log('State v3:');
console.log(stateV3);
```

By the second version of the state, we've added two messages to the state. We then dispatch a `DELETE_MESSAGE` action, specifying the message at index `0`.

Run the file with `babel-node`:

```
./node_modules/.bin/babel-node src/App.js
```

As expected, in the third version of the state the first message has been removed:

```
State v1:
{ messages: [ 'How does it look, Neil?' ] }
State v2:
{ messages: [ 'How does it look, Neil?', 'Looking good.' ] }
State v3:
{ messages: [ 'Looking good.' ] }
```

Subscribing to the store

Our store so far provides methods for the view to dispatch actions and to read the current version of the state.

One important feature is missing before we can connect the store to React, however. While the view can read the state at any time with `getState()`, **the view needs to know when the state has changed**. Constantly polling the store with `getState()` is inefficient.

In our previous apps, when we wanted to modify the state we called `setState()`. Importantly, `setState()` triggers a `render()` call on the component.

Now, state is being modified outside of React and inside of the store. Our views are unaware of when it changes. If we're going to keep our views up to date with the most current state in the store, then our views should receive a notification whenever the state changes.

Our store will use the **observer pattern** to allow the views to immediately update when the state changes. The views will register a callback function that they would like to be invoked when the state changes. The store will keep a list of all of these callback functions. When the state changes, the store will invoke each function, "notifying" the listeners of the change.

The best way to illustrate this pattern is to implement it.

Inside `createStore()`, we will:

1. Define an array called `listeners`
2. Add a `subscribe()` method which adds a new listener to `listeners`
3. Call each listener function when the state is changed

1. Define an array called `listeners`

We declare `listeners` at the top of `createStore()`:

redux/chat_simple/src/complete/App-3.js

```
function createStore(reducer, initialState) {
  let state = initialState;
  const listeners = [];
  // ...
```

2. Add a `subscribe()` method which adds a new listener to `listeners`

Next, below the declaration of `listeners`, let's add `subscribe()`:

redux/chat_simple/src/complete/App-3.js

```
  const subscribe = (listener) => (
    listeners.push(listener)
  );
```

The `listener` argument of `subscribe()` is a function, the function that the view would like invoked whenever the state changes. We add this function to the `listeners` array.

To make `subscribe()` accessible, we need to expose `subscribe` by adding it to the store object returned by `createStore()`:

redux/chat_simple/src/complete/App-3.js

```
  // ...
  return {
    subscribe,
    getState,
    dispatch,
  };
```

3. Call each listener function when the state is changed

Whenever the state changes, we need to invoke all the functions kept in `listeners`. The state may change whenever we dispatch actions. As such, we'll add the invocation logic to `dispatch()`:

redux/chat_simple/src/complete/App-3.js

```
  // ...
  const dispatch = (action) => {
    state = reducer(state, action);
    listeners.forEach(l => l());
  };
  // ...
```

Note that there are no arguments passed to the listeners. This callback is solely a notification that the state changed.

`createStore()` in full

Here's our `createStore()` function, in full:

redux/chat_simple/src/complete/App-4.js

```
function createStore(reducer, initialState) {
  let state = initialState;
  const listeners = [];

  const subscribe = (listener) => (
    listeners.push(listener)
  );

  const getState = () => (state);

  const dispatch = (action) => {
    state = reducer(state, action);
    listeners.forEach(l => l());
  };

  return {
    subscribe,
    getState,
    dispatch,
  };
}
```

Stripped of comments, warnings, and sanity checks, the Redux library's `createStore()` looks and behaves quite like our function.

Try it out

With `subscribe()` in place, our store is complete. Let's test everything out.

In `App.js`, clear out all the previous testing code below this line where we initialize the store:

redux/chat_simple/src/complete/App-4.js

```
const store = createStore(reducer, initialState);
```

We'll dispatch add and delete message actions like before. Except, now we'll use `subscribe()` to register a function that will perform a `console.log()` every time the state changes.

Our listener prints the current state to the console:

redux/chat_simple/src/complete/App-4.js

```
const listener = () => {
  console.log('Current state: ');
  console.log(store.getState());
};
```

Next, let's subscribe this listener:

redux/chat_simple/src/complete/App-4.js

```
store.subscribe(listener);
```

Now, we can dispatch our actions. After every `dispatch()` call, the listening function we passed to `subscribe()` will be called, writing to the console:

redux/chat_simple/src/complete/App-4.js

```
const addMessageAction1 = {
  type: 'ADD_MESSAGE',
  message: 'How do you read?',
};
store.dispatch(addMessageAction1);
    // -> `listener()` is called

const addMessageAction2 = {
  type: 'ADD_MESSAGE',
  message: 'I read you loud and clear, Houston.',
};
store.dispatch(addMessageAction2);
```

```
    // -> `listener()` is called

const deleteMessageAction = {
  type: 'DELETE_MESSAGE',
  index: 0,
};
store.dispatch(deleteMessageAction);
    // -> `listener()` is called
```

Save `App.js` and run it with `babel-node`:

```
$ ./node_modules/.bin/babel-node src/App.js
```

And note the output:

```
Current state:
{ messages: [ 'How do you read?' ] }
Current state:
{ messages: [ 'How do you read?', 'I read you loud and clear, Houston.' ] }
Current state:
{ messages: [ 'I read you loud and clear, Houston.' ] }
```

With our store feature complete, we're prepared to connect our Redux store to some React views and see a complete, working Redux pipeline.

Connecting Redux to React

Revisiting the Flux diagram from earlier, we can now explore the specifics behind how Redux and React work together to fulfill this design pattern:

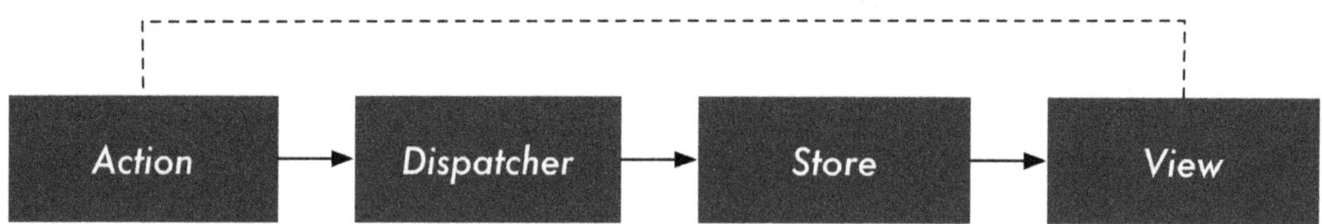

Using `store.getState()`

React is no longer managing state. Redux is. Therefore, top-level React components will use `store.getState()` as opposed to `this.state` to drive their `render()` functions. The state provided by Redux will trickle down from there.

For instance, if we want to render our state's `messages`, we fetch them from our Redux store:

```
// An example top-level component
class App extends React.Component {
  // ...
  render() {
    const messages = store.getState().messages;
    // ...
  }
};
```

Using `store.subscribe()`

When React manages state, we call `setState()` to modify `this.state`. `setState()` will trigger a re-render after the state is modified.

When Redux is managing state, we use `subscribe()` inside the top-level React component to setup a listening function that initiates the re-render.

We can subscribe our component inside of `componentDidMount`. The listening function that we pass to `subscribe()` will call `this.forceUpdate()`, triggering the component (`this`) to re-render.

As an example, subscribing a React component looks like this:

```
// An example top-level component
class App extends React.Component {
  // ...
  componentDidMount() {
    store.subscribe(() => this.forceUpdate());
  }
  // ...
};
```

Using `store.dispatch()`

Lower-level components will dispatch actions in response to events that should modify state. For instance, a React component might dispatch an action to the store whenever a delete button is clicked:

```
// An example leaf component
class Message extends React.Component {
  handleDeleteClick = () => {
    store.dispatch({
      type: 'DELETE_MESSAGE',
      index: this.props.index,
    });
  };
  // ...
};
```

This `dispatch()` call will modify the state. `dispatch()` will then invoke the listener, which we registered with `subscribe()`. This forces the `App` component to re-render. When `render()` is invoked, the `App` component reads from the store again with `getState()`. `App` then passes the latest version of the state down to its child components.

This cycle repeats every time React dispatches an action.

The app's components

The chat app has three React components:

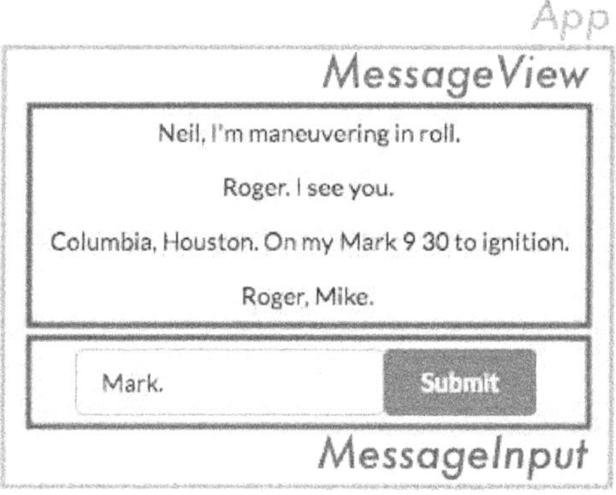

- `App`: The top-level container
- `MessageView`: The list of messages
- `MessageInput`: The input to add new messages

As we saw, the input box enables adding messages. Clicking on a message deletes it.

`MessageView` will render the state's `messages`. It will also dispatch `DELETE_MESSAGE` actions every time the user clicks an individual message.

`MessageInput` will not use state to render. However, it will dispatch `ADD_MESSAGE` actions every time the user submits a new message.

We could have broken `MessageView` into `MessageList` and `Message`. This would follow the pattern from previous apps. However, each message is simple enough at the moment that this is not necessary.

Preparing `App.js`

For this project, the store logic and React components will all be inside `src/App.js`. We will be able to reference `store` directly in each of our components.

In more complex applications, the store will likely be located in a different file than React components. In a later chapter, we'll explore other ways to have React components communicate with a Redux store object.

Clear out all the testing code below the declaration of `store` at the end of `src/App.js`:

redux/chat_simple/src/complete/App-4.js

```
const store = createStore(reducer, initialState);
```

The `App` component

`App` is the top-level React component in our app. `App` will be the component that reads from the store. We'll need it to subscribe to our Redux store.

Subscribing to changes

Like we talked about above, we will `subscribe()` inside of `componentDidMount`. The callback function we give to `subscribe()` calls `this.forceUpdate()`. This will cause the `App` component to re-render every time the state changes:

redux/chat_simple/src/complete/App-5.js

```
class App extends React.Component {
  componentDidMount() {
    store.subscribe(() => this.forceUpdate());
  }
```

Rendering the view

In `render`, we'll first use `getState()` to read `messages` from the store. We'll then render the two children, `MessageView` and `MessageInput`. Only `MessageView` needs the list of messages:

redux/chat_simple/src/complete/App-5.js

```
  render() {
    const messages = store.getState().messages;

    return (
      <div className='ui segment'>
        <MessageView messages={messages} />
        <MessageInput />
      </div>
    );
  }
```

We have our downward data pipeline, from the store through `App` down to `MessageView`. But what about the inverse direction? We want `MessageView` to have the ability to delete messages and `MessageInput` to be able to add them.

When React is managing state, we pass down functions as props from state-managing components to children. This enables children to propagate events up to the parent who modifies the state.

Now, we have a `store` object that we can dispatch actions to. While we could still concentrate all communication with the store inside of `App`, let's explore allowing our child components to dispatch actions to the store directly.

As in previous projects, the two `div` tags (and their `className` attributes) are provided for styling.

The `App` component in full:

redux/chat_simple/src/complete/App-5.js

```
class App extends React.Component {
  componentDidMount() {
    store.subscribe(() => this.forceUpdate());
  }

  render() {
    const messages = store.getState().messages;

    return (
      <div className='ui segment'>
        <MessageView messages={messages} />
        <MessageInput />
```

```
      </div>
    );
  }
}
```

The `MessageInput` component

`MessageInput` will have a single input field and a submit button. When the user clicks the submit button, the component should dispatch an `ADD_MESSAGE` action.

As a controlled component, we'll want to keep track of the value of the input in state somewhere. We *could* keep this state in our Redux store. But it's usually easier to just keep form data in the form component's state.

Let's begin by defining the initial state as well as the `onChange` handler function:

redux/chat_simple/src/complete/App-5.js

```
class MessageInput extends React.Component {
  state = {
    value: '',
  };

  onChange = (e) => {
    this.setState({
      value: e.target.value,
    })
  };
```

For more info on controlled components, see the "Forms" chapter.

Next, we'll define `handleSubmit()`, the function that will call `dispatch()`:

redux/chat_simple/src/complete/App-5.js

```
  handleSubmit = () => {
    store.dispatch({
      type: 'ADD_MESSAGE',
      message: this.state.value,
    });
    this.setState({
      value: '',
    });
  };
```

`render` will contain an `input` and a `button` wrapped in a `div`. `button` will have its `onClick` attribute set to `this.handleSubmit`:

redux/chat_simple/src/complete/App-5.js

```
  render() {
    return (
      <div className='ui input'>
        <input
          onChange={this.onChange}
          value={this.state.value}
          type='text'
        />
        <button
          onClick={this.handleSubmit}
          className='ui primary button'
          type='submit'
        >
          Submit
        </button>
      </div>
    );
  }
```

Do I have to keep *all* my app's state in my Redux store?

We mentioned that we *could* have kept the value of the input inside `MessageInput` in our Redux store. This is a perfectly valid and common approach.

However, we often find that using component state in certain areas is just fine. We like using component state for data that will always be isolated to the component, like form input data or whether or not a drop-down is open. If in the future it ever feels "wrong," it's easy to move that state into Redux.

The `MessageView` component

The `MessageView` component's `messages` prop is an array of strings. `MessageView` will render these messages as a list. Furthermore, whenever the user clicks a message we want to dispatch a `DELETE_-MESSAGE` action.

Let's begin by defining the component and its function `handleClick()`. `handleClick()` will be the function that calls `dispatch()`. `handleClick()` accepts one argument, `index`, which it uses in the action object it dispatches:

redux/chat_simple/src/complete/App-5.js

```
class MessageView extends React.Component {
  handleClick = (index) => {
    store.dispatch({
      type: 'DELETE_MESSAGE',
      index: index,
    });
  };
```

The `render` function will use `map` to create the list of messages to render. We want each individual `message` to be wrapped inside of a `div`:

redux/chat_simple/src/complete/App-5.js

```
  render() {
    const messages = this.props.messages.map((message, index) => (
      <div
        className='comment'
        key={index}
        onClick={() => this.handleClick(index)}
      >
        {message}
      </div>
    ));
```

On this `div` we set the `onClick` attribute. We want this to call a function that calls `handleClick()`, passing in the index of the target message.

Finally, we return `messages` wrapped inside of a `div`:

redux/chat_simple/src/complete/App-5.js

```
    return (
      <div className='ui comments'>
        {messages}
      </div>
    );
```

Finally, we export `App` at the bottom of the file:

redux/chat_simple/src/complete/App-5.js

```
export default App;
```

We already include `App` in `index.js` and mount it to the DOM using `ReactDOM.render()`. Therefore, we're ready to try everything out.

Try it out

Save `App.js`. In your terminal, from the root of the project folder, boot the server:

```
$ npm start
```

Add a few messages, then click on them to see them instantly disappear.

Next up

Redux is a powerful way to manage state in your app. By using a few simple ideas you can get an understandable data architecture that scales well to large apps.

Admittedly, in the current state of our app it's difficult to see how Redux provides any advantage over managing state in React. Indeed, as stated in the introduction of this chapter, using React for state management is a preferable choice for a wide variety of applications.

However, as we'll see as we scale up the complexity of our messaging app, Redux is advantageous as an app's interactivity and state management grows more complicated. This is because:

1. All of the data is in a central data structure
2. Data changes are also centralized
3. The actions that views emit are decoupled from the state mutations that occur
4. One-way data flow makes it easy to trace how changes flow through the system

With the core ideas of Redux behind us, we're prepared to significantly increase the functionality of the messaging app. In doing so, we'll explore solutions for a variety of real-world challenges.

As we evolve the messaging app, we'll cover:

- How to use the Redux library
- How to use the React-Redux library
- How to deal with more complicated state
- How to split up our reducers (and recombine them)
- How to re-organize our React components

React and Redux pair wonderfully, and we'll see first-hand how well they scale to handle our escalating requirements.

Intermediate Redux

In the last chapter, we learned about a specific Flux implementation, Redux. By building our own Redux store from scratch and integrating the store with React components, we got a feel for how data flows through a Redux-powered React app.

In this chapter, we build on these concepts by adding additional features to our chat application. Our chat app will begin to look like a real-world messaging interface.

In the process, we'll explore strategies for handling more complex state management. We'll also use a couple of functions directly from the `redux` library.

Preparation

Inside of the code download that came with the book, navigate to `redux/chat_intermediate`:

```
$ cd redux/chat_intermediate
```

This app is setup identically to the chat app in the last chapter, powered by create-react-app.

```
$ ls
README.md
nightwatch.json
package.json
public
semantic
semantic.json
src
tests
yarn.lock
```

Checking out `src/`:

```
$ ls src/
App.js
complete
index.css
index.js
```

Again, `App.js` is where we'll be working. It contains the app as we left it in the previous chapter. And again, `complete/` contains each iteration of `App.js` as we build it up over the next two chapters. `index.js` currently includes the final version of `App.js` and mounts it to the DOM.

As usual, run `npm install` to install all of the dependencies for the project:

```
$ npm install
```

And then execute `npm start` to boot the server:

```
$ npm start
```

View the completed app by visiting `http://localhost:3000` in your browser.

In this iteration of the chat app, our app has threads. Each message belongs to a particular thread with another user. We can switch between threads using the tabs at the top.

As in the last iteration, note that we can add messages with the text field at the bottom as well as delete messages by clicking on them.

To begin, let's swap in `App.js` in `src/index.js`:

```
import React from "react";
import ReactDOM from "react-dom";
import App from "./App";
```

Using `createStore()` from the `redux` library

In the last chapter, we implemented our own version of `createStore()`. At the top of `src/App.js`, you'll find the `createStore()` function just as we left it. The store object that this function creates has three methods: `getState()`, `dispatch()`, and `subscribe()`.

As we noted in the last chapter, our `createStore()` function is very similar to that which ships with the `redux` library. Let's remove our implementation and use the one from `redux`.

In `package.json`, we already include the `redux` library:

```
"redux": "3.6.0",
```

We can import the `createStore()` function from the library:

redux/chat_intermediate/src/complete/App-1.js

```
import { createStore } from 'redux';
```

Now we can remove our own `createStore()` definition from `App.js`.

Try it out

To verify everything is working properly, ensure the server is running:

```
$ npm start
```

And then check out the app on `http://localhost:3000`.

Behavior for the app will be the same as we left it in the previous chapter. We can add new messages and click on them to delete.

There are a couple subtle behavioral differences between our `createStore()` and the one that ships with the Redux library. Our app has yet to touch on them. We'll address these differences when they come up.

Representing messages as objects in state

Our state up to this point has been simple. State has been an object, with a `messages` property. Each message has been a string:

```
// Example of our state object so far
{
  messages: [
    'Roger. Eagle is undocked',
    'Looking good.',
  ],
}
```

To bring our app closer to a real-world chat app, each message will need to carry more data. For example, we might want each message to specify when it was sent or who sent it. To support this, we can use an object to represent each message as opposed to a string.

For now, we'll add two properties to each message, `timestamp` and `id`:

```
// Example of our new state object
{
  messages: [
    // An example message
    // messages are now objects
    {
      text: 'Roger. Eagle is undocked',
      timestamp: '1461974250213',
      id: '9da98285-4178',
    },
    // ...
  ]
}
```

The `Date.now()` function in JavaScript returns a number representing the number of milliseconds since January 1, 1970 00:00 UTC. This is called "Epoch" or "Unix" time. We're using this representation for the `timestamp` property above.

You can use a JavaScript library like Moment.js[87] to render more human-friendly timestamps.

In order to support messages that are objects, we'll need to tweak our reducer as well as our React components.

Updating `ADD_MESSAGE`

The reducer function we wrote in the last chapter handles two actions, `ADD_MESSAGE` and `DELETE_MESSAGE`. Let's start by updating the `ADD_MESSAGE` action handler.

As you recall, the `ADD_MESSAGE` action currently contains a `message` property:

```
{
  type: 'ADD_MESSAGE',
  message: 'Looking good.',
}
```

`reducer()` receives this action and returns a new object with a `messages` property. `messages` is set to a new array that contains the previous `state.messages` with the new message appended to it:

[87] http://momentjs.com/

redux/chat_intermediate/src/complete/App-1.js

```
function reducer(state, action) {
  if (action.type === 'ADD_MESSAGE') {
    return {
      messages: state.messages.concat(action.message),
    };
```

Let's tweak our ADD_MESSAGE action so that it uses the property name text instead of message:

```
// Example of what our new ADD_MESSAGE will look like
{
  type: 'ADD_MESSAGE',
  text: 'Looking good.',
}
```

text matches the property name that we'll be using for the message object.

Next, let's modify our reducer's ADD_MESSAGE handler so that it uses message objects as opposed to string literals.

We will give each message object a unique identifier. We include the uuid library in our package.json. Let's import it at the top of src/App.js:

redux/chat_intermediate/src/complete/App-2.js

```
import uuid from 'uuid';
```

Next, let's modify ADD_MESSAGE so that it creates a new object to represent the message. It will use action.text for the text property and then generate a timestamp and an id:

redux/chat_intermediate/src/complete/App-2.js

```
  if (action.type === 'ADD_MESSAGE') {
    const newMessage = {
      text: action.text,
      timestamp: Date.now(),
      id: uuid.v4(),
    };
```

Date.now() is part of the JavaScript standard library. It returns the current time in the Unix time format, in milliseconds.

We'll use concat again. This time, we'll use concat to return a new array that contains state.messages and our newMessage object:

redux/chat_intermediate/src/complete/App-2.js

```
    return {
      messages: state.messages.concat(newMessage),
    };
```

Our modified ADD_MESSAGE handler in full:

redux/chat_intermediate/src/complete/App-2.js

```
  if (action.type === 'ADD_MESSAGE') {
    const newMessage = {
      text: action.text,
      timestamp: Date.now(),
      id: uuid.v4(),
    };
    return {
      messages: state.messages.concat(newMessage),
    };
```

Updating DELETE_MESSAGE

The DELETE_MESSAGE action up until now contained an `index`, the index of the message in the `state.messages` array to be deleted:

```
{
  type: 'DELETE_MESSAGE',
  index: 5,
}
```

Now that all of our messages have a unique `id`, we can use that:

```
// Example of what our new DELETE_MESSAGE will look like
{
  type: 'DELETE_MESSAGE',
  id: '9da98285-4178',
}
```

To remove the message from `state.messages`, we can use Array's `filter()` method. `filter()` returns a new array containing all of the elements that "pass" the supplied test function:

redux/chat_intermediate/src/complete/App-2.js

```
} else if (action.type === 'DELETE_MESSAGE') {
  return {
    messages: state.messages.filter((m) => (
      m.id !== action.id
    ))
```

Here, we're building a **new** array containing every object that does **not** have an `id` that corresponds to the action's `id`.

With these changes in place, our reducers are ready to handle our new message objects. We'll update our React components next. We need to update both the actions they emit as well as how they render messages.

Updating the React components

`MessageInput` dispatches an `ADD_MESSAGE` action whenever the user clicks its submit button. We'll need to modify this component so that it uses the property name `text` as opposed to `message` for the action:

redux/chat_intermediate/src/complete/App-2.js

```
handleSubmit = () => {
  store.dispatch({
    type: 'ADD_MESSAGE',
    text: this.state.value,
  });
  this.setState({
    value: '',
  });
};
```

`MessageView` dispatches a `DELETE_MESSAGE` action whenever the user clicks on a message. We need to tweak the action it dispatches so that it uses the property `id` as opposed to `index`:

redux/chat_intermediate/src/complete/App-2.js

```
class MessageView extends React.Component {
  handleClick = (id) => {
    store.dispatch({
      type: 'DELETE_MESSAGE',
      id: id,
    });
  };
```

Then, we need to change the `render()` function for `MessageView`. We'll modify the HTML for each message so that it also includes the `timestamp` property. To render the text of the message, we call `message.text`:

redux/chat_intermediate/src/complete/App-2.js

```
  render() {
    const messages = this.props.messages.map((message, index) => (
      <div
        className='comment'
        key={index}
        onClick={() => this.handleClick(message.id)} // Use `id`
      >
        <div className='text'> {/* Wrap message data in `div` */}
          {message.text}
          <span className='metadata'>@{message.timestamp}</span>
        </div>
      </div>
    ));
```

Note that we now pass in `message.id` as opposed to `index` to `this.handleClick()`. We wrap the display logic for each message inside a `div` with class `text`.

Our reducers and React components are now on the same page. We're using our new representation of both the state and actions.

Save `App.js`. If your server isn't already running, boot it:

```
$ npm start
```

Navigate to `http://localhost:3000`. When you add messages, a timestamp should appear to the right of each message. You can also delete them as before by clicking on them:

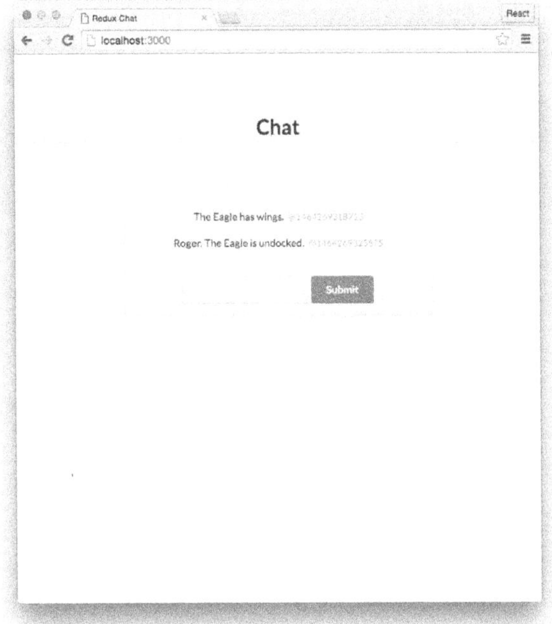

Introducing threads

Our state now uses message objects, which will allow us to carry information about each message in our app (like `timestamp`).

But in order for our app to begin reflecting a real-world chat app, we'll need to introduce another concept: **threads**.

In a chat app, a "thread" is a distinct set of messages. A thread is a conversation between you and one or more other users:

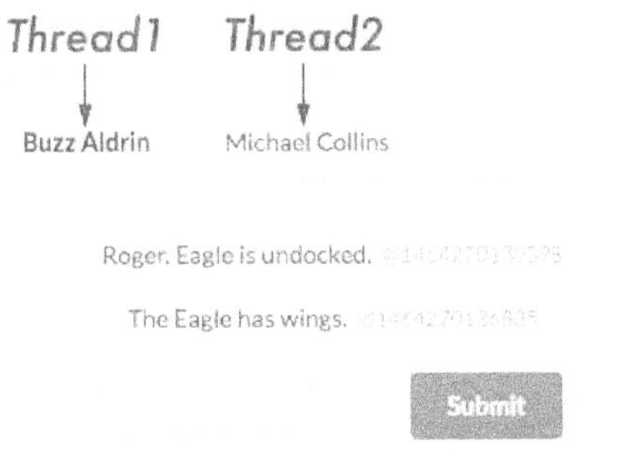

Two threads in the interface

As the completed version of the app demonstrated, our app will use tabs to enable a user to switch between threads. Each message belongs to a single thread:

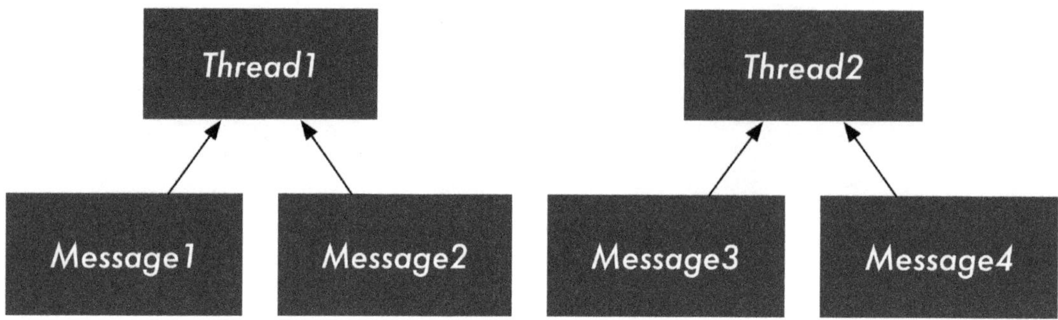

Messages belong to Threads

To support threads, we'll update the shape of our state object. The top-level property will now be `threads`, an array of thread objects. Each thread object will have a `messages` property which will contain the message object we introduced to the system in the previous section:

```
{
  threads: [
    {
      id: 'd7902357-4703', // UUID of the thread
      title: 'Buzz Aldrin', // Who the conversation is with
      messages: [
        {
          id: 'e8596e6b-97cc',
          text: 'Twelve minutes to ignition.',
          timestamp: 1462122634882,
        },
        // ... other messages with Buzz Aldrin
      ]
    },
    // ... other threads (with other users)
  ],
}
```

Supporting threads in `initialState`

To support threads, let's first update our initial state.

At the moment, we're initializing state to an object with a `messages` property:

redux/chat_intermediate/src/complete/App-2.js

```
const initialState = { messages: [] };
```

Now we want our top-level property to be `threads`. We could initialize state to this:

```
{ threads: [] }
```

But that would quickly add a significant amount of complexity to our app. Not only do we need to update our reducers to support our new thread-driven state, but we'd need to also add some way to create new threads.

For our app to reflect a real-world chat app, we'd need the ability to create new threads in the future. But for now, we can take a smaller step by just initializing our state with a hard-coded set of threads.

Modify `initialState` now, initializing it to an object with a `threads` property. We'll have two thread objects in state:

redux/chat_intermediate/src/complete/App-3.js

```
const initialState = {
  activeThreadId: '1-fca2', // New state property
  threads: [ // Two threads in state
    {
      id: '1-fca2', // hardcoded pseudo-UUID
      title: 'Buzz Aldrin',
      messages: [
        { // This thread starts with a single message already
          text: 'Twelve minutes to ignition.',
          timestamp: Date.now(),
          id: uuid.v4(),
        },
      ],
    },
    {
      id: '2-be91',
      title: 'Michael Collins',
      messages: [],
    },
  ],
};
```

Because we're hardcoding the `id` for our threads for now, we're using a clipped version of UUID for each of them.

Notice our initial state object contains another top-level property, `activeThreadId`. Our front-end displays only one thread at a time. Our view needs to know *which* thread to display. In addition to threads and messages, our app should also have this additional piece of state.

Here, we initialize it to our first thread which has an id of `'1-fca2'`.

We now have an initial state object that our React components can use to render a threaded version of our app. We'll update the components first to render from this new state shape.

Our app will be locked at this initial state though; we won't be able to add or delete any messages or switch between tabs. Once we confirm the views look good, we'll update our actions and our reducer to support our new thread-based chat app.

For now, we're initializing the first thread object with a single message already under `messages`. This will enable us to verify our React components are properly rendering a thread with a message ahead of our reducers supporting our updated `ADD_MESSAGE` action.

Supporting threads in the React components

To enable switching between threads in the app, the interface will have tabs above the messages view. We'll need to both add new React components and modify existing ones to support this.

Looking at the completed version of this chapter's chat app, we can identify the following components:

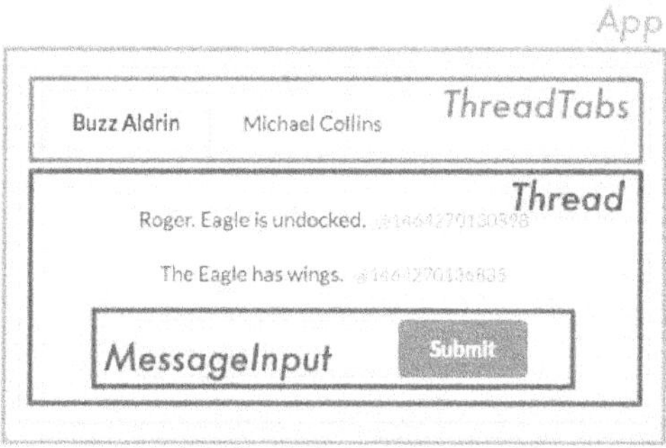

- `App`: The top-level component.
- `ThreadTabs`: The tabs widget for switching between threads.
- `Thread`: Displays all the messages in a thread. This component has been called `MessageView`, but we'll update its name to reflect our new thread-based state paradigm.

- MessageInput: The input to add new messages *to the open thread.* We can have this nested under Thread.

Let's first update our existing components to support our thread-based state. We'll then add our new component, ThreadTabs.

Modifying App

App currently subscribes to the store. App uses getState() to read the messages property and then renders its two children.

We'll have the component use our state's activeThreadId property to deduce which thread is active. The component will then pass the active thread to Thread (formerly MessageView) to render its messages.

First, we read both activeThreadId and threads from the state. We then use Array's find to find the thread object that has an id that matches activeThreadId:

redux/chat_intermediate/src/complete/App-3.js

```
class App extends React.Component {
  componentDidMount() {
    store.subscribe(() => this.forceUpdate());
  }

  render() {
    const state = store.getState();
    const activeThreadId = state.activeThreadId;
    const threads = state.threads;
    const activeThread = threads.find((t) => t.id === activeThreadId);
```

We pass our Thread component the activeThread for it to render. We're removing MessageInput from App as it will now be a child of Thread:

redux/chat_intermediate/src/complete/App-3.js

```
    return (
      <div className='ui segment'>
        <Thread thread={activeThread} />
      </div>
    );
```

The updated App component, in full:

redux/chat_intermediate/src/complete/App-3.js

```
class App extends React.Component {
  componentDidMount() {
    store.subscribe(() => this.forceUpdate());
  }

  render() {
    const state = store.getState();
    const activeThreadId = state.activeThreadId;
    const threads = state.threads;
    const activeThread = threads.find((t) => t.id === activeThreadId);

    return (
      <div className='ui segment'>
        <Thread thread={activeThread} />
      </div>
    );
  }
}
```

Turning `MessageView` into `Thread`

Now that messages are collected under a single thread, our front-end is displaying one thread's messages at a given time. We'll rename `MessageView` to `Thread` to reflect this.

`Thread` will render both the list of messages pertaining to the thread it's rendering as well as the `MessageInput` component for adding new messages to that thread.

First, rename the component:

redux/chat_intermediate/src/complete/App-3.js

```
class Thread extends React.Component {
```

Now, to create `messages` in `render()`, we'll use `this.props.thread.messages` instead of `this.props.messages`

redux/chat_intermediate/src/complete/App-3.js

```
  render() {
    const messages = this.props.thread.messages.map((message, index) => (
```

Last, we'll add `MessageInput` as a child of `Thread`. While we'll eventually need to update `MessageInput` to work properly with our new threaded state paradigm, we'll hold off on that update for now:

redux/chat_intermediate/src/complete/App-3.js

```
    return (
      <div className='ui center aligned basic segment'>
        <div className='ui comments'>
          {messages}
        </div>
        <MessageInput />
      </div>
    );
```

Try it out

Save `App.js`. Navigating to `http://localhost:3000`, we see our app with a single message, the message we set in `initialState`. However, we cannot add or delete any messages:

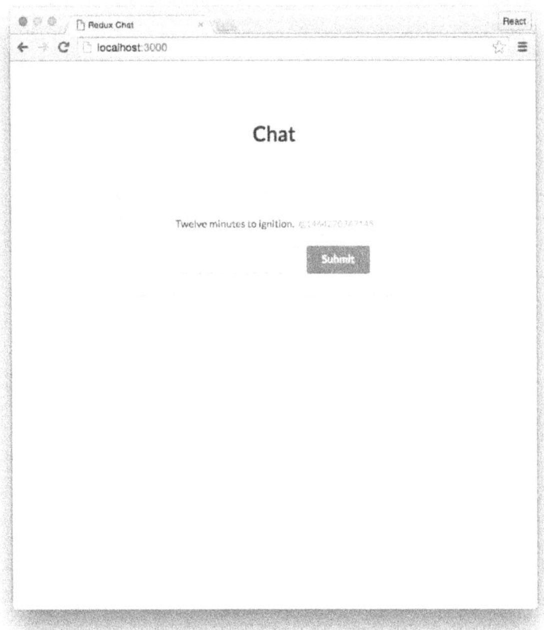

Our actions and our reducer do not yet support our new state shape. Before we update them, though, let's add the `ThreadTabs` component to our app.

Adding the `ThreadTabs` component

Our `App` component will render `ThreadTabs` above its other child components. `ThreadTabs` will need a list of thread titles to render as tabs. We'll eventually have the component dispatch an action to update the `activeThreadId` piece of state whenever a tab is clicked, but for now we'll just have it render the thread titles.

Updating `App`

First, we'll prepare a `tabs` array. This array will contain objects that correspond to the information `ThreadTabs` needs to render each tab.

`ThreadTabs` will need two pieces of information:

- The `title` of each tab
- Whether or not the tab is the "active" tab

Indicating whether or not the tab is active is for style purposes. Here's an example of two tabs. In the markup, the left tab is indicated as active:

Active Tab Inactive Tab

Inside `render` for `App`, we'll create an array of objects, `tabs`. Each object will contain a `title` and an `active` property. `active` will be a boolean:

redux/chat_intermediate/src/complete/App-4.js

```
    const tabs = threads.map(t => (
      { // a "tab" object
        title: t.title,
        active: t.id === activeThreadId,
      }
    ));
```

We add `ThreadTabs` to the `App` component's markup, passing down `tabs` as a prop:

redux/chat_intermediate/src/complete/App-4.js

```
    return (
      <div className='ui segment'>
        <ThreadTabs tabs={tabs} />
        <Thread thread={activeThread} />
      </div>
    );
```

Creating `ThreadTabs`

Next, let's add the `ThreadTabs` component right beneath the declaration of `App`. While we'll soon dispatch actions from `ThreadTabs` whenever a tab is clicked, for now it will just render the HTML for our tabs.

We first map over `this.props.tabs`, preparing the markup for each tab. In Semantic UI, we represent each tab as a `div` with a `class` of `item`. The active tab has a `class` of `active item`. We'll use `index` for the React-required `key` prop of each tab:

redux/chat_intermediate/src/complete/App-4.js

```
class ThreadTabs extends React.Component {
  render() {
    const tabs = this.props.tabs.map((tab, index) => (
      <div
        key={index}
        className={tab.active ? 'active item' : 'item'}
      >
        {tab.title}
      </div>
    ));
    return (
      <div className='ui top attached tabular menu'>
        {tabs}
      </div>
    );
  }
}
```

Try it out

Save `App.js`. Ensure the server is still running, and browse to `http://localhost:3000`. Everything is as before — we can't add or delete messages — but we now have tabs in the interface. We can't switch between the tabs yet, though:

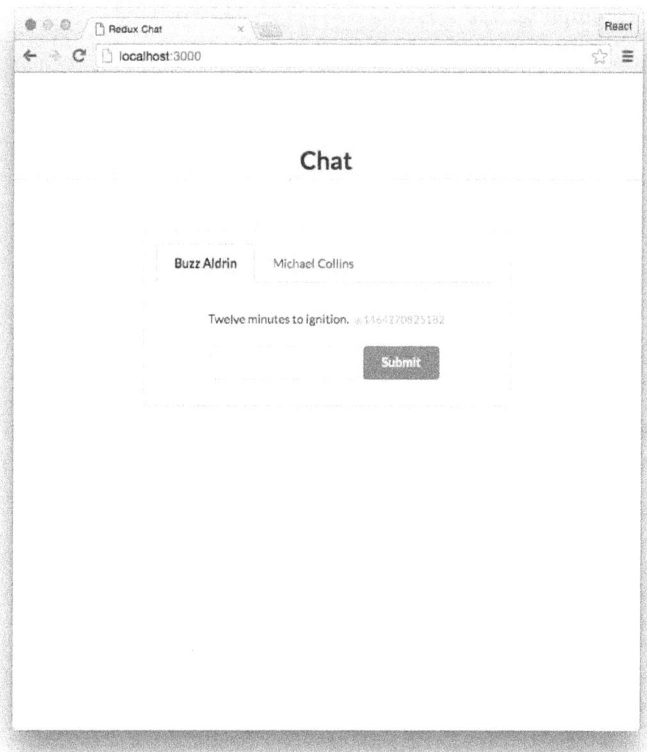

The first thread ("Buzz Aldrin") is our active thread. Its corresponding `tab` object has its `active` property set to `true`. This sets the `class` of the tab to `active item`, which gives us a nice visual indication of the active tab on the interface.

We've updated our state to support threads and our React components are properly rendering based on this new representation. Next, we'll restore interactivity by updating the actions and the reducer to work with this new state model.

Supporting threads in the reducer

Because our representation of state for this app has changed, we'll need to update the action handlers in our reducer.

Updating `ADD_MESSAGE` in the reducer

Because messages now belong to a thread, our `ADD_MESSAGE` action handler will need to add new messages to a specific thread. We'll add a property to this action object, `threadId`:

```
{
  type: 'ADD_MESSAGE',
  text: 'Looking good.',
  threadId: '1-fca2', // <- Or whichever thread is appropriate
}
```

Before, our `ADD_MESSAGE` handler in `reducer()` created a new message object and then used `concat` to append it to `state.messages`.

Now, we need to do the following:

1. Create the new message object `newMessage`
2. Find the corresponding thread (`action.threadId`) in `state.threads`
3. Append `newMessage` to the end of `thread.messages`

Let's modify `reducer()` in `App.js` now.

We keep the instantiation of the `newMessage` object. Next, we define `threadIndex` by hunting through `state.threads` and identifying the thread that corresponds to `action.threadId`:

redux/chat_intermediate/src/complete/App-5.js

```
    const newMessage = {
      text: action.text,
      timestamp: Date.now(),
      id: uuid.v4(),
    };
    const threadIndex = state.threads.findIndex(
      (t) => t.id === action.threadId
    );
```

Now, we might be tempted to just update the `messages` property on the thread like this:

```
// tempting, but flawed
const thread = state.threads[threadIndex];
thread.messages = thread.messages.concat(newMessage);
return state;
```

This would technically work; `thread` is a reference to the thread object sitting in `state.threads`. So by setting `thread.messages` to a new array with the new message included, we're modifying the thread object inside `state.threads`.

But this **mutates `state`**. As we discussed in the last chapter, `reducer()` *must* be a pure function. This means treating the state object as read-only.

We can't, therefore, modify the thread object. Instead, we can create a *new* thread object that contains the updated `thread.messages` property.

So, adding some detail to our plan from before, we actually want to do the following:

1. Create the new message object `newMessage`
2. Find the corresponding thread (`state.activeThreadId`) in `state.threads`
3. **Create a new thread object that contains all of the properties of the original thread object, *plus* an updated `messages` property**
4. **Return `state` with a `threads` property that contains our *new* thread object in place of the *original* one**

We already have step 1 taken care of. We have the `threadIndex` defined. Let's see how we create our new thread object:

redux/chat_intermediate/src/complete/App-5.js

```
    const oldThread = state.threads[threadIndex];
    const newThread = {
      ...oldThread,
      messages: oldThread.messages.concat(newMessage),
    };
```

To create `newThread`, we use an experimental JavaScript feature: the spread syntax *for objects*. We used the spread syntax in the last chapter for arrays, creating a new array based off of chunks of an existing one. The spread syntax for *arrays* was introduced in ES6. Here, we're using it to create a new *object* based on properties of an existing object.

This line *copies* all of the properties from `oldThread` to `newThread`:

redux/chat_intermediate/src/complete/App-5.js

```
      ...oldThread,
```

And then this line sets the `messages` property of `newThread` to the new messages array that contains `newMessage`:

redux/chat_intermediate/src/complete/App-5.js

```
      messages: oldThread.messages.concat(newMessage),
```

Note that by having the property `messages` appear *after* `oldThread`, we're effectively "overwriting" the `messages` property from `oldThread`.

We could have used `Object.assign()` to peform the same operation:

```
Object.assign({}, oldThread, {
  messages: oldThread.messages.concat(newMessage),
});
```

As you may recall, the first argument for `Object.assign()` is the target object. You can pass in as many additional arguments which are all of the objects you would like to copy properties from.

Because we perform lots of operations like this when working with pure reducer functions in Redux, we prefer the terser syntax of object's spread operator.

The spread operator for objects (`...`)

The spread operator was introduced for arrays in ES6. For objects, the spread operator is still a "stage 3" proposal. It is very likely it will be ratified and included in a future version of JavaScript.

We've been careful about using experimental JavaScript features in this book. We've been using property initializers, another experimental feature, elsewhere in the book because the React community has been using them heavily. The same goes for the Redux community and the spread operator for objects. As such, we're using it for this project.

The syntax is supported with the Babel preset `stage-0` which is included in `package.json`. `stage-0` includes all "stage 3" JavaScript proposals.

Usage

The ellipsis `...` operator copies one object into another:

```
const commonDolphin = {
  family: 'Delphinidae',
  genus: 'Delphinus',
};

const longBeakedDolphin = {
  ...commonDolphin,
  species: 'D. capensis',
};
// =>
// {
//   family: 'Delphinidae',
//   genus: 'Delphinus',
//   species: 'D. capensis',
// }

const spottedDolphin = {
  ...commonDolphin,
  genus: 'Stenella',
```

```
  species: 'S. attenuata',
};
// =>
// {
//   family: 'Delphinidae',
//   genus: 'Stenella',
//   species: 'S. attenuata',
// }

const atlanticSpottedDolphin = {
  ...spottedDolphin,
  species: 'S. frontalis',
}
// =>
// {
//   family: 'Delphinidae',
//   genus: 'Stenella',
//   species: 'S. frontalis',
// }
```

The spread operator enables us to succinctly construct new objects by copying over properties from existing ones. Because of this feature, we'll be using this operator often to keep our reducer functions pure.

Now, we have a `newThread` object that contains all of the properties of the original thread except with an updated `messages` property that contains the message being added.

The last step is to return the updated state. We want to return an object which has a `state.threads` that's set to the original list of threads except with our new thread object "subbed-in" for our old one.

We can re-use our strategy for creating a new array that contains chunks of a previous one. We have `threadIndex`, the index of the thread in the array we want to swap out. We want to create a new array that looks like this:

- All of the threads in `state.threads` up to but not including `threadIndex`
- `newThread`
- All of the threads in `state.threads` after `threadIndex`

That would look like this:

```
// Building a new array of threads
[
  ...state.threads.slice(0, threadIndex), // up to the thread
  newThread,                              // insert the new thread object
  ...state.threads.slice(
    threadIndex + 1, state.threads.length // after the thread
  ),
]
```

We can't set `state.threads` to this new array. That would be modifying `state`. Instead, we can create a new object and again use the spread operator to copy over all of the properties of `state` into the new object. Then, we can overwrite the `threads` property with our new array:

redux/chat_intermediate/src/complete/App-5.js

```
    return {
      ...state,
      threads: [
        ...state.threads.slice(0, threadIndex),
        newThread,
        ...state.threads.slice(
          threadIndex + 1, state.threads.length
        ),
      ],
    };
```

Updating `ADD_MESSAGE` required some new concepts, but now we have an important strategy we'll be re-using in the future: how to update state objects while avoiding mutations.

Our new logic for handling the `ADD_MESSAGE` action, in full:

redux/chat_intermediate/src/complete/App-5.js

```
  if (action.type === 'ADD_MESSAGE') {
    const newMessage = {
      text: action.text,
      timestamp: Date.now(),
      id: uuid.v4(),
    };
    const threadIndex = state.threads.findIndex(
      (t) => t.id === action.threadId
    );
    const oldThread = state.threads[threadIndex];
    const newThread = {
```

```
      ...oldThread,
      messages: oldThread.messages.concat(newMessage),
    };

    return {
      ...state,
      threads: [
        ...state.threads.slice(0, threadIndex),
        newThread,
        ...state.threads.slice(
          threadIndex + 1, state.threads.length
        ),
      ],
    };
```

Introducing threads to our state significantly increased the complexity of this action handler. Soon, we'll explore ways to break this action handler apart into smaller pieces. For now, let's update the areas where we're dispatching the `ADD_MESSAGE` action. There's just one: the `MessageInput` component.

Updating the `MessageInput` component

Our action object for `ADD_MESSAGE` should now contain the property `threadId`.

`MessageInput` is the only component that dispatches this action. The component should set `threadId` to the `id` of the active thread. We'll have `Thread` pass `MessageInput` the active thread's `id` as a prop:

redux/chat_intermediate/src/complete/App-5.js

```
    return (
      <div className='ui center aligned basic segment'>
        <div className='ui comments'>
          {messages}
        </div>
        <MessageInput threadId={this.props.thread.id} />
      </div>
    );
  }
```

Then, we can read from `this.props` in `MessageInput` to set `threadId` on the action object:

redux/chat_intermediate/src/complete/App-5.js

```
  handleSubmit = () => {
    store.dispatch({
      type: 'ADD_MESSAGE',
      text: this.state.value,
      threadId: this.props.threadId,
    });
    this.setState({
      value: '',
    });
  };
```

With `MessageInput` dispatching our updated `ADD_MESSAGE` action, let's verify that the functionality for adding messages has returned.

Try it out

Save `App.js`. Refreshing `http://localhost:3000`, we see that we can now submit messages again:

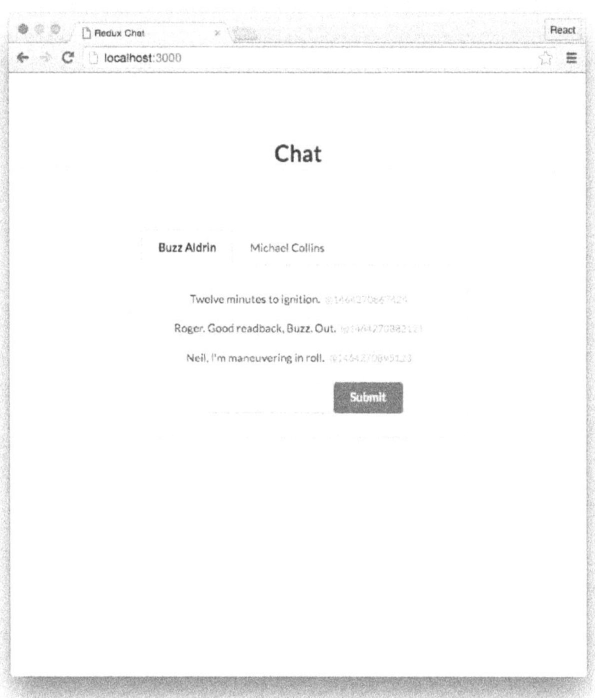

We still can't delete messages or switch between our threads. Let's focus on updating the `DELETE_-MESSAGE` action first.

Updating DELETE_MESSAGE in the reducer

The DELETE_MESSAGE action currently carries the property id which indicates which message should be deleted. While our app at the moment only permits a message to be deleted from the active thread, we'll write our reducer so that it searches all of the threads for the matching message.

When removing a message from state, we face a similar challenge as to the one that we faced with ADD_MESSAGE. The message is sitting in the messages array of a thread. But we can't modify the thread object in state.

We can use a similar strategy:

1. Grab the thread that holds the message we want to remove
2. Create a new thread object that contains all of the properties of the original thread object, plus an updated messages property that does *not* include the message we're removing
3. Return state with a threads property that contains our *new* thread object in place of the *original* one

Let's modify the reducer's DELETE_MESSAGE handler now.

First, we identify the thread that holds the message we're deleting:

redux/chat_intermediate/src/complete/App-6.js

```
} else if (action.type === 'DELETE_MESSAGE') {
  const threadIndex = state.threads.findIndex(
    (t) => t.messages.find((m) => (
      m.id === action.id
    ))
  );
  const oldThread = state.threads[threadIndex];
```

Inside of the findIndex callback, we perform a find against the messages property of that thread. If find finds the message matching the action's id, it returns the message. This satisfies the findIndex testing function, meaning that the thread's index is returned.

Next, we create a new thread object. We use the spread syntax to copy over all of the attributes from oldThread to this new object. We overwrite the messages property by using the filter() function just as before to generate a new array that does not include the deleted message:

redux/chat_intermediate/src/complete/App-6.js

```
    const newThread = {
      ...oldThread,
      messages: oldThread.messages.filter((m) => (
        m.id !== action.id
      )),
    };
```

The `return` statement for `DELETE_MESSAGE` is identical to the one for `ADD_MESSAGE`. We're performing the same operation: We ultimately want to "swap out" the original thread object in `state.threads` with our new one. So we want to:

1. Create a new object and copy over all the attributes from `state`
2. Overwrite the `threads` property with a new array of threads that has our new thread object swapped in for the original one

Again, the code is identical to that of `ADD_MESSAGE`:

redux/chat_intermediate/src/complete/App-6.js

```
    return {
      ...state,
      threads: [
        ...state.threads.slice(0, threadIndex),
        newThread,
        ...state.threads.slice(
          threadIndex + 1, state.threads.length
        ),
      ],
    };
```

In full, our `DELETE_MESSAGE` action handler:

redux/chat_intermediate/src/complete/App-6.js

```
} else if (action.type === 'DELETE_MESSAGE') {
  const threadIndex = state.threads.findIndex(
    (t) => t.messages.find((m) => (
      m.id === action.id
    ))
  );
  const oldThread = state.threads[threadIndex];

  const newThread = {
    ...oldThread,
    messages: oldThread.messages.filter((m) => (
      m.id !== action.id
    )),
  };

  return {
    ...state,
    threads: [
      ...state.threads.slice(0, threadIndex),
      newThread,
      ...state.threads.slice(
        threadIndex + 1, state.threads.length
      ),
    ],
  };
```

The complexity of this action handler, like that of `ADD_MESSAGE`, was significantly complicated by the introduction of threads. What's more, we've witnessed similar patterns emerge between the two action handlers: They both instantiate a new thread object that's a derivative of an existing thread object. And they both swap this thread object in for the thread object being "modified" in state.

Soon, we'll explore a new strategy to share this code and break these procedures down. But for now, let's test out deleting messages again.

Try it out

Save `App.js`. Make sure your server is running and navigate to `http://localhost:3000`. Adding and deleting messages are both working now:

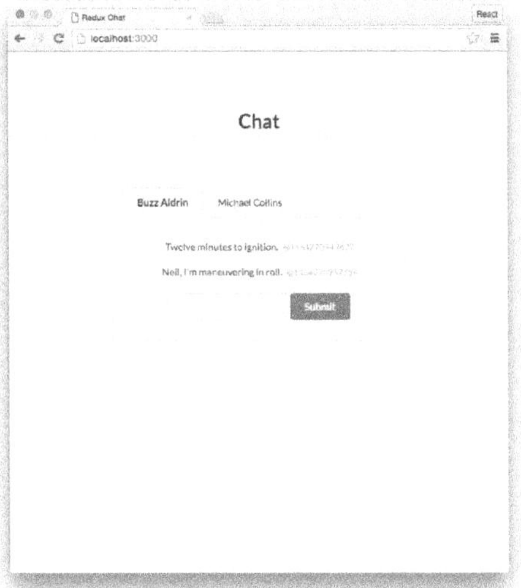

Clicking on the tab to switch threads still does not work, however. We initialize our state with `activeThreadId` set to `'1-fca2'` but have no actions in the system to modify this part of the state.

Adding the action `OPEN_THREAD`

We'll introduce another action, `OPEN_THREAD`, which React will dispatch whenever the user clicks on a thread tab to open it. This action will ultimately modify the `activeThreadId` property on `state`.

The component `ThreadTabs` will be the one to dispatch this action.

The action object

The action object just needs to specify the `id` of the thread the user wants to open:

```
{
  type: 'OPEN_THREAD',
  id: '2-be91', // <- or whichever `id` is appropriate
}
```

Modifying the reducer

Let's add another clause to our reducer to handle this new action. We'll add this clause below the `DELETE_MESSAGE` clause but before the final `else` statement.

We can't modify the state object directly:

```
// Incorrect
} else if (action.type === 'OPEN_THREAD') {
  state.activeThreadId = action.id;
  return state;
}
```

Instead, we'll copy over all of the attributes from `state` into a new object. We'll overwrite the `activeThreadId` property of this new object:

redux/chat_intermediate/src/complete/App-7.js

```
} else if (action.type === 'OPEN_THREAD') {
  return {
    ...state,
    activeThreadId: action.id,
  };
```

Using this strategy, we do not modify state.

Now, we just need to have `ThreadTabs` dispatch this action whenever a tab is clicked.

Dispatching from `ThreadTabs`

In order for `ThreadTabs` to dispatch the `OPEN_THREAD` action, it needs the `id` of the thread that was clicked on.

Right now, the tab object that we're giving to `ThreadTabs` contains the properties `title` and `active`. We'll need to modify the instantiation of `tabs` in `App` to also include the property `id`.

Let's do that first. Inside the `App` component, add this property to the tab object that we create:

redux/chat_intermediate/src/complete/App-7.js

```
    const tabs = threads.map(t => (
      {
        title: t.title,
        active: t.id === activeThreadId,
        id: t.id,
      }
    ));
```

Next, we'll add the component function `handleClick` to `ThreadTabs`. The function accepts `id`:

redux/chat_intermediate/src/complete/App-7.js

```
class ThreadTabs extends React.Component {
  handleClick = (id) => {
    store.dispatch({
      type: 'OPEN_THREAD',
      id: id,
    });
  };
```

Finally, we add an `onClick` attribute to the `div` tag for each tab. We set it to a function that calls `handleClick` with the thread's id:

redux/chat_intermediate/src/complete/App-7.js

```
    const tabs = this.props.tabs.map((tab, index) => (
      <div
        key={index}
        className={tab.active ? 'active item' : 'item'}
        onClick={() => this.handleClick(tab.id)}
      >
```

`ThreadTabs` is now emitting our new action. Let's test everything out.

Try it out

Save `App.js`. Pull up `http://localhost:3000` in your browser. At this point, adding and deleting messages works and we can switch between tabs. If we add a message to one thread, it's added to just that thread:

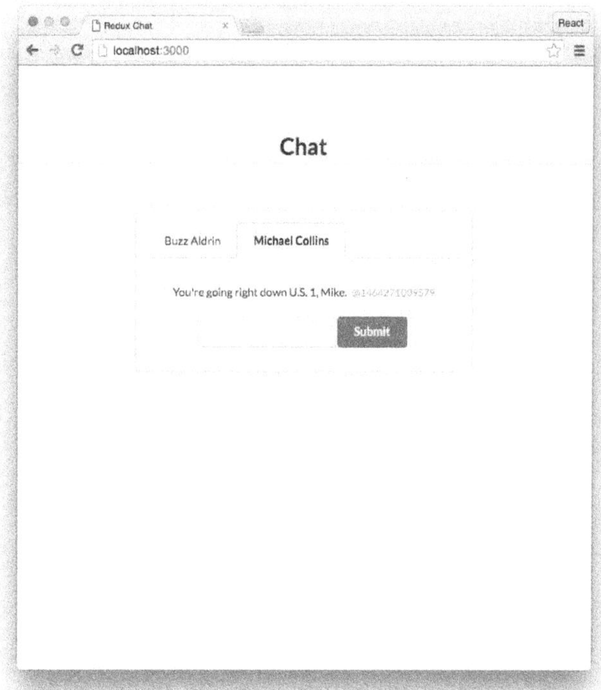

This is starting to look like an actual chat application! We've introduced the concept of threads and now support an interface that can switch between conversations with multiple users.

However, in the process, we significantly complicated our reducer function. While it's nice that all of our state is being managed in a single location, each of our action handlers contain a lot of logic. What's more, our `ADD_MESSAGE` and `DELETE_MESSAGE` handlers duplicate a lot of the same code.

It's also odd that the management of two distinct pieces of state — adding/deleting messages and switching between threads — are both managed in the same place. The idea of having a single reducer function manage the entirety of our state as the complexity of our app grows might feel daunting and even a bit dubious.

Indeed, Redux apps have a strategy for breaking down state management logic: **reducer composition**.

Breaking up the reducer function

With reducer composition, we can break up the state management logic of our app into smaller functions. We'll still pass in a single reducer function to `createStore()`. But this top-level function will then call one or more other functions. Each reducer function will manage a different part of the state tree.

Adding and deleting messages is a distinct piece of functionality from switching between threads. Let's break these two apart first.

A new `reducer()`

We'll still call our top-level function `reducer()`. Except now, we'll have two other reducer functions, each managing their part of the state's top-level properties. We'll name each of these sub-reducers after the property name that they manage:

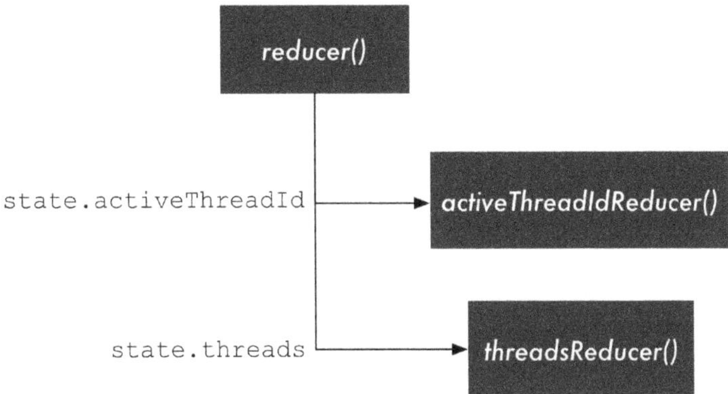

To implement this, let's first see what our new top-level `reducer()` function should look like. We can then create our sub-reducer functions.

To avoid confusion, let's rename our current reducer function from `reducer()` to `threadsReducer()`:

redux/chat_intermediate/src/complete/App-8.js

```
function threadsReducer(state, action) {
```

We still have to tweak this function, but we'll get back to it in a bit.

Now, above `threadsReducer()`, we'll insert our *new* function, `reducer()`:

redux/chat_intermediate/src/complete/App-8.js

```
function reducer(state, action) {
  return {
    activeThreadId: activeThreadIdReducer(state.activeThreadId, action),
    threads: threadsReducer(state.threads, action),
  };
}
```

The function is short but there's a lot going on.

We are returning a brand new object with the keys `activeThreadId` and `threads`. Importantly, we are *delegating the responsibility of how to update* `activeThreadId` *and* `threads` *to their respective reducers.*

Check out this line again:

redux/chat_intermediate/src/complete/App-8.js

```
    activeThreadId: activeThreadIdReducer(state.activeThreadId, action),
```

For the property `activeThreadId` on next state, we're delegating responsibility to the yet-to-be-defined function `activeThreadIdReducer()`. Notice how the first argument is not the whole state — it's only the part of the state that this reducer is responsible for. We pass in the action as the second argument.

Same strategy with `threads`:

redux/chat_intermediate/src/complete/App-8.js

```
    threads: threadsReducer(state.threads, action),
```

We delegate responsibility of the state's `threads` property to `threadsReducer()`. The state that we pass this reducer — the first argument — is the part of the state that `threadsReducer()` is responsible for updating.

This is how sub-reducers work in tandem with the top-level reducer. The top-level reducer breaks up each part of the state tree and delegates the management of those pieces of state to the appropriate reducer.

To get a better idea, let's write `activeThreadIdReducer()` below `reducer()`:

redux/chat_intermediate/src/complete/App-8.js

```
function activeThreadIdReducer(state, action) {
  if (action.type === 'OPEN_THREAD') {
    return action.id;
  } else {
    return state;
  }
}
```

This reducer only handles one type of action, `OPEN_THREAD`. Remember, the `state` argument being passed to the reducer is actually `state.activeThreadId`. This is the only part of the state that this reducer needs to be concerned with. As such, `activeThreadIdReducer()` receives a string as `state` (the id of a thread) and will return a string.

Notice how this simplifies the logic for handling `OPEN_THREAD`. Before, our logic had to consider the *entire* state tree. So we had to create a new object, copy over all of the state's properties, and then overwrite the `activeThreadId` property. Now, our reducer just has to worry about this single property.

If the action is OPEN_THREAD, activeThreadIdReducer() simply returns action.id, the id of the thread to be opened. Otherwise, it returns the same id it was passed.

Up in reducer(), the return value of activeThreadIdReducer() is set to the property activeThreadId in the new state object.

Let's update threadsReducer() next. Before, this function received the entire state object. Now, it's only receiving part of it: state.threads. We'll be able to simplify the code a bit as a result.

Updating threadsReducer()

threadsReducer() is now receiving only part of the state. Its state argument is the array of threads.

As a result, we can simplify our returns like we did with activeThreadIdReducer(). We no longer need to create a new state object, copy all the old values over, then overwrite threads. Instead, we can just return the updated array of threads.

What's more, instead of referencing state.threads everywhere we'll reference state as this is now the array of threads.

Let's make these modifications first for ADD_MESSAGE.

We reference state as opposed to state.threads:

redux/chat_intermediate/src/complete/App-8.js

```
    const threadIndex = state.findIndex(
      (t) => t.id === action.threadId
    );
    const oldThread = state[threadIndex];
    const newThread = {
      ...oldThread,
      messages: oldThread.messages.concat(newMessage),
    };
```

For the return statement, we no longer need to return a full state object, just the array of threads:

redux/chat_intermediate/src/complete/App-8.js

```
    return [
      ...state.slice(0, threadIndex),
      newThread,
      ...state.slice(
        threadIndex + 1, state.length
      ),
    ];
```

`DELETE_MESSAGE` will receive the same treatment.

We first change our references from `state.threads` to `state`:

redux/chat_intermediate/src/complete/App-8.js

```
  } else if (action.type === 'DELETE_MESSAGE') {
    const threadIndex = state.findIndex(
      (t) => t.messages.find((m) => (
        m.id === action.id
      ))
    );
    const oldThread = state[threadIndex];
```

Then, we return just the array as opposed to the whole state object:

redux/chat_intermediate/src/complete/App-8.js

```
    return [
      ...state.slice(0, threadIndex),
      newThread,
      ...state.slice(
        threadIndex + 1, state.length
      ),
    ];
```

Finally, we can remove the `OPEN_THREAD` handler from `threadsReducer()`. This reducer is not concerned about the `OPEN_THREAD` action. That action pertains to a part of the state tree that this reducer does not work with. So, whenever that action is received, the function will reach the last `else` clause and will just return `state` unmodified.

Our updated `threadsReducer()` function, in full:

redux/chat_intermediate/src/complete/App-8.js

```
function threadsReducer(state, action) {
  if (action.type === 'ADD_MESSAGE') {
    const newMessage = {
      text: action.text,
      timestamp: Date.now(),
      id: uuid.v4(),
    };
    const threadIndex = state.findIndex(
      (t) => t.id === action.threadId
    );
    const oldThread = state[threadIndex];
    const newThread = {
      ...oldThread,
      messages: oldThread.messages.concat(newMessage),
    };

    return [
      ...state.slice(0, threadIndex),
      newThread,
      ...state.slice(
        threadIndex + 1, state.length
      ),
    ];
  } else if (action.type === 'DELETE_MESSAGE') {
    const threadIndex = state.findIndex(
      (t) => t.messages.find((m) => (
        m.id === action.id
      ))
    );
    const oldThread = state[threadIndex];

    const newThread = {
      ...oldThread,
      messages: oldThread.messages.filter((m) => (
        m.id !== action.id
      )),
    };

    return [
      ...state.slice(0, threadIndex),
      newThread,
```

```
      ...state.slice(
        threadIndex + 1, state.length
      ),
    ];
  } else {
    return state;
  }
}
```

By focusing this reducer and having it deal with only the `threads` property in state, we were able to simplify our code a little. Our return functions no longer have to worry about the entire state tree and we removed an action handler from this function.

We still duplicate logic between the two action handlers. Notably, their return functions are the same.

In fact, while we simplified the reducer by having it work with only `state.threads`, this reducer is actually dealing with two levels of the state tree: both threads *and* messages. We can further break our reducer logic into smaller pieces and share code by having `threadsReducer()` delegate the responsibility to another reducer: `messagesReducer()`.

We'll explore this in the next section. For now, let's boot up the app and verify our solution so far works.

You might be asking: Why not just rename the first argument in `threadsReducer()` to `threads` as opposed to calling it `state`?

Indeed, doing this could improve readability of the reducer function. You'd no longer need to hold the idea in working memory that `state` is actually `state.threads`.

However, consistently calling the first argument to a Redux reducer `state` can be helpful for avoiding errors. It's a clear reminder that the argument is a part of the state tree and that you should avoid accidentally mutating it.

Ultimately, it's a matter of personal preference.

Try it out

Save `App.js`. Boot the server if it isn't running:

```
$ npm start
```

And then point your browser to `http://localhost:3000`. On the surface, it should appear as though nothing has changed; adding and deleting messages works and we can switch between threads.

Adding `messagesReducer()`

We used the concept of reducer composition to break up the management of our state. Our top-level `reducer()` function delegates the management of the two top-level state properties to their respective reducers.

We can take this concept even further. We've noticed that `threadsReducer()` has the responsibility of managing the state of both threads and messages. What's more, we see an opportunity to share code between the two action handlers.

We can have `threadsReducer()` delegate the management of each thread's `messages` property to another reducer, `messagesReducer()`. In full, the reducer tree will look like this:

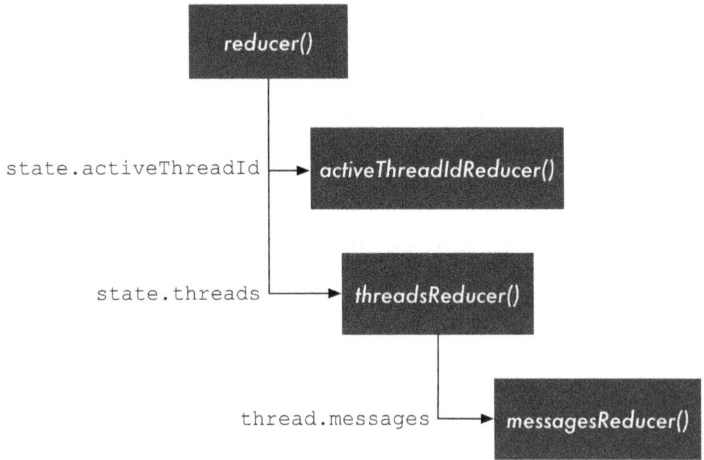

Let's first modify `threadsReducer()`, anticipating this new messages reducer function. We want the threads reducer function to know as little as possible about messages. `threadsReducer()` will rely on `messagesReducer()` to determine how a given thread's messages should be updated based on the action received.

Modifying the `ADD_MESSAGE` action handler

Let's see what happens when we delegate all message handling functionality to our anticipated `messagesReducer()` function.

We'll no longer declare `newMessage`. We expect that `messagesReducer()` will take care of this.

Then, when specifying the `messages` attribute for `newThread`, we'll delegate the creation of this array to `messagesReducer()`:

redux/chat_intermediate/src/complete/App-9.js

```
function threadsReducer(state, action) {
  if (action.type === 'ADD_MESSAGE') {
    const threadIndex = state.findIndex(
      (t) => t.id === action.threadId
    );
    const oldThread = state[threadIndex];
    const newThread = {
      ...oldThread,
      messages: messagesReducer(oldThread.messages, action),
    };
```

We pass `messagesReducer()` the array `oldThread.messages` as the first argument and `action` as the second. This follows our pattern so far: `reducer()` passed `threadsReducer()` `state.threads` as its first argument. `threadsReducer()` passes `thread.messages` as the first argument to `messagesReducer()`. We now know that when we build `messagesReducer()`, the first argument (`state`) will be an array of a given thread's messages.

The full `action` object is passed along in its entirety down the chain.

We do not need to make any modifications to the return value.

At the moment, this might only seem like a minor — perhaps negligible — victory. Before, we were calling `concat` in-line to create a new `messages` array with the new message inside. Now we have the added complexity of calling another function to do this.

We are breaking apart the responsibility of our functions, which is a worthwhile endeavor in its own right. Furthermore, another benefit will become apparent when we give `DELETE_MESSAGE` the same treatment.

Prior to modifying our `DELETE_MESSAGE` action handler, let's start on our `messagesReducer()` function to get an idea of how these reducers will work together.

Creating `messagesReducer()`

We'll write `messagesReducer()` below `threadsReducer()` in `App.js`. We'll start it off with one action handler (`ADD_MESSAGE`).

As we saw above, `threadsReducer()` passes `messagesReducer()` a thread's `messages` array as the first argument. This will be `state` inside of `messagesReducer()`.

`messagesReducer()` needs to:

1. Create the new message
2. Return a new array of messages that includes this new message appended to the end of it

We'll use the same logic that we had previously in `threadsReducer()` to accomplish this:

redux/chat_intermediate/src/complete/App-9.js

```
function messagesReducer(state, action) {
  if (action.type === 'ADD_MESSAGE') {
    const newMessage = {
      text: action.text,
      timestamp: Date.now(),
      id: uuid.v4(),
    };
    return state.concat(newMessage);
  } else {
    return state;
  }
}
```

`messagesReducer()` receives an array of messages as its first argument, `state`. The `ADD_MESSAGE` handler creates a new message using `action.text`. We use `concat` just as before to return a new messages array with our new message appended to it.

Now that we've seen how `threadsReducer()` delegates `ADD_MESSAGE` to `messagesReducer()`, let's take a look at how `DELETE_MESSAGE` can do the same thing.

Modifying the `DELETE_MESSAGE` action handler

As with the `ADD_MESSAGE` action handler, we want our `DELETE_MESSAGE` action handler in `threadsReducer()` to delegate the responsibility of handling the messages property of each thread to `messagesReducer()`.

Instead of invoking the `filter()` function directly, we can call `messagesReducer()` inside of the declaration of `newThread` and have *it* generate the `messages` property, like this:

redux/chat_intermediate/src/complete/App-9.js

```
  } else if (action.type === 'DELETE_MESSAGE') {
    const threadIndex = state.findIndex(
      (t) => t.messages.find((m) => (
        m.id === action.id
      ))
    );
    const oldThread = state[threadIndex];
    const newThread = {
      ...oldThread,
      messages: messagesReducer(oldThread.messages, action),
    };
```

Look familiar? With these modifications, the threads reducer's DELETE_MESSAGE looks almost exactly like its ADD_MESSAGE. The only difference is how the two handlers identify threadIndex.

On reflection, this makes sense. The action that we're dealing with is adding and removing messages. This will only ever affect the messages property on an individual thread. Because the messages property is now being managed by messagesReducer(), the differences between ADD_MESSAGE and DELETE_MESSAGE are expressed in that function. Aside from determining threadIndex, the rest of the ceremony — creating a new thread object with an updated messages property — is identical.

We can define a new function, findThreadIndex(), where we can store the logic to determine threadIndex. Then, we can combine our two action handlers as their code will be identical.

First, we'll write findThreadIndex() above threadsReducer(). This function will take both threads (or state in threadsReducer()) and the action as arguments. We'll copy the logic for finding the index of the affected thread into this function:

redux/chat_intermediate/src/complete/App-10.js

```
function findThreadIndex(threads, action) {
  switch (action.type) {
    case 'ADD_MESSAGE': {
      return threads.findIndex(
        (t) => t.id === action.threadId
      );
    }
    case 'DELETE_MESSAGE': {
      return threads.findIndex(
        (t) => t.messages.find((m) => (
          m.id === action.id
        ))
      );
    }
  }
}
```

We decided to use a switch statement here as opposed to an if/else clause. Using a switch statement in reducers and their helper functions can be slightly easier to read and manage. You'll see it used in many Redux apps. As the actions in a system grows, a single reducer will have to have multiple action handlers. switch is built for this use case.

Another reason for using switch in findThreadIndex() is because we'll use one in our refactored threadsReducer():

redux/chat_intermediate/src/complete/App-10.js

```
function threadsReducer(state, action) {
  switch (action.type) {
    case 'ADD_MESSAGE':
    case 'DELETE_MESSAGE': {
      const threadIndex = findThreadIndex(state, action);

      const oldThread = state[threadIndex];
      const newThread = {
        ...oldThread,
        messages: messagesReducer(oldThread.messages, action),
      };

      return [
        ...state.slice(0, threadIndex),
        newThread,
        ...state.slice(
          threadIndex + 1, state.length
        ),
      ];
    }
    default: {
      return state;
    }
  }
}
```

`switch` is nice here because this:

redux/chat_intermediate/src/complete/App-10.js

```
  switch (action.type) {
    case 'ADD_MESSAGE':
    case 'DELETE_MESSAGE': {
```

Reads a bit clearer than the alternative:

```
if (action.type === 'ADD_MESSAGE' || action.type === 'DELETE_MESSAGE') {
  // ...
}
```

This readability concern will be exacerbated if we continue to introduce more actions to the system that just affect the `messages` property of a given thread (like `UPDATE_MESSAGE`). With a `switch` statement, we can cleanly specify that all of these actions share the same code block.

Other than the call to `findThreadIndex()`, the body of the combined action handler matches what we had individually for each above.

Adding `DELETE_MESSAGE` to `messagesReducer()`

The `threadsReducer()` function now treats `ADD_MESSAGE` and `DELETE_MESSAGE` actions in the exact same way. When the reducer receives a `DELETE_MESSAGE` action, it will call `messagesReducer()` with a list of messages and the action. The list of messages corresponds to an individual thread's `messages` property. The action carries the directive for which message to remove.

Let's add the `DELETE_MESSAGE` logic to `messagesReducer()`. You can keep the `if/else` clause for now or change to `switch`:

redux/chat_intermediate/src/complete/App-10.js

```
function messagesReducer(state, action) {
  switch (action.type) {
    case 'ADD_MESSAGE': {
      const newMessage = {
        text: action.text,
        timestamp: Date.now(),
        id: uuid.v4(),
      };
      return state.concat(newMessage);
    }
    case 'DELETE_MESSAGE': {
      return state.filter(m => m.id !== action.id);
    }
    default: {
      return state;
    }
  }
}
```

Remember, `state` here is the array of messages. The logic for "filtering out" the message is the same that we had in `threadsReducer()`.

At this point, we've broken out the logic to manage state across three reducer functions. Each function manages a different part of the state tree. Our tree of reducer functions is combined up at `reducer()`, which is the function that we pass to `createStore()`.

The complexity of both our app and our state increased significantly in this chapter. We now see how using reducer composition allows us to manage this complexity. We have a pattern for scaling our system to handle the addition of many more actions and pieces of state.

There's one more improvement we can make. While the logic for managing state updates is contained within our reducers, the initial state of the app is defined elsewhere, in `initialState`. Let's bring the parts of this initialization closer to their respective reducers. This will scale better as our state tree grows. In addition, it means *all* of the logic around a particular part of the state tree is contained inside of its reducer.

Defining the initial state in the reducers

Right now, we declare our `initialState` object and then pass it into `createStore()`:

```
const store = createStore(reducer, initialState);
```

This argument is not required. Let's change this line so that we no longer pass in `initialState`:

```
const store = createStore(reducer);
```

What will happen?

The `createStore()` function in the `redux` library contains one key difference from the one we wrote in the last chapter. After the store is initialized but *right before* it's returned, `createStore()` actually dispatches an initialization action. That dispatch call looks like this:

```
  // ...
  // Inside of `createStore()` in `redux`
  dispatch({ type: '@@redux/INIT' });

  return { // returns store object
    dispatch,
    subscribe,
    getState,
  }
}
```

While the *initialization action* has a `type`, chances are you'll never need to use it.

The important part is that because we didn't specify an `initialState`, **`state` will be `undefined` when `createStore()` dispatches the initialization action**. The only time `state` will be `undefined` is for this first dispatch.

Therefore, we can have our reducers specify the initial state for their part of the state tree whenever `state` is `undefined`.

Initial state in `reducer()`

When `createStore()` dispatches the initialization object, `reducer()` will receive a `state` that is `undefined`.

In this situation, we want to set `state` to a blank object (`{}`). This will enable `reducer()` to delegate the initialization of each property in the state object to its reducer. We'll see how this works in practice shortly.

We can use ES6's **default arguments** to achieve this:

redux/chat_intermediate/src/complete/App-11.js

```
function reducer(state = {}, action) {
```

When `reducer()` receives a `state` of `undefined`, `state` is set to `{}`.

Importantly, when `reducer()` then calls each of its sub-reducers, each one of them will receive a `state` argument that is `undefined`.

A `state` that is `undefined` is the canonical way to initialize a reducer in Redux. While we could use this special initialization action object's type, with ES6's default arguments just relying on an `undefined` state is much easier.

For more info on default arguments, see "Appendix B."

Adding initial state to `activeThreadIdReducer()`

We can use default arguments to initialize the state in `activeThreadIdReducer()`. We want the initial state to be `'1-fca2'`, the `id` we'll specify for our first thread:

redux/chat_intermediate/src/complete/App-11.js

```
function activeThreadIdReducer(state = '1-fca2', action) {
```

Let's recap the initialization flow for `activeThreadIdReducer()`.

At the end of `createStore()`, right before the function returns the new store object, it dispatches the initialization action. Then:

1. `reducer()` is called with a `state` of `undefined` and the initialization action object
2. `state` defaults to `{}`
3. `reducer()` calls `activeThreadIdReducer()` with `state.activeThreadId`, which is `undefined`
4. `activeThreadIdReducer()` sets `state` to `'1-fca2'` with its default argument
5. The `else` clause in `activeThreadIdReducer()` returns `state` (`'1-fca2'`)

Adding initial state to `threadsReducer()`

We'll use the same strategy for `threadsReducer()`. Its initial state is more complex, so we'll split it up over multiple lines:

redux/chat_intermediate/src/complete/App-11.js

```
function threadsReducer(state = [
  {
    id: '1-fca2',
    title: 'Buzz Aldrin',
    messages: messagesReducer(undefined, {}),
  },
  {
    id: '2-be91',
    title: 'Michael Collins',
    messages: messagesReducer(undefined, {}),
  },
], action) {
```

If we weren't initializing our app with two threads already in state, the default argument for `threadsReducer()` would just be `[]`:

```
function threadsReducer(state = [], action) {
  // ...
}
```

Now, let's set the default argument in `messagesReducer()`. While we were initializing one of the threads with a message before, we don't need that anymore:

redux/chat_intermediate/src/complete/App-11.js

```
function messagesReducer(state = [], action) {
```

We could have just set the `messages` property in the initial state for threads to `[]`. But by calling `messagesReducer()` with `undefined`, we're still delegating initialization responsibility of `messages` to `messagesReducer()`.

We could have done this too:

```
// ...
{
  id: '2-be91',
  title: 'Michael Collins',
  messages: messagesReducer(
    undefined, { type: '@@redux/INIT' }
  ),
},
// ...
```

But passing along a blank action object is sufficient because we won't ever need to switch off of the special `type` of the initialization action object.

Last, go ahead and remove `initialState` from `App.js`. We don't need it anymore.

Let's kick the tires and make sure things are still working.

Try it out

Save `App.js`. Make sure the server is running, and then load `http://localhost:3000` in your browser.

As expected, everything works as before: we can add and delete messages and switch between tabs. The only difference is that we no longer have a default message initialized with the state.

While on the surface the behavior has not changed, we know that under the hood our code is a lot cleaner.

Using `combineReducers()` from `redux`

The pattern we implemented of combining different reducers to manage distinct parts of the state tree is a common one in Redux. In fact, the `redux` library includes a function `combineReducers()` that can generate a top-level `reducer()` function like the one we wrote by hand.

You can pass `combineReducers()` an object that specifies to which function it should delegate each property of the state object. To see how it works, let's use it now.

First, import the function from the `redux` library:

redux/chat_intermediate/src/complete/App-12.js

```
import { createStore, combineReducers } from 'redux';
```

Then, let's replace our definition of `reducer()`:

redux/chat_intermediate/src/complete/App-12.js

```
const reducer = combineReducers({
  activeThreadId: activeThreadIdReducer,
  threads: threadsReducer,
});
```

We're telling `combineReducers()` that our state object has two properties, `activeThreadId` and `threads`. We set those properties to the functions that handle them.

`combineReducers()` returns a reducer function that behaves exactly like the combinatorial `reducer()` function we wrote by hand.

A common pattern is to have the name of the reducer function match that of the property it manages. If we renamed `activeThreadIdReducer()` to `activeThreadId()` and `threadsReducer()` to `threads()`, we could then use ES6's shorthand notation for maximum terseness:

```
const reducer = combineReducers({
  activeThreadId,
  threads,
});
```

We append `Reducer` to the names of all our reducer functions here because our app is entirely contained in one file. When a Redux app reaches a certain size, it usually makes sense to break out the reducer functions into their own file, like `reducers.js`. At that point, appending `Reducer` to each function name is no longer necessary and you could apply this shorthand.

Next up

After adding complexity to the app and its state with the introduction of threads, we did some significant refactoring with our reducer logic. At first, our single reducer function was managing many different parts of the state tree and was duplicating logic. With the introduction of reducer composition, we managed to break all our state management apart into smaller pieces.

Our app now neatly isolates responsibility. Not only does this make the code easier to read, but it sets us up for scale.

If we wanted to add a new action to the system that deals with messages, we wouldn't have to worry about logic around managing threads. We'd re-use the same code path as `ADD_MESSAGE` and `DELETE_MESSAGE` in `threadsReducer()` and write all action-specific logic in `messagesReducer()`.

If we wanted to add an entirely new piece of state to the system — like a notifications panel — the management of that state would be entirely isolated to its own function. We wouldn't have to tread lightly over existing code.

There's an opportunity to refactor our React components as well. We'll be focusing on our organization of React components in the next chapter.

Using Presentational and Container Components with Redux

In the last chapter, we added complexity to both the state as well as the view-layer of our application. To support threads in our app, we nested message objects inside of thread objects in our state tree. By using reducer composition, we were able to break up the management of our more complex state tree into smaller parts.

We added a new React component to support our threaded model, `ThreadTabs`, which lets the user switch between threads on the view. We also added some complexity to existing components.

At the moment, we have four React components in our app. Every React component interacts directly with the Redux store. `App` subscribes to the store and uses `getState()` to read the state and passes down this state as props to its children. Child components dispatch actions directly to the store.

In this chapter, we'll explore a new paradigm for organizing our React components. We can divide up our React components into two types: **presentational components** and **container components**. We'll see how doing so limits knowledge of our Redux store to container components and provides us with flexible and re-usable presentational components.

Presentational and container components

In React, a **presentational component** is a component that *just renders HTML*. The component's only function is presentational markup. In a Redux-powered app, a presentational component does not interact with the Redux store.

The presentational component accepts props from a **container component**. The container component specifies the data a presentational component should render. The container component also specifies behavior. If the presentational component has any interactivity — like a button — it calls a prop-function given to it by the container component. The container component is the one to dispatch an action to the Redux store:

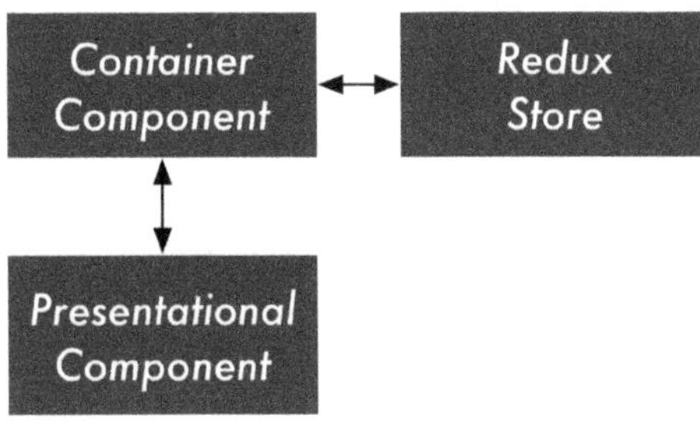

Take a look at the `ThreadTabs` component:

redux/chat_intermediate/src/complete/App-12.js

```
class ThreadTabs extends React.Component {
  handleClick = (id) => {
    store.dispatch({
      type: 'OPEN_THREAD',
      id: id,
    });
  };

  render() {
    const tabs = this.props.tabs.map((tab, index) => (
      <div
        key={index}
        className={tab.active ? 'active item' : 'item'}
        onClick={() => this.handleClick(tab.id)}
      >
        {tab.title}
      </div>
    ));
    return (
      <div className='ui top attached tabular menu'>
        {tabs}
      </div>
    );
  }
}
```

At the moment, this component both renders HTML (the text field input) and communicates with the store. It dispatches the `OPEN_THREAD` action whenever a tab is clicked.

But what if we wanted to have *another* set of tabs in our app? This other set of tabs would probably have to dispatch another type of action. So we'd have to write an entirely different component even though the HTML it renders would be the same.

What if we instead made a generic tabs component, say `Tabs`? This presentational component would not specify what happens when the user clicks a tab. Instead, we could wrap it in a container component wherever we want this particular markup in our app. That container component could then specify what action to take by dispatching to the store.

We'll call our container component `ThreadTabs`. It will do all of the communicating with the store and let `Tabs` handle the markup. In the future, if we wanted to use tabs elsewhere — say, in a "contacts" view that has a tab for each group of contacts — we could re-use our presentational component:

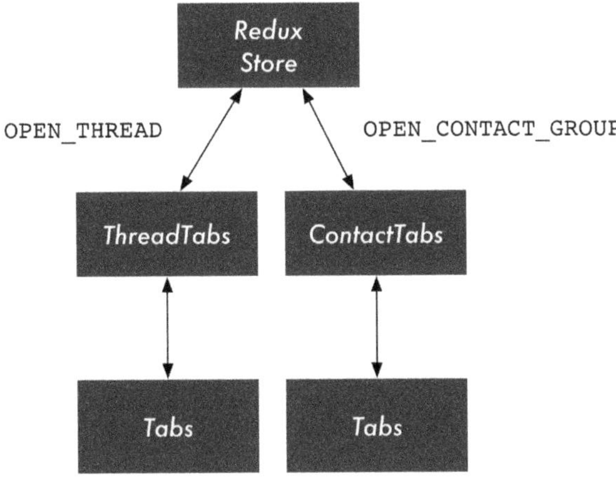

Splitting up `ThreadTabs`

We'll split up `ThreadTabs` by first writing the presentational component `Tabs`. This component will only be concerned with rendering the HTML — the array of horizontal tabs. It will also expect a prop, `onClick`. The presentational component will allow its container component to specify whatever behavior it wants when a tab is clicked.

Let's add `Tabs` to `App.js` now. Write it above the current `ThreadTab` component. The JSX for the HTML markup is the same as before:

redux/chat_intermediate/src/complete/App-13.js

```
const Tabs = (props) => (
  <div className='ui top attached tabular menu'>
    {
      props.tabs.map((tab, index) => (
        <div
          key={index}
          className={tab.active ? 'active item' : 'item'}
          onClick={() => props.onClick(tab.id)}
        >
          {tab.title}
        </div>
      ))
    }
  </div>
);
```

A unique aspect of our new presentational component is how it's declared. So far, we've been using ES6 classes like this:

```
class App extends React.Component {
  // ...
}
```

React components declared in this manner are wrapped in React's component API. This declaration gives the component all of the React-specific features that we've been using, like lifecycle hooks and state management.

However, as we cover in the "Advanced Components" chapter, React also allows you to declare **stateless functional components**. Stateless functional components, like `Tabs`, are just JavaScript functions that return markup. They are not special React objects.

Because `Tabs` does not need any of React's component methods, it can be a stateless component.

In fact, all our presentational components can be stateless components. This reinforces their single responsibility of rendering markup. The syntax is terser. What's more, the React core team recommends using stateless components whenever possible. Because these components are not "dressed up" with any of the capabilities of React component objects, the React team anticipates there will be many performance advantages introduced for stateless components in the near future.

As we can see, the first argument passed in to a stateless component is `props`:

redux/chat_intermediate/src/complete/App-13.js

```
const Tabs = (props) => (
```

Because `Tabs` is not a React component object, it does not have the special property `this.props`. Instead, parents pass props to stateless components as an argument. So we'll access this component's props everywhere using `props` as opposed to `this.props`.

Our map call for `Tabs` is in-line, nested inside of the `div` tag in the function's return value.

You could also put this logic above the function's return statement, like we had before in the `render` function of `ThreadTabs`. It's a matter of stylistic preference.

Our presentational component is ready. Let's see what the container component that uses it looks like. Modify the current `ThreadTabs` component:

redux/chat_intermediate/src/complete/App-13.js

```
class ThreadTabs extends React.Component {
  render() {
    return (
      <Tabs
        tabs={this.props.tabs}
        onClick={(id) => (
          store.dispatch({
            type: 'OPEN_THREAD',
            id: id,
          })
        )}
      />
    );
  }
}
```

Although we don't use any of React's component methods, we're still using an ES6 class component as opposed to declaring a stateless component. We'll see why in a moment.

Our container component specifies the props and behavior for our presentational component. We set the prop `tabs` to `this.props.tabs`, specified by `App`. Next, we set the prop `onClick` to a function that calls `store.dispatch()`. We expect `Tabs` to pass the id of the clicked tab to this function.

If we were to test the app out now, we'd be happy to note that our new container/presentational component combination is working.

However, there's one odd thing about `ThreadTabs`: It sends actions to the store *directly* with dispatch, yet at the moment it's reading from the store *indirectly* through props (through `this.props.tabs`). `App` is the one reading from the store and this data trickles down to `ThreadTabs`. But if `ThreadTabs` is dispatching directly to the store, is this indirection for reading from the store necessary?

Instead, we can have all of our container components be responsible for both sending actions to the store and reading from it.

In order to achieve this with `ThreadTabs`, we can subscribe directly to the store in `componentDidMount`, the same way that `App` does:

redux/chat_intermediate/src/complete/App-14.js

```
class ThreadTabs extends React.Component {
  componentDidMount() {
    store.subscribe(() => this.forceUpdate());
  }
```

Then, inside of `render`, we can read `state.threads` directly from the store with `getState()`. We'll generate `tabs` here using the same logic that we used in `App`:

redux/chat_intermediate/src/complete/App-14.js

```
  render() {
    const state = store.getState();

    const tabs = state.threads.map(t => (
      {
        title: t.title,
        active: t.id === state.activeThreadId,
        id: t.id,
      }
    ));
```

Now we don't need to read from `this.props` at all. We pass `Tabs` the `tabs` variable that we created:

redux/chat_intermediate/src/complete/App-14.js

```
    return (
      <Tabs
        tabs={tabs}
        onClick={(id) => (
          store.dispatch({
            type: 'OPEN_THREAD',
            id: id,
          })
        )}
      />
    );
```

Our `Tabs` component is purely presentational. It specifies no behavior of its own and could be dropped-in anywhere in the app.

The `ThreadTabs` component is a container component. It renders no markup. Instead, it interfaces with the store and specifies which presentational component to render. The container component is the connector of the store to the presentational component.

Our presentational and container component combination, in full:

redux/chat_intermediate/src/complete/App-14.js

```
const Tabs = (props) => (
  <div className='ui top attached tabular menu'>
    {
      props.tabs.map((tab, index) => (
        <div
          key={index}
          className={tab.active ? 'active item' : 'item'}
          onClick={() => props.onClick(tab.id)}
        >
          {tab.title}
        </div>
      ))
    }
  </div>
);

class ThreadTabs extends React.Component {
  componentDidMount() {
    store.subscribe(() => this.forceUpdate());
  }

  render() {
    const state = store.getState();

    const tabs = state.threads.map(t => (
      {
        title: t.title,
        active: t.id === state.activeThreadId,
        id: t.id,
      }
    ));

    return (
      <Tabs
        tabs={tabs}
        onClick={(id) => (
          store.dispatch({
            type: 'OPEN_THREAD',
            id: id,
          })
        )}
```

```
      />
    );
  }
}
```

In addition to the ability to re-use our presentational component elsewhere in the app, this paradigm gives us another significant benefit: We've de-coupled our presentational view code entirely from our state and its actions. As we'll see, this approach isolates all knowledge of Redux and our store to our app's container components. This minimizes the switching costs in the future. If we wanted to move our app to another state management paradigm, we wouldn't need to touch any of our app's presentational components.

Splitting up `Thread`

Let's continue refactoring with our new design pattern.

`Thread` receives the `thread` as a prop and contains all the markup for rendering the messages inside of that thread as well as `MessageInput`. The component will dispatch to the store a `DELETE_MESSAGE` action if a message is clicked.

Part of rendering the view for a thread involves rendering the view for its messages. We could have separate container and presentational components for threads and messages. In this setup, the presentational component for a thread would render the container component for a message.

But because we don't anticipate ever rendering a list of messages *outside* of a thread, it's reasonable to just have the container component for the thread also manage the presentational component for a message.

We can have one container component, `ThreadDisplay`. This container component will render the presentational component `Thread`:

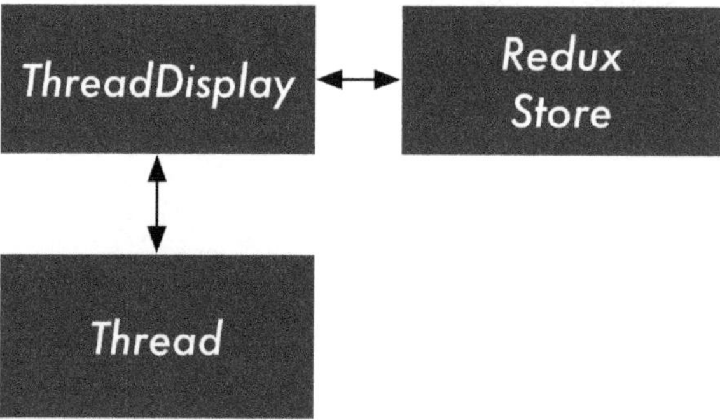

For the list of messages, we can have `Thread` render another presentational component, `MessageList`.

But what about the component `MessageInput`? Like our previous version of `ThreadTabs`, the component contains two responsibilities. The component renders markup, a single text field with a submit button. In addition, it specifies the behavior for what should happen when the form is submitted.

We could, instead, just have a generic presentational component. `TextFieldSubmit` only renders markup and allows its parent to specify what happens when the text field is submitted. `ThreadDisplay`, through `Thread`, could control the behavior of this text field.

With this design, we'd have one container component for a thread up top. The presentational component `Thread` would be a composite of two child presentational components, `MessageList` and `TextFieldSubmit`:

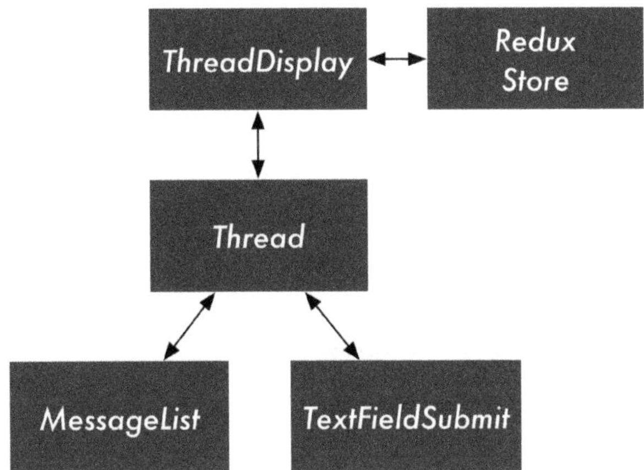

Let's first rename our current `Thread` component to `ThreadDisplay` to avoid confusion:

```
// Rename from `Thread`
class ThreadDisplay extends React.Component {
  // ...
};
```

We'll begin at the bottom, writing the presentational components `TextFieldSubmit` and `MessageList`. We'll work our way up to `Thread` and then `ThreadDisplay`.

TextFieldSubmit

Like with `ThreadTabs`, `MessageInput` has two distinct roles: the component both renders the HTML for an input field but also specifies what the behavior around submitting that input field should be (dispatching `ADD_MESSAGE`).

If we remove the dispatch call from `MessageInput`, we'd be left with a generic component that just rendered markup: a text field with an adjacent submit button. The presentational component will allow its container component to specify whatever behavior it wants when the input field is submitted.

Let's rename `MessageInput` to `TextFieldSubmit` to make it more generic. The only additional change we need to make is in `handleSubmit()`. We'll have `TextFieldSubmit` expect a single prop, `onSubmit`. Instead of dispatching to the store directly, it will invoke this prop-function:

redux/chat_intermediate/src/complete/App-14.js

```
class TextFieldSubmit extends React.Component {
  state = {
    value: '',
  };

  onChange = (e) => {
    this.setState({
      value: e.target.value,
    })
  };

  handleSubmit = () => {
    this.props.onSubmit(this.state.value);
    this.setState({
      value: '',
    });
  };
```

`MessageList`

The `MessageList` component will accept two props: `messages` and `onClick`. As before, this presentational component will not specify any behavior. As a stateless component, it will only render HTML.

Write it below `TextFieldSubmit` and above the `ThreadDisplay` component in `App.js`:

redux/chat_intermediate/src/complete/App-14.js

```
const MessageList = (props) => (
  <div className='ui comments'>
    {
      props.messages.map((m, index) => (
        <div
          className='comment'
          key={index}
          onClick={() => props.onClick(m.id)}
        >
          <div className='text'>
```

```
          {m.text}
          <span className='metadata'>@{m.timestamp}</span>
        </div>
      </div>
    ))
  }
  </div>
);
```

The map that we perform over props.messages is the same logic we had previously in Thread. We perform it in-line, nested inside of the div tag which is responsible for styling. The three changes:

- We perform the map over props.messages as opposed to this.props.threads
- The onClick attribute is now set to props.onClick
- For brevity, we're using the variable m in place of message

You could optionally break this presentational component down further by adding another component, Message. The markup for each message is still simple enough that we opted not to do this just yet here.

Thread

We have two presentational components related to displaying a thread. One is MessageList, which renders all of the messages in that thread. The other is TextFieldSubmit, a generic text field entry that we're going to have submit new messages to the thread.

We're collecting these two presentational components under Thread, another presentational component. The container component ThreadDisplay will render Thread which in turn will render MessageList and TextFieldSubmit.

We anticipate that ThreadDisplay will pass Thread three props:

- thread: The thread itself
- onMessageClick: The message click handler
- onMessageSubmit: The text field submit handler

We'll have Thread pass along the appropriate props to each of its child presentational components:

redux/chat_intermediate/src/complete/App-14.js

```
const Thread = (props) => (
  <div className='ui center aligned basic segment'>
    <MessageList
      messages={props.thread.messages}
      onClick={props.onMessageClick}
    />
    <TextFieldSubmit
      onSubmit={props.onMessageSubmit}
    />
  </div>
);
```

`ThreadDisplay`

`ThreadDisplay` (previously named `Thread`) is our container component. Like with our two previous container components, it will subscribe to the store. The component will be responsible for both reading from the store and dispatching actions to it.

First, subscribe to the store in `componentDidMount`:

redux/chat_intermediate/src/complete/App-14.js

```
class ThreadDisplay extends React.Component {
  componentDidMount() {
    store.subscribe(() => this.forceUpdate());
  }
```

`ThreadDisplay` will read from the store directly to get the active thread. The container component will then render `Thread`, passing in the props `thread` and `onMessageClick`.

Inside of `render`, we'll use the same logic we had used in `App` to grab the active thread:

redux/chat_intermediate/src/complete/App-14.js

```
  render() {
    const state = store.getState();
    const activeThreadId = state.activeThreadId;
    const activeThread = state.threads.find(
      t => t.id === activeThreadId
    );
```

We return `Thread`, passing it `thread` as well as specifying its behavior for `onMessageClick` and `onMessageSubmit`:

redux/chat_intermediate/src/complete/App-14.js

```
    return (
      <Thread
        thread={activeThread}
        onMessageClick={(id) => (
          store.dispatch({
            type: 'DELETE_MESSAGE',
            id: id,
          })
        )}
        onMessageSubmit={(text) => (
          store.dispatch({
            type: 'ADD_MESSAGE',
            text: text,
            threadId: activeThreadId,
          })
        )}
      />
    );
```

Our container component `ThreadDisplay`, in full:

redux/chat_intermediate/src/complete/App-14.js

```
class ThreadDisplay extends React.Component {
  componentDidMount() {
    store.subscribe(() => this.forceUpdate());
  }

  render() {
    const state = store.getState();
    const activeThreadId = state.activeThreadId;
    const activeThread = state.threads.find(
      t => t.id === activeThreadId
    );

    return (
      <Thread
        thread={activeThread}
        onMessageClick={(id) => (
          store.dispatch({
            type: 'DELETE_MESSAGE',
```

```
          id: id,
        })
      )}
      onMessageSubmit={(text) => (
        store.dispatch({
          type: 'ADD_MESSAGE',
          text: text,
          threadId: activeThreadId,
        })
      )}
    />
  );
 }
}
```

We've split up all of our view components into container and presentational components. Our two container components are communicating directly with the store, performing both reads (`getState()`) and sending actions (`dispatch()`).

Because of this, we actually don't need `App` to talk to the store at all. The `render` function for `App` right now reads from the store and then sends props down to its children. Now that its children are communicating with the store, it's no longer necessary that `App` supply them with any props.

Removing store from `App`

Because our container components are now interfacing with the store themselves, we can remove all communication with the store from `App`. In fact, we can just turn `App` into a stateless component:

redux/chat_intermediate/src/complete/App-15.js

```
const App = () => (
  <div className='ui segment'>
    {/* `Thread` changed to `ThreadDisplay` below */}
    <ThreadTabs />
    <ThreadDisplay />
  </div>
);
```

Quite a contrast to the top-level component of some of our previous apps, no?

Due to a combination of our new container and presentational component paradigm and a Redux state manager, the top-level component for this app is just specifying what container components to include on the page. All of the responsibility for reading and writing to state has been pushed down to each one of our container components.

Because we're not dispatching actions directly from our leaf components, we've isolated all knowledge of the Redux store to our container components. We're free to re-use our presentational components in other contexts within our app. What's more, if we wanted to switch state management paradigms from Redux to something else, we would only need to modify our container components.

Our container components all look pretty similar. They subscribe to the store and then map state and actions to props on a presentational component. In the next section, we'll explore an option for reducing some of the ceremony around writing container components.

But for now, let's pause briefly to verify that everything still works as before.

Try it out

Save `App.js`. While we've made some big architectural changes to our React components, viewing the app at `http://localhost:3000` everything is working as before.

Generating containers with `react-redux`

Looking at our two container components (`ThreadTabs` and `ThreadDisplay`), they have similar behavior:

- They subscribe to the store in `componentDidMount`.
- They might have some logic to massage data from state into a format fit as a prop for the presentational component (like `tabs` in `ThreadTabs`).
- They map actions on the presentational component (like click events) to functions that dispatch to the store.

Because container components rely on presentational components to render markup, they just contain "glue" code between the store and presentational components.

A popular library, `react-redux`, gives us a couple conveniences when writing React apps that use a Redux store. The primary convenience is its `connect()` function.

The `connect()` function in `react-redux` **generates container components**. For each presentational component, we can write functions that specify how state should map to props and how events should map to dispatches.

Let's see what this looks like in action.

The `Provider` component

Before we can use `connect()` to generate container components, we need to make a small addition to our app.

Right now, our containers are referencing the store variable directly. This works because we declare this variable inside the same file as our components.

In order for `connect()` to be able to generate container components, it needs some canonical mechanism for containers to access the Redux store. The function can't rely on the `store` variable being declared and available in the same file.

To solve this, the `react-redux` library supplies a special `Provider` component. You can wrap your top-level component in `Provider`. `Provider` will then make the store available to all components via React's context feature.

When we use `connect()` to generate container components, those container components will assume that the `store` is available to them via context.

Context is a React feature that you can use to make certain data available to all React components. We talk about context in the "Advanced Component Configuration" chapter.

With props, data is explicitly passed down the component hierarchy. A parent must specify what data is available to its children.

Context allows you to make data available *implicitly* to all components in a tree. Any component can "opt-in" to receiving context and that component's parent doesn't need to do anything.

While we cover context elsewhere in the book, it is a rarely used feature in React. The React core team actively discourages its use, except in special circumstances.

Wrapping `App` in `Provider`

Inside of `package.json`, we're already including the `react-redux` library:

```
"react-redux": "5.0.4",
```

To use the `Provider` component, we first include it at the top of `App.js`:

redux/chat_intermediate/src/complete/App-15.js

```
import { Provider } from 'react-redux';
```

To allow our generated container components to access the store through context, we need to wrap `App` in `Provider`.

At the bottom of `App.js`, we'll declare a new component, `WrappedApp`. `WrappedApp` will return the `App` component wrapped in the `Provider` component. We'll export `WrappedApp` from the file:

redux/chat_intermediate/src/complete/App-15.js

```
const WrappedApp = () => (
  <Provider store={store}>
    <App />
  </Provider>
);

export default WrappedApp;
```

`Provider` expects to receive the prop `store`. The store is now available anywhere in our component hierarchy under the context variable `store`.

It's also common to import `Provider` into `index.js` and wrap the `App` component in it there.

Using `connect()` to generate `ThreadTabs`

The `ThreadTabs` component connects the presentational component `Tabs` with our Redux store. It does so by:

- Subscribing to the store in `componentDidMount`
- Creating a `tabs` variable based on the store's `threads` property and using that for the prop `tabs` on `Tabs`
- Setting the `onClick` prop on `Tabs` to a function that dispatches an `OPEN_THREAD` action

We can use `connect()` to generate this component.

We need to pass two arguments to `connect()`. The first will be a function that maps the state to the props of `Tabs`. The second will be a function that maps dispatch calls to the component's props.

We'll see how this works by implementing it.

Mapping state to props

First, import the `connect()` function from the `react-redux` library:

redux/chat_intermediate/src/complete/App-16.js

```
import { Provider, connect } from 'react-redux';
```

At the moment, we perform our "mapping" between the state and the props for `Tabs` inside of the render function for `ThreadTabs` by creating the `tabs` variable.

We'll write a function that `connect()` will use to perform this same operation. We'll call this function `mapStateToTabsProps()`.

Whenever the state is changed, this function will be invoked to determine how to map the new state to the props for `Tabs`.

Declare the function above `ThreadTabs` in `App.js`. The function expects to receive the state as an argument:

redux/chat_intermediate/src/complete/App-16.js

```
const mapStateToTabsProps = (state) => {
```

We can copy and paste the logic that we had in `ThreadTabs` to produce the variable `tabs`, based on `state.threads`:

redux/chat_intermediate/src/complete/App-16.js

```
  const tabs = state.threads.map(t => (
    {
      title: t.title,
      active: t.id === state.activeThreadId,
      id: t.id,
    }
  ));
```

Our state-to-props mapping function needs to return an object. The properties on this object are the prop names for `Tabs`. Because the prop is called `tabs` and the variable we're setting it to is also `tabs`, we can use the ES6 object shorthand:

redux/chat_intermediate/src/complete/App-16.js

```
  return {
    tabs,
  };
};
```

Our `mapStateToTabsProps()` function, in full:

redux/chat_intermediate/src/complete/App-16.js

```
const mapStateToTabsProps = (state) => {
  const tabs = state.threads.map(t => (
    {
      title: t.title,
      active: t.id === state.activeThreadId,
      id: t.id,
    }
  ));

  return {
    tabs,
  };
};
```

This function encapsulates the logic that was previously in `ThreadTabs`, describing how the state maps to the prop `tabs` for `Tabs`. Now we have to do the same for the prop `onClick`, which maps to a dispatch call.

Mapping dispatches to props

We'll declare this function below `mapStateToTabsProps()`. We'll call it `mapDispatchToTabsProps()`:

redux/chat_intermediate/src/complete/App-16.js

```
const mapDispatchToTabsProps = (dispatch) => (
```

We'll pass this function second to `connect()`. It will be invoked on setup with `dispatch` passed in as an argument.

Like with `mapStateToTabsProps()`, we'll return an object that maps the prop `onClick` to the function that will perform the dispatching. This function is identical to the one that `ThreadTabs` previously specified:

redux/chat_intermediate/src/complete/App-16.js

```
const mapDispatchToTabsProps = (dispatch) => (
  {
    onClick: (id) => (
      dispatch({
        type: 'OPEN_THREAD',
        id: id,
      })
    ),
  }
);
```

We now have a function that maps the store's state to the prop `tabs` on `Tabs` and another that maps the prop `onClick` to a function that dispatches `OPEN_THREAD`.

We can now replace our `ThreadTabs` component by using `connect()`. Delete the entire `ThreadTabs` component currently in `App.js`.

The first argument to `connect()` is the function that maps the state to props. The second argument is the function that maps props to dispatch functions. `connect()` returns a function that we will immediately invoke with the presentational component we'd like to "connect" to the store with our container component:

```
// Signature of `connect()`
// (Note this is partial, we see the full signature later)
connect(
  mapStateToProps(state),
  mapDispatchToProps(dispatch),
)(PresentationalComponent)
```

Let's use `connect()` to create `ThreadTabs`:

redux/chat_intermediate/src/complete/App-16.js

```
const ThreadTabs = connect(
  mapStateToTabsProps,
  mapDispatchToTabsProps
)(Tabs);
```

On the surface it may not look like it, but `ThreadTabs` is a React container component, not too unlike the one we had before.

Using `connect()` to generate `ThreadDisplay`

The next component we'll generate with `connect()` is `ThreadDisplay`.

The container component specifies three props on `Thread`:

- `thread`
- `onMessageClick`
- `onMessageSubmit`

State to props

We'll call this mapping function `mapStateToThreadProps()`. It maps one prop:

- `thread`: maps to the active thread in state

Dispatch to props

We'll call this mapping function `mapDispatchToThreadProps()`. It maps two props:

- `onMessageClick`: maps to a function that dispatches `DELETE_MESSAGE`
- `onMessageSubmit`: maps to a function that dispaches `ADD_MESSAGE`

`mapStateToThreadProps()`

We'll write our state-to-props glue function above `ThreadDisplay` in `App.js`.

`mapStateToThreadProps()` accepts the argument `state`. We have it return an object that maps the `thread` property to the active thread in state:

redux/chat_intermediate/src/complete/App-16.js

```
const mapStateToThreadProps = (state) => (
  {
    thread: state.threads.find(
      t => t.id === state.activeThreadId
    ),
  }
);
```

This follows from the same logic that `ThreadDisplay` used to set the `thread` property of `Thread`.

`mapDispatchToThreadProps()`

Below `mapStateToThreadProps()`, we'll write our dispatch-to-props glue function.

The first dispatch prop we'll write is that for `onMessageClick`. This function accepts an `id` and dispatches a `DELETE_MESSAGE` action. Again, this logic matches that of `ThreadDisplay`:

redux/chat_intermediate/src/complete/App-16.js

```
const mapDispatchToThreadProps = (dispatch) => (
  {
    onMessageClick: (id) => (
      dispatch({
        type: 'DELETE_MESSAGE',
        id: id,
      })
    ),
```

Next, we need to define the dispatch function for `onMessageSubmit`.

As you recall, inside of `ThreadDisplay`, this function dispatched an `ADD_MESSAGE` action like this:

```
store.dispatch({
  type: 'ADD_MESSAGE',
  text: text,
  threadId: activeThreadId,
})
```

`connect()` will not pass our dispatch-to-props function the state. How do we get the active thread's `id`, then?

We might be tempted to try something like this:

```
store.dispatch({
  type: 'ADD_MESSAGE',
  text: text,
  // just read `activeThreadId` from the store directly
  threadId: store.getState().activeThreadId,
})
```

For the purposes of our app, this will work just fine. `store` is defined in this file, so we could just read from it directly.

But, it's preferable that the mapping functions that you pass to `connect()` **do not access the store directly**.

Why so?

We're about to replace our declaration of `ThreadDisplay` with a container component generated by `connect()`. Powerfully, after we've done so, the only reference to the store from our React components will be right here:

```
<Provider store={store}>
  <App />
</Provider>
```

Isolating the reference to store to just one location has two huge benefits.

The first benefit is one we covered earlier when we discussed container components. The less references we have to store, the less work we'd have to do if we wanted to move from Redux to some other state management paradigm. Our mapping functions are just JavaScript functions and could conceivably perform mapping for some other type of store, so long as the API for the store was somewhat similar to that of our Redux store.

The more immediate benefit is for testing. When writing tests for a React app, you might want to inject a fake store into your app. With a fake store, you could specify what it should return for each spec or assert that certain methods on that store are called.

By passing the `store` as a prop to `Provider` and not referencing it directly anywhere else in the app, we could easily swap in a mock store during tests.

So, we need the `id` of the thread we're displaying in order to dispatch our `ADD_MESSAGE` action. But we don't have access to this property inside our dispatch-to-props function.

`connect()` allows you to pass in a *third* function, what it calls `mergeProps`. So, in full, the three functions you can pass to `connect()`:

```
// Full function signature of `connect()`
connect(
  mapStateToProps(state, [ownProps]),
  mapDispatchToProps(dispatch, [ownProps]),
  mergeProps(stateProps, dispatchProps, [ownProps])
)
```

In `connect()`, `ownProps` refers to the props set on the *container component* that we're generating. In this instance, these would be any props that `App` sets on either of our container components, `ThreadTabs` or `ThreadDisplay`.

Accepting and using `ownProps` is optional. Because `App` does not specify any props on our container components, none of our mapping functions use this second argument.

`mergeProps` is called with two arguments: `stateProps` and `dispatchProps`. These are just the objects that are returned by `mapStateToProps` and `mapDispatchToProps`.

So we can pass `connect()` a third function, `mergeThreadProps()`. This function will be invoked with two arguments:

- The object we return in `mapStateToThreadProps()`
- The object we return in `mapDispatchToThreadProps()`

`connect()` will use the object returned by `mergeThreadProps()` as the final object to determine the props for `Thread`.

In sequence, `connect()` will do the following:

1. Call `mapStateToThreadProps()` with `state`
2. Call `mapDispatchToThreadProps()` with `dispatch`
3. Call `mergeThreadProps()` with the results of the two previous map functions (`stateProps` and `dispatchProps`)
4. Use the object returned by `mergeThreadProps()` to set the props on `Thread`

Inside of `mergeThreadProps()`, we'll need access to two items to create our `ADD_MESSAGE` dispatch function:

- The `id` of the thread
- The `dispatch` function itself

We'll get the `id` of the thread via `stateProps`, as that object has the full thread object under `thread`.

To get access to `dispatch`, we can pass it along in `mapDispatchToThreadProps()`.

As such, our `mapDispatchToThreadProps()` function will define two properties:

- `onMessageClick`
- `dispatch`

The dispatch-to-props function, in full:

redux/chat_intermediate/src/complete/App-16.js

```
const mapDispatchToThreadProps = (dispatch) => (
  {
    onMessageClick: (id) => (
      dispatch({
        type: 'DELETE_MESSAGE',
        id: id,
      })
    ),
    dispatch: dispatch,
  }
);
```

Now we'll define our final mapping function. Again, this "merging" function will be passed the results of our state-to-props mapping function and our dispatch-to-props mapping function. The object it returns is the one that `connect()` will use to bind the props of `Thread`.

We'll declare this function below `mapDispatchToThreadProps()`. Our merging function receives two arguments:

redux/chat_intermediate/src/complete/App-16.js

```
const mergeThreadProps = (stateProps, dispatchProps) => (
```

We want to create a new object that contains:

- All the properties from `stateProps`
- All the properties from `dispatchProps`
- An additional property, `onMessageSubmit`

Let's see what this looks like:

redux/chat_intermediate/src/complete/App-16.js

```
const mergeThreadProps = (stateProps, dispatchProps) => (
  {
    ...stateProps,
    ...dispatchProps,
    onMessageSubmit: (text) => (
      dispatchProps.dispatch({
        type: 'ADD_MESSAGE',
        text: text,
        threadId: stateProps.thread.id,
      })
    ),
  }
);
```

We copy both `stateProps` and `dispatchProps` over to our new object using the spread operator (`...`).

`onMessageSubmit` dispatches the same `ADD_MESSAGE` action that `ThreadDisplay` previously dispatched. Note that we're grabbing the `dispatch` function from `dispatchProps`:

redux/chat_intermediate/src/complete/App-16.js

```
      dispatchProps.dispatch({
```

And then, we're grabbing the thread's `id` from `stateProps`:

redux/chat_intermediate/src/complete/App-16.js

```
        threadId: stateProps.thread.id,
```

With our two mapping functions and one merge function prepared, we can now generate `ThreadDisplay` with `connect()`.

We'll declare `ThreadDisplay` below `mergeThreadProps()`:

redux/chat_intermediate/src/complete/App-16.js

```
const ThreadDisplay = connect(
  mapStateToThreadProps,
  mapDispatchToThreadProps,
  mergeThreadProps
)(Thread);
```

Be sure to remove the old declaration of the `ThreadDisplay` component from `App.js`.

Using the `mergeProps` argument of `connect()` feels like a bit of a workaround. This is because the parameters for using `connect()` are quite strict. This is by design. The library enforces this usage for both performance reasons and to prevent a few possible developer mistakes.

However, with our merge function, we got `connect()` to generate a `ThreadDisplay` component as desired. We removed some of the boilerplate around our container components. And, we've isolated the connection between Redux and React to a single area — as a prop for `Provider`.

Let's verify everything is working properly.

Try it out

Make sure the server is running. Navigate to `http://localhost:3000` and observe that all of the functionality of the app is working.

Action creators

Right now, in every instance where we want to dispatch an action, we declare an action object of a certain `type` as well as its required properties. For example, for the `DELETE_MESSAGE` action:

```
dispatch({
  type: 'DELETE_MESSAGE',
  id: id,
})
```

In the current iteration of the app, we only dispatch each type of action from a single location. As Redux apps grow, it's common for the same action to be dispatched from multiple locations.

A popular pattern is to use **action creators** to create the action objects. An action creator is a function that returns an action object. An action creator for our `DELETE_MESSAGE` action would look like this:

```
// Example action creator for `DELETE_MESSAGE`
function deleteMessage(id) {
    return {
      type: 'DELETE_MESSAGE',
      id: id,
    };
  }
```

Then, anywhere in our app, if we wanted to dispatch a `DELETE_MESSAGE` action, we could just use our action creator:

```
dispatch(deleteMessage(id));
```

It's a light abstraction that hides the action's `type` as well as its property names from React components. More importantly, using action creators enables certain advanced patterns, like coupling an API request with an action dispatch.

Let's swap out our action objects and use action creators instead.

First, we'll write our action creators. Let's declare them below the line where we initialize the store with `createStore()`.

We already saw what the `deleteMessage()` action creator looks like. The action creator is a function that accepts the `id` of the message to be deleted. It then returns an object of type `DELETE_MESSAGE`:

redux/chat_intermediate/src/complete/App-17.js

```
function deleteMessage(id) {
  return {
    type: 'DELETE_MESSAGE',
    id: id,
  };
}
```

The action creator `addMessage()` expects both a `text` and `threadId` argument:

redux/chat_intermediate/src/complete/App-17.js

```
function addMessage(text, threadId) {
  return {
    type: 'ADD_MESSAGE',
    text: text,
    threadId: threadId,
  };
}
```

And `openThread` expects the `id` of the thread to open:

redux/chat_intermediate/src/complete/App-17.js

```
function openThread(id) {
  return {
    type: 'OPEN_THREAD',
    id: id,
  };
}
```

We can now work down `App.js` and replace action objects with our new action creators.

Inside `mapDispatchToTabsProps()`:

redux/chat_intermediate/src/complete/App-17.js

```
const mapDispatchToTabsProps = (dispatch) => (
  {
    onClick: (id) => (
      dispatch(openThread(id))
    ),
  }
);
```

Then `mapDispatchToThreadProps()`:

redux/chat_intermediate/src/complete/App-17.js

```
const mapDispatchToThreadProps = (dispatch) => (
  {
    onMessageClick: (id) => (
      dispatch(deleteMessage(id))
    ),
    dispatch: dispatch,
  }
);
```

And finally `mergeThreadProps()`:

redux/chat_intermediate/src/complete/App-17.js

```
const mergeThreadProps = (stateProps, dispatchProps) => (
  {
    ...stateProps,
    ...dispatchProps,
    onMessageSubmit: (text) => (
      dispatchProps.dispatch(
        addMessage(text, stateProps.thread.id)
      )
    ),
  }
);
```

Another benefit of using action creators is that they list out all of the possible actions in our system in one place. We no longer have to infer the shapes of possible actions by hunting through the reducers or React components. This is exacerbated as the number of actions in a system grows.

Conclusion

Over the last three chapters, we've explored the fundamentals of the Redux design pattern. The architecture of our Redux-powered chat app is a stark difference from what it would be if we'd used React's component state.

We don't have to worry about pipelining props through tons of intermediary components, as we define functionality close to leaf components in our container components. Consider the scenario where we wanted to add more data to each thread, like a profile picture of the user. We'd just have to tweak the state-to-props mapping function in our container component to make the profile picture's URL available to our presentational component.

Furthermore, instead of a heavy top-level component that performs all of our state management, we have a series of reducer functions that each handle their own part of our state tree. The advantage here is accentuated if one action should affect multiple parts of the state tree.

Imagine if we introduced a notifications counter to the chat app. The counter indicates the number of unread threads. Every time the user opened a thread, we'd want to decrement this counter.

In the component-state paradigm, this means that the function — say, `handleThreadOpen()` — would not only affect the `activeThreadId` part of the state tree. It would also be responsible for modifying the notifications counter. In this model, single actions that affect multiple parts of the state tree can become cumbersome, quickly.

With Redux, the affect of a given action on each part of the state tree is isolated to each reducer. In our case, we wouldn't have to touch `activeThreadIdReducer()` to incorporate a new notifications counter. The affect of `OPEN_THREAD` on the notifications counter would be isolated to the reducer for that piece of state.

Asynchronicity and server communication

The last concept you'll need to begin composing real-world applications with Redux is how to handle server communication.

Redux does not have an established mechanism for handling asynchronicity built-in. Instead, there are a variety of tools and patterns within the Redux ecosystem for handling asynchronicity.

While asynchronicity in Redux is outside the scope of this book, with the Redux fundamentals covered in the last few chapters you're equipped to integrate these patterns and libraries into your own applications.

The most popular strategy is to use a light piece of middleware called redux-thunk[88]. Using `redux-thunk`, you can have a `dispatch` call execute a function as opposed to dispatching an action directly to the store. Inside of that function, you can make a network request and dispatch an action when the request finishes.

---

[88] https://github.com/gaearon/redux-thunk

For a detailed example of using `redux-thunk` to handle asynchronicity, check out this tutorial on the Redux site: http://redux.js.org/docs/advanced/AsyncActions.html[89].

[89] http://redux.js.org/docs/advanced/AsyncActions.html

Using GraphQL

Over the last few chapters, we've explored how to build React applications that interact with servers using JSON and HTTP APIs. In this chapter, we're going to explore GraphQL, which is a specific API protocol developed by Facebook that is a natural fit in the React ecosystem.

What is GraphQL? Most literally it means "Graph Query Language", which may sound familiar if you've worked with other query languages like SQL. If your server "speaks" GraphQL, then you can send it a GraphQL query string and expect a GraphQL response. We'll dive into the particulars soon, but the features of GraphQL make it particularly well-suited for cross-platform applications and large product teams.

To discover why, let's start with a little show-and-tell.

Your First GraphQL Query

Typically GraphQL queries are sent using HTTP requests, similar to how we sent API requests in earlier chapters; however, there is usually just **one URL endpoint** per-server that handles all GraphQL requests.

GraphQLHub[90] is a GraphQL service that we'll use throughout this chapter to learn about GraphQL. Its GraphQL endpoint is `https://www.graphqlhub.com/graphql`, and we issue GraphQL queries using an HTTP POST method. Fire up a terminal and issue this cURL command:

```
$ curl -H 'Content-Type:application/graphql' -XPOST https://www.graphqlhub.com/g\
raphql?pretty=true -d '{ hn { topStories(limit: 2) { title url } } }'
{
  "data": {
    "hn": {
      "topStories": [
        {
          "title": "Bank of Japan Is an Estimated Top 10 Holder in 90% of the Ni\
kkei 225",
          "url": "http://www.bloomberg.com/news/articles/2016-04-24/the-tokyo-wh\
ale-is-quietly-buying-up-huge-stakes-in-japan-inc"
        },
        {
          "title": "Dropbox as a Git Server",
```

[90] https://www.graphqlhub.com/

```
          "url": "http://www.anishathalye.com/2016/04/25/dropbox-as-a-true-git-s\
erver/"
        }
      ]
    }
  }
}
```

It may take a second to return, but you should see a JSON object describing the title and url of the top stories on Hacker News[91]. Congratulations, you've just executed your first GraphQL query!

Let's break down what happened in that cURL. We first set the `Content-Type` header to `application/graphql` - this is how the GraphQLHub server knows that we're sending a GraphQL request, which is a common pattern for many GraphQL servers (we'll see later on in "Writing Your GraphQL Server").

Next we specified a POST to the `/graphql?pretty=true` endpoint. The `/graphql` portion is the path, and the `pretty` query parameters instructs the server to return the data in a human-friendly, indented format (instead of returning the JSON in one line of text).

Finally, the `-d` argument to our cURL command is how we specify the **body of the POST request**. For GraphQL requests, the body is often **a GraphQL query**. We had to write our request in one line for cURL, but here's what our query looks like when we expand and indent it properly:

```
// one line
{ hn { topStories(limit: 2) { title url } } }

// expanded
{
  hn {
    topStories(limit: 2) {
      title
      url
    }
  }
}
```

This is a GraphQL query. On the surface it may look similar to JSON, and they do have a tree structure and nested brackets in common, but there are crucial differences in syntax and function.

Notice that the structure of our query is the same structure returned in the JSON response. We specified some properties named `hn`, `topStories`, `title`, and `url`, and the response object has that

[91] https://news.ycombinator.com

exact tree structure - there are no extra or missing entries. This is one of the key features of GraphQL: **you request the specific data you want from the server**, and no other data is returned implicitly.

It isn't obvious from this example, but GraphQL not only tracks the properties **available** to query, but the **type** of each property as well ("type" as in number, string, boolean, etc). This GraphQL server knows that `topStories` will be a list of objects consisting of `title` and `url` entries, and that `title` and `url` are strings. The type system is much more powerful than just strings and objects, and really saves time in the long-run as a product grows more complex.

GraphQL Benefits

Now that we've seen a bit of GraphQL in action, you may be wondering, "why anyone would prefer GraphQL over URL-centric APIs such as REST?" At first glance, it seems like strictly more work and setup than traditional protocols - what do we get for the extra effort?

First, our API calls become easier to understand by **declaring the exact data we want from the server**. For a newcomer to a web app codebase, seeing GraphQL queries makes it immediately obvious what data is coming from the server versus what data is derived on the clients.

GraphQL also opens doors for better unit and integration testing: it's easy to mock data on the client, and it's possible to assert that your server GraphQL changes don't break GraphQL queries in client code.

GraphQL is also designed with performance in mind, especially with respect to mobile clients. Specifying only the data needed in each query prevents over-fetching (i.e., where the server retrieves and transmits data that ultimately goes unused by the client). This reduces network traffic and helps to improve speed on size-sensitive mobile environments.

The development experience for traditional JSON APIs is often acceptable at best (and infuriating more often). Most APIs are lacking in documentation, or worse have documentation that is inconsistent with the behavior of the API. APIs can change and it's not immediately obvious (i.e. with compile-time checks) what parts of your application will break. Very few APIs allow for discovery of properties or new endpoints, and usually it occurs in a bespoke mechanism.

GraphQL dramatically improves the developer experience - its type system provides a **living form of self-documentation**, and tooling like GraphiQL (which we play with in this chapter) allow for natural exploration of a GraphQL server.

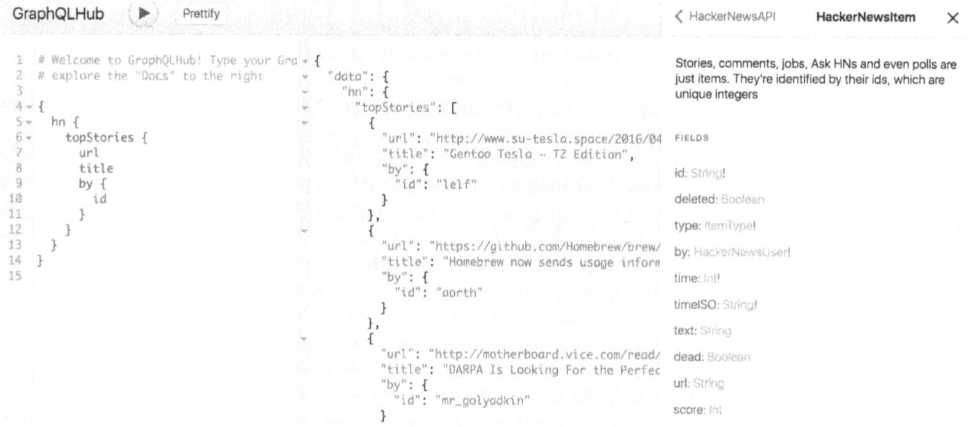

Navigating a Schema with GraphiQL

Finally, the declarative nature of GraphQL pairs nicely with the declarative nature of React. A few projects, including the Relay framework from Facebook, are trying to bring the idea of "colocated queries" in React to life. Imagine writing a React component that automatically fetches the data it needs from the server, with no glue code around issuing API calls or tracking the lifecycle of a request.

All of these benefits compound as your team and product grow, which is why it evolved to be the primary way data is exchanged between client and server at Facebook.

GraphQL vs. REST

We've mentioned alternative protocols a bit, but let's compare GraphQL to REST specifically.

One drawback to REST is "endpoint creep." Imagine you're building a social network app and start with a `/user/:id/profile` endpoint. At first the data this endpoint returns is the same for every platform and every part of the app, but slowly your product evolves and accumulates more features that fit under the "profile" umbrella. This is problematic for new parts of the app that only need *some* profile data, such as tooltips on a news feed. So you might end up creating something like `/user/:id/profile_short`, which is a restricted version of the full profile.

As you run into more cases where new endpoints are required (imagine a `profile_medium`!), you now duplicate some data with calls to `/profile` and `/profile_short`, possibly wasting server and network resources. It also makes the development experience harder to understand - where does a developer find out what data is returned in each variation? Are your docs up-to-date?

An alternative to creating *N* endpoints is to add some GraphQL-esque functionality to query parameters, such as `/user/:id/profile?include=user.name,user.id`. This allows clients to specify the data they want, but still lacks many of the features of GraphQL that make such a system work in the long-run. For example, that sort of API there is still no strong typing information that enables resilient unit testing and long-lived code. This is especially critical for mobile apps, where old binaries might exist in the wild for long periods of time.

Lastly the tooling for developing against and debugging REST APIs is often lack-luster because there are so few commonalities among popular APIs. At the lowest level you have very general purpose tools like cURL and wget, some APIs might support Swagger[92] or other documentation formats, and at the highest level for specific APIs like Elasticsearch or Facebook's Graph API you may find bespoke utilities. GraphQL's type system supports introspection (in other words, you can use GraphQL itself to discover information about a GraphQL server), which enables pluggable and portable developer tools.

GraphQL vs. SQL

It's also worthwhile to compare GraphQL to SQL (in the abstract, not tied to a specific database or implementation). There's some precedent for using SQL for web apps with the Facebook Query Language (FQL)[93] - what makes GraphQL a better choice?

SQL is very helpful for accessing relational databases and works well with the way such databases are structured internally, but it is not how front-end applications are oriented to consume data. Dealing with concepts like joins and aggregations at the browser level feels like an abstraction leak - instead, we usually do want to think of information as a graph. We often think, "Get me this particular user, and then get me the friends of that user," where "friends" could be any type of connection, like photos or financial data.

There's also a security concern - it's awfully tempting to shove SQL from the web apps straight into the underlying databases, which will inevitably lead to security issues. And as we'll see later on, GraphQL also enables precise access control logic around who can see what kinds of data, and is generally more flexible and less likely to be as insecure as using raw SQL.

Remember that using GraphQL does not mean you have to abandon your backend SQL databases - GraphQL servers can sit on top of any data source, whether it's SQL, MongoDB, Redis, or even a third-party API. In fact, one of the benefits of GraphQL is that it is possible to write a single GraphQL sever that serves as an abstraction over several data stores (or other APIs) simultaneously.

Relay and GraphQL Frameworks

We've talked a lot about *why* you should consider GraphQL, but haven't gone much into *how* you use GraphQL. We'll start to uncover more about that very soon, but we should mention Relay.

Relay[94] is Facebook's framework for connecting React components to a GraphQL server. It allows you to write code like this, which shows how an `Item` component can automatically retrieve data from a Hacker News GraphQL server:

---

[92] http://swagger.io/

[93] https://en.wikipedia.org/wiki/Facebook_Query_Language

[94] https://facebook.github.io/relay/

```
class Item extends React.Component {
  render() {
    let item = this.props.item;

    return (
      <div>
        <h1><a href={item.url}>{item.title}</a></h1>
        <h2>{item.score} - {item.by.id}</h2>
        <hr />
      </div>
    );
  }
};

Item = Relay.createContainer(Item, {
  fragments: {
    item: () => Relay.QL`
      fragment on HackerNewsItem {
        id
        title,
        score,
        url
        by {
          id
        }
      }
    `
  },
});
```

Behind the scenes, Relay handles intelligently batching and caching data for improved performance and a consistent user experience. We'll go in-depth on Relay later on, but this should give you an idea of how nicely GraphQL and React can work together.

There are other emerging approaches on how to integrate GraphQL and React, such as Apollo[95] by the Meteor team.

You can also use GraphQL without using React - it's easy to use GraphQL anywhere you'd traditionally use API calls, including with other technologies like Angular or Backbone.

[95] http://www.apollostack.com/

Chapter Preview

There are two sides to using GraphQL: as an author of a client or front-end web application, and as an author of a GraphQL server. We're going to cover both of these aspects in this chapter and the next.

As a GraphQL client, consuming GraphQL is as easy as an HTTP request. We'll cover the syntax and features of the GraphQL language, as well as design patterns for integrating GraphQL into your JavaScript applications. This is what we'll cover in this chapter.

As a GraphQL server, using GraphQL is a powerful way to provide a query layer over any data source in your infrastructure (or even third-party APIs). GraphQL is just a standard for a query language, which means you can implement a GraphQL server in any language you like (such as Java, Ruby, or C). We're going to use Node for our GraphQL server implementation. We'll cover writing GraphQL servers in the next chapter.

Consuming GraphQL

If you're retrieving data from a server using GraphQL - whether it's with React, another JavaScript library, or a native iOS app - we think of that as a GraphQL "client." This means you'll be writing GraphQL queries and sending them up to the server.

Since GraphQL is its own language, we'll spend this chapter getting you familiar with it and learning to write idiomatic GraphQL. We'll also cover some mechanics of querying GraphQL servers, including various libraries and starting off with an in-browser IDE: GraphiQL.

Exploring With GraphiQL

At the start of the chapter we used GraphQLHub with cURL to execute a GraphQL query. This isn't the only way GraphQLHub provides access to its GraphQL endpoint: it also hosts a visual IDE called GraphiQL[96]. GraphiQL is developed by Facebook and can be used hosted on any GraphQL server with minimal configuration.

You can always issue GraphQL requests using tools like cURL or any language that supports HTTP requests, but GraphiQL is particularly helpful while you become familiar with a particular GraphQL server or GraphQL in general. It provides type-ahead support for errors or suggestions, searchable documentation (generated dynamically using the GraphQL introspection queries), and a JSON viewer that supports code folding and syntax highlighting.

Head to https://graphqlhub.com/playground[97] and get your first look at GraphiQL:

[96]https://github.com/graphql/graphiql

[97]https://graphqlhub.com/playground

GraphQLHub ▶ Prettify ‹ Docs

```
# Welcome to GraphQLHub! Type your GraphQL query here, or
# explore the "Docs" to the right
```

Empty GraphiQL

Not much going on yet - go ahead and enter the GraphQL query we cURL'd from earlier:

```
# Welcome to GraphQLHub! Type your GraphQ
# explore the "Docs" to the right

{
  hn {
    topStories(limit: 1) {
      title
      url
    }
  }
}
```

url
id
by
String The URL of the story.

GraphiQL query

As you type the query, you'll notice the helpful typeahead support. If you make mistakes, such as entering a field that doesn't exist, GraphiQL will warn you immediately:

```
{
  hn {
    topStories(limit: 2) {
      titl
      urls
    }
  }
}
```

Cannot query field "urls" on type "HackerNewsItem".

GraphiQL error

This is a great example of GraphQL's type system at work. GraphiQL knows what fields and types exist, and in this case the field `urls` does not exist on the `HackerNewsItem` type. We'll explore how types get their fields and names later on.

Hit the "Play" button in the top navigation bar to execute your query. You'll see the new data appear in the right pane:

GraphQLHub ▶ Prettify < Docs

```
# Welcome to GraphQLHub! Type your GraphQL q
# explore the "Docs" to the right

{
  hn {
    topStories(limit: 2) {
      title
      url
    }
  }
}
```

```
{
  "data": {
    "hn": {
      "topStories": [
        {
          "title": "Bank of Japan Is an Estimated Top 10
          "url": "http://www.bloomberg.com/news/articles/
        },
        {
          "title": "Dropbox as a Git Server",
          "url": "http://www.anishathalye.com/2016/04/25/
        }
      ]
    }
  }
}
```

GraphiQL data

See that "Docs" button in the top right corner of GraphiQL? Give that a click to expand the full documentation browser:

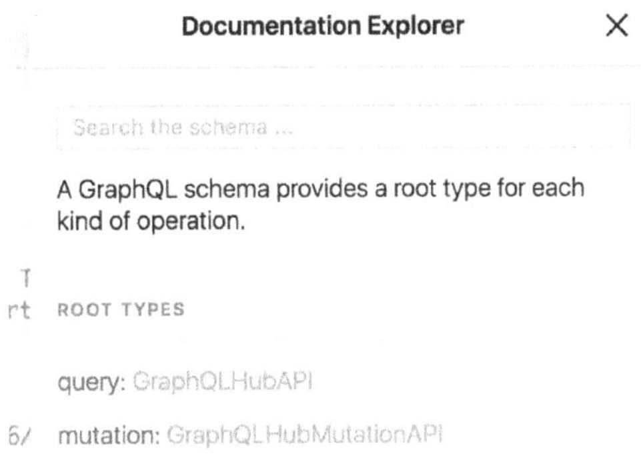

GraphiQL docs

Feel free to click around and choose-your-own-adventure, but eventually come back to the page in the screenshot (the top-level page) and search that `HackerNewsItem` type we ran into trouble with earlier:

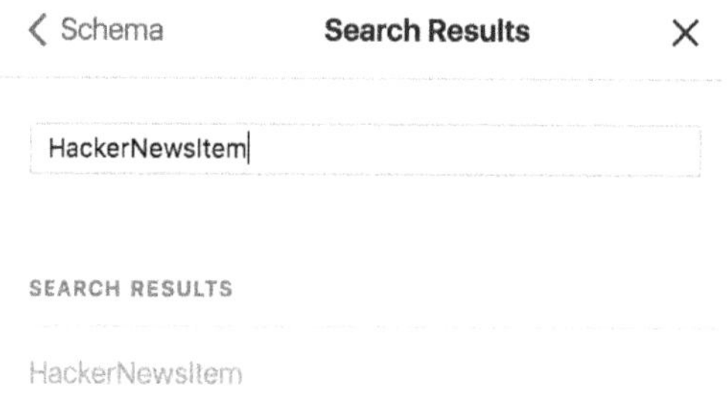

GraphiQL search

Click the matching entry. This takes you to the documentation describing the `HackerNewsItem` type, which includes a description (written by a human, not generated) and a list of all the fields on the type. You can click the fields and their types to find out more information:

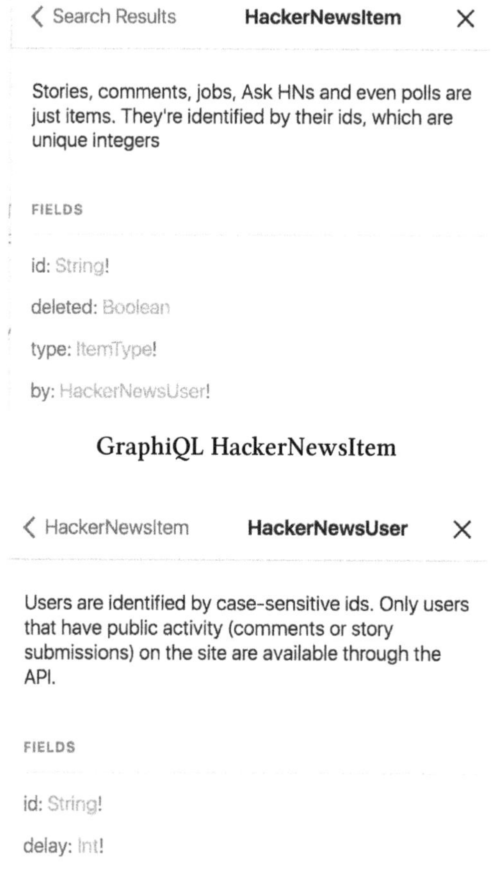

GraphiQL HackerNewsItem

GraphiQL HackerNewsUser

As you can see, the `by` field of `HackerNewsItem` has the type `HackerNewsUser`, which has its own set of fields and links. Let's change our query to grab the information about the author:

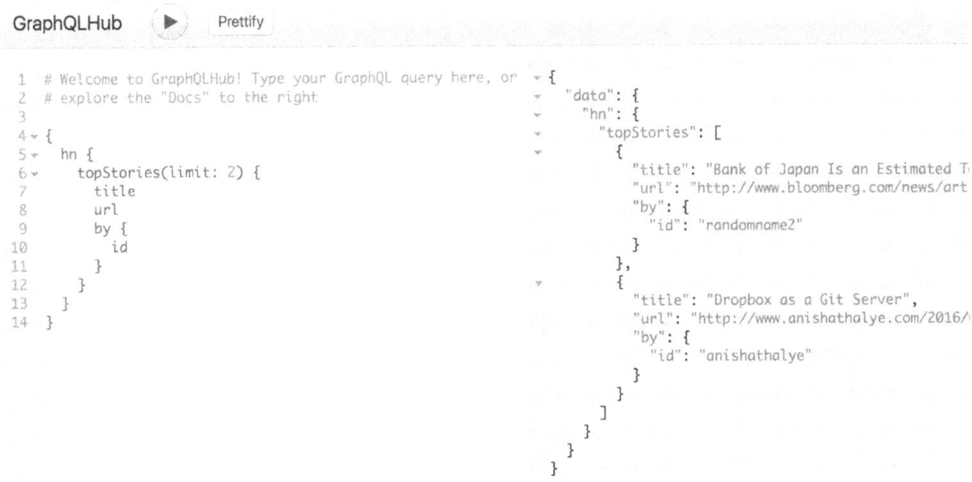

GraphQLHub ▶ Prettify

```
# Welcome to GraphQLHub! Type your GraphQL query here, or
# explore the "Docs" to the right

{
  hn {
    topStories(limit: 2) {
      title
      url
      by {
        id
      }
    }
  }
}
```

```
{
  "data": {
    "hn": {
      "topStories": [
        {
          "title": "Bank of Japan Is an Estimated T
          "url": "http://www.bloomberg.com/news/art
          "by": {
            "id": "randomname2"
          }
        },
        {
          "title": "Dropbox as a Git Server",
          "url": "http://www.anishathalye.com/2016/
          "by": {
            "id": "anishathalye"
          }
        }
      ]
    }
  }
}
```

GraphiQL query with HackerNewsUser

Notice how the `by` field now shows up both in our query and in the final data - ta da!

Keep GraphQLHub's GraphiQL open in a tab as we start to dig into the mechanics of GraphQL.

GraphQL Syntax 101

Let's dig into the semantics of GraphQL. We've used some terms like "query", "field", and "type", but we haven't properly defined them yet, and there are still a few more to cover before we delve further into our work. For a complete and formal examination of these topics, you can always refer to the GraphQL specification[98].

The entire string you send to a GraphQL server is called a *document.* A document can have one or more *operations* - so far our example documents have just only a *query operation*, but you can also send *mutation operations.*

A *query* operation is read-only - when you send a query, you're asking the server to give you some data. A *mutation* is intended to be a write followed by a fetch; in other words, "Change this data, and then give me some other data." We'll explore mutations more in a bit, but they use the same type system and have the same syntax as queries.

Here's an example of a document with just one query:

[98] https://facebook.github.io/graphql/

```
query getTopTwoStories {
  hn {
    topStories(limit: 2) {
      title
      url
    }
  }
}
```

Note that we have prefixed our original query with `query getTopTwoStories`, which is the full and formal way to specify an operation within a document. First we declare the type of operation (`query` or `mutation`) and then the name of the operation (`getTopTwoStories`). If your GraphQL document contains just one operation, you can omit the formal declaration and the GraphQL will assume you mean a query:

```
{
  hn {
    topStories(limit: 2) {
      title
      url
    }
  }
}
```

In the case that your document has multiple operations, you need to give each of them a unique name. Here's an example of a document with several operations:

```
query getTopTwoStories {
  hn {
    topStories(limit: 2) {
      title
      url
    }
  }
}

mutation upvoteStory {
  hn {
    upvoteStory(id: "11565911") {
      id
      score
    }
```

```
  }
}
```

Generally you won't be sending multiple operations to the server, as the GraphQL specification states a server can only run one operation per document.

Multiple operations are allowed in a document for advanced performance optimizations[99] detailed by Facebook.

So that's documents and operations, now let's dig into a typical query. An operation is composed of *selections*, which are generally *fields*. Each field in GraphQL represents a piece of data, which can either be an irreducible *scalar* type (defined below) or a more complex type composed of yet more scalars and complex types.

In our previous examples, `title` and `url` are scalar fields (as `string` is a scalar type), and `hn` and `topStories` are complex types.

A unique trait of GraphQL is that you **must** specify your selection until it is entirely composed of scalar types. In other words, this query is invalid because `hn` and `topStories` are complex types and the query does not end in any scalar fields:

```
{
  hn {
    topStories(limit: 2) {
    }
  }
}
```

If you try this in GraphiQL, it will tell you eagerly that it is invalid:

```
# Wel  Syntax Error GraphQL (7:5) Expected Name, found }
# exp
       6:  topStories(limit: 2) {
{      7:  }
           ^
  hn
    t  8: }
    }
  }
}
```

GraphiQL error without scalar

More philosophically, this means that GraphQL queries must be unambiguous and reinforces the concept that GraphQL is a protocol where you fetch only the data you demand.

[99] https://github.com/facebook/graphql/issues/29#issuecomment-118994619

Scalar types include `Int`, `Float`, `String`, `Boolean` and `ID` (coerced to a string). GraphQL provides ways of composing these scalars into more complex types using `Object`, `Interface`, `Union`, `Enum`, and `List` types. We'll go into each of those later, but it should be intuitive that they allow you to compose different scalar (and complex) types to create powerful type hierarchies.

Additionally, fields can have *arguments*. It's useful to think of all fields as being functions, and some of them happen to take arguments like functions in other programming languages. Arguments are declared between parenthesis after the name of a field, are unordered, and can even be optional. In our previous example, `limit` is an argument to `topStories`:

```
{
  hn {
    topStories(limit: 10) {
      url
    }
  }
}
```

Arguments are also typed in the same way as fields. If we try to use a string, GraphiQL shows us the error in our ways:

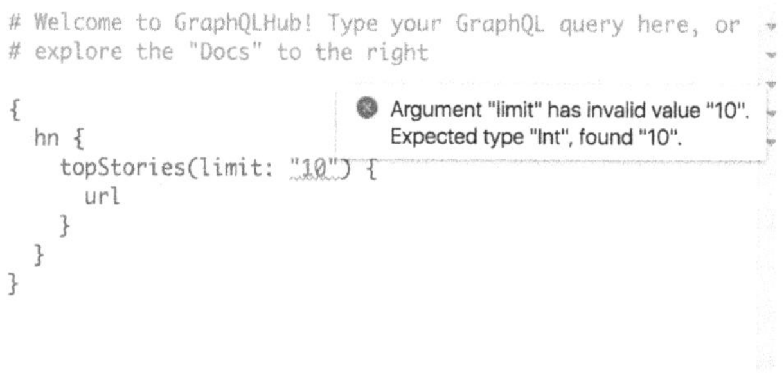

```
# Welcome to GraphQLHub! Type your GraphQL query here, or
# explore the "Docs" to the right

{
  hn {
    topStories(limit: "10") {
      url
    }
  }
}
```

Argument "limit" has invalid value "10".
Expected type "Int", found "10".

GraphiQL error argument type

It turns out that `limit` is actually an optional argument for this GraphQL server, and omitting it is still a perfectly valid query:

```
{
  hn {
    topStories {
      url
    }
  }
}
```

The arguments to a GraphQL field can also be complex objects, referred to as *input objects*. These are not just the string or numeric scalars we've shown, but are arbitrarily deeply nested maps of keys and values. Here's an example where the argument `storyData` takes an input object which has a `url` property:

```
{
  hn {
    createStory(storyData: { url: "http://fullstackreact.com" }) {
      url
    }
  }
}
```

The collection of fields of a GraphQL server is called its *schema*. Tools like GraphiQL can download the entire schema (we'll show how to do that later) and use that for auto-complete and other functionality.

Complex Types

We've discussed scalars but only alluded to complex types, though we've been using them in our examples. The `hn` and `topStories` fields are examples of `Object` and `List` type fields, respectively. In GraphiQL we can explore their exact types - search `HackerNewsAPI` to see details about `hn`:

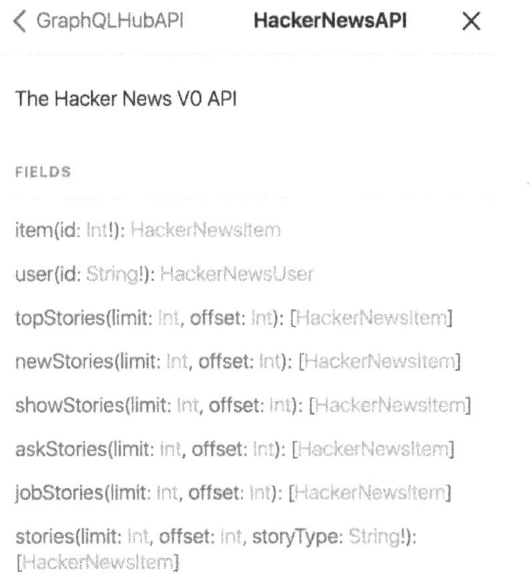

HackerNewsAPI type

Unions

What do you do if your field should actually be more than one type? For example, if your schema has some kind of universal search functionality, it's likely that it will return many different types.

So far we've only seen examples where each field is one type, either a scalar or a complex object - how would we handle something like search?

GraphQL provides a few mechanisms for this use-case. First is *unions*, which allow you to define a new type that is one of a list of other types. This is example of unions comes straight from the GraphQL spec[100]:

```
union SearchResult = Photo | Person

type Person {
  name: String
  age: Int
}

type Photo {
  height: Int
  width: Int
}

type SearchQuery {
  firstSearchResult: SearchResult
}
```

This syntax look unfamiliar? It's an informal variant of pseudo-code used by the GraphQL spec to describe GraphQL schemas - we won't be writing any code using this format, it's purely to make it easier to describe GraphQL types independent of server code.

In that example, the `SearchQuery` type has a `firstSearchResult` field which may either be a `Photo` or `Person` type. The types in a union don't have to be objects - they can be scalars, other unions, or even a mix.

Fragments

If you look closer, you'll notice there are no fields in common between `Person` and `Photo`. How do we write a GraphQL query which handles both cases? In other words, if our search returns a `Photo`, how do we know to return the `height` field?

This is where *fragments* come into play. Fragments allow you to group sets of fields, independent of type, and re-use them throughout your query. Here's what a query with fragments could look like for the above schema:

[100]https://facebook.github.io/graphql/#sec-Unions

```
{
  firstSearchResult {
    ... on Person {
      name
    }
    ... on Photo {
      height
    }
  }
}
```

The `... on Person` bit is referred to as an *inline fragment*. In plain-English we could read this as, "If the `firstSearchResult` is a `Person`, then return the `name`; if it's a `Photo`, then return the height."

Fragments don't have to be inline; they can be named and re-used throughout the document. We could rewrite the above example using *named fragments*:

```
{
  firstSearchResult {
    ... searchPerson
    ... searchPhoto
  }
}

fragment searchPerson on Person {
  name
}

fragment searchPhoto on Photo {
  height
}
```

This would allow us to use `searchPerson` in other parts of the query without duplicating the same inline fragment everywhere.

Interfaces

In addition to unions, GraphQL also supports *interfaces*, which you might be familiar with from programming languages like Java. In GraphQL, if an object type implements an interface, then the GraphQL server enforces that the type will have all the fields the interface requires. A GraphQL type that implements an interface may also have its own fields that are not specified by the interface, and a single GraphQL type can implement multiple interfaces.

To continue the search example, you can imagine our search engine having this type of schema:

```
interface Searchable {
  searchResultPreview: String
}

type Person implements Searchable {
  searchResultPreview: String
  name: String
  age: Int
}

type Photo implements Searchable {
  searchResultPreview: String
  height: Int
  width: Int
}

type SearchQuery {
  firstSearchResult: Searchable
}
```

Let's break this down. Our `firstSearchResult` is now guaranteed to return a type that implements `Searchable`. Because this otherwise unknown type implements `Searchable`,

These are the primitives of GraphQL - operations, types (scalar and complex), and fields - and we can use them to compose higher-order patterns.

Exploring a Graph

We've explored the "QL" of GraphQL, but haven't touched too much on the "Graph" part.

When we say "Graph", we don't mean in the sense of a bar chart or other data visualizations - we mean a graph in the more mathematical sense[101].

A graph is composed of a set of objects that are linked together. Each object is called a *node*, and the link between a pair of objects is called an *edge*. You might not be used to thinking about your product's data with this vocabulary, but it is surprisingly representative of most applications.

Let's consider the graph of a Facebook user:

[101] https://en.wikipedia.org/wiki/Graph_(discrete_mathematics)

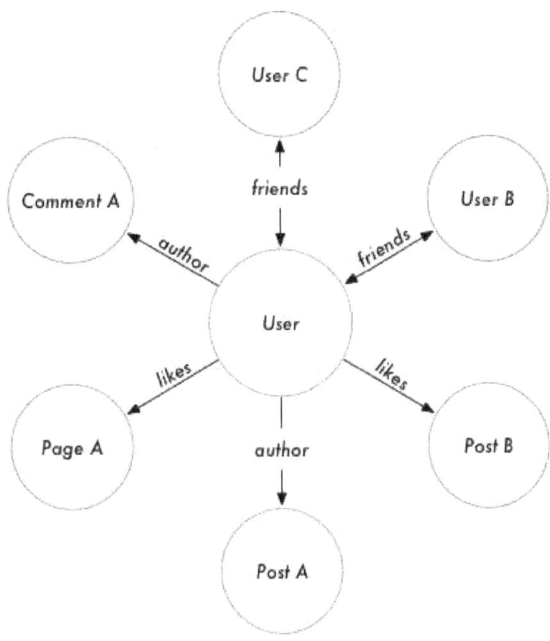

Facebook Graph

But also consider the graph of a productivity application like Asana:

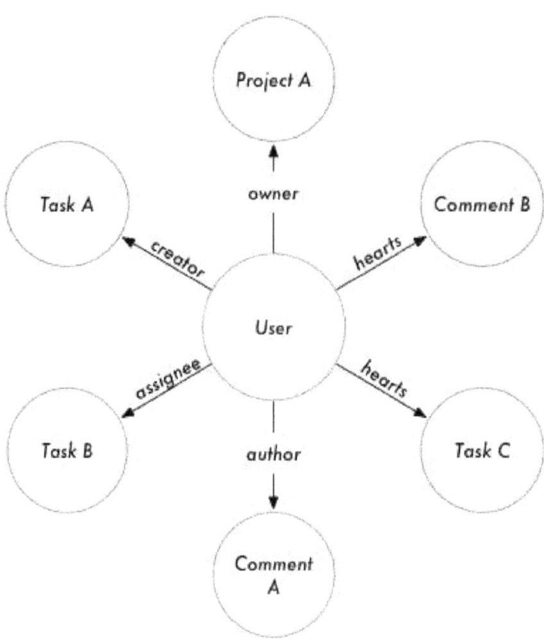

Asana Graph

Even though Asana is not really a social network, the product's data still forms a graph.

Note that just because your product's data resembles a graph structure doesn't mean you need to use a graph database: Facebook and Asana's underlying datastore is often MySQL, which doesn't natively support graph operations. Any data store, whether a relational database, key-value store, or document store, can be exposed as a graph in GraphQL.

The ideal GraphQL schema closely models the shape and terms of a mathematical graph. Here's a preview of the type of graph-like schema we'll be exploring:

```
{
  viewer {
    id
    name
    likes {
      edges {
        cursor
        node {
          id
          name
        }
      }
```

```
      }
    }
    node(id: "123123") {
      id
      name
    }
}
```

Adding these extra layers of fields (`edges`, `node`, etc) may seem like over-engineering when coming from something like REST. However, these patterns emerged from building Facebook and provide a foundation as your product grows and adds new features.

The patterns we're going to describe in the next few sections are derived from the GraphQL patterns required by Relay[102]. Even if you don't use Relay, this way of thinking of your GraphQL schema will prevent you from "fighting the framework" and it wouldn't be surprising if future GraphQL front-end libraries beyond Relay continue to embrace them.

Graph Nodes

When querying a graph, you generally need to start your query with a node. Your app is either fetching fields directly on a node or finding out about what connections it has.

For example, the querying "the current user's feed" in Facebook would start with the current user's node, and explore all "feed item" nodes connected to it.

In idiomatic GraphQL, you generally define a simple Node interface like this:

```
interface Node {
  id: ID
}
```

So anything that implements this interface is expected to have an `id` field - that's it. Remember from earlier that the `ID` scalar type is casted to a `string`. If you're coming from the REST world, this is sort of like when you can query a resource using a URL like `/$nouns/:id`.

One key difference that idiomatic GraphQL and other protocols is all of your node IDs should be globally unique. In other words, it would be invalid to have a User with an ID of "1" and a Photo with an ID of "1", as the IDs would collide.

The reason behind this is that you should also expose a top-level field that lets you query arbitrary nodes by ID, something like this:

[102] https://facebook.github.io/relay/docs/graphql-relay-specification.html

```
{
  node(id: "the_id") {
    id
  }
}
```

If you have IDs that collide across types, it's impossible to determine what to return from that field. If you're using a relational database, this might be puzzling because by default primary keys are only guaranteed to be unique per-table. A common technique is to prefix your database IDs with a string that corresponds to the type and makes the IDs unique again. In pseudo-code:

```
const findNode = (id) => {
  const [ prefix, dbId ] = id.split(":");
  if (prefix === 'users') {
    return database.usersTable.find(dbId);
  }
  else if ( ... ) {
  }
};

const getUser = (id) => {
  let user = database.usersTable.find(id);
  user.id = `users:${user.id}`;
  return user;
};
```

Whenever our GraphQL server returns a user (via `getUser`), it changes the database ID to make it unique. Then when we lookup a node (via `findNode`), we read the "scope" of the ID and act appropriately. This also highlights a benefit of why IDs are strings in GraphQL, because they allow for readable changes like these.

Why do we want the ability to query any node using the `node(id:)` field? It makes it easier for our web applications to "refresh" stale data without having to keep track of where a piece of data comes from in the schema. If we know a todo-list item changed it's state, our app should be able to look-up the latest state from the server without knowing what project or group it belongs to.

Generally our apps don't query global node IDs from the start - how do we describe the "current user's node" in GraphQL? It turns out the *viewer pattern* comes in handy.

Viewer

In addition to the `node(id:)` field, it's very helpful if your GraphQL schema has a top-level `viewer` field. The "viewer" represents the current user and the connections to that user. At the schema-level, the viewer's type should implement the `Node` interface like any other node type.

If you're coming from REST, this either happens implicitly or all of your endpoints are prefixed being with a path like `/users/me/$resources`. GraphQL tends to prefer explicit behaviors, which is why the `viewer` field tends to exist.

Imagine we're writing a Slack app with GraphQL. Everything is viewer-centric in a messaging app ("what messages do *I* have", "what channels am *I* subscribed to", etc), so our queries would look something like this:

```
{
  viewer {
    id
    messages {
      participants {
        id
        name
      }
      unreadCount
    }
    channels {
      name
      unreadCount
    }
  }
}
```

If we didn't have the top-level `viewer` field on its own, we'd either have to make two server calls ("get me the ID of the current user, and then get me the messages for that user") or make top-level `messages` and `channels` fields that implicitly return the data for the current user.

When we implement our own GraphQL server later on, we'll see that using a `viewer` field also makes it easier to implement authorization logic (i.e. prevent one user from seeing another user's messages).

Graph Connections and Edges

In that last example of a `viewer`-centric query, we had two fields that you can think of as *connections* to sets of other nodes (`messages` and `channels`). For simple and small sets of data, we could just return an array of all these nodes - but what happens if the data set is very large? If we were loading something like posts of Reddit, we definitely couldn't fit them into one array.

The usual way to load large sets of data is *pagination*. Many APIs will let you pass some kind of query parameters like `?page=3` or `?limit=25&offset=50` to iterate over a bigger list. This works well for apps where the data is relatively stable, but can accidentally lead to a poor experience in apps where data updates in near-real-time: something like Twitter's feed is may add new tweets while the user is browsing, which will throw off the offset calculations and lead to duplicated data when loading new pages.

Idiomatic GraphQL takes a strong opinion on how to solve that problem using *cursor-based pagination*. Instead of using pages or limits and offsets, GraphQL requests pass *cursors* (usually strings) to specify the location in the list to load next.

In plain-English, a GraphQL request retrieves an initial set of nodes and each node is returned with a unique cursor; when the app needs to load more data, it sends a new request equivalent to, "Give me the 10 nodes after cursor *XYZ*."

Let's try using a GraphQL endpoint that supports cursors. Take a look at this query that you can send to GraphQLHub:

```
{
  hn2 {
    nodeFromHnId(id:"dhouston", isUserId:true) {
      ... on HackerNewsV2User {
        submitted(first: 2) {
          pageInfo {
            hasNextPage
            hasPreviousPage
            startCursor
            endCursor
          }
          edges {
            cursor
            node {
              id
              ... on HackerNewsV2Comment {
                text
              }
            }
          }
        }
      }
    }
  }
}
```

Pretty big query there, let's break it down - first we get our initial node using `nodeFromHnId` (which retrieves the node for Drew Houston[103]'s Hacker News account). We then grab the first two nodes in the `submitted` connection.

[103] https://en.wikipedia.org/wiki/Drew_Houston

A GraphQL connection has two fields, `pageInfo` and `edges`. `pageInfo` is metadata about that particular "page" (remember that this is more of a moving "window" than a page). Your front-end code can use this metadata to determine when and how to load more information - for example, if `hasNextPage` is true then can show the appropriate button to load more items. The `edges` field is a list of the actual nodes. Each entry in `edges` contains the `cursor` for that node, as well as the `node` itself.

Notice that the node `id` and `cursor` are separate fields - in some systems it may be appropriate to use `id` as part of the cursor (such as if your identifiers are atomically incrementing integers), but others may prefer to make `cursor` a function of timestamp, offset, or both. In general, cursors are intended to be opaque strings, and may become invalid after a certain period of time (in the case that the backend is caching search results temporarily).

Let's say this is the data returned by that query:

```
{
  "nodeFromHnId": {
    "submitted": {
      "pageInfo": {
        "hasNextPage": true,
        "hasPreviousPage": false,
        "startCursor": "YXJyYXljb25uZWN0aW9uOjE=",
        "endCursor": "YXJyYXljb25uZWN0aW9uOjI="
      },
      "edges": [
        {
          "cursor": "YXJyYXljb25uZWN0aW9uOjE=",
          "node": {
            "id": "aXRlbTo1MzgxNjk0",
            "text": "it's not going anywhere :)<p>(actually, come work on it: <a\
 href=\"https://www.dropbox.com/jobs\" rel=\"nofollow\">https://www.dropbox.com/\
jobs</a> :))"
          }
        },
        {
          "cursor": "YXJyYXljb25uZWN0aW9uOjI=",
          "node": {
            "id": "aXRlbTo0NjgxMzY2",
            "text": "yes we are :)"
          }
        }
      ]
    }
```

```
  }
}
```

Take a look at how some of the fields match up - the first `cursor` in `edges` matches the `startCursor`, as well as the `endCursor` matching the last node's `cursor`. Our front-end code could use `endCursor` to construct the query to fetch the next set of data using the `after` argument:

```
{
  hn2 {
    nodeFromHnId(id:"dhouston", isUserId:true) {
      ... on HackerNewsV2User {
        submitted(first: 2, after: "YXJyYXljb25uZWN0aW9uOjI=") {
          pageInfo {
            hasNextPage
            hasPreviousPage
            startCursor
            endCursor
          }
          edges {
            cursor
            node {
              id
              ... on HackerNewsV2Comment {
                text
              }
            }
          }
        }
      }
    }
  }
}
```

The other arguments that exist on connections are `before` and `after` (which accept cursors), and `first` and `last` (which accepts integers).

The cursor pattern may come off as verbose if you're used to pagination in REST, but give it five minutes and explore the Hacker News pagination API we demonstrated. Cursors are robust to real-time updates and allow for more reusable app-level code when loading nodes. When we implement our own GraphQL server in a bit, we'll show how to implement this kind of schema and you'll see it isn't as daunting as it may initially appear.

Mutations

When we first introduced operations, we mentioned that `mutation` exists alongside the read-only `query` operation. Most apps will need a way to write data to the server, which is the intended use for mutations.

With REST-like protocols, mutations are generally occur with POST, PUT, and DELETE HTTP requests. In that sense, both GraphQL and REST try to separate read-only requests from writes. So what do we gain with GraphQL? Because GraphQL mutations leverage GraphQL's type system, you can declare the data you want returned following your mutation.

For example, you can try this mutation on GraphQLHub to edit an in-memory key value store:

```
mutation {
 keyValue_setValue(input: {
   clientMutationId: "browser", id: "this-is-a-key", value: "this is a value"
  }) {
   item {
    value
    id
   }
  }
}
```

The mutation field here is `keyValue_setValue`, and it takes an `input` argument that gives information what key and value to set. But we also get to pick and choose the fields returned by the mutation, namely the `item` and whatever set of fields we want from that. If you run that request, you'll get back this sort of payload:

```
{
  "data": {
    "keyValue_setValue": {
      "item": {
        "value": "some value",
        "id": "someKey"
      }
    }
  }
}
```

In a REST world, we would be stuck with whatever data the request returns, and as our product evolves we may have to make many changes to that payload on the client and server. Using GraphQL means that our server and client will be more resilient and flexible in the future.

Other than requiring specifying the `mutation` operation type, everything about mutations is normal GraphQL: you have types, fields, and arguments. As we'll see later on when we implement our own GraphQL schema, implementing them on the server is similar as well.

Subscriptions

We've discussed the two main types of GraphQL operations, `query` and `mutation`, but there is a third type of operation currently in development: `subscription`. The use-case of subscriptions is to handle the kinds of real-time updates seen in apps like Twitter and Facebook, where the number of likes or comments on an item will update without manual refreshing by the user.

This provides a great user experience, but is often complicated to implement on a technical level. GraphQL takes the opinion that the server should publish the set of events that it's possible to subscribe to (such as new likes to a post) and clients can opt-in to subscribing to them. Check out the example subscription that Facebook gives in their documentation[104]:

```
input StoryLikeSubscribeInput {
  storyId: string
  clientSubscriptionId: string
}

subscription StoryLikeSubscription($input: StoryLikeSubscribeInput) {
  storyLikeSubscribe(input: $input) {
    story {
      likers { count }
      likeSentence { text }
    }
  }
}
```

Issuing a GraphQL request with this subscription essentially tells the server, "Hey, here's the data I want whenever a `StoryLikeSubscription` occurs, and here's my `clientSubscriptionId` so you know where to find me." Note that the use of `clientSubscriptionId` or any details about what `subscription` operations should look like is not specific by GraphQL; it merely reserves the `subscription` operation type as an acceptable and defers to each application on how to handle real-time updates.

The mechanics of how the clients subscribe to updates are outside of the scope of GraphQL - Facebook mentions using MQTT[105] with the `clientSubscriptionId`, but other possibilities include

[104]http://graphql.org/blog/subscriptions-in-graphql-and-relay/

[105]https://en.wikipedia.org/wiki/MQTT

WebSockets[106], Server-Sent Events[107], or any of a number of other mechanisms. In pseudo-code, the process looks like:

```
var clientSubscriptionId = generateSubscriptionId();
// this "channel" could be WebSockets, MQTT, etc
connectToRealtimeChannel(clientSubscriptionId, (newData) => {});
// send the GraphQL request to tell the server to start sending updates
sendGraphQLSubscription(clientSubscriptionId);
```

The way GraphQL has decided to implement subscriptions, where a server allows a finite list of possible events, is different than the way other frameworks like Meteor handle updates, where all data is subscribable by default. As Facebook details in their writing[108], that type of system is generally very difficult to engineer, especially at scale.

GraphQL With JavaScript

So far we've been using cURL and GraphiQL for all of our GraphQL queries, but at the end of the day we're going to be writing JavaScript web apps. How do we send GraphQL requests in the browser?

Well, you can use any HTTP library you like - jQuery's AJAX methods will work, or even raw XmlHttpRequests, which enables you to use GraphQL in older non-ES2015 apps. But because we're examining how modern JavaScript apps work in the React ecosystem, we're going to examine ES2015 `fetch`.

Fire up Chrome, open up the GraphQLHub website[109] and open a JavaScript debugger.

You can open the Chrome DevTools JavaScript Debugger by clicking the Chrome "hamburger" icon and picking `More Tools > Developer Tools` or by right-clicking on the page, pick `Inspect`, and then clicking on the `Console` tab.

Modern versions of Chrome support `fetch` out of the box, which makes it handy for prototyping, but you can also use any other tooling that supports poly-filling `fetch`. Give this code a shot:

[106] https://en.wikipedia.org/wiki/WebSocket

[107] https://en.wikipedia.org/wiki/Server-sent_events

[108] http://graphql.org/blog/subscriptions-in-graphql-and-relay/#why-not-live-queries

[109] https://www.graphqlhub.com/

```
var query = ' { graphQLHub } ';
var options = {
  method: 'POST',
  body: query,
  headers: {
    'content-type': 'application/graphql'
  }
};

fetch('https://graphqlhub.com/graphql', options).then((res) => {
  return res.json();
}).then((data) => {
  console.log(JSON.stringify(data, null, 2));
});
```

The configuration here should look similar to our settings for cURL. We use a `POST` method, set the appropriate `content-type` header, and then use our GraphQL query string as the request body. Give your code a moment and you should see this output:

```
{
  "data": {
    "graphQLHub": "Use GraphQLHub to explore popular APIs with GraphQL! Created \
by Clay Allsopp @clayallsopp"
  }
}
```

Congratulations, you just ran a GraphQL query with JavaScript! Because GraphQL requests are Just HTTP at the end of the day, you can incrementally move your API calls over to GraphQL, it doesn't have to be done in one big-bang.

Making API calls is usually a fairly low-level operation, though - how can it integrate into a larger app?

GraphQL With React

This book is all about React, so it's about time we integrate GraphQL with React, right? Almost!

The most promising way of using GraphQL and React is Relay, to which we're dedicating an entire chapter. Relay automates many of the best practices for React/GraphQL applications, such as caching, cache-busting, and batching. It would be a tall-order to cover the mechanics of how Relay does these things, and ultimately using Relay is the better solution than writing your own.

But adopting Relay may have more friction in an existing app, so it's worthwhile to discuss a few techniques for adding GraphQL to an existing React app.

If you're using Redux, you can probably swap out your REST or other API calls with GraphQL calls using the `fetch` technique we showed earlier. You won't get the colocated queries API that Relay or other GraphQL-specific libraries provide, but GraphQL's benefits (such as development experience and testability) will still shine.

There are burgeoning alternatives to Relay as well. Apollo[110] is a collection of projects including `react-apollo`[111]. `react-apollo` allows you to colocate views and their GraphQL queries in a manner similar to Relay, but uses Redux under-the-hood to store your GraphQL cache and data. Here's an example of a simple Apollo component:

```
class AboutGraphQLHub extends React.Component {
  render() {
    return <div>{ this.props.about.graphQLHub }</div>;
  }
}

const mapQueriesToProps = () => {
  return {
    about : {
      query: '{ graphQLHub }'
    }
  };
};

const ConnectedAboutGraphQLHub = connect({
  mapQueriesToProps
})(AboutGraphQLHub);
```

Building upon Redux means you can more easily integrate it into an existing Redux store like any other middleware or reducer:

[110] http://apollostack.com

[111] http://docs.apollostack.com/apollo-client/react.html

```
import ApolloClient from 'apollo-client';
import { createStore, combineReducers, applyMiddleware } from 'redux';


const client = new ApolloClient();

const store = createStore(
  combineReducers({
    apollo: client.reducer(),
    // other reducers here
  }),
  applyMiddleware(client.middleware())
);
```

Check out the Apollo docs[112] if this sounds like it could be a good fit for your project.

Wrapping Up

Now you've written a few GraphQL queries, learned about different its features, and even written a bit of code to get GraphQL in your browser. If you have an existing GraphQL server for your product, it might be okay to move on and jump to the chapter on Relay - but in most cases you'll also need to draft your own GraphQL server. Excelsior!

[112]http://docs.apollostack.com/index.html

GraphQL Server

Writing a GraphQL Server

In order to use Relay or any other GraphQL library, you need a server that speaks GraphQL. In this chapter, we're going to write a backend GraphQL server with NodeJS and other technologies we've used in earlier chapters.

We're using Node because we can leverage the tooling used elsewhere in the React ecosystem, and Facebook targets Node for many of their backend libraries. However, there are GraphQL server libraries in every popular language, such as Ruby[113], Python[114], and Scala[115]. If your existing backend uses a framework in a language other than JavaScript, such as Rails, it might make sense to look into a GraphQL implementation in your current language.

The lessons we'll go over in this section, such as how to design a schema and work with an existing SQL database, are applicable to all GraphQL libraries and languages. We encourage you to follow along with the section and apply what you learn to your own projects, regardless of language.

Let's get to it!

Special setup for Windows users

Windows users require a little additional setup to install the packages for this chapter. Specifically, the `sqlite3` package that we use can be a bit difficult to install on some Windows versions.

1. Install `windows-build-tools`

`windows-build-tools` allows you to compile native Node modules, which is necessary for the `sqlite3` package.

After you've setup Node and npm, install `windows-build-tools` globally:

```
npm install --global --production windows-build-tools
```

2. Add `python` to your PATH

After installing `windows-build-tools`, you need to ensure `python` is in your PATH. This means that typing `python` into your terminal and pressing enter should invoke Python.

`windows-build-tools` installs Python here:

[113] https://github.com/rmosolgo/graphql-ruby

[114] https://github.com/graphql-python/graphene

[115] https://github.com/sangria-graphql/sangria

```
C:\<Your User>\.windows-build-tools\python27
```

Python comes with a script to add itself to your PATH. To run that script in PowerShell:

```
> $env:UserProfile\.windows-build-tools\python27\scripts\win_add2path.py
```

If you're getting an error that this script is not found, verify the version number for Python above is correct by looking inside the `C:\<Your User>\.windows-build-tools` directory.

After running this, **you must restart your computer**. Sometimes just restarting PowerShell works. In any case, you can verify that Python is properly installed by invoking `python` in the terminal. Doing so should start a Python console:

```
> python
```

Game Plan

At a high-level, here's what we're going to do:

- Create an Express[116] HTTP server
- Add an endpoint which accepts GraphQL requests
- Construct our GraphQL schema
- Write the glue-code that resolves data for each GraphQL field in our schema
- Support GraphiQL so we can debug and iterate quickly

The schema we're going to draft is going to be for a social network, a sort of "Facebook-lite," backed by a SQLite database. This will show common GraphQL patterns and techniques to efficiently engineer GraphQL servers talking to existing data stores.

Express HTTP Server

Let's start setting up our web server. Create a new directory called `graphql-server` and run some initial `npm` commands:

[116] http://expressjs.com

```
$ mkdir graphql-server
$ cd ./graphql-server
$ npm init
# hit enter a bunch, accept the defaults
$ npm install babel-register@6.3.13 babel-preset-es2015@6.3.13 express@4.13.3 --\
save --save-exact
$ echo '{ "presets": ["es2015"] }' > .babelrc
```

Let's run through what happened: we created a new folder called `graphql-server` and then jumped inside of it. We ran `npm init`, which creates a `package.json` for us. Then we installed some dependencies, Babel and Express. The name Babel should be familiar from earlier chapters - in this case, we installed `babel-register` to transpile NodeJS files and `babel-preset-es2015` to instruct Babel on how to transpile said files. The final command created a file called `.babelrc`, which configured Babel to use the `babel-preset-es2015` package.

Create a new file named `index.js`, open it, and add these lines:

```
require('babel-register');

require('./server');
```

Not a lot going on here, but it's important. By requiring `babel-register`, every subsequent call to `require` (or `import` when using ES2015) will go through Babel's transpiler. Babel will transpile the files according to the settings in `.babelrc`, which we configured to use the `es2015` settings.

For our next trick, create a new file named `server.js`. Open it and add a quick line to debug that our code is working:

```
console.log({ starting: true });
```

If you run `node index.js`, you should see this happen:

```
$ node index.js
{ starting: true }
```

Wonderful start! Now let's add some HTTP.

Express is a very powerful and extensible HTTP framework, so we're not going to go too in-depth; if you're ever curious to learn more about it, check out their documentation[117].

Open up `server.js` again and add code to configure Express:

[117] http://expressjs.com

```
console.log({ starting: true });

import express from 'express';

const app = express();

app.use('/graphql', (req, res) => {
  res.send({ data: true });
});

app.listen(3000, () => {
  console.log({ running: true });
});
```

The first few lines are straight-forward - we import the `express` package and create a new instance (you can think of this as creating a new server). At the end of the file, we tell that server to start listening for traffic on port 3000 and show some output after that's happening.

But before we start the server, we need to tell it how to handle different kinds of requests. `app.use` is how we're going to do that today. It's first argument is the path to handle, and the second argument is a handler function. `req` and `res` are shorthand for "request" and "response", respectively. By default, paths registered with `app.use` will respond on all HTTP methods, so as of now `GET /graphql` and `POST /graphql` do the same thing.

Let's give a shot and test it out. Run your server again with `node index.js`, and in a separate terminal fire off a cURL:

```
$ node index.js
{ starting: true }
{ running: true }


$ curl -XPOST http://localhost:3000/graphql
{"data":true}
$ curl -XGET http://localhost:3000/graphql
{"date":true}
```

We have a working HTTP server! Now time to "do some GraphQL," so to speak.

Tired of restarting your server after every change? You can setup a tool like Nodemon[118] to automatically restart your server when you make edits. `npm install -g nodemon && nodemon index.js` should do the trick.

[118] https://github.com/remy/nodemon#nodemon

Adding First GraphQL Types

We need to install some GraphQL libraries; stop your server if it's running, and run these commands:

```
$ npm install graphql@0.6.0 express-graphql@0.5.3 --save --save-exact
```

Both have "GraphQL" in their name, so that should sound promising. These are two libraries maintained by Facebook and also serve as reference implementations for GraphQL libraries in other languages.

The `graphql` library[119] exposes APIs that let us construct our schema, and then exposes an API for resolving raw GraphQL document strings against that schema. It can be used in any JavaScript application, whether an Express web server like in this example, or another servers like Koa, or even in the browser itself.

In contrast, the `express-graphql` package[120] is meant to be used only with Express. It handles ensuring that HTTP requests and responses are correctly formatted for GraphQL (such dealing with the `content-type` header), and will eventually allows us to support GraphiQL with very little extra work.

Let's get to it - open up `server.js` and add these lines after you create the `app` instance:

```
const app = express();

import graphqlHTTP from 'express-graphql';
import { GraphQLSchema, GraphQLObjectType, GraphQLString } from 'graphql';

const RootQuery = new GraphQLObjectType({
  name: 'RootQuery',
  description: 'The root query',
  fields: {
    viewer: {
      type: GraphQLString,
      resolve() {
        return 'viewer!';
      }
    }
  }
});

const Schema = new GraphQLSchema({
```

[119] https://github.com/graphql/graphql-js

[120] https://github.com/graphql/express-graphql

```
  query: RootQuery
});

app.use('/graphql', graphqlHTTP({ schema: Schema }));
```

Note that we've changed our previous arguments to `app.use` (this replaces the `app.use` from before).

There's a bunch of interesting things going on here, but let's skip to the good part first. Start up your server (`node index.js`) and run this cURL command:

```
$ curl -XPOST -H 'content-type:application/graphql' http://localhost:3000/graphq\
l -d '{ viewer }'
{"data":{"viewer":"viewer!"}}
```

If you see the above output then your server is configured correctly and resolving GraphQL requests accordingly. Now let's walk through how it actually works.

First we import some dependencies from the GraphQL libraries:

```
import graphqlHTTP from 'express-graphql';
import { GraphQLSchema, GraphQLObjectType, GraphQLString } from 'graphql';
```

The `graphql` library exports many objects and you'll become familiar with them as we write more code. The first two we use are `GraphQLObjectType` and `GraphQLString`:

```
const RootQuery = new GraphQLObjectType({
  name: 'RootQuery',
  description: 'The root query',
  fields: {
    viewer: {
      type: GraphQLString,
      resolve() {
        return 'viewer!';
      }
    }
  }
});
```

When you create a new instance of `GraphQLObjectType`, it's analogous to defining a new class. It's required that we give it a `name` and optional (but very helpful for documentation) that we set a `description`.

The `name` field sets the type name in the GraphQL schema. For instance, if want to define a fragment on this type, we would write `... on RootQuery` in our query. If we changed `name` to something like `AwesomeRootQuery`, we would need to change our fragment to `... on AwesomeRootQuery`, even though the JavaScript variable is still `RootQuery`.

That defines the type, now we need to give it some fields. Each key in the `fields` object defines a new corresponding field, and each field object has some required properties.

We need to give it:

- a `type` - the GraphQL library exports the basic scalar types, such as `GraphQLString`.
- a `resolve` function to return the **value** of the field - for now, we have the hard-coded value `'viewer!'`.

Next we create an instance of `GraphQLSchema`:

```
const Schema = new GraphQLSchema({
  query: RootQuery
});
```

Hopefully the naming makes it clear that this is the top-level GraphQL object.

You can only resolve queries once you have an instance of a schema - you can't resolve query strings against object types by themselves.

Schemas have two properties: `query` and `mutation`, which corresponds to the two types of operations we discussed earlier. Both of these take an instance of a GraphQL type, and for now we just set the `query` to `RootQuery`.

One quick note on naming things (one of the Hard Problems of computer science): we generally refer to the top-level query of a schema as the *root*. You'll see many projects that have similar `RootQuery`-named types.

Finally we hook it all up to Express:

```
app.use('/graphql', graphqlHTTP({ schema: Schema }));
```

Instead of manually writing a handler function, the `graphqlHTTP` function will generate one using our `Schema`. Internally, this will grab our GraphQL query from the request and hand it off to the main GraphQL library's resolving function.

Adding GraphiQL

Earlier we used GraphQLHub's hosted instance of GraphiQL, the GraphQL IDE. What if I told you that you could add GraphiQL to our little GraphQL server with just one change?

Try adding the `graphiql: true` option to `graphqlHTTP`:

```
app.use('/graphql', graphqlHTTP({ schema: Schema, graphiql: true }));
```

Restart your server, head to Chrome, and open `http://localhost:3000/graphql`. You should see something like this:

Empty GraphiQL

If you open the "Docs" sidebar, you'll see all the information we entered about our Schema - the `RootQuery`, the description, and it's `viewer` field:

Server Docs

You'll also get auto-complete for our fields:

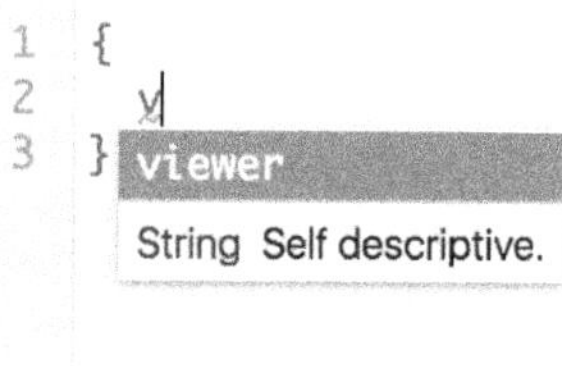

Server Autocomplete

We get all of this goodness for free by using `graphql-express`.

It's also possible to setup GraphiQL if you're using another JavaScript framework or an entirely different language, read GraphiQL's documentation[121] for details.

You'll notice that our typeahead suggests some interesting fields like `__schema`, even though we didn't define that. This is something we've alluded to throughout the chapter: GraphQL's introspection features.

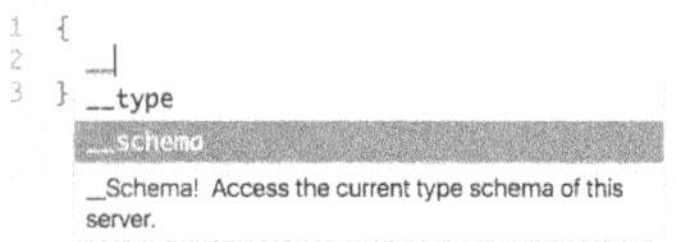

Server Introspection

Let's dig into it a bit further.

Introspection

Go ahead and run this GraphQL query inside of our server's GraphiQL instance:

```
{
  __schema {
    queryType {
      name
      fields {
        name
        type {
          name
        }
      }
    }
  }
}
```

`__schema` is a "meta" field that automatically exists on every GraphQL root query operation. It has a whole tree of its own types and their fields, which you can read about in the GraphQL introspection spec[122]. GraphiQL's auto-complete will also give you helpful information and let you explore the possibilities of `__schema` and the other introspection field, `__type`.

After running that query, you'll get some data back like this:

[121] https://github.com/graphql/graphiql#getting-started

[122] https://facebook.github.io/graphql/#sec-Schema-Introspection

```
{
  "data": {
    "__schema": {
      "queryType": {
        "name": "RootQuery",
        "fields": [
          {
            "name": "viewer",
            "type": {
              "name": "String"
            }
          }
        ]
      }
    }
  }
}
```

This is essentially a JSON description of our server's schema. This is how GraphiQL populates it's documentation and auto-complete, by issuing an introspection query as the IDE boots up. Since every GraphQL server is required to support introspection, tooling is often portable across all GraphQL servers (again, regardless of the language or library they were implemented with).

We won't do anything else with introspection for this chapter, but it's good to know that it exists and how it works.

Mutation

So far we've set the root `query` of our schema, but we mentioned that we can also set the root `mutation`. Remember from earlier that mutations are the correct place for "writes" to happen in GraphQL - whenever you want to add, update, or remove data, it should occur through a mutation operation. As we'll see, mutations differ very little from queries other than the implicit contract that writes should **not** happen in queries.

To demonstrate mutations, we'll create a simple API to get and set in-memory `node` objects, similar to the idiomatic `Node` pattern we described earlier. For now, instead of returning objects that implement a `Node` interface, we're going to return a `string` for our nodes.

Let's start by importing some new dependencies from the GraphQL library:

```
import { GraphQLSchema, GraphQLObjectType, GraphQLString,
  GraphQLNonNull, GraphQLID } from 'graphql';
```

GraphQLID is the JavaScript analog to the ID scalar type, while GraphQLNonNull is something we haven't quite covered yet. It turns out that GraphQL's type system not only tracks the types and interfaces of fields, but also whether or not they can be null. This is especially handy for field arguments, which we'll get to in a second.

Next we need to create a type for our mutation. Take a second to think about what that code will look like, given that it should be fairly similar to our RootQuery type. What kinds of invocations and properties will we need?

After you've given it some thought, compare it to the actual implementation:

```
let inMemoryStore = {};
const RootMutation = new GraphQLObjectType({
  name: 'RootMutation',
  description: 'The root mutation',
  fields: {
    setNode: {
      type: GraphQLString,
      args: {
        id: {
          type: new GraphQLNonNull(GraphQLID)
        },
        value: {
          type: new GraphQLNonNull(GraphQLString),
        }
      },
      resolve(source, args) {
        inMemoryStore[args.key] = args.value;
        return inMemoryStore[args.key];
      }
    }
  }
});
```

At the very top we initialize a "store" for our nodes. This will only live in-memory, so whenever you restart the server it will clear the data - but you can start to imagine this being a key-value service like Redis or Memcached. Creating an instance of GraphQLObjectType, setting the name, description, and fields should all look familiar.

One new thing here is dealing with field arguments using the args property. Similar to how we set the names of fields with the fields property, the keys of the args object are the names of the arguments allowed by the field.

We specify each argument's type, wrapped as an instance of GraphQLNonNull. For arguments, this means that the query **must** specify a non-null value for each argument. Our resolve function takes this into account - `resolve` gets passed several arguments, the second of which is an object containing the field arguments (we'll touch on `source` later on).

When we set a value in `inMemoryStore`, that is the "write" of our mutation. We also return a value in the `resolve` function, to cooperate with the `type` of the `setNode` field. In this case it happens to be a `string`, but you can imagine it being a complex type like `User` or something bespoke for the mutation.

Now that we have our mutation type, we add it to our schema:

```
const Schema = new GraphQLSchema({
  query: RootQuery,
  mutation: RootMutation,
});
```

For one last bit of housekeeping, we'll go ahead and add a `node` field to our query:

```
  fields: {
    viewer: {
      type: GraphQLString,
      resolve() {
        return 'viewer!';
      }
    },
    node: {
      type: GraphQLString,
      args: {
        id: {
          type: new GraphQLNonNull(GraphQLID)
        }
      },
      resolve(source, args) {
        return inMemoryStore[args.key];
      }
    }
  }
```

Restart your server and give this query a run in GraphiQL:

```
mutation {
  setNode(id: "id", value: "a value!")
}
```

Notice that we have to explicitly state the `mutation` operation type, since GraphQL assumes `query` otherwise. Running the mutation should return the new value:

```
{
  "data": {
    "node": "a value!"
  }
}
```

You can then confirm that the mutation worked by running a fresh query:

```
query {
  node(id: "id")
}
```

Mutations aren't too conceptually complicated, and most apps will need them to write data back to the server eventually. Relay has a slightly more rigorous pattern to defining mutations, which we'll get to in due time.

This mutation changed an in-memory data structure, but most products' data lives in datastores like Postgres or MySQL. It's time to explore how we work with those environments.

Rich Schemas and SQL

As we mentioned earlier, we're going to build a small Facebook clone using SQLite. It's going to show how to communicate with a database, how to handle authorization and permissions, and some performance tips to make it runs smoothly.

Before we dive into the code, here's what our database is going to look like:

- A `users` table, which has `id`, `name`, and `about` columns
- A `users_friends` table, which has `user_id_a`, `user_id_b`, and `level` columns
- A `posts` column, which has `body`, `user_id`, `level`, and `created_at` columns

The `level` columns are going to represent a hierarchical "privacy" setting for friendships and posts. The possible levels we'll use are `top`, `friend`, `acquaintance`, and `public`. If a post has a `level` of `acquaintance`, then only friends with that level or "higher" can see it. `public` posts can be seen by anyone, even if the user isn't a friend.

To implement this in NodeJS, we're going to use the `node-sql`[123] and `sqlite3`[124] packages. There are many options when working with database in NodeJS, and you should do your own research before using any mission-critical libraries in production, but these should suffice for our learning.

Setting Up The Database

Time to install some more libraries! Run this to add them to our project:

```
$ npm install sqlite@0.0.4 sqlite3@3.1.3 --save --save-exact
$ mkdir src
```

We'll eventually want three files. On macOS or Linux, you can run:

```
$ touch src/tables.js src/database.js src/seedData.js
```

Windows users can create them as we go.

Now let's create a database. SQLite databases exist in files, so there's no need to start a separate process or install more dependencies. For legibility, we're going to start splitting our code into multiple files, which is the set of files we created with `touch`.

First we define our tables - you can read `node-sql`'s documentation for specifics, but it's pretty legible. Open up `tables.js` and add these definitions:

```
import sql from 'sql';

sql.setDialect('sqlite');

export const users = sql.define({
  name: 'users',
  columns: [{
    name: 'id',
    dataType: 'INTEGER',
    primaryKey: true
  }, {
    name: 'name',
    dataType: 'text'
  }, {
    name: 'about',
    dataType: 'text'
```

[123] https://github.com/brianc/node-sql
[124] https://github.com/mapbox/node-sqlite3

```
  }]
});

export const usersFriends = sql.define({
  name: 'users_friends',
  columns: [{
    name: 'user_id_a',
    dataType: 'int',
  }, {
    name: 'user_id_b',
    dataType: 'int',
  }, {
    name: 'level',
    dataType: 'text',
  }]
});

export const posts = sql.define({
  name: 'posts',
  columns: [{
    name: 'id',
    dataType: 'INTEGER',
    primaryKey: true
  }, {
    name: 'user_id',
    dataType: 'int'
  }, {
    name: 'body',
    dataType: 'text'
  }, {
    name: 'level',
    dataType: 'text'
  }, {
    name: 'created_at',
    dataType: 'datetime'
  }]
});
```

`node-sql` lets us craft and manipulate SQL queries using JavaScript objects, similar to how the GraphQL JavaScript library enables us to work with GraphQL. There's nothing "happening" in this particular file, but we'll consume the objects it exports soon.

Now we need to create the database and load it with some data. Included with the materials for this course, inside the graphql-server/src directory, is a data.json file. Go ahead and copy that into the src directory of the project we're working on. You can also come up with your own data, but the examples we'll work through will assume you're using the included data file.

To copy the data from data.json into the database, we need to write a bit of code. First open up src/database.js and define some simple exports:

```
import sqlite3 from 'sqlite3';

import * as tables from './tables';

export const db = new sqlite3.Database('./db.sqlite');

export const getSql = (query) => {
  return new Promise((resolve, reject) => {
    console.log(query.text);
    console.log(query.values);
    db.all(query.text, query.values, (err, rows) => {
      if (err) {
        reject(err);
      } else {
        resolve(rows);
      }
    });
  });
```

First we define our database file and export it so other code can use it. We also export a getSql function, which will run our queries as asynchronous promises. The GraphQL JS library uses promises to handle asynchronous resolving, which we'll leverage soon.

Then open up the src/seedData.js file we created earlier and start by adding this createDatabase function:

```
import * as data from './data';
import * as tables from './tables';
import * as database from './database';

const sequencePromises = function (promises) {
  return promises.reduce((promise, promiseFunction) => {
    return promise.then(() => {
      return promiseFunction();
    });
  }, Promise.resolve());
```

```
};

const createDatabase = () => {
  let promises = [tables.users, tables.usersFriends, tables.posts].map((table) =\
> {
    return () => database.getSql(table.create().toQuery());
  });

  return sequencePromises(promises);
};
```

Recall that the exports of `tables.js` are the objects created by `node-sql`. When we want to create a database query with `node-sql`, we use the `.toQuery()` function and then pass it into the `getSql` function we just wrote in `database.js`. In plain-English, our new `createDatabase` function runs queries that create each table. We sequence the promises to make sure all of the tables are created before moving on to any next steps in the promise chain.

After the tables are setup, we need to add our data from `data.json`. Write this new `insertData` function next:

```
const insertData = () => {
  let { users, posts, usersFriends } = data;

  let queries = [
    tables.users.insert(users).toQuery(),
    tables.posts.insert(posts).toQuery(),
    tables.usersFriends.insert(usersFriends).toQuery(),
  ];

  let promises = queries.map((query) => {
    return () => database.getSql(query);
  });
  return sequencePromises(promises);
};
```

Similar to `createDatabase`, we create queries using `toQuery` and then execute them using `getSql`. Finally we tie it all together at the end of the file by invoking our two functions:

```
createDatabase().then(() => {
  return insertData();
}).then(() => {
  console.log({ done: true });
});
```

To get this code to run, you can invoke this shell command:

```
$ node -e 'require("babel-register"); require("./src/seedData");'
{ done: true }
```

You should now have a `db.sqlite` file at the top of your project! You can use many graphical tools to explore your SQLite database, such as DBeaver[125], or you can verify that it has some data with this one-line command:

```
$ sqlite3 ./db.sqlite "select count(*) from users"
5
```

Now it's time to hook up the GraphQL schema to our newly created database.

Schema Design

In our earlier examples, the `resolve` functions in our GraphQL schema would just return constant or in-memory values, but now they need to return data from our database. We also need corresponding GraphQL types for our `users` and `posts` table, and to add the corresponding fields to our original root query.

Before we dive into the code, we should take a minute to consider how our final GraphQL queries are going to look. Generally it's a good practice to start with the `viewer`, since most of our data will flow through that field.

In this case, the `viewer` will be the current user. A user has `friends`, so we'll need a list for that, as well as a connection for the `posts` authored by that user. The `viewer` also has a `newsfeed`, which is a connection to posts authored by other users. We'll want all of these connections to be idiomatic GraphQL and include features like proper pagination, in case the entire newsfeed or friends list gets too long to compute or send in one response.

Given all of that information, we expect our `viewer` to enable queries like this:

[125] http://dbeaver.jkiss.org/

```
{
  viewer {
    friends {
      # connection fields for Users
    }

    posts {
      # connection fields for Posts
    }

    newsfeed {
      # connection fields for Posts
    }
  }
}
```

Remember that we want all of our objects to also be nodes in a graph, in accordance with idiomatic GraphQL. Eventually, all of the data returned in `newsfeed` will need to be authorization-aware, taking into account the friendship `level` between the author of a given post and the `viewer`.

We should add support for queries that fetch arbitrary nodes using a top-level `node(id:)` field like this:

```
{
  node(id: "123") {
    ... on User {
      friends {
        # friends
      }
    }

    ... on Post {
      author {
        posts {
          # connection fields
        }
      }

      body
    }
  }
}
```

As we mentioned in an earlier section, this field is valuable to help front-end code re-fetch the current state of any node without knowing it's position in the hierarchy.

This may be surprising, but the GraphQL convention is to fetch lots of different types of objects from the same top-level `node` field. SQL databases usually have a different table for each type, and REST APIs use distinct endpoints per type, but idiomatic GraphQL fetches all objects the same way as long as you have an identifier. This also means that IDs need to be globally unique, or else a GraphQL server can't tell the difference between a `User` with `id: 1` and a `Post` with `id: 1`.

Object and Scalar Types

To start making these queries possible, we'll create a new file to hold these types called `src/types.js`.

The first type we need to define is the `Node` interface. Recall that for a type to be a valid `Node`, it needs to have a globally-unique `id` field. To implement that in JavaScript, we start by importing some APIs and creating an instance of `GraphQLInterfaceType`:

```
import {
  GraphQLInterfaceType,
  GraphQLObjectType,
  GraphQLID,
  GraphQLString,
  GraphQLNonNull,
  GraphQLList,
} from 'graphql';

import * as tables from './tables';

export const NodeInterface = new GraphQLInterfaceType({
  name: 'Node',
  fields: {
    id: {
      type: new GraphQLNonNull(GraphQLID)
    }
```

Aside from using a new class, everything looks familiar to how we create instance of `GraphQLObjectType`. Notice that the `id` field does *not* have a `resolve` function. Fields in interfaces are not expected to have default implementations of `resolve`, and even if you do provide one it will be ignored. Instead, each object type that implements `Node` should define its own `resolve` (we'll get to that in a second).

In addition to defining `fields`, `GraphQLInterfaceType` instances must also define a `resolveType` function. Remember that our top-level `node(id:)` field only guarantees that some kind of `Node` will be returned, it does not make any guarantees about which specific type. In order for GraphQL to do further resolution (such as using partial fragments, i.e. `... on User`), we need to inform the GraphQL engine of the concrete type for a particular object.

We can implement it like this:

```
export const NodeInterface = new GraphQLInterfaceType({
  name: 'Node',
  fields: {
    id: {
      type: new GraphQLNonNull(GraphQLID)
    }
  },
  resolveType: (source) => {
    if (source.__tableName === tables.users.getName()) {
      return UserType;
    }
    return PostType;
  }
});
```

The `resolveType` function takes in raw data as its first argument (in this case, `source` will be the data returned directly from the database), and is expected to return an instance of `GraphQLObjectType` that implement the interface. We use the `__tableName` property of `source`, which isn't an actual column in the database - we'll see how that gets injected later.

We return some objects, `UserType` and `PostType`, that we haven't defined quite yet. Add their definitions below `resolveType`:

```
const resolveId = (source) => {
  return tables.dbIdToNodeId(source.id, source.__tableName);
};

export const UserType = new GraphQLObjectType({
  name: 'User',
  interfaces: [ NodeInterface ],
  fields: {
    id: {
      type: new GraphQLNonNull(GraphQLID),
      resolve: resolveId
    },
    name: {
      type: new GraphQLNonNull(GraphQLString)
    },
```

```
    about: {
      type: new GraphQLNonNull(GraphQLString)
    }
  }
});

export const PostType = new GraphQLObjectType({
  name: 'Post',
  interfaces: [ NodeInterface ],
  fields: {
    id: {
      type: new GraphQLNonNull(GraphQLID),
      resolve: resolveId
    },
    createdAt: {
      type: new GraphQLNonNull(GraphQLString),
    },
    body: {
      type: new GraphQLNonNull(GraphQLString)
    }
  }
```

Most of the code should look similar to everything we've been working with so far. We define new instances of `GraphQLObjectType`, add `NodeInterface` to their `interfaces` property, and implement their `fields`. Some of the `fields` are wrapped in `GraphQLNonNull`, which enforces that they must exist. If you don't provide an implementation of `resolve` to a field, it will do a simple property lookup on the underlying `source` data - for example, the `name` field will invoke `source.name`.

We do provide an implementation of `resolve` for `id` on both of these types, which both use the same `resolveId` function. Even though our `NodeInterface` code couldn't provide a default `resolve`, we can still share code by referencing the same variable.

Our implementation of `resolveId` uses `tables.dbIdToNodeId`, which we haven't defined in `tables.js`. Open up `tables.js` and add these two new exported functions at the bottom:

```
export const dbIdToNodeId = (dbId, tableName) => {
  return `${tableName}:${dbId}`;
};

export const splitNodeId = (nodeId) => {
  const [tableName, dbId] = nodeId.split(':');
  return { tableName, dbId };
};
```

Earlier we mentioned that `Node` IDs must be globally unique, but looking at our `data.json` we have some row ID collisions. This is not uncommon in relational databases like Postgres and MySQL, so we have to write some logic which coerces the row integer ID into a unique string. In a production application, you may want to obfuscate IDs to leak less information about your database, but using the raw table name will make it easier to debug for now.

We're almost ready to run a GraphQL query! Head to `server.js`, import some of the types we just authored, and change the `RootQuery` to have only the new `node` field that we want:

```
import {
  NodeInterface,
  UserType,
  PostType
} from './src/types';

import * as loaders from './src/loaders';

const RootQuery = new GraphQLObjectType({
  name: 'RootQuery',
  description: 'The root query',
  fields: {
    node: {
      type: NodeInterface,
      args: {
        id: {
          type: new GraphQLNonNull(GraphQLID)
        }
      },
      resolve(source, args) {
        return loaders.getNodeById(args.id);
      }
    }
  }
});
```

We also imported a new file, `src/loaders.js`, which we need to edit. Its purpose will be to expose APIs that load data from the source - we don't want to clutter our server or top-level schema code with code that directly accesses the database.

Create that `src/loaders.js` file and add this small function:

```
import * as database from './database';
import * as tables from './tables';

export const getNodeById = (nodeId) => {
  const { tableName, dbId } = tables.splitNodeId(nodeId);

  const table = tables[tableName];
  const query = table
    .select(table.star())
    .where(table.id.equals(dbId))
    .limit(1)
    .toQuery();

  return database.getSql(query).then((rows) => {
    if (rows[0]) {
      rows[0].__tableName = tableName;
    }
    return rows[0];
  });
};
```

This should look similar to the code we wrote in `seedData` - we use the `node-sql` APIs to construct a SQL query based on the `nodeId` provided. Remember that this `nodeId` is the globally-unique node ID, not a row ID, so we extract the database-specific information with `tables.splitNodeId`.

One trick we perform is attaching the `__tableName` property. This helps us in our earlier `resolveType` function, and anywhere else we may need to tie an object back to its underlying table. It's safe to add this because we don't expose the `__tableName` property explicitly in the GraphQL schema, so malicious consumers can't access it.

A very subtle but important thing happening with all of this code is that `loaders.getNodeById` returns a `Promise` (which is why we can attach the `__tableName` using `.then`), and ultimately that promise is returned in `resolve`. Promises are how GraphQL handles asynchronous field resolution, which usually occurs with database queries and any third-party API calls. If you're using an API that doesn't natively support promises, you can refer to the Promise API[126] to convert callback-based APIs to promises.

[126] https://developer.mozilla.org/en-US/docs/Web/JavaScript/Reference/Global_Objects/Promise#Creating_a_Promise

One last step, we need to tell our `GraphQLSchema` about all the possible types in our schema. You have to do this if you use interfaces, so GraphQL can compute the list of types that implement any interfaces.

```
const Schema = new GraphQLSchema({
  types: [UserType, PostType],
  query: RootQuery,
  mutation: RootMutation,
});
```

And that's it! Restart your server, open up GraphiQL (still available at `http://localhost:3000/graphql`), and try this query:

```
{
  node(id:"users:4") {
    id
    ... on User {
      name
    }
  }
}
```

You should see this data returned:

```
{
  "data": {
    "node": {
      "id": "users:4",
      "name": "Roger"
    }
  }
}
```

You can play around with other node IDs, such as `"posts:4"` and `... on Post`. Before we move on, reflect on what's going on under the hood: we request a particular node ID, which invokes a database call, and then each field gets `resolve`'d against the database `source` data.

We could write a very simple front-end app against our current server at this point, but we have more of our schema to fill-out. Let's work on some of those `friends` list and `posts` connections.

Lists

We mentioned earlier that the `friends` field should return a list of `User` types. Let's take baby steps towards that goal and return a simple list of IDs for now.

First let's edit our `UserType`. Open up `types.js` and a new `friends` field:

```
    about: {
      type: new GraphQLNonNull(GraphQLString)
    },
    friends: {
      type: new GraphQLList(GraphQLID),
      resolve(source) {
        return loaders.getFriendIdsForUser(source).then((rows) => {
          return rows.map((row) => {
            return tables.dbIdToNodeId(row.user_id_b, row.__tableName);
          });
        })
      }
    }
```

We set the `friends` field to return a `GraphQLList` of IDs. `GraphQLList` works similarly to the `GraphQLNonNull` we saw earlier, wrapping an inner type in its constructor. Inside `resolve` we invoke a new loader (to-be-written), and then coerce its results to the globally-unique IDs we expect.

Add an `import` at the top of the file to prepare for our new loader:

```
import * as tables from './tables';
import * as loaders from './loaders';
```

Edit `loaders.js` with that new `getFriendIdsForUser` function:

```
export const getFriendIdsForUser = (userSource) => {
  const table = tables.usersFriends;
  const query = table
    .select(table.user_id_b)
    .where(table.user_id_a.equals(userSource.id))
    .toQuery();

  return database.getSql(query).then((rows) => {
    rows.forEach((row) => {
      row.__tableName = tables.users.getName();
    });
    return rows;
  });
};
```

That's all the new code we have to write - fire up GraphiQL and run this query:

```
{
  node(id:"users:4") {
    id
    ... on User {
      name
      friends
    }
  }
}
```

Confirm that your results are equal to this:

```
{
  "data": {
    "node": {
      "id": "users:4",
      "name": "Roger",
      "friends": [
        "users:1",
        "users:3",
        "users:2"
      ]
    }
  }
}
```

Performance: Look-Ahead Optimizations

This is great, but there's some sneaky business going on under-the-hood that we should explore. When we resolve the original `node` field, that executes one database query (`loaders.getNodeById`). Then after that node is resolved, we execute *another* database query (`loaders.getFriendIdsForUser`). If you extend this pattern to a larger application, you can imagine lots of database queries getting fired - at worst, one per field. But we know that in SQL it's possible to express these two queries with one efficient SQL query.

It turns out the GraphQL library provides a way of doing these sort of optimizations, where we want to "look ahead" at the rest of the GraphQL query and perform more efficient resolution calls. It may not be appropriate to do this in every case, but certain products and workloads may benefit tremendously.

Open up `server.js` and let's do a bit of work on the `node` field's `resolve` function. Aside from `source` and `args`, GraphQL passes two more variables to `resolve`: `context` and `info`. We'll use `context` later to help with authentication and authorization; `info` is a bag of objects, including an *abstract syntax tree (AST)* of the entire GraphQL query. We'll do a simple traversal of the AST and determine if we should run a more efficient loader:

```
    node: {
      type: NodeInterface,
      args: {
        id: {
          type: new GraphQLNonNull(GraphQLID)
        }
      },
      resolve(source, args, context, info) {
        let includeFriends = false;

        const selectionFragments = info.fieldASTs[0].selectionSet.selections;
        const userSelections = selectionFragments.filter((selection) => {
          return selection.kind === 'InlineFragment' && selection.typeCondition.\
name.value === 'User';
        })

        userSelections.forEach((selection) => {
          selection.selectionSet.selections.forEach((innerSelection) => {
            if (innerSelection.name.value === 'friends') {
              includeFriends = true;
            }
          });
        });

        if (includeFriends) {
          return loaders.getUserNodeWithFriends(args.id);
        }
        else {
          return loaders.getNodeById(args.id);
        }
      }
    }
```

There's a lot happening as we traverse the AST, and we won't go into detail on most of the specifics. If you end up performing these look-ahead optimizations in your code, you can `console.log` each level of the tree and determine what information you can access.

Essentially we look for `User` fragments on the `node` field's selection set, and determine if the fragment accesses the `friends` field. If it does, then we run a new loader; else, we fall back to the original loader.

Now let's take a look at the new `loaders.getUserNodeWithFriends` function:

```
export const getUserNodeWithFriends = (nodeId) => {
  const { tableName, dbId } = tables.splitNodeId(nodeId);

  const query = tables.users
    .select(tables.usersFriends.user_id_b, tables.users.star())
    .from(
      tables.users.leftJoin(tables.usersFriends)
      .on(tables.usersFriends.user_id_a.equals(tables.users.id))
    )
    .where(tables.users.id.equals(dbId))
    .toQuery();


  return database.getSql(query).then((rows) => {
    if (!rows[0]) {
      return undefined;
    }

    const __friends = rows.map((row) => {
      return {
        user_id_b: row.user_id_b,
        __tableName: tables.users.getName()
      }
    });

    const source = {
      id: rows[0].id,
      name: rows[0].name,
      about: rows[0].about,
      __tableName: tableName,
      __friends: __friends
    };
    return source;
  });
};
```

This starts getting a bit complicated, and very specific to this product and the frameworks we chose - which is a common pattern when working on performance optimizations. Our SQL query now grabs all of the friends and the user's profile simultaneously, eliminating a database round-trip. We then load those friends into a `__friends` property (we've chosen to continue the __ prefix for "private" properties), and can access it inside of `types.js`:

```
    friends: {
      type: new GraphQLList(GraphQLID),
      resolve(source) {
        if (source.__friends) {
          return source.__friends.map((row) => {
            return tables.dbIdToNodeId(row.user_id_b, row.__tableName);
          });
        }

        return loaders.getFriendIdsForUser(source).then((rows) => {
          return rows.map((row) => {
            return tables.dbIdToNodeId(row.user_id_b, row.__tableName);
          });
        })
      }
    }
```

Other applications might perform look-ahead optimizations differently - instead of making globbing multiple SQL queries into one, they might warm a cache in the background. The important takeaway is that `resolve` accepts many arguments which let you short-circuit the usual recursive resolution flow.

Lists Continued

Our `friends` field returns a complete list of IDs (performantly, might I add), but what we really want is a list to their full `User` types. For large lists, we'd probably want to use an idiomatic GraphQL connection (which we'll implement soon) but we'll allow the `friends` field to return all entries on each query.

We'll start by removing the logic we added for performance optimization. Since our application is about to change a bit, we can revisit performance once its capabilities have stabilized.

```
      resolve(source, args, context, info) {
        return loaders.getNodeById(args.id);
      }
```

Next we need to change the `type` returned by our `friends` field to a list of `User`. Since we already have a loader for loading arbitrary nodes by ID, there's not much code we need to write:

```
export const UserType = new GraphQLObjectType({
  name: 'User',
  interfaces: [ NodeInterface ],
  // Note that this is now a function
  fields: () => {
    return {
      id: {
        type: new GraphQLNonNull(GraphQLID),
        resolve: resolveId
      },
      name: { type: new GraphQLNonNull(GraphQLString) },
      about: { type: new GraphQLNonNull(GraphQLString) },
      friends: {
        type: new GraphQLList(UserType),
        resolve(source) {
          return loaders.getFriendIdsForUser(source).then((rows) => {
            const promises = rows.map((row) => {
              const friendNodeId = tables.dbIdToNodeId(row.user_id_b, row.__tabl\
eName);
              return loaders.getNodeById(friendNodeId);
            });
            return Promise.all(promises);
          })
        }
      }
    };
  }
});
```

We now set the `friends` type to `GraphQLList(UserType)`. Because of how JavaScript variable hoisting works, we have to change the `fields` property to a function instead of an object in order to pick up a "recursive" type definition (where a type returns a field of itself). We invoke `loaders.getNodeById` on all of the IDs we previously retrieved and voila! Restart your server and execute this kind of query in GraphiQL:

```
{
  node(id:"users:4") {
    ... on User {
      friends {
        id
        about
        name
      }
    }
  }
}
```

Which should return this data:

```
{
  "data": {
    "node": {
      "friends": [
        {
          "id": "users:1",
          "about": "Sports!",
          "name": "Harry"
        },
        {
          "id": "users:3",
          "about": "Love books",
          "name": "Hannah"
        },
        {
          "id": "users:2",
          "about": "I'm the best",
          "name": "David"
        }
      ]
    }
  }
}
```

You can even go a step further and query the `friends` of `friends`!

Connections

Now we want to implement idiomatic connection fields. Instead of returning a simple list, we're going to return a more complicated (but powerful) structure. Although there is additional work, connections fields are most appropriate for lists that would otherwise be large or unbounded. It might be prohibitive or wasteful to return a huge list in one query, so GraphQL schemas prefer to break up these fields into smaller paginated chunks.

Instead of using literal page numbers, recall from the last chapter that idiomatic GraphQL uses opaque strings called *cursors*. Cursors are more resilient to real-time changes to your data, which might lead to duplicates in simple page-based systems. The `pageInfo` field of a connection gives metadata to help with making new requests, while the `edges` field will hold the actual data for each item.

Instead of the previous query which used lists for `friends`, we want something like this for `posts`:

```
{
  node(id:"users:1") {
    ... on User {
      posts(first: 1) {
        pageInfo {
          hasNextPage
          hasPreviousPage
          startCursor
          endCursor
        }
        edges {
          cursor
          node {
            id
            body
          }
        }
      }
    }
  }
}
```

Instead of just returning a list of `PostType`, the `posts` field will now return a `PostsConnection` type.

Define the `PageInfo`, `PostEdge`, and `PostsConnection` types in your `types.js`, in addition to importing more types from the `graphql` library:

```
import {
  GraphQLInterfaceType,
  GraphQLObjectType,
  GraphQLID,
  GraphQLString,
  GraphQLNonNull,
  GraphQLList,
  GraphQLBoolean,
  GraphQLInt,
} from 'graphql';
```

```
const PageInfoType = new GraphQLObjectType({
  name: 'PageInfo',
  fields: {
    hasNextPage: {
      type: new GraphQLNonNull(GraphQLBoolean)
    },
    hasPreviousPage: {
      type: new GraphQLNonNull(GraphQLBoolean)
    },
    startCursor: {
      type: GraphQLString,
    },
    endCursor: {
      type: GraphQLString,
    }
  }
});

const PostEdgeType = new GraphQLObjectType({
  name: 'PostEdge',
  fields: () => {
    return {
      cursor: {
        type: new GraphQLNonNull(GraphQLString)
      },
      node: {
        type: new GraphQLNonNull(PostType)
      }
    }
  }
});
```

```

const PostsConnectionType = new GraphQLObjectType({
  name: 'PostsConnection',
  fields: {
    pageInfo: {
      type: new GraphQLNonNull(PageInfoType)
    },
    edges: {
      type: new GraphQLList(PostEdgeType)
    }
  }
```

These are mostly just type definitions with no inherent `resolve` functions for now. Different applications will have different ways and patterns for resolving connections, so don't consider some of the implementation details here as the gospel for your own work.

Now we need to hook up our `UserType` to the new types we created and actually create the `posts` field.

```
        }
      },
      posts: {
        type: PostsConnectionType,
        args: {
          after: {
            type: GraphQLString
          },
          first: {
            type: GraphQLInt
          },
        },
        resolve(source, args) {
          return loaders.getPostIdsForUser(source, args).then(({ rows, pageInfo \
}) => {
            const promises = rows.map((row) => {
              const postNodeId = tables.dbIdToNodeId(row.id, row.__tableName);
              return loaders.getNodeById(postNodeId).then((node) => {
                const edge = {
                  node,
                  cursor: row.__cursor,
                };
                return edge;
              });
```

```
            });

            return Promise.all(promises).then((edges) => {
              return {
                edges,
                pageInfo
              }
            });

          })
        }
      }
    };
  }
});
```

This should look familiar to how we implement our `friends` field, aside from the new arguments. Remember that this field does not return a list of `PostType` - it returns a `PostsConnectionType`, which is an object with `pageInfo` and `edges` keys.

We use a new `loader` method, `getPostIdsForUser`, and pass it the `args` to our resolver. We'll implement this loader very soon, and it will not only return the associated `rows` but also a `pageInfo` structure that corresponds to the `PageInfoType`. We then load the nodes for each of the identifiers and create the wrap them into a `PostEdgeType` with the row's cursor.

There are ways to make this more efficient at the JavaScript and database levels, but for now let's focus on making our code work by implementing `getPostIdsForUser`.

This loader will determine what data to fetch based on the pagination arguments and what cursors to assign the rows returned. The algorithm for slicing and pagination through your data based on the arguments is rather complex when supporting all possibilities, and you can read about it in detail in the Relay specification[127]. For brevity, we're only going to support the `after` and `first` arguments.

We start by defining the new function and parsing the arguments:

```
export const getPostIdsForUser = (userSource, args) => {
  let { after, first } = args;
  if (!first) {
    first = 2;
  }
```

In other words, if the user does not supply an argument for `first`, then we will return two posts. Then we start to construct our SQL query:

[127]https://facebook.github.io/relay/graphql/connections.htm#sec-Pagination-algorithm

```
const table = tables.posts;
let query = table
  .select(table.id, table.created_at)
  .where(table.user_id.equals(userSource.id))
  .order(table.created_at.asc)
  .limit(first + 1);
```

We grab `first + 1` rows as a cheap method to determine if there are any more rows beyond what the user wants. Our query is ordered by `created_at ASC`, which is important in order to get deterministic data upon successive queries.

Next we account for an `after` cursor that may be passed:

```
if (after) {
  // parse cursor
  const [id, created_at] = after.split(':');
  query = query
    .where(table.created_at.gt(after))
    .where(table.id.gt(id));
```

Our cursors in this example are strings composed of row IDs and row dates. Generally cursors will be based upon some date in most systems, since keeping IDs as incrementing integers is less common when working with high scale data.

We can finally execute our database query:

```
return database.getSql(query.toQuery()).then((allRows) => {
  const rows = allRows.slice(0, first);

  rows.forEach((row) => {
    row.__tableName = tables.posts.getName();
    row.__cursor = row.id + ':' + row.created_at;
```

Remember that we actually queried one more row than the user requested, which is why we have to `slice` the rows returned. We also construct the cursor for each row and set the `__tableName` property so that our future `JOIN` queries will work.

Now that we have our rows, we execute it and start to create our `pageInfo` object:

```
    const hasNextPage = allRows.length > first;
    const hasPreviousPage = false;

    const pageInfo = {
      hasNextPage: hasNextPage,
      hasPreviousPage: hasPreviousPage,
    };

    if (rows.length > 0) {
      pageInfo.startCursor = rows[0].__cursor;
      pageInfo.endCursor = rows[rows.length - 1].__cursor;
    }
```

Keeping a reference to `allRows` lets us calculate `hasNextPage`; because we don't support the `before` and `last` arguments, we always set `hasPreviousPage` to false. Setting `startCursor` and `endCursor` is as simple as grabbing the first and last elements of our `rows` array.

We return both the `rows` and `pageInfo` objects to finish the loader - finally! Restart your server and try the query we described at the start of the section:

```
{
  node(id:"users:1") {
    ... on User {
      posts(first: 1) {
        pageInfo {
          hasNextPage
          hasPreviousPage
          startCursor
          endCursor
        }
        edges {
          cursor
          node {
            id
            body
          }
        }
      }
    }
  }
}
```

In response you should get the first post by this user:

```
{
  "data": {
    "node": {
      "posts": {
        "pageInfo": {
          "hasNextPage": true,
          "hasPreviousPage": false,
          "startCursor": "1:2016-04-01",
          "endCursor": "1:2016-04-01"
        },
        "edges": [
          {
            "cursor": "1:2016-04-01",
            "node": {
              "id": "posts:1",
              "body": "The team played a great game today!"
            }
          }
        ]
      }
    }
  }
}
```


See that `endCursor`? Now try running a query with that cursor as the `after` value:

```
{
  node(id:"users:1") {
    ... on User {
      posts(first: 1, after:"1:2016-04-01") {
        pageInfo {
          hasNextPage
          hasPreviousPage
          startCursor
          endCursor
        }
        edges {
          cursor
          node {
            id
            body
          }
```

```
          }
        }
      }
    }
}
```

This returns the next (and final, judging from `hasNextPage`) post in the series:

```
{
  "data": {
    "node": {
      "posts": {
        "pageInfo": {
          "hasNextPage": false,
          "hasPreviousPage": false,
          "startCursor": "2:2016-04-02",
          "endCursor": "2:2016-04-02"
        },
        "edges": [
          {
            "cursor": "2:2016-04-02",
            "node": {
              "id": "posts:2",
              "body": "Honestly I didn't do so well at yesterday's game, but eve\
ryone else did."
            }
          }
        ]
      }
    }
  }
}
```

Congratulations, you've now implemented cursor-based pagination! You might be able to use simple lists for static data, but using cursors prevents all kinds of frontend bugs and complexity for data that updates relatively often. It also allows you to leverage Relay's understanding of pagination and build paginated or infinite-scrolling UIs very quickly.

Authentication

Earlier we noted that in our social network the friendships have "levels," which posts should respect. For example, if a post has a level of `friend`, then only my friends with a level of `friend` or higher (instead of `acquaintance` or a lower level) should see it.

This topic is generally referred to as *authorization*. GraphQL has no inherit notion or opinions on authorization, which makes it quite flexible for implementing controls on who can see what data in your schemas. This also means you need to take care to ensure that youâ€™re not accidentally exposing data that should be hidden to the user.

We're going to add a small *authentication* layer to our server, which verifies that the GraphQL query is allowed to be processed, as well as the authorization logic to control who can see the different posts. The techniques we'll use are definitely not the only ways to implement these features with GraphQL, but should spark some ideas that might apply to your product.

For authentication, we're going to use HTTP basic authentication[128]. There are a myriad of protocols for authentication, such as OAuth, JSON web tokens, and cookies, and the choice is ultimately very unique to each product. HTTP basic auth is fairly simple to add to our current NodeJS server, which is the primary reason in this case.

First, install the `basic-auth-connect` package, which provides a very simple API to allow certain credentials access:

```
$ npm i basic-auth-connect@1.0.0 --save --save-exact
```

Then in our server code, import the module:

```
import express from 'express';
import basicAuth from 'basic-auth-connect';

const app = express();
```

Right before we add our GraphQL endpoint, add a new call to `app.use`. Remember that Express will trigger each `app.use` function in the order they are added - if we put the new `basicAuth` function *after* our `graphqlHTTP` function, the ordering would be incorrect.

```
app.use(basicAuth(function(user, pass) {
  return pass === 'mypassword1';
}));

app.use('/graphql', graphqlHTTP({ schema: Schema, graphiql: true }));
```

For now, we'll allow any user with the right password. Restart your server and try running this cURL command to test a simple query:

---

[128] https://en.wikipedia.org/wiki/Basic_access_authentication

```
$ curl -XPOST -H 'content-type:application/graphql' http://localhost:3000/graphq\
l -d '{ node(id:"users:4") { id } }'
Unauthorized
```

Since we didn't specify a username or password, our query fails. Try this next command to correctly pass our credentials:

```
$ curl -XPOST -H 'content-type:application/graphql' --user 1:mypassword1 http://\
localhost:3000/graphql -d '{ node(id:"users:4") { id } }'
{"data":{"node":{"id":"users:4"}}}
```

Great, now our authentication is working. You can also try this in Chrome and Firefox, which allow a GUI for entering the username and password.

The important concept here is that authentication is generally decoupled from a GraphQL schema. It's definitely possible to pass the username and password into a GraphQL query to authenticate the user (over HTTPS of course), but idiomatic GraphQL tends to separate the concerns.

Authorization

Now, onto tackling authorization. Remember in the last chapter we brought up the idea of a `viewer` field, which represents the logged-in users node in the data graph. We're going to add that field to our schema and allow our resolution code to be aware of the viewer's permissions.

By using `basic-auth-connect`, we can access to a `user` property on every Express request. The specifics on how you determine the user making each request will vary depending on your authentication library, but we simple need to take that `request.user` property and forward to our GraphQL resolver:

```
app.use('/graphql', graphqlHTTP((req) => {
  const context = 'users:' + req.user;
  return { schema: Schema, graphiql: true, context: context, pretty: true };
}));
```

Instead of always returning the same `schema` and `graphiql` settings for all requests, we now return a different configuration object for each GraphQL query. This new configuration has the `context` property set to the username, like the `user1` from the example earlier.

The next question is how do we access that `context` inside our GraphQL fields? Recall from earlier in the chapter that each `resolve` function gets passed some arguments. We've become very familiar with the `args` argument, but it turns out the `context` is also passed.

Here's how we add the `viewer` field with that knowledge:

```
const RootQuery = new GraphQLObjectType({
  name: 'RootQuery',
  description: 'The root query',
  fields: {
    viewer: {
      type: NodeInterface,
      resolve(source, args, context) {
        return loaders.getNodeById(context);
      }
    },
```

If you restart your server, you should be able to cURL the endpoint like so:

```
$ curl -XPOST -H 'content-type:application/graphql' --user 1:mypassword1 http://\
localhost:3000/graphql -d '{ viewer { id } }'
{
  "data": {
    "viewer": {
      "id": "users:1"
    }
  }
}
```

You can explore using the `... on User` inline fragment to query more properties. We are able to provide this sort of consistent API with minimal code changes because we modeled our application data as a graph - neat!

Not only can top-level `viewer` field access the `context`, but *all* `resolve` functions have access, regardless of their depth in the hierarchy. This makes it very simple to add authorization checks to our `posts` field.

We start by forwarding the `context` argument in our `resolve` function:

```
        resolve(source, args, context) {
          return loaders.getPostIdsForUser(source, args, context).then(({ rows, \
pageInfo }) => {
```

GraphQL schemas should not handle authorization logic directly, which is likely to duplicate logic from your main codebase. Instead, that responsibility should fall into the underlying data loading libraries or services, as we show here.

Inside our `getPostIdsForUser`, we need to load each post's `level` from the database before we can use it. All we have to do is add it to our `select` arguments:

```
  let query = table
    .select(table.id, table.created_at, table.level)
    .where(table.user_id.equals(userSource.id))
    .order(table.created_at.asc)
    .limit(first + 10);
```

In addition to running the database query to get all of the posts, we're also going to run another query to get all of the user access levels for our `context`. We'll use that list of levels to filter down the results our database query.

```
  return Promise.all([
    database.getSql(query.toQuery()),
    getFriendshipLevels(context)
  ]).then(([ allRows, friendshipLevels ]) => {
    allRows = allRows.filter((row) => {
      return canAccessLevel(friendshipLevels[userSource.id], row.level);
    });
    const rows = allRows.slice(0, first);
```

We're referencing two new functions that have yet to be implemented, `getFriendshipLevels` and `canAccessLevel`. Before we get to that, note that this does potentially introduce a bug into our system. We were calculating `hasNextPage` based on the length of `allRows`, but now `allRows` can be truncated depending on privacy settings. This highlights some of the complexity of systems that are highly aware of authorization; a naive mitigation of this is to just read more rows eagerly from the database, which we changed above (`first + 10`).

The `getFriendshipLevels` definition is similar to our other queries:

```
const getFriendshipLevels = (nodeId) => {
  const { dbId } = tables.splitNodeId(nodeId);

  const table = tables.usersFriends;
  let query = table
    .select(table.star())
    .where(table.user_id_a.equals(dbId));

  return database.getSql(query.toQuery()).then((rows) => {
    const levelMap = {};
    rows.forEach((row) => {
      levelMap[row.user_id_b] = row.level;
    });
    return levelMap;
  });
};
```

At the end we transform the array of rows into an object for a slightly more efficient API (you can also implement this transformation using a single `reduce` function if you'd like).

The last piece is `canAccessLevel`. Because our privacy settings are totally linear, we can represent the settings as an array and use the indices as a simple comparison:

```
const canAccessLevel = (viewerLevel, contentLevel) => {
  const levels = ['public', 'acquaintance', 'friend', 'top'];
  const viewerLevelIndex = levels.indexOf(viewerLevel);
  const contentLevelIndex = levels.indexOf(contentLevel);

  return viewerLevelIndex >= contentLevelIndex;
};
```

That all wasn't too bad, was it? We can test this out with some queries. Login as user `1` (so username `1` and password `mypassword1`) and run this query:

```
{
  node(id:"users:2") {
    ... on User {
      posts {
        edges {
          node {
            id
            ... on Post {
              body
            }
          }
        }
      }
    }
  }
}
```

In return, you'll see no posts. This is because our `context` (user 1) is not friends with the node we're accessing (user 2), and their posts have a level of `friend`.

Now open an incognito window, login as user `5`, run that same query. You'll see a post!

```
{
  "data": {
    "node": {
      "posts": {
        "edges": [
          {
            "node": {
              "id": "posts:3",
              "body": "Hard at work studying for finals..."
            }
          }
        ]
      }
    }
  }
}
```

This is because user 5 is actually a friend of user 2.

This is a simple example, but highlights a few points about GraphQL.

- GraphQL server libraries typically allow you to forward on some kind of query-level `context`
- Your GraphQL schema code should not concern itself with authorization logic, instead deferring to your underlying data code

We've been reading data from our server for a bit, but now we should try out changing some of it with mutations.

Rich Mutations

There's only so much your application can do if it can only read data from the server - more often than not, we have to upload some new data. Recall from the last chapter that in GraphQL, we call these updates *mutations*.

We're going to add a mutation to our schema which creates a new post. The field will have a string arguments for the post body and a friendship privacy level, and it will allow us to query more information about the resulting post object.

Earlier in this chapter we added a simple key-value mutation in our `server.js` file. Let's update that definition to use the arguments and types we expect for creating a new post:

```
import { GraphQLSchema, GraphQLObjectType, GraphQLString,
  GraphQLNonNull, GraphQLID, GraphQLEnumType } from 'graphql';
```

```
const LevelEnum = new GraphQLEnumType({
  name: 'PrivacyLevel',
  values: {
    PUBLIC: {
      value: 'public'
    },
    ACQUAINTANCE: {
      value: 'acquaintance'
    },
    FRIEND: {
      value: 'friend'
    },
    TOP: {
      value: 'top'
    }
  }
});

const RootMutation = new GraphQLObjectType({
  name: 'RootMutation',
  description: 'The root mutation',
  fields: {
    createPost: {
      type: PostType,
      args: {
        body: {
          type: new GraphQLNonNull(GraphQLString)
        },
        level: {
          type: new GraphQLNonNull(LevelEnum),
        }
      },
      resolve(source, args, context) {
        return loaders.createPost(args.body, args.level, context).then((nodeId) \
=> {
          return loaders.getNodeById(nodeId);
        });
      }
    }
```

```
  }
});
```

First we instantiate a new kind of object, a `GraphQLEnumType`. We only briefly mentioned the `Enum` GraphQL type in previous chapter, but it works similarly to how enums work in many programming languages. Because our `level` argument should only be one of a fixed amount of options, we enforce that contract at the schema level with an enum. By convention, enums in GraphQL are `ALL_CAPS`.

After creating our enum, we use it in the `args` property of our new `createPost` mutation. Note that in addition to the arguments, `createPost` has a `type` of `PostType`, which means we eventually need to return a post object after performing our mutating code. That work is actually deferred to a new `createPost` loader, which looks like this:

```
export const createPost = (body, level, context) => {
  const { dbId } = tables.splitNodeId(context);
  const created_at = new Date().toISOString().split('T')[0];
  const posts = [{ body, level, created_at, user_id: dbId }];

  let query = tables.posts.insert(posts).toQuery();
  return database.getSql(query).then(() => {
    return database.getSql({ text: 'SELECT last_insert_rowid() AS id FROM posts'\
 });
  }).then((ids) => {
    return tables.dbIdToNodeId(ids[0].id, tables.posts.getName());
  });
};
```

This is mostly specific to our SQLite database, but you can imagine how this would work in other frameworks or data stores. We construct our database row, insert it, and then retrieve the newly inserted ID.

If you open up GraphiQL, you should be able to give this mutation a try:

```
mutation {
  createPost(body:"First post!", level:PUBLIC) {
    id
    body
  }
}
```

In the wild, you may run into more complex scenarios for updating data such as uploading files. The specifics will depend on what server language and library you use, but it's supported with Relay and GraphQL-JS. The Relay documentation[129] discusses how files are handled, and you can find examples elsewhere[130] of how to leverage those within your GraphQL schema.

Relay and GraphQL

The "Facebook-lite" schema we've developed may be small, but it should give you an idea of how to structure common operations in a GraphQL server. It also happens to be compatible with Relay[131], Facebook's frontend React library for working with a GraphQL server.

In addition to publishing Relay itself, Facebook publishes a library to help you more easily construct a Relay-compatible GraphQL server with Node. This GraphQL-Relay-JS[132] package reduces much of the boilerplate we've experienced, especially for some of Relay's more powerful features.

You should read over the docs for all the details, but we're briefly going to convert some of our code to use this library. First we need to install it via npm:

```
$ npm install graphql-relay@0.4.1 --save --save-exact
```

GraphQL-Relay is particularly helpful with connection fields. Although we only had one proper connection field in our schema (`posts`), you can imagine that repeating the types and code for each connection in a larger app would become tiresome. Luckily, all we need is a quick import:

```
import {
  connectionDefinitions
} from 'graphql-relay';
```

Then delete all of our existing connection types, so that we skip straight to the `UserType`:

```
const resolveId = (source) => {
  return tables.dbIdToNodeId(source.id, source.__tableName);
};

export const UserType = new GraphQLObjectType({
  name: 'User',
```

And at the very bottom, add this one-liner to define `PostsConnectionType`:

---

[129] https://facebook.github.io/relay/docs/api-reference-relay-mutation.html#getfiles

[130] http://stackoverflow.com/a/35585482

[131] https://facebook.github.io/relay/

[132] https://github.com/graphql/graphql-relay-js

```
const { connectionType: PostsConnectionType } = connectionDefinitions({ nodeType\
: PostType });
```

Internally, this generates all the types we crafted by hand - `PageInfo`, `PostEdge`, and `PostConnection`. You can confirm this if you load up the GraphiQL documentation:

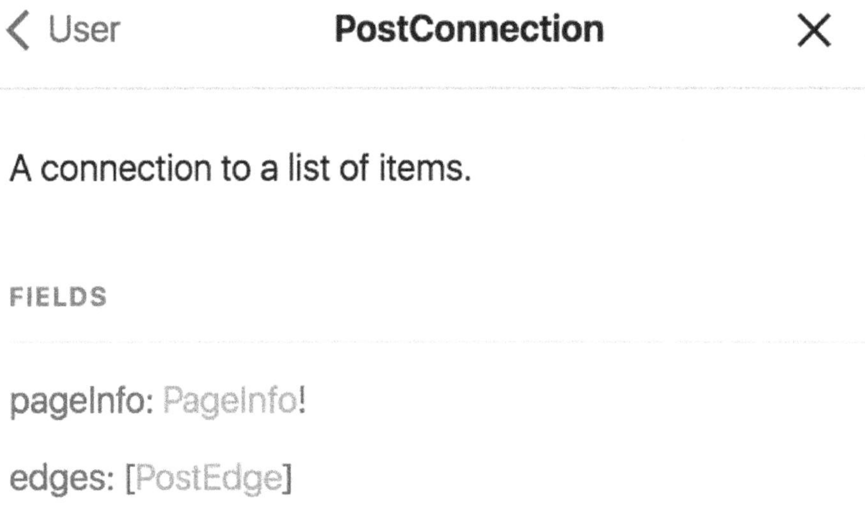

GraphQL Relay

In addition to connections, the GraphQL-Relay library also has functions for simplifying how node types are structured[133] and working with Relay-compatible mutations[134]. We'll explore this more in the upcoming Relay chapter, but Relay imposes some rules on how mutations work, similar to the way that certain types and arguments required for connections.

None of the GraphQL server changes required for Relay are specific to GraphQL-JS or JavaScript in general. Any language GraphQL server can be made compatible with Relay, and hopefully this chapter has made you more familiar with the basic building blocks of any GraphQL schema.

Performance: N+1 Queries

Now that our schema has settled, we can reconsider performance. Before we dive in, remember that the performance needs of different products can be incredibly disparate. Engineers should carefully consider the costs and benefits of writing code that is more performant at the risk of additional complexity.

Let's consider a query like this:

[133] https://github.com/graphql/graphql-relay-js#object-identification
[134] https://github.com/graphql/graphql-relay-js#mutations

```
{
  node(id:"users:4") {
    ... on User {
      friends {
        edges {
          node {
            id
            about
            name
          }
        }
      }
    }
  }
}
```

Under the hood, our current GraphQL resolution code will trigger one database query to get the node for `"users:4"`, one query to get the list of friend IDs, and N database queries for each of the `friends` edges. This is commonly referred to as the N+1 Query Problem[135] and can easily occur using any web framework or ORM. You can imagine that for a slow database or a large number of edges, this will cause degraded performance. We can visualize this with the following raw SQL:

```
SELECT "users".* FROM "users" WHERE ("users"."id" = 4) LIMIT 1
SELECT "users_friends"."user_id_b" FROM "users_friends" WHERE ("users_friends"."\
user_id_a" = 4)
SELECT "users".* FROM "users" WHERE ("users"."id" = 1) LIMIT 1
SELECT "users".* FROM "users" WHERE ("users"."id" = 3) LIMIT 1
SELECT "users".* FROM "users" WHERE ("users"."id" = 2) LIMIT 1
```

In a perfect world, we would only need two database queries: one to retrieve the initial node, and then one to retrieve **all** of the friends in one query (or within whatever paging limits we need) - in other words, we batch all of the queries for friends. Something more like this would not:

```
SELECT "users".* FROM "users" WHERE ("users"."id" = 4) LIMIT 1
SELECT "users_friends"."user_id_b" FROM "users_friends" WHERE ("users_friends"."\
user_id_a" = 4)
SELECT "users".* FROM "users" WHERE ("users"."id" in (1, 3, 2)) LIMIT 3
```

Consider how loading a user works: it's a call to `loaders.getNodeById`. Currently that function immediately triggers a database query, but what if we could "wait" for some small amount of

[135] https://secure.phabricator.com/book/phabcontrib/article/n_plus_one/

time, collect node IDs that need to be loaded, and then trigger a database query like the one above? GraphQL and JavaScript enable intuitive techniques for batching alike queries, which we'll implement.

Facebook maintains a library called DataLoader[136] to help, which is a generic JavaScript library independent of React or GraphQL. You use the library to create *loaders*, which are objects that automatically batch fetching of similar data. For example, you would instantiate a `UserLoader` to load users from the database:

```
const UserLoader = new DataLoader((userIds) => {
  const query = table
    .select(table.star())
    .where(table.id.in(userIds))
    .toQuery();

  return database.getSql(query.toQuery());
});

// elsewhere, loading a single user
function resolveUser(userId) {
  return UserLoader.load(userId);
}
```

Notice how `UserLoader.load` takes a single `userId` as an argument, but the argument to it's internal function is an array of `userIds`. This means if we call `UserLoader.load` from multiple places in rapid succession, we have the option of crafting a more efficient database query.

In our app, most of our code touches `loaders.getNodeById` which makes it a strong candidate for automatic batching. None of the code that invokes `getNodeById` has to change; instead, we're going to internally batch node fetches using DataLoader.

First, install DataLoader from npm:

```
$ npm install dataloader@1.2.0 --save --save-exact
```

Now onto our changes to `loaders.js`. We're going to make one data loader per table, which is a reasonable way to start optimizing. The code starts like this:

136 https://github.com/facebook/dataloader

```
import * as database from './database';
import * as tables from './tables';

import DataLoader from 'dataloader';

const createNodeLoader = (table) => {
  return new DataLoader((ids) => {
    const query = table
      .select(table.star())
      .where(table.id.in(ids))
      .toQuery();

    return database.getSql(query).then((rows) => {
      rows.forEach((row) => {
        row.__tableName = table.getName();
      });
      return rows;
    });
  });
};
```

Our `createNodeLoader` is a factory function which returns a new instance of `DataLoader`. We craft a query of the form `SELECT * FROM $TABLE WHERE ID IN($IDS)`, which lets us select multiple nodes with a single query.

Now we need to invoke our factory function, which we'll store in a constant:

```
const nodeLoaders = {
  users: createNodeLoader(tables.users),
  posts: createNodeLoader(tables.posts),
  usersFriends: createNodeLoader(tables.usersFriends),
};
```

Finally, we change our definition of `getNodeById` to use the appropriate loader:

```
export const getNodeById = (nodeId) => {
  const { tableName, dbId } = tables.splitNodeId(nodeId);
  return nodeLoaders[tableName].load(dbId);
};
```

If you open up GraphiQL and try this query, you'll notice the SQL logs in the server console are appropriately batching our database fetches:

```
{
  user3: node(id:"users:3") {
    id
  }
  user4: node(id:"users:4") {
    id
  }
}
```

```
$ node index.js
{ starting: true }
{ running: true }
SELECT "users".* FROM "users" WHERE ("users"."id" IN ($1, $2))
[ '3', '4' ]
```

Note that our higher-level GraphQL schema code is totally unaware of this optimization and didn't have to change at all. In general, you should prefer keeping optimizations at the loader and data service level so all consumers can enjoy the benefits.

DataLoader is simple but powerful tool. Although we showed off its batching abilities, it can also act as a cache - if you'd like to learn more, check out its documentation[137] and consider watching this talk by its maintainer[138].

Summary

We covered a lot of ground in this chapter. We designed a schema, created a GraphQL server from scratch, connected it to a relational database, and explored some performance optimizations. Regardless of your production language and stack, these concepts will apply to all GraphQL server implementations. Additionally, this should give you some more understanding and context whenever you connect to a GraphQL server from the frontend.

We used the Facebook-maintained GraphQL-JS library in this chapter, but the GraphQL ecosystem is exploding. Here some more popular options and technologies you might want to explore:

- GraphQL[139] for Ruby
- Graphene[140] for Python
- Sangria[141] for Scala

[137] https://github.com/facebook/dataloader#getting-started
[138] https://www.youtube.com/watch?v=OQTnXNCDywA
[139] https://github.com/rmosolgo/graphql-ruby
[140] https://github.com/graphql-python/graphene
[141] https://github.com/sangria-graphql/sangria

- Apollo Server[142] for Node
- Graffiti-Mongoose[143] for Node and MongoDB
- Services like Reindex[144] and Graphcool[145] for hosting GraphQL servers

Now that we've learned about consuming GraphQL and authoring a GraphQL server, it's time to put everything we've covered thus far and learn about Relay.

[142]http://docs.apollostack.com/apollo-server/tools.html

[143]https://github.com/RisingStack/graffiti-mongoose

[144]https://www.reindex.io/

[145]https://graph.cool/

Relay

Introduction

Picking the right data architecture in a client-server web app can be difficult. There are a myriad of decisions to be made when you try to implement a data architecture. For example:

- How will we fetch data from the server?
- What do we do if that fetch fails?
- How do we query dependencies and relationships between data
- How do we keep data consistent across the app?
- How can we keep developers from breaking each others' components accidentally?
- How can we move faster and write our app-specific functionality rather than spending our time pushing data back and forth from our server?

Thankfully, Relay has a theory on all of these issues. Even better: it's an implementation of that theory and it's a joy to use, once you get it set up. But it's natural to ask: What *is* Relay?

Relay is a library which connects your React components to your API server.

We talked about GraphQL earlier in the book and it may not be immediately clear what the relationship is between Relay, GraphQL, and React. You can think of Relay as the glue between GraphQL and React.

Relay is great because:

- components declare the data they need to operate
- it manages *how* and *when* we fetch data
- it intelligently aggregates queries, so we don't fetch more than we need
- it gives us clear patterns for navigating relationships between our objects and mutating them

One of the most helpful things about Relay that we'll see in this chapter is that the GraphQL queries are **co-located with the component**. This gives us the benefit of being able to see a clear specification of the values needed to render a component directly alongside the component itself.

Each component specifies what it needs and Relay figures out if there's any duplication, before making the query. Relay will aggregate the queries, process the responses, and then hand back to each component just the data it asked for.

GraphQL can be used independent of Relay. You can, in theory, create a GraphQL server to have more-or-less any schema you want. However, Relay has a specification that your GraphQL server must follow in order to be Relay-compatible. We'll talk about those constraints.

What We're Going to Cover

In this chapter we're going to walk through a practical tutorial on **how to setup and use Relay in a client app**.

Relay depends on a GraphQL server, which we've provided in the sample code, but we're not going to talk about the implementation details of that server.

In this chapter we're going to:

- explain the various concepts of Relay
- describe how to setup Relay in our app (with routing)
- show how to fetch data from Relay into our components
- show how to update data on our server using mutations
- highlight tips and tricks about Relay along the way

By the end of this chapter you'll understand what Relay is, how to use it, and have a firm foundation for integrating Relay into your own apps.

What We're Building

The Client

In this chapter, we're going to build a simple bookstore. We'll have three pages:

- A book listing page, which shows all of the books we have for sale.

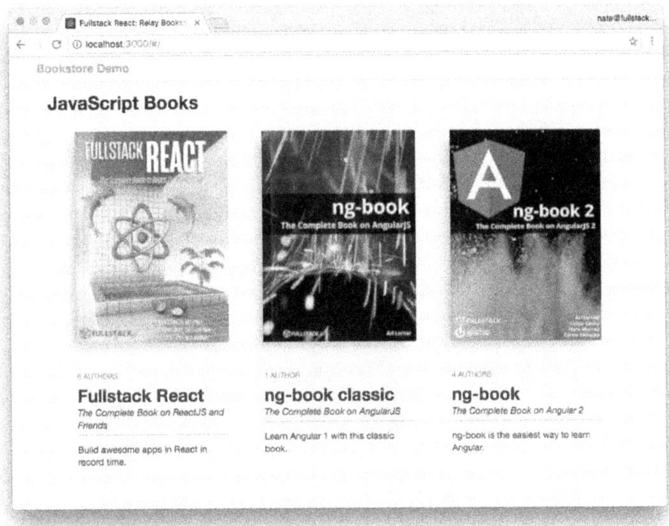

Books Store Page

- An author bio page, which shows an author's information and the books they've authored.

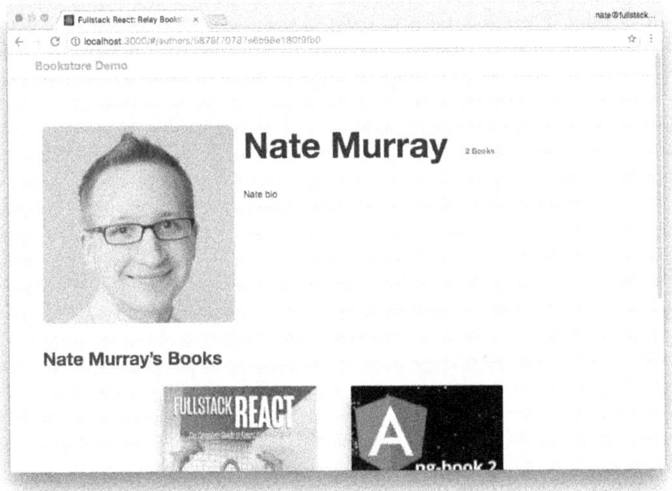

Author Page

- A book listing page, which shows a single book and the authors for that book. We'll also **edit** a book on this page.

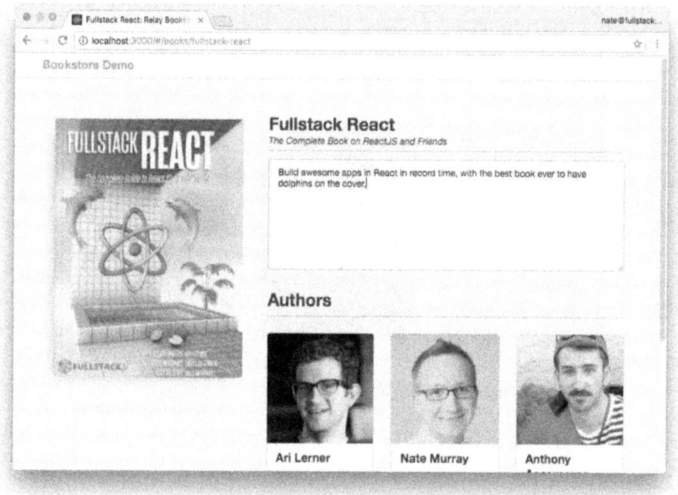

Book Listing Page

The data model here is straightforward: a book has (and belongs to) many authors.

This data is provided to our app via an API server.

The Server

We've provided a Relay-compatible GraphQL demo server in the sample code with this app. In this chapter **we aren't going to discuss the implementation details of the server**. If you're interested in building GraphQL servers, checkout the chapter "GraphQL Server."

This server was created with the library graffiti-mongoose[146]. If you're using MongoDB and mongoose[147], then `graffiti-mongoose` is a fantastic choice for adapting your models to GraphQL. `graffiti-mongoose` takes your `mongoose` models and automatically generates a Relay-compatible GraphQL server.

That said, there are libraries that can help you generate GraphQL from your models for every popular language. Checkout the list awesome-graphql[148] to see what libraries are available.

Try The App

You can find the project for this chapter inside the `relay` folder of the code download:

146 https://github.com/RisingStack/graffiti-mongoose

147 http://mongoosejs.com/

148 https://github.com/chentsulin/awesome-graphql

```
$ cd relay/bookstore
```

We've included the completed server and completed client. Before we can run them, we need to run `npm install` on both the client and the server:

```
$ npm install
$ cd client
$ npm install
$ cd ..
```

Next, you can run them individually in two separate tabs with:

```
# tab one
$ npm run server
# tab two
$ npm run client
```

Or we've provided a convenience command that will run them both with:

```
$ npm start
```

When they're running, you should be able to access the GraphQL server at `http://localhost:3001` and the client app at `http://localhost:3000`.

In this chapter, we're going to be spending time in our browser looking at **both the client and the server**. We've installed the GraphQL GUI tool "GraphiQL" on this demo server.

Relay is based on GraphQL, and so to get a better understanding of how it works, we're going to be running a few queries "by hand" in this GraphiQL interface.

How to Use This Chapter

While we will *introduce* all of the terminology of Relay, this chapter is intended to be a guide to working with Relay and not the API documentation.

As you're reading this chapter, feel free to cross-reference the official docs[149] to dig in to the details.

Prerequisites

This is an advanced chapter. We're going to focus on using Relay and not re-cover the basics of writing React apps. It's assumed that you're somewhat comfortable with writing components, using props, JSX, and loading third party libraries. Relay also requires GraphQL, and so we assume you have some familiarity with GraphQL as well.

If you don't feel comfortable with these things, we cover all of them earlier in the book.

---

149 https://facebook.github.io/relay/

Relay 1

Currently this chapter covers Relay 1.x. There is a new version of Relay in the works, but don't let that stop you from learning Relay 1. There is no public release date and Facebook employee Jaseph Savona stated on GitHub[150] that Relay 2 has "definite API differences, but the core concepts are the same and the API changes serve to make Relay simpler and more predictable"

Some good news here is that the underlying GraphQL specification doesn't change[151]. So while, yes, Relay will have a v2 in the future. We can still use Relay 1 in our production apps today.

If you're interested more in the future of Relay, checkout Relay: State of the State[152].

Guide to the Code Structure

In this chapter, we've provided the **completed** version of the app in `relay/bookstore`.

In order to break up the concepts in to more digestible bites, we've broken up some of the components into steps. We've included these intermediate files in `relay/bookstore/client/steps`.

Our Relay app contains a server, a client, and several build tools – these all add up to quite a lot of files and directories. Here's a brief overview of some of the directories and files you'll find in our project. (Don't worry if some of this is unfamiliar, we'll explain everything you need to know in this chapter):

```
-- bookstore
    |-- README.md
    |-- client
    |   |-- config                          // client configuration
    |   |   |-- babelRelayPlugin.js         // our custom babel plugin
    |   |   |-- webpack.config.dev.js       // webpack configuration
    |   |   `-- webpack.config.prod.js
    |   |-- package.json
    |   |-- public                          // images and index.html
    |   |   |-- images/
    |   |   `-- index.html
    |   |-- scripts                         // helper scripts
    |   |   |-- build.js
    |   |   |-- start.js
    |   |   `-- test.js
```

[150] https://github.com/facebook/relay/issues/1369

[151] https://github.com/facebook/relay/issues/1369#issuecomment-266647767

[152] https://facebook.github.io/react/blog/2016/08/05/relay-state-of-the-state.html

```
|   `-- src
|       |-- components              // our components are here
|       |   |-- App.js
|       |   |-- AuthorPage.js
|       |   |-- BookItem.js
|       |   |-- BookPage.js
|       |   |-- BooksPage.js
|       |   |-- FancyBook.js
|       |   `-- TopBar.js
|       |-- data                    // graphql metadata
|       |   |-- schema.graphql
|       |   `-- schema.json
|       |-- index.js
|       |-- mutations               // mutations make changes
|       |   `-- UpdateBookMutation.js
|       |-- routes.js               // our routes
|       |-- steps/                  // intermediate files
|       `-- styles                  // css styles here
|-- models.js                       // server models
|-- package.json
|-- schema.js                       // graphql schema on the server
|-- server.js                       // our server definition
|-- start-client.js
|-- start-server.js
`-- tools
    `-- update-schema.js            // a helper for generating the schema
```

Feel free to poke around at the sample code we've provided, but don't worry about understanding every file just yet. We'll cover all of the important parts.

Relay is a Data Architecture

Relay is a JavaScript library that runs on the client-side. You connect Relay to your React components and then Relay will fetch data from your server. Of course, your server also needs to conform to Relay's protocol, and we'll talk about that, too.

Relay is designed to be the data-backbone for your React app. This means that, ideally, we'd use Relay for all of our data loading and for maintaining the central, authoritative state for our application.

Because Relay has its own store it's able to cache data and resolve queries efficiently. If you have two components that are concerned with the same data, Relay will combine the two queries into one and then distribute the appropriate data to each component. This has the duel benefit of minimizing the number of server calls we need but still allowing the individual components the ability to specify locally what data they need.

Because Relay holds a central store of your data, this means it's not really compatible with other data architectures that keep a central store, like Redux. You can't have two central stores of state and so this makes the current versions of Redux and Relay essentially incompatible.

Apollo

If you're already using Redux but you'd like to try Relay, there's still hope: the Apollo project[153] is a Relay-inspired library that is based on Redux. If you're careful, you can retrofit Apollo into your existing Redux app.

We're not going to talk about Apollo in this chapter, but it's a fantastic library and it's absolutely worth looking into for your app.

Relay GraphQL Conventions

One thing we need to clarify is the relationship between Relay and GraphQL.

Our GraphQL server defines our GraphQL schema and how to resolve queries against that schema. GraphQL itself lets you define a wide variety of schemas. For the most part, it doesn't dictate what the structure of your schema should be.

Relay defines a set of conventions on top of GraphQL. In order to use Relay, your GraphQL server must adhere to a specific set of guidelines.

At a high level, these conventions are:

1. A way to fetch **any object by ID** (regardless of type)
2. A way to **traverse relationships** between objects (called "connections") with pagination
3. A structure around changing data with **mutations**

These three requirements allow us to build sophisticated, efficient apps. In this chapter, we'll make these generic guidelines concrete.

Let's explore implementations of these three Relay conventions directly on our GraphQL server. Then later in the chapter we'll implement them in our client app.

Relay Specification Official Docs

You can checkout Facebook's Official Documentation on the Relay/GraphQL specification here[154]

[153] http://www.apollodata.com/

[154] https://facebook.github.io/relay/docs/graphql-relay-specification.html

Exploring Relay Conventions in GraphQL

Make sure you have the GraphQL server running, as described above, and open it in your browser at the address `localhost:3001`.

Remember that GraphiQL reads our schema and provides a documentation explorer to navigate the types. Click on the "Docs" link in GraphiQL to show the "Root Types" of our schema.

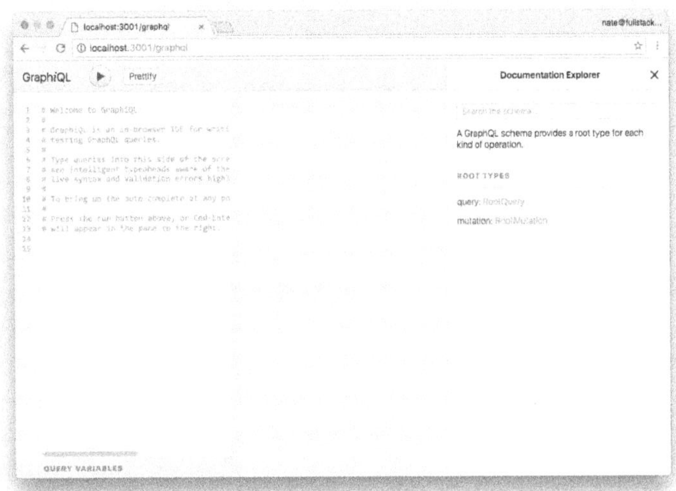

GraphiQL Interface with Docs

Fetching Objects By ID

In our server we have two models: `Author` and `Book`. The first thing we're going to do is look-up a specific object by ID.

Imagine that we want to create a page that shows the information about a particular author. We might have a URL such as `/authors/abc123`, where `abc123` is the ID of the author. We'd want Relay to ask our server "what is the information for the author `abc123`?" In that case, we'd use a GraphQL query like we're going to define below.

However, we have a bit of a chicken and egg problem at the moment: we don't know the IDs of any individual record.

So let's load the entire list of authors' `names` and `ids` and then take note of one of the IDs.

Enter the following query into GraphiQL:

```
query {
  authors {
    id
    name
  }
}
```

And click the play button:

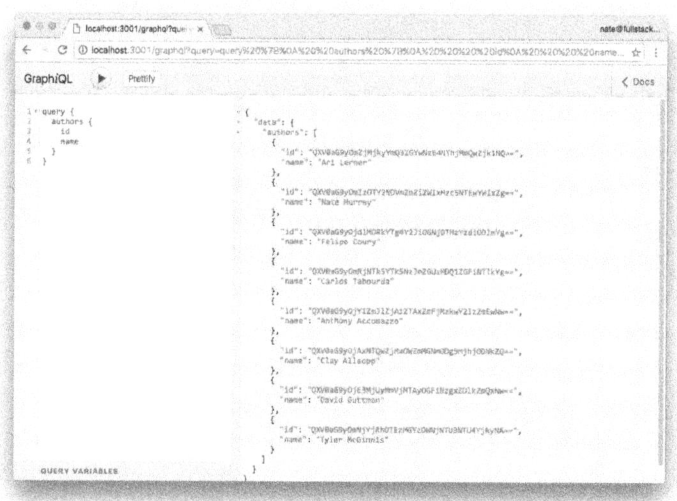

GraphiQL Authors with IDs

Now that we have an author ID, we can query `author` to get the author with a *specific* id:

Query:

```
query {
  author(id: "QXV0aG9yOjY1ZmJlZjA1ZTAxZmFjMzkwY2IzZmEwNw==") {
    id
    name
  }
}
```

Response:

```
{
  "data": {
    "author": {
      "id": "QXV0aG9yOjY1ZmJlZjA1ZTAxZmFjMzkwY2IzZmEwNw==",
      "name": "Anthony Accomazzo"
    }
  }
}
```

While this is handy, from the `author` query we can only receive an object of type `Author`, so it doesn't fulfill the requirement of the Relay specification. The Relay specification says that we need to have a way to query **any object** (`Node`) via the `node` query.

We'll talk more about our GraphQL schema later in the chapter, but it's worth pointing out that both `Author` and `Book` types implement the `Node`-type interface.

We've implemented the ability to lookup a `Node` via `node` on our server, so let's try it out. First, let's query just the `id` from `node`:

Query:

```
query {
  node(id: "QXV0aG9yOjY1ZmJlZjA1ZTAxZmFjMzkwY2IzZmEwNw==") {
    id
  }
}
```

Response:

```
{
  "data": {
    "node": {
      "id": "QXV0aG9yOjY1ZmJlZjA1ZTAxZmFjMzkwY2IzZmEwNw=="
    }
  }
}
```

This works! But it isn't very useful because we don't have any other data about the author. Let's try fetching the name:

Query:

```
query {
  node(id: "QXV0aG9yOjY1ZmJlZjA1ZTAxZmFjMzkwY2IzZmEwNw==") {
    id
    name
  }
}
```

This fails with the error:

```
Cannot query field "name" on type "Node". Did you mean to use an inline fragment\
 on "Author" or "Book"?
```

What happened here? Because `Node` is a generic type, we can't query the `name` field. Instead we need to provide a *fragment* which says, if we're querying an `Author`, then return `Author` specific fields. So we can adjust our query like so:

Query:

```
query {
  node(id: "QXV0aG9yOjY1ZmJlZjA1ZTAxZmFjMzkwY2IzZmEwNw==") {
    id
    ... on Author {
      name
    }
  }
}
```

Response

```
{
  "data": {
    "node": {
      "id": "QXV0aG9yOjY1ZmJlZjA1ZTAxZmFjMzkwY2IzZmEwNw==",
      "name": "Anthony Accomazzo"
    }
  }
}
```

It works! We're able to fetch an author using their `ID`. The key idea here is that we can query **any object** in our system by using the `node` query by ID (which is a Relay requirement). For instance, if we had a `Book` ID, we could also look up a book using the `node` query as well.

A useful exercise would be to try looking up a `Book` by ID using `node`. Hint: You'll need to add a fragment `on Book` using the syntax: `... on Book` and then specifying the `Book` fields you wish to retrieve.

Globally Unique IDs

The implications here are that we actually have a globally unique ID for each object. If, for instance, you were using a traditional SQL database (like Postgres) with auto-incrementing IDs per-table, you may have an `Author` with ID `2` and a `Book` with ID `2`. How do we resolve this?

This issue is resolved by the GraphQL server. The idea is that you'll have to come up with a convention that, say, embeds the table name and numeric ID into a GUID. Then your GraphQL server would encode and decode these IDs.

This actually is happening with the server we've provided. You may have noticed that our schema models have both an `id` field and an `_id` field. What's the difference?

The `_id` field is the MongoDB ID. The `id` field is the *Relay GUID*, a composite of the table name and the `_id` field.

Relay uses the `node` interface particularly for *re-fetching objects*. When writing our apps, we can have dozens of ways of loading various objects. The idea behind the `node` interface is to give a consistent, easy way for Relay to ask the server "what's the most current value for this object, given this ID?"

Now that we can query individual `Node`s, we need to talk about how we traverse relationships *between* them. In our example app we're going to show a list of books on the homepage, and we want to be able to load the authors who wrote that book.

In Relay we will indicate a relationship between an `Author` and `Book` by using a *connection*.

Walking Connections

An `Author` may have contributed to several `Book`s.

If you're familiar with traditional relational databases, maybe you've seen this relationship modeled with:

- An `authors` table which has an `id`
- A `books` table which has an `id`
- and an `authorships` table which holds both an `author_id` and a `book_id`

The idea in this scenario would be that for every `Author`/`Book` pair, you'd create this new "join model" called an `Authorship` which represents an `Author` who contributed to a particular `Book`. This idea is sometimes referred to as "has-and-belongs-to-many".

Analogously, Relay also defines a "join model" that should be used to denote a relationship between two models. To be precise, Relay specifies **two**:

1. The "connection" model which specifies a relationship between two models and keeps pagination data and
2. The "edge" model which wraps a cursor as well as the node- (model-) specific data.

This might seem a bit of overkill the first time you come to it, but recognize that this is a powerful and flexible model that provides consistent pagination across your models.

What's a *cursor*?

When we're traversing a large set of items, we need to keep track of where we are in that traversal. For instance, imagine that we're doing pagination through a list of products. The simplest "cursor" could be the current **page number** (e.g. page number `3`).

Of course, in real applications you may have items being added and removed to the list all the time and so you might find that by the time you load page `4` you miss some records (because some records have been added or deleted).

So what can we do in this case? This is where a *cursor* comes in. A *cursor* is a value take indicates where we "are" in traversing a list. Implementations vary, but the idea is that you can send the cursor to the server and the server give you the next page of results.

For example Twitter's API uses cursoring and you can checkout their docs here[155]

Let's try a few queries where we traverse these connections.

Here's a query that will get an author along with all of their book names:

```
query {
  author(id: "QXV0aG9yOmZjMjkyYmQ3ZGYwNzE4NThjMmQwZjk1NQ==") {
    id
    name
    books {
      count
      edges {
        node {
          id
          name
        }
      }
    }
  }
}
```

[155]https://dev.twitter.com/overview/api/cursoring

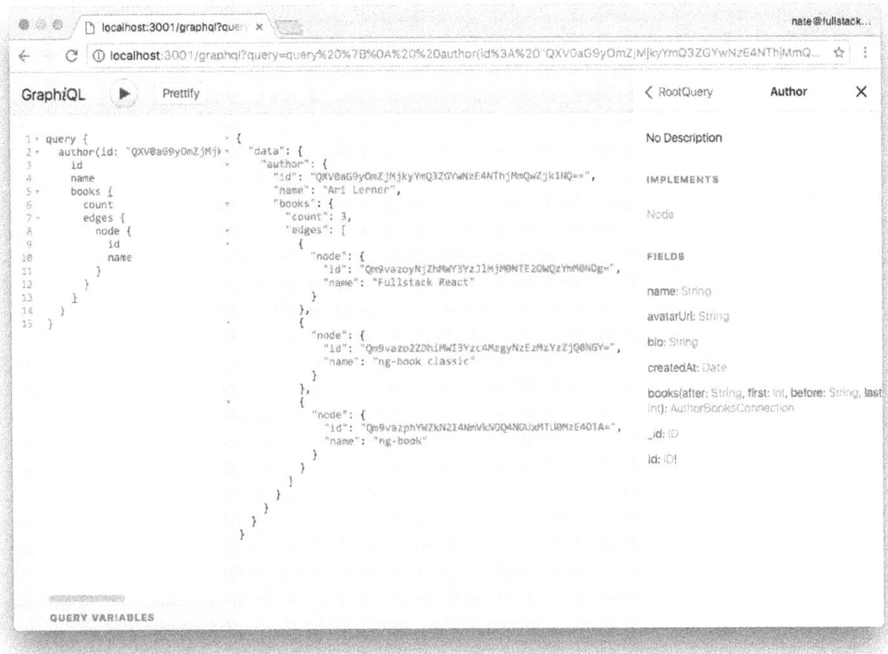

GraphiQL Author with Books

Click through the documentation for `Author` in the GraphiQL interface. Notice that on the `Author` type `books` doesn't return an array of `Book`, but rather it:

1. accepts arguments, such as `first` or `last` and
2. Returns an `AuthorBooksConnection`

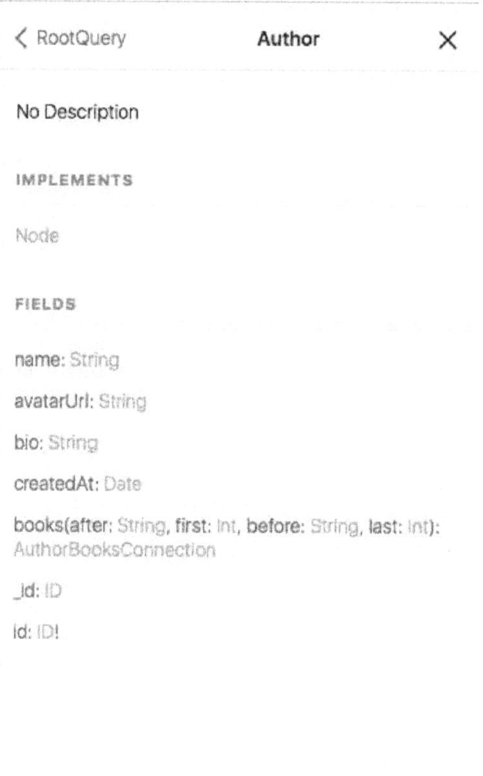

GraphiQL Author Type

Relay was designed to handle relationships that have a huge number of items. In the case where we have too many `Books` to load at once, we could use these arguments to limit the number of results that returned. We use the `first` and `last` arguments to denote the number of items we want to retrieve.

The `AuthorBooksConnection` has three fields:

- `pageInfo`
- `edges` and
- `count`

`count` gives us the total number of `edges` we have (the number of `Books` this person has authored, in this case).

`pageInfo` gives us information such as if there is a previous or next page and what the start and end cursor for this page are. We could use these cursors later on to ask for the next (or previous) page.

`edges` contains the list of `AuthorBooksEdge`. Look at the `AuthorBooksEdge` type in the GraphiQL interface.

GraphiQL `AuthorBooksEdge` Type

The `AuthorBooksEdge` has two fields:

- `node` and
- `cursor`

The `cursor` is a string we can use for pagination, from this record. Here we can see that the `node` is of type `Book`. Within that `node` is the hard data that we're looking for.

While we are using these connections for many-to-many relationships, you'd navigate one-to-many relationships the same way. By using this standard for traversing relationships between models it's easy to know how to get access to related models, regardless of the type of relationship. Everything is nodes and edges in a graph.

Additionally, by making pagination part of the standard, we're making accommodations for real-world data sets where we're not going to load every piece of data in a relationship (or table) at the same time.

Having standardized pagination as a part of Relay make it that much easier to standardize pagination in our React apps.

Which part is Relay and which part is GraphQL?

Relay vs. GraphQL with connections and edges

To be clear, here we're talking about Relay specification that we implement on our GraphQL server.

The pattern of connections and edges, with the fields defined above, is part of the Relay specification. Anytime we need a relationship between two objects (that goes beyond a simple array) we'll use the edge/connection paradigm.

Relay specifies the convention (e.g. that we specify `first` or `last` when retrieving a connection, and a connection returns `edges`) and our GraphQL server implements how we actually fetch those records (from the database).

Changing Data with Mutations

Mutations are how we change data in Relay/GraphQL. To change data with mutations we need to:

1. Locate the mutation we want to call
2. Specify the input arguments and
3. Specify what data we want to be returned after the mutation is finished.

Say, for instance, that we want to change an author's bio. We could perform the following:

Query:

```
mutation {
  updateAuthor(input: {
    id: "QXV0aG9yOmZjMjkyYmQ3ZGYwNzE4NThjMmQwZjk1NQ==",
    bio: "all around great guy"
  }) {
    changedAuthor {
      id
      name
      bio
    }
  }
}
```

Now we can see in the response that the `bio` has been changed to `"all around great guy"`.

Response:

```
{
  "data": {
    "updateAuthor": {
      "changedAuthor": {
        "id": "QXV0aG9yOmZjMjkyYmQ3ZGYwNzE4NThjMmQwZjk1NQ==",
        "name": "Ari Lerner",
        "bio": "all around great guy"
      }
    }
  }
}
```

In this case, the *mutation* is `updateAuthor`. As you may recall from the GraphQL chapter, we change data in GraphQL by creating a *mutation query*. Our server defines a mutation query for common data operations.

For instance, if you're familiar with the REST paradigm of Create-Read-Update-Delete (CRUD), we might define similar mutations for our models here: `createAuthor`, `updateAuthor`, `deleteAuthor`.

While mutations are used generally in GraphQL, Relay, unsurprisingly, specifies some constraints around how it expects *mutations* to be defined.

Mutations on the client-side can be a bit daunting. We'll talk more about them later in the chapter.

Relay GraphQL Queries Summary

Above, we've just covered the three types of queries we'll use when writing Relay apps:

1. Fetching individual records from our server
2. Traversing relationships between records, using connections and edges
3. Mutating data with mutation queries.

Now that we've explored our data and reviewed the conventions on our server, let's take a look at how Relay works inside our app.

Adding Relay to Our App

Quick Look at the Goal

Now let's switching gears into writing our React app.

There are quite a few steps to installing Relay into our app. Before we walk through them, let's take a look at the goal: a basic Relay container component that loads data from our server and renders it.

Once we have one component that can load data from Relay, building our app gets much easier from there.

Below we'll walk through how to build out a fully working Relay app, but it can also be helpful to take a look at a **single-file, "hello world" example**. Below is the code for a minimal, but working Relay app. Many of the specifics will be unfamilar, and the rest of the chapter is dedicated to explaining in detail how to use each idea. For now, just skim this code to get an idea of the different parts involved in working with Relay.

relay/bookstore/client/src/steps/index.minimal.js

```
/* eslint-disable react/prefer-stateless-function */
import React from 'react';
import ReactDOM from 'react-dom';
import Relay from 'react-relay';

import '../semantic/dist/semantic.css';
import './styles/index.css';

// Customize this based on your server's URL
const graphQLUrl = 'http://localhost:3001/graphql';

// Configure Relay with a "NetworkLayer"
Relay.injectNetworkLayer(
  new Relay.DefaultNetworkLayer(graphQLUrl)
);

// Create the top-level query that we'll execute
class AppQueries extends Relay.Route {
  static routeName = 'AppQueries';
  static queries = {
    viewer: () => Relay.QL`
      query {
        viewer
      }
    `,
  };
}

// A basic component that renders the list of authors
class App extends React.Component {
  render() {
    return (
      <div>
```

```
        <h1>Authors list</h1>
        <ul>
          {this.props.viewer.authors.edges.map(edge =>
            <li key={edge.node.id}>{edge.node.name}</li>
          )}
        </ul>
      </div>
    );
  }
}

// A Relay Container that specifies the fragment to be used in our query above
const AppContainer = Relay.createContainer(App, {
  fragments: {
    viewer: () => Relay.QL`
      fragment on Viewer {
        authors(first: 100) {
          edges {
            node {
              id
              name
            }
          }
        }
      }
    `,
  },
});

ReactDOM.render(
  <Relay.Renderer
    environment={Relay.Store}
    Container={AppContainer}
    queryConfig={new AppQueries()}
  />,
  document.getElementById('root')
);
```

In the example above, our `AppContainer` fetches a collection of authors and renders them in a list. Notice that this code is *declarative*. That is, there's no part of the code where we're saying "make a post request to the server and interpret it as JSON" etc. Instead, our component declares the data it needs, and Relay fetches it from the server and provides it to our component.

A Preview of the Author Page

Let's look at another example, taken from our Bookstore app. Here's a version of the `AuthorPage` component:

relay/bookstore/client/src/steps/AuthorPage.minimal.js

```
class AuthorPage extends React.Component {
  render() {
    const { author } = this.props;

    return (
      <div>
        <img src={author.avatarUrl} />
        <h1>{author.name}</h1>
        <p>
          {/* e.g. '2 Books' or '1 Book' */}
          {author.books.count}
          {author.books.count > 1 ? ' Books' : ' Book'}
        </p>
        <p>{author.bio}</p>
      </div>
    );
  }
}

export default Relay.createContainer(AuthorPage, {
  fragments: {
    author: () => Relay.QL`
    fragment on Author {
      name
      avatarUrl
      bio
      books {
        count
      }
    }`,
  },
});
```

There are two parts: 1. the `Relay.createContainer` statement (with a `Relay.QL` query) and 2. the `render()` function.

At a high level, what's happening here is that our `Relay.QL` query specifies the data we want to load for this author. Then the `author` is passed in to the component via `props` and we `render` the data.

We haven't yet talked about all of the setup that goes in to getting our app to this point. We will. For now, just notice that once we have everything setup, it becomes extremely easy to load data into our components (and **it's easy to modify our queries if we change our mind**).

Notice that when we use `Relay` on our component, we have two things: 1. the `createContainer` and 2. a `fragment`.

Minimal Author

Containers, Queries, and Fragments

Components that need to load data from Relay are called *containers*. Containers specify *fragments* that are essentially "partial queries". Fragments **specify the data this component needs to render properly**.

We create a Relay container using `Relay.createContainer`. We pass in our component and the required fragments as arguments.

Your containers specify the `fragments` that they need to render properly but you have to **execute the queries to render the fragments**. You can think of this sort of like components needing to be rendered into the DOM. **Fragments aren't rendered until they're pulled in by a query**.

Each container specifies a fragment (or several) and at some point later we execute a query which will use this fragment to fetch data.

That is, before this data will become available to the component, you have to **execute a query that contains this fragment**. We'll talk about executing queries in a few minutes.

But first, let's talk about the `Relay.QL` query.

Validating Our Relay Queries at Compile Time

One of the great things about GraphQL is that we have a type-schema for our API. We can use this to our advantage when writing client side code.

When we write query fragments in our components, it looks like this:

code/relay/bookstore/client/src/steps/AuthorPage.minimal.js

```
  fragments: {
    author: () => Relay.QL`
    fragment on Author {
      name
      avatarUrl
      bio
      books {
        count
      }
    }`,
  },
```

But notice that we're putting the query in a long JavaScript string. It's easy to write, but in a naive implementation of handling these queries, typos could be the source of many bugs because there's no way to validate that the contents are well formed. In the case where something was mis-typed, we wouldn't even know there was a typo until one of these queries was run.

However, the good news is that there is a custom Babel plugin which will verify these queries against our schema **at compile time**.

For this we'll use the `babel-relay-plugin`[156]. This plugin:

1. reads these `Relay.QL` backtick strings
2. parses the GraphQL query
3. validates them against our schema
4. and converts our `Relay.QL` queries to a expanded function calls[157]

But in order to verify our schema, **we need to have the schema available to our client-side build tools.**

Remember that our schema is **defined by our server**. It's our GraphQL *server* that defines the data models (Books and Authors, in this case) and the corresponding GraphQL schema.

So how do we make our server's schema available to our client build-tools? **We export the schema from the server as a JSON file and copy it over.**

[156]https://www.npmjs.com/package/babel-relay-plugin

[157]This is similar to how JSX works

Building the `schema.json`

To provide the schema to our client build tools we'll write a script **in the server** that will export the schema to a JSON file.

We'll then configure `babel-relay-plugin` to use this JSON file when we compile our client code. It's a little bit of work up-front, but the benefit is that we'll get compile-time validation of or Relay queries in our client app. This can save our team tons of time trying to track down bugs because of invalid queries.

Here's the script we're using to generate our `schema.json`:

relay/bookstore/tools/update-schema.js

```
import fs from 'fs';
import path from 'path';
import { graphql } from 'graphql';
import { introspectionQuery, printSchema } from 'graphql/utilities';
import schema from '../schema';

// Save JSON of full schema introspection for the Babel Relay Plugin to use
const generateJSONSchema = async () => {
  var result = await (graphql(schema, introspectionQuery));
  if (result.errors) {
    console.error(
      'ERROR introspecting schema: ',
      JSON.stringify(result.errors, null, 2)
    );
  } else {
    fs.writeFileSync(
      path.join(__dirname, '../client/src/data/schema.json'),
      JSON.stringify(result, null, 2)
    );
  }

  // Save user readable type system shorthand of schema
  fs.writeFileSync(
    path.join(__dirname, '../client/src/data/schema.graphql'),
    printSchema(schema)
  );
};

generateJSONSchema().then(() => {
  console.log("Saved to client/src/data/schema.{json,graphql}");
})
```

Take a look at the dependencies we're loading here. Besides `fs` and `path`, we have:

1. `graphql`, `introspectionQuery`, `printSchema` from `graphql` and
2. `schema` from `../schema`.

One thing to notice is that we're not loading anything from the `relay` library. This is all GraphQL. The `relay` library isn't involved. Our GraphQL schema *conforms* to the Relay standard, but we don't depend on any Relay-specific functionality. This process of exporting your schema can be done with **any** GraphQL server.

We aren't going to look deeply into the implementation of our `schema`. In this case, we're using the helper library `graffiti-mongoose`, but that's really an implementation detail. This `schema` can be any `GraphQLSchema` object.

So to use this script for your app, simply change the paths to the `schema` as well as the output paths.

What's happening here is that we're telling the `graphql` library to take our `schema` and then `introspectionQuery` and print out our schema into two files:

The `introspectionQuery` is a query which asks GraphQL information about what queries it supports. You can read more about GraphQL Introspection here[158]

1. a machine-readable `schema.json` file (for our client) and
2. a human-readable `schema.graphql` file

Here's a sample from the `schema.graphql` file:

relay/bookstore/client/src/data/schema.graphql

```
type Author implements Node {
  name: String
  avatarUrl: String
  bio: String
  createdAt: Date
  books(after: String, first: Int, before: String, last: Int): AuthorBooksConnec\
tion
  _id: ID
```

[158] http://graphql.org/learn/introspection/

```
  # The ID of an object
  id: ID!
}

# A connection to a list of items.
type AuthorBooksConnection {
  # Information to aid in pagination.
  pageInfo: PageInfo!

  # A list of edges.
  edges: [AuthorBooksEdge]
  count: Float
}
```

If we're in the root directory for this project (`relay`) then we can generate this schema by running:

```
npm run generateSchema
```

If we ever change our schema (like adding a field to a model or adding a new model) then we need to run this script to regenerate our schema. If we don't regenerate the schema and try to use the new data in our client app then `babel-relay-plugin` will throw compiler errors because it will using the old schema. So make sure if you change your models, you regenerate your schema.

Watch out for schema caching

Some webpack configurations (such as the default that is generated when you eject from `create-react-app`) cache compiled scripts. If you're using such a feature (as we are in this app) then your **schema is also cached**.

This means that when you update your schema, you have to clear your `react-scripts` cache. On my machine, this folder is kept in `node_modules/.cache/react-scripts`. So whenever we regenerate the schema we run the following command as well to clear the cache:

```
rm -rf client/node_modules/.cache/react-scripts/
```

Failure to clear this cache when regenerating your schema may result in your client loading the old, cached schema which can be confusing.

Installing `babel-relay-plugin`

To use `babel-relay-plugin` we have to:

1. `npm install babel-relay-plugin`
2. Tell `babel-relay-plugin` about our `schema.json`
3. Configure `babel` to use our plugin

To do #2, see the file `client/config/babelRelayPlugin.js` like so:

relay/bookstore/client/config/babelRelayPlugin.js

```
var getBabelRelayPlugin = require('babel-relay-plugin');
var schema = require('../src/data/schema.json');

module.exports = getBabelRelayPlugin(schema.data, {
  debug: true,
  suppressWarnings: false,
  enforceSchema: true
});
```

What we're doing here is just configuring the `babel-relay-plugin` by adding in our own schema and setting a few options. Now we need to add this script as a plugin to our `babel` config.

To do this, we've added the following to the *client's* `package.json`:

```
"babel": {
  "presets": [
    "react-app"
  ],
  "plugins": [
    "./config/babelRelayPlugin"
  ]
},
```

Above, we've added `"./config/babelRelayPlugin"` to the `plugins` section of our `babel` configuration in the `package.json`.

When you're setting up your own app to use Relay, it's fine if you have a different set of `presets` and `plugins` in your app, just add this custom `babelRelayPlugin` to the list.

Also, if you configure babel via a `.babelrc` or some other way, the core idea here is to add our custom `babelRelayPlugin` script to the list of `plugins`.

Setting Up Routing

Now that we have our build tools in place, we can start integrating Relay with React. Because we're building a multi-page app, we're going to need a router. For this app we're going to use `react-router` with `react-router-relay`.

If you'd like to see an example of a Relay app that uses Relay directly (without using `react-router` then checkout the `relay-starter-kit`[159].

`react-router-relay` uses `react-router` v2.8 (**not router v4**, which we covered in the chapter "Routing."

Unfortunately, as you can see here[160], there are no plans to directly support Relay in React-Router v4.

That said, it is possible to integrate Relay with any routing framework including React Router v4. Doing so is beyond the scope of this chapter.

In this chapter, we'll provide all of the route configuration needed to run the app, but we're not going to be discussing the React Router API . If you need to look it up, you can find the docs for Router here[161].

`react-router-relay` provides a convenient way to execute Relay queries whenever the route changes. `react-router-relay` also will read parameters from the URL and pass them as parameters to our Relay queries. We'll take a close look at this feature in a it.

To install `react-router-relay` into our app, we'll do the following:

1. Configure Relay
2. Configure our `Router`
3. Use the `react-router-relay` middleware to connect Relay to our `Router`.

Let's look at the code we use to do this:

[159] https://github.com/relayjs/relay-starter-kit
[160] https://github.com/relay-tools/react-router-relay/issues/193
[161] https://github.com/ReactTraining/react-router

relay/bookstore/client/src/index.js

```
import React from 'react';
import ReactDOM from 'react-dom';
import createHashHistory from 'history/lib/createHashHistory';
import Relay from 'react-relay';
import applyRouterMiddleware from 'react-router/lib/applyRouterMiddleware';
import Router from 'react-router/lib/Router';
import useRouterHistory from 'react-router/lib/useRouterHistory';
import useRelay from 'react-router-relay';

import routes from './routes';

import './semantic-dist/semantic.min.css';
import './styles/index.css';

// Customize this based on your server's URL
const graphQLUrl = 'http://localhost:3001/graphql';

// Configure Relay with a "NetworkLayer"
Relay.injectNetworkLayer(
  new Relay.DefaultNetworkLayer(graphQLUrl)
);

const history = useRouterHistory(createHashHistory)({ queryKey: false });

ReactDOM.render(
  <Router
    history={history}
    routes={routes}
    render={applyRouterMiddleware(useRelay)}
    environment={Relay.Store}
  />,
  document.getElementById('root')
);
```

The first section `imports` our dependencies.

Next we configure the URL to our server in the variable `graphQLUrl`. If your server is at a different URL, configure it here. For instance, we'll often use an environment-specific variable here.

Next we configure Relay with a "Network Layer". In this case, we're using `DefaultNetworkLayer` which will make HTTP requests, but you could use this to, say, mock out a Relay server for testing or use a different protocol entirely.

We're going to use hash-based routing for this app, so we configure `history` to use `createHashHistory`.

We tie our `Router` root component to Relay by:

1. Using `applyRouterMiddleware(useRelay)` – which comes from `react-router-relay` and
2. Setting our `Relay.Store` onto the `Router environment`.

Setting up our Router this way makes Relay *available* to our app, but to actually perform Relay queries we have one more step: we need to configure Relay queries on our routes.

Adding Relay to Our Routes

Let's take a look at our `routes.js`:

relay/bookstore/client/src/steps/routes.author.js

```
import Relay from 'react-relay';
import React from 'react';
import IndexRoute from 'react-router/lib/IndexRoute';
import Route from 'react-router/lib/Route';

import App from './components/App';
import AuthorPage from './components/AuthorPage';

const AuthorQueries = {
  author: () => Relay.QL`
  query {
    author(id: $authorId)
  }`,
};

export default (
  <Route
    path='/'
    component={App}
  >
    <Route
      path='/authors/:authorId'
      component={AuthorPage}
      queries={AuthorQueries}
    />
  </Route>
);
```

For these initial routes we have a **parent** route that uses the App component and a **child** route that uses the AuthorPage component. Eventually we will have a child component for each page in our app, but for now let's look at the following in order:

1. Our parent App Component
2. The AuthorQueries and how the relate to the AuthorPage then
3. Dig in to the AuthorPage component.

App Component

Our top-level App component establishes the wrapper for the rest of the app:

relay/bookstore/client/src/components/App.js

```
import React, { Component } from 'react';
import { withRouter } from 'react-router';

import TopBar from './TopBar';
import '../styles/App.css';

class App extends React.Component {
  render() {
    return (
      <div className='ui grid'>
        <TopBar />
        <div className='ui grid container'>
          { React.cloneElement(this.props.children) }
        </div>
      </div>
    );
  }
}

export default withRouter(App);
```

Here we render the TopBar and the markup that will wrap any child components (this.props.children).

Before we export App, we wrap it using withRouter from react-router. withRouter is a helper function[162] that provides props.router on our component.

We *could* make the App component a Relay container if we needed to, but in this case we don't need any Relay data in the App component.

[162] https://github.com/ReactTraining/react-router/blob/master/docs/API.md#withroutercomponent-options

AuthorQueries Component

Now that we understand the App component, hop back into routes.js and look at the AuthorQueries:

relay/bookstore/client/src/steps/routes.author.js

```
const AuthorQueries = {
  author: () => Relay.QL`
  query {
    author(id: $authorId)
  }`,
};
```

Remember that in Relay in order to fetch the data that we need for our components we have to execute *queries*. When using react-router-relay we specify that when a particular route is visited, **the queries defined on that route will be executed.**

Notice that the AuthorQueries has one query: author. This query also has a variable $authorId. Where does the $authorId variable come from? It comes from the route path parameter:

relay/bookstore/client/src/steps/routes.author.js

```
    <Route
      path='/authors/:authorId'
      component={AuthorPage}
      queries={AuthorQueries}
    />
```

Here in this route we're saying that we'll match the route /authors/ and whatever follows will be interpreted as the authorId. This authorId is passed as a variable to the Relay query.

Notice something else odd about the author query: it doesn't specify any "leaf nodes" of data to fetch. The query stops at author(id: $authorId). This is because the query is leaving the decision of what particular data to fetch to the component.

It is in our **component** (well, our Relay Container, to be precise), that we will specify the fields that are needed to render that component.

With that in mind, let's turn our attention to the AuthorPage component and look at the Relay query there.

AuthorPage Component

Here's the code that specifies what fields we need to render the minimal AuthorPage:

relay/bookstore/client/src/steps/AuthorPage.minimal.js

```
export default Relay.createContainer(AuthorPage, {
  fragments: {
    author: () => Relay.QL`
    fragment on Author {
      name
      avatarUrl
      bio
      books {
        count
      }
    }`,
  },
});
```

On the "inside" of the query it's easy to see that we're asking for the `name`, `avatarUrl`, and `bio` of the author. We're even able to dip into the `books` relationship and get the `count` of the number of books this person has authored.

However, it may not be clear how this ties into the query above. There are two constraints we need to follow.

The first is that the key names of these `fragments` must match the keys names of the queries. In this case, because this component is being rendered with a query key name of `author` (in `AuthorQueries`) the fragment key name must also be `author` (in `AuthorPage fragments`).

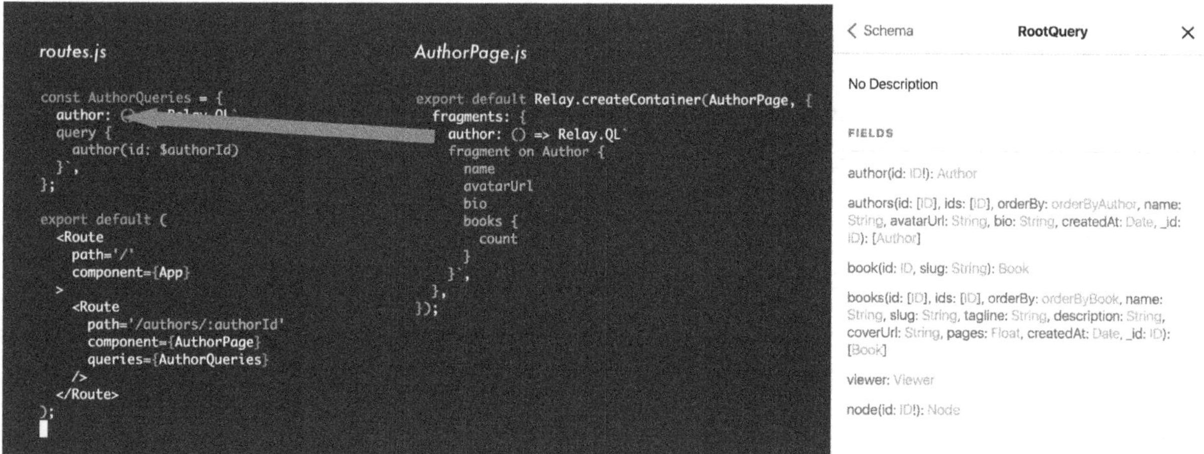

Relay Fragment Naming

The second constraint is that **this fragment will be a `fragment on` the type of the inner field of `query`**. That is, we wouldn't put `fragment on Book` here, because the containing query "ends" on an `Author`. We can see this by looking at the GraphQL schema in GraphiQL.

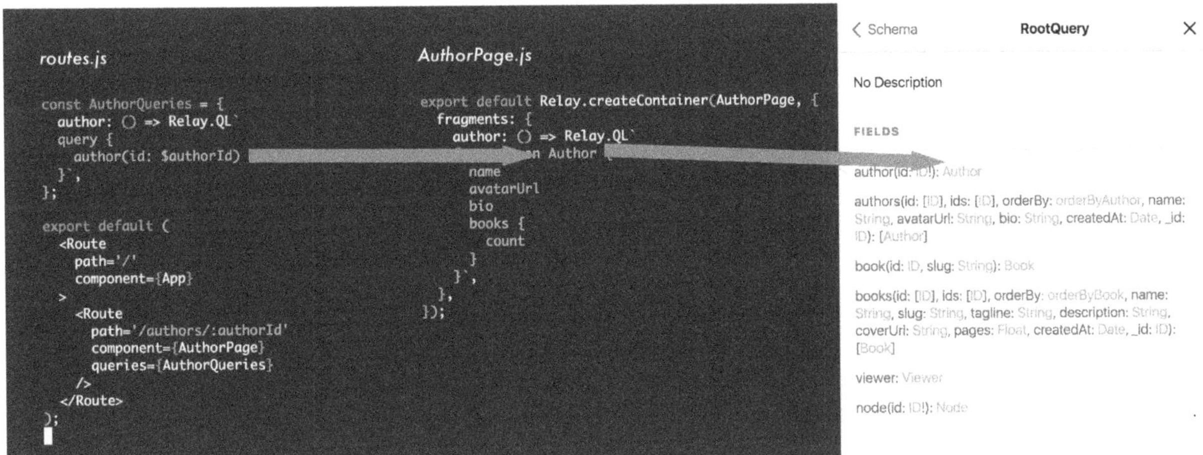

Relay Fragment on Type

When a route matching `/authors/:authorId` is visited, the `AuthorPage` `author` fragment will be pulled into the `AuthorQueries` and results will be fetched from the server and passed down into our component.

Try It Out

We've only setup the `AuthorPage` so far, but it's enough for us to try out.

To do this, ensure you have both the GraphQL server started, as well as the client, as described above.

Then visit the GraphiQL server at `http://localhost:3001/graphql` and try the following query:

```
query {
  authors {
    id
    name
  }
}
```

Copy an author ID and then visit the client app with that ID. Something like:

```
http://localhost:3000/#/authors/QXV0aG9yOmIzOTY2NDVmZmZiZWIxMzc5NTEwYWIxZg==
```

In our browser, if we look at our network pane we can see the GraphQL query that was called:

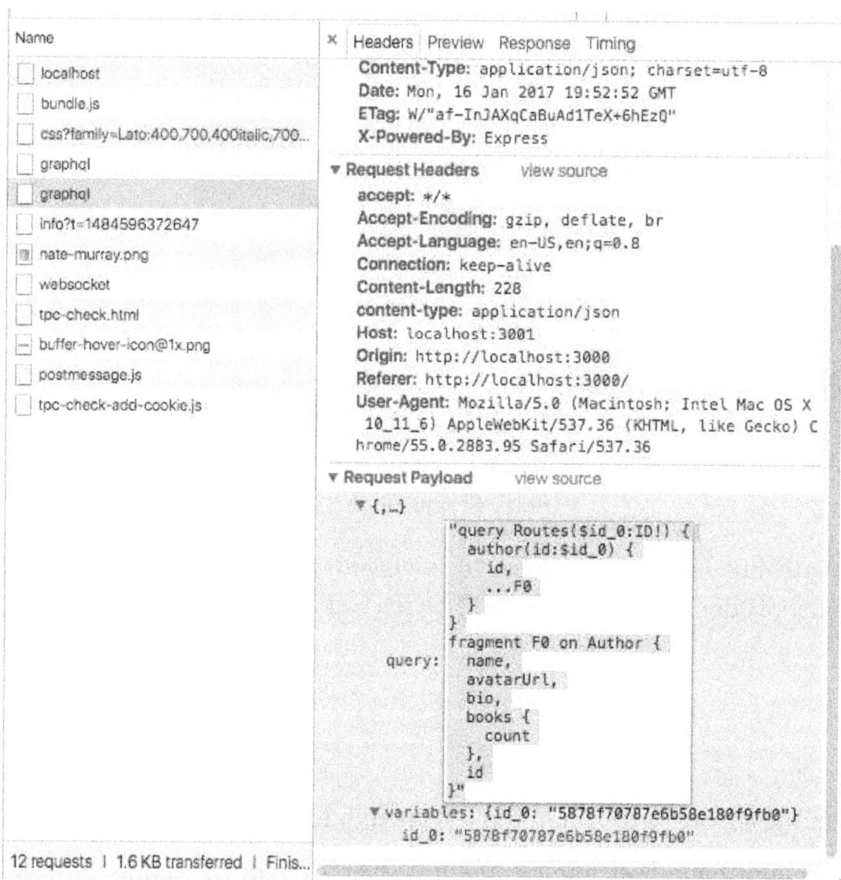

Relay GraphQL Call in Network Pane

In this case, the query sent over the wire looks something like:

```
query Routes($id_0:ID!) {
  author(id:$id_0) {
    id,
    ...F0
  }
}
fragment F0 on Author {
  name,
  avatarUrl,
  bio,
  books {
    count
  },
  id
}
```

The first part of the query (`query Routes...`) comes from `AuthorQueries` and the fragment `F0` comes from our `author` fragment on `AuthorPage`. Again, note that it wouldn't make any sense for this fragment `F0` to be on any type *other than* `Author` because the child of `query > author` is of type `Author`. Trying to put a `Book`- or any other-typed fragment here would be invalid.

`AuthorPage` with Styles

The minimal `AuthorPage` we've rendered so far doesn't look so great. Let's quickly add a bit of markup so that the page looks better.

> Like many of the examples in this book, we're using Semantic UI[163] for the CSS framework. When you see CSS `class` names like `sixteen wide column` or `ui grid centered` these are coming from Semantic UI.

Keeping the same Relay query, we're going to change the `AuthorPage` markup to the following:

relay/bookstore/client/src/steps/AuthorPage.styled.js

```
class AuthorPage extends React.Component {
  render() {
    const { author } = this.props;

    return (
      <div className='authorPage bookPage sixteen wide column'>
        <div className='spacer row' />

        <div className='ui divided items'>
          <div className='item'>
            <div className='ui'>
              <img src={author.avatarUrl}
                alt={author.name}
                className='ui medium rounded bordered image'
              />
            </div>
            <div className='content'>
              <div className='header authorName'>
                <h1>{ author.name }</h1>
                <div className='extra'>
                  <div className='ui label'>
                    { author.books.count }
                    { author.books.count > 1 ? ' Books' : ' Book' }
```

163 http://semantic-ui.com/

```
                  </div>
                </div>
              </div>
              <div className='description'>
                <p> { author.bio } </p>
              </div>

            </div>
          </div>
        </div>

      </div>
    );
  }
}
```

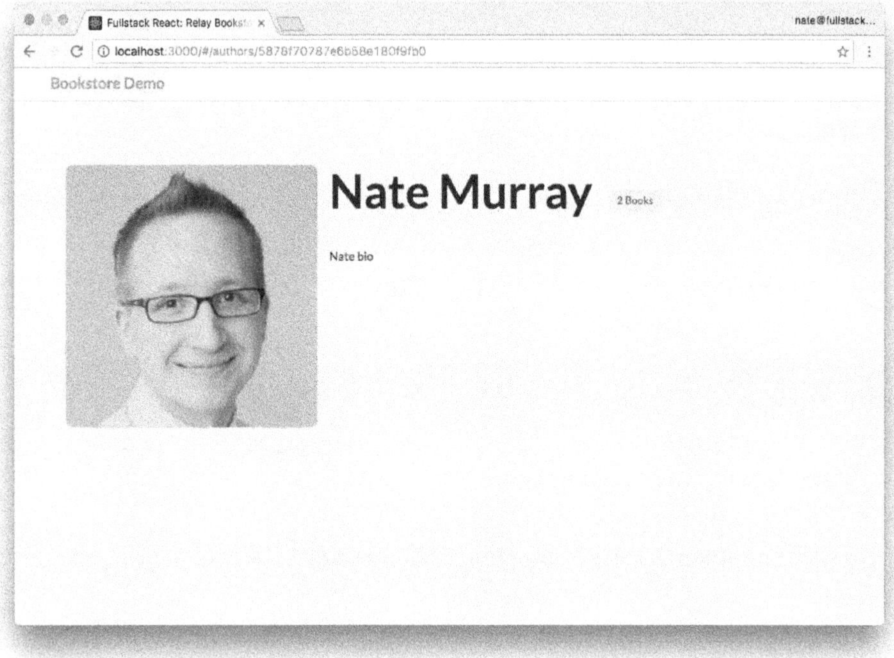

Author Page with Styling

We'll add the list of this author's books to this page later, but for now let's build the "index" page of the site, which will show the list of all of the books available.

BooksPage

Here's what the list of books page will look like when we're finished:

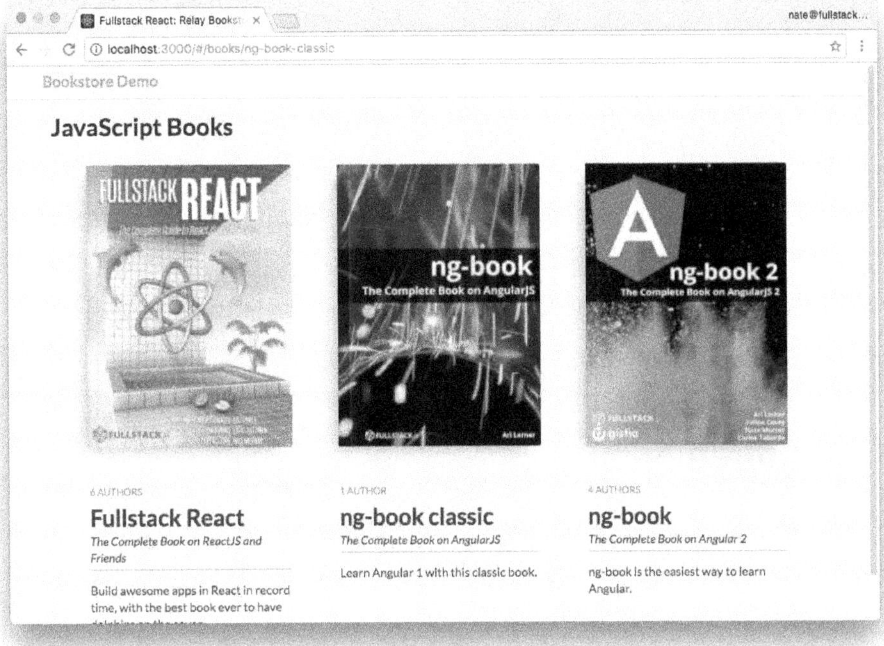

Books Page

The first thing we need to do is create the route for the `BooksPage` and the queries for that route.

`BooksPage` Route

The `BooksPage` is going to be the default page for our app so we will use the `IndexRoute` helper to define this route:

relay/bookstore/client/src/routes.js

```
    <IndexRoute
      component={BooksPage}
      queries={ViewerQueries}
    />
```

Let's take a look at the `ViewerQueries`:

relay/bookstore/client/src/routes.js

```
const ViewerQueries = {
  viewer: () => Relay.QL`query { viewer }`,
};
```

On this page, we're going to be looking up the list of books via the `viewer` node.

The `viewer` node is not strictly part of Relay but it's a pattern that you see in many GraphQL apps. The idea is that **the "viewer" is the current user of the app**. So, often in a real application you'd see that the `viewer` field accepts a user-identity field as an argument, such as an authentication token.

Imagine creating an app with a social feed. We could use the `viewer` field to get the feed for a particular user as opposed to the "firehose" feed for *all* users.

In this case, we're going to use the `Viewer` to load a list of `Books`.

`BooksPage` Component

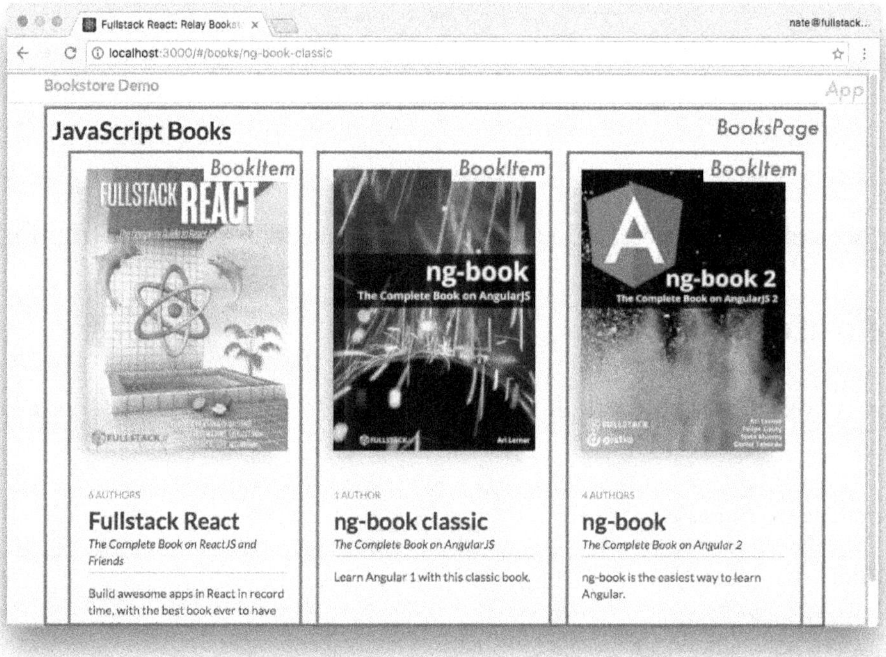

Books Page Components

Here we have **two** Relay containers:

1. the `BooksPage` which holds all the books

2. a `BookItem` which renders a particular book

Because our `BooksPage` route specified queries on `viewer` we're going to specify a fragment on the key `viewer` (on the `Viewer`-type). Let's take a look at the query:

relay/bookstore/client/src/components/BooksPage.js

```
export default Relay.createContainer(BooksPage, {
  initialVariables: {
    count: 100,
  },
  fragments: {
    viewer: () => Relay.QL`
    fragment on Viewer {
      books(first: $count) {
        count
        edges {
          node {
            slug
            ${BookItem.getFragment('book')}
          }
        }
      }
    }
    `,
  },
});
```

There's a couple of new things here:

1. `initialVariables`
2. Composing a fragment, using `getFragment()`

Fragment Variables

We can set variables for our queries by using the `initialVariables` field. Here you can see that we're telling Relay we want to set `$count` to `100`. In the query you can see that we're asking for the first 100 books.

By using this `viewer` we can't say "I want **all** the books". The reason for this is that this server is designed for large apps and you generally don't want to load every single item in your database. Typically we would use pagination.

In this case though, we're just going to set the `count` to `100` because that's more than enough for this simple app. But say that we wanted to change the variable `count`. How would we do it?

You use `this.props.relay.setVariables` like this:

```
this.props.relay.setVariables({count: 2});
```

If we called the above function you would see that we load only 2 books instead of the whole set.

More generally, we can use Relay variables when we want our component to be able to change parameters about the query that's being executed.

If you forget to set the proper variables (e.g. no `first` field) when trying to get a list of items through a connection, you might get an error like the following: {lang=text,line-numbers=off} Uncaught Error: Relay transform error `You supplied the `edges` field on a connection named `authors`, but you did not supply an argument necessary to do so. Use either the `find`, `first`, or `last` argument.` in file `code/relay/bookstore/client/src/components/BookPage.js`. Try updating your GraphQL schema if an argument/field/type was recently added.

Fragment Composition

This is important: if you use a child Relay component you need to embed the child's fragment in the parent's query by using `getFragment()`.

Remember that fragments are parts of queries and they aren't realized until they're part of an executed query. If you want a child component like `BookItem` to be able to render each book, **you have to include the `BookItem` fragment in the `BooksPage` query**.

This takes a little getting used to, and we haven't even looked at the `render` function of `BooksPage` yet, so let's do that and come back to this idea of fragment composition when we have a bit more context.

BooksPage render()

Here's the rendering for `BooksPage`:

relay/bookstore/client/src/components/BooksPage.js

```
class BooksPage extends React.Component {
  render() {
    const books = this.props.viewer.books.edges.map(this.renderBook);

    return (
      <div className='sixteen wide column'>
        <h1>JavaScript Books</h1>
        <div className='ui grid centered'>
          { books }
```

```
        </div>
      </div>
    );
  }

  renderBook(bookEdge) {
    return (
      <Link
        to={`/books/${bookEdge.node.slug}`}
        key={bookEdge.node.slug}
        className='five wide column book'
      >
        <BookItem
          book={bookEdge.node}
        />
      </Link>
    );
  }
}
```

Our `render` function has a basic wrapper. We're taking `this.props.viewer.books.edges` and calling `renderBook` on each **edge**.

Notice that we're not calling `renderBook` on the book itself (`node`), but on the `edge`.

Within `renderBook`, we render a:

1. `Link` to `/books/${bookEdge.node.slug}` with a
2. `BookItem` component, populating it with a book, found in `bookEdge.node`

Let's dig deeper into `BookItem` and then we'll pop back up to `BooksPage` to take a closer look at how Relay manages parent/child fragment values.

`BookItem`

Here's our Relay Query for `BookItem`:

relay/bookstore/client/src/components/BookItem.js

```
export default Relay.createContainer(BookItem, {
  fragments: {
    book: () => Relay.QL`
    fragment on Book {
      name
      slug
      tagline
      coverUrl
      pages
      description
      authors {
        count
      }
    }
    `,
  },
});
```

We're defining a fragment with the key of `book` on type `Book`. This query is asking for basic book information like the `name`, the `slug`, the number of `pages`, and we also dip into `authors` to get the `count`.

Here's the component definition:

relay/bookstore/client/src/components/BookItem.js

```
class BookItem extends React.Component {
  render() {
    return (
      <div className='bookItem'>
        <FancyBook book={this.props.book} />

        <div className='bookMeta'>
          <div className='authors'>
            { this.props.book.authors.count }
            { this.props.book.authors.count > 1 ? ' Authors' : ' Author' }
          </div>
          <h2>{ this.props.book.name }</h2>
          <div className='tagline'>{ this.props.book.tagline }</div>
          <div className='description'>{ this.props.book.description }</div>
        </div>
```

```
        </div>
      );
    }
}
```

Inside the `div` `bookMeta` we show the basic information such as the number of `authors`, the book `name`, `tagline` and `description`.

We also pass `this.props.book` to a pure component `FancyBook`, which simply provides the markup for the fancy 3D CSS effect on the book.

`BookItem Fragment`

What's interesting about the `BookItem` fragment `book` is that **it isn't tied to a particular query**. Remember that the query we're using in `BooksPage` starts on a `Viewer`.

What we're doing here is saying, to use this component, it's concern is with something on a `Book` type. As long as we compose this `Book` fragment into the parent's fragment at a location where a `Book` fragment is valid then we'll be able to use this `BootItem` component.

The rule of thumb here is that if you are composing Relay components, make sure you compose their fragments.

If you get a warning that reads like the following:

`warning.js:36 Warning: RelayContainer: component` BookItem `was rendered with variables that differ from the variables used to fetch fragment` book.

This means that you forgot to include the child fragment in parent's query.

Fragment Value Masking

There's another important feature of Relay that we haven't talked about yet: data masking.

The idea is **components can only see data they asked for explicitly**. If the component didn't ask for a specific field, Relay will actively hide that field from the component **even if that data was loaded**.

For instance, look at the queries on `BookItem` and `BooksPage` side-by-side . Notice that:

- `BookItem` loads the `slug` field for the book and
- `BooksPage` uses the `slug` field for the `Link` URL

For review, here's `BookItem`'s `Relay.QL` query:

relay/bookstore/client/src/components/BookItem.js

```
export default Relay.createContainer(BookItem, {
  fragments: {
    book: () => Relay.QL`
    fragment on Book {
      name
      slug
      tagline
      coverUrl
      pages
      description
      authors {
        count
      }
    }
    `,
  },
});
```

And `BooksPage`'s `Relay.QL` query:

relay/bookstore/client/src/components/BooksPage.js

```
export default Relay.createContainer(BooksPage, {
  initialVariables: {
    count: 100,
  },
  fragments: {
    viewer: () => Relay.QL`
    fragment on Viewer {
      books(first: $count) {
        count
        edges {
          node {
            slug
            ${BookItem.getFragment('book')}
          }
        }
      }
    }
    `,
  },
});
```

You might think that because we're calling `${BookItem.getFragment('book')}` in the `BooksPage` query that means that `slug` would be available to the `BooksPage` component, but **this is not the case**.

Fragment composition **does not** make that child-fragment's data available to our parent query. We must **explicitly** list the `slug` field in the `BooksPage` query if we want to be able to use that field in our `render` function of `BooksPage`.

Data masking is one of those features that can feel like an inconvenience at first, but it turns out to be super helpful as your app (and team) grows because it prevents bugs that result from changes outside of your component.

For instance, say that `BooksPage` was depending on the `slug` field from `BookItem` to be loaded. But, somewhere down the line, someone is cleaning up `BookItem` and they remove the `slug` field. What would happen? `BooksPage` would now break.

The idea is that **it is bad to have this coupling between components**. Each component should define everything it needs to render properly. Data masking is a way to ensure that every component explicitly defines the set of data it needs to operate.

Masking Works Both Ways

This masking also goes the other way: since we **do** define that `BooksPage` (the parent) needs the `slug` field, even though we pass the book (via `<BookItem book={bookEdge.node}/>`) **the child cannot access `slug`** if it does not ask for it explicitly.

Any Relay manged props will have masking applied to them according to the queries. So be mindful of data masking when writing your applications – if you find that you unexpectedly have missing data (that you know you loaded somewhere else), check your queries to make sure you've explicitly request those specific fields in the component where they're needed.

Improving the `AuthorPage`

Now that we can render a list of books, a nice touch to the author's page would be to show a list of the books that person has authored.

Given what we've just covered, we know that we can add this list of books by doing the following:

1. Request the author's `books` in our Relay query
2. Include the `BookItem` fragment in this query
3. Take the list of the author's books and render a `BookItem` for each one

Let's do this now.

Requesting an Author's Books

Right now the `AuthorPage` only includes the `count` of the number of books an author appears on. Let's change the `AuthorPage` query to include more data on author's books in order to show a complete book thumbnail and link to them:

relay/bookstore/client/src/components/AuthorPage.js

```
export default Relay.createContainer(AuthorPage, {
  fragments: {
    author: () => Relay.QL`
    fragment on Author {
      _id
      name
      avatarUrl
      bio
      books(first: 100) {
        count
        edges {
          node {
            slug
            ${BookItem.getFragment('book')}
          }
        }
      }
    }`,
  },
});
```

This change shows one of the things that's great about Relay and GraphQL. Consider what this type of change might look like if we were working with a traditional REST-based API. We'd have to write code that looks up the author's `id` and makes a request to the server asking for that author's books. We'd have to add code to gracefully handle errors. Here, with Relay, all we have to do is add a `books()` section to the query and populate it with the fields we want.

Notice that we just hard-code that we want the first 100 books. In a real app, we'd probably set a variable like we did on the `BooksPage`.

The other thing we have to remember to do is include the `BookItem` fragment `book`. Again, note that the "parent" query here is `author`. You might recall that this is on an `Author` type up in the router. But, you don't really need to remember that. All you need to know is that `BookItem`'s `book` fragment is on type `Book` and so you can place it in your query wherever a `Book` type is allowed.

How do I know what fragments my child components need?

If you're building your first Relay app it might not be immediately clear how you even know what fragments to request. Essentially, it should be part of the documentation of the component. In the same way that in order to use a "regular" component, you're probably going to know what `props` it needs, in the same way, the author of the component you're using needs to document what fragments you'll use to render that component.

AuthorPage renderBook

Now that we have the books we can render them like so:

relay/bookstore/client/src/components/AuthorPage.js

```
class AuthorPage extends React.Component {
  renderBook(bookEdge) {
    return (
      <Link
        to={`/books/${bookEdge.node.slug}`}
        key={bookEdge.node.slug}
        className='five wide column book'
      >
        <BookItem
          book={bookEdge.node}
        />
      </Link>
    );
  }
```

and in the `render()` function:

```
render() {
  const author = this.props.author;
  const books = this.props.author.books.edges.map(this.renderBook);

  return (
    {/* ... truncated  */}

      <div className='sixteen wide column'>
        <h1>{ author.name }&rsquo;s Books</h1>
        <div className='ui grid centered'>
          { books }
```

```
      </div>
    </div>

  {/* ... truncated */}
  );
}
```

Here's a screenshot of what our author page looks like now that we have the books added in:

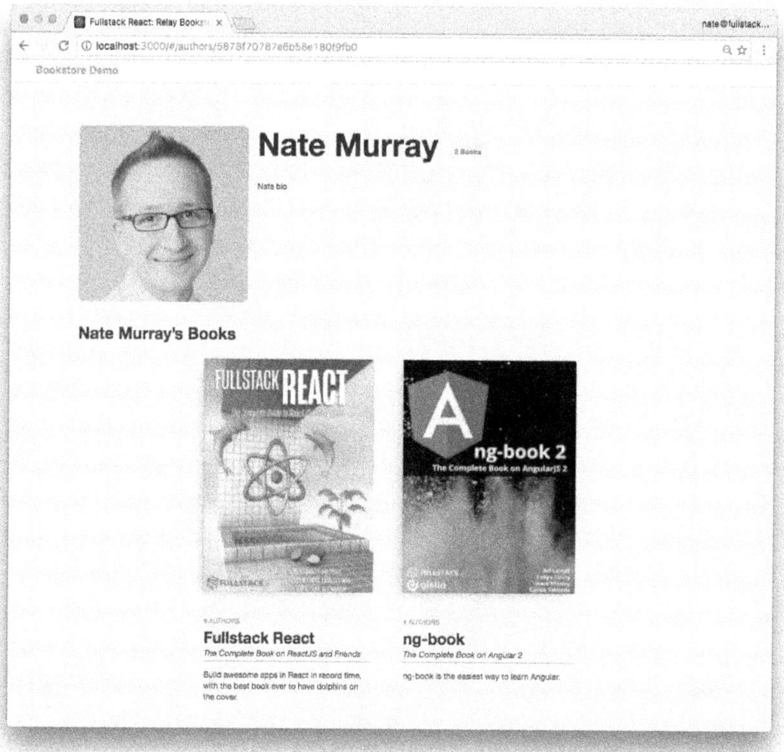

Author with Books Page

Changing Data With Mutations

Now we've seen how to:

1. **read a single record** of data from Relay
2. **read a list** of data from Relay
3. load data from **child components**

There's one critical issue we haven't covered: **changing data**. In Relay, changing data is done through *mutations.*

We're going to add the ability to edit the metadata of a book.

First, let's create a new page for an individual book. We'll read the initial data from Relay, as have been doing. Then we'll talk about how to change the data with mutations.

Building a Book's Page

The read-only version of the individual book page doesn't have a lot of new ideas in it, so let's talk through it briefly.

First, here's a screenshot:

Individual Book Page, Read Only

You can see that we show the basic book image, each author, and the book cover.

Here's the Relay container:

relay/bookstore/client/src/steps/BookPage.reads.js

```
export default Relay.createContainer(BookPage, {
  fragments: {
    book: () => Relay.QL`
    fragment on Book {
      id
      name
      tagline
      coverUrl
      description
      pages
      authors(first: 100) {
        edges {
          node {
            _id
            name
            avatarUrl
            bio
          }
        }
      }
    }`,
  },
});
```

In this fragment we're loading the `Book` metadata as well as the first 100 authors.

Let's look at the `render()` function:

relay/bookstore/client/src/steps/BookPage.reads.js

```
  render() {
    const { book } = this.props;
    const authors = book.authors.edges.map(this.renderAuthor);
    return (
      <div className='bookPage sixteen wide column'>
        <div className='spacer row' />

        <div className='ui grid row'>
          <div className='six wide column'>
            <FancyBook book={book} />
          </div>
```

```
          <div className='ten wide column'>
            <div className='content ui form'>

              <h2>{book.name}</h2>

              <div className='tagline hr'>
                {book.tagline}
              </div>

              <div className='description'>
                <p>
                  {book.description}
                </p>
              </div>

            </div>

            <div className='ten wide column authorsSection'>
              <h2 className='hr'>Authors</h2>
              <div className='ui three column grid link cards'>
                {authors}
              </div>
            </div>

          </div>
        </div>

      </div>
    );
  }
```

Most of the markup here is `divs` with Semantic UI classes. Basically we're just show the book information with a reasonable layout.

For each author edge we call `renderAuthor`:

relay/bookstore/client/src/steps/BookPage.reads.js

```
  renderAuthor(authorEdge) {
    return (
      <Link
        key={authorEdge.node._id}
        to={`/authors/${authorEdge.node._id}`}
        className='column'
      >
        <div className='ui fluid card'>
          <div className='image'>
            <img src={authorEdge.node.avatarUrl}
              alt={authorEdge.node.name}
            />
          </div>
          <div className='content'>
            <div className='header'>{authorEdge.node.name}</div>
          </div>
        </div>
      </Link>
    );
  }
```

Book Page Editing

Now let's add in some basic editing for this book's data. What we'd like to be able to do is click on any field like the title or description and edit it in-place. To make this simple, let's use the existing inline-edit component React Edit Inline Kit[164].

React Edit Inline Kit (or RIEK for short) has a simple API. We specify:

1. The original value
2. The property name of this value
3. A callback to run when this value changes

You can view the docs for RIEK here[165] and you can view the demos here[166]

[164]https://github.com/kaivi/riek
[165]https://github.com/kaivi/riek
[166]http://kaivi.github.io/riek/

So that we can isolate what we're doing, let's integrate RIEK into our app **without changing the data in Relay**. The first step is just to get the inline form editing working and then we'll deal with what to do with the changes once we have them.

Here's our new `render()` function on `BookPage` with `RIEK`:

relay/bookstore/client/src/steps/BookPage.iek.js

```
  render() {
    const { book } = this.props;
    const authors = book.authors.edges.map(this.renderAuthor);
    return (
      <div className='bookPage sixteen wide column'>
        <div className='spacer row' />

        <div className='ui grid row'>
          <div className='six wide column'>
            <FancyBook book={book} />
          </div>

          <div className='ten wide column'>
            <div className='content ui form'>

              <h2>
                <RIEInput
                  value={book.name}
                  propName={'name'}
                  change={this.handleBookChange}
                />
              </h2>

              <div className='tagline hr'>
                <RIEInput
                  value={book.tagline}
                  propName={'tagline'}
                  change={this.handleBookChange}
                />
              </div>

              <div className='description'>
                <p>
                  <RIETextArea
                    value={book.description}
                    propName={'description'}
```

```
                  change={this.handleBookChange}
                />
              </p>
            </div>

          </div>

          <div className='ten wide column authorsSection'>
            <h2 className='hr'>Authors</h2>
            <div className='ui three column grid link cards'>
              {authors}
            </div>
          </div>

        </div>
      </div>

    </div>
  );
}
```

We've added three new components using `RIEInput` and `RIETextArea`. All three will call `handleBookChange` when the data changes. Here's the current implementation:

relay/bookstore/client/src/steps/BookPage.iek.js

```
handleBookChange(newState) {
  console.log('bookChanged', newState, this.props.book);
}
```

All we're going to do at this point is **log out the changes to `console`**.

Here's a screenshot of what happens when I change the tagline to `"The Complete Book on ReactJS and Dolpins"`:

```
bookChanged ▶ Object {description: "The Complete Book on ReactJS and Dolphins"}  BookPage.js:121
▼ Object
    __dataID__: "Qm9vazoyNjZhMWY3YzJlMjM0NTE2OWQzYmM0NDg="
  ▶ __fragments__: Object
  ▶ authors: Object
    coverUrl: "/images/books/fullstack_react_book_cover.png"
    description: "The Complete Book on ReactJS and Friends"
    id: "Qm9vazoyNjZhMWY3YzJlMjM0NTE2OWQzYmM0NDg="
    name: "Fullstack React"
    pages: 760
    tagline: "The Complete Book on ReactJS and Friends"
  ▶ __proto__: Object
```

`console.log` the tagline

You can see here that `newState` has the **new** values we need to update the `book`. Our task at hand is to **tell Relay about this change via a *mutation***.

Just to be clear, `RIEK` is a completely arbitrary choice for a forms library, selected here for convenience. It has nothing to do with Relay. The steps that we're about to take to create mutations in Relay could be done with any form library. If you'd like to build your own forms, that's perfectly fine. Checkout the chapter "Forms."

Mutations

A *mutation* in Relay is an object that describes a change. Mutations are one of the most difficult aspects to get used to in Relay. That said, the complexity of mutations comes trade-offs that are inherent to building client-server applications. Let's take a look at the steps necessary to create mutations in Relay:

To mutate data in Relay:

1. We define a **mutation object**
2. We create an instance of that object, passing configuration variables and then
3. We send it to Relay using `Relay.Store.commitUpdate`

There are 5 major types of mutations in Relay:

- `FIELDS_CHANGE`
- `NODE_DELETE`
- `RANGE_ADD`
- `RANGE_DELETE`
- `REQUIRED_CHILDREN`

We are going to update the fields for an existing object, and so we will write a `FIELDS_CHANGE` mutation.

We're not going to cover every type of mutation in depth in this chapter.

If you want to view the official documentation that describes each of these mutations, checkout the Official Mutations Guide[167].

It's also worth noting that mutations can be a bit difficult to understand the first time. Making mutations easier to use is one of the major goals of Relay 2.

Defining a Mutation Object

Mutations in Relay are objects. To define a new mutation we subclass `Relay.Mutation`. Then when we want to *execute* a mutation, we create an instance of this class, configure it with the appropriate properties, and give it to Relay (which handles communicating with the server and updating the Relay store).

When we create a `Relay.Mutation` subclass, we have to define 6 things that describe the behavior of the mutation:

1. What GraphQL method are we using for this mutation?
2. What variables will be used as the **input** to this mutation?
3. What fields does this mutation depend on in order to run properly?
4. What fields could change as a result of this mutation?
5. If everything goes smoothly, what's the expected outcome of this mutation?
6. How should Relay handle the actual response that comes back from the server?

We specify each of these things by **defining a function for each one**.

This might be more care than we usually take when we're using a fire-and-forget API, but remember, by specifically describing each of these steps in our mutation we get the benefits of Relay managing the bookkeeping for our data.

This is much easier if we walk through a concrete example, so lets make an "update" with `FIELDS_-CHANGE`.

Open up `client/src/mutations/UpdateBookMutation.js`. Starting at the top let's look at `.getMu-tation`:

[167] https://facebook.github.io/relay/docs/guides-mutations.html#content

relay/bookstore/client/src/mutations/UpdateBookMutation.js

```
export default class UpdateBookMutation extends Relay.Mutation {
  getMutation() {
    return Relay.QL`mutation { updateBook }`;
  }
```

The first thing we need to specify when we create a `Relay.Mutation` subclass is the node of the GraphQL mutation. Here we've specified that we're using the `updateBook` mutation.

You can find this mutation in the schema by using GraphiQL and picking the `mutation` field at the root.

We can see here that `updateBook` takes a single argument `input`, which is of type `updateBookInput`, and it returns an item of type `updateBookPayload`.

For `updateBook`, the values that we use for `updateBookInput` will be used as the **new values for the book** we specify.

That is, we'll send an `id`, which will be used to look up the specific `Book` we're changing, and we'll send new values such as the `name`, `tagline`, or `description`.

When it comes time to send this mutation, the values passed in to `updateBookInput` will come from the function `getVariables`:

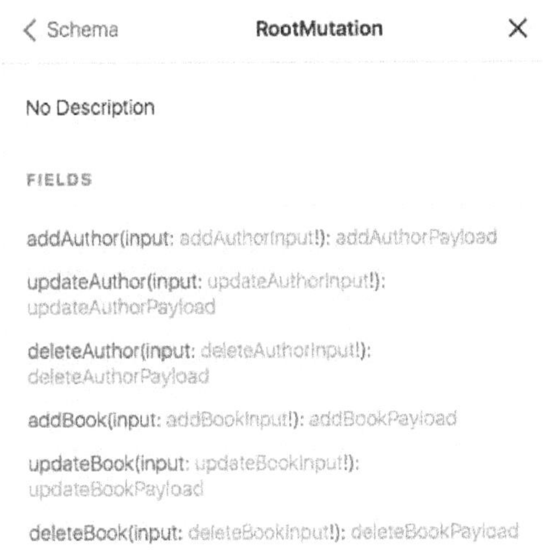

< Schema RootMutation ×

No Description

FIELDS

addAuthor(input: addAuthorInput!): addAuthorPayload

updateAuthor(input: updateAuthorInput!): updateAuthorPayload

deleteAuthor(input: deleteAuthorInput!): deleteAuthorPayload

addBook(input: addBookInput!): addBookPayload

updateBook(input: updateBookInput!): updateBookPayload

deleteBook(input: deleteBookInput!): deleteBookPayload

updateBook Mutation

relay/bookstore/client/src/mutations/UpdateBookMutation.js

```
  getVariables() {
    return {
      id: this.props.id,
      name: this.props.name,
      tagline: this.props.tagline,
      description: this.props.description,
    };
  }
```

This function describes how to create the arguments for `updateBookInput` – in this case we're going to look at `this.props` for values for the `id`, `name`, `tagline`, and `description`.

One of the things we have to be careful of is to ensure that this mutation has all of the fields it needs to operate properly. For instance, this mutation especially needs a `Book id` because that's how we're going to reference the object we're changing.

To do this, we specify `fragments`, much like we do for Relay container components:

relay/bookstore/client/src/mutations/UpdateBookMutation.js

```
  static fragments = {
    book: () => Relay.QL`
      fragment on Book {
        id
        name
        tagline
        description
      }
    `,
  }
```

Notice that in `getVariables` we're also sending along the `name`, `tagline`, and `description` – without checking if they have any value.

Relay will mask `prop` values from mutations just like components. So there's a subtle bug that could be introduced here. If we forget to specify the proper fragment, the mutation can accidentally set values to `null`.

What's the solution? In the same way that parent components need to include their child components' fragments, any component that uses a mutation also needs to include that mutation's fragments. We'll show how to do this when we use the `UpdateBookMutation` in our app below.

After we send this mutation it will be evaluated on the server. In this case, what changes on the server is pretty simple: we're updating the field values for **one object**.

That said, for many mutations the effects are probably more nuanced – we can't always know the full set of side effects that will occur from a mutation operation.

Furthermore, we don't actually have confirmation that this operation succeeded at all.

To deal with this, we're going to ask the server to send back to us all the fields that we think might have changed. To do this, we'll specify what's called a "fat query". It's "fat" because we're trying to capture everything that might have changed:

relay/bookstore/client/src/mutations/UpdateBookMutation.js

```
  getFatQuery() {
    return Relay.QL`
      fragment on updateBookPayload {
        changedBook
      }
    `;
  }
```

The fat query is a GraphQL query. In this case, we're just asking for the `changedBook`. So once the mutation is run on the server we're asking the server to send us back the new, updated values for the book that we (hopefully) changed.

Relay will take that `changedBook` (which is an object of type `Book`), look at its ID, and update the Relay Store accordingly.

However, before the server returns our *actual* response, we have the option to make a performance optimization and specify an "optimistic" response. The optimistic response answers the question: assuming this mutation executed successfully, what would be the response?

Here's our implementation of `getOptimisticResponse`:

relay/bookstore/client/src/mutations/UpdateBookMutation.js

```
  getOptimisticResponse() {
    const { book, id, name, tagline, description } = this.props;

    const newBook = Object.assign({}, book, { id, name, tagline, description });

    const optimisticResponse = {
      changedBook: newBook,
    };
    console.log('optimisticResponse', optimisticResponse);
    return optimisticResponse;
  }
```

In this function we're merging together the old `book` with the argument values. Our optimistic response returns a `newBook` that looks like the response we're about to get from `getFatQuery`.

This mutation is straightforward: we have the original book and we have the updated fields. In this case, we know what the result of the mutation is going to be **without even asking the server**.

So what we can do is fake to the user that their operation was successful. This can give our user the feeling of a super-responsive app, because they're able to see the effects of their changes **immediately** without waiting for a network call.

If the mutation succeeds, the user is none the wiser.

If the mutation fails, then we've given the user false confirmation. But we'll still have the opportunity to handle that case and inform the user, perhaps telling them that they need to try again.

If the consistency trade-offs are acceptable to your application, optimistic responses can greatly improve the feel of the response time of your app.

When the real response is returned from the server, Relay needs to be told how to handle that data.

Because there are several different ways to mutate data, Relay mutations must implement a `getConfigs` method which describes the *way* Relay is going to handle the actual data that changed.

relay/bookstore/client/src/mutations/UpdateBookMutation.js

```
  getConfigs() {
    return [ {
      type: 'FIELDS_CHANGE',
      fieldIDs: {
        changedBook: this.props.book.id,
      },
    } ];
  }
```

In this case, because we're using a `FIELDS_CHANGE` mutation, we're specifying that we'll look at `changedBook` to find an ID that matches the `Book` we're talking about.

Inline Editing

Now that we have our mutation defined, we're now prepared to implement click-to-edit on our `BookPage`.

Remember that our mutation is going to be making a query to check with the server for the current value of the `Books` data after the mutation finishes. Because of this, we need to **compose our mutation's fragment into our `BookPage` query**.

Just like a child Relay component needs its fragments composed, any mutations a component uses also needs to have its fragments composed.

Here is our `BookPage` query now that we're adding in the mutation's fragments:

relay/bookstore/client/src/components/BookPage.js

```
  fragments: {
    book: () => Relay.QL`
    fragment on Book {
      id
      name
      tagline
      coverUrl
      description
      pages
      authors(first: 100) {
        edges {
          node {
            _id
            name
            avatarUrl
            bio
          }
        }
      }
      ${UpdateBookMutation.getFragment('book')}
    }`,
  },
```

In the future, if you forget to add your mutation fragment to your query, you might get this:

```
Warning: RelayMutation: Expected prop `book` supplied to `UpdateBookMutation` to\
 be data fetched by Relay. This is likely an error unless you are purposely pass\
ing in mock data that conforms to the shape of this mutation's fragment.
```

The solution: add your mutation fragment to the calling component's query.

Now we have everything in place to actually execute our mutation! Let's update `handleBookChange` to send out the mutation:

relay/bookstore/client/src/components/BookPage.js

```
  handleBookChange(newState) {
    console.log('bookChanged', newState, this.props.book);
    const book = Object.assign({}, this.props.book, newState);
    Relay.Store.commitUpdate(
      new UpdateBookMutation({
        id: book.id,
        name: book.name,
        tagline: book.tagline,
        description: book.description,
        book: this.props.book,
      })
    );
  }
```

Here we create a *new* object that is the merger of `this.props.book` and `newState` by using `Object.assign`. Next we execute our mutation by calling `Relay.Store.commitUpdate` and passing a new `UpdateBookMutation` to it.

Behind the scenes, Relay will:

- immediately update our view (and the Relay store) using the optimistic response
- call out to the GraphQL server and try to execute our mutation
- receive the reply from the GraphQL server and update the Relay store

Hopefully, at this point our optimistic response matches the actual response. But if not, the actual value will be represented on our page.

Conclusion

Once we have the foundation in place, using Relay is a fantastic developer experience compared to hand-managing a traditional REST API.

Relay and GraphQL give a strong, typed structure to our data while giving us unmatched flexibility in changing our component data requirements.

Relay 2 is on the horizon and it promises to have even better performance, and a better developer experience (particularly around mutations). That said, Relay 1 is powerful enough to write apps with today.

Where to Go From Here

If you want to learn more about Relay, here's a few resources:

- Learn Relay[168] – This is an introductory tutorial to Relay.
- `relay-starter-kit`[169] is a bare-bones implementation of Relay with a React app
- `relay-todomvc`[170] is an implementation of the popular TodoMVC app using Relay. If you're looking for more examples of mutations, this is a good place to start.
- `react-router-relay`[171] is the integration library we used in this chapter to use React Router with Relay
- A guide to authentication in GraphQL[172] - at some point you'll probably want to add authenticated pages to your server. Checkout this post for a good starting point
- Relay 2: simpler, faster, more predictable[173] – if you want to see where Relay is going, checkout these slides by Greg Hurrell

[168] https://www.learnrelay.org/
[169] https://github.com/relayjs/relay-starter-kit
[170] https://github.com/taion/relay-todomvc
[171] https://github.com/relay-tools/react-router-relay
[172] https://dev-blog.apollodata.com/a-guide-to-authentication-in-graphql-e002a4039d1#.z0vnf3846
[173] https://speakerdeck.com/wincent/relay-2-simpler-faster-more-predictable

React Native

In this chapter, we're going to walk through how to build your first React Native app. We won't get to cover React Native in-depth in this chapter. React Native is a *huge* topic that warrants its own book.

We're going to explain React Native for the React Developer. By the end of this chapter you'll be able to take your React web app and have the foundation to turn it into a React Native app.

As we've seen so far, React is both fun and powerful. In this chapter, the goal is to get an idea of how everything we love about React can be used to build a native iOS or Android application using React Native.

Without getting too deep into the technicalities of how React Native works under the hood, the high-level summary looks like this:

When we build React components, we're actually building representations of our React components, not actual DOM elements using the *Virtual DOM*. In the browser, React takes this virtual DOM and pre-computes what the elements should look like in a web browser and then hands it over to the browser to handle the layout.

The idea behind React Native is that we can take the tree of object representations from our React components and rather than mapping it to the web browser's DOM, we map it to iOS's UIView[174] or Android's android.view[175]. Theoretically, we can use the same idea behind React in the web browser to build native iOS and Android applications. This is the fundamental idea behind React-Native.

In this section, we're going to work through building React components for the native renderers and highlight the differences between React for Native vs. React for the web.

Before we dive into the details, let's start off high level. It's crucial to understand that we're no longer building for the web environment, which means we have different UX, UI, and no URL locations. Despite the fact that the thought processes we've built around building UIs for the web help, they aren't enough to translate to building a great user experience in the mobile native environment.

Let's take a second and look at some of the most popular native applications and play around with them. Rather than use the application from a user perspective, try imagining building the application, taking note of the details. For instance, look for the micro-animations, how the views are setup, the page transitions, the caching, how data is passed around from screen to screen, what happens when we're waiting for information to load.

In general, we can get away with less deliberately designed UI on the web. On mobile however, where our screen-size and data details are more constrained and focused, we are forced to focus on

[174]https://developer.apple.com/reference/uikit/uiview

[175]https://developer.android.com/reference/android/view/View.html

the experience of our application. Building a great UX for a native app requires deliberate execution and attention to detail.

In this chapter one of our goals is to highlight both the syntactic differences as well as the aesthetic differences that exist between both platforms.

Init

As we're focused on getting directly to the code as we work through this section, we'll want to have an application bootstrapped for us so we can experiment and test out building native applications. We'll need to *bootstrap* our application so we have a basic application we can work with as we are learning the different components of React-Native.

In order to bootstrap a React-Native application, we can use the `react-native-cli` tool. We'll need to install the React-Native cli tool by using the Node Package Manager (`npm`). Let's install the `react-native-cli` tool globally so we can access it anywhere on our system:

```
npm i -g react-native-cli@2.0.1
```

Installation documentation

For formal instructions on getting set up with React Native for your specific development environment, check out the official Getting started[176] docs.

With the `react-native-cli` tool installed, we will have the `react-native` command available in our terminal. If this returns a "not recognized" error, check the getting started docs from above for your development platform.

```
$ react-native
```

To create a new React-Native project, we'll run the `react-native init` command with the name of the application we want to generate. For example, let's generate a React-Native application called `Playground`:

```
$ react-native init Playground
```

[176] http://facebook.github.io/react-native/releases/0.31/docs/getting-started.html

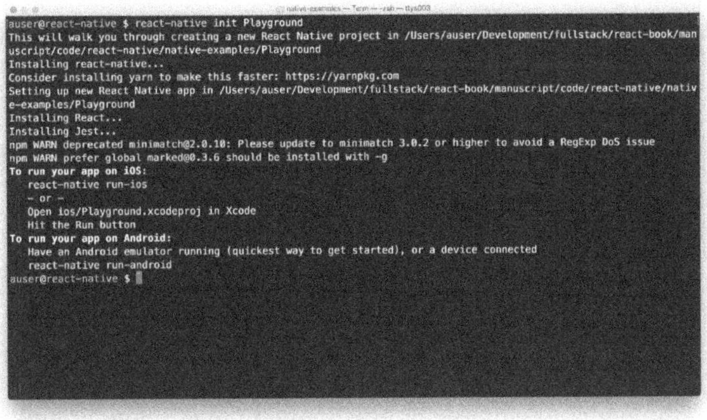

```
auser@react-native $ react-native init Playground
This will walk you through creating a new React Native project in /Users/auser/Development/fullstack/react-book/man
uscript/code/react-native/native-examples/Playground
Installing react-native...
Consider installing yarn to make this faster: https://yarnpkg.com
Setting up new React Native app in /Users/auser/Development/fullstack/react-book/manuscript/code/react-native/nativ
e-examples/Playground
Installing React...
Installing Jest...
npm WARN deprecated minimatch@2.0.10: Please update to minimatch 3.0.2 or higher to avoid a RegExp DoS issue
npm WARN prefer global marked@0.3.6 should be installed with -g
To run your app on iOS:
   react-native run-ios
   - or -
   Open ios/Playground.xcodeproj in Xcode
   Hit the Run button
To run your app on Android:
   Have an Android emulator running (quickest way to get started), or a device connected
   react-native run-android
auser@react-native $
```

> Your output of the command might look a bit different from above, but as long as you see the instructions on how to launch it. If you see an error, check the Troubleshooting[177] documentation for more instructions on launching the application.

Now we can use our `Playground` app we just created to test and run the code we'll create throughout this section.

Routing

Let's start off our application with routing as it's foundational to nearly every application.

When we implement routing in the web, we're typically mapping a URL to a particular UI. For example, let's take a game that might be written for the web with multiple screens written using the React Router V2 API:

When we implement routing on the web, we're typically mapping some URL to a specific UI. Here's how that looks with React Router V2 with the URLs mapped to the active components:

src/routes.js

```
export const Routes = (
  <Router history={hashHistory}>
    <Route path='/' component={Main}>
      <IndexRoute component={Home} />
      <Route
        path='players/:playerOne?'
        component={PromptContainer}
      />
```

[177] http://facebook.github.io/react-native/releases/0.31/docs/troubleshooting.html#content

```
      <Route
        path='battle'
        component={ConfirmBattleContainer}
      />
      <Route
        path='results'
        component={ResultsContainer}
      />
    </Route>
  </Router>
);
```

URL	Active Component
foo.com	Main -> Home
foo.com/players	Main -> PromptContainer
foo.com/players/ari	Main -> PromptContainer
foo.com/battle	Main -> ConfirmBattleContainer
foo.com/results	Main -> ResultsContainer

React Router lays out this mapping between URL and UI beautifully (i.e. declaratively).

As our user navigates to different URLs in our applications, different components become *active.* The URL is so foundational to React Router that it's mentioned twice in the opening description:

> React Router keeps your UI in sync with the **URL.** **...**Make the** **URL** your first thought, not an after-thought.

This is a clean, well-understood paradigm and one that has made React Router as popular as it is. However, what if we're developing for a native app? There is no URL we can refer. There's not really even a similar conceptual mapping of a URL in a native application.

Paradigm shift #1—when building a React Native app, we need to think of our routes in terms of *layers* rather than URL to UI mappings.

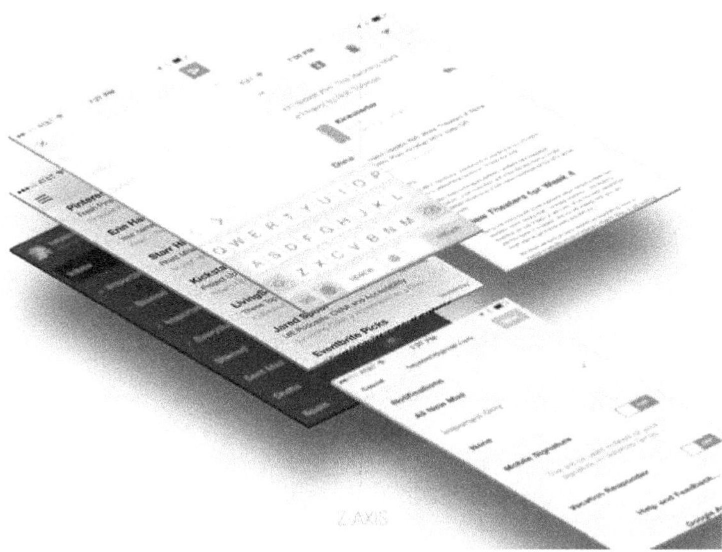

The routing layers in a native application structure themselves in a stack format, which roughly speaking is basically an array. When we transition between routes in React Native, we're simply pushing (navigating *into* a view) or popping (navigating *out of* a view) a route onto or from our *route stack*.

What is a route stack?

A *route stack* refers to an array of views a user visits throughout the application. When the user first opens the application, the route stack is going to have a length of 1 (the initial screen). Let's say that the user navigates to a *my account* screen next. The route stack will have two entries, the initial screen and the account screen.

When the user navigates back to the home screen in our fictitious application, the route stack will *pop* (or remove the latest) view leaving the route stack to contain one entry again: the initial screen.

Coming from the web browser, this is a different paradigm than mapping a discrete URL. Instead of mapping to a unique URL, we will be managing an array mapping to a route stack.

In addition, we're not just mapping view components to a view, we'll also be working through how to make transitions between routes. Unlike the web, where we *typically* have independent route transitions, native apps generally need to know about each other as we navigate from one screen to the next.

For example, we'll usually have animations once our view renders, but not have a transition between routes themselves. However, in a native application, we'll still have these animations once our view renders as well as needing to devise a method that one route transitions into the next in the navigation stack.

Most route transitions on native devices are naturally hierarchical and should *generally* appropriately reflect our user's journey through each phase of the app.

In React Native, we can configure these route transitions through *scene configurations*. We'll take a look at how we can customize our *scene transitions* a little bit later, but for now we'll note that different platforms require different route transitions.

On the iOS platform, we're usually handling one of three different transitions between routes:

- Right to left
- Left to right
- Bottom to top

Typically when we push a route on iOS from the right when we're drilling deeper into the same hierarchy, we'll present a view from the bottom when it's a modal screen that is in a different hierarchy. We'll usually `push` a new view in the same hierarchy with the left to right transition and `pop` from the right to left transition after leaving a previous route.

The Android paradigm is slightly different, however. We'll still have the idea of drilling into more content, but rather than a hard left to right transition, we'll have a concept of creating an *elevation* change.

Play around with it

Regardless of the device we're building for, it's a good idea to open popular apps for the platform we're working with and taking note of what the route transitions look like between screens.

Enough theory. Let's get back to implementation. React Native routing has several options. At the time of writing, Facebook has indicated it's working on a new router component for React Native. For now, we'll stick with the tried and tested `Navigator` component to handle routing in our application.

`<Navigator />`

Just like the web version of the router, where we have React components that render to handle routing, the `<Navigator />` component is *just a React component*. This means we'll use it just like any other component in the view.

```
<Navigator />
```

Knowing the `<Navigator />` component is just a react component, we'll want to know:

1. What `props` does it accept?
2. Is it necessary to wrap it in a Higher Order Component?
3. How do we navigate with a single component?

Let's start off with #1, what `props` does it accept?

The `<Navigator />` only requires two `props`, both of them are functions:

- `configureScene()`
- `renderScene()`

Every time we change routes in our application, both the `configureScene()` and `renderScene()` functions will be called.

The `renderScene()` function is responsible for determining which UI (or component) to render next, while the `configureScene()` function is responsible for detailing out which transition type to make (as we looked at earlier).

In order to do their job, we'll need to receive some information about the specific route change that is *about to occur*. Naturally, since these are functions, they will be called with this information as an *argument* to the function.

Rather than talk about it, let's look at what this looks like in code. Starting with the boilerplate, we know now we'll be rendering a component:

src/app/index.js

```
export default class App extends Component {
  configureScene(route) {
    // Handle configuring scene
  }

  renderScene(route, navigator) {
    // handle rendering scene
  }

  render() {
    return (
      <Navigator
        renderScene={this.renderScene}
        configureScene={this.configureScene}
      />
    );
  }
}
```

Beautiful. We'll notice that this answers our second question from above. Typically when we're using the `<Navigator />` component, we'll wrap it in a *Higher Order Function* in order to handle our `renderScene()` and `configureScene()` methods.

`renderScene()`

Now let's take a look at how the `renderScene()` method needs to be implemented. We currently know two things about the `renderScene()` function:

1. It's purpose is to figure out which UI (or component) to render when transitioning into a new scene.
2. It receives an object which represent the route change that is going to occur.

With these two things in mind, let's look at an example of how a `renderScene()` might be implemented:

src/app/index.js

```
renderScene(route) {
  if (route.home === true) {
    return <HomeContainer />
  } else if (route.notifications === true) {
    return <NotificationsContainer />
  } else {
    return <FooterTabsContainer />
  }
}
```

Since the entire purpose of the `renderScene()` function is to determine which UI (or component) to render next, it makes sense that the `renderScene()` function is just one big *if* statement which renders different components based on a property of the `route` object.

The next natural question is "where is the `route` object coming from and how did it get the `home` and `notifications` properties on it?

This is where the react native configuration things get a little bit weird. Remember from above, we mentioned *every time we change routes in our applications, both `configureScene()` and `renderScene()` will be called*? Well, we still haven't answered just *how* we *change routes in our applications.* To answer that question, we'll need to look at the second argument the `renderScene()` function receives: the `navigator`:

```
renderScene(route, navigator) {
  // render scene
}
```

The `navigator` object is an instance object we can use to manipulate our current routing from within our application. The object itself contains some pretty handy methods, including the `push()` and `pop()` methods. The `push()` and `pop()` methods are how we're actually handling manipulating our route changes from within our app by pushing to or popping from the route stack.

Notice that we're receiving the `navigator` object inside our `renderScene()` method here, but the `renderScene()` method is for picking the next scene, not *invoking* route changes. In order to actually *use* the `navigator` object in our rendered scene, we'll need to pass it along to our new route as a `prop`:

src/app/index.js

```
renderScene(route, navigator) {
  if (route.home === true) {
    return <HomeContainer navigator={navigator} />
  } else if (route.notifications === true) {
    return <NotificationsContainer navigator={navigator} />
  } else {
    return <FooterTabsContainer navigator={navigator} />
  }
}
```

With this update, the `<HomeContainer />`, `<NotificationsContainer />`, and the `<FooterTabsContainer />` all have access to the `navigator` instance and can each call out to `push()` or `pop()` from the route stack using `this.props.navigator`.

For instance, let's say that we're working on our home route and we want to navigate to the notifications route. We can *push* to the navigation's route in a method like so:

src/app/containers/home.js

```
handleToNotifications() {
  this.props.navigator.push({
    notifications: true,
  });
}
```

Once we invoke the `handleToNotifications()` method inside the `<HomeContainer />` component, our `renderScene()` method will be called with the `route` argument, which is passed down through the `object` *pushed* onto by the `this.props.navigator.push()` method. When the `renderScene()`

sees the `route` object contains the `notifications` property as true, it returns the `<NotificationsContainer />` as the next component to render.

Don't worry quite yet if this didn't *click* right away. We'll be working with the `<Navigator />` component often. With some more experience under our belts, it will make more sense as we move along.

`configureScene()`

Now that we know how we'll change our routes in our app, we'll need to be able to tell our app *which* transition type to make based on the specific route change that will occur (where the transition type is *left to right, right to left, modal,* etc). From our discussion above, recall this takes place inside the `configureScene()` method we defined earlier:

```
configureScene(route) {
  // Configure the scene
}
```

The same route object passed to the `renderScene()` method is passed to the `configureScene()` method as well. We can use the same logic from inside the `configureScene()` method as we used in the `renderScene()` method:

src/app/index.js

```
  configureScene(route) {
    if (route.home === true) {
      // Transitioning to HomeContainer
    } else if (route.notifications === true) {
      // Transitioning to NotificationsContainer
    } else {
      // Showing FooterTabsContainer
    }
  }
```

Instead of rendering components here, we'll tell the `<Navigator />` component which transition type we want to use when transitioning to the new UI. The `<Navigator />` object comes with 10 different types of scene configurations[178], all of which are located on the `Navigator.SceneConfigs` object.

- `Navigator.SceneConfigs.PushFromRight` (default)
- `Navigator.SceneConfigs.FloatFromRight`

[178] http://facebook.github.io/react-native/releases/0.31/docs/navigator.html#configurescene

- `Navigator.SceneConfigs.FloatFromLeft`
- `Navigator.SceneConfigs.FloatFromBottom`
- `Navigator.SceneConfigs.FloatFromBottomAndroid`
- `Navigator.SceneConfigs.FadeAndroid`
- `Navigator.SceneConfigs.HorizontalSwipeJump`
- `Navigator.SceneConfigs.HorizontalSwipeJumpFromRight`
- `Navigator.SceneConfigs.VerticalUpSwipeJump`
- `Navigator.SceneConfigs.VerticalDownSwipeJump`

The configuration we return from the `configureScene()` method will be the transition type that will be used for the specific route change.

For instance, say our user is on iOS and we want every route besides our notifications route to have the standard *left to right* transition and we want the notifications route to come up from the bottom as a *modal* transition. We can implement this behavior with an update the `configureScene()` method like so:

src/app/index.js

```
configureScene(route) {
  if (route.notifications === true) {
    return Navigator.SceneConfigs.FloatFromBottom;
  }

  return Navigator.SceneConfigs.FloatFromRight;
}

renderScene(route, navigator) {
  if (route.home === true) {
    return <HomeContainer navigator={navigator} />
  } else if (route.notifications === true) {
    return <NotificationsContainer navigator={navigator} />
  } else {
    return <FooterTabsContainer navigator={navigator} />
  }
}

render() {
  return (
    <Navigator
      renderScene={this.renderScene}
      configureScene={this.configureScene}
    />
```

```
  );
}
```

Now, when our user navigates to our notifications view, we'll see a nice `FloatFromBottom` transition. For any other route, we'll get the default `FloatFromRight` transition as it's what we specified inside the `configureScene()` method.

Earlier, we talked about how Android has a fundamentally different route transition than iOS. Let's see how we can implement this as well.

In order to detect what platform our app is currently running on, we can use the `Platform` object exported by the `react-native` package. First, we need to get a hold of the `Platform` export from react-native:

src/app/index.js

```
import { Platform } from 'react-native';
```

The `Platform` object has a property called `OS` which has a string that shows which platform the app is currently using. For iOS, the string is `'ios'` and for android it is `'android'`.

src/app/index.js

```
  configureScene(route) {
    if (route.notifications === true) {
      if (Platform.OS === 'android') {
        return Navigator.SceneConfigs.FloatFromBottomAndroid;
      } else {
        return Navigator.SceneConfigs.FloatFromBottom;
      }
    }

    return Navigator.SceneConfigs.FloatFromRight;
  }

  renderScene(route, navigator) {
    if (route.home === true) {
      return <HomeContainer navigator={navigator} />
    } else if (route.notifications === true) {
      return <NotificationsContainer navigator={navigator} />
    } else {
      return <FooterTabsContainer navigator={navigator} />
    }
  }
```

```
  render() {
    return (
      <Navigator
        renderScene={this.renderScene}
        configureScene={this.configureScene}
      />
    );
  }
```

Now if we navigate to the notifications route while on an Android device (or the simulator), we'll get the `FloatFromBottomAndroid` transition and still get the `FloatFromBottom` while on an iOS device.

With the `<Navigator />` component in place, we now have routing working in our React Native app that works for both Android and iOS.

Web components vs. Native components

The first difference we'll encounter between React and React-Native is the difference of built-in components.

On the web, we can use the native browser components, such as `<div />`, `<a />`, `<span />`, etc. However, in a native application these elements don't exist. As we're relying on the underlying native UI layer to render our layouts, we can't use native web elements, instead we have to use elements that the UI builder knows how to render. Luckily for us, React-Native exports a bunch of these view elements for us out of the box that the underlying view managers understand (and they've made it pretty easy to create our own as well).

These elements aren't a huge conceptual difference for the most part, so we won't dive deep into the differences, but we'll look at a few of the built-in components which are most commonly used in creating a React Native application.

> The following list of built-in components are the most commonly used components. The React-Native ecosystem is active and engaged, so if your application needs a specific component, it may have already been built for you to use, if it's not already implemented into the React Native core.
>
> Before implementing your own component, check to see if it has been built either through https://www.npmjs.com/search?q=react-native[179] or js.coach/react-native[180].

[179] www.npmjs.com/search?q=react-native

[180] https://js.coach/react-native

`<View />`

The `<View />` component is the most fundamental component for building UIs with React Native. The `<View />` component maps directly to the native equivalent for the current platform where our app is running. It maps to the `UIView` on iOS, `android.view` on Android, and even (yes) `<div />` in the web. It's fair to use the `<View />` component the same way we would with a `<div />` on the web.

`<Text />`

The `<Text />` component is used for displaying text in a React Native app. It's important to note that we can't render any plain text that is *not* wrapped in a `<Text>text component</Text>`. The view layers don't know what to do with it, so we have to be explicit when adding plain text to the view.

`<Image />`

The `<Image />` component is used when we want to display any type of image, including network images, static resources, temporary local images, and images from the local device (such as the camera roll/library).

`<TextInput />`

Just like on the web, we can get user input from our users using an input field called `<TextInput />`. The `<TextInput />` component is the main way we can get input from a keyboard on the device. One particular `prop` it accepts is the `onChangeText()` property which is a function that it will call anytime the text in the input field changes.

`<TouchableHighlight />`, `<TouchableOpacity />`, and `<TouchableWithoutFeedback />`

When we want to listen for any press events in React Native, we'll need to use one of the *touchable* components. These *touchable* components are often a point of confusion when we first start out with React Native because in the web, we can just add an `onClick()` prop to any element and it becomes "touchable"."

However, in React Native not only is the component *not* `onClick()` (it's `onPress()`), but most components in React Native don't know what to do with the `onPress()` property. Because of this, we'll need to wrap any module we're interested in having a *touchable* property in one of these touchable components.

Each of the different touchable components has a slightly different effect when it's touched.

- `<TouchableHighlight />` component will decrease the opacity of the component, which will allow the underlay color to shine through.
- `<TouchableOpacity />` decreases the opacity of a component, but does not display an underlay color.
- `<TouchableWithoutFeedback />` invokes the component when it's pressed, but does not give any user feedback on the component itself.

We'll want to use the `<TouchableWithoutFeedback />` component sparingly as we'll most often want to give the user feedback when a *touchable* component is pressed.

Use `<TouchableWithoutFeedback />` sparingly

More often than not, we'll want to give the user feedback that a *touchable* component has been pressed. This is one of the main reasons mobile web browsers don't feel *native*.

`<ActivityIndicator />`

The default loading indicator for React Native is the `<ActivityIndicator />` component. This component works on multiple platforms as it's implemented entirely in JavaScript. One side benefit we get with a component entirely written in JavaScript is that the default styling is updated based upon the platform the app is operating on without any customization required.

`<WebView />`

The `<WebView />` component allows us to display some web content in our React Native application.

`<ScrollView />`

The `<ScrollView />` component allows us to *scroll* along a view. In the web, this is generally handled automatically (and can be controlled/defined in CSS). In a native app, however if our content goes off screen, we won't be able to see it. In a native app, our users expect to be able to scroll content when this happens. This is where we use the `<ScrollView />` component.

If our content is larger than the screen (meaning we'll have to scroll to see it), we'll wrap our `<View />` in a `<ScrollView />` component.

Keep in mind that the `<ScrollView />` component works best for a relatively small list of items since performant lists are critical for a good UX on mobile. The `<ScrollView />` component renders *all* the elements and views of a `<ScrollView />` are rendered regardless if they are shown on screen or not. Because of this, React Native providers another, more performant way to render larger lists with the `<ListView />`.

<ListView />

The `<ListView />` component is a performance-focused option for rendering long lists of data. Unlike the `<ScrollView />` component, the `<ListView />` only renders elements that are currently showing on the screen. One interesting note is that the `<ListView />` uses the `<ScrollView />` under the hood, but it adds a lot of nice performance abstractions for us to leverage.

As performant lists are fundamental in building native apps, and the ListView is a bit different than what we're used to in the web, let's dive into how to use the `<ListView />` in more detail.

Let's say that we're building an app similar to Twitter and we want to create a Feed component which will receive an array of tweets and render those tweets to the view. Let's look at how we'd do this on the Web, with ScrollView, then with ListView. (We'll purposefully neglect styling, as that's not the focus of this exercise).

We might implement this on the web like so:

Web version

src/feed.js

```
import PropTypes from 'prop-types';
import React from 'react';

Feed.propTypes = {
  tweets: PropTypes.arrayOf(PropTypes.shape({
    name: PropTypes.string.isRequired,
    user_id: PropTypes.string.isRequired,
    avatar: PropTypes.string.isRequired,
    text: PropTypes.string.isRequired,
    numberOfFavorites: PropTypes.number.isRequired,
    numberOfRetweets: PropTypes.number.isRequired,
  })).isRequired,
};

function Feed ({ tweets }) {
  return (
    <div>
      {tweets.map((tweet) => (
        <div>
          <div>
            <img alt="tweet" src={tweet.avatar} />
            <span>{tweet.name}</span>
          </div>
          <p>{tweet.text}</p>
```

```
          <div>
            <div>Favs: {tweet.numberOfFavorites}</div>
            <div>RTs: {tweet.numberOfRetweets}</div>
          </div>
        </div>
      )
      )}
    </div>
  );
}
```

We have a stateless functional component named Feed which takes in an array of tweets, maps over each of those, and displays some UI for each tweet (in this case, a `<div />` element with some children).

`<ScrollView />` version

We can implement the *same* functionality using the `<ScrollView />` component like so:

src/app/twitter-scrollview.js

```
import React, { PropTypes } from 'react';
import { View, Text, ScrollView, Image } from 'react-native';

Feed.propTypes = {
  tweets: PropTypes.arrayOf(PropTypes.shape({
    name: PropTypes.string.isRequired,
    user_id: PropTypes.string.isRequired,
    avatar: PropTypes.string.isRequired,
    text: PropTypes.string.isRequired,
    numberOfFavorites: PropTypes.number.isRequired,
    numberOfRetweets: PropTypes.number.isRequired,
  })).isRequired,
};

function Feed ({ tweets }) {
  return (
    <ScrollView>
      {tweets.map((tweet) => (
        <View>
          <View>
            <Image src={tweet.avatar} />
            <Text>{tweet.name}</Text>
```

```
          </View>
          <Text>{tweet.text}</Text>
          <View>
            <Text>Favs: {tweet.numberOfFavorites}</Text>
            <Text>RTs: {tweet.numberOfRetweets}</Text>
          </View>
        </View>
      )
      )}
    </ScrollView>
  );
}
```

Notice this implementation is pretty similar to what we're used to on the web. We've just swapped out the specific web components for their React Native counterpart, but the actual logic of mapping over each tweet is the same.

Now, let's look at how we can implement the same functionality using the more performant `<ListView />` element:

> Don't sweat the details here as we'll go over everything we need to know about *how* to use the `<ListView />` component shortly. We're using this as an example to highlight the differences between how we can think about implementing the same functionality.

src/app/twitter-listview.js

```
import React, { PropTypes, Component } from 'react';
import { View, Text, ScrollView, Image, ListView } from 'react-native';

class Feed extends Component {
  static props = {
    tweets: PropTypes.arrayOf(PropTypes.shape({
      name: PropTypes.string.isRequired,
      user_id: PropTypes.string.isRequired,
      avatar: PropTypes.string.isRequired,
      text: PropTypes.string.isRequired,
      numberOfFavorites: PropTypes.number.isRequired,
      numberOfRetweets: PropTypes.number.isRequired,
    })).isRequired,
  }

  constructor(props) {
```

```
    super(props);

    this.ds = new ListView.DataSource({
      rowHasChanged: (r1, r2) => r1 !== r2,
    });

    this.state = {
      dataSource: this.ds.cloneWithRows(this.props.tweets),
    };
  }

  componentWillReceiveProps(nextProps) {
    if (nextProps.tweets !== this.props.tweets) {
      this.setState({
        dataSource: this.ds.cloneWithRows(nextProps.tweets),
      });
    }
  }
  renderRow = ({ tweet }) => {
    return (
      <View>
        <View>
          <Image src={tweet.avatar} />
          <Text>{tweet.name}</Text>
        </View>
        <Text>{tweet.text}</Text>
        <View>
          <Text>Favs: {tweet.numberOfFavorites}</Text>
          <Text>RTs: {tweet.numberOfRetweets}</Text>
        </View>
      </View>
    );
  }
  render() {
    return (
      <ListView
        renderRow={this.renderRow}
        dataSource={this.state.dataSource}
      />
    );
  }
}
```

The `<ListView />` implementation a *lot* different. Let's walk through the differences.

The first thing we'll see is that we've switched from a stateless functional component to a Class component which allows us to keep `state`. Since our component needs to keep track of the data that's currently rendered on screen as well as listen for anytime we get a request to update the data through the `shouldComponentUpdate()` lifecycle hook.

When using a `<ListView />` component, we'll need two things to properly implement a `<ListView />` component:

- `ListView.DataSource` instance
- `renderRow()` function defined in our component

The `ListView.DataSource` instance is a bit out of left-field, so let's look at that first. We'll see that we start off by creating a new instance of the type `ListView.DataSource`. We'll pass it and object that allows us to customize how it works under the hood. Here, we've passed it a `rowHasChanged()` method, which is a function that the `<ListView />` uses to determine if the list needs to be re-rendered.

src/app/twitter-listview.js

```
    this.ds = new ListView.DataSource({
      rowHasChanged: (r1, r2) => r1 !== r2,
    });
```

Taking a step back for a moment, if we think about the fundamental aspect of creating a high-performance list view, making it easy to detect when a row in the list has changed in order to avoid re-rendering rows that haven't changed is pretty important. This is the first optimization that the `<ListView />` handles for us automatically.

The next step is to actually give our `ListView.DataSource` instance data to keep track of and show to the user. This is where the `ds.cloneWithRows()` method works. The `ds.cloneWithRows()` method will set (or update) the data kept internally by the `ListView.DataSource` instance.

src/app/twitter-listview.js

```
    this.state = {
      dataSource: this.ds.cloneWithRows(this.props.tweets),
    };
```

Notice that we're using the `ds.cloneWithRows()` method in both the `constructor()` function as well as the `componentWillReceiveProps()` methods.

src/app/twitter-listview.js

```
componentWillReceiveProps(nextProps) {
  if (nextProps.tweets !== this.props.tweets) {
    this.setState({
      dataSource: this.ds.cloneWithRows(nextProps.tweets),
    });
  }
}
```

In both cases, we are receiving tweets we want to show on the screen, so we'll need to make sure we add them to our `dataSource` instance variable, which means in both cases we'll need to call the `cloneWithRows()` method. Without calling the `cloneWithRows()` (or other relatives of the method – more on that later), the data won't be updates on the `ListView.DataSource` instance.

Immutable data

The data keeps by the `dataSource` instance object is *immutable. Immutable* objects cannot be updated or changed. Once it's created, it cannot be modified or updated.

When we do want to change the data, we'll have to create a separate copy of the data elsewhere so we can update a local copy and call `cloneWithRows()` with that data. Although this might seem like a limitation, it is a huge performance optimization and it's how we have to interact with the `ListView.DataSource` object.

In the previous example, we're not keeping a copy of the previous tweets because we're receiving a brand new array of tweets on every change. If these changes are incremental, however (adding/removing tweets) we would need to keep a copy of the *unDataSourced* data elsewhere.

Now that we have data kept inside the `dataSource` instance object, we'll need to implement a `renderRow()` function. This is a bit more straight-forward. The `renderRow()` method is called for every single row inside the `dataSource` instance's copy of the data and is responsible for providing a UI component to be rendered for every row.

src/app/twitter-listview.js

```
renderRow = (tweet) => {
  return (
    <View>
      <View>
        <Image source={{ uri: tweet.avatar }} />
        <Text>{tweet.name}</Text>
      </View>
      <View>
        <Text>{tweet.text}</Text>
        <Text>Favs: {tweet.numberOfFavorites}</Text>
        <Text>RTs: {tweet.numberOfRetweets}</Text>
      </View>
    </View>
  );
}
```

Notice that in converting from the `<ScrollView />` to the `<ListView />` implementation, we've take the `.map()` call from the `data` *out* of the `render()` function and into the `renderRow()` function. We can treat the JSX inside the `renderRow()` function just like it's the JSX from the `.map()` function as it is called for each item in the `dataSource` instance.

The `<ListView />` component accepts a few other props that we won't go "too" much into detail about here, but it's useful to know they exist. We'll look at the `renderSeparator()`, `renderHeader()`, and `renderFooter()`.

These extra `props` are pretty self-explanatory, but let's look at each one:

`renderSeparator()`

When a `renderSeparator()` prop is passed as a `prop` to the `<ListView />` component, it is expected to be a function that will be responsible for returning a component that will be rendered as a separator between each item in the `<ListView />`.

Rather than adding a border to the component's styles, using the `renderSeparator()` prop is intelligent and won't add a border to the last rendered row.

src/app/twitter-listview.js

```
renderSeparator = (sectionId, rowId) => {
  return (
    <View key={rowId} style={styles.separator} />
  );
}

render() {
  return (
    <ListView
      renderRow={this.renderRow}
      dataSource={this.state.dataSource}
      renderSeparator={this.renderSeparator}
    />
  );
}
```

`renderHeader()`

The `renderHeader()` prop accepts a function that is expected to return a component which will be used as the header for the `<ListView />` component. For instance, let's say we wanted to add a search bar at the top of our feed for filtering content. We can use the `renderHeader()` method as a way to achieve this.

src/app/twitter-listview.js

```
renderHeader = () => <SearchBar />

render() {
  return (
    <ListView
      renderRow={this.renderRow}
      dataSource={this.state.dataSource}
      renderHeader={this.renderHeader}
    />
  );
}
```

`renderFooter()`

The `renderFooter()` prop allows us to add a footer to our ListView. For instance, we might want to show a button to allow the user to fetch more tweets from our tweet list, for example.

src/app/twitter-listview.js

```
  renderFooter = () => <ShowMoreTweets />

  render() {
    return (
      <ListView
        renderRow={this.renderRow}
        dataSource={this.state.dataSource}
        renderFooter={this.renderFooter}
      />
    );
  }
```

Styles

Styling in React Native is not as straight-forward as it is in the web. React Native takes the idea of styling with Cascading StyleSheets (or CSS, for short) to the native app world where we apply styling declarations to a component. As we've seen through our work with React throughout this course, we can apply CSS rules within a React component using the `style` prop on most elements. React Native follows this same approach with React Native elements.

Before we jump too much into *how* we style React Native components, it's important to note that React Native takes the `100%` of styling is done in JavaScript approach. That is, every core component accepts a `style` prop that accepts an object (or an array of objects) that contain a component's styles. As we're in JavaScript, properties that contain a -, however must be handled slightly differently. Rather than `background-color` or `margin-left`, we need to camel-case[181] the style name property.

For instance, if we want to add a style of a background color to a component we can add it

src/app/styledViews.js

```
  <View style={{ backgroundColor: 'green', padding: 10 }}>
    <Text style={{ color: 'blue', fontSize: 25 }}>
      Hello world
    </Text>
  </View>
```

One nice feature that React Native introduces that we don't have with the web version of React is the ability to pass an array to the style prop (without a separate library), which React Native will merge into a single style.

[181] https://en.wikipedia.org/wiki/Camel_case

src/app/styledViews.js

```
const ContainerComponent = () => {
  const getBackgroundColor = () => {
    return { backgroundColor: 'red' };
  };

  return (
    <View style={[ getBackgroundColor(), { padding: 10 } ]}>
      <Text style={{ color: 'blue', fontSize: 25 }}>
        Hello world
      </Text>
    </View>
  );
};
```

As it is right now, this is pretty simple. What if we have more than 2-3 style properties for a component? React Native exports a helper for just this case called `StyleSheet`. The `StyleSheet` export allows us to create an abstraction just like we can do with web-based CSS stylesheets.

StyleSheet

The `StyleSheet` object has a `create()` method on it which accepts an object that contains a list of our styles. We can then use the `styles` object the `create()` method returns rather than a raw styles object.

For example, let's decorate a few components:

src/app/styledViews.js

```
const styles = StyleSheet.create({
  container: {
    padding: 10,
  },
  containerText: {
    color: 'blue',
    fontSize: 20,
  },
});

class ExampleComponent extends Component {
  getBackgroundColor() {
    return {
```

```
      backgroundColor: 'yellow'
    };
  }

  render() {
    return (
      <View style={[
        this.getBackgroundColor(),
        styles.container
      ]}>
        <Text style={styles.containerText}>
          Hello world
        </Text>
      </View>
    );
  }
}
```

We get a few benefits to using the `StyleSheet` approach. One is that our components are more readable. Even more important is that `StyleSheet` gives us some performance gains that we don't get when applying an object directly to the `styles` prop.

Now that we've seen how to apply styles, let's jump into the architecture of our styles and using Flexbox.

Flexbox

Flexbox as a technology exists gives us the ability to define a layout in an efficient way. We can *lay out*, *align*, and *distribute space* among items in a container, even when the size of the components are unknown or are dynamic. Where creating a dynamic, all-purpose layout with CSS can be cumbersome, flexbox makes this much easier.

In other words, flexbox is all about creating dynamic layouts.

The main concept behind flexbox is that we give a parent element the ability to control the layout of all their child elements rather than having each child element control their own layout. When we give the parent this control, the parent element becomes a *flex container* where the child elements are referred to as *flex items*.

An example of this is instead of having to float all of the element's children left and add a margin to each, we can instead just have the parent element specify having all of its children to be laid out in a row with even space between them. In this way, the layout responsibilities move from the child to the parent component, which overall gives us more fine-tuned control over the layout of our apps.

The *most important* concept to understand about flexbox is that it's based on different axes. We have a *main* axis and a *cross* axis.

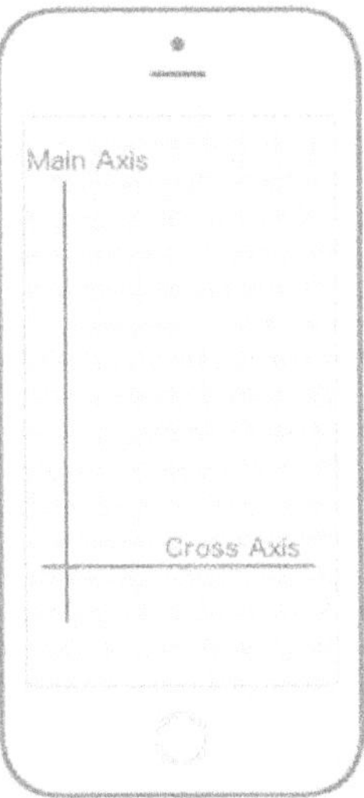

By default, in React Native the *main axis* is vertical while the *cross axis* is horizontal. Everything from here on out is built upon the concept of the axes. When we say "which will align all the child elements along the *main* axis," we mean that, by default the children of the parent element will be laid out vertically from top to bottom. When we say that this will align all the child elements on the *cross* axis, we mean, by default the children elements will be laid out horizontally from left to right.

The rest of the flexbox concepts is deciding how we want to align, position, stretch, spread, shrink, center, and wrap child elements along the main and cross axis.

Let's look at the flexbox properties.

`flex-direction`

We have been very deliberate in saying the *default behavior* when talking about the main and cross axis. This is because we can actually change which axis is the main axis and which is the cross. We can use the `flex-direction` (in React Native, this is `flexDirection`) property to specify this property.

It can accept one of two values:

- `column`
- `row`

By default, React Native sets all elements to have the `flexDirection: column` property. This is to say that the element's main axis is vertical and it's cross axis is horizontal; just as we saw in the image above. However, if we define the `flexDirection: row` to be *row*, the axes switch. The main axis becomes horizontal, while the cross axis is vertical.

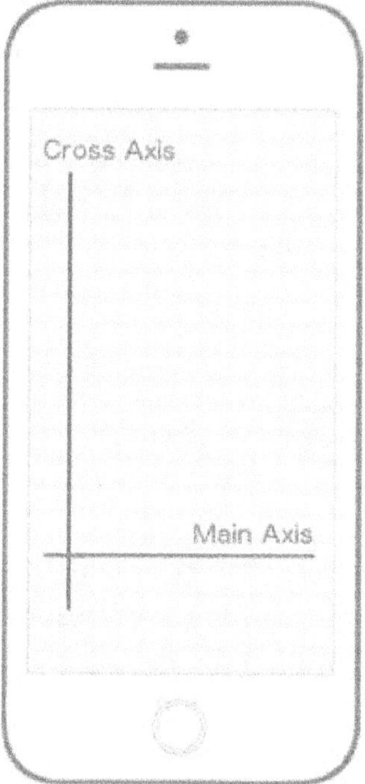

It's crucial to understand the concepts of the *main* and *cross* axes as our *entire layout* depends upon these different settings.

Let's dive into a few different properties we can use to align child elements along these axes.

Focusing on the *main* axis first, in order to specify how children align themselves along the main axis, we can use the `justifyContent` property.

The `justifyContent` property can accept one of five different values we can use in order to change how the children align themselves along the main axis:

- `flex-start`
- `center`
- `flex-end`
- `space-around`
- `space-between`

Let's walk through what each of these mean.

Follow along

In this section, we *highly* recommend following along by building an application *with* us as we walk through this flexbox introduction.

We've included the sample applications with this book, or you can create your own simply and replace the `index.ios.js` and `index.android.js` code from the sample project with the following code sample.

To create a sample app for yourself, use the `react-native-cli` package:

```
react-native init FlexboxExamples
```

For the following examples, we'll use the following code to demonstrate how flexbox works with laying out child elements.

src/app/styledViews.js

```
import React, { Component } from 'react';
import { StyleSheet, Text, View } from 'react-native';

export class FlexboxExamples extends Component {
  render() {
    return (
      <View style={ styles.container }>
        <View style={ styles.box } />
        <View style={ styles.box } />
        <View style={ styles.box } />
      </View>
    );
  }
}

const styles = StyleSheet.create({
  container: {
    flex: 1,
  },
  box: {
    height: 50,
    width: 50,
    backgroundColor: '#e76e63',
    margin: 10,
  },
});
```

```
export default FlexboxExamples;
```

If you're creating your own example and replacing the `index.[platform].js` files, add the following code to make sure the app is *registered* with React native as the app:

```
import { AppRegistry } from 'react-native'; // at the top of the file
// ...
// at the end of the file
AppRegistry.registerComponent('FlexboxExamples', () => FlexboxExamples);
```

In this code, the only thing we'll be changing for every example is the `container` key of the `styles` object. We can ignore the `flex: 1;` for now (we'll come back to it later).

With the code above, we have an app that aligns the content along the main, vertical axis, adding the key `justifyContent: 'flex-start'` results in an app with every child element towards the start of the main axis:

justifyContent: 'flex-start'

```
container: {
  flex: 1;
  justifyContent: 'flex-start';
}
```

The default value for `flexDirection` is `column`, so when we don't have a value for our flex direction, it is set to `column`. Since `justifyContent` targets the *main* axis, our child elements align themselves towards the start of the *main* axis, which is the top left and work their way down.

When we set the value to `justifyContent: 'center'`, our child elements will align themselves towards the center of the main axis:

justifyContent: 'flex-center'

```
container: {
  flex: 1;
  justifyContent: 'center';
}
```

When we set `justifyContent` value to `flex-end`, our child elements align themselves toward the end of the main axis:

justifyContent: 'flex-end'

```
container: {
  flex: 1;
  justifyContent: 'flex-end';
}
```

We can also set our `justifyContent` to be `space-between`, which will align every child so that the space between each child item is even along the main axis:

justifyContent: 'space-between'

```
container: {
  flex: 1;
  justifyContent: 'space-between';
}
```

Finally, we can set our `justifyContent` value to `space-around`, which aligns every child elements so there is even space *around* each element on the main axis:

justifyContent: 'space-around'

```
container: {
  flex: 1;
  justifyContent: 'space-around';
}
```

What happens if we change the value of `flexDirection` of our container to `row` instead of to `column`?

The *main* axis switches to the *horizontal* axis and all of our child elements will still align themselves to the *main axis*, which is now vertical, rather than the *vertical* axis.

flexDirection: 'row'

```
container: {
  flex: 1;
  flexDirection: 'row',
  justifyContent: 'space-around';
}
```

Notice that all we did was change the `flexDirection` value and our layout is a completely new, updated layout. The ability to dynamically update our layout makes flexbox incredibly powerful.

Let's take a look at the cross axis. In order to specify how children align themselves along the cross axis, we'll use the `align-items` (or `alignItems` in React Native) property.

Unlike the `justifyContent` values, we only have four available values to set our `alignItems` property to:

- `flex-start`
- `center`
- `flex-end`
- `stretch`

Let's walk through these as well.

When our container's `alignItems` value is set to `flex-start`, all of our child elements will align themselves towards the start of the cross axis:

alignItems: 'flex-start'

```
container: {
  flex: 1;
  alignItems: 'flex-start';
}
```

When our container's `alignItems` value is set to `center`, all of our child elements will align themselves towards the middle of the cross axis:

alignItems: 'center'

```
container: {
  flex: 1;
  alignItems: 'center';
}
```

When our container's `alignItems` value is set to `flex-end`, all of our child elements will align themselves towards the end of the cross axis:

alignItems: 'flex-end'

```
container: {
  flex: 1;
  alignItems: 'flex-end';
}
```

When we set our container's `alignItems` value to `stretch`, every child element along the cross axis will be stretched to the entire width of the cross-axis (provided there is not a specified `width` when our `flexDirection: row` or a `height` when our `flexDirection: column`).

Whenever we set `alignItems` to stretch, each child will *stretch* across the full width or height of the parent container, but only if the child element does *not* set a width. This makes sense as flexbox will try to set the width for our child elements automatically if the child doesn't try to override it.

To see this in action, check out the following screen-shots. Notice that we're including the `box` styles here as well to see that we've updated the `box` styles as well.

With the container set to: `flexDirection: column`, our layout will look like the following diagram. Notice we've removed the static `width` when we're using `flexDirection: column`:

alignItems: 'stretch'

```
container: {
  flex: 1;
  flexDirection: 'column',
  alignItems: 'stretch';
},
box: {
  height: 50,
  backgroundColor: '#e76e63',
  margin: 10
}
```

With the container set to: `flexDirection: row`, our layout will look like the following diagram. Notice we've removed the static `height` when we're using `flexDirection: row`:

alignItems: 'stretch'

```
container: {
  flex: 1;
  flexDirection: 'row',
  alignItems: 'stretch';
},
box: {
  width: 50,
  backgroundColor: '#e76e63',
  margin: 10
}
```

Breaking this down a bit, the main axis now runs horizontally since our `flexDirection: row` is set to `row`. This means the `alignItems` aligns the child elements along the vertical axis (the new *cross* axis). Since we've removed the height of the child elements and set the `alignItems` to `stretch`, the elements are now going to stretch along the vertical axis for the entire length of the parent component's entire cross axis view. For this example here, this is the entire view.

Through this point, we've been working with a single *flex container* or parent element. If we create nested *flex containers*, the *same logic* applies for the nested container child elements (flex items). Instead of being relative to the entire view (like in our previous examples), they'll position themselves according to the nested parent component. Our *entire UI will be built upon nesting flex containers.*

Other dynamic layouts

In flexbox, there is no such thing as a percentage-based styling. Although this *can* make things a bit more difficult, using flexbox to layout our UI is powerful as our layouts will look the way we want regardless of screen-size.

Recall in our earlier example, we set the `flex: 1` value to 1? The `flex` property allows us to specify *relative* widths for our flex containers.

As we've seen over and over, Flexbox is concerned with giving control over to the parent element to handle the layout of its children elements. The `flex` property is a bit different as it allows child elements to specify their height or width in comparison to their sibling elements. The best way to explain flex is to look at some examples,

Let's start with a view that looks like this:

This is implemented using the following styles:

src/app/styledViews.js

```
const styles = StyleSheet.create({
  container: {
    flex: 1,
    flexDirection: 'row',
    justifyContent: 'center',
    alignItems: 'center',
  },
  box: {
    backgroundColor: '#e76e63',
    margin: 10,
    width: 50,
    height: 50,
  },
});
```

What if we want the UI to have two smaller boxes surrounding one larger box, like so:

We can use the *exact same* layout, but now the middle section is twice as wide as the two surrounding it. The `flex` property allows us to set this dynamically.

src/app/styledViews.js

```
import React, { Component } from 'react';
import { StyleSheet, View } from 'react-native';

const styles = StyleSheet.create({
  container: {
    flex: 1,
    flexDirection: 'row',
    justifyContent: 'center',
    alignItems: 'center',
  },
  box: {
    backgroundColor: '#e76e63',
    margin: 10,
    width: 50,
    height: 50,
  },
});

export class FlexboxLayouts extends Component {
  render() {
    return (
      <View style={[ styles.container ]}>
        <View style={[ styles.box, { flex: 1 } ]} />
        <View style={[ styles.box, { flex: 2 } ]} />
```

```
        <View style={[ styles.box, { flex: 1 } ]} />
      </View>
    );
  }
}

export default FlexboxLayouts;
```

Notice that we didn't add to our styles, we just set the middle sibling's `flex` property to have a `flex: 2`, while the other siblings have a `flex: 1`.

We can read this like the flexbox layout is saying: "make sure the middle sibling is twice as large along the main axis as the first and third children." This is the reason why `flex` can replace percentage-based layouts. In a percentage-based layout, generally is one where the specific elements are relative in size to other elements, which is exactly what we're doing above.

It's important to note that if we place `flex: 1` on an element, the element is going to try to take up as much space as its parent takes up. In most our examples above, we want the "layout area" to be the size of the parent, which in our initial examples was the entire viewport.

Let's go deeeeeeper.

What if we wanted a layout like this:

It's as if the first and third elements are centered both vertically and horizontally, but the second element is aligned all the way at the bottom.

Breaking the layout down in flexbox terms, we basically have the first and third elements are aligned on the main axis, both `center`, while the second element uses `flex-end` along the cross axis, which is vertical. To implement this design, we'll need a way to have the child element override a specific positioning received from it's parent.

Good news! We have the `align-self` (`alignSelf` in React Native) property that allows us to have the child specify it's alignment directly. The `alignSelf` property positions itself among the *cross* axis and has the *same* options as `alignItems` (which makes sense, as it's the child telling the parent what to set it's `alignItems` property is for a single element).

src/app/styledViews.js

```
import React, { Component } from 'react';
import { StyleSheet, View } from 'react-native';

const styles = StyleSheet.create({
  container: {
    flex: 1,
    flexDirection: 'row',
    justifyContent: 'center',
    alignItems: 'center',
  },
  box: {
    backgroundColor: '#e76e63',
    margin: 10,
    width: 50,
    height: 50,
  },
});

export class FlexboxLayouts extends Component {
  render() {
    return (
      <View style={[ styles.container ]}>
        <View style={styles.box} />
        <View style={[ styles.box, { alignSelf: 'flex-end' } ]} />
        <View style={styles.box} />
      </View>
    );
  }
}

export default FlexboxLayouts;
```

Note that all we did to implement this layout was add a single `alignSelf: flex-end` property to the second child element which overrides the instruction set by the parent element (which is set to `center` in `styles.container`).

Let's look at the differences between flexbox for the web and for React Native.

When we hear the phrase "React Native uses Flexbox for styling," what this really means is that "React Native has its own Flexbox (and CSS) implementation[182] which is *similar* to Flexbox, but it isn't an exact clone."

These differences can be summed up in two parts, *defaults* and *excluded* properties, where *defaults* which are automatically applied to every element and *excluded* properties are properties that exist in CSS/Flexbox that don't exist in React Native's implementation.

Let's look at the default values that are applied to every element for React Native;

```
box-sizing: border-box;
position: relative;

display: flex;
flex-direction: column;
align-items: stretch;
flex-shrink: 0;
align-content: flex-start;

border: 0 solid black;
margin: 0;
padding: 0;
min-width: 0;
```

Let's walk through some of the non-obvious ones.

`box-sizing: border-box`

The `box-sizing` property makes it so an element's specified width and height are *not* affected by padding or borders – which is what we expect to happen naturally, but browser implementations are weird and this isn't the case by default.

`flex-direction: column`

The `flex-direction` on the web is set to `row`, but the default for `flexDirection` in React Native is `column`.

`align-items: stretch`

The default `alignItems` property is set to `stretch`, whereas in the web it's set to `flex-start`.

[182] https://github.com/facebook/yoga

`position: relative`

By having every element set to relative positioning by default, it makes absolute positioned child elements target the direct parent rather than the typical "closest parent with position relative or absolute". This makes using absolute positioning more consistent while also allowing for left, right, top, and bottom values by default.

`display: flex`

Unlike the web implementation, there is no need to set `display: flex` ever as every element in a React Native app is already set to `display: flex` by default.

Now let's look at the properties that exist on the web, but don't exist for React Native's implementation.

`flex-grow, flex-shrink, flex-basis`

The three properties available in the web flexbox, which allow an element to grow or shrink a flex item. React Native has a similar property called `flex`, but don't have the same three elements that *do* exist in CSS. It's also important to note that the `flex` property in React Native works differently than in the web.

`flex` on React Native is a number rather than a string and is used to make a specific component larger or smaller than its sibling components. A component with flex set to `2` will take twice the space (either vertically or horizontally depending on its primary axis) as a component with flex set to `1`. If flex is set to `0`, that component will be sized according to its width and height. This brings us to our next "exclude" which is any size unit besides `px`.

In order to accomplish percentage-based layouts, we'll have to use `flex` as we just talked about in the previous section.

Although we did not talk about them directly, React Native allows us to use CSS properties that we're already used to in CSS, like position, zIndex, minWidth, etc. A full list of all the available properties that React Native knows about are available at https://facebook.github.io/react-native/docs/layout-props.html[183].

HTTP requests

We're only going to get so far in building a React Native app without needing to make an HTTP request and fetch some data from an external API. React Native includes an abstraction to make HTTP requests using the `fetch` API. The fetch[184] API provides an interface for fetching resources, which will seem pretty familiar for anyone who has used _XMLHttpRequest' or other clients such as axios[185] and superagent[186].

[183]https://facebook.github.io/react-native/docs/layout-props.html
[184]https://developer.mozilla.org/en-US/docs/Web/API/Fetch_API
[185]https://www.npmjs.com/package/axios
[186]https://github.com/visionmedia/superagent

The `fetch` API uses promises, so before we get to jumping into using the `fetch` API with React Native, let's take a detour and talk about Promises.

What is a promise

As defined by the Mozilla, a `Promise` object is used for handling asynchronous computations which has some important guarantees that are difficult to handle with the callback method (the more old-school method of handling asynchronous code).

A `Promise` object is simply a wrapper around a value that may or may not be known when the object is instantiated and provides a method for handling the value *after* it is known (also known as `resolved`) or is unavailable for a failure reason (we'll refer to this as `rejected`).

Using a `Promise` object gives us the opportunity to associate functionality for an asynchronous operation's eventual success or failure (for whatever reason). It also allows us to treat these complex scenarios by using synchronous-like code.

For instance, consider the following synchronous code where we print out the current time in the JavaScript console:

```
var currentTime = new Date();
console.log('The current time is: ' + currentTime);
```

This is pretty straight-forward and works as the `new Date()` object represents the time the browser knows about. Now consider that we're using a different clock on some other remote machine. For instance, if we're making a Happy New Years clock, it would be great to be able to synchronize the user's browser with everyone Else's using a single time value for everyone so no-one misses the ball dropping ceremony.

Suppose we have a method that handles getting the current time for the clock called `getCurrentTime()` that fetches the current time from a remote server. We'll represent this now with a `setTimeout()` that returns the time (like it's making a request to a slow API):

```
function getCurrentTime() {
  // Get the current 'global' time from an API
  return setTimeout(function() {
    return new Date();
  }, 2000);
}
var currentTime = getCurrentTime()
console.log('The current time is: ' + currentTime);
```

Our `console.log()` log value will return the timeout handler id, which is definitely *not* the current time. Traditionally, we can update the code using a callback to get called when the time is available:

```
function getCurrentTime(callback) {
  // Get the current 'global' time from an API
  return setTimeout(function() {
    var currentTime = new Date();
    callback(currentTime);
  }, 2000);
}
getCurrentTime(function(currentTime) {
  console.log('The current time is: ' + currentTime);
});
```

What if there is an error with the rest? How do we catch the error and define a retry or error state?

```
function getCurrentTime(onSuccess, onFail) {
  // Get the current 'global' time from an API
  return setTimeout(function() {
    // randomly decide if the date is retrieved or not
    var didSucceed = Math.random() >= 0.5;
    if (didSucceed) {
      var currentTime = new Date();
      onSuccess(currentTime);
    } else {
      onFail('Unknown error');
    }
  }, 2000);
}
getCurrentTime(function(currentTime) {
  console.log('The current time is: ' + currentTime);
}, function(error) {
  console.log('There was an error fetching the time');
});
```

Now, what if we want to make a request based upon the first requests value? As a short example, let's reuse the `getCurrentTime()` function inside again (as though it were a second method, but allows us to avoid adding another complex-looking function):

```
function getCurrentTime(onSuccess, onFail) {
  // Get the current 'global' time from an API
  return setTimeout(function() {
    // randomly decide if the date is retrieved or not
    var didSucceed = Math.random() >= 0.5;
    console.log(didSucceed);
    if (didSucceed) {
      var currentTime = new Date();
      onSuccess(currentTime);
    } else {
      onFail('Unknown error');
    }
  }, 2000);
}
getCurrentTime(function(currentTime) {
  getCurrentTime(function(newCurrentTime) {
    console.log('The real current time is: ' + currentTime);
  }, function(nestedError) {
    console.log('There was an error fetching the second time');
  })
}, function(error) {
  console.log('There was an error fetching the time');
});
```

Dealing with asynchronousity in this way can get complex quickly. In addition, we could be fetching values from a previous function call, what if we only want to get one… there are a lot of tricky cases to deal with when dealing with values that are not yet available when our app starts.

Enter Promises

Using promises, on the other hand helps us avoid a lot of this complexity (although is not a silver bullet solution). The previous code, which could be called spaghetti code can be turned into a neater, more synchronous-looking version:

```
function getCurrentTime(onSuccess, onFail) {
  // Get the current 'global' time from an API using Promise
  return new Promise((resolve, reject) => {
    setTimeout(function() {
      var didSucceed = Math.random() >= 0.5;
      didSucceed ? resolve(new Date()) : reject('Error');
    }, 2000);
  })
}
getCurrentTime()
  .then(currentTime => getCurrentTime())
  .then(currentTime => {
    console.log('The current time is: ' + currentTime);
    return true;
  })
  .catch(err => console.log('There was an error:' + err))
```

This previous source example is a bit cleaner and clear as to what's going on and avoids a lot of tricky error handling/catching.

To catch the value on success, we'll use the `then()` function available on the `Promise` instance object. The `then()` function is called with whatever the return value is of the promise itself. For instance, in the example above, the `getCurrentTime()` function resolves with the `currentTime()` value (on successful completion) and calls the `then()` function on the return value (which is another promise) and so on and so forth.

To catch an error that occurs anywhere in the promise chain, we can use the `catch()` method.

> We're using a promise chain in the above example to create a *chain* of actions to be called one after another. A promise chain sounds complex, but it's fundamentally simple. Essentially, we can "synchronize" a call to multiple asynchronous operations in succession. Each call to `then()` is called with the previous `then()` function's return value.
>
> For instance, if we wanted to manipulate the value of the `getCurrentTime()` call, we can add a link in the chain, like so:

```
getCurrentTime()
  .then(currentTime => getCurrentTime())
  .then(currentTime => {
    return 'It is now: ' + currentTime;
  })
  // this logs: "It is now: [current time]"
  .then(currentTimeMessage => console.log(currentTimeMessage))
  .catch(err => console.log('There was an error:' + err))
```

Single-use guarantee

A promise only ever has one of three states at any given time:

- pending
- fulfilled (resolved)
- rejected (error)

A *pending* promise can only every lead to either a fulfilled state or a rejected state *once and only once*, which can avoid some pretty complex error scenarios. This means that we can only ever return a promise once. If we want to rerun a function that uses promises, we need to create a *new* one.

Creating a promise

We can create new promises (as the example shows above) using the `Promise` constructor. It accepts a function that will get run with two parameters:

- The `onSuccess` (or `resolve`) function to be called on success resolution
- The `onFail` (or `reject`) function to be called on failure rejection

Recalling our function from above, we can see that we call the `resolve()` function if the request succeeded and call the `reject()` function if the method returns an error condition.

```
var promise = new Promise(function(resolve, reject) {
  // call resolve if the method succeeds
  resolve(true);
})
promise.then(bool => console.log('Bool is true'))
```

Now that we have a familiarity with promises, let's use this in a React Native app. The simplest possible GET implementation to make an HTTP request, the `fetch` method accepts a URL as it's first argument and returns a promise which, when resolved, contains the response object.

For instance, let's say we have a `getGithubUsers()` function where we want to make an API call to fetch some users from github. This `fetch` call could be implemented like so:

src/app/styledViews.js

```
const baseUrl = 'https://api.github.com';

export const getGithubUsers = ({ offset }) => {
  return fetch(`${baseUrl}/users?since=${offset}`)
          .then(response => response.json())
          .catch(console.warn);
};
```

It's possible to use `fetch` for more than just GET requests, of course. We can specify more details for our requests by passing a second argument which contains more details along with the request.

For example, let's say we wanted to create a `gist` on github using the github API. We can easily handle this by using the `fetch` API with a second parameter. We might implement this like so:

src/app/styledViews.js

```
export const makeGist = (
  activity,
  { description = '', isPublic = true } = {}
  ) => fetch(`${baseUrl}/gists`, {
    method: 'POST',
    body: JSON.stringify({
      files: {
        'activity.json': {
          content: JSON.stringify(activity),
        },
      },
      description,
      public: isPublic,
    }),
  })
  .then(response => response.json());
```

The fetch API has a lot of possibilities and can be used across platforms with React Native's implementation. For more details about the API, check out the docs on MDN at https://developer.mozilla.org/en-US/docs/Web/API/Fetch_API/Using_Fetch[187].

[187] https://developer.mozilla.org/en-US/docs/Web/API/Fetch_API/Using_Fetch

Debugging with React Native

One of the nicest features that comes along with writing a React Native app is the debugging experience. A primary goal of the React Native team is to take the development workflow we're used to working with on the web and bring it to native development.

When we're running our app on the simulator, we can open the debugging menu by platform by pressing:

- iOS: `Cmd + D` (or `CTRL + D` on a PC)
- Android: Cmd + M (or `CTRL + M` on a PC)

If this works, this will bring up the in-app developer menu:

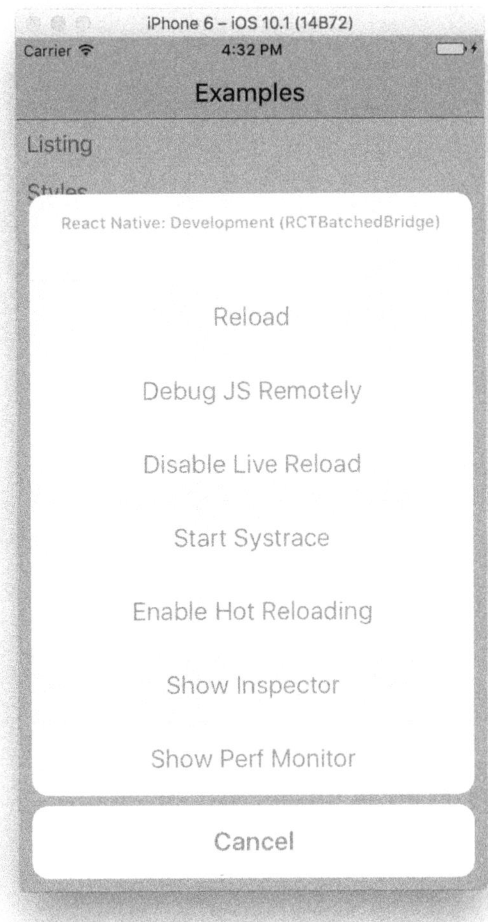

From this menu, we have a bunch of different options for debugging. The one we'll work with directly is the menu item with the label: `Debug JS Remotely`. Clicking on this menu item will bring up a window in Chrome[188].

If we open the developer console on the page it opens, we'll see that we can actually debug out native application using the Chrome dev tools!

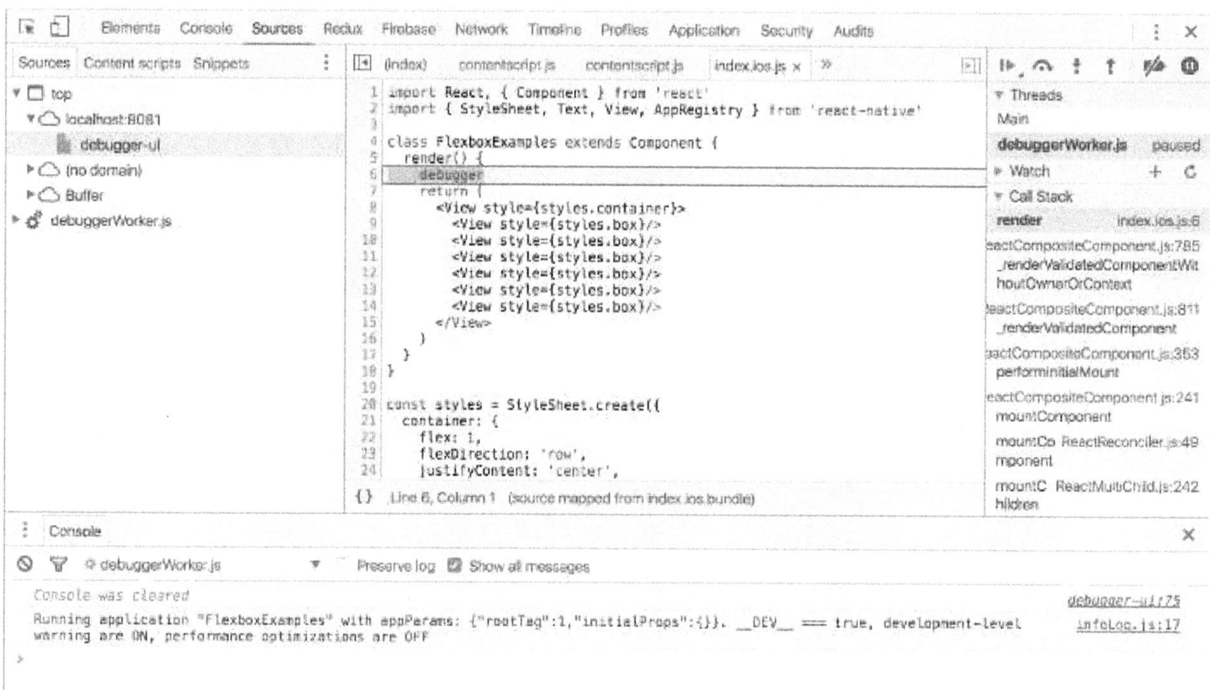

Where to go from here

The React Native community is active and growing all the time.

The number of React Native meetups is growing all the time and we highly recommend checking one out. The list of world-wide React Native meetups can be found on meetup.com at:

[188] https://google.com/chrome

https://www.meetup.com/topics/react-native/[189].

The React Native team has an open React Native chat channel available through Discord, which can be found at: https://discordapp.com/invite/0ZcbPKXt5bZjGY5n[190].

Community resources can be found on npmjs.org at https://www.npmjs.com/search?q=react-native[191].

---

[189] https://www.meetup.com/topics/react-native/

[190] https://discordapp.com/invite/0ZcbPKXt5bZjGY5n

[191] https://www.npmjs.com/search?q=react-native

Appendix A: PropTypes

PropTypes are a way to validate the values that are passed in through a component's props. Well-defined interfaces provide us with a layer of safety at the run time of our apps. They also provide a layer of documentation to the consumer of our components.

To use PropTypes, install the package with npm:

```
$ npm i --save prop-types
```

And then import the library in whichever files you need it:

```
import PropTypes from 'prop-types';
```

In versions of React earlier than 15.5.0, you'd access PropTypes via the main React library. This behavior is staged for deprecation.

We define PropTypes by passing defining them as a static property of the component class. We can either do this by setting the propTypes as a static property on the class or by setting them after the class is defined.

code/appendix/proptypes/Component.js

```
class Component extends React.Component {
  static propTypes = {
    name: PropTypes.string
  }
  // ...
  render() {
    return (<div>{this.props.name}</div>)
  }
}
```

We can also set the propTypes as a static property on the component after the class is defined.

code/appendix/proptypes/Component.js

```
class Component extends React.Component {
  // ...
  render() {
    return (<div>{this.props.name}</div>)
  }
  // ...
Component.propTypes = {
  name: PropTypes.string
}
```

`createClass()` proptypes

When using the `createClass()` method to define a component, we pass the `propTypes` as a key with the value as the propTypes:

```
const Component = React.createClass({
 propTypes: {
   // propType definitions go here
 },
 render: function() {}

});
```

The `key` of the `propTypes` object defines the name of the prop we are validating, while the value is the types defined by the `PropTypes` object (which we discuss below) *or* a custom one through a custom function.

The `PropTypes` object exports a lot of validators that cover the most of the cases we'll encounter. For the not-so common cases, React allows us to define our own `PropType` validators as well.

Validators

The `PropTypes` object contains a list of common validators (but we can also define our own. More on that later).

When a `prop` is passed in with an invalid type or fails the prop type, a warning is passed into the JavaScript console. These warnings will *only* be shown in development mode, so if we accidentally deploy our app into production with an improper use of a component, our users won't see the warning.

The built in validators are:

- `string`
- `number`
- `boolean`
- `function`
- `object`
- `shape`
- `oneOf`
- `instanceOf`
- `array`
- `arrayOf`
- `node`
- `element`
- `any`
- `required`

string

To define a prop as a string, we can use `PropTypes.string`.

code/appendix/proptypes/string.js

```
class Component extends React.Component {
  static propTypes = {
    name: PropTypes.string
  }
  // ...
  render() {
    return (<div>{this.props.name}</div>)
  }
}
```

To pass a string as a prop we can either just pass the string itself as an attribute or use the `{}` braces to define a string variable. These are all *functionally* equivalent:

```
<Component name={"Ari"} />
<Component name="Ari" />
```

number

To specify a prop should be a number, we can use `PropTypes.number`.

code/appendix/proptypes/number.js

```
class Component extends React.Component {
  static propTypes = {
    totalCount: PropTypes.number
  }
  // ...
  render() {
    return (<div>{this.props.totalCount}</div>)
  }
}
```

Passing in a number, we must pass it as a JavaScript value or the value of a variable using braces:

```
var x = 20;

<Component totalCount={20} />
<Component totalCount={x} />
```

boolean

To specify a prop should be a boolean (true or false), we can use `PropTypes.bool`.

code/appendix/proptypes/bool.js

```
class Component extends React.Component {
  static propTypes = {
    on: PropTypes.bool
  }
  // ...
  render() {
    return (
      <div>
        {this.props.on ? 'On' : 'Off'}
      </div>
    )
  }
}
```

To use a boolean in a JSX expression, we can pass it as a JavaScript value.

```
var isOn = true;

<Component on={true} />
<Component on={false} />
<Component on={isOn} />
```

A trick for using booleans to show or hide content is to use the `&&` expression.

For instance, inside our `Component.render()` function, if we want to show content only when the `on` proptype is true, we can do so like: {lang=text,line-numbers=off} render() { return (<div> {this.props.on && <p>This component is on</p>} </div>) }

---

function

We can pass a function as a `prop` as well. To define a prop to be a function, we can use `PropTypes.func`. Often times when we write a `Form` component, we'll pass a function as a prop to be called when the form is submitted (i.e. `onSubmit()`). It's common to define a prop as a required function on a component.

code/appendix/proptypes/func.js

```
class Component extends React.Component {
  static propTypes = {
    onPress: PropTypes.func
  }
  // ...
  render() {
    return (
      <div onClick={this.props.onPress}>
        Press me
      </div>
    )
  }
}
```

We can pass a function as a prop by using the JavaScript expression syntax, like so:

```
const x = function(name) {};
const fn = value => alert("Value: " + value);

<Component onComplete={x} />
<Component onComplete={fn} />
```

object

We can require a prop should be a JavaScript object through the `PropTypes.object`:

code/appendix/proptypes/object.js

```
class Component extends React.Component {
  static propTypes = {
    user: PropTypes.object
  }
  // ...
  render() {
    const { user } = this.props
    return (
      <div>
        <h1>{user.name}</h1>
        <h5>{user.profile}</h5>
      </div>
    )
  }
}
```

Sending an object through as a prop, we'll need to use the JavaScript expression `{}` syntax:

```
const user = {
  name: 'Ari'
}

<Component user={user} />
<Component user={{name: 'Anthony'}} />
```

object shape

React allows us to define the shape of an object we expect to receive by using `PropTypes.shape()`. The `PropTypes.shape()` function accepts an object with a list of key-value pairs that dictate the keys an object is expected to have as well as the value type:

code/appendix/proptypes/objectOfShape.js

```
class Component extends React.Component {
  static propTypes = {
    user: PropTypes.shape({
      name: PropTypes.string,
      profile: PropTypes.string
    })
  }
  // ...
  render() {
    const { user } = this.props
    return (
      <div>
        <h1>{user.name}</h1>
        <h5>{user.profile}</h5>
      </div>
    )
  }
}
```

multiple types

Sometimes we don't know in advance what kind a particular prop will be, but we can accept one or other type. React gives us the propTypes of `oneOf()` and `oneOfType()` for these situations.

Using `oneOf()` requires that the propType be a discrete value of values, for instance to require a component to specify a log level value:

code/appendix/proptypes/oneOf.js

```
class Component extends React.Component {
  static propTypes = {
    level: PropTypes.oneOf([
      'debug', 'info', 'warning', 'error'
    ])
  }
  // ...
  render() {
    return (
      <div>
        <p>{this.props.level}</p>
      </div>
```

```
    )
  }
}
```

Using `oneOfType()` says that a prop can be one of any number of types. For instance, a phone number may either be passed to a component as a string or an integer:

code/appendix/proptypes/oneOfType.js

```
class Component extends React.Component {
  static propTypes = {
    phoneNumber: PropTypes.oneOfType([
      PropTypes.number,
      PropTypes.string
    ])
  }
  // ...
  render() {
    return (
      <div>
        <p>{this.props.phoneNumber}</p>
      </div>
    )
  }
}
```

instanceOf

We can dictate that a component *must* be an instance of a JavaScript class using `PropTypes.instanceOf()` as the value of the propType:

code/appendix/proptypes/instanceOf.js

```
class Component extends React.Component {
  static propTypes = {
    user: PropTypes.instanceOf(User)
  }
  // ...
  render() {
    const { user } = this.props

    return (
```

```
      <div>
        <h3>{user.name}</h3>
      </div>
    )
  }
}
```

We'll use the JavaScript expression syntax to pass in a particular prop.

code/appendix/proptypes/instanceOf.js

```
class User {
  constructor(name) {
    this.name = name
  }
}
```

```
const ari = new User('Ari');

<Component user={ari} />
```

array

On occasion we'll want to send in an array as a prop. To set an array, we'll use the `PropTypes.array` as the value.

code/appendix/proptypes/array.js

```
class Component extends React.Component {
  static propTypes = {
    authors: PropTypes.array
  }
  // ...
  render() {
    const { authors } = this.props
    return (
      <div>
        {authors && authors.map(author => {
          <AuthorCard author={author} />
        })}
      </div>
```

```
    )
  }
}
```

Sending an object through as a prop, we'll need to use the JavaScript expression {} syntax:

```
const users = [
  {name: 'Ari'}
  {name: 'Anthony'}
];
```

```
<Component authors={[{name: 'Anthony'}]} />
<Component authors={users} />
```

array of type

React allows us to dictate the type of values each member of an array should be using `PropTypes.arrayOf()`.

code/appendix/proptypes/arrayOfType.js

```
class Component extends React.Component {
  static propTypes = {
    authors: PropTypes.arrayOf(PropTypes.object)
  }
  // ...
  render() {
    const { authors } = this.props
    return (
      <div>
        {authors && authors.map(author => {
          <AuthorCard author={author} />
        })}
      </div>
    )
  }
}
```

We'll use the JavaScript expression syntax {} to pass in an array:

```
const users = [
  {name: 'Ari'}
  {name: 'Anthony'}
];
```

```
<Component authors={[{name: 'Anthony'}]} />
<Component authors={users} />
```

node

We can also pass anything that can be rendered, such as numbers, string, DOM elements, arrays, or fragments that contain them using the `PropTypes.node`.

code/appendix/proptypes/node.js

```
class Component extends React.Component {
  static propTypes = {
    icon: PropTypes.node
  }
  // ...
  render() {
    const { icon } = this.props
    return (
      <div>
        {icon}
      </div>
    )
  }
}
```

Passing a *node* as a prop is straightforward as well. Passing a node as a value is often useful when requiring a component to have children or setting a custom element. For instance, if we want to allow our user to pass in either the name of an icon or a custom component, we can use the node `propType`.

```
const icon = <FontAwesomeIcon name="user" />


<Component icon={icon} />
<Component icon={"fa fa-cog"} />
```

element

React's flexibility allows us to pass another React element in as a prop as well by using the `PropTypes.element`.

We can build our components so that the interface they allow our users to specify a custom component. For instance, we might have a `<List />` component who's responsibility is to output a list of elements. Without custom components, we would have to build a separate `<List />` React component for each type of list we want to render (which might be appropriate, depending on the behavior of the element). By passing a component type, we can reuse the `<List />` component.

For instance, a list component might look like:

code/appendix/proptypes/element.js

```
class Component extends React.Component {
  static propTypes = {
    listComponent: PropTypes.element,
    list: PropTypes.array
  }
  // ...
  render() {
    const { list } = this.props
    return (
      <ul>
        {list.map(this.renderListItem)}
      </ul>
    )
  }
}
```

We can use this list component with or without specifying a custom component:

code/appendix/proptypes/element.js

```
const Item = function(props) {
  return (
    <div>{props.children}</div>
  )
}
```

```
<List list={[1, 2, 3]} />
<List list={[1, 2, 3]} listComponent={Item} />
```

any type

React also allows us to specify that a prop must be present, regardless of it's type. We can do this by using the `PropTypes.any` validator.

code/appendix/proptypes/any.js

```
class Component extends React.Component {
  static propTypes = {
    mustBePresent: PropTypes.any
  }
  // ...
  render() {
    return (
      <div>
        Is here: {this.props.mustBePresent}
      </div>
    )
  }
}
```

Optional & required props

All props are considered optional unless otherwise specified. To require a prop be passed to a component and validated, we can append every propType validation with `.isRequired`.

For instance, if we must have a function to get called after some action when a `Loading` component has completed, we can specify it like this:

code/appendix/proptypes/optional.js

```
class Component extends React.Component {
  static propTypes = {
    // Optional props:
    onStart: PropTypes.func,
    // Required props:
    onComplete: PropTypes.func.isRequired,
    name: PropTypes.string.isRequired
  }
  // ...
  startTimer = (seconds=5) => {
    const { onStart, onComplete } = this.props
    onStart()
    setTimeout(() => onComplete(), seconds)
  }
  // ...
  render() {
    const { name } = this.props
    return (
      <div onClick={this.startTimer}>
        {name}
      </div>
    )
  }
}
```

custom validator

React allows us to specify a custom validation function for all of the other situations where the default validation functions don't cover it. In order to run a write a custom validation we'll specify a function that accepts 3 arguments:

1. The `props` passed to the component
2. The `propName` being validated
3. The `componentName` we're validating against

If our validation passes, we can run through the function and return anything. The validation function will only fail if an `Error` object is raised (i.e. `new Error()`).

For instance, if we have a loader that accepts validated users, we can run a custom function against the prop.

code/appendix/proptypes/custom.js

```
class Component extends React.Component {
  static propTypes = {
    user: function(props, propName, componentName) {
      const user = props[propName];
      if (!user.isValid()) {
        return new Error('Invalid user');
      }
    }
  }
  // ...
  render() {
    const { user } = this.props
    return (
      <div>
        {user.name}
      </div>
    )
  }
}
```

Where the `User` class might look something like this:

code/appendix/proptypes/custom.js

```
class User {
  constructor(name) {
    this.name = name
  }
  isValid() {
    // must have a name
    return !!this.name && new Error('Name must be present')
  }
}
```

Appendix B: ES6

This appendix is a non-exhaustive list of new syntactic features and methods that were added to JavaScript in ES6. These features are the most commonly used and most helpful.

While this appendix doesn't cover ES6 classes, we go over the basics while learning about components in the book. In addition, this appendix doesn't include descriptions of some larger new features like promises and generators. If you'd like more info on those or on any topic below, we encourage you to reference the Mozilla Developer Network's website[192] (MDN).

Prefer `const` and `let` over `var`

If you've worked with ES5 JavaScript before, you're likely used to seeing variables declared with `var`:

appendix/es6/const_let.js

```
var myVariable = 5;
```

Both the `const` and `let` statements also declare variables. They were introduced in ES6.

Use `const` in cases where a variable is never re-assigned. Using `const` makes this clear to whoever is reading your code. It refers to the "constant" state of the variable in the context it is defined within.

If the variable will be re-assigned, use `let`.

We encourage the use of `const` and `let` instead of `var`. In addition to the restriction introduced by `const`, both `const` and `let` are *block scoped* as opposed to *function scoped*. This scoping can help avoid unexpected bugs.

Arrow functions

There are three ways to write arrow function bodies. For the examples below, let's say we have an array of city objects:

[192] https://developer.mozilla.org

appendix/es6/arrow_funcs.js

```
const cities = [
  { name: 'Cairo', pop: 7764700 },
  { name: 'Lagos', pop: 8029200 },
];
```

If we write an arrow function that spans multiple lines, we must use braces to delimit the function body like this:

appendix/es6/arrow_funcs.js

```
const formattedPopulations = cities.map((city) => {
  const popMM = (city.pop / 1000000).toFixed(2);
  return popMM + ' million';
});
console.log(formattedPopulations);
// -> [ "7.76 million", "8.03 million" ]
```

Note that we must also explicitly specify a `return` for the function.

However, if we write a function body that is only a single line (or single expression) we can use parentheses to delimit it:

appendix/es6/arrow_funcs.js

```
const formattedPopulations2 = cities.map((city) => (
  (city.pop / 1000000).toFixed(2) + ' million'
));
```

Notably, we don't use `return` as it's implied.

Furthermore, if your function body is terse you can write it like so:

appendix/es6/arrow_funcs.js

```
const pops = cities.map(city => city.pop);
console.log(pops);
// [ 7764700, 8029200 ]
```

The terseness of arrow functions is one of two reasons that we use them. Compare the one-liner above to this:

appendix/es6/arrow_funcs.js

```
const popsNoArrow = cities.map(function(city) { return city.pop });
```

Of greater benefit, though, is how arrow functions bind the `this` object.

The traditional JavaScript function declaration syntax (`function () {}`) will bind `this` in anonymous functions to the global object. To illustrate the confusion this causes, consider the following example:

appendix/es6/arrow_funcs_jukebox_1.js

```
function printSong() {
  console.log("Oops - The Global Object");
}

const jukebox = {
  songs: [
    {
      title: "Wanna Be Startin' Somethin'",
      artist: "Michael Jackson",
    },
    {
      title: "Superstar",
      artist: "Madonna",
    },
  ],
  printSong: function (song) {
    console.log(song.title + " - " + song.artist);
  },
  printSongs: function () {
    // `this` bound to the object (OK)
    this.songs.forEach(function(song) {
      // `this` bound to global object (bad)
      this.printSong(song);
    });
  },
}

jukebox.printSongs();
// > "Oops - The Global Object"
// > "Oops - The Global Object"
```

The method `printSongs()` iterates over `this.songs` with `forEach()`. In this context, `this` is bound to the object (`jukebox`) as expected. However, the anonymous function passed to `forEach()` binds its internal `this` to the global object. As such, `this.printSong(song)` calls the function declared at the top of the example, *not* the method on `jukebox`.

JavaScript developers have traditionally used workarounds for this behavior, but arrow functions solve the problem by **capturing the `this` value of the enclosing context**. Using an arrow function for `printSongs()` has the expected result:

appendix/es6/arrow_funcs_jukebox_2.js

```
  printSongs: function () {
    this.songs.forEach((song) => {
      // `this` bound to same `this` as `printSongs()` (`jukebox`)
      this.printSong(song);
    });
  },
}

jukebox.printSongs();
// > "Wanna Be Startin' Somethin' - Michael Jackson"
// > "Superstar - Madonna"
```

For this reason, throughout the book we use arrow functions for all anonymous functions.

Modules

ES6 formally supports modules using the `import`/`export` syntax.

Named exports

Inside any file, you can use `export` to specify a variable the module should expose. Here's an example of a file that exports two functions:

```
// greetings.js

export const sayHi = () => (console.log('Hi!'));
export const sayBye = () => (console.log('Bye!'));

const saySomething = () => (console.log('Something!'));
```

Now, anywhere we wanted to use these functions we could use `import`. We need to specify which functions we want to import. A common way of doing this is using ES6's destructuring assignment syntax to list them out like this:

```
// app.js

import { sayHi, sayBye } from './greetings';

sayHi(); // -> Hi!
sayBye(); // => Bye!
```

Importantly, the function that was *not* exported (`saySomething`) is unavailable outside of the module.

Also note that we supply a **relative path** to `from`, indicating that the ES6 module is a local file as opposed to an npm package.

Instead of inserting an `export` before each variable you'd like to export, you can use this syntax to list off all the exposed variables in one area:

```
// greetings.js

const sayHi = () => (console.log('Hi!'));
const sayBye = () => (console.log('Bye!'));

const saySomething = () => (console.log('Something!'));

export { sayHi, sayBye };
```

We can also specify that we'd like to import all of a module's functionality underneath a given namespace with the `import * as <Namespace>` syntax:

```
// app.js

import * as Greetings from './greetings';

Greetings.sayHi();
  // -> Hi!
Greetings.sayBye();
  // => Bye!
Greetings.saySomething();
  // => TypeError: Greetings.saySomething is not a function
```

Default export

The other type of export is a default export. A module can only contain one default export:

```
// greetings.js

const sayHi = () => (console.log('Hi!'));
const sayBye = () => (console.log('Bye!'));

const saySomething = () => (console.log('Something!'));

const Greetings = { sayHi, sayBye };

export default Greetings;
```

This is a common pattern for libraries. It means you can easily import the library wholesale without specifying what individual functions you want:

```
// app.js

import Greetings from './greetings';

Greetings.sayHi(); // -> Hi!
Greetings.sayBye(); // => Bye!
```

It's not uncommon for a module to use a mix of both named exports and default exports. For instance, with `react-dom`, you can import `ReactDOM` (a default export) like this:

```
import ReactDOM from 'react-dom';

ReactDOM.render(
  // ...
);
```

Or, if you're only going to use the `render()` function, you can import the named `render()` function like this:

```
import { render } from 'react-dom';

render(
  // ...
);
```

To achieve this flexibility, the export implementation for `react-dom` looks something like this:

```
// a fake react-dom.js

export const render = (component, target) => {
  // ...
};

const ReactDOM = {
  render,
  // ... other functions
};

export default ReactDOM;
```

If you want to play around with the module syntax, check out the folder `code/webpack/es6-modules`.

For more reading on ES6 modules, see this article from Mozilla: "ES6 in Depth: Modules[193]".

`Object.assign()`

We use `Object.assign()` often throughout the book. We use it in areas where we want to create a modified version of an existing object.

`Object.assign()` accepts any number of objects as arguments. When the function receives two arguments, it *copies* the properties of the second object onto the first, like so:

appendix/es6/object_assign.js

```
const coffee = { };
const noCream = { cream: false };
const noMilk = { milk: false };
Object.assign(coffee, noCream);
// coffee is now: `{ cream: false }`
```

It is idiomatic to pass in three arguments to `Object.assign()`. The first argument is a new JavaScript object, the one that `Object.assign()` will ultimately return. The second is the object whose properties we'd like to build off of. The last is the changes we'd like to apply:

[193] https://hacks.mozilla.org/2015/08/es6-in-depth-modules/

appendix/es6/object_assign.js

```
const coffeeWithMilk = Object.assign({}, coffee, { milk: true });
// coffeeWithMilk is: `{ cream: false, milk: true }`
// coffee was not modified: `{ cream: false, milk: false }`
```

`Object.assign()` is a handy method for working with "immutable" JavaScript objects.

Template literals

In ES5 JavaScript, you'd interpolate variables into strings like this:

appendix/es6/template_literals_1.js

```
var greeting = 'Hello, ' + user + '! It is ' + degF + ' degrees outside.';
```

With ES6 template literals, we can create the same string like this:

appendix/es6/template_literals_2.js

```
const greeting = `Hello, ${user}! It is ${degF} degrees outside.`;
```

The spread operator (`...`)

In arrays, the ellipsis `...` operator will *expand* the array that follows into the parent array. The spread operator enables us to succinctly construct new arrays as a composite of existing arrays.

Here is an example:

appendix/es6/spread_operator_arrays.js

```
const a = [ 1, 2, 3 ];
const b = [ 4, 5, 6 ];
const c = [ ...a, ...b, 7, 8, 9 ];

console.log(c); // -> [ 1, 2, 3, 4, 5, 6, 7, 8, 9 ]
```

Notice how this is different than if we wrote:

appendix/es6/spread_operator_arrays.js

```
const d = [ a, b, 7, 8, 9 ];
console.log(d); // -> [ [ 1, 2, 3 ], [ 4, 5, 6 ], 7, 8, 9 ]
```

Enhanced object literals

In ES5, all objects were required to have explicit key and value declarations:

appendix/es6/enhanced_object_literals.js

```
const explicit = {
  getState: getState,
  dispatch: dispatch,
};
```

In ES6, you can use this terser syntax whenever the property name and variable name are the same:

appendix/es6/enhanced_object_literals.js

```
const implicit = {
  getState,
  dispatch,
};
```

Lots of open source libraries use this syntax, so it's good to be familiar with it. But whether you use it in your own code is a matter of stylistic preference.

Default arguments

With ES6, you can specify a default value for an argument in the case that it is `undefined` when the function is called.

This:

appendix/es6/default_args.js

```
function divide(a, b) {
  // Default divisor to `1`
  const divisor = typeof b === 'undefined' ? 1 : b;

  return a / divisor;
}
```

Can be written as this:

appendix/es6/default_args.js

```
function divide(a, b = 1) {
  return a / b;
}
```

In both cases, using the function looks like this:

appendix/es6/default_args.js

```
divide(14, 2);
// => 7
divide(14, undefined);
// => 14
divide(14);
// => 14
```

Whenever the argument `b` in the example above is `undefined`, the default argument is used. Note that `null` will not use the default argument:

appendix/es6/default_args.js

```
divide(14, null); // `null` is used as divisor
// => Infinity    // 14 / null
```

Destructuring assignments

For arrays

In ES5, extracting and assigning multiple elements from an array looked like this:

appendix/es6/destructuring_assignments.js

```
var fruits = [ 'apples', 'bananas', 'oranges' ];
var fruit1 = fruits[0];
var fruit2 = fruits[1];
```

In ES6, we can use the destructuring syntax to accomplish the same task like this:

appendix/es6/destructuring_assignments.js

```
const [ veg1, veg2 ] = [ 'asparagus', 'broccoli', 'onion' ];
console.log(veg1); // -> 'asparagus'
console.log(veg2); // -> 'broccoli'
```

The variables in the array on the left are "matched" and assigned to the corresponding elements in the array on the right. Note that `'onion'` is ignored and has no variable bound to it.

For objects

We can do something similar for extracting object properties into variables:

appendix/es6/destructuring_assignments.js

```
const smoothie = {
  fats: [ 'avocado', 'peanut butter', 'greek yogurt' ],
  liquids: [ 'almond milk' ],
  greens: [ 'spinach' ],
  fruits: [ 'blueberry', 'banana' ],
};

const { liquids, fruits } = smoothie;

console.log(liquids); // -> [ 'almond milk' ]
console.log(fruits); // -> [ 'blueberry', 'banana' ]
```

Parameter context matching

We can use these same principles to bind arguments inside a function to properties of an object supplied as an argument:

appendix/es6/destructuring_assignments.js

```
const containsSpinach = ({ greens }) => {
  if (greens.find(g => g === 'spinach')) {
    return true;
  } else {
    return false;
  }
};

containsSpinach(smoothie); // -> true
```

We do this often with functional React components:

appendix/es6/destructuring_assignments.js

```
const IngredientList = ({ ingredients, onClick }) => (
  <ul className='IngredientList'>
    {
      ingredients.map(i => (
        <li
          key={i.id}
          onClick={() => onClick(i.id)}
          className='item'
        >
          {i.name}
        </li>
      ))
    }
  </ul>
)
```

Here, we use destructuring to extract the props into variables (`ingredients` and `onClick`) that we then use inside the component's function body.